Power and Resistance
in an African Society

Les Switzer

Power and Resistance in an African Society

The Ciskei Xhosa and the Making of South Africa

The University of Wisconsin Press

The University of Wisconsin Press
114 North Murray Street
Madison, Wisconsin 53715

3 Henrietta Street
London WC2E 8LU, England

5   4   3   2   1

Printed in the United States of America

Library of Congress Cataloging-in-Publication Data
Switzer, Les.
    Power and resistance in an African society : the Ciskei Xhosa and
the making of South Africa / Les Switzer.
    470 p.   cm.
    Includes bibliographical references (p. 367) and index.
    ISBN 0-299-13380-X   ISBN 0-299-13384-2 (pbk.)
    1. Ciskei (South Africa)—Politics and government.   2. Xhosa
(African people)   3. Nationalism—Ciskei (South Africa)   I. Title.
DT2400.C58S95   1993
968.7'92—dc20   93-10085

To my children

and

To the children of the Ciskei

Contents

Illustrations

Tables

Abbreviations

1882 Imbumba	Imbumba Yama Nyama (South African Aborigines Association)
1887 Imbumba	Imbumba Eliliso Lomzi Yabantsundu (Union of Native Vigilance Associations)
1898 Imbumba	Imbumba Eliliso Lomzi Yabantsundu
1912 Imbumba	Imbumba Yezizwe Zomzantsi Afrika (South African Races Congress)
AAC or Convention	All-African Convention
AFCWU	African Food and Canning Workers' Union
AME church	American Methodist Episcopal church
ANC or Congress	African National Congress
APO	African Political (People's) Organisation
BC	Black Consciousness
BCP	Black Community Programmes
BPC	Black People's Convention
CGC or Ciskei Bunga	Ciskeian General Council
CAD	Coloured Affairs Department
CATA	Cape African Teachers' Association
CLA	Ciskei Legislative Assembly
CNDC	Ciskei National Development Corporation
CNETU	Council for Non-European Trade Unions
CNIP	Ciskei National Independence Party
CNP	Ciskei National Party
CNVC	Cape Native Voters' Convention
CPSA	Communist Party of South Africa
CTA	Ciskei Territorial Authority
FTS	Federal Theological Seminary of Southern Africa
GMS	Glasgow Missionary Society
GWU	General Workers' Union

ICU	Industrial and Commercial Workers' Union of Africa
IDC	Industrial Development Corporation
Iliso Lomzi(s)	Vigilance Association(s)
Imvo or *IZ*	*Imvo Zabantsundu* (Native Opinion)
Independent ICU	Independent Industrial and Commercial Workers' Union of Africa
IOTT	Independent Order of True Templars
LMS	London Missionary Society
NAD	Native Affairs Department
NEA	Native Educational Association
NEUM or Unity	Non-European Unity Movement
NRC	Natives' Representative Council
NRFA	Non-Racial Franchise Association
NUSAS	National Union of South African Students
PAC	Pan-Africanist Congress
PCA	Presbyterian Church of Africa
SAAWU	South African Allied Workers' Union
SAIC	South African Indian Congress
SAIRR	South African Institute of Race Relations
SANA	South African Native Association
SANAC	South African Native Affairs Commission
SANC	South African Native Congress
SANNC	South African Native National Congress
SASM	South African Students' Movement
SASO	South African Students' Organisation
Spro-Cas	Study Project of Christianity in Apartheid Society
UCM	University Christian Movement

Preface

The sons of Noah who came out of the ark were Shem, Ham, and Japheth . . . and their descendants spread over the whole earth. . . . Ham, father of Canaan, saw his father naked. . . . Noah . . . learnt what his youngest son had done to him, and said: "Cursed be Canaan, slave of slaves shall he be to his brothers."

Genesis 9:18–25

Africa was of God given to the race of Ham. . . . Until the Negro is doomed against all history and experience—until his God-given inheritance of Africa be taken finally from him, I shall never believe in the total extinction of his brethren . . . of the land of Ham.

Rev. Tiyo Soga, 1865

This book has been almost fifteen years in the making. My interest in the Ciskei region began while I was teaching at Rhodes University in Grahamstown in the 1970s and early 1980s. My focus in those years was on the media of communication, and the Ciskei became a window through which I began to explore the revisionist historiography of South Africa. I wrote my first essay on colonial Ciskei in 1979, but it was abandoned as I became more and more immersed in critical theory and in the work of critical scholars in South African studies.

For several years the Ciskei was on the back burner in terms of my research priorities, but in two summers at Yale University in 1983 and 1987 the project gradually began to take shape. The African peoples who live in this region offered a unique case study in the ambiguities of power and resistance in South Africa. The Ciskei and the eastern Cape in general have been the subject of numerous scholarly books, monographs, and articles as well as unpublished theses, reports, and conference and seminar papers. More research has probably been done on this region than on any other in South Africa, but the literature is uneven in quality and there are still crucial gaps in the historical narrative. This study offers a critical interpretation and synthesis of the primary and secondary sources in telling the Ciskei story and analyzing its significance for South Africa.

The project could not have been done without the advice and encouragement of numerous colleagues at Rhodes University. Nancy Charton first stimulated my interest in the region, and Simon Bekker, Rodney Davenport, Michael Ashley, Phil Black, Cecil Manona, Gordon kaTywakadi, Oakley West (who first drafted and later corrected two of the maps), Mike Berning, Sandy Rowoldt, and Jackson Vena, among others, helped me at various times along the way. My efforts were also informed by a history honors seminar on the eastern Cape that Colin Bundy offered at Rhodes in 1984. Fraser Mzalazala, the journalism department's messenger for many years, did more than he will ever know to make me aware of what was needed in writing this book.

I am grateful to the University of Houston, which provided a number of grants to complete the project, and to Barry Brown, former director of our college's computer center, who always knew the answer to my computer woes, to student assistant Duke Baldauf, who helped reformat some of the chapters, to artist Darlene Hanks and her successor Joel Powell in University Media Services, who prepared and revised the maps, to Martha Steele and her staff in University Access Services, who got essential materials to me quickly when I most needed them. My thanks to Bob Edgar for the photograph of Enoch Mgijima (Figure 8.1), to Catherine Higgs and the University of South Africa Documentation Centre for African Studies for the photographs of John Tengo Jabavu and D. D. T. Jabavu (Figures 5.1 and 8.2), and to the staff of Rhodes University's Cory Library for the remaining photographs. My thanks also to Surplus People Project, Rhodes University Department of Geography, and the University Press of New England for allowing me to reproduce all or part of three maps used in the text, and to Elizabeth Cunningham for preparing the index.

I owe a special debt of gratitude to John McNamara, who read the introduction and has helped to broaden and clarify my approach to critical theory over the years, to Richard Elphick, who scrutinized Chapter 7, and to Jeff Peires and Hunt Davis, who offered detailed critiques of the manuscript as a whole. I could not have completed this book without the support of my wife, Hazel, who helped with the proofreading and was always there to offer encouragement and share the burden.

Power and Resistance
in an African Society

Introduction: A Case Study of the Ciskei Region

The current generation of critical scholars in South African history has not yet produced a general study that explores the relationship between economic, political, and cultural phenomena over time and demonstrates how they emerge as manifestations of a single historical process. This book addresses the problem by examining these phenomena as expressions of power and resistance at work in a single region. The whole, as it were, is read in relation to the sum of one of its parts.

The Ciskei in the eastern Cape Province was selected as the case study. The region is situated roughly between the Fish and Kei rivers along the Indian Ocean and extends inland to an area of low mountains centering on the Stormberg (Map 3). The term Ciskei—meaning on this side of the Kei River (or the side closest to Cape Town)—was in use as early as the 1840s when it referred to Bantu-speaking Africans west of this geographical boundary.[1] It was being used in a more restricted sense—to describe the truncated African locations established in the region during the European conquest—even before South Africa's reserves were officially delineated in the 1913 Land Act. In terms of human settlement, the history of the Ciskei region before the arrival of the Europeans resembles that of South Africa as a whole. It had been continuously inhabited by various population groups for at least 15,000 years,[2] and in common with the rest of the subcontinent was apparently an area of hominid occupation extending back 1.5–2 million years.[3]

The Ciskei was the historic zone of conflict between European and Bantu-speaking African in South Africa; the Cape-Xhosa wars in this region lasted one hundred years. The contemporary African nationalist movement first emerged in a variety of organizational forms in the Ciskei during the 1870s and 1880s. The strategy of petitionary protest probably persisted longer here than anywhere else in South Africa in the postcolonial period, but popular resistance found a variety of windows outside organized African politics. The Ciskei and its environs became a militant base of operations for protest groups in the 1940s and 1950s, when the gap between urban and rural dissidents in South Africa was first bridged during the Defiance Campaign. Finally, the

Ciskei reserve emerged as a primary site of struggle in South Africa's periphery in the 1970s and 1980s.

The Ciskei, then, offers a benchmark for exploring the ambiguities of power and resistance in the struggle for South Africa. I wanted to show how these complex categories were transmuted in an African society over time, so the focus of this study is on the Xhosa-speaking peoples who lived in the Ciskei region in the first century after conquest. I also wanted to highlight the linkages between regional and national issues, so the Ciskei region is examined in the context of unfolding events in the Cape Colony and in the unified settler state of South Africa after 1910. Finally, I wanted to offer readers of African history a study "from below"—from the perspective of a subaltern society in transition and transformation—that would be readable, comprehensive, and in the critical scholarly tradition. These readers must judge the extent to which I have succeeded.

No introduction to a book on a subject as fraught with controversy as South Africa would be complete without examining its main theoretical assumptions: (1) the material and symbolic manifestations of power were both represented and resisted in the Ciskei as elsewhere in South Africa during the colonial and postcolonial periods, and (2) resistance was generated in an environment that was largely conditioned but not controlled by South Africa's dominant cultural order.

The Material Manifestations of Power

In part, power was manifested in a material form through a new economic system that gradually undermined and destroyed the reproductive capacity of African homestead production. As modes-of-production theorist Jairus Banaji has expressed it, capitalism imposes its own "laws of motion" on the forces of precapitalist production and exchange. Nevertheless, archaic social relations are retained and rejuvenated to promote capitalist development.[4] In South Africa, these precapitalist social structures played a distorted but crucial role in capitalist development. Precolonial African hierarchies were revived in a neutered form after initial efforts to destroy them, colonial definitions of "communal" tenure in the African reserves were affirmed and procedures of "native law and custom" codified, and relations between landowner and tenant on white farms assumed a feudal-like status.

Archaic structures of stratification and exploitation were propped up, redefined, and reempowered to ensure control over the labor power of the subjugated African population. Initially unmarried men, later heads of households, and eventually unmarried and married females lost their economic independence and became migrant wage laborers in the ongoing process of capitalist expansion and development. Nevertheless, this proletarianization of the African population was slow, uneven, and probably still incomplete even a century after conquest.[5]

The pattern of capitalist production and of the economic reorganization of African society as a whole did appear to conform to underdevelopment theory, as the capitalist sector expanded in articulation with, and at the expense of, the indigenous African population.[6] The underdevelopment of South Africa's peripheral African reserves, for example, had its roots in the Ciskei region in the dramatic events of the frontier-war generation between ca. 1830 and ca. 1860.

As a mode of production, capitalism took specific forms and functioned in specific ways in South Africa just as it did elsewhere in the non-Western world. Class relations, however, were structured from the beginning in a racial discourse that became ever more elaborate and more pervasive as modernization proceeded. Color consciousness united an otherwise fractionalized white capitalist class or *national bourgeoisie* and eventually forced those who ruled to accommodate white workers, divided a multiracial and potentially mediating *petty bourgeoisie,* and ultimately polarized the mass of the black working classes.

A growing proportion of the African population—landless peasants, agricultural workers, urbanites who did not participate formally in the capitalist sector and were not employed by the government, and women in a variety of occupations—operated on the fringes of the wage-labor economy and collectively composed the most disorganized and repressed social category. The vast majority of blacks would eventually be reduced to these superexploited "excluded classes."[7] A distinct blend of accommodating and oppositional discourses would be formed in the complex interplay between color, consciousness, and class in South Africa.

The Symbolic Manifestations of Power

In part, power was manifested in a symbolic form through dominating cultural mechanisms that gradually matured with the emergence of a racially stratified, industrial capitalist state. The role of culture in the context of capitalist development, however, has been the source of considerable debate.

Antonio Gramsci offers a point of departure with his notion of the hegemonic state. Writing from prison in Mussolini's Italy, Gramsci sought to explain why a dominant "historical bloc" in a contemporary capitalist state must rely on consensus as well as coercion to contain dissent. He concluded that the state was more than the governing political, administrative, legislative, and judicial apparatus: it also embraced the dominant cultural forces that accompanied the rise of industrial capitalism. The modern authoritarian as well as the liberal democratic state played an active and positive role in trying "to raise the great mass of the population to a particular cultural . . . level . . . which corresponds to the needs of the productive forces for development, and hence to the interests of the ruling classes."[8]

The cultural institutions in a given society were the arbiters of a hegemonic consensus. These agencies were private as well as public, and they included the family, schools, churches, political parties, labor unions, sports and other recreational associations, and the mass media of communication. They represented the agencies of persuasion in "civil society," and they could be contrasted with the agencies of coercion controlled more directly by the state—the administrative bureaucracy, military, police, judiciary and penal authorities, and the tax system.

The main task of cultural institutions was to legitimate the social order in the consciousness and in the actions of the subordinate social classes. Gramsci's vision of the hegemonic state, however, also embraced the concept of ambiguity. This process of legitimation, which he called "abstract consciousness," was often in conflict with a person's lived experiences, which he called "situational consciousness." The resulting "contradictory consciousness" of "man-in-the-mass" was an expression both of commitment to and of ambivalence about the social order. For Gramsci, hegemony did not require the active support of the subordinate masses. Compliance was sufficient. The seeds of accommodation to and resistance against the hegemonic state, however, could be discerned in an individual or group's "situational consciousness."[9]

In the Gramscian schema, the term culture is a complex category that embraces all social activity. For some Gramscian interpreters, moreover, hegemonic cultures are situated in a continuum. In "closed" hegemonic cultures, dissenting groups may lack even the language necessary to organize resistance. In "open" hegemonic cultures, "the capability for resistance flourishes and may lead to the creation of counterhegemonic alternatives."[10]

The mechanisms of coercion and consensus are both used to win the allegiance of the dominated masses, and one or the other might feature more prominently in any given historical epoch. Ruling power blocs in virtually all contemporary capitalist societies, however, are dependent to at least some degree on the consent of the governed. For Gramsci, the hegemonic state was a unifying force, mediating conflict while actively and positively seeking to gain support from all the constituted groups in a given social formation. In essence, the modern capitalist state functioned through "hegemony protected by coercion."[11]

In contrast to what happened in much of sub-Saharan Africa, the state in South Africa developed into a powerful and well-organized instrument of persuasion as well as coercion that served the interests of a segmented but relatively stable racial alliance of white middle- and working-class interests.

Conceptualizing the activities of those who control the state in South Africa, however, has been the source of some controversy.

The "instrumentalist" theory of the state—and of ideology as the dominant discourse—is derived mainly from the classical marxist position.[12] This position focuses on the ways in which the state serves the interests and needs of the ruling alliance. The state is viewed essentially as the tool of the people in power. Conflicts exist between competitive fractions within the ruling order, but the state itself is not generally perceived as a focal point of class struggle, and the powerbrokers are rarely inhibited, much less neutralized, by other, contradictory forces in the social formation.

An alternative, "structuralist" position argues that the level of capitalist development and its corresponding class relations determine the nature of the state and the way it functions to promote unity and sustain the capitalist system. If the state is to represent the capitalist class, it has to appear to be independent of specific class interests. Only an autonomous state—one that seeks to be neutral or impartial in terms of class interests—can appeal to the public interest and thereby attempt to harmonize conflicts within the ruling bloc, disorganize the opposition, and orchestrate the class struggle.[13]

For the structuralist, then, the state is not perceived to be the embodiment of relatively homogeneous ruling-class interests. At any given historical moment, the structures of the state—the way it is organized and operates—are being shaped by the ongoing struggle between, as well as within, dominant and dominated classes. Oppositional cultures exist as a potential if not an actual threat to all hegemonic states. At the same time, hegemonic interests seek to neutralize, manipulate, and ultimately incorporate dissent. The structuralist perspective also implies that, at least in open hegemonic societies or in societies undergoing a hegemonic crisis, passive consent is no longer enough. Those who control the state are forced to make a real attempt to bring about the active consent of those who are governed.

Instrumentalist and structuralist positions on the hegemonic state are not necessarily in opposition to each other: one focuses on how effectively the state rules in the interests of capital and the other focuses on why it does so, how it is able to do so, and with what effect. Both positions are useful in conceptualizing the role of the state in South Africa.[14]

Although scholars have generally depicted the South African state as monolithic, repressive, and all-powerful in terms of its control over the subordinate black population, in crucial areas of activity the ruling historical bloc was actually unable to implement changes in its own interests. The boundaries of state power can be discerned, for example, in the attempts that were repeatedly made to alter prevailing patterns of land use and tenure in the reserves, accelerate the commercialization of white agriculture, and proletarianize black farm workers.

While the state was relatively closed to mediation from below, it was nevertheless actively involved in developing mechanisms of ideological consensus that embraced fractions of the subordinate black as well as the dominant white population. Cape liberalism in its various forms was perhaps the best-known and longest-lasting legitimating discourse as far as the emerging African petty bourgeoisie was concerned, but independent African nationalist organizations—political, trade union, religious, educational, and agricultural—were also engaged in organizing consent. At the same time, the state sought to intervene more directly in African society to preserve and later expand the authority of urban- and rural-based collaborative structures.

Hegemonic crises would occur particularly when the existing racial order was threatened. The legitimacy of ruling power blocs was periodically compromised and sometimes even shattered, as in the armed conflict that pitted English against Afrikaner at the end of the nineteenth century; in the industrial unrest that temporarily galvanized black workers and pitted capital against white labor after World War I (especially in the so-called 1922 Rand rebellion) and again after World War II; in the reaction against apartheid that precipitated the turn to armed struggle in the early 1960s; and in periodic breakdowns of civil authority following the Soweto uprising in 1976.

The Configurations of Power and Resistance

The mechanisms that ultimately confirm or deny a given hegemonic state, then, are cultural as well as material. The configurations of power and resistance are to be found in the interrelationship between material forces and their ideological forms.

For Gramsci, ideology was "spontaneous philosophy"—the symbolic discourse of popular consciousness embedded in language itself—that sought to make sense of and come to terms with human existence. In essence, the world we live in—our culture—is expressed as ideological discourse. Inheritors of the Gramscian schema returned to the ambiguities of ideology in the postwar era, and it has now become a central issue in the field of critical cultural studies.[15]

French structuralist Louis Althusser was among the first to establish conditions for an autonomous ideology, and the reading of ideology by Stuart Hall, a lucid interpreter as well as critic of the Althusserian position, will be employed in this study:

> By ideology I mean the mental frameworks—the languages, the concepts, categories, imagery of thought, and the systems of representation—which different classes and social groups deploy in order to make sense of, define, figure out and render intelligible the way society works. [But ideology also involves] the processes by which new forms of consciousness, new conceptions of the world, arise,

which move the masses of the people into historical action against the prevailing system.[16]

Hall breaks away from the classical marxist position that the material conditions of our existence have a fundamental reality of their own—in other words, that they exist apart from the ways in which we represent these conditions to ourselves and others. He rejects the view that each social class, for example, has a distinct ideology (if not manifested, it is "false consciousness"), or that the position of a social class in the relations of production shapes, sets boundaries, or otherwise gives expression to its own ideology.

But Hall also apparently stops short of postmarxist positions that assume there are no conditions of being apart from the ways in which we experience these conditions. For cultural theorists who adopt this point of view, social reality has no fixed meanings. Thus ideology, for example, has limited explanatory power because it is used mainly in a pejorative sense with reference to the language of the ruling class.[17]

Hall occupies a middle position in this debate. Class relations in capitalist formations—and I shall argue that this perspective is also applicable to precapitalist formations—exist as an objective reality "independent of mind, independent of thought," but "they can only be conceptualized in thought, in the head," as an ideological representation.[18]

Ideologies are revealed in the language of personal discourse ("signifying practices") and inscribed in the language of public discourse ("social practices"). Numerous ideologies are present in a hegemonic culture, and these discourses compete with and borrow from each other in the struggle to confer meaning on human experience. The ideologies of a dominant class struggle to represent and hopefully secure a hegemonic culture, but a ruling bloc cannot guarantee ideological consensus:

> a variety of different ideological systems . . . are available in any social formation. The notion of *the* dominant ideology and *the* subordinated ideology is an inadequate way of representing the complex interplay of different ideological discourses. . . . They contest one another, often drawing on a common, shared repertoire of concepts.

Hall maintains that while our experiences can be represented in a variety of ways, all lived experiences are ideological representations:

> It is not possible to bring ideology to an end and simply live the real. . . . when we contrast ideology to experience, or illusion to authentic truth, we are failing to recognize that there is no way of experiencing the "real relations" of a particular society outside of its cultural and ideological categories.

Language itself—"the medium of thought and ideological calculation"— is the arena of struggle, a "war of position" (following Gramsci) between ideological referents that may uphold or deny a given cultural order.[19] In the process, individuals and communities consume and interpolate fragments of numerous ideologies in the ongoing process of trying to make sense of the world to themselves and to others.

Ideological discourses are formed initially in infancy and centered in the family,[20] but the relationship between ideology and social class is not predetermined. The power to consign meaning to our lived experiences is realized only through ideological struggle, but these signifying practices and their accompanying social practices are necessarily pragmatic, ambiguous, and even contradictory. There are preferred meanings in ideological discourse, but no ideological meaning is immutable.

The lived experiences of the African population in South Africa provide considerable support for this position. The racial, ethnic, gender, and religious experiences of the mass of the people, for example, were influenced but not predetermined by their relationship to the changing mode of capitalist production. The cultural mechanisms that structured consent, moreover, did not guarantee consent. While Cape liberalism was a dominant ideological discourse for the African petty bourgeoisie between the 1880s and the 1930s, the political activities of these elites cannot be interpreted simply as a prolonged reformist attempt to gain entry into white middle-class society. While the state made a concerted attempt to develop mechanisms of ideological consensus that would embrace the majority population in the 1970s and 1980s, the struggle to secure a hegemonic cultural order split the ruling power bloc and created new opportunities for the expression of counterhegemonic dissent.

Dominating and accommodating ideologies have been continually contested by ideologies of resistance in South Africa. Africans denied the world they were forced to live in even while they confirmed it, and these negotiated ideologies were concretized in social practices that at some level challenged the racial order. Resistance, moreover, occurred outside as well as inside the fabric of organized African politics, and it was expressed in the protocols, etiquettes, rituals, ceremonies, festivals, and other routines of everyday life.

This study is concerned almost exclusively with resistance as a community experience, but one cannot ignore discursive approaches that conceive of the power struggle as a personal experience. Resistance is positioned in individual daily practices: the struggle for power is centered in the struggle for control of the physical body, the primary system of organization.[21]

The classic expression of resistance at the personal level in rural eastern Cape was the cleavage between Red (*amaqaba*) and School (*amagqoboka*) folk cultures.[22] A division between those who came to be identified with the literate Christian community and those who sought a strategy for survival that was actively antagonistic to modernization had existed in embryo from the earliest period of contact with the mission enterprise. It had solidified during the

Cape-Xhosa wars—especially in the cattle-killing event—and in the policies pursued by various colonial administrators. It was maintained when the School community emerged as a political and ideological force in African society in the 1880s and 1890s. As the limited options open to School people became more limited, the Red community became more unyielding to change. Resistance to the School tradition, which for Reds was a symbol of dependence on a culture dominated by whites, seemed to be endemic in the eastern Cape by the early 1900s.

Social anthropologists Monica Hunter, David Hammond-Tooke, Bonnie Keller, and Philip Mayer, among others, have commented at length on the persistence of this phenomenon in the region.[23] The cleavages between School and Red ideologies were polarized in the everyday discourse of white observers and of Africans associated with both cultures. Red and School homesteads in the rural areas were perceived to represent distinct and antagonistic lifestyles— in speech and mannerisms, in dress, food, housing and furniture, and in vocational status. It was assumed that Reds would not convert to Christianity, go to church, or attend school. As poverty levels deepened, Red communities clung more tenaciously to their traditionalist values. They adhered to chiefly authority figures even in the Ciskei where the chiefship had been all but destroyed. As peasants, they refused to accept individual tenure, and they would not comply with restrictions placed on them by government officials seeking to halt the deterioriation of land in the reserves.

The Red-School dichotomy, however, has recently been under fire.[24] Critics have suggested that these divisions were not mutually exclusive. Cultural differences between the two communities in the nineteenth century, moreover, were perceived as ethnic differences by many contemporary observers. Mfengu in the Ciskei were often associated with the "progressive" School community, while Xhosa were perceived as "primitive" Reds. As the Christian community became more diverse, these ethnic associations fell away.

Poverty was the crucial factor that obviated cultural distinctions in the region. Large numbers of Christians, with little or no land and virtually no formal education, were often more alienated from the mission-educated elites than the Reds. While individuals did perceive themselves as belonging to the Red and School communities, they also collaborated against the governing authorities in attempting to redress mutual grievances. The Reds did not remain silent as a conquered people. They lived a privatized existence—generally removed from public scrutiny—but resistance continued, as we shall see, at various levels in the century after the conquest.[25]

In essence, the Red-School division was only one among many other divisions segmenting the rural population in the eastern Cape. The peasantry as a whole constituted a proletarian class in the making, but there were numerous gradations between semicommercial farmers and agricultural workers who didn't have access to land, between migrant laborers in town and tenants on white farms, between urbanites with few ties and urbanites with firm ties to the reserves. Women in School as well as Red communities, moreover, collectively formed an increasingly exploited fraction of the peasant population.

The focus on ideological discourse ultimately has important implications for conceptualizing resistance. The signifying systems that sanctioned obedience were also sites of struggle. The historian, however, must deconstruct these systems in order to locate the inchoate voices that sought to free the African from the domain of South Africa's ruling culture.

The story of the Ciskei begins with the peoples who inhabited southern Africa before the Europeans arrived. Chapter 1 offers a typology of hunting, herding, and farming societies occupying the landscape during a period that scholars have divided rather arbitrarily into a Later Stone Age, an Early Iron Age, and a Later Iron Age. The focus of the chapter is on the peoples who inhabited the Ciskei region during the period associated with the Later Iron Age.

Chapter 2 begins with the era of European conquest, which many culturally insensitive scholars—in homage to the veracity of the written word—still refer to as the beginning of the historical period. The Ciskei region formed part of a vast frontier of converging European and African populations that stretched roughly eight hundred miles along the Indian Ocean from the southwestern Cape to the eastern Cape as far as the Mbashe River in what was to become the Transkei (meaning across the Kei River or on the other side of the river from Cape Town), and inland to various mountain ranges and semidesert plateaus stretching to the Orange River. The populations that inhabited this area are placed in the context of two unfolding frontier zones located in the Cape coastal lowlands during the eighteenth and nineteenth centuries. The focus of this chapter is on the activities of the Xhosa chiefdoms in the Ciskei frontier zone.

The next four chapters examine the African reaction and response to the dominant European political, economic, and cultural forces at work in Cape colonial society. Chapter 3 focuses on the economic manifestations of colonial rule in the Ciskei region as the precapitalist mode of homestead production broke down, fractions of the peasantry struggled to gain access to commercial markets, and capitalist South Africa gradually shifted from a mercantile to a mining economy. The chapter ends with an attempt to describe and periodize the process of proletarianization in the Ciskei region during the colonial period.

Chapter 4 describes the religious and educational manifestations of colonial rule as embodied in the mission enterprise. Chapter 5 chronicles the role that African Christian modernizers played in settler politics, and it highlights African attempts in the 1880s and 1890s to mobilize public opinion and develop indigenous political organizations that were essentially independent of settler control. The beginnings of African nationalism at the Cape are considered in Chapter 6. Particular attention is paid to the involvement of Ciskeian political, educational, and religious bodies in the events leading to the creation of South Africa in 1910, to the founding of the South African Native National Congress in 1912, to the campaign to establish an African university, and to the creation of the first African independent churches.

The dominant themes in this book are taken up again in Chapter 7, which focuses on the political economy of the truncated Ciskei reserve—the most underdeveloped area in South Africa—from the formation of the Union of South Africa in 1910 to the apartheid era. Chapters 8 and 9 are concerned with African politics and popular resistance in the Ciskei and South Africa between 1910 and the banning of the main opposition groups in 1960. African politics was the preserve of an expanding petty bourgeoisie—a largely mission-educated elite whose stronghold was increasingly in the urban areas and outside the eastern Cape and southern Natal, where the first African political groups were established. Peasants and industrial workers with roots in modern as well as premodern cultures played only a marginal role in organized politics until the 1940s and 1950s, when a gradual shift from petitionary protest to various forms of nonviolent resistance became evident in African nationalist politics. The struggles of the working poor before the 1940s are recorded in the activities of certain trade unions, millenarian churches, and community action groups.

Chapter 10 examines the struggle for control over African labor in the apartheid era. The South African state attempted to reorganize the labor control system and intervene decisively in the peripheral reserves in the 1950s and 1960s. The decentralization of this system in the 1970s was accompanied by renewed attempts to win African support for the existing social order. The Ciskei was a focal point of concern as it evolved from a fragmented reserve to a so-called national state in December 1981.

Chapter 11 offers a final evaluation of the Ciskei as a case study in the manifestations of power and resistance in South Africa. It ends with a brief summary of events that foreshadowed the close of the apartheid era.

Part 1
From Independence to Conquest

1
The Precolonial Past

In the Ciskei, as elsewhere in southern Africa, the precolonial populations have been traditionally divided into three groups—hunters, herders, and farmers—and distinguished primarily by physical type, language, and material culture. The occupation of southern Africa by herders and farmers, however, has been pushed back more than a millennium in the past twenty years, and contemporary scholars have demonstrated that the criteria separating these groups are relative rather than absolute. The terms conventionally used to divide these communities in space and time have become less tenable as more and more evidence suggests intensive interaction at all three levels.

This chapter briefly examines the precolonial hunting, herding, and farming populations in southern Africa before narrowing the focus of inquiry to the eastern Cape region.

Section 1.1 describes the hunting and herding groups traditionally associated with the Later Stone Age in southern Africa.

Section 1.2 offers a critical analysis of farming groups during the period traditionally associated with the Iron Age in southern Africa.

Section 1.3 considers the implications of this analysis for the Xhosa and their neighbors in the eastern Cape.

1.1. Khoisan Hunters and Herders

Most specialists concerned with the precolonial history of southern Africa assume that Stone Age hunting and foraging groups had occupied the whole of the subcontinent by 8000 B.C. at the latest.[1] During the last glacial epoch, however, portions of the northern interior were even drier than they are today, while portions of the coastline were drowned with the rise in the sea level. Some areas were apparently depopulated. Existing populations retreated to areas where the environment was more hospitable, and they achieved a relatively advanced material culture based on the manufacture of stone tools and weapons.

Hunting and foraging groups associated with the Later Stone Age will be identified as San rather than Bushman, a colonial term that has pejorative connotations.[2] As indicated by skeletal remains and as recorded by early European observers, the San were small—the men rarely above five feet in height and the women several inches shorter—with relatively long slender arms and legs and small hands and feet in relation to their body size. Their skin color was yellowish brown, and they had little body hair except for the hair on their head. Their faces were triangular in shape with high cheekbones and frequently oriental eyefolds. *Steatopygia* (pronounced buttocks) was a feature among the women.

They were organized in minimal groups or bands—usually several family households related by blood or marriage—and they occupied specific territories and spoke numerous distinct languages based on four consonantal "click" sounds. Social anthropologists suggest that a hunter band today has to have at least ten persons actively hunting and gathering food if it is to remain independent of other bands. There is a division of labor, but neither men nor women are accorded higher status. Men do all the hunting, women do most of the gathering and contribute up to two-thirds of the food. Hunting and foraging for twenty hours a week provides enough food to feed the band; families consume the food they gather, but products of the hunt are shared equally among band members.

While all bands have leaders, they are only marginally more important than other family members. What power they have, moreover, cannot be inherited by others. Some scholars believe there were language-related minimum and maximum bands. Minimum bands may have comprised up to twenty-five people, while maximum bands may have comprised up to five hundred people. Maximum bands would have been formed irregularly for religious or ritual purposes, to exchange technology and seek marriage partners, and perhaps more often during crises when more labor was needed to gather food.

San hunters used a variety of materials—wood, ivory, shell, bone, plant fibers, animal skins, and clay as well as several types of stone—in fashioning the artifacts of their culture. They were also capable of modifying the natural landscape to a minor extent to obtain food and improve living conditions: this is evidenced by pits that have been found especially in the interior, by artificial tidal pools along the South African coast and small rock dams formed in the rivers, and by the alteration of cave dwellings.

While they lived in a relatively rich plant and animal environment, the territories they inhabited were by no means uniform. Hunters in the drier grassland plateau regions of the interior were nomadic; they generally lived in open settlements near water, and they probably depended more on foraging than on hunting. Hunters in wetter coastal regions had a greater variety of resources, adopted more sedentary lifestyles, and with their counterparts in mountainous areas apparently used caves and rock shelters more frequently. They shifted between fixed sites or occupied one site more or less permanently with seasonal departures by members of the band. Coastal populations adapting to a marine environment also had a more predictable food supply that was high in calories and proteins.

Migrational patterns conformed to the requirements of the band as it followed various animal herds, encountered unexpected climatic changes, or moved with the seasons. San groups along the Atlantic Ocean in the western Cape, for example, are known to have migrated between the coast and the upland interior for centuries. The extent of land occupied by a single band was dictated by the availability of food and water, but in times of necessity or in the pursuance of some desirable object there was undoubtedly movement beyond specified territories. Hunters who moved frequently—as did those in the drier plateau regions—apparently had fewer possessions and practiced more severe methods of birth control (including infanticide). The San population during the Later Stone Age is unknown, but it must have been low in terms of what the land could bear because the evidence suggests that these communities had achieved a pretty successful lifestyle in response to their environment.

Some scholars now believe San groups in southern Africa acquired domesticated stock from agropastoralists in central Africa, and a click language servicing a pastoral economy spread to the region north of the Cunene-Okavango–Upper Zambezi river systems between 2,000 and 2,500 years ago. Herders began to penetrate southern Africa's relatively arid western zone (comprising what is today Namibia, Botswana, and South Africa's Cape Province), punctuated by the Namib and Kalahari deserts, between about 200 B.C. and 400 A.D.—in other words, several centuries before the beginnings of farming in the subcontinent. While rainfall in most areas today is considerably less than twenty inches a year, there is evidence that in Botswana at least it was higher (as much as three times higher in some areas) and the grasslands more extensive between 1,500 and 2,500 years ago.

The archeological and linguistic evidence suggests that pastoral communities moved in a southerly direction from a dispersal center in northern Botswana. Herders from northern Botswana and western Zimbabwe had occupied all the grassland areas of the western zone by 1000 A.D. The main routes seem to have been along the western and eastern margins of the Kalahari basin and through the pan, lake, and river systems and permanent springs in the wetter grassland areas (Map 1). Pastoralists who made and used pottery were in the coastal and inland grazing areas of the Ciskei region, for example, by the eleventh century at the latest.

The pastoralists called themselves Khoikhoi ("men of men" or "the genuine people"), which again is preferable to the pejorative colonial term Hottentot. Herders could be distinguished physically from hunters—presumably because their regular diet included milk and meat obtained from domesticated

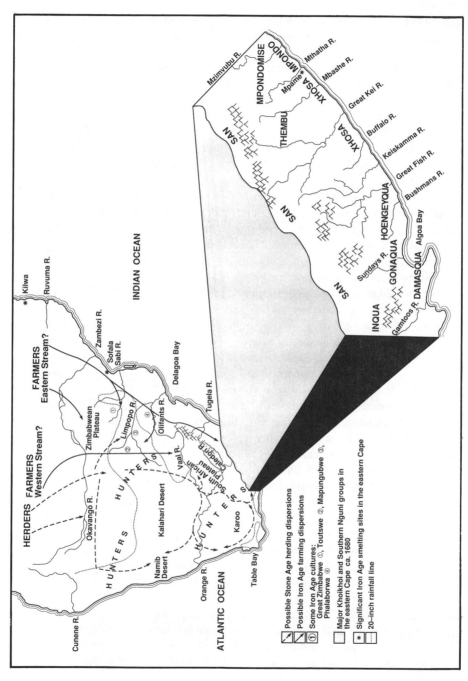

Map 1. Hunters, herders, and farmers in the Eastern Cape and Southern Africa before the European colonial epoch.

Possible Stone Age herding dispersions

Possible Iron Age farming dispersions

Some Iron Age cultures:
Great Zimbabwe ①, Toutswe ②, Mapungubwe ③,
Phalaborwa ④

Major Khoikhoi and Southern Nguni groups in
the eastern Cape ca. 1680

Significant Iron Age smelting sites in the eastern Cape

20-inch rainfall line

stock—but in many respects the two groups shared a common lifestyle. In pastoralist groups, family involvement in activities other than herding remained much the same. The two groups had similar views about their universe, and they adopted the same religious rites and healing rituals using the same types of medicine men. When the pastoralists arrived, however, there was a marked decline in stone tool technology. Both groups are referred to collectively as the Khoisan.

The Khoikhoi, then, were hunters and foragers who domesticated stock—probably sheep, goats, and dogs initially—and also became skilled in the making of charcoal-tempered pottery. All herders spoke recognizably the same language and understood one another, whereas hunter languages were limited to specific territories and were usually distinct from one another. Individual families owned their domesticated animals and related possessions and did not share their goods to the same extent as the San. They also lived a more settled existence than the hunters: they were organized in larger settlements (up to two hundred people), and they possessed more complex social units. Men controlled the livestock, which was their principal source of wealth, and they ranked higher than women.

While the hunters of southern Africa's western zone were in contact with herders for thousands of years, it seems probable that the transition to a pastoral culture was no easy task. Khoikhoi social practices, for example, encouraged the acquisition of personal wealth and competition for livestock and grazing rights, whereas the San slaughtered animals for food and shared the meat with all members of the community. Thus it would have been difficult for hunters to maintain enough sheep or cattle to become independent producers.

The levels of contact between Cape hunters and herders as revealed in early colonial texts ranged from open warfare to various forms of political, economic, and cultural interaction. Civil strife seems to have been rare among the San, although they fiercely defended their territories against outsiders. Khoikhoi herding groups on the other hand fought each other as well as the San and gradually forced the hunters out of grassland areas suitable for pastoralism. The San in response raided Khoikhoi sheep and cattle, but they also helped procure food for the Khoikhoi (staples would have included wild honey, roots, fruit, vegetables, and especially meat) as well as the animal skins favored by Khoikhoi leaders. In return, the herders offered milk, mutton and probably beef, and eventually beads, tobacco, and iron acquired in part from trade with the whites.

The herders used the same weapons and tools as the hunters—bows and arrows, spears, fishing equipment, snares, traps, and digging sticks for gathering roots and bulbs—but they clearly perceived themselves to be superior. They possessed livestock, wore clothing made of dressed sheepskin, and greased their bodies as evidence of their riches. Intermarriage, moreover, apparently took place primarily between Khoikhoi men and San women. San men were usually absorbed as subordinate clients and employed, for example, as hunters, guards, trackers, spies, and messengers. In time, they would be elevated to herders, soldiers, and even envoys and become full-fledged members of Khoikhoi communities.

Khoikhoi polities were patrilineal—social relationships were derived through the male line—and the primary unit of organization was the lineage-based clan that could vary in size and complexity from a single extended family to an elaborate cluster of related kinship groups. Every person belonged to a lineage—a family tree, in essence, with a forefather presumed to be common to all who were members of the lineage—and several lineages claiming descent through a common male ancestor composed a clan. There were dominant and subordinate clans and loose federations of clans that resembled chiefdoms. But the clan heads—they were called captains during the colonial period—constituted the leadership cadre. The eldest son of a chief could normally expect to inherit the chiefship, but the chiefdoms themselves were fragile. Among the Cape Khoikhoi, they may have split at regular intervals since most chiefs had confidants who were virtually equal to them in rank.

Individual clans had considerable autonomy, and the chief was effectively under the jurisdiction of a council comprising the heads of individual clans. Since wealth was measured in personal terms, chiefdoms were continually fluctuating as individuals gained or lost livestock. Khoikhoi chiefs often had more than one wife, but it was rare among commoners. There is some doubt as to whether any chiefship was strong enough to survive during periods of even moderate hardship.

Herders had apparently displaced hunters as the dominant population group in the southwestern Cape when the first permanent European settlement was established in the region in the last half of the seventeenth century. Whites recording the settlement patterns of the Khoisan found that the herders generally occupied the well-watered coastal grazing areas and river valleys, and the hunters had retreated to the more mountainous interior. Nevertheless, hunters also inhabited the river valleys and were fishing and shell collecting along the Cape coast. While Khoikhoi apparently did not depend as much on seafood as the coastal San did, they continued to exploit the natural environment as hunters and foragers.

1.2. Bantu-speaking Farmers during the Iron Age

Farming groups began to settle in southern Africa's eastern zone (embracing Zimbabwe, Mozambique, and eastern South Africa, including Lesotho and Swaziland) perhaps two hundred to four hundred years after some hunting groups in southern Africa's western zone had begun to shift to a pastoral way of life.[3] They are associated with the Iron Age, and until recently most scholars have accepted the hypothesis that they were immigrants who could be distinguished from the Khoisan in terms of physical traits, languages, and material cultures.

They were perceived as racially distinct, and in contrast to Stone Age hunters and herders they cultivated the soil and grew a variety of domesticated plants. Unlike the Khoisan, they knew how to smelt and forge iron and other metals or had access to metal tools and weapons. The languages they spoke stemmed from a different parent family than the languages spoken by hunters and herders, and they possessed more complex sociopolitical organizations. They also kept domesticated stock, made and used ceramic pottery to store, cook, and serve their food, and lived in permanent settlements.

This Iron Age package has been under attack, however, by a new generation of physical anthropologists, archeologists, linguists, and historians. The conventional view that "negroid" peoples from the north moved into southern Africa and absorbed or displaced nonnegroid hunters and herders, for example, has been virtually abandoned. Distinctions between population groups based on physical appearance have been rendered obsolete as scientists have gained greater insight into the complexity of the human genetic structure. Race is now perceived as a social rather than a physical category, one's racial identity being determined by one's culture. Arbitrary racial characteristics like skin color, hair texture, facial structure, or alleged cranial capacity—which according to one study account for only 10 percent of human differences— have been replaced by the concept of gene pools, breeding populations, and the geographical distribution of specific genetic traits.

All African ethnic groups in southern Africa today have a number of genetic elements in common with each other. Although the Khoisan were apparently isolated from other groups for long periods of time during the Later Stone Age, they still share major genetic traits with other breeding populations in the subcontinent. Questions relating to physical differences between the various African population groups cannot be resolved because not enough skeletal remains have been recovered to determine the potential significance of physical type in the migration of peoples into southern Africa during the Iron Age.[4]

Scholars seem to agree only on the evidence that the African peoples of southern, central, and eastern Africa today share a common ancestral language that apparently originated in the region of southeastern Nigeria and southern Cameroon on the western margins of the equatorial rain forest. They have christened the languages spoken throughout the area as Bantu (meaning People) languages. After a long period of gestation, Bantu-speaking Africans adopted farming and spread rapidly in an easterly and southerly direction. (Experts estimate that sorghum-based crop farmers facing relatively poor climatic and soil conditions in Africa advanced cultivation perhaps five kilometers a year, whereas wheat- and barley-based crop farmers in Europe advanced about one kilometer a year).

There is no agreement on the routes favored by Bantu speakers across sub-Saharan Africa or when the migrations took place, on the physical appearance of these immigrants, on where and when they acquired the rudiments of an Iron Age culture, on how Iron Age technologies were acquired and whether they came as a package, on the possibility that pastoralists and cultivators were present in central Africa centuries before the arrival of Bantu-speaking communities, or even on the necessity for assuming that the coming of the Iron Age to sub-Saharan Africa was conditioned by significant migrations of existing population groups. Nevertheless, the expansion of herding and farming populations south of the equator seems to have occurred fairly rapidly.

Bantu-speaking Iron Age groups were moving into areas suitable for cultivation in southern Africa by the beginning of the Christian era (Map 1). Scholars assume that they settled mainly in the subcontinent's eastern zone, where the rainfall pattern is above twenty inches a year in most areas and enough rain falls in the summer to support subtropical Iron Age crops. Iron Age peoples crossed the Zambezi River and occupied parts of present-day Zimbabwe between ca. 100 A.D. and ca. 300 A.D., and they crossed the Limpopo River into present-day South Africa about 200 A.D. Within two hundred years or so, there were numerous Iron Age settlements in what is today the South African province of the Transvaal.

Khoisan hunters and herders apparently continued to dominate southern Africa's western zone, where the climate was generally unsuitable for agriculturalists except along the coast. Rainfall was sufficient in coastal areas of the southwestern Cape, but the dry summer months would not sustain sorghum and millet, the main Iron Age cereal plants.

Subsistence Production Systems

Early Iron Age farming communities tended to avoid the drier plateau regions and settle in low-lying areas and especially in river valleys where there was more rain, more wood, and the soil was more fertile. Indeed, in eastern South Africa the lush coastal lowland between the Drakensberg and the sea (with its dependable supply of fish and shell food) was apparently favored over the interior plateau. Iron Age farmers had already spread south into what is now the province of Natal by 300 A.D. The southwestern extremity of the eastern zone—the coastal lowlands of the eastern Cape—was occupied by ca. 600 A.D. east of the Kei River.[5] In essence, Bantu speakers had populated most of the areas suitable for tropical agriculture well before the traditional close of the Early Iron Age in southern Africa in ca. 1000 A.D.

Farming populations increased rapidly in relation to existing hunting and herding populations. Subsistence farming provided a better and more reliable supply of food, and shifting agricultural economies—new fields were cleared every four or five years—led to a more thorough exploitation of the natural environment. Subsistence farming was also a labor-intensive enterprise: many workers were required to clear the woodlands that initially covered most of the lowland eastern zone as well as sow, weed, protect, and harvest crops. As the forest cover was removed, more land was made available for grazing, and the cultivators were given an opportunity to diversify production. Small stock like sheep and goats along with hunting, fishing, and shellfish collecting initially supplemented cereal cultivation. Surpluses would have been possible if some groups had gained unequal access to land and labor, but there is no evidence to suggest disparities in food production among these small-scale agropastoralists.

Iron Age communities in southern Africa were mainly patrilineal, and male polygamy was practiced. There was a pronounced division of labor: females cultivated the fields and foraged while males tended the stock and hunted. The farmers possessed the tools to exploit their environment, including iron hoes and axes as well as stones for grinding grain, and built relatively substantial dwellings. Houses were generally round with thatched roofs attached to a central pole; floors were made with daga (a mixture of water, dung, and mud or sand); and branches stuffed with grass formed a scaffolding for the walls that were then plastered with daga. In some areas, the farmers adopted Khoikhoi techniques: saplings were placed in the ground in a circle and bent to meet in the center where they were tied together and then covered with woven reed mats. Small villages—often situated on the ridges of hills for protection— would consist of several huts constructed in a circular pattern with stock and grain-storage facilities enclosed in the center.

The dominance of these agropastoralists over existing populations in southern Africa's eastern zone was certainly established gradually. Low population density, a limited technology, and abundant space between areas occupied by various population groups would have been factors in limiting competition and conflict. It is also believed that the hunter population in eastern South Africa was relatively sparse in the millennium preceding the Iron Age, and except for a few rock paintings depicting sheep in western Zimbabwe there is no evidence that herders actually competed for livestock and grazing land with Bantu-speaking agropastoralists during the Early Iron Age.

Scholars can only speculate about the extent of economic interaction between the various population groups inhabiting southern Africa at this time. Hunters apparently maintained a separate existence in semidesert regions, mountainous areas, tsetse-fly-infested swamps, coastal forests, and estuaries that were inhospitable to herders and farmers, but Iron Age sites have been found alongside Stone Age sites in Namibia, for example, dating from ca. 600 A.D. and in Botswana dating from ca. 400 A.D.

Opportunities to accumulate wealth in either individual or group terms

were limited in the subsistence hunting, herding, and farming household production systems associated with the Later Stone Age and Early Iron Age. New
food sources, more permanent settlements, or even new technologies did not
really alter existing social relations. These communities were obliged to maintain a network of reciprocal relationships that would ensure survival, so work
was apparently shared and goods were distributed equally. Evidence of specific
sharing practices has been perceived in the rock paintings and engravings that
make southern Africa one of the world's great treasure houses of precolonial
art. The similarity in designs and decorations on ceramic ware from Mozambique to the eastern Cape during the first thousand years or so of the Iron Age
may also be a sign of the reciprocal obligations so essential to the preservation
of these cultures.[6]

Surplus Production Systems

The Iron Age in South Africa is traditionally divided into two epochs—an
Early Iron Age that ends about 1000 A.D. and a Later Iron Age that ends
somewhat arbitrarily between the beginnings of European colonial penetration
into areas occupied by Bantu speakers toward the end of the eighteenth century
and the mineral revolution in the last three decades of the nineteenth century.

Until recently it was hypothesized that new Iron Age groups moved into
southern Africa's eastern zone and eventually supplanted their predecessors as
well as the remaining Stone Age peoples. These assumptions were based in
part on what appeared to be a distinct break in Iron Age ceramic traditions, in
part on what appeared to be a major increase in surplus cattle-keeping communities after 1000 A.D., and in part on the oral genealogies of Bantu-speaking
populations today that don't go back much earlier than the fifteenth or sixteenth
centuries.

As scholars have gained greater insight into the dynamics of change in
precolonial Africa, however, the assumptions that traditionally guided research
have been increasingly difficult to maintain. Hunting, herding, and farming
technologies associated with the Stone Age and Iron Age were not mutually
exclusive. Hunters made use of cattle and iron as well as food grown by
farmers, and farmers made use of hunting and building practices associated
with Khoisan communities. Stone Age herders made pottery, and Stone Age
hunters made use of pottery. The degree of similarity between Bantu language groups in southern Africa today, moreover, would suggest that linguistic
evidence to support new waves of migrants after 1000 A.D. is lacking.

The break in ceramic tradition that appears to have taken place in southern
Africa's eastern zone between the Early and Later Iron Age apparently did
not take place in areas like eastern Botswana or elsewhere among the herding
communities of the western zone. Women were responsible for making pottery
in African households by the colonial period, and some scholars speculate the

distinction could have come about if women had replaced men as the principal potters sometime during the precolonial period. In parts of central Africa where men are still responsible for ceramic production, there have been no major changes in pottery making and decorating since the beginning of the Iron Age.

There were also no distinctions between the Early and Later Iron Ages in other areas of production. Mining intensified and there were some refinements in existing techniques, but basic metal smelting and forging technologies did not change. Cultivators continued to rely on iron hoes and axes, and when iron was not available they continued to use stone axes and hoes and wooden digging sticks. Grain storage facilities remained virtually the same in design and effectiveness, whether they were bins raised above the ground on stones or wooden poles (as in parts of the interior plateau) or pits constructed below the ground (as in the coastal areas).

The types of food cultivated would not change significantly until the colonial era. Farmers in Zimbabwe, for example, did adopt imported crops like bananas from southeast Asia (as early as the tenth century), Asian rice and American maize (from the sixteenth century), wheat and even vegetables like potatoes (cultivated in Jesuit estates in the lower Zambezi valley region during the seventeenth and early eighteenth centuries). But original Iron Age crops like sorghum and millet remained the main food crops until the early twentieth century except in southeastern Africa, where maize (which offers a higher yield and does not require as much labor as sorghum or millet) gradually became dominant from the eighteenth century.

The crucial economic and political changes observed in the Later Iron Age, comprising (1) a shift in emphasis from cereal cultivation to cattle keeping and a parallel dispersion of peoples from lowland cultivating areas to upland grazing areas, (2) increases in population and trade and increased occupational specialization, and (3) the development of more powerful polities (stratified clan lineages, chiefdoms, and ultimately various kinds of centralized states), are now believed to have been well under way before the end of the first millennium.

Critical scholars today are challenging models that assume it is possible or even meaningful to distinguish between Iron Age societies or between the Later Stone Age and the Iron Age. In place of these arbitrary divisions, they are offering a new paradigm that focuses on the processes of production and exchange and on how power was naturalized in the material cultures of these precapitalist formations. Archeologist Martin Hall, among others, argues that there were two transformations in the mode of production during the precolonial era. All societies in southern Africa were eventually influenced by these transformations, although they did not experience them in the same way, to the same degree, or at the same time.

The first transformation came about when existing subsistance economies in southern Africa's western and eastern zones shifted to cattle keeping and surplus production, and lowland communities began moving into the drier plateau grassland regions. For example, cattle-keeping sites in eastern Botswana's upper Limpopo River valley date from 500 A.D. and in parts of the Cape from 600 A.D. Cattle raising did not require as much labor as crop farming. Stock farmers could accumlate wealth if they concentrated on cattle, where the surplus was measured in terms of the number of beasts they owned. Thus surplus cattle became the new symbols signifying power relations during the Later Iron Age. They served three major needs: as a source of food, as a bridal dowry, and as loan capital.

While Bantu-speaking cultivators continued to obtain most of their food from cereal crops, and hunting, foraging, fishing, and shell collecting were still important, milk products played an increasingly significant role in their diet. The more cattle one had, the more possible it was to have milk all year round. Thus cattle became much more valuable as dairy herds than they were as a source of meat. Bride price was normally paid in cattle so that the more cattle one had the more wives one could possess. Men had as many wives as they could afford to increase the size of their families and hence the potential labor force. Men who were temporarily impoverished or were seeking wives and lacked the requisite bride price (young men seeking cattle for marriage purposes were usually dependent on older men who had cattle) might herd the cattle of a wealthy patron in return for stock. Those who had lost their herds might acquire cattle on loan and thereby receive a portion of the milk and the calves born thereafter.

Surplus cattle production in the western and eastern zones of South Africa in the Later Iron Age was accompanied by increasing fragmentation as well as stratification within the lineage-based clans, the building blocks of African society. Dominant lineages under leaders who inherited their power base emerged, and there was a gradual expansion of the territories occupied by these lineages. This transformation occurred between about 700 and 1200 A.D.

The key political-cum-territorial unit in the development of these surplus cattle-keeping economies was the chiefdom.[7] Although its origins are unknown, the chiefship in Bantu-speaking communities was rooted in patrilineal clan lineages that bore at least some resemblance to the clan lineages of the Khoikhoi herders. The chiefship was derived from a dominant lineage claiming precedence over other lineages in what would constitute the royal clan. The subordinated lineages in the royal clan claimed descent from the royal line even when they could not demonstrate a genealogical relationship. Commoner clans with their own distinct lineages occupying territory claimed by the royal clan could also be absorbed as full members of the chiefdom. Thus the chiefdom comprised a royal clan (with a royal lineage and a number of other lineages aligned with the royal family) and various commoner clans (with lineages that were not linked to the royal descent line).

Bantu-speaking as well as Khoikhoi chiefs were restricted by numerous checks and balances, and the chiefdoms themselves were unstable. A host of factors, as we shall see, caused these political units to expand, contract, and split apart at irregular intervals as leaders and rivals gained or lost followers. Wealth was measured in terms of cattle, which the senior members of the royal lineage tried to control, but the commoners also had access to this commodity and therefore could place considerable constraints on the central authority.

The second transformation occurred when a significant proportion of surplus goods and services was formally directed to and retained by a distinct ruling class. Their power base was expanded and made permanent by exacting various forms of tribute from their increasingly powerless subjects. Trade may well have been essential to this process. Hall suggests that the shift from a lineage to a tributary mode of production and power came about in part because the ruling class gained control over goods that had little use value and could not be procured as easily as cattle. The obvious source of wealth was luxury goods that could be obtained only through regional or interregional trading or through control over a specialized labor force producing these commodities.

The accumulation of wealth and power in the hands of the few was also enhanced by pressure from European mercantile capitalists beginning with the Portuguese in the sixteenth century. Powerlessness would be expressed in a variety of forms with the rise of city-states and kingdoms in various parts of southern Africa during the Later Iron Age: independent chiefs became tributaries to kings, and their followers were removed from the land, forced into servile labor, or conscripted into slave armies. This transformation led to the emergence of centralized states in various parts of southern Africa. It was apparently initiated in the Limpopo River valley between the tenth and twelfth centuries—in other words, before the first stage of European colonialism—and it was brought to an end in the early twentieth century when the Europeans gained hegemony over the whole of the subcontinent.

The earliest known centralized states were located along the upper and lower reaches of the Limpopo River system at clusters of sites designated as Toutswe and Mapungubwe, respectively (Map 1). Mapungubwe apparently played a key role in the movement of goods between the interior and the coast during this period, and it may have been the first region in southern Africa to be absorbed into the Indian Ocean trade network. The city-states or kingdoms of the Toutswe declined rapidly after ca. 1250 A.D. for reasons that were probably related to overgrazing, drought, or possibly a change in climate, and these sites were abandoned about 1300 A.D. Similar environmental factors may have contributed to the decline of Mapungubwe, but apparently trading networks also shifted north to take advantage of the expanding gold market in

Zimbabwe. The spread of cattle-keeping communities across Zimbabwe and the South Africa plateau may well have been augmented by refugees from these dying states along the Limpopo River.

Gold and other metals helped finance Zimbabwe's long-distance trade in luxury goods with the outside world. Regional and interregional exchange networks linked the ancestors of the Shona to other peoples in the interior of central and eastern Africa, and from about the fourteenth century to trading cities like Kilwa and Sofala (Map 1) along the Indian Ocean coast.[8] The Portuguese apparently became dominant intermediaries in the external trade soon after they arrived early in the sixteenth century. Long-distance commerce helped sustain the wealth and power of the centralized states of Zimbabwe during the Later Iron Age, centering on Great Zimbabwe (ca. 1250–ca. 1450) (Map 1), Torwa (ca. 1450–ca. 1650), and Changamire (ca. 1680–ca. 1840) in the southern plateau and Mutapa (ca. 1450–ca. 1880) in the northern plateau.[9]

Iron Age stock farmers in South Africa initially occupied the Transvaal plateau—known locally as the highveld—about 700 A.D., but apparently they did not move across the Vaal River into the southern highveld in what is now the Orange Free State until about 1400 A.D. Cattle keepers then dispersed south and east into the foothills of the Drakensberg in Lesotho and the eastern Transvaal, where they were absorbing or displacing surviving bands of hunters and foragers by the sixteenth century.

The shift to surplus cattle production and the development of more centralized polities must have contributed considerably to the breakdown of those reciprocal relations that had previously bound individuals, families, and villages together. Variations in the design and decoration of pottery are associated with the growing importance of cattle, and they begin to appear in Iron Age sites in the eastern Transvaal and in Natal's Tugela River basin, for example, by 900 A.D.

The shift to surplus cattle production was accompanied by a marked change in the spatial environment—especially in the arrangement of building materials—as stock keepers moved onto the interior plateau. In the Transvaal highveld, the villages tended to be built in areas where there was enough water for agriculture. They were larger (some extending over several miles), more compact, and more densely populated than villages in lower-lying, higher-rainfall areas. The cultivated fields surrounded the settlements, and the cattle grazed beyond the fields. Thus residential areas tended to be some distance away from the food production areas. In the Orange Free State highveld, villages tended to be smaller—hence the Iron Age population in this region was probably lower—with fields and grazing land much nearer the residences. Stone was now the preferred building material: thousands of paved foundations and stone-walled enclosures have been found across the grassland plateau regions of Zimbabwe and eastern South Africa.

Cattle-keeping settlements between the Drakensberg and the Indian Ocean during the Later Iron Age showed greater variation in size, in the arrangement of buildings, and in the types of building materials used. Although some were essentially extensions of the stone-walled villages of the interior plateau (as in the Tugela River basin), most were more akin to Khoikhoi dwellings with beehive-shaped huts built of wood, clay, or cattle dung, and thatched grass (as in the eastern Cape, the Natal lowlands, Zululand, and Swaziland). Settlements facing the ocean south of the Drakensberg, moreover, were much more fragmented than settlements in the interior plateau. Individual homesteads and groups of family-related homesteads organized in villages were separated from each other and scattered across the landscape.

Metal working in South Africa during the Later Iron Age seems to have taken place outside rather than inside the villages as was the case during the Early Iron Age, and it became more concentrated—the major areas being the Natal lowlands, Zululand, and the northeastern Transvaal. The ancient mining site at Phalaborwa, for example, has been continuously worked from at least the tenth century (Map 1). Shafts were sunk to depths of eighty feet in some places, with branching horizontal galleries, and hundreds of small smelters have been uncovered. Skilled metal workers bartered their wares (which included bracelets, beads and arm bands, wire, various farming and woodworking tools, and weapons) for grain and especially cattle with the outside world.

The shift from lineage-based chiefdoms to centralized, tributary-based states in southeastern Africa began in the mid-eighteenth century, and it resulted in the emergence of several African kingdoms between the eastern Cape and southern Mozambique in the early nineteenth century. Scholars have suggested a number of factors that might account for this phenomenon, including famine and periodic ecological crises resulting from population pressure, soil erosion and overgrazing, increases in cattle production, extensions in the range of locally produced commodities and a more specialized labor force, more diversified regional and interregional hunting and trading practices, and increasing commercial and cultural interaction with Europeans operating mainly from the Cape, from the settler community at Port Natal (today the port of Durban), and from Portuguese-controlled coastal towns in southern Mozambique and especially at Delagoa Bay (which was developing as a trade diffusion center fed by Portuguese, British, Dutch, and French mercantile interests during this period).

These processes culminated in the rise of Shaka and the Zulu state and the destabilization of vast areas of southern Africa as well as parts of the interior of central and eastern Africa in the first forty years or so of the nineteenth century. Scholars have accepted with little qualification the paradigm of the *Mfecane,*[10] which portrayed Shaka as a bloodthirsty tyrant who wreaked havoc on his own people,[11] unleashed the power of the Zulu kingdom against his neighbors, and thereby set in motion a chain of events that ultimately led to the European colonization of the subcontinent.

This paradigm is now being challenged by a number of South African historians, led by Julian Cobbing (Rhodes University) and John Wright (University of Natal), who argue that an Afrocentric interpretation of these events effectively ignores the enormous impact an expansionist European material culture had on African Iron Age societies nominally outside its orbit. They have attacked a wide range of settler writings that formed the primary sources for the *Mfecane* paradigm and generated a settler-inspired historiography of African as well as European societies in southern Africa immediately before and during the period of the European conquest.[12]

This critique has some specific implications for African communities in the Ciskei region during the early colonial period and some general implications for African communities in the interior during the precolonial period. Cobbing, for example, suggests that the key to an understanding of the causes of the *Mfecane* lies in the European demand for labor. As evidence, he points to the Portuguese trade at Delagoa Bay, to the activities of raiding communities in the interior,[13] and to the upheavals that accompanied Dutch and British advances in the eastern Cape in the later eighteenth and early nineteenth centuries. We shall return to this point in the next chapter.

1.3. The Xhosa and Their Neighbors in the Eastern Cape

The history of southern Africa before the colonial era remains inadequate and incomplete, but it does provide a context for the focal point of this study.[14] Linguists use the term Nguni to refer to the family of Bantu languages spoken between the Drakensberg and the Indian Ocean, and the African peoples who occupied the southern portion of this area—the eastern Cape—during the Later Iron Age comprised the southern branch of the Nguni.

The term Nguni has been subjected to critical scrutiny in recent years,[15] but it does convey the idea that the African peoples of southeast Africa today have lived in the same geographical region and shared for at least a millennium a common economic, political, linguistic, and cultural tradition, with certain regional variations. Nguni languages can be distinguished from the family of Bantu languages known as Sotho-Tswana, which is spoken by peoples who inhabit the interior plateau regions of eastern South Africa and adjacent territories. The languages of the northern Nguni today are Zulu and Swazi; the language of the southern Nguni today is Xhosa, which is also the name of one of the main southern Nguni ethnic groups.

There is no evidence to suggest that the Nguni were Later Iron Age migrants who moved down the coast until they eventually reached the eastern Cape. It seems most likely that existing population groups, speaking related languages now identified as Nguni and organized in patrilineal lineage-based clans, developed territorially based chiefdoms sometime after 1000 A.D.

The Xhosa Vanguard

Scholars have arbitrarily suggested a date between the twelfth and fifteenth centuries for the earliest chiefdoms in the eastern Cape. According to oral tradition at least four—Xhosa, Thembu, Mpondo, and Mpondomise—were operating in the region by the sixteenth century. The Xhosa, in particular, were in the forefront of Nguni expansion westward, and much of the Ciskei's subsequent history revolves around the activities of this group (Map 1).

European observers noted that Bantu-speaking agropastoralists were strongly entrenched northeast of the Mthatha River by the mid-sixteenth century, and they are known to have occupied territory in what is now southern Transkei by the early seventeenth century (Map 1). Few if any were living near the sea or were dependent on it for food at this time. The Cape coastal shoreline as well as inland areas west of the southern Nguni in the eastern Cape were occupied by the Khoisan.

Social relations between hunters, herders, and farmers in the eastern Cape before the Europeans arrived remain unclear, but the evidence suggests a long period of interaction. Economic, linguistic, ritual, and other ties formed lasting bonds between these societies. Climate and ecology certainly slowed down the movement of stock-farming peoples into southern Africa's western zone: the southwestern boundary of the summer rainfall area, for example, is in the vicinity of the Gamtoos River valley, while the cultivation of subtropical crops used by Early Iron Age agriculturalists becomes more problematic west of the Kei River because rainfall is erratic and the region as a whole is subject to periodic drought. Nevertheless, it is also possible that the westward dispersion of the Xhosa vanguard was constrained by relatively dense populations of Khoisan hunters and herders.

The survivors of Portuguese, Dutch, and English shipwrecks, the accounts of traders and hunters, and reports of official and unofficial traveling expeditions provide most of the primary written sources for the history of the eastern Cape in the two hundred years or so before contact between Dutch and Nguni stock farmers was established in the eighteenth century. These data are supplemented by the oral traditions of the principal Nguni groups together with oral evidence concerning the Khoisan as recorded by various European observers. The picture that emerges from these records is blurred but revealing: the balance of power between the various peoples who had occupied the eastern Cape for centuries was breaking down in favor of the Nguni.

Written sources suggest that by the late seventeenth century the Xhosa vanguard had penetrated much of the area between the Fish and Kei rivers in what is now the Ciskei region, where apparently the first large-scale assimilation of Khoikhoi pastoralists took place. By the early eighteenth century, the Xhosa had advanced as far as the Gamtoos River, and by the mid-eighteenth century they were in permanent occupation of grazing land between Algoa Bay, in the vicinity of present-day Port Elizabeth, and the Fish River. From the 1770s, they were more or less in continuous contact with Dutch farmers in this area, who were expanding their own frontier along the coastal belt from Cape Town (Map 2). The Xhosa continued to push westward: according to Heinrich Lichtenstein, a German traveler in the Cape during the early nineteenth century, small groups were moving "all over the colony, coming sometimes even to Cape Town." [16]

The Xhosa and their Bantu-speaking neighbors were organized in three hierarchical tiers: the chiefs of the royal lineage and the heads of aligned lineages in the royal clan, the councillors and other elders of the commoner lineages, and their followers, who composed the mass of subject commoners organized in homestead production units. The Nguni, as opposed to the Sotho-Tswana, were obliged to observe exogamy taboos whereby a person could marry only outside his or her clan lineage. Obligations to one's lineage and, to a lesser extent, one's clan assured a considerable degree of solidarity, but power rested with the clan lineages rather than the clans themselves. Members of the royal lineage, for example, formed only a small component of the royal clan. Every person acknowledged family kinship ties that included relatives on the mother's as well as the father's side of the family, but these ties did not extend beyond four or five generations. The commoner clans apparently did not maintain extensive genealogies, and leadership rarely extended beyond the authority of elders of individual kinship groups.

The Bantu-speaking chiefdoms of the eastern Cape never developed centralized states to the degree that the Zulu and Swazi did in the early nineteenth century, but the exact nature of the state and its role in these African societies have been the source of considerable controversy. According to social anthropologist David Hammond-Tooke, the Xhosa polity, for example, resembled a "tribal cluster" of genealogically related but politically independent chiefdoms. Historian Jeff Peires, however, maintains the Xhosa polity was more like a segmentary state that had supplanted earlier, clan-based polities. Individual Xhosa political units may have been autonomous, but they were never independent of the paramount chief or of the genealogically related chiefdom. The paramount was the head of a discernible Xhosa "nation" sharing a common language, royal lineage, and geographical origin.

Further disputes have arisen over the processes by which southern Nguni states like the Xhosa expanded their territories. In every Xhosa family, the wives were divided into two main "houses," the Great House and Right-Hand House. In theory, the heir to a chiefdom was the eldest son of the first-ranked wife of the Great House, and the eldest son of the second-ranked wife who controlled the Right-Hand House was the heir apparent. After the marriage of the Great Wife, other wives were allocated to one or the other of these houses and ranked accordingly.

Hammond-Tooke maintains that this dual family structure was designed to divide into independent political units—he calls the process fission—at regular intervals. Cleavages normally occurred between the two main houses, and any number of reasons could cause a division. A chief, unlike a commoner, usually married his Great Wife late in life. The chief's councillors selected her from a foreign chiefdom, Thembu women being preferred by the Xhosa. Succession disputes were inevitable if the chief died before marrying a Great Wife, if she did not bear an heir, or if the chief died before the heir was of age. Personal greed or ambition by a regent or a member of a minor house, the weakness or brutality of an incumbent chief or his heir, pressure from alien chiefdoms, the sheer weight of numbers and the need for more land have also been cited as factors causing segmentation.

Peires insists that these cleavages did not lead to political secession. He stresses the complexity of alliances that subsequently might be formed around favored claimants to the chiefship. The chiefs' sons inherited an equal power base from their mothers, who were of noble birth, and in practice house origin—cleavages occurring in minor as well as major houses—did not necessarily dictate political allegiance. The segmentation process eased rather than aggravated conflicts within the chiefdom because it enabled the sons of a chief to leave with their followers and establish new chiefships. Segmentation provided the crucial social mechanism for expansion in a genealogically related chiefdom like the Xhosa, but it never threatened the essential unity of the Xhosa people before the colonial era.[17]

Most scholars today would accept the view that southern Nguni groups like the Xhosa were essentially segmentary states containing a varying number of autonomous political units under chiefs who were members of the same royal lineage. As the embodiment of the state, the Xhosa chief was the guardian of his people. He protected them from their enemies and had custody of their environment, resolving internal disputes over cultivation, grazing, and hunting land, for example, and acting as a patron for those who needed food or cattle to acquire a wife. To carry out these responsibilities, he needed an income that was provided largely through various kinds of tribute, special fees, and emergency levies, and especially the fines he received in court matters requiring his judgment.

The chief's main task was to ensure that everyone had an equal share of the available resources. He guaranteed individual and communal rights while regulating access to and use of the land. To maintain control, the chief and his deputies allocated land for pasture and for fields, supervised hunting privileges, and declared the beginning and ending of the agricultural cycle with rainmaking and first-fruit ceremonies. Thus theoretically all households started and ended work in the fields at the same time, thereby regulating the supply of labor and helping to ensure that no one would gain an unfair advantage by working outside the time allotted to sow and reap the crops.

Chiefs could not prevent their subjects from cultivating their fields or grazing their stock, and they could not transfer ownership of the land because the southern Nguni had no concept of private property in land. Every adult male—he usually had to be married—had a right to the land, but it was a right to use the land that was held in trust for him by the chief. The Xhosa commoner occupied the land and like the serfs of feudal Europe he was protected from expropriation. He grazed his cattle, cultivated his fields, and consumed the products of his labor under the protection of his chief.

The chief's power ultimately depended on obtaining the consensus of his subjects. This was accomplished by relying on the senior members of the commoner clans, who were the chief's councillors and the real mediators between the chief and his people. They were also usually the chief's age mates as they had undergone the rite of manhood with the chief. Together with the chief's personal followers, the councillors constituted the state bureaucracy, carrying out the tasks assigned to them by the chief. But the authority of the councillors was derived from their own followers, not from the chief.

Because all sons of chiefs had the potential to establish chiefships, the councillors could also further their own interests by exploiting the internal dynastic rivalries that were endemic in Xhosa society. The chief's powers were severely circumscribed by his councillors: they might leave their chief and, with followers and cattle, desert to a rival chief. In rare cases, they could force a chief to resign, even though the institution of the chiefship was sacrosanct. They remained autonomous when their chief died, and they could exert considerable influence over his successor, especially if he was a regent. Chiefs could manipulate councillors and they were often skilled in influencing policy, but councillors were the main decision makers in these polities.

The Dynamics of Power and Privilege

Segmentary states like the Xhosa, then, were stronger than the loosely organized chiefdoms of the Khoikhoi but weaker than the centralized kingdoms that developed along the upper and lower reaches of the Limpopo River, in Zimbabwe, or in the region embraced by northern Natal and southern Mozambique toward the end of the Iron Age. Important constraints were placed on the chief's authority, and his councillors exercised considerable political power within the chiefdom.

Economic power was rooted in the struggle to control labor within the individual homestead, the centers of production in all cattle-keeping cultures. As Jeff Guy describes it:

the process took place within the production community—the homestead—in the charge of the homestead-head, and supported by the labor of women and children who were obtained in exchange for cattle, and whose productive and reproductive capacities were released in exchange for cattle.[18]

Married men within the homestead controlled the means of production in cattle and land, and they appropriated the labor power of women and children—indeed, all unmarried adults—who were not allowed to possess cattle and land. Conflicts between contenders for power in segmentary states like the Xhosa—between chiefs and councillors who represented the richer homesteads or between the representatives of dominant and dominated lineages—were essentially conflicts between members of the same dominant social class. The real powerbrokers were the men who controlled the homestead production units.

The precise nature of the Xhosa homestead has been the source of some confusion in the literature. As the key element in the production process, the homestead or *umzi* needs to be distinguished from individual households consisting of the family head, his wives, and their children. The homestead was made up of a varying number of households. The head of one of these households was the acknowledged leader of the homestead. The central dynamic in power relations, then, was the tendency of some homesteads to acquire client households at the expense of other homesteads. Homestead heads who had acquired a number of vassal households and thus had control over a larger portion of labor and production were in a powerful position in the chiefdom.

The extent to which homestead production units differed in size and in wealth in the precolonial period is unknown, but social stratification does not seem to have been as pronounced among the Xhosa as it was among the Zulu or Swazi. Before the mid-eighteenth century, there was apparently a plentiful supply of unoccupied land for cultivation and pasture as well as for hunting close to the homesteads. In essence, land provided a safety valve against potential friction between homesteads.

The homestead production units, moreover, appear to have been generally small in size and rudimentary in technology. Each household was allotted ground to cultivate that was more or less equal to its needs, and its members were fully occupied in working the land. There was apparently no labor surplus among the Xhosa, and it seems most unlikely that households produced large surpluses of food in the precolonial period. Wealthy individuals would have been conspicuous and thereby rendered vulnerable to accusations of witchcraft by envious members of the community. Neighboring homesteads usually linked by bonds of kinship, moreover, were duty-bound in time of need to share their goods and services through redistribution networks and communal work parties. It was unnecessary to save for a rainy day, as it were, if one could rely on one's kin or one's neighbors for aid.

Xhosa-speaking peoples had the same divisions of labor within each household as their Bantu-speaking counterparts elsewhere in southern Africa. Males tended the stock, did the milking, and provided labor for short intensive tasks like clearing the land for crops; females and their children were the cultivators and foragers, and they prepared and cooked the food. Crops included varieties of millet, sorghum, beans, pumpkins, melons, sweetcane, dagga, and eventually maize, potatoes, bananas, and tobacco.

Possession of cattle, as we have seen, offered a household head far more status than a well-cultivated field. Homestead heads who possessed large herds of cattle had a distinct political, social, and economic advantage over those who did not. The head of the homestead would be the head of the wealthiest household in terms of his control over cattle and household labor. The heads of the richer households and homestead production units were patronized by the chief, who needed their support to secure the loyalty of their followers.

It is important to recognize that southern Nguni chiefs never gained control over household labor as did the northern Nguni chiefs. The commoners maintained their political and economic rights centered on their households in the homestead production units. There was obviously some stratification between richer and poorer homesteads among the Xhosa in the precolonial period, but these distortions were not severe until the nineteenth century. Although Xhosa chiefs were wealthier than their subjects, Peires maintains that their living standard was "still so close to that of the commoners that less perceptive outside observers remained under the impression that there was no difference at all." [19]

Xhosa chiefs never achieved conspicuous economic advantages over their subjects in the precolonial period. They could and did exact tribute, which was undoubtedly redistributed unequally to the more wealthy homestead units. The councillors were chosen from the richer homestead heads, and in return they ensured that the men in their households would serve the chief and fight for him in battle. But there was no permanent bureaucracy apart from the chief's personal retinue and his councillors. If the chief did not satisfy their needs, he could forfeit their loyalty. Fighting between chiefdoms, moreover, increased as these segmentary states expanded.

European settlers, soldiers, administrators, and missionaries during the nineteenth century habitually ignored the realities of life in these African societies. They persisted in holding the paramount chief responsible for the actions of other chiefdoms in the segmented state, and they disregarded the dynamics of power and privilege within individual chiefdoms. Once their military position was secure, they also tried with some success to manufacture the grievances that inevitably ended in war.

The Xhosa State before the Colonial Era

The oral genealogies of Xhosa chiefs are difficult sources to interpret when it comes to chronicling Xhosa history. Tshawe, legendary founder of the Xhosa royal lineage, is impossible to place in any meaningful historical context. Togu, the third chief after Tshawe who is recorded in oral tradition, is supposed to have been alive in 1686 and firmly established on the Kei River, but Peires maintains that Togu's son Ngconde is the earliest Xhosa chief who can be dated with any degree of confidence.[20] Ngconde's reign is placed in the mid-seventeenth century when the Xhosa, under the Tshawe royal lineage, were in permanent occupation of territory centering on the Mbashe River, east of the Kei River, in what is now the Transkei (Map 1).

The original Xhosa chiefdom, experiencing a rapid increase in population, segmented into ten different chiefdoms in six generations during the seventeenth and eighteenth centuries. As a result of these cleavages, rival chiefs of the Tshawe royal lineage moved into new territories west of the Kei River. Permanent occupation of areas beyond the Kei was relatively slow. Some Xhosa chiefdoms had dispersed as far as the Buffalo River near present-day East London by the 1680s, but apparently they did not settle permanently in the Sundays-Fish river area 65 miles further south until the 1760s—roughly eighty years later (Map 2).[21]

The Xhosa segmentary state experienced two major schisms during the eighteenth century, and both are shrouded in the ambiguities of oral tradition. The most serious of the two occurred in the last half of the century, and it involved two major protagonists—Gcaleka and Rharhabe—whose descendants would dominate Xhosa history during the era of the European conquest.

J. H. Soga, an influential Xhosa historian writing in the 1920s and 1930s, suggested that Gcaleka, who represented the Great House and was therefore the legitimate heir, tried to usurp the chiefship and was defeated by his father, Phalo, and Rharhabe, son of the Right-Hand House. Nevertheless, Gcaleka was supported by the Xhosa majority. Thus Phalo and Rharhabe left the Xhosa nucleus (then near present-day Butterworth in the southern Transkei) and crossed the Kei River. As sons of the Great House, Gcaleka and his heirs who remained in the Transkei were recognized as rulers of the senior Xhosa chiefdom.[22]

Peires supports another version of oral tradition that focuses on the rivalry between Phalo's sons Gcaleka and Rharhabe. The brothers together with their followers confronted each other in battle, and Rharhabe was defeated and captured. Gcaleka kept him as a hostage for some years, but eventually Rharhabe was released and allowed to move across the Kei River, where he settled in the vicinity of present-day Stutterheim. Gcaleka remained with Phalo as his chosen successor, and he became the paramount chief of the Xhosa when Phalo died about 1775.

Rharhabe (1725?–ca. 1782) sought to establish himself as the dominant Xhosa chief west of the Kei River, subjugating various Khoisan groups and extending his territory between the Kei and Buffalo rivers (Map 2). When Gcaleka died in 1778, Rharhabe tried to stage a coup against Gcaleka's son

Khawuta, but again he was defeated. Rharhabe and his designated heir, Mlawu, then moved north against the Thembu, where they were killed in battle about 1782. The paramount Khawuta selected Mlawu's son Ngqika, who was still a child, as heir to the Rharhabe chiefship and appointed Ndlambe, a brother of Mlawu, as regent.[23]

However one interprets these events, the fact remains that this time the Xhosa schism was irreversible. While the Gcaleka Xhosa maintained a relatively stable polity east of the Kei River in the later eighteenth and early nineteenth centuries, the Rharhabe Xhosa became involved in a struggle for power with numerous other Xhosa and Khoikhoi groups west of the Kei River. At least six autonomous Xhosa chiefdoms—Ntinde, Gwali, Mdange, Hleke, Mbalu, and Gqunukhwebe—and some smaller Xhosa units without chiefs were already operating in the territory between the Gamtoos and Kei rivers when the Rharhabe Xhosa moved into the region (Map 2). These chiefdoms contained varying numbers of Khoikhoi within their ranks, but all were cleavages of the Tshawe royal clan except the Gqunukhwebe, a commoner chiefdom that was in the vanguard of the Xhosa dispersal across the Kei River. White observers recorded Gqunukhwebe, for example, between the Keiskamma and Fish rivers (1750s), Fish and Bushmans rivers (1760s, 1780s), and west of the Gamtoos River (1770s).

As the Xhosa were expanding down the coast of the eastern Cape, European trading ships on their way to the eastern coast of Africa, India, and Indonesia began sailing into Table Bay in the southwestern Cape to obtain fresh water and food supplies.[24] Dutch traders associated with a private merchant company called the Dutch East India Company established a permanent supply depot for their ships in 1652 at a site that is now Cape Town. The settlement soon included a fort, hospital, and vegetable garden, and company officials began trading with local Khoikhoi communities, who had been involved in barter with Europeans since the first ships arrived in Table Bay sixty years earlier.

The Khoikhoi exchanged their sheep and cattle mainly for iron, copper, and tobacco (as a substitute for dagga). Company officials, fearful the Khoikhoi might use iron-tipped spears against them, stopped the trade in iron and offered other luxuries like brass, beads, and alcohol. As the demand for livestock grew, the Khoikhoi became increasingly reluctant to sell the basis of their livelihood for goods that were not required for survival. Relations with the Dutch deteriorated, and hostilities broke out when the company released a number of its employees from their contracts in 1657 and allowed them to establish their own farms on Khoikhoi grazing land.

The pattern of European domination over the Khoisan was established in the occupation of the southwestern Cape during the last half of the seventeenth

Figure 1.1. Xhosa nationalists of the old order: Ciskei chiefs, *left*, Ngqika, and, *right*, Sandile.

century. Pastoralists and foragers were destroyed by three wars and several armed expeditions, disease (culminating in a smallpox epidemic in 1713 that resulted in the death of most Khoikhoi still living in the region), and above all by the loss of hunting and grazing land and livestock. The survivors were pressed into service mainly as domestic servants and farm laborers by the settlers in Cape Town and the surrounding countryside. Although most were subjected to forms of subordination that approximated slavery, the Khoisan were not slaves in the legal sense. African and Asian slaves, however, were imported in significant numbers beginning in 1658.

About fifteen hundred white settlers had dispersed across the southwestern Cape by the end of the century, and small groups were moving north into the interior and east along the Indian Ocean coast beyond the perimeters of the Dutch East India Company. These migrating stockfarmers or trekboers, as they were called, were essentially pastoralists who supplemented their needs with subsistence farming and hunting. They were issued with grazing permits from 1703 so they could rent large tracts of grazing land (a minimum of six thousand acres), known as loan farms, at a token price (equivalent to two cows a year from 1714) for their exclusive use. Thus the trekboers retained the concept of private property, and their movement beyond the borders of the settled European community was accelerated.

The trekboers dispersed in several directions, but the main route was easterly along the coast and interior valleys of the southern Cape, where they gradually established a new life for themselves beyond the control of Dutch East India Company officials. In seventy years, they had moved from within fifty miles of Cape Town to the Fish River, more than five hundred miles away (Map 2), where they came into permanent contact with the Xhosa and neighboring peoples who inhabited the region that would eventually be known as the Ciskei.[25]

2
Frontier Zones in a Colonial Setting

Eurocentric versions of South African history—Afrikaner nationalist, British imperial and settler versions—were forged in the crucible of the Cape's northern and eastern frontiers during the eighteenth and nineteenth centuries. Although scholars may differ in their interpretation of these experiences, they generally agree that the frontier tradition played a crucial role in the making of modern South Africa.[1]

As in the United States, the frontier thesis in South Africa has been written and narrated by the conquerors: it usually refers to boundary lines drawn by intruding white populations between themselves and the indigenous peoples they came to dominate. The present study will employ the definition of a frontier zone proposed by Howard Lamar and Leonard Thompson in a recent comparison of frontier traditions in North America and southern Africa:

> a territory or zone of interpenetration between two [or more] previously distinct societies. Usually, one of the societies is indigenous to the region, or at least has occupied it for many generations; the other is intrusive. The frontier "opens" in a given zone when the first representatives of the intrusive society arrive; it "closes" when a single political authority has established hegemony over the zone.[2]

This chapter examines the history of two designated frontier zones in the eastern Cape. The first one was opened between the 1750s and the 1770s when Dutch and Xhosa stockfarmers began moving into a region bounded by the Gamtoos and Fish rivers on the coast and extending inland to the vicinity of the Sneeuwberg Mountains (Map 2). The second one, and the focal point of this chapter, was opened by the British in stages between 1812 and 1878. It embraced the Ciskei region between the Fish and Kei rivers (Map 3).

Section 2.1 focuses on relations between the various communities that occupied the Gamtoos-Fish frontier zone. Contact between the intruding Dutch and Xhosa stockfarmers had degenerated into conflict by the 1770s. Indigenous Khoisan hunters and herders were caught between these advancing groups and largely overrun and absorbed, killed or driven out of the region by the

1780s. The British initially gained control of the Cape in 1795. The trekboers effectively relinquished their autonomy during the 1790s, and the Xhosa were expelled from this frontier zone in 1812.

Section 2.2 focuses on relations between the intruding British and the indigenous Xhosa in the Ciskei frontier zone, which would be closed essentially in three stages after more than two generations of conflict. The areas set aside for the African population in this region during the conquest period would form the nucleus of the Ciskei's African reserve.

2.1. The Gamtoos-Fish Frontier Zone

At least four separate Khoikhoi chiefdoms occupied the land between the Gamtoos and Fish rivers when Dutch and Xhosa stockfarmers began to move into this frontier zone in the 1760s. The first contacts with the Khoikhoi in the region were probably initiated through trade. The Inqua, for example, were regarded as the most powerful Khoikhoi chiefdom in the southern Cape during the seventeenth century, and to the south and east of the Inqua were the Damasqua, Gonaqua, and Hoengeyqua Khoi (Map 1).

Economic and Social Interaction with the Khoisan

Extensive trading networks during the seventeenth and eighteenth centuries linked Khoisan living in the western Cape and southern Cape coastal belt with Khoisan in Namibia and in the Cape interior, with the Dutch in the Cape peninsula, with various Bantu-speaking groups in eastern South Africa, and possibly even with the Portuguese at Delagoa Bay.[3] Metal, cattle, dagga, and beads formed the major items of exchange. In the western and southwestern Cape, Khoikhoi obtained metal and other goods from the Dutch in exchange for cattle, and metal was also obtained through Khoikhoi living along the Orange River or directly from the Tswana north of the river in exchange for cattle. In the southern and eastern Cape, the Khoikhoi traded metal and beads for dagga and later tobacco obtained mainly from the Xhosa.

The Inqua Khoi, whose territory lay near the headwaters of the Gamtoos River, were key intermediaries in these exchanges. Since there are virtually no mineral deposits in the eastern Cape and iron in particular was a precious commodity, the Inqua (together with the Gonaqua Khoi) traded iron and copper to the Xhosa. The Xhosa, in turn, traded part of the copper they received to the Thembu (in exchange for iron) and to the Mpondo. Local networks were undoubtedly involved in these transactions as well.[4]

Trade between the Khoikhoi, Dutch, and Xhosa provided an opening for political and social intercourse that had major consequences for the peoples of the frontier zone. The Xhosa clearly regarded themselves as superior to the Khoikhoi, but they rarely established their suzereignty over the herders by force. The Xhosa absorbed them into their lineage-based polities in stages just as herders had absorbed hunters.[5] The incorporation of Khoisan and independent Nguni units meant that Xhosa society became more heterogeneous as it expanded, but as Peires points out Xhosa nationhood was a political concept, not an ethnic or geographical one. Anyone who accepted the suzereignty of the Tshawe lineage was regarded as a Xhosa.[6]

Khoisan languages, for example, directly influenced Nguni languages, especially the dialects spoken by the southern Nguni. Clicks can be found in one-sixth of all Xhosa words today, and there are also numerous nonclick consonants of Khoisan origin. Few Xhosa click words have Zulu cognates, which implies that the southern Nguni absorbed these Khoisan words after settling in the eastern Cape. There are also numerous Khoisan place names for mountains and rivers in the region. The word *Xhosa* itself is derived from a Khoikhoi word that meant "angry men." [7]

The Xhosa had apparently succeeded in imposing a measure of political authority over Khoikhoi pastoral communities from the Kei River to the Cape peninsula by the mid-seventeenth century,[8] but significant control leading to loss of independence and absorption into the Xhosa polity occurred in the eastern Cape only during the eighteenth century. Khoikhoi leaders often retained their followers and became councillors to Xhosa chiefs, and they would sometimes play an important role as policymakers in the chiefdoms they were compelled to join. Even economic discrimination lasted no more than a generation, and the additional cattle and expertise in stock keeping must have advanced Xhosa homestead production.

The Xhosa were much harder on the San—at least from the eighteenth century when the San were stereotyped as cattle thieves—but there are examples of San bands being absorbed by the Xhosa or paying tribute to Xhosa chiefs. And San bands also absorbed Xhosa refugees. Xhosa men married San women, and San were employed as diviners and rainmakers in Xhosa religious ceremonies. San were also active in trade with the Xhosa, obtaining cattle and dagga in exchange for ivory.

The trekboers regarded the Khoikhoi as culturally inferior, but their skills as pastoralists were coveted as well as their grazing land and stock. Conflict was not inevitable: there were alliances between Khoikhoi and trekboer groups, Khoikhoi herders were offered protection from San raiders and employed as soldiers to fight them, and free Khoikhoi were sometimes allowed to pasture their herds and flocks on land acquired by the whites in return for labor service. Nevertheless, the western Cape Khoikhoi had virtually vanished as an independent people by the 1720s, and in the next fifty years or so the eastern Cape Khoikhoi would suffer the same fate. By the late 1760s, the trekboers were laying claim to all Khoikhoi grazing land between the Gamtoos and Fish rivers. Those who would not be subjugated on trekboer terms would be forced to seek refuge with other African peoples temporarily beyond the reach of the expanding Europeans, or they would be driven from the frontier zone altogether.

The trekboers regarded the aboriginal San as subhuman, and there were few if any mediating factors in relations between the two groups. Dutch stock-farmers held the San collectively responsible for stock theft, and they initiated numerous expeditions against hunting groups in the later seventeenth and eighteenth centuries. These raiders did not discriminate between San hunters, Khoikhoi without cattle who had reverted to a hunting lifestyle, and fragmented hunting-herding units who had joined together to protect themselves against the trekboers. Raids against independent Khoisan hunters and herders would eventually escalate into virtual wars of extermination: the adults would be killed and the children and youth coerced into a lifetime of labor on white farms.[9]

Economic and Social Interaction between
Xhosa and Dutch Stockfarmers

Contact between Dutch stockfarmers and frontier Xhosa chiefdoms like the Gqunukhwebe was established early in the eighteenth century.[10] Attempts by succeeding Dutch East India Company administrators to limit and/or regulate interaction between the two groups proved futile, because Dutch officials were never strong enough to dictate policy in what constituted their eastern frontier zone. They had to be conciliatory in their negotiations with the Xhosa, and interaction was generally peaceful for the first two generations. Company officials arbitrarily extended their eastern frontier to Mossel Bay in 1743, to the Gamtoos River and inland to the Bruintjeshoogte Mountains in 1770, and to the length of the Great Fish River in 1778 (Map 2), but Dutch and Xhosa frontiersmen alike ignored these phantom barriers.[11]

Trade relations apparently remained undeveloped, however, even after permanent relations were established in the 1770s. Part of the reason was mistrust on both sides. The earliest known contact was an unprovoked raid by Dutch frontiersmen on a group of Xhosa near the Bruintjeshoogte in 1702. Hunting expeditions by both groups ranged all over the frontier zone, and trade before the 1750s consisted largely of bartering for ivory, meat, and skins. The frequency of direct communication increased thereafter as Khoikhoi groups like the Gonaqua and Hoengeyqua, who had previously acted as intermediaries, were eliminated. The trekboers made contact in the 1770s with the Ntinde and Mdange Xhosa in the upper Fish River area. When the trekboers moved across the Sundays and Bushmans rivers in the 1780s and developed farms near the lower Fish River, they also came into contact with the Gqunukhwebe, Gwali, and Mbalu Xhosa.

Dutch and Xhosa stockfarmers actually had much in common with each other. They ate the same kinds of food and lived in the same kinds of huts.

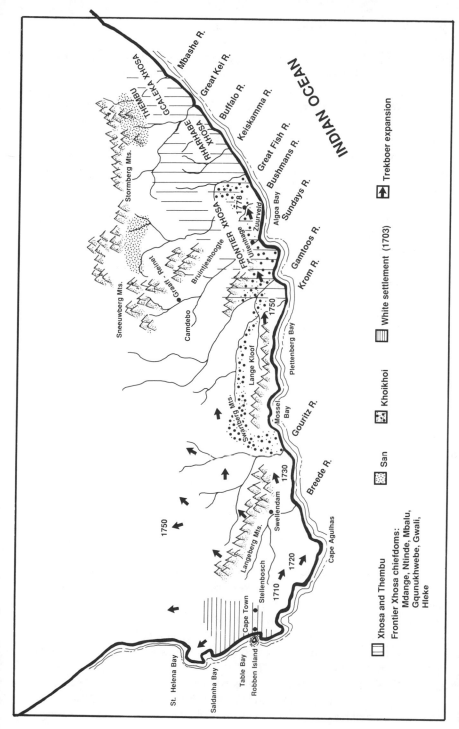

Map 2. Cape frontier zones in the eighteenth century. Courtesy of Richard Elphick and Hermann Giliomee (eds.), *The Shaping of South African Society, 1652–1840,* fig. 2.1: Trekboer expansion, 1703–1780 (as adapted), copyright 1979, 1988 by Maskew Miller Longman Ltd.

47

Boer children, at least, were usually dressed in animal skins like the Xhosa. The trekboers were less effective as cultivators, but livestock exhibited a socio-cultural dimension in Dutch frontier society that bore some resemblance to the role of cattle in Nguni society. Both groups depended on cattle as their principal source of wealth, and there was a degree of cooperation, for example, in their mutual efforts to eliminate San stock raiders. Life centered on the family, or extended family, and decision making by both groups was a highly personalized process. Frontier Dutch and Xhosa alike were essentially pragmatists in relations with other groups: disputes were resolved as they occurred, without recourse to broader alliances.

If anything, the Xhosa dominated relations with the trekboers during this period. They did not fear the Dutch, and they saw no reason why these stockfarmers should not be absorbed, when Xhosa polities were already absorbing refugees and adventurers from Cape Dutch society. The expansion of the frontier Xhosa westward across the Sundays River and beyond continued unabated.

White stockfarmers were very thinly scattered across the landscape and still partially dependent on Cape Town for survival. The total trekboer population (including servants and slaves) between the Gamtoos and Fish rivers extending inland to the Camdebo-Bruintjeshoogte area numbered only about a thousand persons in the 1770s. However much they wished to escape the rule of Dutch (and later British) administrators, they depended on Cape Town as a market for their livestock and as a resource base where they could buy weapons, ammunition, and other essential supplies. In addition, they needed to legitimize and solemnize their social relationships, such as baptism and marriage, and acquire ministers, teachers, and other guardians of the social order to preserve their way of life apart from the dominant Bantu speakers.

The Crisis in the Zuurveld, ca. 1770–1812

Competition for land between white and black in the Gamtoos-Fish frontier zone was not a serious matter except where the Xhosa were already entrenched along the coast between the Sundays and Fish rivers. This well-watered region—roughly eighty miles long and forty to fifty miles wide—was known as the *zuurveld* (sour grass), and it was prime grazing land (Map 2). Xhosa stockfarmers pastured their cattle in upland pastures for about four months in the spring and summer and in lowland pastures where the grass retained its flavor and nutritional value during the drier fall and winter. Increasing numbers of Dutch trekboers began moving into the zuurveld and contesting the Xhosa for control of the land from the 1770s.

Settler-inspired histories of the first two Cape-Xhosa wars have generally pitted virtuous Dutch trekboers against cattle-thieving Xhosa who had no respect for colonial boundaries. In reality, the trekboers sought to take advantage of a struggle for power by leaders of the Rharhabe Xhosa for control over Xhosa living west of the Kei River. The trekboers participated in the spoils of war as allies of the Rharhabe Xhosa, but they did not play a major role in these events. The third war (1799–1803) was far more frightening from the point of view of the colonial authorities, because it involved rebellious Dutch stock-farmers, independent San hunting bands in the mountainous interior, Xhosa chiefdoms east as well as west of the Fish River, and the subjugated Khoisan population in the frontier districts who were desperately seeking to reclaim land that had once belonged to them. The area of conflict ranged from the Fish to Mossel Bay along the coast and inland from the Camdebo-Bruintjeshoogte to the Swartberg Mountains (Map 2).[12]

Meanwhile, the Dutch East India Company, which was nominally responsible for administering the Cape, lost control of the territory to Britain in 1795. The merchant company itself ceased functioning three years later during the Napoleonic Wars, but the British had occupied the Cape for only about seven years when it reverted to Dutch control—Holland at this time was called the Batavian Republic of United Netherlands—under the Treaty of Amiens signed in March 1802. The third Cape-Xhosa war was far from over—Khoikhoi/Xhosa units were actually on the offensive—when British military forces left the colony six months later. A representative of the Batavian government reached Cape Town in December and immediately declared a ceasefire. The new governor arrived in February 1803, and two months later he was on his way to the town of Graaff-Reinet (headquarters of the colony's huge eastern frontier district) to sue for peace.

The Batavians sought to reestablish a policy of territorial segregation in the aftermath of this war. Dutch administrators assumed that conflict had come about because the trekboers had mistreated the Khoikhoi and Xhosa in the absence of strong governmental authority in the frontier districts. Therefore they tried to prevent public and private trade in commodities and labor between the trekboers and the Xhosa, encourage the Xhosa to accept the Fish River as the boundary line, and stop the trekboers from intruding on what was deemed to be Xhosa territory east of the Fish River. The Batavians also tried to increase administrative control over their eastern frontier by splitting Graaff-Reinet into two separate districts. The southern portion along the coast between the Krom and Fish rivers and extending inland to the Upper Gamtoos River–Bruintjeshoogte Mountain region was established as the district of Uitenhage in 1804. The northern portion—the old district of Graaff-Reinet—would be limited to the inland mountain and plateau region north and east of the district of Uitenhage (Map 2).

Desperate to make the colony pay for itself, the Batavians also tried to promote sheep farming in hopes of developing a commercial wool industry. Attempts to stimulate the economy and maintain the status quo on the Cape's eastern frontier, however, were doomed to failure: the Batavians did not have the financial resources to develop sheep ranching or the military resources to enforce territorial segregation and remove the Xhosa threat from the zuurveld.

The main achievement of the Batavian interlude was to reestablish colonial control over the dispirited Khoikhoi in the frontier zone, convincing them to return to service with the stockfarmers, remain on mission stations established for them in the western Cape and at Bethelsdorp and Theopolis in the eastern Cape (Map 3), or enlist in a separate military unit that had been established for the Khoikhoi called the Cape Regiment. A tenuous peace on the frontier was maintained under the Batavians because the rebellious trekboers were too weak to challenge their authority, the Khoisan had either been subordinated by the Dutch, absorbed by the Xhosa, or had fled the frontier districts, and the frontier Xhosa were preoccupied with their warring neighbors—the Rharhabe Xhosa—across the Fish River.

Two events beginning in the new century, however, would have profound consequences for all concerned in this frontier zone. Britain had originally seized the Cape to prevent it from falling into the hands of the French: the territory was reoccupied in 1806, and permanent occupation was confirmed following the Treaty of Vienna in 1814. For the first time, Dutch and Xhosa alike were faced with the power of a European state that was determined to rule the Cape's eastern frontier. Meanwhile, a dispute between Rharhabe's grandson Ngqika and his uncle Ndlambe, the ex-regent of the Rharhabe Xhosa, split the chiefdom and embroiled the Xhosa nation in more than twenty years of civil war.

British officials accepted the Fish River as the boundary between the Cape Colony and Xhosaland, but they could not contain the movement of Xhosa into the zuurveld. Stock theft and increasing violence between Xhosa and Dutch stockfarmers plagued those who administered the Cape's eastern frontier during the early 1800s.

These problems were aggravated when the slave trade was abolished in 1807 and the demand for labor rose sharply. A proclamation two years later attempted to alleviate the shortage of workers by placing severe restrictions on the movement of Khoisan men, women, and children within the colony. The authorities then tried to segregate the Xhosa from the whites and subjugated Khoikhoi by forcing Xhosa units operating west of the Sundays River to return to the zuurveld, by prohibiting marriage between Khoikhoi and Xhosa, and by denying settlers the right to employ Xhosa labor. Troops were also dispatched to the border area in 1810 as a show of force against the Xhosa and to placate the trekboers who were demanding protection.

Although frontier farmers were leaving their farms by this time, their reasons for doing so were not always dictated by the alleged Xhosa threat.

A drought in the zuurveld's coastal lowlands, for example, drove away most stockfarmers from this region. Others, especially those in the upland Bruintje-shoogte area, could not tolerate the Xhosa version of reciprocal hospitality, which was usually interpreted as begging or stealing. (Xhosa were duty bound to provide food and shelter to European travelers in Xhosaland, and they demanded the same treatment when passing through European farming areas.)

Unoccupied white homesteads, however, were being burned by Xhosa cattle raiders, and by the early months of 1811 they were becoming much bolder, striking as far west as the Gamtoos River valley. The killing of several Dutch farmers and their Khoisan servants actually sealed the fate of the zuurveld Xhosa. The British concluded that a policy of segregation could be maintained only if all the chiefs and their followers were expelled from the Gamtoos-Fish frontier zone.

Ndlambe (ca. 1738–1828) and Ngqika (ca. 1778–1829)—the two contenders for power over the Xhosa west of the Kei River—seemed oblivious to the threat posed by the new colonial authority in their midst. About 1807, Ngqika provoked a confrontation with Ndlambe by inexplicably abducting one of his uncle's wives. In Xhosa society this act constituted the serious crime of incest, and numerous chiefdoms supported Ndlambe when he punished Ngqika in the resulting War of Thuthula. After the battle was over, they switched sides in hopes that a balance could be maintained between the two Rharhabe chiefs. Ndlambe remained in the zuurveld, but he agreed that Ngqika was the senior chief and did not challenge his sovereignty across the Fish.

Ngqika, however, was determined to subordinate Ndlambe and the other zuurveld chiefs, and at this critical juncture in Xhosa history he declared his support for the Fish River as the boundary between the Cape and Xhosaland. The colonial authorities, having already organized a commando of more than thirteen hundred British army regulars, farmers, and Khoikhoi recruits (the Cape Regiment) to expel all Xhosa found west of the Fish River, now had Ngqika's neutrality.

The commando leaders waited until December 1811—when the cornfields had been planted and were almost ready for harvest—before they attacked. They sought to confront the enemy, but the zuurveld chiefs offered no resistance. Chungwa, aged chief of the Gqunukhwebe, was shot while he lay sleeping, but Ndlambe, his brother Mnyaluza, and the other frontier chiefs eluded the commando and crossed the lower Fish River in mid-January 1812. Mdange and Ntinde Xhosa living in the interior fought back, but they were fewer in number and the chiefdoms fragmented.

By the end of February, the Gamtoos-Fish frontier zone had been cleared of Xhosa and roughly four thousand square miles of territory opened up to white settlement. About twenty thousand Xhosa men, women, and children

were deliberately and ruthlessly driven off the land, most of their cattle confiscated, and their crops and homesteads destroyed in the War of 1811–12, a war
that was without precedent in the Xhosa experience.[13]

2.2. The Ciskei Frontier Zone

The Cape-Xhosa wars—nine were fought over a period of a hundred years
between 1779 and 1878—were the most protracted in southern Africa during
the period of primary resistance against colonial rule. Four of these wars were
fought for control of the Ciskei frontier zone, and the final war completed the
subjugation of the Xhosa people east as well as west of the Kei River.

The wars associated with the conquest of the Xhosa in the eastern Cape
form the nucleus of a settler-inspired frontier tradition in South African historiography.[14] The discourse of the dominant culture—the setting, sequence, and
significance of the European conquest—was naturalized in the texts of these
frontier-war experiences. Settler historians allotted primary roles to whites,
marginalized blacks, and projected a negative stereotyped image of their role
in frontier history. They highlighted white political and administrative practices
and downplayed economic practices. They established narrative structures that
in some respects have remained intact for more than a hundred fifty years.
They determined what the frontier wars would be called,[15] for example, when
they would begin and how they would end, who the main combatants were and
how they would be portrayed.

Key elements of the settler thesis were addressed by revisionists of the
liberal school between the 1920s and the publication of the two-volume *Oxford
History of South Africa* in 1969 and 1971,[16] but a new paradigm began to
emerge only in the 1970s, and it was inspired largely by scholars influenced
by the marxist tradition.[17] These revisionists assumed that the frontier was
invented by the settlers to serve their own ends, and they inverted the frontier thesis to focus on white rather than black aggression in the frontier zone.
The settlers sought British military protection against the alleged Xhosa threat
while continuing to attack all Africans still capable of resisting their demands.

Settler demands for African land and labor constituted the major themes
in the frontier experience. The settlers conspired with successive Cape colonial
administrators in pursuit of these interests, even when these interests conflicted
with policies being pursued by the British Colonial Office in London. As we
shall see, settler apologists created "tribes," codified "native law," and in other
ways sought to invent an African tradition to conform to the world they had
created for themselves. Like their counterparts elsewhere in colonial Africa,
they also invented a European tradition, as Terence Ranger puts it, to provide
"Africans a series of clearly defined points of entry into the colonial world."[18]

A critical reading of the settler thesis provides a context for periodizing the subjugation of the African population in the Ciskei frontier zone after 1812. In the first stage, which ends with the War of 1834–35, the Xhosa were pushed beyond the Keiskamma River and forced to compete for survival with various other African communities now living in the frontier zone. In the second stage, which ends with the War of 1850–53, the Ciskei Xhosa and their allies were completely subjugated, restricted to segregated "locations," or expelled from the frontier zone. In the third stage, the Xhosa nation embarked on the cattle killing—the most dramatic event in the history of African resistance during this period—and in the wake of this catastrophe the Cape settlers completed their conquest of Xhosaland.

In Retreat to the Keiskamma

Ngqika would pay a heavy price for collaborating with the British in expelling his rivals from the zuurveld in 1812. Thirty small forts were built along the Fish River, and the soldiers had orders to shoot Xhosa who attempted to cross this boundary. Although British officials were well aware of the limitations of Ngqika's authority, they would now hold him responsible for all acts perpetrated against the colonists by the Ciskei Xhosa. Settlers who had cattle stolen, moreover, would have the right to enter Xhosaland and seize whatever stock they could find as compensation. The colonial governor, Lord Charles Somerset (April 1814–March 1826), met Ngqika on the Kat River in March 1817 and outlined the chief's obligations, in return for which he would receive some military aid and trading rights. Ngqika himself was appeased with a shower of presents, but he was thoroughly compromised in the eyes of his peers.

The Gcaleka Xhosa east of the Kei River were now led by Hintsa (1789–1835), and he recognized Ndlambe as the dominant Xhosa chief west of the Kei River. Ndlambe's military potential improved when his estranged son Mdushane, the designated heir and a formidable warrior in his own right, returned to the chiefdom with his followers. Ndlambe's credibility was also enhanced with the rise of the war prophet Nxele, who rallied the dissident Ciskei Xhosa behind the aging chief. Hintsa and Ndlambe joined forces and under Nxele's leadership they defeated Ngqika decisively in the Battle of Amalinde (October 1818). Ngqika managed to escape and fled to the mountain stronghold of the Winterberg, where he appealed to the colonial authorities for support. Again the British intervened, despite repeated attempts by Ndlambe to maintain peace with the whites, and arbitrarily demanded that the victors submit to their vanquished foe. Thus British interference in a purely Xhosa dynastic quarrel served as a major cause of the War of 1818–19.[19]

A British-Boer commando crossed the Fish River in December 1818: the Ndlambe Xhosa did not offer resistance, but Ngqika's men attacked them so savagely that the British commander was eventually forced to confiscate the weapons of his erstwhile Xhosa allies. Ndlambe's people lost twenty-three thousand head of cattle in the raid, and Ngqika's people returned to the land they had occupied before the Amalinde defeat. The Ndlambe, impoverished by the loss of their cattle and a drought that persisted almost three years, had little choice but to fight back. They attacked Ngqika again, forcing him to vacate his home territory between the Fish and Keiskamma rivers, and then they entered the colony to reclaim their cattle. Xhosa patrols crossed the Fish River during the early months of 1819 and began raiding for cattle and killing those farmers who tried to stop them.

The Cape authorities organized a force of 3,315 British army regulars, Boer militia, and Khoikhoi scouts and sharpshooters from the Cape Regiment—the largest ever assembled by a Cape colonial government up to that time—to punish Ndlambe, but he decided not to wait until he was attacked. His chiefs had raised an army of about six thousand men (and several thousand noncombatant women and children who supplied food to the soldiers), which was also the largest force ever before assembled by Africans against the Cape. Led by the charismatic Nxele, they crossed the Fish in April and launched an attack on Grahamstown (founded in 1812), military headquarters of the colony's eastern frontier at the time (Map 3). They chose to fight en masse during the day, a suicidal tactic against a fortified position armed with cannon and infantry equipped with modern weapons. The battle lasted about five hours before the surviving Xhosa broke ranks and fled.

Once Grahamstown was made secure against further attacks, the commando force moved slowly and methodically into the Ciskei. The countryside between the Fish and Keiskamma rivers was virtually cleared of Xhosa; huts and food supplies were destroyed and cattle were seized as compensation. The campaign was extended across the Kei, and Hintsa actually fled as far as the Mbashe River before the war was brought to an end in October 1819. Ngqika had finally bested his principal rivals, but he was now virtually a puppet of the colonial government.

Having won the war, the British dictated the peace. In the next fifteen years a settlement would be implemented, primarily in two phases, with irrevocable consequences for those living in the Ciskei frontier zone. In the first phase, the colonial authorities insisted on establishing a neutral zone stretching from the Fish to the Keiskamma River along the coast and inland to the Kat and Tyhume rivers below the Winterberg (Map 3). This area embraced virtually all of Ngqika's territory, the Cape's erstwhile Xhosa ally and the most powerful chief in the Ciskei. When talking to Ngqika and other Xhosa chiefs, government officials claimed that with the exception of a few forts to maintain peace whites as well as blacks would be barred from settling there. When talking among themselves or to their superiors in London, however, these same officials regarded the area as "ceded" territory. Dutch-speaking settlers (mainly from the vicinity of Somerset East) began crossing the Fish to farm in the disputed area from the early 1820s.

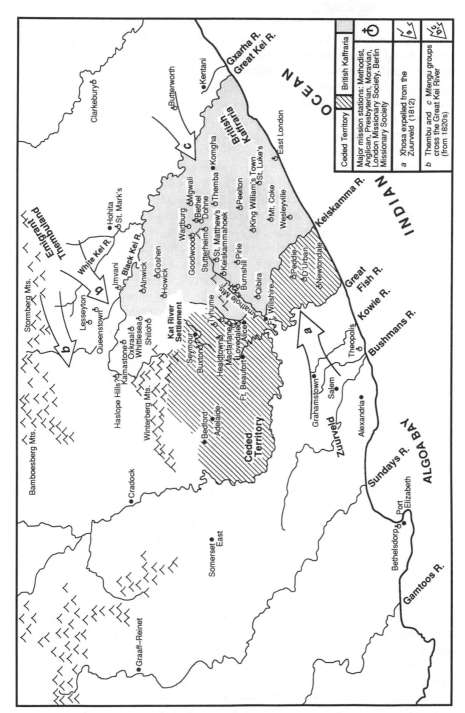

Map 3. The Ciskei region in the nineteenth century.

55

Maqoma (1798–1873), the most popular warrior chief and Ngqika's eldest son, refused to leave his home, and he was joined in this act of defiance by his brothers Tyhali, Nqeno, and Bhotumane and their followers. The British military authorities reluctantly allowed them to live in the northern portion along the Kat and Tyhume rivers, but they sought every means at their disposal short of declaring war to drive Ngqika's people off the land. The expulsion of the Xhosa from the zuurveld would be reenacted in the expulsion of the Xhosa from the "ceded" territory. Maqoma was forced to leave in the middle of a drought in 1829, and his land was given to Khoi/Coloureds from over-crowded mission stations at Bethelsdorp and Theopolis west of the Fish. The 400-square-mile Kat River Settlement, as it was called, was immediately in-corporated into the colony as a buffer against the Xhosa (Map 3). Ngqika also died in 1829, virtually a pariah among his own people.[20]

The Cape government, having established with British Colonial Office approval the so-called neutral zone, inaugurated the second phase in their campaign to establish hegemony over the Ciskei region with a divide-and-rule policy that was intended to isolate individual chiefdoms from each other and render each one defenseless in so far as that was possible. The Ndlambe and Gqunukhwebe Xhosa, expelled from the zuurveld in 1812, were pushed beyond the Keiskamma after 1819, and both chiefdoms became much weaker and more fragmented thereafter. Nxele, exiled to Robben Island off the coast of Cape Town, was drowned while trying to escape in 1820; Ndlambe died at the age of about ninety in 1828 and his heir, Mdushane, a year later.

Meanwhile, five thousand English immigrants, accompanied by a number of British officials and missionaries, arrived in the zuurveld in 1820. The area between the Bushmans and Fish rivers had already been proclaimed the sepa-rate district of Albany six years earlier (Map 3). The Cape authorities hoped white stockfarmers would have some incentive to improve the land, and with this in mind they took up the Batavian idea of developing a wool industry. The farmers were encouraged to replace indigenous fat-tailed Cape sheep with imported wool-bearing Spanish merino, and the old Gamtoos-Fish frontier zone had become the major sheep ranching region in the colony by the 1840s. The demand for labor increased considerably. Hitherto stockfarmers had only needed herders to tend their stock; now workers would be needed to wash and shear the wool as well as grade and pack it for marketing.

The War of 1834–35 and the "Fingo/Mfengu" Story. The demand for land, then, was coupled with a growing labor shortage in the Cape's eastern frontier districts during the 1820s and 1830s, and Alan Webster claims this was a major factor contributing to the War of 1834–35.[21] The settlement imposed on the Xhosa in 1819, however, was almost guaranteed to provoke hostility. Having virtually forced the Xhosa into the two previous Cape-Xhosa wars, colonial rule in the next fifteen years seemed designed to provoke another war.

British military and settler patrols invaded Xhosa territory with impunity during this period and greatly aggravated existing tensions, intimidating older chiefs and alienating younger militants. Cattle raiding increased on both sides, but the Xhosa were almost always held responsible and the settlers generally took as many cattle as they could find in compensation. The chiefs were under surveillance,[22] their land was being taken away from them, their cattle were seized without compensation, their villages were attacked at random, their subjects and sometimes even they themselves were the victims of unprovoked assaults.

Maqoma and his brother chiefs were finally provoked into action in December 1834. Marauding patrols had repeatedly pushed them off the land (Tyhali and Nqeno, for example, had been uprooted three times in fourteen months), burned miles of huts and crops, seized women and children as well as cattle, and shot several chiefs (killing at least one as well as Nqeno's son) in the process of driving the Ngqika Xhosa out of the "ceded" territory during another drought in 1833–34. Maqoma, Tyhali, and Nqeno initiated the first "counter-attacks," as Webster describes them, in what was "a desperate attempt to halt the settler advance." [23]

The chiefs conducted a guerrilla-type campaign, in contrast to the War of 1818–19, moving in small units and using hit-and-run tactics as they reclaimed the "ceded" territory and crossed the Fish River into the zuurveld. They kept clear of the towns and raided and burned selected farms, seizing cattle and killing about twenty-five men but as always leaving the women and children unharmed. Within a month, the British-colonial army had regained the initiative: Maqoma and his allies had retreated back to the Keiskamma River, and the new Cape governor, Sir Benjamin D'Urban (January 1834–January 1838), was contemplating the annexation of the entire Ciskei region between the Fish and Kei rivers.[24]

The logistical support system of the British-colonial army—unlimited quantities of food, clothing, medical supplies, guns and ammunition—could not be challenged by the Xhosa. Search-and-destroy tactics were ruthlessly applied to homesteads, crops, and stock as well as warriors. Maqoma, Tyhali, and their allies retreated to the relatively impenetrable mountain area of the Amathole east of the Tyhume River (Map 3), but they were simply bypassed as half of the British-colonial force was now deployed against the Gcaleka Xhosa. Governor D'Urban had demanded that Hintsa and his people join the war on the side of the British, but as the Xhosa paramount he wished to remain neutral. In response, D'Urban's army crossed the Kei River, burning huts and crops, seizing cattle, women, and children, and killing all who tried to resist.

Hintsa was virtually surrounded by hostile forces, as the governor had secured the support of the Thembu and Mpondo against him. Assured he would not be harmed, he entered D'Urban's camp headquarters to sue for peace. Instead, Hintsa was taken prisoner, eventually shot, and his ears cut off as souvenirs. British troops drove through Gcaleka territory and even raided for cattle among the Bomvana, allies of the Gcaleka who lived between the Mbashe and Mthatha rivers. D'Urban's invasion force returned to the Ciskei in May 1835, the Rharhabe chiefs sued for peace, and the war was finally brought to an end in September.

The War of 1834–35 was a turning point in the conquest of the Ciskei. The British lost less than a hundred men in this war; the Xhosa lost at least four thousand warriors and an unknown number of noncombatants, sixty thousand cattle as well as other stock, a large portion of their grain supplies, and their land west of the Tyhume/Keiskamma rivers. "At some point in the 1830s," according to Peires, "Xhosaland [the Xhosa people east and west of the Kei River] became unable to provide for its population." [25] The British had replaced the Rharhabe Xhosa as the real power brokers in the Ciskei region. In twenty-five years, the expansion of Xhosa polity westward had been halted and reversed by a military force that could now dictate the nature as well as the pace of change in this frontier zone.

The British also introduced a new African ethnic group into the Ciskei. The "Fingo" as they were christened at the time, or the "Mfengu" as they were rechristened by Africanist historians in the 1960s, were part of the folklore of Mfecane historiography.[26] According to the settler version, several northern Nguni groups, known collectively as the Fingo/Mfengu, had fled Natal during the destructive military campaigns initiated by Shaka, founder of the Zulu kingdom, between 1817 and 1828. These refugees settled among the southern Nguni as far south as the zuurveld, fighting in some areas but generally living peacefully among the Thembu, Mpondo, and Xhosa with whom they came into contact.

Most of these Mfengu groups settled with the Gcaleka Xhosa, but they were treated badly until they found a benefactor by the name of John Ayliff, a Methodist missionary who was in charge of a mission station established in 1826 at Butterworth in Gcaleka territory. Ayliff was convinced the Mfengu were "slaves" of Hintsa's people, and he asked the British invasion forces to "rescue" the Mfengu when they crossed the Kei River during the War of 1835. Ayliff claimed there were 16,800 Mfengu at Butterworth, and they were moved voluntarily (along with about 22,000 cattle taken from the Gcaleka) to Peddie west of the Keiskamma River in May 1835. They were allowed to occupy about half of the "ceded" territory, where they provided a strategic buffer between the Cape Colony and the Rharhabe Xhosa.

While historians have revised parts of the settler version, the basic assumptions underlying the story of the Mfengu were not challenged until the Mfecane thesis itself came under attack. Webster examined the primary sources and has tried to validate a hypothesis initially offered by Julian Cobbing: the Africans held hostage by Hintsa's people and "liberated" by the British were largely Gcaleka and Rharhabe Xhosa refugees, who were brought into the Cape Colony as indentured labor.[27]

The War of 1834–35 triggered serious upheavals in Xhosa society, and according to Webster the invasion force across the Kei River actually encountered three groups of refugees "willing to co-operate with the Colony in exchange for land." The first group were military collaborators, who provided about a thousand men to serve the British-colonial army during the remaining months of the war (as spies, messengers, foot soldiers, stock herders, and to assist the troops in raiding expeditions). The second group were the missionaries and about five hundred of their followers, who had congregated at Butterworth. The third group had been captured by raiding parties or had sought safety with the British. The three groups together comprised about seventeen thousand people—most of whom were women and children—or more than 20 percent of the Gcaleka Xhosa population estimated at eighty thousand in 1837.[28]

Webster claims that "merely a few hundred" of the refugees picked up by D'Urban could be identified as "Fingo"—the term he prefers because it is "the anglicised word for a British creation." [29] Most of these people, moreover, had moved from the interior plateau trying to escape the slave and cattle raiders—they were not fleeing Shaka's Zulu from the future colony of Natal. Scattered groups of "Fingo" were living all over the eastern Cape between the Sundays and Mzimvubu rivers (Map 1) before 1835. Some were absorbed as laborers inside the Cape, and some found a haven with Xhosa, Thembu, and Mpondo chiefdoms outside the colony. There were people described as "Fingo" living among the Rharhabe as well as the Gcaleka Xhosa east of the Kei River. They were treated well and would in time have been fully absorbed into these communities.

Webster believes the term "Fingo" was applied by the settlers to all these groups only after D'Urban's army had relocated some of them in the Ciskei at Peddie and Tyhume in the "ceded" territory and at King William's Town, a new military settlement being built by D'Urban near the site of a mission station east of the Keiskamma River. Most refugees from the 1834–35 war, however, were sent as indentured farm labor to the settler towns of Grahamstown, Cradock, Fort Beaufort, and Somerset East inside the colony (Map 3). These Mfengu refugees brought very few cattle with them. As Webseter puts it: "The Fingo did not take the cattle. The British did." The "Fingo," moreover, never formed the buffer between the Cape Colony and the Xhosa that settler historians have claimed for them.[30]

The Cobbing-Webster hypothesis has triggered considerable debate among specialists in the early colonial period in South African history. It seems quite probable that groups of refugees identified as Mfengu were living in Bantu-speaking communities outside as well as inside Xhosaland before the 1834–35 war, and D'Urban's army unquestionably encountered refugees in Xhosaland during the war who were not linked to missionaries like Ayliff and his flock at Butterworth. But it seems much less probable that virtually all of them were really impoverished Xhosa. Is it reasonable to suppose that thousands of Xhosa—however desperate—would have converted overnight, as it were, to a new identity as Mfengu? Is it reasonable to suppose that the "Fingo" were merely a figment of the colonial imagination, when such a large population in the eastern Cape have identified themselves as Mfengu and believe they have a history as a people that predates this war? In essence, there is not enough evidence at this point to support the hypothesis.

The Mfengu, however, would now become a crucial factor in the history of the Ciskei. While Khoikhoi and Xhosa groups had been military allies of the Europeans at one time or another in all previous Cape-Xhosa wars,[31] it was the people identified collectively as the Mfengu who became invaluable collaborators in the last four wars—so crucial to the survival of the Xhosa nation.[32] In return, they were given more and more land at the expense of the Xhosa and their allies. The Mfengu would become the vanguard of a new African elite in the colonial order.

The Subjugation of the Ciskei Xhosa

The Ciskei frontier zone was now home to numerous peoples besides the Rharhabe Xhosa. Mfengu and white settler farms dotted parts of the landscape; Thembu units arrived during the 1820s and settled below the Stormberg. San hunters could still be found in isolated pockets of the Winterberg, Amathole, and Stormberg mountain ranges, and Khoi/Coloured communities were positioned along the Kat River (Map 3).

The British were now the dominant authority in the Ciskei, and D'Urban actually annexed the whole region up to the Kei River in May 1835. He called it the Province of Queen Adelaide and allowed more settler farms to be established inside and outside the "ceded" territory near their new source of labor—the Mfengu living at Peddie, Tyhume, and King William's Town. A Xhosa police force called the Kaffir Police was also created to help the military authorities monitor the activities of the Rharhabe Xhosa. Although Queen Adelaide proved to be unacceptable to the Colonial Office in London and the province was formally dissolved in February 1837, it was a portent of the future.

The British Colonial Office refused initially to annex more territory in the Ciskei and ordered the local authorities to draw up a series of treaties with the Rharhabe Xhosa, now represented by the senior chiefs of the Ngqika lineage. The British would maintain effective control over the "ceded" territory, more forts would be built, and settler farms already established beyond the borders of the colony would be retained. The chiefdoms were confined to specific "locations" with their boundaries virtually frozen, and those who had been dispossessed before 1836 when the treaties were being negotiated could not reclaim their land. The ubiquitous practice of sending marauding commandos into Xhosaland, however, was forbidden; colonial farmers were told to hire more herders and protect their own stock; some of the cattle stolen from various Xhosa chiefdoms was returned; and Maqoma's people were allowed to reoccupy part of their land in the "ceded" territory. British interests were represented by a few "diplomatic agents" stationed near the residences of the principal chiefs.

Nevertheless, the treaty system was doomed almost from the beginning: it was simply not in the settlers' interest to observe these treaties. They wanted more land, and the continuing labor shortage in the Cape's eastern frontier districts militated against any policy that would inhibit access to African workers beyond the border. In any event, the British would not provide money or personnel to police the frontier: this responsibility was left to the chiefs. Although their authority was being steadily undermined, the chiefs were obliged to discipline their increasingly impoverished people and in particular stop the theft of colonial stock—an explosive issue that English settlers, like the Dutch before them, continually exploited. Since it was in the chiefs' interests to observe the treaties, they carefully ensured that this was done. Violence was contained, and stock theft, when it occurred, was punished. Cattle were returned or full compensation was paid.

The treaty system began to fall apart when Andries Stockenström, one of the few government officials trusted by the Xhosa, was forced out of office by the settlers in 1839. He had been the lieutenant governor in charge of the eastern frontier districts and the person responsible for drafting the treaties. Succeeding government agents revised the treaties without consulting the chiefs. In 1841, for example, "unarmed" patrols were allowed to cross the Fish in search of "stolen" stock and, if found, to confiscate more stock as "compensation." Three years later under a new Cape governor, Sir Peregrine Maitland (March 1844–January 1847), new treaties were drawn up. Xhosa accused of crimes were to be tried in the colony, and Christian converts (most of them identified as Mfengu) would not be subject to chiefly authority. The chiefs were also obliged to accept the government's right to erect more forts in the "ceded" territory. The rights of settlers to recover their stock and be compensated for theft were strengthened, and a court of sorts was created where they could air their grievances against the chiefs.

In the end, the new treaties were made obsolete as the British reverted to a military solution to complete their conquest of the Ciskei frontier zone. The Cape authorities launched a "pre-emptive strike," as Peires puts it, in March 1846 against the embittered Ngqika Xhosa, now led by Ngqika's designated successor, Sandile (1820–79).[33] His elder brother Maqoma, who had held the post of regent until Sandile came of age, was still the main warrior chief. Other Xhosa chiefs joined the Ngqika as well as some Thembu units living near the Stormberg in the northeastern quadrant of the frontier zone. Sarhili (ca. 1810–93), the Gcaleka paramount who had succeeded Hintsa, was technically neutral but sympathetic to the plight of the Xhosa in the Ciskei. Like Hintsa, he offered refuge to men, women, children, and cattle.

The Xhosa counterattacked on two fronts. The main body of the Ngqika Xhosa together with their Thembu allies swept through the northern portion of the "ceded" territory, across the Fish and into the Bruintjeshoogte to the head-waters of the Sundays River (Map 3). The Gqunukhwebe under Chungwa's son Phatho swept through the southern portion of the "ceded" territory, across the Fish and into the zuurveld along the coast to the lower Sundays River. In both strikes, they again avoided the towns and fought in small units against selected targets. Within two months, however, British regular and colonial troops, along with Khoikhoi and Mfengu recruits and with plenty of logistical support, had returned to the offensive. Warriors allied to the Ndlambe Xhosa got caught in the open and about five hundred were killed in what became known as the Battle of Gwangpa. Once again, the chiefs retreated across the Fish and Keiskamma to their mountain stronghold in the Amathole. Once again, British-colonial troops avoided a confrontation, rampaged through the Ciskei, crossed the Kei River and attacked the Gcaleka Xhosa.

The British-colonial army, however, was now in some disarray. Stockenström, field commander of the commando units, resigned and most of the settlers serving with him returned to their homes when the governor refused to accept a peace agreement he had made with the paramount Sarhili. The Khoikhoi conscripts were angry because their families had received inadequate rations, while British regulars were sick with dysentery and dispirited because they had hardly made contact with the enemy during the campaign. The Xhosa were becoming more skilled at guerrilla warfare, making extensive use of firearms for the first time and learning to employ some of their enemy's tactics (they burned pastures, for example, to prevent the British from using the grass to feed their horses and oxen). The Xhosa were not yet beaten, but they had been reduced to near starvation. Maqoma gave up in October 1847, and Sandile was taken into custody in December when he thought he was negotiating for peace. Phatho finally gave up, and the British concluded the war in late December 1847.

The Ciskei frontier zone was to be divided into three parts. The Cape Colony annexed the rest of the "ceded" territory between the Fish and Keiskamma rivers. The Xhosa were expelled altogether from the region, and the land was given to settlers and Mfengu. A northern portion below the Stormberg range occupied by the Thembu since the 1820s was also incorporated into the colony. A few locations were created for "loyal" Thembu and Mfengu, but most of the land went to white settlers. Thembu who had joined the Xhosa in the war were pushed across the Kei River.

Xhosa chiefdoms in the Ciskei were squeezed into about 3,050 square miles of specified locations between the Keiskamma and Kei rivers. The region was called British Kaffraria, and it was to be administered separately as a Crown Colony with its own high commissioner—Sir Harry Smith, who had helped D'Urban administer the abortive Province of Queen Adelaide—and its own capital in King William's Town (Map 3). Even British Kaffraria, however, was dotted with settler enclaves: King William's Town; East London, the port being built on the coast at the mouth of the Buffalo River; eight forts sited on some of the best land between the Xhosa locations; and the mission stations. The territory was carved up into counties, each with its own English name, and a detailed census was taken of the Xhosa population. Commissioners were appointed to oversee locations set aside for the Xhosa, and the boundaries of each were surveyed. The chiefs were still in authority, but their decisions could now be challenged by the commissioners.

Xhosa work seekers wishing to enter the colony were obliged to sign contracts before leaving British Kaffraria (Ordinance 3 of 1848), and they could be indentured to unknown employers and at unspecified wages in areas far removed from the Ciskei region. More than half of the 922 officially indentured laborers from the territory in 1848, moreover, were classified as women and children. White traders soon established a permanent presence in the region and were buying and selling goods across the Kei as far as the Umzimkulu River on the Natal border. Six mission agencies had established fifteen stations in British Kaffraria by 1850. The Ciskei Xhosa now faced the full force of colonization as a veritable army of administrators, soldiers, missionaries, traders, and labor recruiters descended on the truncated locations.

The War of 1850–53. Settler demands for more land and labor were not satiated in the aftermath of the 1846–47 war. Within three years, the chiefs had been forced into a position where they had no choice but to fight again for the survival of their people.

Smith, who was now governor of the Cape Colony (December 1847– March 1852), bears a major share of personal responsibility for manufacturing the events that led to war—the eighth frontier war as it is designated in South African historiography (or more popularly, Mlanjeni's War)—between December 1850 and February 1853.[34] Openly contemptuous of Xhosa tradition and with an arrogance unmatched even by the other overweening colonial officials of the day, he systematically humiliated the chiefs and denigrated their authority. Ultimately, he deposed Sandile and then declared the senior chief of the Rharhabe Xhosa an outlaw among his own people. Government administrators, goaded by the settlers and their press, seemed determined to strip

the poverty-stricken Xhosa, Thembu, and even staunch allies like the Khoi/
Coloured farmers of the Kat River Settlement[35] of their remaining dignity and
self-respect. Having done their utmost to alienate most of the subject peoples
in the frontier zone, the colonists thus prepared the stage for what would be
the longest and most bitterly fought of all the Cape-Xhosa wars.

Inspired by Sandile's war doctor Mlanjeni who, like Nxele in 1818, was
the principal prophet of resistance, most of the Xhosa chiefs in the Ciskei
(some Ndlambe and Gqunukhwebe chiefdoms were technically neutral), the
Thembu under Chief Maphasa north of British Kaffraria, the Khoi/Coloureds
from Kat River, members of Smith's supposedly loyal Kaffir Police, and even
some whites (one of whom was appointed an officer in the Xhosa army) joined
in the war against the British.

The Gcaleka Xhosa under Sarhili also got involved in the fighting. The
annexation of Xhosa and Thembu land at the end of the 1846–47 war had
brought the Cape Colony to the northern edge of Sarhili's territory. The boundary, in fact, was now very close to a new capital, named Hohita, the paramount
had built on land taken from the Thembu east of the White Kei River (Map 3).
Sarhili committed all his military resources to the war north of the Amathole
Mountains in a vain effort to block further colonial annexations in this area,
and he suffered relatively heavy casualties as a result because his warriors were
forced to fight mainly in flat, open grassland country. He tried repeatedly to
seize the fortified village of Whittlesea, for example, and lost hundreds of men
when he was drawn into open combat at the Battle of Imvane in April 1851.

The British strategy of starving the Xhosa into submission was carried out
with brutal efficiency during this war, and, as Peires carefully documents, both
sides reached a level of dehumanization that was unprecedented. Thousands of
British soldiers were sent to the Cape to fight what was essentially a guerrilla
operation with scores of small engagements erupting all over the Ciskei frontier
zone and into the zuurveld. In one thickly wooded mountain area west of the
Kat River, for example, four thousand troops were tied down for more than
eighteen months trying to dislodge a Xhosa-Khoi force that probably did not
number more than two hundred ill-equipped men. Smith was sent home in
disgrace after failing to drive them from this stronghold.

The British-colonial army, along with their Mfengu auxiliaries, had still
not forced the Xhosa out of their hiding places in the Amathole Mountains
when Smith's successor, Sir George Cathcart (March 1852–December 1854),
finally met the chiefs east of the Kei River and reached a verbal agreement that
the fighting was over. The death toll on both sides—an estimated sixteen thousand Xhosa and fourteen hundred British-colonial troops—was the highest in
the history of the Cape-Xhosa wars.

While the Xhosa were waiting for a signed peace treaty that would allow
them to return to their locations in the Ciskei and govern their people, Cathcart

made preparations to remove some from their land. The Ngqika Xhosa were finally expelled from their stronghold in the Amathole Mountains—which was proclaimed a Crown Reserve and repopulated with white settlers and Mfengu— and confined to the rest of British Kaffraria between the Amathole and the Kei River. The Khoi/Coloureds were removed from the Kat River Settlement, and their land, along with land occupied by Thembu in the region of present-day Queenstown (founded in 1853), was sold mainly to settlers (Map 3).

Thembu expelled from the Ciskei during the 1846–47 and 1850–53 wars now sought to claim territory occupied by the Gcaleka Xhosa east of the Kei River. This land dispute triggered a series of armed clashes that would last more than twenty years. It would also be used by the Cape authorities as an excuse to precipitate another war in the eastern Cape and expel the Gcaleka Xhosa from their nuclear homeland.

The Cattle-killing and Its Aftermath

Cathcart was replaced by a new governor, Sir George Grey (December 1854– January 1862). Grey, an arch imperialist, was the final architect in the conquest of Xhosaland. While the Xhosa had lost much land and the majority were destitute, their social institutions were still largely intact. Grey's mission was to "undermine and destroy"[36] these institutions, as he himself put it, and position the Xhosa as a subordinate people in Cape colonial society. His principal biographer, who was very sympathetic to the man and his methods, leaves no one in doubt about his goals:

> Grey's policy was to undermine the power of the chiefs, break up the larger tribes into smaller more manageable units, overawe them by a show of military force, remove large numbers of natives out of the province [British Kaffraria] altogether, concentrate the rest in village settlements under European officers, and convey large tracts of the best land to European farmers. . . . It was only the Kafirs [i.e., the Xhosa] who disliked it, and some of them derived some benefits from it.[37]

Grey succeeded in convincing colonial officials in London that more costly wars could be averted (he used the bogus threat of a possible Mfengu-Xhosa alliance to strengthen his argument) and the Xhosa converted to British rule if they agreed to subsidize a plan he had devised to provide "public works projects"—schools and hospitals for the Xhosa—and reorganize the administration of British Kaffraria. Grey was given forty thousand pounds a year to "civilise" the Xhosa along these lines, and the commissioners in British Kaffraria, who had been looking after British and Cape colonial interests in the locations since the end of the 1846–47 war, would be his agents.[38]

The Xhosa were put to work digging irrigation channels to improve local water supplies and building roads through the Amathole and other hitherto inaccessible areas that had been strongholds of resistance during previous

Cape-Xhosa wars. The wages were less than one-third the going rate in the colony, but most Xhosa had little choice in the matter. The war itself and the loss of land and cattle after the war had left them deeply impoverished, and few Xhosa at this time were given the necessary travel documents to enter the colony, this privilege being reserved for the Mfengu.

The missionaries, as we shall see, rejoiced at the prospect of getting money for schools, even if Grey was more interested in training the Xhosa to be carpenters and shoemakers than teachers and evangelists. The attempt to introduce Western medicine to the Xhosa—in the person of Dr. J. P. Fitzgerald, an eye specialist brought to the Cape from New Zealand where Grey had previously been governor—was actually a qualified success. Fitzgerald apparently treated the Xhosa medicine men as professional equals, and he gained a considerable reputation as a physician among Ngqika's people.

The success of Grey's plan, however, hinged on how effective he could be in permanently undermining the authority of the chiefs. He believed Xhosa resistance would not finally be broken until the chiefs were deprived of the material basis of their power, which lay primarily in their right to levy judicial fees and fines and receive gifts as the arbiters of Xhosa law and custom. Grey took this right away from them and replaced it with a fixed government stipend. The chief's councillors were also placed on the government payroll, since they had been his advisers in judicial and other matters and they had received a portion of these payments for their services. Chiefs and councillors could still judge cases, but from now on they would be assisted by white magistrates attached to the main locations. Although some councillors argued vigorously against this ruling, the initial salaries were high, and for the impoverished chiefs there seemed to be no alternative but to accept the new dispensation.

The basis of political power in Xhosa society was now in real jeopardy, while the cumulative impact of more than forty years of disruptive, discriminatory, and generally violent contact with British-colonial rule had shaken its economic and cultural foundations. The Xhosa response was to seek release from bondage through an act of atonement—as much a spiritual as a physical catharsis—that proved to be the single, most decisive event in their history. It is known as the cattle killing, and it consumed much of the nation between May 1856 and June 1857. While not unique in the history of resistance to colonial rule, the cattle killing remains one of the most extraordinary manifestations of its kind in sub-Saharan Africa.

Peires has provided a compelling and convincing reconstruction of this catastrophe.[39] The Xhosa were plagued by a series of economic reverses following the 1850–53 war. A Dutch ship carrying Friesland bulls infected with lungsickness arrived in South Africa in 1853, and the disease spread inexorably through the colony and into Xhosaland. Lungsickness was virtually impossible to contain, and it was a particularly agonizing death to observe for a cattle-keeping people like the Xhosa. They sought in every way to stop the spread of the disease, but it was to no avail. The death toll had risen to about five thousand beasts a month by 1855–56, and some chiefdoms lost virtually all their herds.

Maize, now the Xhosa's primary food staple, was also under attack by a species of grub that destroyed the stalks before the corncobs were edible. Birds, insects, and excessive rains that rotted the grain fields also hampered food production. There was virtually no game left to hunt and no unclaimed land for new chiefdoms in Xhosaland. Some evidence of the degree of tension within Xhosa society can be gleaned from the rise in witchcraft killings; more than twenty were recorded among the Gcaleka Xhosa east of the Kei, for example, in the first six months of 1855.

The prophetic witness loomed large in the midst of a people whose world was falling apart. Xhosa religion had traditionally been pragmatic rather than transcendental: it was concerned with the way people behaved in the existing world, but it was essentially ambivalent on the subject of death and life after death. Consequently, the Xhosa response to death and dying was dictated in large measure by previous experiences. A major smallpox epidemic about 1770, for example, had been so devastating that funeral rituals were abandoned, and the dying were removed from their huts and abandoned in the bush.

The fear of death had greatly intensified during the Cape-Xhosa wars, which were accompanied by hitherto unprecedented hardships on the civil population. Therefore it is not surprising that the Christian message concerning the Crucifixion and especially the resurrection of the dead would appeal to many Xhosa: it seemed to fill a spiritual void in their own religion. The missionaries, who perceived the Xhosa way of life as essentially evil and were determined to mold their converts in the colonial image, never appreciated the implications of the Gospel from this perspective.

In Xhosa society, as in other societies, when military prowess failed attempts were made to resolve crises by employing spiritual leaders whose revelationary messages generated a sense of unity and purpose that conventional political leaders could not provide. During the first half of the nineteenth century, a number of Xhosa prophets fused elements of Christianity with Xhosa religion in an attempt to find meaning in the colonial experience and offer hope for their people. Nxele was one such prophet.[40] Chief Ndlambe had turned to him after the debacle of 1812, and he rose to become the chief strategist in the 1819 war. Nxele appeared during the period when European intrusion into Xhosa affairs first began to threaten the integrity of the nation, and his fusion of Christian and pre-Christian visions of the future survived both defeat in war and his own death. Others took his place as the Xhosa way of life slowly unraveled in the next generation.

Nxele's mantle as a prophet, miracle worker, and war doctor for all the Xhosa was conferred on the seer Mlanjeni during the decisive 1850–53 war. Mlanjeni urged his followers to forsake witchcraft and kill all dun- and yellow-colored cattle (these colors were deemed to be evil, and the settlers were probably correct in fearing they were meant to represent the English). His millennial promises included the imminent return of the ancestors and a final battle between the forces of good and evil. Mlanjeni died six months after the war ended, but it was commonly believed that he, Nxele, and other prophets had risen from the dead and would lead the ancestral forces in restoring the nation.

The prophetic vision, as Peires emphasizes, was perfectly compatible with existing Xhosa beliefs. The ancestors were ever present in the land of the living, bringing health and prosperity to those who were good and misfortune to those who were bad. As intermediaries, Xhosa diviners were supposed to have experienced death and rebirth as part of their apprenticeship in communicating with the invisible world. The restoration of past and present, moreover, was gradually perceived as a manifestation of an even larger event that encompassed the redemption of humankind. The creation event would be repeated: when the prophecies came to pass, all non-Xhosa as well as Xhosa would return to *uHlanga,* a concept that meant both the creator and the source of creation.

Nongqawuse, the main prophet of the cattle-killing movement, was a young woman about fifteen years of age when she began to proclaim her gospel in Sarhili's domains east of the Kei River. Her uncle and guardian as well as the principal interpreter of her visionary messages was a man named Mhlakaza, who had worked for some years in the colony and spoke English and Dutch fluently. Peires has established that Mhlakaza apparently lived in Grahamstown under the name of Wilhelm Goliath. He joined a Methodist congregation, married an Mfengu by Christian rites, and in June 1849 he became the personal servant of one Nathaniel Merriman, the newly appointed Anglican archdeacon for Grahamstown and the frontier districts. For more than a year he accompanied Merriman on a walking tour of his vast parish, and the two apparently became close friends; Goliath gained a knowledge of the Bible and Anglican liturgy, and in essence he was the clergyman's African evangelist.

Under Merriman's tutelage, Goliath was apparently the first Xhosa to receive the Anglican communion and be confirmed as a full member of this church. The relationship began to deteriorate, however, when the pair returned to Grahamstown and Goliath resumed his duties as a servant in the Merriman household. The clergyman's wife regarded him as a nuisance who did not earn his keep, and Merriman was obliged to find his protegé a teaching position in a Xhosa farm school near the settler city. The school closed down with the outbreak of war in 1850 and Goliath was again employed by the Merrimans, but he refused to work as a servant. His religious experiences, apparently increasing in intensity, were now regarded as pretentious nonsense by the family that had once encouraged him to believe he had a life in the church.

Goliath left the Merriman household soon after the war ended in 1853, reassumed his African name Mhlakaza, and returned to Xhosaland where he established a homestead on the Gxarha River just east of the Kei (Map 3). He brought with him a child he had adopted, whose parents had been killed during the war. It seems reasonable to believe that this orphan was none other than Nongqawuse.

Nongqawuse's first eschatological vision occurred in April 1856, but the messages she and her contemporaries[41] received then and later were very similar to those received by the earlier prophets. The people must kill all their cattle because they were contaminated and they could not mix with the cattle that would be brought by the ancestors of the Xhosa—the New People, as they were called—who would inaugurate the millennium. The Xhosa must abandon witchcraft, and all charms and medicines associated with witchcraft had to be destroyed. Virtually everything the Xhosa possessed—much of it now European-made goods—was deemed to be contaminated: food (including cattle, sheep, goats, and other livestock), clothing, blankets, ornaments, cooking pots, hoes, spades and other household items, and weapons had to be destroyed, given away, or sold. The people were told to purify themselves through seclusion and special sacrifices and construct new houses, cattle enclosures, grain pits, and milk sacks for the New People.

The cattle-killing prophets appeared initially in those British Kaffrarian chiefdoms that were first affected by the cattle-killing disease. Lungsickness crossed the Kei River early in 1856 and spread through the southern half of Sarhili's territory, where Mhlakaza and his niece lived. It then radiated northward and by August at the latest it had reached Sarhili's capital at Hohita (Map 3) and was decimating the royal herds.

Sarhili at this point in time was perhaps the most influential of all the Xhosa leaders—among the commoners as well as the demoralized chiefs— east and west of the Kei River. Thus the king's response to the prophecy would be a crucial factor in determining its credibility with the mass of the Xhosa. Mhlakaza's father had been one of Sarhili's councillors, and the king himself decided to go to Mhlakaza's homestead on the Gxarha River in July 1856 to ascertain the truth of the oracle. He came away convinced that the prophecy must be obeyed and sent messages to his brother chiefs urging them to comply.

The first Resurrection Day was set for the full moon in August 1856, and when nothing happened Sarhili and other prominent believers tried to enlist support from the leading Mpondo, Mpondomise, and Thembu chiefs, the Sotho king Moshoeshoe, the Mfengu who had also suffered greatly from lungsickness, and the African mission station community. Now even whites were to be included in the new creation, and the settlers were urged to dispose of their worldly goods and cleanse themselves in anticipation of *uHlanga*. Unbelieving Xhosa were warned that their selfishness could jeopardize the coming millennium and they would be gathered up by Satan if they refused to adhere to the prophecies. Settler antagonism, however, soon prompted the believers to declare that whites were not eligible to enter the promised land (they had killed the Son of God). Virtually the only non-Xhosa who responded to the prophecies were those Thembu who had been followers of Maphasa and had lost their land as well as their chief in the 1850–53 war.

Sandile's vote would be decisive for the success or failure of the cattle-killing movement among the Ciskei Xhosa just as Sarhili's vote had been for the Gcaleka Xhosa. Between August and December 1856, as lungsickness began to infect his district, Sandile moved from being a passive unbeliever to being an ardent believer. Most of his people had planted crops during the sowing season (between August and December) in 1855, but they did not do so in 1856.

The prophets assigned dates for Resurrection Days in December 1856 and again in February 1857, but the New People did not appear. Near Hohita a new prophet named Tsimbi rose to rally the people. He set another Resurrection Day in April and predicted the New People would rise from beneath Sarhili's capital, but again they did not appear. A "moon of wonders" set for June 1857 also did not bring back the dead, but now the believers had nothing left to slaughter. The cattle-killing sacrifice had been carried out to the bitter end.

The Xhosa faced mass starvation. The first reported death—the child of a diviner—had already occurred in October 1856. The prophet Tsimbi died in August 1857 and Mhlakaza in November, and between 35,000 and 50,000 others also died as a direct result of the cattle killing. At least 150,000 would be displaced from their homes within a year of the event. According to one estimate, 400,000 cattle had been killed by January 1857, and this did not include the ones that succumbed to lungsickness. Nongqawuse was transported to Cape Town and placed under confinement with other females seized in the aftermath of the cattle killing. When the prisoners were released and sent to East London in August 1859, her name was not among them. A woman claiming to be Nongqawuse was reportedly living on a farm near Port Elizabeth in 1905, but thereafter she disappears from history.

Individual households, homesteads, and chiefdoms split over the validity of Nongqawuse's vision. Most Xhosa women were ardent believers: the future kingdom held out hope to those who had an inferior position in the present one. While the men were apparently more divided, at least 85 percent of them in the seven main cattle-killing chiefdoms in British Kaffraria eventually joined the cause. The impoverished, subject commoners were the driving force behind the movement. They were sincerely motivated by the vision of a new redemptive order embracing all of humanity. The millennial apocalypse was a synthesis of Christian and pre-Christian revelations: if their world was utterly corrupt, the only legitimate response was to cleanse themselves of corruption. If their sin was fundamental, their sacrifice must be equally fundamental. Only then would the millennial promise be fulfilled.

The unbelievers included several prominent councillors, the richer home-stead heads (5–10 percent, for example, in Sandile's chiefdom), and a few chiefs (notably the Christian chiefs Khama and Dyani Tshatshu, and the Ngqika chief Anta, whose people lived high in the mountains and were the only group in Xhosaland not affected by the lungsickness epidemic). Those who for one reason or another were outcasts from Xhosa society and most of the mission station community were also in this group.

For most believers, the cattle-killing movement was their last hope to preserve the old way of life. They reasserted the traditional values of loyalty and sacrifice for the good of the community as a whole, and they condemned the unbelievers as selfish individuals who were interested only in enriching themselves. The antagonistic Red and School folk cultures that became such an enduring feature of everyday life in rural eastern Cape in later generations stem essentially from this period in Xhosa history. Peires points out that the un-believers often did represent those householders who were already competing in the colonial market economy and seeking to improve their living standards, sending their children to mission schools and adopting other aspects of Euro-pean culture. The chiefs, as we shall see, were losing not only their political power but also their economic power over the homesteads.

Relations between the believers and unbelievers had turned to violence by the early months of 1857. The colonial authorities did not support the unbeliev-ers when they might have convinced the wavering majority not to participate in the cattle killing, and they did not protect them when their property and even their lives were at stake in the aftermath of this event. Instead, Grey and his officials compiled a cattle-killing narrative designed to support the hypothesis that it was a plot hatched by the Xhosa chiefs and their allies to make war on the colony. The colonial authorities essentially rewrote this cataclysmic event to suit their own purposes. They manufactured a so-called chiefs' plot to destroy the power of the chiefs, force the Xhosa into migrant labor, and open up their territories to white settlement.[42]

The chiefs, their councillors, and many subject commoners who had promoted the cattle killing were detained, placed on trial, found guilty, and de-ported. The chiefs were incarcerated on Robben Island off Cape Town (South Africa's Alcatraz), while the commoners were employed as laborers in the colony or in some cases sent to labor camps (the "public works projects") in British Kaffraria. The court verdicts served a twofold purpose: they tempo-rarily expelled most of the chiefs as well as hundreds of destitute Xhosa from British Kaffraria (more than nine hundred prisoners, for example, had been transported to Cape Town by the end of 1857) and at the same time supplied the settlers with convict labor. It was an act of frontier justice without precedent in the history of the Cape-Xhosa wars.

Emergency rations offered by the colonial authorities were given almost exclusively to Xhosa who agreed to register as laborers and work in the colony once they were deemed fit.[43] A total of 29,142 Xhosa had registered for work in the Cape by February 1858, and Peires suggests at least an equal number had entered the colony as unregistered migrants. The eastern Cape's labor requirements had been temporarily satisfied by the end of 1858, and even in the western Cape there were fears that perhaps too many Xhosa had been absorbed into the colonial economy. They now formed a permanent segment of the population in most Cape midland and border towns west of the Kei River.

The starving Xhosa had few other alternatives. Some fled to the Mpondo, and others sought sanctuary with the Sotho under their paramount Moshoeshoe. Still others tried to survive among the unbelieving Thembu and Mfengu, who had profited during the early phase of the cattle killing when the Xhosa were practically giving away everything they owned. They also sent their children to the mission stations, and the chiefs now welcomed missionaries in their districts in the vain hope that the presence of white clergy might serve to protect their people from predatory officials and settlers. Grey, however, forced the Mfengu to expel the Xhosa in their midst, and the Thembu used the occasion to wage war against the weakened Xhosa in a bid to regain land Sarhili's father had seized nearly thirty years earlier. Mission agencies did not have the financial resources to cope with the influx of migrants, and Grey would not grant government funds for this purpose.

The Xhosa population in British Kaffraria dropped from about 105,000 to 37,200 between January and July 1857 and to a low of 25,916 by the end of 1858. Having temporarily removed thousands of Xhosa from this territory, Grey moved quickly to ensure that as much of their land as possible would be turned over to settlers. The number of whites in British Kaffraria rose from 949 in October 1856 (the beginning of the cattle killing) to 5,388 in December 1858—from less than 1 percent to 12.5 percent of the total population.[44] The Rharhabe Xhosa never recovered from the land losses, which were upward of two thousand square miles in British Kaffraria alone.

Meanwhile, across the Kei River war broke out between the Thembu and the Gcaleka Xhosa in June 1857. The fighting increased in intensity in subsequent months as Sarhili's emaciated warriors fought savagely to retain their homesteads. Grey saw the dispute as another opportunity to intervene on behalf of an ally, and in February 1858 a commando force was dispatched to punish the hapless Gcaleka. Sarhili and his "army" of perhaps five hundred men were chased out of their ancient homeland. Colonial troops seized five hundred head of cattle (virtually all the Gcaleka had left) and destroyed all homes and gardens they could find. Sarhili's people gained sanctuary with their Bomvana allies east of the Mbashe River.

The homeland of the Gcaleka Xhosa between the Kei and Mbashe rivers was virtually depopulated for several years while the Cape tried without success to get London to underwrite the costs of moving white immigrants into the region. Attempts to squeeze more Xhosa out of British Kaffraria by offering Sandile's people a slice of land in Sarhili's country also failed. Grey's successor, Sir Philip Wodehouse (January 1862–May 1867), finally persuaded four Thembu chiefs near Queenstown to resettle in the northern third of the Gcaleka homeland. This area, which became known as Emigrant Thembuland, was in the foothills of the Drakensberg near the Indwe River and included Sarhili's capital, Hohita. Mfengu living in overcrowded locations between the Fish and Keiskamma rivers in the Ciskei were resettled in the central portion, known as Fingoland, which included Hintsa's old capital near the mission station at Butterworth.

Sarhili and his people were finally allowed to reoccupy the southern third of their ancestral homeland in 1865. This area, to be known as Gcalekaland, comprised the coastal lowlands facing the Indian Ocean and included Mhlakaza's old homestead on the Gxarha River. The previous division of British Kaffraria into counties with English names was withdrawn and the territory incorporated into the Cape Colony as the districts of East London and King William's Town in April 1866. Chiefs still imprisoned on Robben Island were released three years later.[45]

With the annexation of British Kaffraria, the whole of the Ciskei between the Fish and Kei rivers was finally incorporated into the Cape. Two-thirds of the old Gcaleka Xhosa homeland between the Kei and Mbashe rivers was now occupied by the Mfengu and Thembu, the two Bantu-speaking groups that had sided most consistently with the British against the Xhosa since the 1830s.[46] The Cape also extended its authority over the Bhaca and Mpondomise east of the Mbashe, and the Gcaleka Xhosa found themselves virtually surrounded by people who were subject to the Cape and therefore protected by British military authority. In August 1877, a group of Gcaleka Xhosa and Mfengu clashed during a beer drink, and when Sarhili retaliated the Cape quickly rushed to the defense of their ally. The king tried to avoid conflict with the whites but finally concluded: "I intend to fight the English. I am in a corner. The country is too small and I may as well die as be pushed in a corner." [47]

The last Cape-Xhosa war (popularly known as the War of Ngcayecibi) was officially initiated when Sarhili's warriors attacked a colonial police force in September 1877, but by the end of November they had been pushed across the Mbashe River. Cape military officials thought the war was over, and preparations were made for opening up Gcalekaland to white settlers. Sarhili, however, had merely removed the women, children, and cattle from the war zone. His warriors recrossed the Mbashe in December, and an emissary was sent into the Ciskei to persuade Sandile to enter the war. A month later, Thembu groups near Queenstown who had participated in the 1850–53 war also joined the Xhosa.

Sarhili's forces had no hope of victory, but they might have prolonged the fighting if they had not abandoned the guerrilla tactics that had tied up colonial troops so effectively in previous wars. Instead, the Xhosa again listened to their wardoctors and chose to fight in close formation in open terrain and attack British-colonial troops entrenched in fortified positions. The Battle of Centane (February 1878) was one of the more tragic acts of desperation in the history of the Cape-Xhosa wars. For the first time, the Xhosa were relatively well equipped with firearms—many acquired from workers in the Kimberley diamond fields—but they were old and outdated and there was little ammunition. Nearly four hundred of Sarhili's warriors lay dead when the fighting finally stopped. The British-colonial force lost two men.

With the authorities offering a reward of a thousand pounds and five hundred cattle for his capture, Sarhili again retreated across the Mbashe, and the Gcaleka Xhosa effectively withdrew from the war. Sarhili himself found a home in a remote area deep in Bomvana territory that was virtually inaccessible to outsiders. Colonial officials declined to pursue him further, and he eventually died there in self-imposed exile.

Sandile, however, refused to surrender: he would fight until he died, and the cattle-killing chiefs who had been imprisoned on Robben Island joined him in this final sacrificial act. Sandile was killed in a skirmish north of King William's Town in May, and in June 1878 the last Cape-Xhosa war came to an end. Sixty white and 137 black soldiers in the colonial army had been killed. The Xhosa lost 3,680 warriors—perhaps one-half of the men who actually participated in the war (but this figure excludes women and children and those warriors who died of wounds and starvation)—and more than 45,000 head of cattle.[48]

The progovernment chiefs, most of the unbelievers in the cattle killing, and a considerable number of Sandile's own people did not participate in the war. Nevertheless, the colonial authorities decided to expel all Ngqika Xhosa across the Kei and sell the land they still occupied in British Kaffraria to white settlers. Perhaps one-half of Sandile's people escaped removal by seeking work on white farms in the Ciskei; the rest were transported as indentured labor to Cape Town[49] or forced to move to locations carved out for them along the coast east of the Kei River in southern Gcalekaland. Most of Sarhili's people were also resettled in Gcalekaland next to the Ngqika Xhosa.

The widespread use of firearms during the War of 1877–78 alarmed the Cape authorities, and they tried to force Africans outside the colony and in Basutoland (under Cape administration from 1871 to 1884) to surrender their weapons. The Peace Preservation Act of 1878 (known as the Gun Act) provoked a so-called Gun War with Basutoland and a "rebellion" east of the Kei in 1880–81 that involved a number of groups (Mpondomise, Sotho living south of the Drakensberg, and various Thembu units) who had never fought against the colony. In the aftermath of these disturbances, the Cape Colony extended its control over the remaining independent African chiefdoms east of the Kei River without resorting to armed conflict.

Further attempts to grab land for white settlers east of the Kei River, however, were abandoned: this area would be administered as one vast African reservation called the Transkei. The chiefs were allowed more authority than their counterparts in the Ciskei, but they were also placed on government salaries, subordinated to local magistrates, restricted to specified locations, and their people subjected to taxes. With the annexation of Pondoland in 1894, all chiefdoms between the Kei and the Natal border had been absorbed by the Cape.

The region between the Fish and Kei rivers known as the Ciskei would ultimately comprise thirteen magisterial districts. In most cases, the name of the district and that of the main settler town were the same. The districts of Peddie, Fort Beaufort, and Stockenstrom (district headquarters was the town of Seymour) would comprise roughly the same area as the old "ceded" territory. British Kaffraria, as noted earlier, was divided initially into the districts of East London and King William's Town. Three other districts—Stutterheim, Cathcart, and Komgha—would be created out of the Crown Colony, and eventually King William's Town was further subdivided into the districts of Middledrift and Keiskammahoek. The district of Victoria East (the main town was Alice) was carved partly from the "ceded" territory and partly from British Kaffraria. Finally, Queenstown and Glen Grey districts were carved out of former Thembu areas north of British Kaffraria (Map 4).

The Mfengu were now apparently the dominant African ethnic group in the Ciskei. They had received land in the Peddie, Victoria East, King William's Town, and Queenstown districts and in the Wittebergen Native Reserve, renamed Herschel in the 1870s, which lay on the border between the future South African province of the Orange Free State and the British protectorate of Basutoland (Lesotho). They also occupied more than one-third of Sarhili's old territory east of the Kei River as well as smaller enclaves further north in Thembuland and East Griqualand.

The boundaries of the surviving Mfengu, Xhosa, and Thembu locations in the Ciskei would remain largely unchanged from the 1870s to the 1970s. Most of them were located between the Fish and Buffalo rivers on the coast. The rest extended inland to include parts of the Queenstown District as well as the districts of Glen Grey and Herschel, a fragmented African reserve in the old Ciskei frontier zone.

Part 2
Conflict, Accommodation, and Subordination in Cape Colonial Society

3

Peasants and Proletarians in a Transitional Economy

British metropolitan control over the Cape Colony was solidified in stages during the first half of the nineteenth century as British administrators gradually supplanted the Dutch both in the older established southwestern Cape and on the volatile northern and eastern frontiers. The Afrikaners—those who spoke the Cape Dutch dialect that had been the language of communication under Dutch rule—continued to migrate periodically beyond the boundaries of British suzereignty into the interior of the subcontinent. Unprecedented numbers of Afrikaner farmers in the eastern Cape, for example, left the colony from the early 1830s in the so-called Great Trek. As a result of this exodus, English-speaking settlers effectively supplanted Dutch speakers as the dominant European ethnic group on the eastern frontier in the last half of the nineteenth century.

This chapter focuses on the economic implications of Cape colonial rule for the Xhosa-speaking peoples of the Ciskei region.

Section 3.1 summarizes the main developments in the expansion of mercantile capitalism in the Cape Colony before the mineral revolution.

Section 3.2 outlines the African peasant's responses to mercantile capitalism in the Ciskei between the 1820s and the 1870s.

Section 3.3 examines the impact of the shift in power relations from chiefs to government-appointed headmen in the Ciskei during the last half of the nineteenth century.

Section 3.4 looks at the consequences of the mineral revolution for Africans in general and in particular for the modernizing peasant sector in the Ciskei.

Section 3.5 considers some of the dynamics in the process of African proletarianization in the Ciskei following the mineral revolution.

3.1. Mercantile Trade in Commodities, Labor, and Land before the Mineral Revolution

The Cape was incorporated into the world economy long before the mineral discoveries of the 1870s and 1880s.[1] Agricultural production—based mainly on wheat, meat, and wine—grew steadily during the eighteenth and early nineteenth centuries. The Dutch East India Company could not isolate the Cape from the world market, and import-export controls generally did not impede the flow of goods into and out of the merchant colony. Nevertheless, most surplus production was absorbed by the local market, and imports greatly exceeded exports throughout this period.[2]

The Cape had to rely increasingly on imported grain from the 1780s, as farmers in the southwestern Cape (they produced most of the wheat and other cereal crops) could not satisfy the demand. The trekboers consumed their own meat or traded for breeding stock and draft oxen in local agricultural markets: only 3–5 percent of the Cape's cattle and sheep were being butchered in Cape Town in the late eighteenth century. Wine was not exported in quantity until the British arrived, and thereafter it was vulnerable to price fluctuations. Production soared, for example, when Cape wines were protected by imperial tariffs in the 1810s and 1820s. When these preferential tariffs were removed in 1830 and the local market could not absorb the surplus, many wine farmers then went bankrupt.

Nevertheless, prices for agricultural commodities (including wine) were generally favorable during most of the period of Dutch and early British rule at the Cape. Surplus production was limited primarily by poor transportation and distribution networks, lack of capital, and lack of markets. A relatively small nonagrarian population—including the administrative bureaucracy, merchants, traders, and artisans—serviced the rural economy and easily absorbed the surplus of an agrarian population that was still engaged primarily in subsistence production.

Economic conditions improved as the boundaries of colonial settlement expanded, more capital was accumulated, and new markets were opened up during the course of the eighteenth century. Harbor towns, for example, were established along the southern Cape coast closer to meat-production centers in the eastern frontier. Stockfarmers in the interior were no longer dependent on Cape Town to buy surplus meat, and now they could export cattle hides and horns as well as meat.

An indigenous merchant class had emerged in Cape Town by the 1770s with the capacity to fund increasing numbers of traders into the interior. Itinerant peddlers or *smousen,* as they were called by the Dutch, were already in contact with the Xhosa by this time. Trading practices became more stratified with the arrival of the British. Merchant houses established in Cape Town had direct representation in London by the 1820s and were gradually integrated into the British Empire's trading networks (through agencies like the Cape of Good Hope Trade Society and through British firms that specialized in trading with the Cape). Outside Cape Town in the eastern frontier districts, traders were also established in larger settlements along the coast (like Port Elizabeth on Algoa Bay) and the interior (like Graaff-Reinet, Grahamstown, and later Cradock); they now supplied the *smousen* with most of their goods and also competed with them in the frontier trade.

The Cape under the Dutch and early British administrations provides a classic example of how mercantile capitalism in its early stages operated on the colonial periphery. The center of economic and cultural activity and the seat of government was Cape Town, the gateway between the African interior and the outside world. Most banking and credit facilities—and most of the money in circulation—were located in Cape Town and its immediate environs. Transactions were conducted informally between a few individuals and institutions representing the mercantile, clerical, and governing establishment.

Cape Town, in turn, was linked to the monetary system then in use by Dutch and other mercantile interests around the world: it was based primarily on silver coins (preferably Spanish) that were easily converted into Dutch currency. The Cape authorities began issuing paper notes in the early 1780s to offset a sharp decline in silver coinage (brought about in part because silver from Spanish America was temporarily cut off during the 1780–84 Anglo-Dutch War). Dutch currency (based on the rixdollar) was steadily devalued as Dutch and later British officials relied increasingly on paper money to stimulate the economy and get themselves out of periodic financial crises.[3]

Cape Town was involved in the slave trade, and slaves from Madagascar, Mozambique, and the East African coast, the East Indies, and India played a crucial role in the local economy.[4] As Cape Town expanded, numbers of slaves as well as freemen became skilled artisans servicing the port city and other settlements. Conditions for slaves and indentured labor (mainly Khoisan until the 1820s) were best in urban areas engaged in commodity production and trade with the outside world; they were worst in the undercapitalized, subsistence-oriented trekboer communities in the northern and eastern frontier districts.[5]

Corruption was endemic at all levels of colonial administration. The governing authorities were in close collusion with landed proprietors and the merchant elite in Cape Town and its hinterland. Dutch East India Company officials appointed administrative and judicial officers and controlled the courts. The same individuals were responsible for civil and criminal proceedings, and one official could hold several public offices at the same time. Those in power regarded the business of government as a means to make money for themselves, their relatives, and their clients, and for the most part they were not accountable for their actions. The abuses associated with the governing elite in Cape Town were replicated on a smaller scale in the frontier districts, where officials exploited the system as best they could in the quest for personal wealth.[6]

The mercantilist system perpetuated by Dutch and early British governors at the Cape was finally dismantled during the 1820s. As depicted by Jeff Peires, it was a "revolution in government" that would have wide repercussions throughout the colony and beyond.[7] The urgency of these reforms was dictated in part by a weakening monetary system. The British had also relied increasingly on paper money to finance the colony, and inflation had seriously undermined the value of Dutch currency. The Cape switched to British currency as legal tender in 1825, and this decision (and the loss of export markets like the British wine trade) almost immediately sent the economy into a tailspin.

The Commission of Eastern Inquiry, appointed in 1822, had already recommmended a series of reforms in the administrative, legal, and economic system that would effectively integrate the Cape into the British Empire. The colony was to be freed from all constraints that had been placed on free trade and competition. Numerous local tithes and taxes as well as monopolies on producing and selling meat, bread, wine, and other commodities were abolished. New roads were built and postal services expanded in an attempt to improve the distribution and marketing of products to and from the interior.

The governor was forced to refer all matters of significance in the colony to the Council of Advice (created in 1825), although in practice no member was prepared to challenge his decisions. The commissioners tried unsuccessfully to create an autonomous Eastern Province with its own lieutenant governor (it failed due to lack of funds), but important civil appointments would now be made directly from London.

A major attempt was made to isolate the civil service from the patronage system and make colonial administration in general more efficient and more responsible for its actions. Officials could no longer hold conflicting posts simultaneously or augment their salaries with cash fees for services rendered. Other reforms were directed at the administration of the frontier districts: the traditional institutions of local government—the Landdrosts and Heemraden—were abolished in 1827 and replaced with resident magistrates and civil commissioners. Thus Afrikaner stockfarmers, who were still the dominant European ethnic group in the eastern Cape, immediately lost their principal access to power and privilege under the old system.

The courts were reorganized and an independent judiciary was guaranteed. Cape lawyers now had to get their law degrees from an English university, the main officers of the court would be appointed from England, and the language of the court would be English. The prevailing system of Roman-

Dutch law was made subordinate to the laws of England. A jury system was introduced, and even the jurors were supposed to speak English, although this provision was dropped in 1834. While it was never completely implemented, the language of communication in the court system, as in the civil service and in the political and military hierarchy, was to be English.

The key obstacles to economic reform were in the allocation of land and labor, especially in the frontier districts. The Cape authorities had attempted to phase out loan farms—the system that had virtually given away unoccupied land to the trekboers in the eighteenth century—in favor of quitrent tenure in 1813. New farms would not exceed 3,000 morgen (6,360 acres), and stock-farmers would be required to cultivate at least some of the ground. The land itself would be surveyed and titles issued, and landholders would now have the right to sell their property. Officials responsible for implementing quitrent tenure, however, were unwilling or unable to collect the rent. Cash-starved farmers manipulated local governing bodies into giving them provisional occu-pation of land as "request places." All the farmer had to do was formally request a piece of land and he could occupy it without title: most farms in the eastern frontier districts in fact were now held as "request places."

Following the recommendations of the commissioners of inquiry, a new urgency was given to implementing the quitrent system. The Cape Land Board with qualified surveyors was established in 1828, and landowners in subse-quent years were pressured into adopting quitrent tenure and paying off arrears in rent. This policy again discriminated against the cash-starved Afrikaner farmers, who did not have the money to pay for land surveys and titles and the yearly quitrent.

The forced labor system also came under attack during the 1820s. The Dutch authorities had required slaves to carry identity documents, or passes as they would be called in South Africa, from the 1760s when traveling between town and countryside. When the slave trade between Britain and its overseas possessions was abolished in 1807, British authorities at the Cape enacted measures in 1809 and 1812 (the "Hottentot Proclamation") that would tighten control over nonslave labor. The pass laws were rewritten: Khoisan not em-ployed by the government were compelled to work for the colonists, and the children of Khoisan servants were required to serve as "apprentices" for ten years—in some cases until they were twenty-five years old. Khoisan were also prevented from owning or leasing land outside their mission stations.

The Khoisan labor force, however, was too small to meet the needs of an expanding Afrikaner farming community and thousands of newly arrived British immigrants. Agriculture was still based mainly on meat, grain, wine, and a limited range of fruits and vegetables, but wool was already becoming a factor in the eastern Cape economy by the 1820s. Wool would replace wine as the colony's major source of export revenue between the 1840s and the 1870s.[8]

Ostrich farming would expand dramatically from the late 1860s, which was also the beginning of the sugar boom in the adjoining British colony of Natal.

The Cape imported indentured labor from Britain and Ireland between 1817 and 1823, but these efforts failed because Europeans could not be compelled to work at low wages or in undesirable occupations. The 1820 Settlers refused to work the land, and the majority migrated to the towns soon after arrival. Many were artisans with a little capital, products of England's new urban industrial culture, who believed trading or manufacturing would be more profitable than agriculture.

Bantu-speaking Africans were regarded as the most desirable laborers, but it was still technically illegal to employ them inside the colony. Nevertheless, the movement of Sotho speakers across the border was apparent by the 1820s. The Afrikaners claimed the Sotho were either "apprentices" (orphaned or impoverished children could be offered apprenticeships under the 1812 "Proclamation") or "Mantatees," a collective term used by the missionaries and colonists to refer to Sotho-Tswana warriors-cum-refugees allegedly fleeing the Mfecane wars. Some scholars now suggest that these refugees—like the Mfengu who followed some years later—were mainly women and children seized by local commandos or raiding parties operating in the interior and acquired by the stockfarmers to supplement their labor force. Whatever the merits of these arguments, the trekboers were indeed supplementing their labor force with Bantu speakers by the early 1820s.[9]

The Cape authorities started dismantling the existing labor control system in the late 1820s. Ordinances 49 and 50 of 1828 (enacted within three days of each other) lifted restrictions on the mobility of Khoisan labor inside the Cape. They no longer had to carry passes, and they were now allowed to own land (which resulted in the Kat River Settlement scheme). They could also avoid apprenticing their children or entering into long-term labor agreements. Most verbal and written agreements were limited to one month—in the case of registered contracts, to a maximum of one year—and local authorities could no longer impose corporal punishment. Bantu-speaking Africans were now officially allowed to enter the colony as work seekers, but they had to carry passes. Failure to do so could mean a term of forced labor for up to one year. Bantu speakers entering the Cape after 1837 could be expelled if they did not work for the settlers (Ordinance 2 of 1837).

The main motive behind these ordinances was to stimulate the economy by encouraging free blacks within and beyond the borders of the Cape to enter the colonial labor market. The same conditions applied to unfree labor soon after the slaves were emancipated in 1834. Four years later they were released from obligatory terms of indentured labor to their former masters and given the right to demand wages for work performed. Statutory discrimination between white and black employees was prohibited in 1841.

In practice, the stick as well as the carrot was used to control and manipulate labor at the Cape. Measures designed to coerce indentured Khoisan
labor in the southwestern Cape in the early 1800s were eased between the
1820s and 1840s because they were not increasing the supply of black workers,
especially in the eastern frontier districts where they were most needed. Once
the Cape gained permanent access to Bantu-speaking African labor with the
subordination of the Xhosa and their neighbors in the eastern Cape, the regulations would be amended to give white employers more control over their black
employees.

Relatively large numbers of impoverished Bantu speakers sought work in
the Cape for the first time in the aftermath of the War of 1834–35. The number
of "native foreigners" (Xhosa and Mfengu) in the Albany District immediately
west of the Fish River, for example, soared to six thousand or 30 percent of
the population. Nevertheless, Peires suggests the employment of Xhosa in the
colony "was still partial, temporary and to a certain extent voluntary" until
the momentous events that precipitated the closing of the Ciskei frontier zone
between 1846 and 1857.[10]

The attempt to surmount the labor crisis by allowing blacks to sell their
labor on the open market triggered an enormous backlash from cash-starved
Afrikaners, who still bartered for goods and services and depended on coerced
labor to maintain a fragile foothold in the mercantile economy.[11] Afrikaner
stockfarming communities in the eastern Cape were most vulnerable to the implementation of the reform program, because they were enmeshed in a political
and economic system that was not yet fully capitalist. They wanted to retain
the old system where they had some influence in local administration and in
the allocation of land and labor.

The Great Trek, as Peires suggests, was primarily a response to specific reforms initiated by the Cape government during the 1820s.[12] Afrikaner farmers
were especially concerned that they were losing control over their labor. They
wanted a vagrancy law to curb the mobility of black workers inside the colony,
and they wanted to stop Xhosa work seekers from being allowed to cross the
border. They were understandably fearful the Xhosa would seek to reclaim as
theirs the pasture land and stock that had only recently been taken from them.
The Cape authorities did temporarily ban Xhosa from entering the colony in
1829, and the governor approved a vagrancy law, but it was overturned by
the Colonial Office in the same year that the proclamation freeing the slaves
was implemented. The first organized Afrikaner trek parties left the eastern
frontier districts in 1834—several months before the outbreak of war—and
moved into the interior: roughtly fifteen thousand Afrikaners would join this
exodus in the next two decades.

As participants in the new social order, the newly arrived British immigrants were better educated and better placed to take advantage of the reform

program than the trekboers. They had more capital, they could exploit the local market more effectively, and they were not so dependent on the direct exchange of services. They had better relations with the merchant elites in Cape Town and the frontier districts, and they could take better advantage of trading opportunities because they could offer Afrikaner and Xhosa stockfarmers alike a much wider range of cheap manufactured goods. They also launched local newspapers like the *Graham's Town Journal* to promote their economic and political interests.

British settlers in the eastern Cape were able to take advantage of the shift from cattle raising to wool production for the British market between the 1820s and 1840s. They put their money into land to raise sheep, and land prices soared. Land speculation became almost as important as wool production for the emerging English-speaking gentry in the eastern Cape,[13] enriching the sheep farmers and their merchant allies, who loaned them money and invested in land as well. British speculators offered land as a commodity, a concept that was as alien to the Afrikaner as it was to the African. The land could be sold and resold without actually possessing it or using it in any way.

Increasing numbers of English-speaking hunters, farmers and land speculators, traders and merchants, administrators, soldiers, and missionaries were moving into the Ciskei frontier zone and beyond from the 1820s. The creation of Port Elizabeth, Grahamstown, and other settlements west and east of the Fish River also helped revive trade relations disrupted during the early Cape-Xhosa wars and the expulsion of the Xhosa from the Gamtoos-Fish frontier zone.

The settlers set up a limited number of trade fairs in 1822 east of Grahamstown in colonial territory, near some clay pits that produced a red ochre much favored by the Xhosa when they had lived there. Two years later, these fairs were moved to Fort Willshire in the "ceded" territory and held once a week. Trade with the Xhosa soared: the demand for ivory soon exhausted the supply of elephants in the region, but the export of cattle hides and horns rose dramatically during the 1820s.[14] This frontier trade averaged £34,000 a year for ten years until the War of 1834–35—the one bright spot in an otherwise depressed economy.

Licensed traders were allowed to establish fairs beyond the colony's borders in 1827, and all restrictions prohibiting trade with Africans outside the Cape were lifted in 1830. Within four years, between one hundred fifty and two hundred European traders had established commercial links directly with the Xhosa and were operating virtually without restrictions in their territory, often bypassing the chiefs in the quest for ivory, hides, and rare animal skins. Xhosa intermediaries in this trade were gradually neutralized by the settlers, who controlled the supply of manufactured goods as well as the supply wagons and were able to manipulate the trade fairs to the point where the Xhosa could not bargain effectively.

Currencies no longer favored were soon eliminated. The traders flooded the market with beads, for example, so they were worthless and could not be used by Africans in commercial transactions. Nevertheless, almost every traveler crossing the Fish River from the 1830s was in contact with Africans seeking to exchange whatever they had for European goods. The British-made Witney blanket, for example, supplanted the Xhosa rawhide kaross as a staple item of clothing in a single generation. Although numbers of traders were killed during the War of 1834–35 and frontier trade for some time thereafter slumped to below twenty thousand pounds a year, the Xhosa were now firmly in the colony's economic orbit. Women, for example, would spend less time in the gardens with the introduction of plow agriculture, and they gradually stopped making household utensils, clothing, or ornaments. European-made goods would supply the basic necessities, and among the Ciskei Xhosa at least most indigenous crafts were no longer being practiced by the 1880s.

3.2. Strategies for Survival in a Rural African Society

War, disease, and drought, coupled with the loss of territory and the exigencies of Cape colonial rule, wreaked havoc on the forces of precapitalist production centered in the Xhosa *umzi* or homestead. As the segmentary Xhosa state was undermined and destroyed in the 1840s and 1850s, the homestead production units fragmented. Heads of households were left to survive as best they could in truncated locations set aside for the Rharhabe Xhosa, Mfengu, and Thembu in the Ciskei between the 1830s and the 1870s.

The beginnings of an African peasantry linked to the colonial economy dates from this period. The term peasant in the present context refers to rural cultivators who had access to a specific portion of land either in the reserves, on white-owned farms, or on unoccupied crown land. Peasants depended mainly on family labor (or extended family labor, in which the immediate family co-ordinated work activities with close relatives), produced most of the foodstuffs they consumed, and were also involved in the production of commodities for an external market. In other words, they sold at least a portion of what they produced to meet the obligations placed on them as participants in an emerging capitalist economy. Peasants, however, were proletarians in the making. They were locked in an unequal struggle with the forces of capitalist production from the beginning. All peasants—and these included white as well as black peasants—were being denied the right to an independent rural existence and ultimately subordinated to the industrial labor process by the same economic system that had created them in the first place.[15]

Colin Bundy, a pioneer in peasant studies in South Africa, located an emergent African peasantry in the eastern Cape between the 1840s and 1870s.[16] Using primary sources drawn mainly from Ciskeian magisterial districts (including Glen Grey and Herschel), he showed how effectively they responded to the market economy. Bundy traced the expansion of the peasantry from the Ciskei into the Transkei and Natal and into the interior northeastern Cape, Orange Free State, and Transvaal during the course of the later nineteenth and early twentieth centuries. Other scholars extended his rough periodization to colonial Basutoland, Rhodesia, and other regions of southern Africa. The decline in the prosperity of peasant communities in the Ciskei region was linked to the impact of the mineral discoveries.

It is impossible to determine with any degree of accuracy exactly how many African households were involved in commercial agriculture between the 1830s, when homesteads in the Ciskei seemed no longer capable of regeneration as subsistence production units, and the 1870s, when a minority of peasant farmers were apparently playing a significant role in the eastern Cape's market economy. But Bundy suggests that by 1870 virtually every African household in the region was at some level linked to mercantile capitalist production as a producer of surplus agricultural goods and a consumer of European manufactured goods.

The range of Xhosa agricultural goods being marketed in the colony included maize, sorghum, wheat, barley, oat hay, tobacco, mimosa gum (for reexport to North America), and wool in addition to hides, horns, skins, and ivory. Wool and maize were generally the major cash crops by the 1860s, but cattle and goats played an important role in the peasant exchange economy. Much to the consternation of the chiefs, the essential products of Xhosa economic life were being exchanged for cheap blankets and clothes, metal tools and cooking utensils, tea, sugar, and other nonessential goods of the new economic order.

Social Stratification in Peasant Communities

Social stratification, as we have seen, was a dynamic of the precapitalist mode of homestead production and not a by-product of colonialism. But colonialism in its various forms greatly accelerated the pace of stratification in African societies that were already structured in terms of dominance.

The upper-ranked rural peasantry were small in number—Bundy estimates that there were between one and two thousand African commercial farmers in this category in the eastern Cape in 1890—but powerful as individuals in the influence they had over other peasant modernizers. They had sufficient capital and/or political clout to gain access to land of good quality, employ tenant or wage laborers in addition to their families, and develop the cash crop potential of their holdings. Although not necessarily Christian or even formally educated, "they were often conspicuously 'loyal' to the colonial government," as Bundy puts it, and their lifestyle "in its material and ideological aspects closely resembled that of solvent and advancing farmers of other races in South Africa." [17]

The Cape was the only colony in South Africa where African residents could buy land in freehold anywhere they could find it, but land prices for Africans were almost always inflated and blatantly discriminatory. Most individual plots were held in the form of quitrent tenure: homesteaders received title to the land on payment of a quitrent that was initially set at one pound a year.[18] While Africans obtained quitrent allotments elsewhere in South Africa during the last half of the nineteenth century, the Ciskei region remained the focal point of these activities. The first individual land grants were issued between 1849 and 1855 to residents of mission stations and to Mfengu and Khoi-Coloureds who had served the British during the Cape-Xhosa wars. Hundreds of Mfengu and Thembu (and some Xhosa), often in syndicates, would acquire land on these terms in the Ciskei.

Most individual plots ranged from 19 to 38 morgen (40 to 80 acres) in size between the 1850s and 1880s, although some were above 47 morgen (100 acres), and a few granted to senior chiefs were between 472 and 1,416 morgen (1,000–3,000 acres).[19] Land grants before the 1894 Glen Grey Act were proportionately bigger in size, and they could be used to qualify for the vote. In addition, household heads were not limited to one lot. Consequently, prior to 1894 some householders owned or controlled a disproportionate share of land under individual tenure.[20]

Most of the landowner villages were located in Mfengu locations west and east of the Keiskamma River (in what the Cape Colony had once termed the "ceded" territory and British Kaffraria) and in Mfengu and Thembu locations in the Queenstown District, where the biggest African land survey in South Africa prior to the Glen Grey Act of 1894 was carried out. Congregational and Methodist mission communities at Oxkraal and Kamastone (Map 3) were allotted 3,780 garden and building lots in quitrent tenure during the early 1860s.

These surveys were generally haphazard before the 1894 act. Residential, grazing, and garden areas were laid out without regard to the quality of the land or the desires of the landowner. Surveyors rarely consulted their African clients, and many allotments had to be canceled because the garden plots could not be cultivated. Since building lots were often placed too far away from garden lots, householders abandoned these sites and built their huts next to their gardens. Africans had to pay for the surveys and title deeds: these costs were usually prohibitive (even after 1881 when the Cape government agreed to pay one-half of the survey costs), and sometimes they amounted to more than the land was worth.[21]

African peasants also became tenants on white-owned farms—often on the same land that had been taken from them and sold to the settlers during the Cape-Xhosa wars. Tenant producers relied almost exclusively on their families for labor, and they looked to the peasant capitalists as role models. In addition, white farmers and land speculators in the Cape found it very profitable to participate in what they called "kaffir farming"—the leasing of white-owned property (usually of little commercial value at the time) to blacks. Tenant "squatters," as they were called, paid rent in the form of cash, labor, and/or a percentage of the crops produced. The more prosperous of these peasants became sharecroppers, paying up to 50 percent of their crops to white (often absentee) landlords. The practice of "farming on the halves" was widespread in such border and Ciskei districts as Alexandria, Bathurst, Somerset East, Bedford, Adelaide, Stutterheim, Fort Beaufort, Cathcart, and Peddie in the last half of the nineteenth century. As we shall see, the success of the mission-educated political elite was dependent on the welfare of these middle-sector peasants, who were potential if not actual voters.

The poorest peasants were most closely identified with the precolonial authority structure and most vulnerable to proletarianization. They lived mainly in the segregated locations and were subject to traditional methods of allocating and utilizing land. These were often subsubsistence producers who participated on the margins of the mercantile economy. Although some worked as wage or tenant labor on farms owned by the African commercial elite, most survived as participants in the migrant labor system. Most Ciskei peasant households would descend to this level of existence before 1910.

The Contradictions in Peasant Commercial Activity

As one who shared a belief in the value of private ownership of land and was convinced of the necessity to participate in a market-oriented economy, the peasant modernizer was a welcome ally of the settler merchant-trader. Existing links with merchant-trading houses in Graaff-Reinet, Grahamstown, Port Elizabeth, East London, and elsewhere in the eastern Cape were changed dramatically as Mfengu and other Bantu speakers, along with Khoi-Coloured and white (virtually all Afrikaner) peasant farmers, entered commercial agriculture. Mercantile brokers and peasant farmers were dependent on each other, and they had a stake in maintaining these economic relationships. The merchant-traders provided credit and goods obtained mainly from Britain, and they transformed what was bartered into commodities to be sold elsewhere in the colony or exported overseas.

African farmers were winning prizes at agricultural fairs in competition with European farmers by the 1860s, and numerous reports of African peasant enterprise were recorded in Victoria East, Keiskammahoek, King William's Town, Stutterheim, Bedford, Herschel, and other Ciskei and border districts during the 1870s. A colonial statistician, for example, noted in 1870 that "the native district of Peddie surpasses the European district of Albany in its productive powers." [22] Queenstown and King William's Town were major market towns for African farmers in the northern and southern districts of the

Ciskei at this time, and there were numerous smaller trading venues in villages like Fort Beaufort, Alice, Peddie, Komgha, Keiskammahoek, and Bensonville (Herschel District) (Map 3). The first African farmers' cooperatives, moreover, were started in the mid-1870s in districts like Queenstown and King William's Town.

The number of plows—a key tool for increasing surplus production—rose rapidly as did the number of wagons and carts. Many peasants could now get their produce to market, and some could hire themselves out as transport drivers and earn extra money to buy land or stock. As peasant farming developed, moreover, crop production diversified as well as increased. Vegetables, fruit, and dairy products, and a wider variety of grains, for example, were being cultivated as cash crops by many African peasants west and east of the Kei River by the 1870s and 1880s.

The Bundy thesis was originally put forward in the early 1970s, and it was consistent with other examples of peasant commercial activity in Africa during the colonial period. Scholars since the 1970s, however, have been more critical of the role peasants played historically in the market economy.[23] Bundy has now acknowledged that he and others "relied too heavily on production for the market as a gauge for the existence of a peasantry: they failed to ask who was producing the goods, when they were being marketed, nor what was the proportion of the marketed produce to total production."[24]

Bundy's main critic as far as the Ciskei peasantry is concerned was a young Ph.D. student in the early 1980s by the name of Jack Lewis.[25] Among other things, he insisted that the capacity of individual households to compete in the new market economy was unequal from the beginning, and only a minority of households actually benefited from the experience. The precolonial homestead production units were finally broken in the cattle-killing catastrophe, which paved the way for the widespread adoption of European farm implements and the production of cash crops for the colonial market. The most active peasant innovators were the Mfengu, the refugee-collaborator group that some scholars have suggested was actually a creation of settler apologists.

Lewis offers a new periodization of peasant commercial activity in the region and suggests that the Ciskei peasant's success as a would-be commercial farmer was limited essentially to a single decade between 1865 and 1875. He also claims that the surplus produced for the market was actually an "economic surplus." In other words, the marketed (or commodity) product was not the surplus left over when minimum domestic needs were met. As in late feudal Europe, the peasants were actually selling part of their subsistence rations in order to survive in the commercial market.

Lewis provided an analysis of the first census of British Kaffraria taken in 1848—eight years before the cattle killing—to illustrate the poverty of most Xhosa households in the Ciskei locations. The 20,928 Ngqika Xhosa under

Sandile enumerated in the census were divided into 1,090 homesteads and 5,765 households. Only 20 percent of the households surveyed were polygamous, and 76 percent of the polygamous households contained only two wives. Most monogamous and many polygamous households were incorporated in larger homesteads. More than 40 percent of the Ngqika Xhosa, in fact, were under the suzerainty of 213 heads of the largest homesteads. Homesteads and households were also polarized in terms of the size and number of cattle. About 80 percent of the Xhosa households in British Kaffraria had less than five cattle and almost one-third had no cattle at all. Household heads with the most cattle were generally the heads of the larger homesteads, and 20 percent of the households in this survey had acquired between 5 and 160 cattle.

The Cape government took advantage of the cattle killing by encouraging its clients—the Mfengu and unbelieving Xhosa—to increase crop production to feed the starving millennialists. The colony would be relieved of having to pay for a massive relief effort, while the Mfengu in particular would be anchored more securely in the market economy. Local grain prices soared in 1857–58 as a result of food shortages, but Lewis believes most grain during these years was marketed by "a mass of small producers with small surpluses most of which went on paying the hut tax." [26]

The cattle killing accelerated the gap between richer and poorer households just at the time when the mission enterprise was taking root in many chiefdoms west and east of the Kei River. The residents of mission station communities, it will be remembered, opposed the cattle killing. Missionaries had been operating across the Fish River since 1799, and they had extensive commercial relations with Africans in the Ciskei frontier zone. They were not bound by colonial regulations regarding trade with the Xhosa (except for the ban on liquor, guns, and ammunition), and at least one scholar suggests they played the dominant role in bringing the Xhosa and their neighbors into the colony's economic orbit during the first three decades of the nineteenth century.[27]

Cape missionary societies had acquired about 225,000 acres by 1848.[28] The mission stations were the only areas in Xhosaland prior to the cattle killing where cultivation had overtaken stockraising as the main economic activity. Missionary admonitions to buy European plows, wagons, and processed iron tools, cultivate more land more intensively, and use male labor in the fields received a positive response from those elements in African society—refugees, outcasts and collaborators from various ethnic groups—in a position to benefit from such advice. The main beneficiaries were the Mfengu.

The capacity to participate in a market economy even among the Mfengu, however, varied enormously. Lewis used as evidence census data obtained from 512 Mfengu households in Oxkraal and Kamastone locations in the Queenstown District in 1861, four years after the cattle killing. This was regarded as a relatively prosperous farming area—38 percent or 184 households were polygamous, a high figure for the Ciskei—and home to many members of the modernizing peasant elite. The top 25 percent of the 512 households surveyed cultivated 57 percent and the bottom 25 percent cultivated 6 percent of the land. Only 25 percent of the households (124 out of 512) owned plows.

The larger households in this survey were those with the most labor and those most likely to cultivate more land. The larger households were also those with the most stock. While 39 percent of the households in the 1861 survey owned from 11 to 840 sheep, 20 percent owned no sheep. Most sheep (more than 50 per household) were owned by 45 households—9 percent of those surveyed. While 25 percent of the households had more than 7 head of cattle, 28 percent had no cattle.[29]

The Mfengu were the first Bantu speakers in the Cape to be subjected to taxation: a tax of ten shillings a hut (in other words, a family) per year was initially imposed in 1848 on Mfengu in the Victoria East District.[30] Hut taxes, in turn, were linked to the resettlement of Africans in villages. The first planned villages organized around individual allotments were imposed on Mfengu resettled in the Amathole Mountains area of British Kaffraria (the Crown Reserve) after the 1850–53 war. Xhosa living in the rest of British Kaffraria were also resettled in villages beginning in February–March 1858 immediately after the cattle killing. Although the precolonial system of communal land tenure still prevailed, the village system would be imposed eventually on all Africans living in the Ciskei. Local magistrates selected the sites for the villages, and householders were required to register with them for permission to occupy land in the village. In theory, the village system made it easier for the authorities to police the locations, monitor the flow of migrants moving in and out of them, and collect taxes.[31]

The hut taxes in communal settlement areas, the quitrents paid by those who held land in individual tenure, and various other taxes (which would eventually include hut taxes for those who lived on grazing land in landowner villages, wheel taxes for those who had wagons, and horse and dog taxes) were to be paid in British currency. Cape governments spent virtually nothing on the locations during the colonial period, since they had a reliable source of revenue obtained entirely from the African population. Thus the Mfengu, Xhosa, and Thembu were not so much attracted as compelled to participate in the market economy to pay their taxes.

Lewis offers a further corrective to the Bundy thesis by suggesting that Mfengu and Thembu from upper-ranked and middle-ranked households were major beneficiaries in the population shifts that occurred in the Ciskei and southern Transkei in the aftermath of the cattle killing. About thirty thousand Mfengu (mainly from the old "ceded" territory) and perhaps twenty thousand Thembu (from the Queenstown District) left their overcrowded locations in the Ciskei and occupied the former homeland of the Gcaleka Xhosa east of the Kei River during the 1860s and 1870s. The most prosperous householders came from these groups, while middle-ranking household heads left behind in the Ciskei—those owning, for example, five to seven head of cattle—took advantage of the situation and increased their land holdings. The biggest losers were lower-ranked household heads owning four head of cattle or less, now a majority of the Ciskei's peasant population.

This period of prosperity in the Ciskei, then, came about primarily because the Mfengu and to a lesser extent the Thembu were able to take advantage of the situation offered by the expulsion of the Gcaleka Xhosa from the southern Transkei. They obtained more land west and east of the Kei River, grew more crops, and increased their stock. The cattle killing was followed by twenty years of relative peace and stability, but the boom was over for most peasant entrepreneurs by the War of 1877–78.

As far as the Ciskei is concerned, the most controversial claim made by Lewis in his critique of the Bundy thesis is the notion of an economic surplus. Although most African households in the region were at least partially dependent on the Cape economy by the 1830s, he insists only a small elite were ever really involved in commercial production. The majority were selling an economic surplus even during the years of relative prosperity between the late 1850s and late 1870s. According to Lewis, no more than 20–30 percent of the household heads in any African location in the Ciskei owned plows during the 1860s, and only about one-third of the households were polygamous or had surplus cattle. Peasant production in the Ciskei region, moreover, had virtually ceased making a significant contribution to the market economy before the mineral discoveries made any noticeable impact on the African population.

The validity of the economic surplus argument must await further research, but it seems unlikely that Ciskeian peasants were producing only subsistence rations for the market economy before the 1880s. After all, one of the major cash crops was wool, which was not being consumed in the home. While most rural cultivators may have been only marginally involved in commercial agriculture, it does not necessarily follow that they were capable of producing only an economic surplus for the market.

3.3. A New Political Order inside the Ciskei Locations

The new economic order was accompanied by a new political order inside the Ciskei's segregated African locations. Cattle had been the lynchpin of economy and society in the precolonial epoch, and the chiefs were the guardians of cattle-keeping cultures. Most peasant households, however, had been forced to shift from stockfarming to cultivation between the 1850s and 1870s. As Sandile told his magistrate, Charles Brownlee, in 1865: "we have no cattle; our cattle are our gardens." [32] With the shift in the mode of production to subsistence gardening, there was an equally important shift in power relations from chiefs to government-designated headmen, the first of whom were appointed during Governor Grey's administration in the mid-1850s.

The chiefs and their councillors were virtually stripped of authority and replaced by men who had not participated in the cattle killing. They were answerable only to the resident magistrate, who selected them and paid their salaries. Headmen were the main instruments of the colonial surveillance system in the Ciskei's rural African locations in the postconquest era. They helped collect the hut tax,[33] and they helped locate stolen stock and apprehend fugitives who broke the law. Above all, headmen kept the magistrates informed about any African perceived as a threat to the colonial order in the countryside.

Since headmen in practice controlled the allocation of land for cultivation and grazing, they were the real arbiters of wealth and status in the locations. Headmen were usually the heads of the biggest and richest households in terms of land, stock, and labor. They maintained a network of social practices on a day-to-day basis: they received payments for land allotments, loaned stock and farm implements, and sometimes set up their own courts (exacting punishment for wrongdoing and claiming fees to settle minor disputes). Some were also involved in illegal practices like receiving payoffs from the sale of illicit homemade beer and laundering stolen cattle.

Headmen were the key intermediaries between colonial officials, labor recruiters, and householders in the locations. Headmen and local traders mobilized laborers, directed them to the recruiting centers, and sometimes even sent personal representatives to supervise workers on the job. Headmen also acted as sounding boards for complaints and grievances, and occasionally they could appeal to employers on behalf of the migrants. In essence, they controlled access to labor.

The headmanship was a highly politicized office in the location with numerous factions competing for power at this level. Headmen were at the center of a complex set of patron-client relationships in an environment where households were increasingly differentiated in terms of wealth, size, and status. As more household economic activities revolved around debt obligations, for example, headmen played a key role in helping to service loans and arbitrate claims before they were taken to the magistrate's court. As debt relations were monetarized in the later nineteenth century, payments in kind for other activities were also monetarized. Headmen negotiated the prices to be paid for such services as hiring out cattle and plows, supplying milk for those who didn't have cows, fencing gardens and cattle kraals, and obtaining wood and other building materials.

Headmen were actually taking land away from householders by the 1880s for not cultivating garden plots, for failing to pay taxes, or in the case of contract labor for being absent from the location for more than six months. The authorities tried to stop these practices in 1890 by insisting that headmen had no legal status unless their appointments were confirmed by the government. They could not decide criminal cases or receive fees for services rendered, and they had no power to allocate land or to deprive anyone of land unless directed to do so by the resident magistrate. The duties of headmen were also specified: they were to report on all persons entering and leaving the location, furnish crime reports and help collect evidence against persons accused of crimes, help collect taxes, enforce forest regulations (mainly to protect the few trees that remained from woodcutters), and monitor the illicit brewing of beer.

Colonial officials, however, were simply not strong enough to impose their will on headmen inside the locations during this period. Headmen were the key organizers of public opinion, and colonial laws could not be implemented in African locations without their support.[34] The resident magistrates were almost completely dependent on headmen, and they urged that the right to allocate land be made legal. The 1890 regulations were not enforced, and headmen were granted authority to allocate land (although contract workers were protected from having their land repossessed) in amending legislation enacted in 1899.

3.4. The Impact of the Mineral Discoveries

The decline in peasant production in the Ciskei, and eventually elsewhere in southern Africa, is associated with economic and political processes set in motion by the mineral revolution. There was a dramatic shift in the nature as well as the pace of capitalist penetration in the wake of diamond and gold discoveries in the South African interior between the 1860s and 1880s.

The political implications were profound. Britain took over the Kimberley diamond fields in 1871 (as the colony of Griqualand West), and the area was absorbed by the Cape Colony in 1880. The idea of a confederation of settler states in southern Africa, originally mooted by Cape governor Sir George Grey in the 1850s, was raised again by British colonial secretary Lord Carnarvon in the 1870s. Although Carnarvon's scheme was opposed by the Cape and the Boer republics (the Orange Free State and Transvaal), Britain temporarily annexed the Transvaal in 1877 and became inextricably involved in the struggles for power in the South African interior.

The fate of the indigenous Bantu-speaking and mixed Khoisan/Coloured societies of the plateau regions was sealed in the 1880s, when gold was discovered in the Transvaal (or rediscovered, since Africans had been involved in surface mining for centuries) and the Boers regained their independence. African kingdoms still independent of settler regimes in the Cape and Natal were either beaten in war (the Zulu in 1879) or otherwise absorbed in the last two decades of the nineteenth century. Imperial control over South Africa was completed with the conquest of the Boer republics between 1899 and 1902 and the incorporation of the Afrikaners into a unified South African settler state in 1910.

The economic implications were equally profound. Enormous injections of capital were needed to satisfy the technological demands of the mining industry, to build the necessary infrastructure (the ports, railways, and goods depots) so that food and machinery could be transported to the new markets in the interior, and to house the thousands of people now concentrated in the Kimberley diamond fields and in Johannesburg and other urban settlements established along the gold-laden Witwatersrand.

British metropolitan capital played a major role in funding development of the mining sector. The production of minerals, in turn, transformed social relations between conqueror and conquered in the subcontinent. Preindustrial societies everywhere were to be subjugated to the requirements of an industrial economy. The mineral discoveries triggered an unprecedented demand for cheap, unskilled, and docile labor to extract the minerals, produce food for the market, build the ports and railways, and erect the buildings to house both ruler and ruled.

The migrant male laborer would be the major component in this labor force. For the migrant labor system to work, the mining industry had to control the source as well as the supply of labor and the deployment of laborers once they were recruited. The mining compound initially solved the latter problem. Compounds effectively regimented the worker's life and prevented him from acting collectively against his employer or from leaving the mines once he was recruited.

It was much more difficult, however, to control the source of labor and hence ensure a steady and reliable supply of laborers. The mine owners were looking for workers primarily in colonial Mozambique and Basutoland and in the segregated locations—or reserves as they would soon be called—set aside for Africans in the South African colonies by the end of the nineteenth century. As regards South Africa, the migrant labor system assumed (1) the reserves could not support the resident population for any length of time, so workers would be forced to migrate to the employment centers in the capital sector; (2) the reserves would nurture a surplus of potentially able-bodied workers (the "reserve army") to replace those who could no longer work; and (3) the reserves would maintain the families of the workers and the sick, disabled, and redundant laborers themselves at little or no cost to their employers. The migrant laborer would work for a specific contract period at a wage that would provide for his individual needs only. He returned to the reserves after fulfilling his contract and was recruited again if he was fit to work or was replaced by another if he was no longer employable.

The mine owners, however, had to compete with white commercial farmers, who also wanted access to this labor source, as well as business and financial interests outside the mining industry. To establish and maintain effective recruiting networks, they also had to come to terms with the pre-colonial authority figures—chiefs and headmen—who continued to exercise real control over their followers. Mine owners and commercial farmers alike, moreover, had to face the problem of recruiting workers who still had more lucrative sources of income derived mainly from the land.

Thus African peasant modernizers were now seen as a threat to settler commercial interests. The Cape authorities had encouraged peasant production in part to wean the African population away from the chiefs, but colonial attitudes changed once the military threat was removed. Like other African modernizers in politics, education, and the church, the would-be commercial farmers were now subjected to a variety of pressures that would eventually block any possibility of competing successfully in a market economy.

The mineral discoveries unquestionably undermined the material basis for cooperation between merchant-traders and peasant farmers. As the urban population increased, the expanding market for produce was absorbed by white commercial farmers. While African farmers received virtually no public or private funding, British settler and Boer republican governments along with various mining and mercantile interests were relatively generous in their support of white commercial agriculture. Discrimination against African farmers in other areas of the production and marketing process—imposing customs and excise duties that effectively marked up goods earmarked for African consumers, artificially raising the price of land bought or leased by Africans, and even refusing to buy African produce—also became more blatant toward the end of the nineteenth century.[35]

3.5. The Dynamics of Proletarianization Following the Mineral Revolution

Bantu speakers were first incorporated into the Cape Colony in large numbers and forced to seek permanent employment on terms set by the settlers in the generation between the 1830s and 1850s.[36] The number of laborers who could be absorbed in an agrarian economy that was still only partially involved in surplus production, however, was limited. Towns were few in number and low in population: by the end of the century, the only urban areas of any size in the eastern Cape, for example, were Port Elizabeth, East London, King William's Town, Grahamstown, and Queenstown (Map 3).

The Conditions of Household Production in the Ciskei's African Locations

The effects of depopulation associated with the cattle killing and its aftermath were virtually over by the end of the 1860s, and new household heads were soon experiencing difficulty in obtaining land in the Ciskei's locations. Except for four years between 1886 and 1890, moreover, drought was endemic in the region during the last two decades of the nineteenth century. According to Lewis, a two-year drought on the eve of the gold discoveries between 1884 and 1886 was "most decisive," wiping out many surviving peasant capitalists and sharply increasing the debt burden and the number of absentee migrant workers.[37]

Richer households had turned increasingly to cultivating winter cash crops like wheat and oats because winter rains often persisted even when summer rains failed. Landowners with stock outside the locations also sought pasture for their herds and flocks on location land. These activities aggravated the competition for land. The poorest householders thought all arable land should be utilized for subsistence crops, while householders without stock demanded that they be allowed to build homes and gardens on grazing land. Headmen were pressured into allocating more and more plots to landless followers on the commonage.

Although African householders in the Ciskei still obtained much food from family gardens, the percentage of a peasant family's income derived from agricultural production apparently declined dramatically between 1880 and 1910. In addition to drought, marginal peasant households in the Ciskei region were especially vulnerable to plant and animal diseases. The rinderpest epidemic that swept through southeastern Africa in 1896–97, for example, killed more than 80 percent of the cattle alone in the Ciskei and Transkei.[38] Since large numbers of goats were also dying from foot rot and other ailments, there was virtually no milk for the vast majority of households. Rinderpest was followed by outbreaks of another stock-killing disease, East Coast fever, after the South African War. Recurring epidemics of locusts (especially in the mid-1890s) and other pests were a continuing threat to subsistence crop production.

Hitherto accessible markets in the Ciskei region were lost as the rapidly developing infrastructure of roads and railways linked town and countryside in white Ciskei and bypassed the African locations. The East London–Berlin–King William's Town rail link was completed in 1877, and the railway line from East London to the diamond and gold fields in Kimberley and Johannesburg was finally finished in 1892. Numerous branch lines thereafter gradually penetrated the region's white farming areas.[39] Freight costs were prohibitive, and peasant ox wagons could not compete with steam engines in transporting agricultural goods to the new urban markets opened up by the mineral discoveries. Price fluctuations in grain and wool (an average of 10 percent a year in the last half of the nineteenth century) also weakened attempts to survive in a market economy.

African peasants inside the locations were dependent on local white traders to store and sell their produce and to sell them the necessities produced in the outside world. Traders would remain the principal intermediary between the producer and the market for generations to come, because they controlled the extension of credit and the prices of goods that were bought and sold. Most traders by the 1890s were no longer offering cash for grain or stock received from the peasants. Payment was made in credit vouchers that could be redeemed only by the traders who issued them. Peasants sometimes had to pay ten or fifteen times as much for grain in a drought year as they received for grain sold in a year when the harvest yielded a surplus.[40] Most African peasants in the Ciskei were probably in debt to traders by the end of the century. The trading store would also become the main source of information and rumor concerning events in the outside world, a venue for communicating news between families, and the local post office, there being no home-delivered post. Thus traders were in a powerful position to monitor the social activities of the location community.

Increased pressure was also placed on peasants to pay their hut taxes, which were now imposed on all African households within the boundaries of the Cape Colony (Act 2 of 1869). Magistrates were allowed to confiscate stock and charge grazing fees in lieu of tax payments (Act 20 of 1878, Act 37 of 1884), but many peasants no longer had stock. Tax collectors were then given permission to seize land and other property and even evict householders from their homes (Proclamation 140 of 1885), and they were exercising this authority by the 1890s.[41]

There were few African commercial farmers left in the Ciskei by 1910. Those who could still afford to be modernizers were putting their money, as Bundy put it, "not in agricultural improvements, but in education and the acquisition of skills for the younger generation."[42] By the 1920s, as we shall see, the mission-educated community was not able to avoid poverty even with advanced schooling. The decline in the fortunes of African farmers in the Ciskei would be a preview for peasant communities elsewhere in the subcontinent.[43]

The failure of peasant capitalism had profound implications for the African population as a whole because there would be few other opportunities to gain even partial access to the means of production in a developing industrial economy. The absence of an independent economic base would cripple African nationalist attempts to challenge the South African state in the twentieth century.

The Glen Grey Act of 1894

The Cape settlers were granted representative government with their own parliament in 1853, and nineteen years later they were granted responsible government, which meant they had virtual home rule and were in a much stronger position to push through discriminatory legislation in their own interests. The most significant attempt by Cape legislators to intervene in the segregated African locations during the later colonial period was the Glen Grey Act of 1894. The measure was endorsed by the 1903–5 South African Native Affairs Commission, and crucial sections were incorporated in subsequent legislation affecting South Africa's reserves in the generation after union in 1910.

The Glen Grey District was adjacent to the Queenstown District (Map 4), and it had been a source of conflict between land-hungry settlers and Thembu residents since the 1850s.[44] There were thirty thousand people in the district in 1870, most of them Thembu, and hundreds of peasant households held land in quitrent tenure and were profitably engaged in commercial activities. Agricultural production in Glen Grey in the 1870s and early 1880s was high when compared to adjoining, white-owned farming districts, and a wide range of cash crops was marketed (including wheat, barley, oats, fruit, and dairy products in addition to maize and sorghum). Africans were raising horses and pigs as well as cattle and sheep, and a few landowners had farms up to 1,500 morgen (3,180 acres) in size. Most men engaged in migrant labor were not doing it out of necessity, and only a few of these were employed at long distances from home.

This scenario changed dramatically in little more than a decade. Glen Grey's resident population had risen to forty thousand by the beginning of the 1890s, and now land was at a premium in the district. The demand for labor in the South African interior, moreover, soared after the gold discoveries in 1886. The Glen Grey Commission was appointed in 1892 to consider the land problem in the district, and the Cape Labour Commission began hearing evidence in 1893. It was no coincidence when the reports of both commissions were published almost simultaneously. As Elsie Wagenaar points out, there was an "intimate link" between overpopulation in the locations, land tenure, and the need for black labor in the deliberations of both commissions and in the parliamentary debates.[45] Cape legislators sought to introduce a system of land tenure that would reduce the size of individual plots inside the locations and force a greater proportion of the male population into the migrant labor market.

The prime minister of the Cape at this time was Cecil Rhodes, the arch-capitalist and empire builder of his day, who was convinced that Africans could have no significant voice in the Cape if English- and Dutch-speaking settlers were to be united in a future South African state. The Glen Grey Act is a case study of the white supremacist policies of Rhodes and his political contemporaries, "a Native Bill for Africa" rammed through Parliament in its first all-night session.[46]

Rhodes wanted to maintain segregated territories for Africans and ensure that those not suitable as labor would be contained in these areas. He wanted the peasants to be restricted to one limited plot of land so they couldn't compete in the market with white farmers, and he wanted a labor tax to process Africans more quickly into the migrant labor force: "Every black man could not have three acres and a cow. . . . It must be brought home to them that in the future nine-tenths of them would have to spend their lives in manual labour, and the sooner that was brought home to them the better." [47] Finally, he wanted to create and coopt a small ruling elite to administer the locations at no cost to the government. The experiment was to be carried out initially in Glen Grey, and it would be extended to several districts in the Transkei by the end of the nineteenth century.

The Meaning of Individual Land Tenure. The Glen Grey District, populated almost entirely by Africans, was divided into eighteen locations. These locations, in turn, were to be surveyed and divided into individual plots. Each Thembu farmer would be limited to one plot of four morgen (8.44 acres). Each plot was to be demarcated by beacons, and each farmer was to have grazing rights to specific pasture land in the location where the plot was situated. Individual tenure with a quitrent of fifteen shillings a year replaced the hut tax of five shillings a year.[48]

The mission-educated community was initially supportive of the individual tenure provision, until they realized that these plots were regarded as communal land so that African landowners in Glen Grey would not qualify for the franchise.[49] Those outside the mission community who preferred some land in communal tenure to no land in individual tenure were even less enthusiastic.[50] The landowner's security of tenure, moreover, was very fragile. The personal goods of household heads who were three months in arrears could be sold off to pay the rent. Those who were one year late could lose title to their land. In the first ten years after the 1894 act, almost all titles confiscated by the colonial authorities were for failure to pay the quitrent (the measure was amended in 1905 so that plots could no longer be confiscated for debt). Titles could also be confiscated in cases of rebellion or in cases where the title holder was convicted of the crime of theft (changed to a second conviction in 1905) or for failing to cultivate the land for one year (changed to three years in 1905).

Allotments in theory could not be mortgaged, leased, or sublet to tenants, and they could not be subdivided or sold to other farmers. Property would be inherited in the first instance by the oldest son of the household head or another male heir (providing the heir held no other property in the district) if there were no sons. The one-man-one-lot principle, as it was called, would effectively prevent the accumulation of capital in land.

Virtually all the land was surveyed within four years after the legislation was passed, and individual titles were issued to virtually all the plot holders in the district.[51] There were barely enough plots, however, for the existing households. The survey cost of five pounds for a four-morgen holding was prohibitive for many farmers and well above the market value of the land. Since only the oldest son could inherit the property, moreover, other male members of the family were rendered officially landless.[52] Allotments still favored the more privileged members of the district—headmen, their relatives, policemen, and other functionaries in the local bureaucracy—who in some cases were given plots up to thirty morgen in size (a quitrent of three shillings a year was charged for each additional morgen above five morgen). Predictably, angry residents produced a stream of petitions protesting discrimination in the allocation of individual plots.

Africans who did not qualify for land moved to the commonage (the grazing area) or left the community. Lack of personnel, however, prevented officials from monitoring use of the land once individual title had been granted. Allotments were soon being cultivated beyond the boundaries of individual plots, and the survey beacons were torn down or bypassed. The distinction between arable land and commonage would be increasingly blurred as the plight of landless family members prevailed over the rights of individual property holders. Thus an amendment to the Glen Grey Act in 1899 accepted reality and imposed a yearly ten-shilling hut tax for those householders allowed to occupy land on the commonage.

The Meaning of Local Government. The Glen Grey Act also provided for limited local government in the form of location boards and a district council. All surveyed and commonage land in the African locations would be administered by location boards. Each of the nineteen boards in the Glen Grey District was made up of three persons—all landholders resident in the location. Although they were officially appointed by the governor for one year (which could be renewed), in practice they were chosen by local magistrates, who were influenced by the headmen. The Glen Grey District Council consisted of twelve African members, six nominated by the governor and six elected by the location boards. Members were given a stipend as councillors. They served for three years, and like location board members they could be renominated or reelected to the council. The resident magistrate of the district was ex officio chairman of the council, which met four times a year. The district councils in Ciskei and Transkei (a general council representing all the districts in the Transkei that had councils was also created in 1903) merely advised the resident magistrates. They had no real power.

District councils would be dominated by headmen and their allies. As one observer wrote in July 1895 with reference to the Transkei district councils:

> The whole council consists of paid Government agents and it is difficult to see how the people are represented. For the headmen as a class have long since lost the confidence of the people. It is only too well known that many of them have used their powers for their personal interests. They, their sons and nephews, have by degrees got into their own hands the very pick of the arable land in the various locations, while the unfortunates who have no means of exercising influence on the headman are left to plough wretched scraps of the poorest land. . . . I fear that there is only too much ground for the people's charges of injustice and selfishness against the majority.[53]

Although Glen Grey's School people were reluctant initially to participate in the location boards or the district council—they did not want to be classified politically with illiterate non-Christians, and they feared their franchise rights might be compromised—many others did try to make the most of these opportunities. For the first time since conquest, nonvoting Africans now had an official forum in which to express their opinions, and those who gained access to the district council would become patrons of considerable influence in the locations.

All registered landholders and other adult males in the district paid a special ratepayers' tax of five shillings a year, which apparently was complied with. The money would be spent largely on projects in the district—building roads and dams, erecting bridges, constructing water storage facilities, establishing schools and paying teachers, planting trees and eliminating poisonous weeds and plants, enacting animal disease-control measures and treating infectious diseases—and it was administered by the council. The magistrates' reports, at least, were full of praise for the district councils during this period.

The location boards, however, were a disaster. They were supposed to regulate the farmers' use of the surveyed land—limiting stock (twenty-five were allowed initially for each landholder in Glen Grey District), providing fencing, maintaining plot beacons, and controlling use of the commonage—but they did nothing. Most boardmen were illiterate (regulations promulgated under the Glen Grey Act were not even translated into Xhosa until after 1903) and subject to bribes. The regulations, moreover, often conflicted with decisions made by the headmen.

The magistrate for Glen Grey wrote to the location boards in his district in an attempt to determine how effective the boardmen were in implementing the regulations. He received fifteen replies and told the South African Native Affairs Commission in 1903:

> The majority of them said that they were not acquainted with the regulations, that they had never seen them, that they never held meetings, and had practically done nothing. . . . They said to me: "We are ignorant men; we cannot write down minutes and we do not keep books." [54]

The location boards were eliminated in 1906 in the Transkei, and a more representative electoral system was inaugurated. In Glen Grey, the district council was made responsible for the activities of the location boards, but as Tim Keegan put it, administration at this level "remained in a twilight world." [55]

The Meaning of an African Labor Tax. All adult males deemed fit for labor by the resident magistrate were obliged to pay an additional tax of ten shillings a year. Men who could prove they had been employed for specified months or years outside their location or district were exempt. If a man did not pay the tax, he could be declared a vagrant and under the colony's vagrancy laws would be punished accordingly. As John Tengo Jabavu, the pioneer African journalist and political leader in the eastern Cape at the time, declared in his newspaper *Imvo Zabantsundu* (Native Opinion):

> At the bottom of the benevolent intention there lies an ugly sediment which appears as soon as the mixture is stirred. Its name is cheap labour secured not by natural or economic laws such as the pressure of the population and the market value of labour, but by an Act of Parliament.[56]

Jabavu called the tax "qualified slavery." [57] Petitions were sent to Cape Town and even to London protesting the proposed legislation.

In the Glen Grey District, however, 63 percent of the men deemed liable for the tax were exempted in 1896 and 74 percent in 1897. And many who were not exempted refused to pay it: by the end of 1895, only £87 10s. had been collected out of the estimated labor tax base of £675 for the district. By the late 1890s, no further attempts were being made to collect labor taxes in Glen Grey, and no more lists of tax defaulters were compiled. Results were equally disastrous from the colonial point of view in four Transkeian districts where the labor tax was applied. Jabavu and others mobilized public opinion against the labor tax: *Imvo Zabantsundu* was particularly conspicuous in the stream of articles, letters, and editorials denouncing this legislation, and even missionary organs like the *Christian Express* got involved in the protest campaign.[58]

The hated labor tax was finally abolished after a decade of protest in 1905, but in truth it was never really needed. Glen Grey—like other districts in the Ciskei and Transkei—was now producing a steady stream of landless and subsubsistence peasants willing to enter the migrant labor market. The uneconomic size of the plots would effectively eliminate any chance the peasant householder might have of entering the market economy.[59]

Prominent white liberals at the Cape seem to have accepted the key provisions of the Glen Grey Act with alacrity. Some Africans would get security of tenure while the rest would be commodities in a supply-and-demand economy. Richard Rose-Innes, a King William's Town lawyer and electoral agent and one of Jabavu's major supporters, spoke for the next settler generation in a paper forwarded to the South African Native Affairs Commission in 1903:

> We shall in time be compelled to create more of such areas . . . as "reservoirs of labour" and homes for these people into which the Native will be free to come and go. He requires this for his sake and we require it for our own. . . . The segregation of the races within certain limits and under safeguards, but without compulsion, is the policy to aim at for the future.[60]

The Glen Grey Act was perceived by white politicians as a milestone on the road to controlling African labor at its source in the segregated locations-cum-reserves. Those who acquired individual tenure, it was presumed, would be hardworking because they now had their own land—private property being an icon of modernization for the Victorian middle class. Fewer and more efficient peasants, it was argued, would increase production and thus be more capable of bearing the burden of feeding and caring for the rest of the reserve population—in other words, those not needed by the settlers as workers in an emerging industrial economy.

The Cape Colony's Labor-Control System

The Cape authorities also tried to tighten up the pass laws. In labor regulations consolidated in 1867, all "native foreigners" were required to carry work permits, and all permanent residents (non-Mfengu as well as Mfengu) were required to carry "certificates of citizenship." As the boundaries of the Cape expanded, however, it became increasingly difficult to distinguish Bantu-speaking citizens from noncitizens. Special provisions in service contracts between resident and nonresident Africans were finally dropped, and the 1883 Native Laws and Customs Commission recommended that the pass system be abolished. According to Sheila van der Horst, the pass laws were not generally applied in the colony between the 1880s and 1910.[61]

While African workers in the Cape might avoid the pass system, they were bound to their employers once they signed a contract. The authorities sought to give white employers more control over their black employees with the Masters and Servants Act of 1856. Breach of contract was made a criminal offense (those who defied their employers could be imprisoned without the option of a fine), and the terms of labor service were made more specific and lengthened to five years. This measure was a prototype for the other settler colonies and for South Africa after 1910. Although it was designed originally to protect both parties in a contractual agreement, it was steadily amended (e.g., in 1873, 1874, 1875, 1889, 1895) in favor of the employer. In the Cape Colony these acts did not discriminate between races, but in practice the categories of employment subsumed by "servants" were invariably occupied by blacks.

The only area where Cape authorities partially succeeded in controlling the supply and deployment of black workers before union in 1910 was on white-owned farms. Settler control over independent African tenants tightened up considerably once the mining industry's need for cheap food made commercial crops feasible even in hitherto marginal areas of the eastern Cape. Land prices soared as speculators, financed by mercantile interests, bought property occupied by African (and white Afrikaner) tenants and sold it to commercial farmers.

Earlier attempts to control African sharecroppers in the Cape Colony—the Location Acts of 1869, 1876, and 1884—had been generally evaded, although they probably slowed down the number of peasants who sought this option. Before the 1890s, there was little incentive in evicting these tenants: they worked the land and made money for the landowner, who needed to invest virtually nothing in return. Tougher location acts in 1892, 1899, and especially 1909, however, were more stringently enforced. Long before the 1913 Land Act, African tenants on white-owned farms in the Cape were in jeopardy. They were driven off the land, often losing their stock in the process, or they were obliged to pay higher rentals in the form of more labor or a bigger percentage of their crops.

The aim of the location acts was to compel African sharecroppers to work entirely for the landowner as labor tenants and eventually to convert these tenants to wage laborers. The official tenant population (white as well as black) on white-owned farms in the Cape, in fact, would decline rapidly in the early 1900s. By 1909, it was estimated at 40,000, the lowest in South Africa. Of 2,000 white-owned farms occupied by black tenants in 1930, for example, only about 74 (with about 7,000 tenants) were in the Cape.

Periodizing the Pattern of Labor Migration

The response of rural cultivators to the demand for wage labor, and its consequences, varied from region to region. But the experiences of Africans in Ciskei and southern Transkei, who were the first in southern Africa to enter the migrant labor force in significant numbers, would be shared by those who followed them.

While the topic awaits further research, it is possible to discern at least five stages in the pattern of labor migration before union in 1910. As noted earlier, the first occurred during the period of conquest between the 1830s and 1860s, when refugees from Xhosaland entered the colony in force in search of work. Most were temporary migrants employed on settler farms or on various public works projects and were paid in stock and grain. Nevertheless, numbers of Africans also worked as wage laborers in building harbors at East London and Port Alfred, for example, and in constructing port facilities at Port Elizabeth.[62] Others worked as laborers in the first phase of railway building in the 1860s.

The second wave of migrants coincided with an upturn in the Cape Colony's economy occasioned by the discovery of diamonds. Earlier labor migration patterns were reinforced as Africans were recruited primarily to work in the port towns and on the railways. The colony experienced serious labor shortages in the 1870s that drove up wages, and this period coincided with the most significant decade of peasant prosperity in the Ciskei. Many peasants found a lucrative source of alternative employment as transport drivers or railway workers. They received 48s.–72s. a month on the railways, for example, compared with men who earned 10s.–15s. a month on white farms. Ten of fourteen strikes recorded in the colony in the 1870s occurred in the eastern Cape, and they all involved migrants working on the docks, railways, roads, and wool-washing plants in Port Elizabeth, Uitenhage, King William's Town, and East London. In a tight labor market, these sporadic work stoppages were at least partially successful in maintaining competitive wages and improved working conditions.

Peasant migrants, then, could still be somewhat selective in their choice and conditions of employment. Lewis argues that African householders in the Ciskei resisted any wage that was below the thirty-six-shillings-a-month-plus-food wage that had been paid for labor on public works projects during Governor Grey's administration in the 1850s. They were prepared to remain impoverished at home rather than work as contract labor at wages that would not improve their standard of living.[63] Few peasants could be induced to work permanently as tenant labor on settler farms or as contract labor on the mines before the 1890s. A number went to Kimberley—Gwayi Tyamzashe, a pioneer church leader and political figure from the Ciskei, was the last African to own a mining claim in 1883—but they generally avoided more menial forms of labor and resisted incarceration in mining compounds.

The bargaining position of the migrant worker steadily worsened in the third stage of the proletarianization process during the 1880s and 1890s. The war years between 1877 and 1881 forced numbers of new refugees into the labor market at the same time as peasant production in the Ciskei was losing momentum. Peasant prosperity was now heavily dependent on access to non-farming sources of income. The 1880s, moreover, were a period of economic recession for the Cape as a whole. Wages dropped for unskilled workers, and employers gained more control over their employees. Cape Africans working on the railways and in the port cities still received relatively higher wages than

African labor on white farms or on the diamond and gold mines during the 1880s, but these preferred sectors of employment were much less competitive in the 1890s. The wages of African gold miners actually rose during the first half of the 1890s, and when the rail line from the Cape to the goldfields was completed in 1892 large numbers of Africans from the Ciskei migrated to the mines.

Collective action by striking European and African miners at Kimberley in the early 1880s, where eight of fourteen strikes recorded in the colony during the decade occurred, was viewed with alarm by the mine owners. As a concession to white workers, they agreed that only blacks should have to live in compounds. The white workers responded by joining the police in smashing a black workers' strike in 1894. In the waning years of the nineteenth century white workers became ever more organized and entrenched in skilled positions while black migrants remained unorganized and relatively unskilled.

The struggle to maintain wage rates for contract workers was over by the late 1890s. The Chamber of Mines, for example, set up its own Native Labour Supply Organisation in 1897, and mine wages were immediately reduced by 30 percent. Most Africans in the Ciskei region, however, were no longer able to withhold their labor and survive on the land as subsistence farmers. Nor could they participate in any meaningful way as producers in the developing industrial economy.

The South African War, 1899–1902. The fourth stage in the pattern of labor migration occurred with the outbreak of the South African War in October 1899. The war had both negative and positive consequences for Africans in the eastern Cape. Thousands of migrants from the Ciskei and Transkei left the war zones to the north and returned to their homes, placing more pressure on food resources at a time when drought had resulted in another season of poor harvests. Grain stocks were severely depleted, and famine conditions actually prevailed in some districts by the end of 1900, even though the region as a whole was not a zone of conflict. Many families were also deprived of income in the form of remittances from migrant wages, and in these circumstances the British military authorities provided an essential source of employment for the local and expatriate African population.

About four thousand Africans (mainly Mfengu and Thembu) were recruited between December 1899 and March 1900 to help defend the northern Transkei and East Griqualand border area following a British defeat in the Stormberg mountains and the Boer occupation of Barkly East in the Transkei. African troops were armed but under the control of white officers. The decision to employ African soldiers helped provoke a political crisis in the Cape Colony, and most recruits were disbanded in March 1900. But African levies (volunteers now included Sotho, Bhaca, and Griqua as well as Mfengu and Thembu) were mobilized and armed again during the extended and devastating guerrilla phase of the war in the northern Cape between December 1900 and May 1902.

Most Cape Africans involved in the war effort, however, were noncombatant workers in various categories. These included translators, scouts, transport personnel, blacksmiths and other artisans, and unskilled laborers who worked directly for the military as well as peasants who were hired to carry food and equipment. Labor depots were established at De Aar (an important rail junction in the northern Cape), Bloemfontein, and Johannesburg, after the goldfields were reoccupied by the British in March 1900. Thousands of Africans left the Ciskei and border districts to enlist as workers: De Aar, for example, recruited most of its initial contingent from the King William's Town District.

The terms of employment were reasonably attractive: unskilled workers received at least 49s. 9d. a month (almost £30 a year) plus rations, the prevailing rate on the gold mines immediately before the war, and many (such as those working at De Aar and later in the Bloemfontein labor depot) up to 60s. a month (or £36 a year). Clothing and blankets, moreover, were sometimes also supplied by the army. Contracts were generally for three months rather than six months (the prevailing length of service for migrants before the war), which was especially attractive to peasants who still gained their livelihood from the land. Most semiskilled/skilled workers in the Cape and Natal, however, could earn at least 90s. a month (£54 a year), including rations and fringe benefits such as overtime and length of service. At least a hundred thousand Africans in South Africa as a whole were employed by British military authorities during the war.

Military employment was not the only option open to peasant householders. The demand for labor was also acute on the railways, on the docks, in road building and other construction work, and on white-owned farms. Some Africans were able to gain additional benefits in the competition for labor between military and civilian authorities, and the wages of even the most exploited of unskilled workers—domestics and casual labor on white farms—apparently increased slightly during the war years. African migrants from the Ciskei, then, may have been better paid and more widely dispersed during and immediately after the war than in any previous period of colonial history.

Upper-ranked peasants who did not depend on migrant wages and who possessed surplus stock and cartage facilities and could afford to cultivate more land seem to have prospered the most during the hostilities. They could supply at least part of the army's demand for grain, vegetables, fruit, and meat and take advantage of the rise in food prices. They had horses for remounts and the oxen or mule teams and wagons or carts to transport the goods needed by the military. When the war ended, a few peasant capitalists would be in a position to sell cattle and sheep to destitute white farmers in the ex-Boer republics and buy more land.[64]

The Cape, however, suffered a serious postwar depression between 1903 and 1909. Trade slumped and revenue figures even in 1908 were half of what they had been in 1902. Recovery thereafter was slow until World War I. Droughts in 1904 and 1908 accelerated the growth of a landless peasantry and forced more indigent Africans into wage labor. Headmen, moreover, no longer played a pivotal role in the recruiting process. Migrant workers were now developing their own networks of communication and establishing new patterns of leadership, as was an aspirant African middle class in the urban areas. These networks were maintained when the migrants returned to the reserves.

Cape Town, a mecca for migrants from the Ciskei and southern Transkei from the 1880s, had a large surplus of workers in the years of recession following the South African War. The fifth and final stage in the pattern of labor migration during the British colonial era occurred between 1904 and 1912, when African subrecruiters drawn mainly from the mission-educated community mobilized these men to migrate to German South-West Africa. They were initially employed on the railways and as transport drivers and construction workers in the German army's campaign to quell the Herero and Nama uprisings between 1904 and 1907. Efforts were later made to supplement this contingent by recruiting laborers from their home districts in the Ciskei (at centers in King William's Town and East London) and southern Transkei.

As many as ten thousand migrants found their way or were brought to the German colony in peak years during this period. Despite severe hardships punctuated by outbreaks of extreme brutality on the part of their colonial overseers, the workers (many of whom were semiliterate Christians from separatist churches) persevered in the hope of gaining a measure of economic independence. The German option, however, was over by 1912, and it had absorbed only a small percentage of the thousands of householders now being pushed or pulled from the Ciskei locations each year in search of work.

Preferred job categories had become much less attractive during the prolonged economic slump of the early 1900s, and as poverty levels deepened in the segregated locations large numbers of work seekers were forced into the lowest levels of employment in white South Africa. While Africans from the Ciskei region had been living in Johannesburg, for example, since at least the 1880s, few were employed underground in the mines before the end of the century. Now they had no choice but to enter the subterranean world of Igoli, the African name for the city of gold.

4

The Mission Enterprise

The mission enterprise in southern Africa formed a distinct variant in a larger and more heterogeneous culture of modernity that was molded in the lived experiences of the middling classes in Britain during the agonizing transformation from a mercantile to an industrial capitalist state. The apostles of the new economic system forged a new symbolic system during the course of the nineteenth century that would explain and justify this transformation to themselves and the alienated majority. The language they used to empower the agents of capital was based essentially on the reification of the individual.

The new discourse was framed early in the century by libertarians like Jeremy Bentham, Adam Smith, and Richard Cobden and by other apostles of individual rights, free trade, and competition in a supply-and-demand economy. The ideology of the middle class was also expressed in the right to private property and to free speech, freedom of religion and of individual conscience, and a free press. The central government would be constrained from interfering with personal rights, and the rule of law would be guaranteed. Individuals would have access to parliament and the right to a constitutional government, and to a permanent corps of civil servants promoted on merit. Once the middle class gained control of parliament and expanded their power base in the last half of the nineteenth century, the liberal program was institutionalized and sustained by the state both in the metropole and in the expanding colonial periphery. The interests and needs of the entire population would be recast within the framework of middle-class culture.

British Protestant missionaries—all of them male—were among the earliest interpreters of the new cultural order in the Cape Colony's eastern frontier zone. Although divided by denomination, they had been observers—if not participants—in the evangelical revivals that had swept through Britain and parts of Western Europe (and North America) during the late eighteenth and early nineteenth centuries and inaugurated a new era in "foreign" missions. These were Evangelical nonconformists driven by the belief that Christ's second coming would not take place until the Gospel was communicated throughout

112

the world. They were also refugees—virtually all in modest economic circumstances clinging to the lower ranks of the middling classes—who had left England in the throes of industrial change to plant the Good News in one corner of the British Empire.[1]

The principal bearers of the new cultural order to the Xhosa before the 1850s were three mission agencies: the Wesleyan Methodists, Scots Presbyterians, and the Congregationalists (the Moravians and the London Missionary Society). As we have seen, missionaries played a crucial role in the political and commercial penetration of Xhosaland, and the chiefs rightly regarded the mission enterprise as a challenge to their authority. Thus the first missionaries to the Xhosa—represented by Johannes van der Kemp and other members of the pioneering London Missionary Society (LMS)—failed to establish a permanent station among Ngqika's people between 1799 and 1801 and again between 1816 and 1818. As British influence became more pervasive, however, the chiefs became more amenable to the missionaries in the vain hope they would intercede on behalf of the Xhosa and somehow contain the expansionist settler community.

Most pioneer mission stations in Xhosaland were built on land that had been allocated to the missionaries by the chiefs. When the Cape began to annex this territory, colonial authorities tried to limit and standardize subsequent mission grants to circular tracts of land two miles in radius. The missionaries in practice continued to ask permission from the chief to occupy the land, but by agreement they were not generally subject to chiefly authority. The treaty system set up after the War of 1834–35 also exempted African preachers and teachers and those who lived on station land from the legal and social obligations associated with precolonial African culture.

The first permanent mission stations in the Ciskei were built in the 1820s. The Wesleyan Methodists established congregations for the 1820 settlers in the zuurveld, and in 1823 they entered the Ciskei and started a mission among the Gqunukhwebe Xhosa at Wesleyville east of the Keiskamma River. Missionary strategist William Shaw envisaged a chain of stations from the Cape frontier to Port Natal (the future Durban), and within seven years the Wesleyans were well on the way to achieving this goal. Five more stations—one in the Ciskei (Mount Coke) and four in the Transkei—were built in the two hundred miles between Wesleyville and Buntingville north of the Mthatha River, about half the distance to Port Natal. Other Methodist stations established between the Fish and Kei rivers during the pioneer generation included Newtondale, D'Urban, and Peddie (in the southern part of the "ceded" territory), Lesseyton (near Queenstown), and Healdtown (near Fort Beaufort) (Map 3).

The Scots Presbyterians—initially the Glasgow Missionary Society (GMS)—established their first stations in the northern part of the "ceded" territory. John Brownlee, an ex-LMS missionary who was also employed as a government agent, built a station at a site on the Tyhume River in 1820. It was located about six miles north of the future town of Alice (in what would become the Victoria East District). Two GMS missionaries joined him within a year, and in 1824 another station was built about eight miles from Tyhume and named Lovedale after the secretary of the Glasgow home mission board. Lovedale was destroyed in the 1834–35 war and rebuilt at another site on the Tyhume River in 1841, and eventually it would become the centerpiece of the mission enterprise in the Ciskei. Other Presbyterian stations established in the region included Pirie and Burnshill between the Keiskamma and Buffalo rivers (Map 3).

The Congregationalists and Lutherans (Berlin Missionary Society) also built a few stations in the Ciskei during this period. The Moravian stations at Shiloh, Goshen, and Ngotini, for example, were located in the northern interior of the frontier zone (in what would become the Queenstown District). The LMS finally built a permanent station at Peelton on the Buffalo River (in what would become the King William's Town District). The Berlin mission built stations at Bethel (adjoining the future town of Stutterheim) and later at Dohne and Wartburg (Map 3), but converts were few and most of the German missionaries moved to Natal. The Lutherans remained a relatively insignificant mission in the region.

The Anglicans, encouraged and aided by Governor Grey, established mission stations west and east of the Kei River from the 1850s. Three were located in British Kaffraria—St. Luke's east of King William's Town, St. Matthew's below the Amathole Mountains near Keiskammahoek, and St. John's at Komgha. Two others—St. Peter's and St. John the Baptist—were built in a large location created for the Thembu that would eventually form part of Glen Grey District, and St. Mark's was built near Sarhili's residence at Hohita close to the confluence of the Great Kei and White Kei rivers (Map 3). The Methodists, Presbyterians, Congregationalists, and Anglicans would have virtually no competition from other missionary agencies in the eastern Cape until the 1890s.[2]

Missionary activity among Bantu-speaking peoples in South Africa during the nineteenth century was concentrated most heavily in the Ciskei and in Natal below the Tugela River,[3] and the mission experience had profound consequences for African converts in both regions. This chapter focuses on the English-language missions in the Ciskei.

Section 4.1 considers the impact of the mission enterprise on precolonial African culture.

Sections 4.2 and 4.3 examine the impact of the mission's African churches and schools on the making of an African Christian community.

4.1. The Missionaries and African Culture

Africans rarely joined mission communities before the 1850s because they were seeking a new religious experience, and even on the stations only a small proportion of the population was converted to Christianity before the cattle killing.[4] Africans sought asylum with the missionaries for a variety of reasons. Some refused to conform to what was expected of them in precolonial African society: young women unwilling to participate in arranged marriages and widows who would not follow custom and marry their brothers-in-law were apparently the most significant proportion in this group. Some were physically disfigured, some were called to be diviners and rejected their vocation, and some had been expelled for the crime of witchcraft. It is understandable that missionaries who welcomed outcasts of this sort would be feared by ordinary Xhosa.

Other refugees were generated by the ongoing Cape-Xhosa wars. These included orphans and the sick, disabled, aged, and homeless, and those who could no longer provide food for themselves or their families. Relatives of converts would come if their kinsmen were seen to be safe and prospering, and occasionally larger groups—those people designated as Mfengu under the guardianship of the missionary John Ayliff are a classic example—would seek the protection of the mission station.

The station communities in the Ciskei and elsewhere were isolated from each other and from most settler communities before the 1860s.[5] The missionaries assumed a chiefly role, allocating the land and exhorting their people to obey the codes and rituals of belief and behavior that were characteristic of Victorian Christianity. Since Xhosa-speaking peoples traditionally lived in scattered homesteads, it was not always possible for Christians to live on the station, but the station gradually became their spiritual if not their temporal home.

The missionaries were passive and sometimes active participants in the struggle to undermine and destroy the authority of the chiefdoms. Only a few were actually paid government agents, but many others reported on the activities of the chiefs in their areas. They also organized and led wartime commando units against the Xhosa, helped establish segregated African locations and create the administrative apparatus for taxing Africans who came under colonial jurisdiction, and occasionally acted as de facto recruiters of African labor. Nevertheless, everyday life for most missionaries of the pioneer generation was a life spent working with the small number of converts who had been recruited at some cost on the stations.

Cultural Discrimination

The missionaries were motivated primarily by ideological conviction, and in this context the mission station was a Trojan horse in these precolonial cultures. For those under mission authority, conversion to Christianity had to be a personal and not a group decision. Christians were to be separated from non-Christians, the saved from the unsaved, and Christianity would be promoted as a superior way of life.

Like their counterparts in Natal, the pioneer missionaries in the Ciskei discriminated on the basis of culture rather than race. Thus in theory they regarded all humankind as potentially equal, but they did not differentiate between Christianity and the accepted norms of their culture. Plows and wagons, cotton clothes, Western medicine, square, upright furniture, square houses built along straight lines,[6] and, above all, formal literacy were regarded as the fruits of the Gospel. Traditional doctors and diviners, clothes, charms, and amulets to ward off evil, traditional dancing, beer drinking, and expressions of what the missionaries regarded as nudity and open sexual behavior were condemned. Male and female initiation rites, male polygamy and the exchange of women against cattle (now referred to as the *lobola* system), and the role of ancestors in worship were rejected as anti-Christian. This missionary generation would expel Africans from the church and even from the land in an effort to gain compliance with the new moral order.

Cattle herding as a male activity was discouraged in favor of tilling the soil, which was deemed to be more suitable for developing a middle-class work ethic. This change in occupational role—cultivation in an African stock-farming community being women's work—signaled yet another assault on the precolonial economic system. The introduction of the Western concept of time—the seven-day week with every Sunday and certain other days of the year set aside for rest, prayer, and contemplation—also helped to alter the prevailing pattern of work and recreation.[7] Traders were encouraged to establish stores on mission land, and the station economies were gradually monetarized.

Communal habits of thinking and living were continually discouraged in favor of individual enterprise and self-sufficiency. The missionaries accepted the dictates of a laissez-faire political economy and actively promoted habits of work and thrift that they believed would enable individual Africans to progress in the station communities. Perceptions of economic advancement in the next generation, for example, were based on acquiring the necessary skills to become teachers, tradesmen, or peasant farmers who worked the land in individual tenure. When Africans complied with these demands, they saw themselves, and they were seen by the settlers as well as the missionaries, as representatives of the Christian community.

God was at the center of this universe and the source of all power in a world where there was no distinction in practice between the sacred and the secular. Every thought and every act was imbued with a specifically Christian significance. The mission took over and sanctified every stage of the life cycle—birth, initiation into manhood and womanhood, marriage, last rites, and burial. The church's sovereignty was invoked in Christian homes and in the fields at harvest time, and its temporal base—the church building—was inevitably the biggest and most imposing on the station. Virtually every activity in the life of the Christian community became institutionalized in the church.

Women constituted a disproportionate number of the converts on most mission stations in the nineteenth century, and the missionaries were especially concerned about their welfare. Precolonial power relations had subordinated women in the production process, and they remained subordinate after the homesteads disintegrated. Thus the missionaries condemned female initiation rites, because they believed the young initiates were sexually exploited (especially by married men) during these ceremonies. They condemned *lobola* especially because they believed the custom exploited women. Male guardians (they might be husbands, fathers, uncles, or any adult male who was the designated guardian) sought to enrich themselves by marrying off their wards to collect the bridewealth.[8]

As the missionaries sought to shift social responsibility from communities to individuals and from extended families to nuclear families, they became more and more concerned with the domestication of women in the home and the church. The new morality sought an alternative to precolonial sexual codes—especially for women. For example, the concern with female purity, reinforced in dress codes, sermons, school reading material, mothers' prayer groups, and even celibate guilds for girls (at least among the Anglicans), would become an important theme in the life of the Christian community by the end of the century.[9]

Mission views on cultural discrimination, however, were not endorsed by the colonial state in the postconquest era. Frontier officials as early as 1856 had compiled a summary of what was acceptable in "native law and custom" as a guideline to the magistrates. In an attempt to resurrect emasculated African patriarchal authority structures in the locations, the Cape in subsequent years recognized numerous precolonial social practices relating to initiation and marriage rites, including male polygamy, the *lobola* system, and the laws of inheritance. The mission's assault on African culture in the postconquest era, then, would be made largely without the support of colonial authority.[10]

The Subordination of Popular Culture

The strength of the mission enterprise stemmed, in part, from its ability to shape the convert's perceptions of reality in such a way that its authority was legitimated. The missionary's construction of reality was to be accepted as objective reality. The Christian community was to be subordinated to a new social order with its framework articulated by the mission.

Nonverbal as well as verbal and written modes of communication were employed by the missionaries in establishing a consensus for the Christian community. The cross, for example, came to occupy a central position in all the churches. New charms and amulets were created—badges, strips, or bands of cloth in different colors—and the wearing of uniforms formed a regular part of the church's many and varied activities.[11] The rites of confession and the use of "holy" water and incense did not feature formally in the liturgy of these pioneer nonconformists, but they certainly heard confessions informally, and the symbolic interpretation of such rituals as the Eucharist, for example, would have had much the same effect as the literal interpretation as far as their audiences were concerned.

Other icons of the new culture—religious paintings, sculptures, and stained glass in church buildings and even homes—were probably exploited more successfully by missionaries from the hierarchical, established state churches of Western Europe, the Lutherans, Anglicans, and ultimately the Roman Catholics, who arrived briefly in Port Elizabeth in the early 1880s and returned permanently to the eastern Cape in the early 1900s. Independent African churches in the region, moreover, were to use symbolic devices extensively and effectively from the 1890s.

Preaching and evangelizing, choral singing and the ritual of daily prayer (both public and private) were encouraged from the beginning, and the effect of these and other verbal modes of communication on pre-Christian oral cultures cannot be overestimated. African converts, recruited initially before the 1850s, embraced these techniques and were primarily responsible for the spectacular impact the tiny Christian community would have on the non-Christian majority in the later Victorian period.

Precolonial songs, dances, stories, and poetry continued to exist independently of mission influence even on the stations, but increasingly the mission appropriated these messages and altered or transformed their meaning in the ongoing task of constructing a consensus that would win the approval of the African Christian community. The mission did not control all oral media, and it did not always or inevitably undermine these traditions. What the missionaries did was to recast oral history in a new framework. In essence, they created a new universe. Conversion for the first generation of converts involved nothing less than a complete break with the old way of life.

The mission's success in establishing a new universe depended in part on its monopoly over the written word. Mission station communities were centered on the church, school, and either possession of or access to a printing press. Churches and schools were inseparable even on the more primitive stations, because the education of an African Christian community imbued with certain moral, emotional, and intellectual qualities was deemed essential for the preservation and expansion of the church. The preaching and teaching ministry, in turn, were dependent on the mission's control and manipulation of literate culture.

The mission agency had a virtual monopoly over the production of both permanent and ephemeral literature in English and Xhosa until the 1880s. The normative framework of Victorian Christianity and culture as interpreted by the missionaries was reflected and reinforced in these mission publications. The dialect spoken by the Ngqika Xhosa, for example, was accepted by the missionaries as the standard to be followed in developing a written language. Once it was frozen in type, the written form of Xhosa as spoken by Ngqika's people was gradually established as the lingua franca of the southern Nguni. Early texts in Xhosa—the first printed material was produced by the Presbyterians on their press in 1823 and the first book in 1824—were written phonetically using African informants. The missionaries did not really begin to master the language until the 1830s when the first grammars were published.

Missionary publications in Xhosa were devotional, evangelical, and educational in content. The missionaries concentrated on producing translations of the Gospels and other portions of the Bible, catechisms, prayer books, religious homilies, hymns and primary school instructional materials, dictionaries and other works concerned with the language. The goal of all the mission societies was to produce the whole of the Bible—the centerpiece of literate culture— in Xhosa. The first translation of the New Testament appeared in 1846, and this was followed by the Old Testament in 1857. The Presbyterian mission undertook to revise the Xhosa Bible in the 1860s, and this was completed in 1887. The possession of books in the Christian home—ideally the Bible, hymnbook or catechism, and perhaps one or two other religious publications— came to symbolize the Christian's commitment to the new cultural order in much the same way as did square houses, European clothing, or the use of the plow.

Printing presses were acquired by several mission societies in the Ciskei between the 1820s and 1870s, including the Methodists at Mt. Coke, the Anglicans at St. Matthews, and the Presbyterians at Lovedale, but by the 1880s it was apparent that the missionaries could not compete with foreign or domestic commercial printing firms. It was cheaper and more efficient to publish material of interest to the African Christian community outside the mission stations. By the early 1900s only a few missionary societies west or east of the Kei River had significant publishing facilities. The exception in the Ciskei was Lovedale, which became one of the major mission publishing centers in sub-Saharan Africa.

The impact of the written word on the developing Christian station communities is exemplified in the Lovedale experience. Lovedale had printing and bookbinding departments (opened in 1861), a retail and wholesale bookstore, and South Africa's oldest continuous mission journal. The *Kaffir Express* (October 1870–December 1875) was renamed the *Christian Express* (January 1876–December 1921) and finally the *South African Outlook* (January 1921–).[12]

The Presbyterians and Methodists jointly published *Ikwezi* (Morning Star), one of the first newspapers aimed at the African Christian community, between August 1844 and December 1845. Although only four issues were produced, *Ikwezi* contains the earliest known writing in Xhosa by Xhosa writers.

Among the contributors were William Kobe Ntsikana and Zaze Soga. William Kobe's father was the legendary Ntsikana, who in 1815 had a vision that changed his life and ultimately the lives of his people. Ntsikana is believed to have been the first African Christian in the eastern Cape, and to this day the Xhosa believe he received the Gospel independently of the missionaries. Although Ntsikana himself attracted very few followers, his disciples were to be key mediators in making Christianity comprehensible to the Xhosa. Ntsikana composed four hymns—including the "Great Hymn" of the Xhosa people, *Ulo Thixo omkhulu ngosezulwine* (He, the Great God in Heaven)— which exemplified his conversion experience.[13] Zaze Soga was a son of Soga, a friend and companion of the prophet Ntsikana and councillor to chiefs Ngqika and Tyhali. Zaze Soga's father was reputedly the first Xhosa to use a plow, irrigate the land, and grow cash crops for the market,[14] and his family would become one of the most influential in the eastern Cape.

By the 1850s, English as well as the vernacular was being used as a medium of communication in the station communities.[15] English versions of the Xhosa Bible, for example, were selling well in the more prominent Ciskei stations by the 1860s and 1870s. The most influential mission newspaper to adopt the trend was *Indaba* (The News), which was published monthly at Lovedale between August 1862 and February 1865. One-third of the journal, which had an estimated 500–600 readers, was in English for the "intellectual advancement" in particular of school-going youth. It contained news of general interest as well as religious news, a pattern that would become characteristic of the more influential periodicals in future decades. *Indaba* tried to avoid "local and party politics," but it covered Cape parliamentary news— especially legislation affecting Africans—and overseas news.[16]

Indaba's correspondents were the vanguard of an educated elite. Among its contributors were men like Ntibane Mzimba, father of Pambini Mzimba, probably the most successful independent church leader in the eastern Cape during the colonial era; and Nikani Mantsayi, father of Robert Mantsayi, a prominent political activist in the region. Gwayi Tyamzashe was a pioneer missionary to the Pedi and a founder of the church in Kimberley, two of his sons would become editors of major African newspapers. Simon Gasa, another correspondent, became a prominent political and educational figure in the Transkei. Govan Koboka, also a political activist, dispensed medicine and prepared surgical dressings at Grey Hospital, built in 1856 in King William's Town as part of Governor Grey's African assimilation policy.[17]

The most prominent writer for *Indaba* was Tiyo Soga (1829–71), another son of Soga, the royal councillor. Educated initially at Lovedale, Tiyo Soga was such a promising pupil that the mission eventually sent him to Scotland to study for the ministry. He was ordained there in 1856, the first African clergyman to achieve this status in southern Africa. He married a Scots woman and returned to the Presbyterian mission, where he preached to Europeans as well as Africans while launching new stations among the Ngqika Xhosa at Mgwali (about thirty miles north of King William's Town) and later at Thuthura east of the Kei River among Sarhili's people.

As far as written literature in Xhosa is concerned, Tiyo Soga was unquestionably the pioneer literary figure. The first book in Xhosa by an African was his translation of the first part of *Pilgrim's Progress,* John Bunyan's extended allegory in prose of the search for a Christian utopia. It was published by Lovedale Press in 1867. He worked on the revision of the Xhosa Bible and also composed several hymns, which were first published by the Presbyterians in 1864 and later included in most other Protestant hymnals. One entitled *Lizalis' idinga lakho, Thixa Nkosi yenyaniso* (Fulfill Thy Promise Lord, God of Truth) has been described as "almost a national anthem." [18] As Soga and other African writers demonstrate, devotional, evangelical, and primary educational themes acceptable to the missionaries continued to dominate book and pamphlet production in the vernacular at Lovedale.[19]

Nevertheless, increasing numbers of Africans were becoming literate in Xhosa, and in postprimary schools like Lovedale, Healdtown, Lesseyton, and St. Matthew's an elite was being educated in English. Mission journals in Xhosa and English, moreover, were reporting ever more confidently on events in the secular world outside these communities by the 1860s and 1870s.

Undoubtedly the most important periodical produced in the first fifty years of the mission press in the eastern Cape was *Isigidimi Sama Xosa* (The Xhosa Messenger), initially a supplement in *Kaffir Express,* the Presbyterian mission's flagship journal. *Isigidimi* was launched as an independent publication aimed exclusively at the Xhosa Christian community in July 1873. It was to appear as a regular monthly—and at intervals between 1879 and 1884 as a fortnightly—until its demise in December 1888.

Elijah Makiwane, an editorial assistant to James Stewart, principal of the secondary school at Lovedale and editor of the *Kaffir Express,* was placed in charge of the new publication. For eight years he was responsible for the newspaper, the first African editor of a mission journal in the subcontinent. In 1881 Makiwane, now an ordained minister, was succeeded by John Tengo Jabavu, a teacher and Methodist lay preacher who had attended Healdtown and was continuing his studies at Lovedale. William Wellington Gqoba, a contemporary of Tiyo Soga, succeeded Jabavu as editor of *Isigidimi* in 1884.

Makiwane, later a founder member of several important African political and educational organizations, Jabavu, soon to emerge as the most prominent

African political figure in the colony, and Gqoba, an accomplished essay writer and poet, set the tone of the publication. In addition to the editors, *Isigidimi* had more than twenty named correspondents representing at least thirty rural settlements and towns in the eastern Cape and in the colony of Natal. The newspaper received contributions from a broad section of the educated elite, many of whom had been writers for *Indaba* and other mission publications.

The African editors and contributors to *Isigidimi* were politically conscious and covered topical news and opinion of concern to their readers. André Odendaal, one of the first scholars to examine the contents of *Isigidimi*, has shown the extent to which the newspaper acted as a vehicle for mobilizing African opinion during this period. A sustained, albeit muted, level of protest could be discerned in the news and letters-to-the-editor pages that was to have important implications for the literate African community.[20]

The development of a specifically Xhosa literature, with a coterie of African authors and an established audience, was a product of the twentieth century. Samuel Edward Krune Mqhayi (1875–1945) was the first major Xhosa literary figure to gain recognition through his published works. As a historian, playwright, novelist, translator, journalist, and, above all, the *imbongi yesizwe* (poet of the nation) he holds a special status in Xhosa literature that has never been superseded. As an *imbongi* (praise poet), Mqhayi tried to capture in writing the essence of the *izibongo* (praise poems) that had formed part of the core of Xhosa oral tradition. He was the first writer to make a serious attempt to syncretize the old and the new cultures that were embodied in oral and written literature.[21]

Outside of Mqhayi and a few others, very few original works in Xhosa were printed before World War I. Lovedale Press had published an estimated 238 Xhosa manuscripts by 1939—second in sub-Saharan Africa only to Swahili—but most of these were produced from the 1920s. The printing of original manuscripts, moreover, was virtually dependent on the goodwill of those missionaries who controlled the mission press. There is evidence that Lovedale effectively manipulated its control over the production of Xhosa manuscripts until its monopoly was broken by the state in the 1950s.[22]

4.2. The Growth of an African Church

An identifiable African Christian community began to emerge in and around the mission stations and outstations in the Ciskei region in the generation after the cattle killing.[23] The scale of conversions was unprecedented, and apparently all the pioneer missions experienced a rapid growth in African church membership.

Very little research has been done on the African church between the 1850s and 1880s, but the expansion in membership seems to have stemmed in part from a series of cathartic revivals within the fledgling congregations.[24] Out of these revivals came hundreds, possibly thousands, of fervent believers who turned to the mission field. On the whole, the European missionaries were unprepared for these events and somewhat fearful that the reformation might weaken their control over the church. Nevertheless, temperance crusades, healing services, prayer meetings, and mass open-air evangelical revivals continued for many years. By 1884, for example, there were more than a hundred mission stations in the eastern Cape—about fifty in the Ciskei and fifty-two in the Transkei—in addition to an unknown number of outstations and preaching and teaching places.[25] The vast majority were founded by Africans emanating from the mission's expanded "native agency" program.

The growth of the church had several ramifications for the Christian community. The mission station lost its status as a haven for refugees and as a closed universe for Christians bound together under the priestly rule of the European missionary. In subsequent decades, African Christian households became more widely scattered among the non-Christian majority and further removed from the civil and religious authority of the mission.

The African clergy everywhere were zealous in enforcing mission codes of belief and behavior, but the further removed one was from the stations, the greater the potential for interaction between the old and the new lifestyles. Rank-and-file members of the African clergy were operating alone and mainly in non-Christian communities by the 1870s. Certain aspects of precolonial culture, at least, did not seem so incompatible to second-generation Christians as to their parents. Congregational support for the pioneer missionary's wholesale negation of precolonial culture was generally less militant in the wake of the relatively massive growth in church membership.

The recognized African clergy—preachers, evangelists, catechists and lay readers—increased rapidly as the church expanded, and they sought to upgrade their status within the mission enterprise. Financially strapped parent boards of several mission societies also began urging their missionaries to establish autonomous "self-supporting, self-governing, self-propagating" African churches. To grant ordination to the African clergy, however, was to signal their ecclesiastical equality with the white missionaries. It had been done only in the case of Tiyo Soga before 1870, and he had been ordained by the United Presbyterian Church in Scotland.

Ordained ministers possessed the exclusive right to sanction baptisms, solemnize marriages, and inter the dead. They could take charge of churches and raise funds on behalf of their congregations. They were also recognized by the government, which brought them a measure of security and mobility in Cape society. The ordained ministry would be among the best paid—between roughly forty and a hundred pounds a year by the 1880s—and most prestigious vocations open to the upwardly mobile elite during the colonial period. As the best-educated men in the Christian community, ordained clergymen were expected to best represent the interests of the community to missionary and settler alike.

The Wesleyan Methodists were the leaders in the eastern Cape in ordaining African pastors during the later nineteenth century. They had the largest mission church—an estimated 63,400 African members, for example, in 1891—and a majority of the individual congregations that in theory could support African ministers. The Methodists established a theological school for Africans at Healdtown in 1867, only thirty-two years after the first Methodist theological school had been established in Britain, and four "native assistant missionaries" were ordained in 1870.[26] About 150 Africans would be trained for the pastorate by the Methodist mission between 1867 and 1910, and more than 125 of these were ordained, most of them being the children of Christian parents. Virtually all of these pastors were commoners, as educated members of royal lineages usually entered secular employment. Men like Charles Pamla (1834–1917),[27] William Shaw Kama,[28] James and John Lwana, and Boyce Mama would become household names in the African Christian community during the colonial period.

Although the Anglicans were the last of the pioneer missionary societies to arrive in the eastern Cape, they were second to the Methodists in number of church members (with more than thirteen thousand in 1897) and African clergymen. The Anglicans were key agents in Governor Grey's "assimilation" plans for the Xhosa after the cattle killing. The children of chiefs and councillors, for example, were to be educated at a special institution originally known as Kaffir College (later renamed Zonnebloem) in Cape Town, which was supposed to remake its pupils into industrious Victorian middle-class men and women.[29]

Theological training before the 1870s was available at Zonnebloem and St. Augustine's College in Canterbury (England). The Zonnebloem course (introduced in 1864), however, was not a success. And since African clergy educated at Canterbury would have been qualified to minister to white congregations, something that South African Anglicans were not in favor of, the Canterbury option was phased out.[30] Most candidates for the Anglican ministry in the Cape between 1870 and 1910 were sent to a theological school established at St. Matthew's in the Ciskei. The Anglicans created a number of licensed ecclesiastical offices within the church, including nonordained readers and catechists and ordained deacons and priests. About sixty Africans were ordained in the Cape Colony during this period.

The Presbyterians had by far the highest educational qualifications for its clergy. The theological school established at Lovedale in 1872 was the only institution of its kind in the Cape that attempted to train African students for service in white as well as black congregations (although no African from this mission except Tiyo Soga is known to have ministered to white communicants in the Cape Colony).[31] Nevertheless, only about twenty-two African Presbyterians were ordained between 1856 and 1910. The failure of denominations other than the Congregational Union of South Africa to support this venture, and the Presbyterian mission's refusal to lower standards in the absence of resources, contributed to the failure to produce more pastors.

The Congregationalists (LMS and Moravian) lagged even further behind. The first African ordination in the LMS mission did not occur until 1873, and only about nine others had been ordained by 1910. The Moravian mission ordained only one African clergyman (1883) before 1900, and in the next fourteen years only eight more were ordained. The most prominent Congregational pastor during this period was Walter B. Rubusana (1858–1936), who was raised by the resident missionary at Peelton near King William's Town and educated at Lovedale. He completed the theological course in 1882 and was ordained in 1886. A well-known writer and translator,[32] Rubusana would emerge as one of the leading political figures in the eastern Cape in the early decades of the twentieth century. Few Africans were ordained by other European missionary agencies in the eastern Cape until after union in 1910.

The African clergy during the 1860s and 1870s were "stunningly hopeful and expectant," as Wallace Mills put it, "that prejudice and inequality would disappear" from the mission enterprise.[33] They had abandoned the old ways and internalized the new: they were not uncritical, but on the whole they accepted the mission's vision of reality as their own. Most missionary societies, including the Methodists, Anglicans, and Congregationalists (the Moravian and LMS mission churches were eventually absorbed by the Congregational Union of South Africa), however, were administered by local settler-dominated church bodies and dependent on them for financial support.

The Presbyterians were an exception to the rule: the parent church in Scotland had suffered a schism in 1843, and their missionaries were forced to choose between two competing church bodies, the Free Church of Scotland and the United Presbyterian Church of Scotland (formed in 1847). Most Presbyterian missionaries in the eastern Cape were members of the Free Church, and there were virtually no links between settler and African churches other than at ministerial level. The African mission churches of the Free Church mission were organized as the Synod of Kaffraria, which was controlled by the missionaries.[34]

Missionary enthusiasm for ordaining African pastors was on the wane by the 1880s, as the arbiters of a segregationist culture began to separate church congregations and limit contact between white and black clergy. The Methodists began raising the qualifications for ordination in the late 1880s to bring them more in line with the standards set by the Presbyterians, a decision that virtually eliminated prospective candidates for ten years. Ordained African clergy in the Anglican church were almost entirely lower-status deacons until the mid-1880s, and those who managed to become priests thereafter were kept in the lowest ranks of the ecclesiastical hierarchy. The Presbyterian missionaries waited twenty years after Tiyo Soga before ordaining Pambini Jeremiah Mzimba (1850–1911) and Elijah Makiwane (1850–1928), among the most widely respected men in the mission-educated community, in the mid-1870s.[35] Thereafter there were apparently no ordinations—the theological seminary had one student, for example, in 1892—until the end of the century. While the African clergy had been largely responsible for establishing the Presbyterian church's Livingstonia mission in what is now Malawi in 1876, few willing candidates could be found to go there a decade later.

Presbyterian and Congregationalist missionaries had less clearly defined lines of authority than the Anglican and Methodist missionaries did as far as the African churches were concerned, but European control remained dominant and pervasive. All-white missionary agencies continued to subordinate the African clergy and exclude them from power. Few Africans were allowed to attend mission meetings, much less be office bearers. Even the Congregationalists, with the longest tradition of local church autonomy, maintained white control over their segregated congregations.

Africans themselves, however, were learning organizational skills in the churches that would be put to good use in the political arena. Men's and women's groups as well as youth groups of every description were being established at the congregational level by the 1860s and 1870s, and men's and women's guilds, choral societies, sports clubs, and Young Men's (and Women's) Christian Associations were being established at the regional level between the 1880s and early 1900s. More Africans were involved in local and regional associations centered on the churches than in any other organized activity during the colonial period.

Among the most popular organizations outside as well as inside the church were those linked to the temperance movement.[36] The temperance forces included a variety of settler interests (government officials, liberal politicians, local farmers and other employers of black labor, churchmen and missionaries) as well as African church leaders. They favored taxes particularly on brandy and urged that alcoholic beverages not be sold to the black population. African temperance leaders also opposed the consumption of relatively mild *utywala* or *amarewu,* the traditional African beer. The war on drink spilled over into settler politics because it impinged on the vested interests of the wine farmers in the southwestern Cape and those merchants who were involved in the wine and liquor trade. The Afrikaner Bond, an Afrikaner political and cultural organization formed in 1879, did not want to restrict or prohibit sales to Africans and Coloureds and rejected a tax on alcoholic drink.

It is perhaps difficult today to appreciate the importance mission-educated

Africans attached to the crusade against drink, but many believed alcohol had been a more effective weapon of colonialism than the soldiers, magistrates, merchants, and missionaries combined. Drink had weakened the will to resist during the Cape-Xhosa wars (Ngqika, the most powerful chief of the Ciskei Xhosa in the early 1800s, is a classic example) and had undermined the moral foundations of the nation. African political organizations and the fledgling black press in the eastern Cape were solidly behind the temperance movement, which in its most intensive phase lasted from the 1870s to the early 1900s. Temperance groups were probably formed in every African congregation, and the crusade against drink was apparently approved by non-Christian tradition-alists. Few other issues generated more deputations, petitions, and letters of protest to colonial and missionary authorities.

The Independent Order of Good Templars, the South African branch of an overseas temperance organization that had originated in North America in the early 1850s and spread to Britain, Western Europe, and several European colonies, gained a foothold in the Cape Colony during the 1870s. Although in theory the Good Templars were interracial, in practice it was a white organization. Africans and Coloureds involved in the temperance movement were only nominally represented in the colony by this settler-dominated body.

LMS and Presbyterian missionaries together with their African clergy began to organize separate African and Coloured temples from the mid-1870s. African temperance groups, for example, were formed in Port Elizabeth in 1875 (Ark of Refuge Temple) and at Lovedale (the Endeavor Temple) in 1876.

A separate interdenominational black temperance society entitled the Independent Order of True Templars (IOTT) was established in 1879, and it had thirty-five hundred members in forty temples in the eastern Cape by 1882. But these temperance groups were mainly Coloured, and most of them were in urban areas like Port Elizabeth, Uitenhage, Graaff-Reinet, and Grahamstown.

Cape Africans became fully involved in the temperance movement from the later 1880s and 1890s. An autonomous Eastern or Kaffrarian Grand Temple of the IOTT, composed almost entirely of Africans, was launched in 1891. This organization had sixty-six temples and 6,000 adherents (with about 2,000 paying members) throughout the eastern Cape by 1900. A youth program—the Band of Hope—was also started which by 1907 had 1,296 members in twenty-seven different bands. Most African modernizers were associated with the Eastern Grand Temple, and it was used as a center for political, educational, and social as well as temperance activities.[37]

4.3. Educating the African Christian Community

The missionaries in the Cape's eastern frontier districts had virtually total control over African education until the mid-1850s.[38] The African had to be literate to participate in a literate culture, so formal education was a priority of the mission enterprise. The primary schools were first confined to the station communities, and the students were either the children of converts or non-Christians who had come under the authority of the missionary. The initial response was enthusiastic, but numbers soon dropped when it became clear that formal education would play a central role in the conversion process.

The mission schools also developed slowly because the teaching ministry was only one of many activities on the station. The missionary teachers could spend only part of their time in this activity, and for some years the mission resisted the appointment of nonmissionary teachers. The Methodists, for example, did not appoint their first white lay teacher until 1828, which was the same year the Presbyterians employed the first Africans to teach in the primary school at Lovedale. Robert Balfour and Charles Henry were evangelists who had been followers of Ntsikana. Their appointment as teachers signaled an important shift in mission educational policy.[39]

African teachers and preachers began to expand the missionary enterprise beyond the central stations in the Ciskei in the late 1830s and 1840s, when the first outstation schools and preaching circuits were established.[40] The number of salaried and "volunteer" (unpaid) African teachers and preachers increased dramatically with the development of the outstations, but the quality of these instructors varied considerably. At best, education in the outstation schools enabled one to gain an elementary reading knowledge of Xhosa. If successful, the pupil could continue his or her education (there were more female than male students during this period) in the station primary schools. Instruction at these institutions was deemed to be on a par "with the mass of European children in the humbler walks of life," according to one contemporary observer.[41] Mission schools during this period, however, were not accommodating the majority of school-age children even in the station communities, and most pupils left school without being able to read and write.

The missionaries began to establish more specialized educational facilities centering on boarding schools to upgrade the training of African teachers, preachers, and evangelists from the end of the 1830s. The boarding school was to become the key institution in the development of an educated Christian elite. Curriculum was to conform to the prevailing norm in English and Scottish schools at the same level—more intensive tutoring in reading, writing, and arithmetic together with literature and science courses and religious instruction. The Methodists and Presbyterians were the early leaders in developing boarding schools in the Ciskei, and they were followed by the Anglicans.

Watson Institutions, as the Methodist schools were called, specialized in teacher training but also included agriculture (several model farms were established) and special courses for preachers, evangelists, and the sons of chiefs. The program eventually faltered in 1865 because too many stations were involved, and money and personnel were spread too thin. The Methodists gradually focused on Healdtown as the main center for postprimary education in the Ciskei, and by the turn of the century it was regarded as the best teacher-training institution of its kind in the Cape.

The Presbyterians established a boarding school at Lovedale in 1841. The major innovation during the early years was to encourage the children of missionaries and settlers to attend the school. This policy would have important implications for the African Christian community because it meant that European as well as African parents had a direct interest in preserving the quality of education at Lovedale. William Govan, a minister and classicist who also had some business experience, was appointed the first principal. Although initially for males only, Lovedale Seminary, as it was then called, admitted European females a few years later, and in 1868 it became the first boarding school in the eastern Cape to admit African females.

Govan, who was head of Lovedale Seminary for twenty-nine years, developed courses to promote functional literacy and initiated "advanced" courses for postprimary students. Instruction at this boarding school, unlike that at the Watson Institutes, was in English only. All students shared the same classroom and dining hall, attended the same clubs, and played sport together. Europeans and Africans, however, ate at separate tables and slept in different rooms. Few if any European schools in the Cape were superior to Lovedale until the 1880s, when they began to receive relatively massive grants-in-aid from the colonial government.

The Scots Presbyterians were the trendsetters in boarding-school education. They established relatively high standards and maintained them as an example for the other missionary societies. If African teachers and preachers managed to meet the criteria established by the missionaries in the boarding schools, they were placed in positions of equal responsibility. Only a few converts met these qualifications before the 1850s—Tiyo Soga and John Muir Vimbe[42] are examples from the original class at Lovedale Seminary—but they made an enormous impression on the African Christian community.

The Anglicans were pioneers in establishing missions for Africans in town as well as the countryside, and African teachers were employed in their schools at an early date. The Grahamstown diocese, which embraced the Ciskei region, established its first postprimary boarding school for Africans in Grahamstown in 1860 (it was called the Kafir Institution), and within nine years twenty-two of the thirty students who had attended the school were employed by the mission as teachers.[43]

The Cape Colony's African Education Policy

Mission schools began to receive regular grants from the Cape when Grey was the colonial governor between 1855 and 1863.[44] The main beneficiaries of the Grey Plan, as it was called, were Lovedale and four boarding schools founded by the Wesleyans at Healdtown, Salem, Lesseyton, and D'Urban. The Moravian stations at Shiloh and Goshen and the LMS station at Peelton were also funded together with schools established by the Anglicans for the children of chiefs and councillors at Zonnebloem in Cape Town, at the Kafir Institution in Grahamstown, and several others in the eastern Cape. The trend toward expanding elementary education in the outstation schools, which would channel the better students to the station's primary ("day") schools and boarding schools, was encouraged and the value of teacher training recognized.

The key to government aid under the Grey Plan, however, was industrial training. Manual labor disguised as industrial training (which included agriculture) would promote "habits of work" appropriate to living in Cape colonial society. This was the real motive behind Grey's desire to promote African education: the settlers needed a dependent labor force that was also disciplined and productive. Thus they tended to think of this training in the most rudimentary terms—learning how to use simple tools and developing work habits appropriate to survival in the new economic order.

The missionaries generally grafted industrial training onto the existing boarding schools. Instruction in various trades, farming techniques, and homemaking (for girls) became one of the areas of specialization alongside courses for teachers, the clergy, and others who sought a more advanced academic education. Lovedale took the greatest advantage of the scheme, and by the early 1860s the boarding school was offering apprenticeships equivalent to the level of journeyman in wagon making, blacksmithing, carpentry, building, printing, and bookbinding.[45]

Although government aid in the form of the Grey Plan was unquestionably beneficial for the mission's primary day and boarding schools, the Africans themselves were paying for much of their education. The colonial budget at this time was derived in part from duties on imported goods, and Africans were increasingly heavy consumers of these goods. Some were already paying school taxes, and a portion of the quitrent fees (for those who held land under individual tenure) was also earmarked for the schools.

While the Presbyterians were the major innovators in African education, the Methodists had the largest number of students and schools. By 1863, for example, they had fifty-one schools with twenty-three hundred students in the Ciskei and eight schools with eight hundred students east of the Kei River. The quality of education in the primary schools varied with the missionary society. The older, established missions, especially those with teachers trained at Lovedale or Healdtown, generally had better teachers. The newer missions—the Anglicans, for example, in the 1850s and 1860s—had less-educated teachers and higher absentee rates among the pupils. Instruction was conducted mainly through the medium of Xhosa and focused on acquiring a reading knowledge of the language, although English only and dual-medium instruction was also employed in many station schools. Less than one-quarter of the students in the primary schools were studying arithmetic, and only about one-third were learning how to write.

African teachers during Grey's administration received between £3 and £50 a year from the Methodists, between £20 and £40 from the Presbyterians, and between £18 and £60 a year from the Anglicans. White teachers at the time received about £150 a year with subsidized housing. Mission school buildings and supplies were deemed inadequate, and the missionaries complained that pupils attended school but remained (like their parents) unresponsive to mission education.

The expansion in the number and variety of schools under the Grey Plan benefited mainly the Mfengu and to a lesser extent the Thembu in the Ciskei. Even Xhosa teachers had little impact on their people before the 1870s. Several missionary societies adopted alternative strategies of informal education centered on the Sunday school (a by-product of the later eighteenth-century Anglo-American revivals), which adults as well as children attended. Instruction was even more elementary in the Sunday schools—learning the alphabet, simple reading exercises, and religious lessons—but the response was apparently enthusiastic. In fact, the Sunday schools competed very successfully for pupils with the station and outstation primary schools during this period.[46]

The Grey Plan ended abruptly in 1863 when colonial grants to African schools were cut by almost one-half. From now on, settler governments would channel aid primarily to European schools. Colonial aid to African schools would be spent essentially on salaries for European and African teachers, but these were reduced drastically as were the grants for pupils attending the boarding schools and undergoing industrial training. The mission societies were essentially responsible for buildings, equipment, and most of the educational materials used in the schools.

The Education Act of 1865 created three categories of aided schools. Order A schools, as they were called, were almost exclusively for white children. Order B schools were aimed at poor whites and Coloureds, mainly in the rural areas, although some African boarding schools in the Ciskei were also included. Order C schools were almost exclusively for Africans. English was required as the medium of instruction in all government-aided schools. The 1863 grant for African (Order C) schools was not surpassed until 1875. On a per capita basis, settler support for African education in the Cape steadily declined. Schools that remained in the same category, and most African schools remained in the Order C category, received the same or lower government grants year after year.[47]

Nevertheless, the missionaries were now dependent on this aid, small as it was, and colonial legislators and education officials who were indifferent and even hostile to African interests increasingly interfered in African educational policy. When the settlers gained control over their own legislative affairs in 1872, the limited funds available for African education were channeled more and more into the elementary schools. The missionaries were encouraged to limit African schooling to Standard IV (sixth grade) and offer "advanced" training only to those who could be employed as elementary teachers, semiskilled artisans, and domestic servants.

Colonial policies in African as well as European education were implemented by a superintendent-general and translated into practice by school inspectors (the first of whom were appointed in 1873) and the missionaries. Continuity was maintained in large part because the individuals appointed to these positions served for long periods of time. The top administrative post, for example, was held by only two men before union in 1910—Langham Dale (1859–92) and Thomas Muir (1892–1915)—and they believed African education should not be supported beyond the primary level except in the case of teacher training.[48]

The collapse of the Grey Plan, aggravated by indifferent support from parent mission boards overseas, forced most missionary societies in the Ciskei to cut back on their educational operations. The boarding schools declined sharply in both numbers of students and quality of education received.[49] Lacking money and personnel, European missionaries on the stations virtually ceased to play a role in supervising and subsidizing the elementary schools and preaching circuits in the outstations.

African Responses to Mission Education

Prompted by the evangelical revivals, the unprecedented growth in church membership, and the cutback in colonial and mission aid to education, the Africans themselves became increasingly responsible for their own schools. Voluntary contributions in cash and kind rose steadily from the 1870s, and in the case of the boarding schools contributions were sometimes spectacular. In the Transkei, for example, the Mfengu contributed £5,600 of £7,000 needed to build Blythswood (sister school of Lovedale Seminary near Butterworth), and the Thembu contributed £1,000 of £1,500 needed to expand the Methodist school at Clarkebury (near the Mbashe River) (Map 3). The students also began paying boarding school fees, which at Lovedale Seminary amounted to £14,372 in twelve years (about £1,200 a year between 1871 and 1883).

The shift in African attitudes toward education was most evident in the expansion of station and outstation primary schools. The magnitude of growth in African primary schools and pupils in the last quarter of the nineteenth century can be seen in the government-aided Order C schools (see Table 4.1). These figures also reveal the extent to which African education conformed to settler demands. Almost all Order C schools were primary schools, and more

Table 4.1. Cape Colony Order C schools, 1874–1900

Year	Aided schools	Students	Students inspected	Below any standard (%)	Std. II plus (%)	Std. IV plus (%)
1864	35[a]	2,000	—	—	—	—
1874	87[b]	6,337	—	—	—	—
1886	201[b]	7,653	5,897	52.7	32.3	5.9
1895	351[b]	20,873	17,383	48.8	33.0	5.3
1900	552[b]	37,442	33,040	53.2	28.8	7.0

SOURCE: R. H. Davis, "Nineteenth-century African education in the Cape colony: a historical analysis," Ph.D. diss., University of Wisconsin, Madison, 1969, 250 (Table 14), 282 (Table 21), 302 (Appendix C, Table 1).
[a] This figure does not include 12 African schools with an unknown number of students in British Kaffraria.
[b] These figures include postprimary boarding schools, of which there were 9 in 1874, 21 in 1886, 13 in 1895 and 11 in 1900.

than 90 percent of the aided pupils were below Standard IV (sixth grade). Inspectors who examined the students in aided schools in 1873, for example, found that only 23 percent of the African pupils tested could pass any standard at all. By 1885 the position had improved to the point where about 47 percent of the pupils tested were passing some standard, but few Africans had more than the equivalent of five years of school.[50]

Aid to African schools was cut even more drastically from the late 1880s as settler hostility to African education mounted and the colonial government, as Richard Hunt Davis put it, "sought to provide instruction for every white student which was more advanced than that available to any African."[51] Government inspectors were examining African students only at the elementary level and in the teacher-training programs by 1900. Mission-aided schools tended to limit instruction to this level, and very few Africans advanced beyond Standard V (seventh grade). With the exception of Lovedale and a few other mission institutions, African education in junior and senior high schools at the Cape did not really begin to improve until the 1940s.

African education under mission agencies in the Cape actually developed at three different levels during the later colonial period. Lower-elementary aided and unaided schools (two to four years) were usually outstation schools, and the most spectacular growth occurred at this level. Unaided Sunday schools also continued to play an important role in lower-elementary education because for many adults and children it was still the only formal schooling they received. Government-aided higher-elementary and lower-secondary day and boarding schools (four to seven years) were mainly station schools, and the most significant developments in African "higher" education occurred at this intermediate level. The massive growth in aided and unaided elementary schools generated a desperate need for teachers, which meant that educational facilities at the advanced level favored teacher training over all other forms of specialized education, including industrial training.

Teacher Education

In line with the need for more teachers, the Cape Education Department began issuing teaching certificates in 1867. Africans sought these certificates because they were one of the few legitimized expressions of academic achievement available to them. Limited success was achieved in the 1870s and 1880s, but the number of certificated teachers dropped in the 1890s as preferential treatment for white schools accelerated. In 1894 the Education Department devised a three-year training course for teachers with a minimum admission requirement of Standard IV (sixth grade) and examinations at the end of each year. Although performance levels by African teachers rose considerably in subsequent years, almost all students above Standard IV were now obliged to undergo teacher training or the missions would lose the government subsidy.[52]

The pay for teachers was not much if at all higher in the 1880s than it had been under the Grey Plan twenty-five years earlier—between £30 and £40 a year for those who had certificates and £20 a year for those who had no certificates. Some teachers were too poor even to qualify for the right to vote in the colony. In fact, the teacher-training certificate seems to have been used to qualify for clerical and other positions outside teaching, such as court interpreters (with salaries as high as £140 a year) and policemen (as high as £95 a year).

The Mfengu, and to a lesser extent the Thembu, benefited the most from missionary education in the later colonial period because they were the first to respond to Christianity. The 1891 Cape census returns are particularly revealing in this context. More Mfengu (19,020), for example, could read and write than all other African ethnic groups combined (16,554), and 28 percent claimed to be Christians as opposed to 15 percent for all other African ethnic groups combined.[53] The percentage of literate Africans of Xhosa origin, beginning with those living in the Ciskei region, did not become significant until the early 1900s.

At least some members of the educated Christian elite, however, were moving beyond the boundaries of denomination and ethnic group. Nowhere was this more apparent than in places like Healdtown, perhaps the leading teacher-training institution for Africans, and Lovedale, the crown jewel among the mission's educational institutions in the Cape.[54] Between the founding of Lovedale Seminary in 1841 and 1870, only 380 pupils had attended the school. In the next ten years, enrollment jumped to almost 1,000 pupils and then leveled off until the early 1900s. There were 889 students at the school in 1896, for example, and they represented fourteen African ethnic groups (in addition to whites and Coloureds) and seven religious denominations. These students paid a total of £2,559 in school fees in 1896, the highest figure up to that point in the history of the institution and one that exceeded the fees paid at every other African school in southern Africa. Lovedale Seminary was the only full-fledged secondary school with matriculation status for Africans in the Cape Colony, and the central building in the complex was reputedly the biggest mission structure in the subcontinent.

By 1902 Lovedale mission station was a village consisting of more than thirty buildings, including missionary houses and student dormitories. Woodworking, horseshoeing, brick-making and wagon-building cottage industries had been created on the station in the wake of the industrial training program. Lovedale had a printing works, bookstore and post and telegraph office, in addition to the trading store and central church, and it was surrounded by developed, mainly mission-owned farmland. Alice, the adjacent settler town and headquarters of the magisterial district of Victoria East, depended for survival on the growth of Lovedale and on trade with African farmers in the surrounding area.

On the surface, Lovedale was a harmonious community that prized education above all. Students drawn from a variety of racial, ethnic, cultural, and religious backgrounds spent years living, working, playing, studying, and praying together. In this atmosphere, they certainly articulated many of the ideas and issues that would be advanced by the African Christian community in the eastern Cape and beyond in generations to come.

Beneath the surface, however, all was not well either at Lovedale or in the African Christian community. There was a stirring of discontent on the Presbyterian mission's central station in the 1880s and 1890s that for many observers seemed to symbolize the tensions developing between European missionaries and African Christians throughout southern Africa. The mission no longer had a captive audience.

5
African Christians and the Cape Liberal Tradition

African Christians emerging from one or at the most two generations of immersion in mission culture in the 1860s and 1870s found themselves increasingly isolated in a hostile, white-dominated world. It was inevitable that they would seek allies among Cape settlers who identified themselves with the mission experience, and it was equally inevitable that they would seek allies among the representatives of mission culture at its source in Britain.

For mid-Victorian mission apologists at the Cape, the principle of a qualified but nonracial franchise was the most important political manifestation of the new cultural order. Individual rights would be restricted to the "civilised" population, but these rights would be enshrined in 1853, when the settlers were granted representative government with their own parliament, and in 1872, when they were granted responsible government. This also meant that African and Coloured voters were able to participate in the political process. This was the political birth of the Cape liberal tradition, as it was called, in South Africa.[1]

Cape African voters were composed mainly but not exclusively of mission-educated Christians who had responded positively to the changes wrought by the impact of British colonialism on the eastern Cape. Christianity and formal education were key facilitators of change, and an indigenous African church overriding ethnic and denominational boundaries was in the making by the 1870s. Economic links between white and black modernizers had been firmly established at least a decade earlier, and loose political alliances were being formed by the 1880s.

The white political allies of Cape African voters stemmed from three main sources in the later colonial period:

1. Representatives of British humanitarian and missionary agencies such as the Anti-Slavery and Aborigines Protection Society, South African Native Races Committee, London Missionary Society, and the Brotherhood Movement;

2. Politicians elected to the Cape Legislative Assembly after the granting of responsible government in 1872;

3. A number of individuals, including merchants, lawyers, newspaper editors, and missionaries, who served as the mission-educated community's secular and spiritual councillors, and as mediators at various levels in the eastern Cape, in Cape Town, and in London.

Settler politicians representing rural and urban constituencies with numbers of African and Coloured voters formed the crucial component in this alliance. Black participation in Cape colonial politics, however, was conditioned in large part by a struggle for supremacy in parliament between the Afrikaners and the English, representing mainly the settlers of Dutch and British origin, between 1872 and 1910. Afrikaners outnumbered English speakers two to one in the Cape Colony during the 1880s. The Afrikaner Bond, launched in 1879, was enlarged and reorganized in 1883 to provide an organizational base to unify and direct the Afrikaners' political aspirations.[2]

The rise of Afrikaner nationalism would have a decisive impact on Cape colonial politics during this period. The Bond comprised the largest single political grouping—at least 40 percent of the total in both houses of parliament—between 1884 and 1910. While Afrikaners never formed a government on their own during this period, J. H. Hofmeyr, leader of the Afrikaner Bond, and his colleagues effectively controlled parliamentary politics by granting and withdrawing support to successive English coalitions in proportion to whether or not they implemented the Bond's policies.[3] English-speaking politicians represented so many conflicting interest groups that it was impossible to forge a single party to challenge the supremacy of the Afrikaner Bond until the late 1890s. In the interim, they sought allies from a variety of sources, including the modernizing African elite.

Reactions to Conquest. A series of events at the end of the frontier-war era between 1877 and 1881 also served to promote African participation in Cape politics. There was widespread opposition to colonial intervention in the dispute between the Mfengu and Gcaleka Xhosa that had resulted in the War of 1877–78, to the 1878 Gun Act that had attempted to disarm Africans west and east of the Kei River and in Basutoland, and to the resulting Gun War of 1880–81. British colonial forces were also active against Africans elsewhere in southern Africa; for example, in 1879 they had destroyed the Zulu kingdom, subjugated the Pedi in the Transvaal, and put down a rebellion by a Sotho chiefdom in southern Basutoland.

The mission-educated children of several Xhosa chiefs and councillors participated in the 1877–78 war, including Edmund (Gonya) and Bisset (Mlindazwe) Sandile, sons of Sandile, the Ngqika chief; Nathaniel Cyril (Kondile)

Umhalla, son of Mhala, the Ndlambe chief; and Dukwana Ntsikana, son of the prophet Ntsikana.[4] The mission-educated community sought unsuccessfully to petition the government to remove the Gun Act, and on this occasion even the missionaries denounced the legislation. According to the *Christian Express*, it had done "more to create anger, disaffection, and a sense of injustice among the natives than any single thing of the kind has ever done."[5]

Mission-educated Christians in the eastern Cape were in a vulnerable position by the 1880s. The missionaries were trying to maintain their authority over African churches, education officials were trying to downgrade African schools, settler newspapers were waging a campaign against mission-educated Africans, and settler legislators were passing laws that discriminated against them. African modernizers were finding themselves increasingly marginalized in colonial society. As Odendaal put it, "their dream of equality and Christian brotherhood in a state dominated by mid-Victorian political liberalism [was turning] into an existential nightmare."[6]

A major grievance was education, where the missionaries seemed unwilling to oppose settler demands that they abandon the effort to educate an elite and concentrate instead on educating as many Africans as possible to the lowest levels of functional literacy. The debate over this issue was particularly intense at Lovedale, where James Stewart had replaced William Govan as principal in 1870.[7] Govan had adopted a policy of advanced training for Africans so they could compete with Europeans in a middle-class culture. He believed higher education would neutralize the social disadvantages of living in a settler-dominated society.

Stewart, who virtually ruled the Presbyterian mission for thirty-five years, was representative of prevailing missionary attitudes toward African education in the later colonial period. He urged that Lovedale focus on training preachers for the churches and teachers for the elementary schools, and as Sheila Brock puts it, "skilled workmen, honest clerks and reliable female domestic servants."[8] The general thrust of Lovedale's educational efforts should be at the primary level because this would best meet the needs of the African community. As Stewart told the students at Lovedale: "Any education which is not practical in its character is of no real value to you at your present stage of civilisation."[9] Stewart's ideas, of course, were fully endorsed by Langham Dale, the Cape superintendent-general of education: "The Rev. Dr. Stewart is desirous to enlarge the sphere of training both of the lads and young women. All cannot become teachers; many have no aptitude either for that occupation or for trades. Agricultural labour offers to Native boys a wider field, and one very necessary."[10]

Although very few Africans had taken advanced courses, they believed that continued access to a classical education offered the only real possibility of achieving equality of opportunity with the European. Stewart's paternalism angered and frustrated those who were now seeking to establish themselves as power brokers among their own people.[11] His increasingly segregationist pronouncements had so alarmed leaders of the Christian community by the 1880s, according to Brock, that they "could no longer trust Lovedale and Stewart to act or speak in their best interests." [12]

The Govan-Stewart rift was a reflection of a much broader debate among missionaries in the eastern Cape and beyond over the role of the African Christian community and its future status in colonial society. Stewart believed it was essential for Lovedale to win the approval of the settlers and to do this effectively African mission policy had to be in harmony with their interests. His ideas signaled a shift in missionary attitudes from the pioneer generation, which had sought to "civilise" the African to the level of the "civilised" European, to the new generation, which sought to legitimate an inferior role for African Christians in a racially stratified society. In line with social Darwinist thinking in other parts of the British Empire, subordination by race in a segregated society rather than incorporation of individuals by class in a potentially integrated society was more acceptable to the mission enterprise in the later colonial period.[13]

African modernizers in the Ciskei and beyond would respond in a variety of ways to these developments. This chapter is concerned primarily with political responses that were associated with the Cape liberal tradition at the time.

Section 5.1 considers the role of the mission-educated community in Cape politics and in the first African pressure groups independent of settler or missionary control. These modernizers were guided primarily by the belief that if they participated in parliamentary politics they would influence the enactment of legislation more favorable to their interests.

Section 5.2 profiles the emergence in the eastern Cape of an African *petty bourgeoisie*. Special attention is paid to the role of the fledgling *petty bourgeois* press as it sought to represent and mobilize African political opinion in the last three decades of Cape colonial rule.

Section 5.3 traces the growth of African political pressure groups in the Ciskei during the 1880s and 1890s, and Section 5.4 chronicles the decline in African participation in Cape liberal politics in the last decade or so of the colonial period.

5.1. Strategies of Participation in Colonial Politics

Mfengu in the Ciskei were the first African ethnic group to acquire a power base in the Cape political system.[14] They had been given documents stating they were British subjects from the 1830s, when pass laws were gradually extended to areas in the Ciskei frontier zone incorporated into the Cape. They occupied much of the best land in the African locations, and they had apparently over-

Figure 5.1. African modernizers of the new order before 1910. John Tengo Jabavu with his eldest son D. D. T. Jabavu, about 1903; *on facing page left*, John Knox Bokwe and, *facing page right*, Alan Kirkland Soga.

taken the Rharhabe Xhosa as the biggest African ethnic group between the Fish and Kei rivers by the 1880s. The African Christian community was dominated by mission-educated Mfengu at this time, and Mfengu headmen were key intermediaries between colonial administrators and the mass of rural African householders. Their cooperation was essential, since they were empowered to allocate land, maintain order, and help administer the locations.

African Voters in the Cape

To be eligible to vote in the colony, one had to be a male of twenty-one years or older who was accepted as a British subject, owned property valued at twenty-five pounds, or received a wage or salary of fifty pounds a year (or twenty-five pounds a year plus food and housing). There was no educational test. Although the 1853 constitution had given Africans who resided permanently in the colony the same franchise rights as the rest of the population, few qualified at the time. Attempts by headmen to register African voters en bloc after the granting of responsible government in 1872, moreover, had been challenged successfully in court by the settlers, and individuals of color who tried to vote were easily intimidated. Africans were still inexperienced in settler politics and not yet actively canvassed by liberal white politicians.

Africans in the frontier districts of the eastern Cape began registering as voters in large numbers only in the 1880s. Whites would always dominate the

Figure 5.2. Key figures in the South African Native Congress included: *above left to right*, Robert R. Mantsayi, Chief Nathaniel Umhalla, Walter B. Rubusana, Daniel Dwanya, and Thomas J. Mqanda and, *below left to right*, Paul Xiniwe, Attwell Maci, William D. Soga, F. Jonas, George Tyamzashe.

Table 5.1. African voters in six constituencies in the 1880s

	1882		1886	
	Number	% of vote	Number	% of vote
Aliwal North	260	20.3	800	53.8
Fort Beaufort	160	13.6	400	21.8
King William's Town	370	22.1	1300	39.4
Queenstown	220	10.6	1700	45.1
Victoria East	90	14.3	520	50.8
Wodehouse	50	3.5	1325	48.9
Total	1150	13.9	6045	42.8

SOURCE: A. Odendaal, "African political mobilisation in the eastern Cape, 1880–1910," Ph.D. thesis, University of Cambridge, 1983, 95.

Cape voters' rolls, but the African vote between 1880 and 1910 was of some significance in seventeen constituencies (out of seventy-four constituencies, for example, in 1891), of which fourteen were in the eastern Cape (including the Transkeian territories). It was crucial in four Ciskei districts (Fort Beaufort, King William's Town, Queenstown, and Victoria East), and in the Wodehouse and Aliwal North districts north of the old Ciskei frontier zone (See Table 5.1). African voters in these six districts increased by more than 500 percent, whereas white voters increased by about 12 percent (from 7,117 to 8,077) during these years. The African vote was also significant in constituencies with relatively large towns like Port Elizabeth and Uitenhage, and in rural Ciskei and Transkei constituencies like Glen Grey, Thembuland, and East Griqualand.

No African at this time, however, felt confident enough to stand for election. Instead, the mission-educated elite in alliance with headmen and other persons of authority in the locations acted as mediators in bringing together African voters and white political candidates or "friends of the natives," as they were called, who would be sympathetic to their interests. African election committees were organized, and African politicians became increasingly more sophisticated in their understanding of how political power was acquired in a parliamentary democracy. They helped select and tutor liberal white candidates and ensure that they had access to black voters in the constituencies. The fledgling black press was mobilized in the effort to gain popular support for electoral politics, and African politicians began to communicate their grievances and aspirations to an ever-widening audience of white sympathizers.

Early Independent African Organizations

African organizations independent of missionary or settler control were also formed during this period. They focused on religious, educational and farming as well as political activities that were mainly of interest to the mission-educated community.

One of the earliest African regional organizations in South Africa was the Native Educational Association (NEA), which was launched in 1880. John Gawler, an African teacher at St. Matthew's mission station, had started a local teachers' association in 1876 but it lasted only a few years. He decided to establish the NEA with an enlarged membership and an expanded program, but the Cape Education Department refused to recognize the organization unless its president was a European. Although a white herbalist from Fort Beaufort was given the post, it was a nominal appointment, and he had no influence in the NEA. John Tengo Jabavu, who was named vice president, was the dominant figure. Gawler was a poor secretary-treasurer, and John Knox Bokwe (1855–1922), an ordained minister who was highly respected in the Lovedale community as a dramatist (his play *Vuka Deborah* is considered a minor classic) and composer of hymns, was placed in charge of the accounts. Under Jabavu's leadership, the NEA was reorganized in 1882 with a new constitution dedicated to "the improvement and elevation of the native races," their "social morality," and their "general and domestic welfare." [15]

The NEA initially represented a small group of teachers from Lovedale, Healdtown, and St. Matthew's, but membership soon expanded to include ministers, traders, peasant farmers, court interpreters, wagon makers, labor-recruiting agents, and schooled headmen, in other words, the Ciskei's mission-educated elite. Ministers and teachers dominated the organization. Elijah Makiwane, the ordained minister from Lovedale, was elected president in 1885.

The NEA held its meetings at Fort Beaufort, King William's Town, and at various rural mission stations in the Ciskei. More than thirty were held between 1881 and 1900. NEA activities were given wide coverage in *Isigidimi* and other African journals and occasionally even in the local settler press. Membership stood at 110 in 1885, but attendance at its half-yearly meetings averaged 30–35 and rarely exceeded 70 members. As a teachers' organization, the NEA was concerned initially with educational matters such as the deterioration in government grants to African education, low teachers' salaries, low pass rates, and problems relating to the curriculum in the schools. The NEA was particularly worried about the Afrikaner Bond. As Makiwane put it in his 1885 inaugural address: "The very expression 'native education' seems to be hateful to this party or movement." [16]

Under Jabavu's tutelage, the NEA became more politicized, registering voters, protesting the pass laws, and urging that Africans be allowed to sit on juries in cases involving Africans. An NEA delegation met Prime Minister Sir Gordon Sprigg, a known hardliner in African matters, in 1887 and presented him with a list of demands that included a ban on liquor in African locations, an end to the pass laws, and parliamentary representation for qualified Africans in Transkeian areas annexed to the colony. The protest delegation was not successful, and apparently there was dissension within the NEA over its political agenda.[17] Jabavu hoped to broaden the NEA's political base with a new constitution, but his efforts were thwarted. The NEA returned to its primary role as a teachers' organization in 1887, and it was eventually reorganized as the South African Native Teachers' Association in 1906.

The first explicitly African political organization to emerge in the eastern Cape was the Imbumba Yama Nyama (South African Aborigines Association), which was launched in Port Elizabeth in September 1882, again in part to counter the activities of the Afrikaner Bond.[18] The name of the organization was derived from a saying of the prophet Ntsikana, who had urged his people to be *imbumba yamanyama* (inseparably united). The 1882 Imbumba was inspired by his example:

> They are white under the soil
> The bones of the thing [son] of Gaba
> Grass has grown over that grave
> Of the great hero of the nation
> Yet he is still alive, he still speaks. . . .[19]

Among the founders of the 1882 Imbumba were several teachers, including Simon P. Sihlali (1856–1910), a graduate of Lovedale and the first African in the colony to pass the matriculation examination (in 1880), and Isaac Wauchope (1852–1917), another Lovedale alumnus who had served briefly as a teacher in the Free Church's Livingstonia mission in British Nyasaland (Malawi) before becoming a clerk and court interpreter in Port Elizabeth. Sihlali was elected president of the organization and Wauchope chairman of the Port Elizabeth branch. Like the NEA, the Imbumba comprised a cross section of the modernizing elite, many of whom were members of both organizations. Its constitution urged members to fight for the rights of Africans throughout the subcontinent and to encourage political participation at all levels of government.

As a political pressure group, the 1882 Imbumba would monitor governmental activities, especially with regard to discriminatory legislation, land (Africans were urged "to withhold the ground of our fathers by buying land in these bad times"), and education (the translation of foreign works into Xhosa was particularly encouraged). Members were also urged to overcome ethnic and denominational barriers, inspire "the nation" to register as voters, and support *Isigidimi* (and later *Imvo Zabantsundu*), the "national newspaper."[20] Membership rose from 40 in September 1882 to 300 in May 1883. Port Elizabeth remained the focal point of activity under the energetic chairmanship of Wauchope, but branches were also established in Graaff-Reinet, Cradock,

Colesberg, and other towns in the Cape's eastern frontier districts. Graaff-Reinet, where Sihlali and W. P. Momoti (another founder of the Imbumba) lived, was actually the biggest branch with 140 members by July 1883, and many were Afrikaans-speaking Coloureds. The Imbumba vied for followers with the NEA in the 1880s and tried without success to absorb the rural-based teachers' body.

Other African organizations, divided along ethnic lines, were also established at district level in the Ciskei and Transkei. Glen Grey's Thembu Association, formally organized in 1884, was made up of alienated non-Christians as well as Christians seeking to prevent white farmers from grabbing African land. It was soon absorbed by the South African Native Association (SANA), a smaller body representing essentially the Thembu educated elite. The president and vice president of SANA, David Malasi and Richard Kawa, were teachers. Malasi was president of the Glen Grey Teachers' Association (also known as the Thembu Teachers' Association). Kawa, an Mfengu, was a writer (he produced a history of the Mfengu), who had taught for many years at Healdtown and was apparently highly influential as an educator (one of his students was Tengo Jabavu). The other non-Thembu leader was James Pelem, an Ngqika Xhosa who had also trained as a teacher at Healdtown. Pelem became the dominant figure in SANA, which would continue to fight for African land rights in the district until the 1894 Glen Grey Act.

Odendaal suggests that district organizations created by Mfengu, Xhosa, and Thembu activists during the 1880s and 1890s evolved at three fairly distinct levels. The first groups were formed at mission stations with major educational facilities like Lovedale, Healdtown, and St. Matthew's, and they ranged from literary and debating societies to teachers' groups. When the students left school, they tended to form "mutual improvement" associations modeled more or less on the clubs they had left behind. More explicit political organizations were also started at the grassroots level. These included one in the Victoria East District in 1883 that sought "to uplift the black nation," the Stockenstrom Original Africander Association formed in the Stockenstrom District in 1884, the Peddie Native Association (also called the Fingo Association or Manyano Lwabantsundu) formed in the Peddie District, and the Native Vigilance Association formed in King William's Town in 1885.[21]

These groups were the primary political catalysts between white candidates and black voters at the local level. Loose alliances of mission-educated Christians, headmen, and other authority figures in the locations (who were usually semiliterate or even illiterate) organized election committees, registered voters, and mobilized opinion. They set the agenda for political, economic, and cultural issues of interest to their constituents. Communication between towns, villages, and rural hamlets in the eastern Cape, however, was slow and cumbersome, and organized political activity was generally uncoordinated. Groups met infrequently, lacking funds and administrative expertise, and membership was small and apparently floating except at election time.

The infrastructure of these fledgling African political groups, then, was still weak and tenuous, but white settler politicians recognized the importance of the African vote and were beginning to compete for African support by the 1880s. The driving force behind the mobilization of African political opinion, however, seems to have stemmed not so much from organizations as from the activities of a few opinion leaders.

5.2. African Political Opinion and the Petty Bourgeoisie

The single most important barometer of African political opinion in the 1880s and 1890s was John Tengo Jabavu (1859–1921).[22] He had been one of *Isigidimi*'s more militant correspondents in the late 1870s and early 1880s. As editor from 1881 to 1884, Jabavu sensed that the depths of protest had hardly been tapped. He brought his readers' grievances nearer the surface and got the newspaper involved in settler politics by openly canvassing African voters and promoting white politicians deemed to be sympathetic to African interests.

Tengo Jabavu and Imvo Zabantsundu

The 1884 election was the first political event in which *Isigidimi* tried to mobilize African voters, but this was too much for James Stewart, the missionary in charge of the newspaper. Jabavu resigned, and in November 1884 the twenty-five-year-old ex-teacher launched *Imvo Zabantsundu* (Native Opinion) in King William's Town, the first newspaper owned and controlled by an African in southern Africa. Jabavu's publication soon eclipsed *Isigidimi* and other mission journals in offering a more effective platform for the educated African community. It was the beginning of a new era.

Jabavu launched *Imvo* as a journal that was committed to libertarian values but independent of specific political interests. It was to be nonpartisan politically but dedicated to "moderate men within all parties," which in practice meant all politicians who were opposed to the Afrikaner Bond.[23] Jabavu was certainly aware of the fact that the English-speaking settlers were no more sympathetic to African interests than were the Afrikaners. But he saw that if the English-Afrikaner split was deliberately polarized, his readers could more easily identify with the issues involved in settler politics. Jabavu also hoped that editorial support for the liberal platform would lend credence to the popular myth that political differences between the two settler groups represented genuine ideological differences.

Jabavu was immensely powerful during the 1880s and 1890s. He was the éminence grise behind the formation of several independent African organizations, and his newspaper expanded the agenda for discussion on the options available to redress African grievances.

Imvo Zabantsundu was a protest journal at two levels. On the one hand, it sought to articulate and unify the interests and needs of the modernizing elite, which by this time had emerged as a distinct social class—an African petty bourgeoisie—in Cape African society. Some idea of its composition in terms of formal education and occupational specialization can be discerned from a book produced by Stewart in 1887 in defense of mission policy at Lovedale Seminary. More than 2,000 African students (1,520 males and 538 females) had been enrolled in postprimary classes since the boarding school was established in 1841. The subsequent occupations of roughly 70 percent of these students were tracked, and they represented a cross section of the modernizing sector. These included teachers, ordained and nonordained clergy, transport riders and peasant farmers with land in individual tenure, law agents, police constables, journalists, magistrate's clerks and court interpreters, and semiskilled and skilled craftsmen such as carpenters, blacksmiths, sewing mistresses and dressmakers, telegraph operators, printers, bookbinders, wagon makers, masons, shoemakers, shop clerks, drugstore assistants, small traders, and storemen.[24]

The communicators and consumers of news and opinion in protest journals like *Imvo* stemmed from the same social strata. They were the "organic intellectuals" (following Gramsci) of their generation, the thinkers and organizers who constructed the ideas and attitudes of the social class to which they belonged. They remained, however, a very small segment of the African population as a whole. The newspaper's circulation, for example, probably did not rise above four thousand before 1910, even though, in addition to the Cape, it was distributed in the colonies of Natal and Basutoland, and in the Afrikaner republics north of the Orange River. One can safely assume that functional literacy rates were still very low, probably less than 10 percent of the Bantu-speaking population even in entrenched mission areas like the Ciskei. Thus there would be few readers for each newspaper sold, even though there may have been many more who heard the news read to them.

Imvo was a medium of mass communication for this modernizing elite, a marketplace for information, ideas, and attitudes, but it also sought to represent the majority population. Although the petty bourgeoisie constituted an insignificant proportion of the African population, they judged themselves to be the primary mediating force between rulers and ruled. They tried to organize public discourse and provide a platform that would embrace the imagined interests of the majority population. They would inform the masses of their rights and school them in the principles of political etiquette and parliamentary democracy. The needs of all Africans, then, were to be expressed within a framework imposed on them by the petty bourgeoisie. As Jabavu himself put it, *Imvo* would provide "a rope to tow these stragglers to the desired shore." [25]

Jabavu's links with prestigious mission schools in the Ciskei and Transkei were instrumental in developing a cadre of subscribers to *Imvo*. His brother-in-law, Benjamin Sakuba, then secretary of the NEA, was probably the first subeditor. When he left in 1887 to start a coffee shop, William D. Soga, a member of one of the Ciskei's leading mission-educated families, replaced him. The subeditors were apparently responsible for the Xhosa columns, within which are embedded the social history of the modernizing elite in the eastern Cape. Jabavu seems to have concentrated on the English section, including the editorial page, and focused on topics of political interest to the African petty bourgeoisie.

White liberals in parliament, who had a political and often a material interest in cultivating African voters, helped fund the newspaper. Jabavu was the election agent, for example, in a successful campaign to get James Rose-Innes a seat in the legislative assembly as a representative of the Victoria East District in 1884. It was Rose-Innes, his brother Richard, and some liberal King William's Town merchant-traders, including T. J. Irvine (a former member of the Cape Legislative Assembly), James Weir, and William Lord, who furnished the capital and connections to enable Jabavu to launch *Imvo*. Richard Rose-Innes, one of the main attorneys involved in court disputes over registering Africans as voters, was the newspaper's first advertising manager. The Mercury Printing Company, which printed the *Mercury,* King William's Town's settler newspaper, agreed to print *Imvo*.

To Jabavu and his contemporaries, men like the Rose-Innes brothers, John X. Merriman, John Molteno, J. W. Sauer, Thomas Scanlen, Saul Solomon, W. P. Schreiner, and Charles Stretch seemed absolutely essential to the democratic process.[26] These "friends of the natives" could make parliamentary politics work on behalf of the African in the colony, and Jabavu became the principal mediator between liberal African and European politicians in the eastern Cape during this period.

African politicians, however, also wanted to retain their links with the British metropole. They preferred indirect rule from London to direct rule from Cape Town, and the Colonial Office was bombarded with letters and petitions seeking imperial intervention on issues that ranged from land disputes to discriminatory legislation. Several attempts were made in the 1880s and 1890s, for example, to form African branches of the Empire League, launched by mining magnate Cecil Rhodes in a bid to mobilize public opinion in favor of a British takeover of the South African Republic. The Africans wanted to use the League not only against Afrikaner nationalism but also as a pressure group to press for the reintroduction of imperial rule at the Cape. British trusteeship became one of the most cherished allegiances of the African petty bourgeoisie. They would continue to rely on imperial intervention on behalf of the African—enshrined in periodic litanies of allegiance to a foreign monarch in a foreign country—until the 1930s.

Jabavu's identification with the liberal tradition also meant that the politics of protest would be conducted strictly within the framework of the laws of the colony. Like Mohandas K. Gandhi, the apostle of Indian passive resistance in Natal, Jabavu was a master publicist who maintained a wide-ranging correspondence with influential lobbyists in and out of parliament in Cape Town and London. He believed in and relied on the tactics of constitutional protest, creating and legitimizing pressure groups, forming delegations and writing petitions to colonial authorities, and exploiting the media of mass communication in the form of letters, editorials, and news reports in the black and, wherever possible, white press.

African modernizers formed a nexus of bonded social and economic as well as political relationships in their pursuit of Victorian middle-class culture. They participated in choral and reading groups, debating societies, sewing and singing groups, and in Victorian-model sports like tennis, croquet, cricket (where in Port Elizabeth, for example, they more than held their own against white clubs), rugby, and even horse racing.[27] Temperance societies and various church-related associations continued to be a powerful social as well as religious force in community life. The "old boy" boarding-school networks, moreover, included increasing numbers of educated girls by the 1880s. Intermarriage between mission-educated men and women was now the rule in African Christian communities. Personal and professional ties, cemented in the rural areas, were recreated after migration to the urban areas.

Africans from the Ciskei began to settle permanently in towns like Port Elizabeth as early as the 1830s,[28] and an urban African petty bourgeoisie from this region could be found in all the settler states of South Africa by the end of the century. The social bonds that linked the mission-educated elites in the Ciskei were retained when they moved to places like East London and Port Elizabeth, and even to new and alienating environments like Cape Town, Johannesburg, and Pretoria, far removed from the rural heartland.

5.3. Regional African Politics in the 1880s and 1890s

African political groups at the district level during the 1880s operated mainly on their own, and the 1882 Imbumba operated mainly in a few towns west of the Fish River.[29] The NEA, which was the best-known rural organization in the Ciskei, was moving away from protest politics. Nevertheless, a number of African political organizers had surfaced in the region besides Tengo Jabavu by the end of the decade.

They included men like Nathaniel Umhalla, the veteran of the last Cape-

Xhosa war; William Kobe Ntsikana, grandson of the prophet Ntsikana and the son and namesake of a founding father of the Christian community; Paul Xiniwe, the best-known African entrepreneur in the Ciskei at the time (he opened the first African hotel in the Cape Colony); Meshach Pelem, who had helped found the 1882 Imbumba; Walter Rubusana, who would soon emerge as Jabavu's main political rival; and Elijah Makiwane, Pambini Mzimba, John Knox Bokwe, Charles Pamla, and a number of other ordained clergymen. Pamla's brother George was a political leader in the southern Transkei along with men like James Pelem (who was Meshach's elder brother), Richard Kawa, and Andrew Gontshi, all leaders of the South African Native Association. Gontshi (1856–1930s?), a graduate of Lovedale and the first African to sit on a jury and be recognized as a law agent in the Cape, helped launch the first political organization in Fingoland, the Manyano nge Mvo Zabantsundu (Union for Native Opinion), in 1887.

The event that served to propel this group into more concerted political action was the Parliamentary Voters Registration Act of 1887 (known by Xhosa speakers as *Tung' umlomo* or "sewing up of the mouth"). The settlers were determined that Africans in newly acquired territories in the Transkei would not be eligible for the franchise, so land that was not secured by individual tenure was declared invalid as far as voting rights were concerned. The act extended the franchise to the Transkei, but Africans living on communal "tribal" land could not use it to satisfy the property qualification when registering as voters. The Registration Act of 1887 eliminated about 20,000 voters, most of whom were African. In the eastern Cape where the African vote was concentrated, about one-third lost the franchise. In the six key frontier districts noted in Table 5.1, there were 4,152 African voters in 1891, or almost 2,000 less than there had been five years earlier.

Imvo mobilized African opinion to fight the legislation. Meetings were held in African communities throughout the eastern Cape, resolutions were passed, and petitions to Cape Town and London were drafted and signed by hundreds of people, many of whom were illiterate. African voters sought legal advice (which initially indicated the legislation might be unconstitutional) and wrote to liberal sympathizers in the colony and in England in a futile bid to get them to influence the imperial authorities to intervene.

The 1887 Imbumba

The first regional African political body in southern Africa was forged in the Ciskei in protest against the 1887 Registration Act. About a hundred delegates from thirteen magisterial districts representing various pressure groups operating west and east of the Kei River met in King William's Town in October 1887. A new organization called the Imbumba Eliliso Lomzi Yabantsundu (or Union of Native Vigilance Associations) was established with affiliated *iliso lomzis* (or vigilance associations, meaning literally "eyes of the house") at the local level. Existing political groups would be converted into these grassroots *iliso lomzis*. They would be coordinated and their activities publicized through the 1887 Imbumba and the medium of Jabavu's newspaper *Imvo*. A permanent executive committee headed by Jabavu was formed in King William's Town. The first members of this committee were Nathaniel Umhalla, Paul Xiniwe, Cobus Mpondo, and Benjamin Sakuba. All except perhaps Umhalla were close associates of Jabavu at this time.

The 1887 Imbumba and the iliso lomzis created a permanent infrastructure for the conduct of African politics in the eastern Cape. Although the new Imbumba did not meet again formally until 1898, the local iliso lomzi in King William's Town, also headed by Jabavu, became a kind of de facto executive for the other iliso lomzis, especially in the Ciskei. According to Odendaal, the iliso lomzis were the prototypes of hundreds of similar bodies to be organized in future decades elsewhere in southern Africa.

The King William's Town conference had planned to send an African delegation to England to protest the 1887 Registration Act, but this was never carried out. The drive to register African voters, however, was renewed with vigor in the late 1880s, and test cases were sent to the courts in a bid to reinstate those voters who had been disqualified. The African vote was still decisive in several districts during the 1888 parliamentary elections, although cracks were already beginning to appear in the facade of unity that had been in evidence during the formation of the 1887 Imbumba. Charles Pamla and Nathaniel Umhalla split the African vote in the King William's Town District, and James Pelem did the same thing in the Queenstown District. In both cases, they and their followers opted for candidates favoring the illiberal coalition government headed by Sir Gordon Sprigg. These splits were a forerunner of future divisions in the African response to Cape settler politics.[30]

Africans were in fact added to the voters' rolls in the aftermath of the 1887 Registration Act. Four years later, for example, they still represented 30 percent of the electorate in twelve constituencies and 20–29 percent in ten constituencies in the eastern Cape. Consequently, the settlers, and especially the Afrikaner Bond, renewed their demands for more legislation restricting access to the franchise.

The Cape government succeeded in raising the property qualification from fifty to seventy-five pounds and imposing a basic literacy test (ability to write one's name, address, and occupation) in the 1892 Franchise and Ballot Act. Jabavu was forced to accept the legislation because his liberal allies, James Rose-Innes, Sauer, and Merriman, were members of a coalition government under the premiership of Rhodes that also included members of the Afrikaner Bond. Jabavu condemned Coloured voters, for example, for supporting a petition to the Colonial Office in London urging imperial intervention, and he effectively prevented any organized African opposition to the 1892 act.

This legislation had a dramatic impact on black voters: 4,291 Africans and Coloureds in twenty-five constituencies had lost their voting rights by 1893, while only 943 were added to the rolls. Although 1,861 whites also lost the vote in eight constituencies, 6,367 whites gained the vote in twenty-nine constituencies. For the colony as a whole, registered African and Coloured voters dropped from 21,960 to 18,612 between 1891 and 1893, while the number of white voters rose from 68,757 to 73,263 during the same period. In subsequent elections, it became increasingly clear that black voters would not offer a serious challenge to white supremacy in the colony.

Nevertheless, Jabavu remained the reigning power broker in regional African politics. His views were reported widely in the settler press and discussed in parliament, and he was the authentic African voice in African matters as far as white liberals were concerned. Jabavu continued to monitor the legislative records of those who were dependent, at least in part, on African voters, and they continued to seek his support in mobilizing the African vote at election time.

The South African Native Congress

Several African modernizers were beginning to question Jabavu's leadership, however, by the early 1890s. One of the contentious issues concerned the 1887 Imbumba. Although Jabavu was the organization's most important official, he did not schedule any more conferences after the inaugural event, and apparently not even the executive committee in King William's Town held any meetings. Jonathan Tunyiswa, a teacher at Mount Coke (the Methodist mission station near King William's Town), wrote to *Imvo* urging that a conference be held in 1889, but Jabavu rejected the idea. Africans did not have the "spirit" for organization and responded only when there was a major event.[31]

Tunyiswa persisted, and in May 1890 he organized two meetings in King William's Town to discuss the possibility of creating a new organization. Jabavu and allies like Elijah Makiwane and Isaac Wauchope refused to attend, but Nathaniel Umhalla (who had already run afoul of Jabavu in the 1888 elections), together with Tunyiswa, William Kobe Ntsikana, and a few others, made plans for a conference that was eventually held in King William's Town in July 1890. Only members of the King William's Town iliso lomzi, which included East London, Stutterheim, Peddie, and Alice, were invited to attend. If the idea of a new organization was supported by the strongest vigilance association in the Ciskei, it would probably be supported by other bodies in the Ciskei and Transkei. The July conference was attended by fifty-eight people, and a committee was given the task of drawing up a constitution—the source of some concern because the 1887 Imbumba did not have one. In the next eighteen months the pros and cons of forming a new regional political organization were hotly debated in the Xhosa-language columns of *Imvo*, while Jabavu, as Odendaal puts it, "remained disapprovingly aloof."[32]

The South African Native Congress (SANC) was formed in King William's Town at the end of December 1891. In attendance at the inaugural conference were thirty-four delegates from fifteen areas in the eastern Cape and one from Basutoland. Tunyiswa, Umhalla, and Ntsikana were joined by James Pelem, who had also defied Jabavu in the 1888 elections, William D. Soga, the erstwhile subeditor of *Imvo,* and even Jabavu's brother-in-law Benjamin Sakuba, the former secretary of the 1887 Imbumba. Other Ciskei delegates included Walter Rubusana, the Congregationalist minister from Peelton, Robert Mantsayi, Bikani Soga (another member of the prominent Soga family) from King William's Town, and Nana Ganya, chief templar of King William's Town, who was the conference chairman. The delegate from Basutoland was Shad B. Mama, whose family was also prominent among the modernizing elite in the Ciskei. Other delegates came from Herschel, Fingoland in the Transkei, and the town of Burgersdorp north of the Stormberg mountains. A constitution was approved, and Thomas Mqanda, a farmer, Methodist lay preacher, and headman from Peddie, was elected president of the executive committee. Tunyiswa and William Soga were appointed secretaries, and Nana Ganya was made the treasurer with Robert Mantsayi as his assistant. Other members of the executive committee included Umhalla, James Pelem, and Richard Nukuna, who was a leading member of the Queenstown iliso lomzi.

The SANC or Congress (Ingqungqutela), as it was called, was dominated by delegates from the old Ciskei frontier zone, just as the 1887 Imbumba had been, and there were many personal and professional links between members of both organizations. The split was probably inevitable given the steady expansion of the African petty bourgeoisie in the 1880s and 1890s. As more and more organizations were created, African politics became more divisive. There is no evidence, however, to suggest that settler politicians were involved in African divisional politics before the late 1890s. Those who supported the SANC did so primarily because they wanted an effective regional organization to represent African interests. Jabavu agreed in principle, as evidenced by the fact that he was the main architect of the 1887 Imbumba, but apparently he could not reconcile himself to the reality of having to share power or prestige with his rivals.

Although Jabavu himself was only in his early thirties, he referred to the organizers of the SANC as "young bloods" who were not yet skilled enough to play a leadership role in African politics.[33] He believed African political interests could best be served by maintaining the small but potent personal power base he had erected in the King William's Town iliso lomzi and in his newspaper *Imvo.* SANC leaders sought a regional power base that they believed would be less dependent on one person and more representative of African interests.

There were apparently no substantive differences, ideological or otherwise, however, between Jabavu and his rivals. They employed the same strategies in seeking redress to African grievances. They used the same political avenues that were open to them in Cape society and operated strictly within the legal and legislative framework imposed on them by the colonial government.

The SANC held conferences at Queenstown in July 1893 and at Wartburg mission station near Stutterheim in May 1895, but its activities were not covered by *Imvo* and its role in African as well as settler politics was apparently marginal before the late 1890s. The SANC did communicate its views to the Cape authorities, but it could not yet offer a serious challenge to Jabavu as the arbiter of African public opinion in the eastern Cape.

5.4. The Decline of African Participation in Colonial Politics

Meanwhile, events were occurring elsewhere in southern Africa that would have a profound impact on settler politics at the Cape. British foreign policy in this corner of the Empire during the later stages of Victorian rule was dictated in part by various economic interest groups intent on gaining control over the mineral deposits in the interior.[34] The cheapest and quickest way to ensure British control over the mineral wealth was to encourage the existing white settler populations in the Cape and Natal to expand northward.

Cecil Rhodes, the Cape's prime minister since 1890 and the wealthiest and most powerful politician in the colony, was ready to embark on a scheme to unify the settler states of the subcontinent under British rule by 1895.[35] Only the recalcitrant Afrikaner republicans in the Transvaal seemed likely to offer serious opposition to his plans, and so he dispatched his lieutenant, Leander Starr Jameson, to subdue them in 1896. The Jameson raid, as it was called, was a disaster and Rhodes was forced to resign from office. The coalition government he headed fell apart, and several independent English liberal politicians, including Sauer, Merriman, and other "friends of the natives," joined the Afrikaner Bond against Rhodes and his supporters.

White Party Politics

The new alignment of forces in settler politics split the liberal alliance. James Rose-Innes and other liberals joined Sprigg and his hardliners in supporting Rhodes. The new coalition launched the South African League, later renamed the Progressive party, in 1897. The Afrikaners and their English liberal allies began referring to themselves as members of the South African party in 1898. Settler politics in the colony would now be organized along party lines.

Jabavu was placed in a most difficult position. He had always believed that an alliance largely comprising English-speaking lawmakers would best serve African interests. But Rhodes and Sprigg, who had dominated the settler coalition governments of the 1880s and 1890s, were responsible for most of the legislation that discriminated against Africans, in particular, the 1878 Gun Act, the 1887 and 1892 Franchise Acts, and the 1894 Glen Grey Act. The

Afrikaner Bond, which had consistently attacked African franchise rights and tried to limit educational advancement, now changed tactics and sought to woo the African vote on behalf of its liberal allies.

Jabavu tried initially to campaign for "friends of the natives" in both parties, but in the end he sided with the Afrikaner Bond, alienating a significant proportion of his supporters and ensuring that African voters in future would also be divided along white party political lines. Even though support from Cape liberals became more tenuous during the 1890s, Jabavu seems to have become more dependent on the vacillations of his white allies.

SANC officials now embarked on a fund-raising campaign to establish a newspaper that would serve their interests. A private company (Eagle Printing Press Company) was formed, and in November 1897 *Izwi Labantu* (Voice of the People) was launched in East London. Umhalla and George Tyamzashe, a son of Gwayi Tyamzashe and a Lovedale graduate who had started his career as a journalist with *Imvo,* were the first editors. Within fifteen months, Umhalla was succeeded by Tiyo Soga's youngest son, Alan (also spelled Allan or Allen) Kirkland Soga (died 1938). He rivaled Jabavu as a protest journalist and virtually ran *Izwi* for the next ten years.[36] Richard Kawa replaced Tyamzashe in 1900, and he, in turn, was succeeded by J. N. J. Tulwana, another veteran political organizer, and S. E. Krune Mqhayi, the Xhosa praise poet.

Since *Imvo* was now perceived to be an organ of the Afrikaner Bond, the Progressive party sought another African newspaper that would support its interests. Rhodes offered to help fund the launching of *Izwi,* and the offer was gratefully accepted. The Progressives continued to provide a subsidy thereafter, but Rhodes and his colleagues had no more success in influencing *Izwi*'s editorial policy than Rose-Innes and Weir, for example, had had with *Imvo.* SANC supporters campaigned for the Progressive party out of conviction. Like Jabavu, they believed in parliamentary democracy and hoped that Rhodes, who in 1898 had declared himself publicly in favor of "equal rights for every civilised man," [37] and his allies would best serve African interests.

The 1898 Imbumba. Jabavu, alarmed at the support the SANC was receiving from the mission-educated community, called a meeting of the King William's Town iliso lomzi and revived the Imbumba. A conference was held at Indwe in the southern Transkei in July 1898—the first in eleven years— and the delegates who attended declared themselves in favor of campaigning for those "friends of the natives" who had joined the Afrikaner Bond. Jabavu's supporters were drawn mainly from Mfengu locations in the Ciskei and southern Transkei. His lieutenants at this time included Green Sikundla, a leading member of the King William's Town iliso lomzi from its inception in the 1880s; John Knox Bokwe, who had left Lovedale after many years as a minister and teacher to join *Imvo*'s staff in 1897; John Sishuba, the organizer from Kamastone location near Queenstown; and Isaac Wauchope, the veteran politician who entered the ministry in 1888 and was now an ordained pastor with a parish near Fort Beaufort.

The Imbumba met again at Pirie, the old Presbyterian mission station near King William's Town, in August 1899. Those who attended came mainly from the southern Ciskeian districts of King William's Town, Peddie, Fort Beaufort, and Stutterheim. The delegates drew up a constitution and made plans to organize Imbumba-affiliated vigilance associations throughout the eastern Cape. The revived Imbumba (designated the 1898 Imbumba to distinguish this organization from its predecessors) now seemed ready to compete with the SANC as a regional body.

These efforts were disrupted, however, when the South African War broke out in October 1899. *Imvo* and *Izwi* embarked on their own war of words over African participation in the hostilities. Jabavu assumed a pacifist, antiwar perspective and urged the British to adopt a policy of reconciliation with the Afrikaners. *Izwi* heaped scorn on *Imvo*'s editorial position and trumpeted the support that Africans in the eastern Cape were giving to the British war effort.

Jabavu's independent stand on the war was rejected by his supporters and attacked by his enemies. *Izwi* and other African journals, for example, cited the sufferings of the African population in areas controlled by the insurgents, which in the northern Cape included attempts to take away African voting rights, and Jabavu's prestige among African politicians melted away. Many white political allies also disassociated themselves from Jabavu and his newspaper. The press in King William's Town that printed *Imvo* withdrew its contract, and the newspaper was actually banned by the military authorities for fifteen months soon after martial law was declared in 1901.[38]

The Cape Franchise before Union in 1910

African politics in the Ciskei region immediately following the South African War was largely the story of the 1898 Imbumba, the SANC, and the personalities who dominated these organizations. Jabavu's stature in protest politics has been somewhat clouded by his actions during these years, but the critics do him an injustice. Jabavu regarded himself as an African liberal who remained nonpartisan politically but committed to redressing the grievances of his people—a position no different from that of any other African political leader at the time. He does seem to have become ever more dependent on the vacillations of white liberals both before and after the war, but his political contemporaries were equally vulnerable. SANC officials made the same kinds of compromises in the face of racial politics at the Cape.

Nevertheless, the leaders of the SANC, as we shall see, would be more aware of the dynamics of change in African national politics than were Jabavu and his allies. They would pursue an indigenous African scheme to establish a black university, whereas Jabavu would refuse to cooperate with his rivals and opt instead for an alternative plan sponsored by the missionaries at Lovedale.

They would accept the independent African church movement and defend its leaders in representations made to the Cape government, even though most of the SANC hierarchy remained loyal to mission churches. Jabavu and *Imvo* would condemn the separatists as a disaster for those who sought a nonracial, nondenominational Christian society at the Cape.

Ethnic rivalries also helped to harden existing political allegiances. The conquered and dispossessed Thembu, Rharhabe, and Gcaleka Xhosa were increasingly qualified for the franchise, and by the early 1900s they outnumbered the Mfengu on the Cape voters' rolls. Those Africans who were members of the 1898 Imbumba and followed Jabavu in supporting the Afrikaner Bond were mainly Mfengu. Those who were members of the SANC and supported the Progressive party were mainly Xhosa and Thembu. Block voting, the Africans' most effective tactic during election campaigns in the 1880s and 1890s, was no longer possible.

Existing political and ethnic differences would now be sustained in separate cultural traditions. The founding father of Mfengu politics in the Transkei, Veldtman Bikitsha (ca. 1828–1912), who as a child had made the flight in 1835 across the Kei River with the missionary John Ayliff, campaigned for a special holiday to commemorate the event. Colonial officials were happy to oblige, and the myth of the Mfengu as slaves of the Gcaleka Xhosa was institutionalized in the eastern Cape.

Fingo Emancipation Day, as it was called, was first celebrated on May 14, 1908. Despite disclaimers that the holiday was not meant to antagonize other ethnic groups, meetings were held all over the eastern Cape, centering on Peddie where the Mfengu had made a pledge of loyalty to Britain following the exodus, and as far north as Kimberley. This event provoked the Xhosa, and a parallel campaign was launched to establish a Xhosa day of celebration. Ntsikana Remembrance Day, as it was called, was first celebrated in King William's Town on April 10, 1909, in honor of the legendary prophet. *Imvo* and the 1898 Imbumba supported Fingo Day just as *Izwi* and the SANC supported Ntsikana Day.

The economic, political, and social options open to the mission-educated community to establish a power base within the colony were essentially closed off by the 1890s, and one reaction to these discriminatory practices was ethnic factionalism. The distinctions between the various African chiefdoms in the precolonial era "created fault lines," as Wilbur Mills puts it, "and under pressure the school community tended to fracture along those ethnic fault lines." [39] Since the Mfengu had responded first to the opportunities available to Africans under the colonial system, the main lines of division were between the Mfengu and the Xhosa-Thembu. Although ethnicity apparently was not significant in this region before the 1890s, it became an important factor in the political and religious conflicts dividing the Christian community in the early decades of the new century.

The 1908 Elections. Afrikaners who had participated in the South African War temporarily lost the right to vote, and the Progressive party, with help from SANC electoral agents and *Izwi*, won the 1904 Cape elections.[40] When the ban was lifted in 1907, all white males twenty-one years or older in the Cape as well as Natal and the ex-Boer republics were given unqualified franchise rights. As a result, the South African party won a landslide victory in the 1908 elections. The SANC maintained its support for the opposition, which was now called the Unionist party after an electoral alliance between the Progressives and a group of independents, while Jabavu and his allies campaigned for liberal candidates representing the South African party. Merriman, a defender of the old Cape liberal tradition, became the new prime minister; for Jabavu, the decision he had made years before to support the Afrikaner Bond now seemed to be vindicated. Merriman would lead the Cape delegation to a national convention that would decide, among other things, the fate of the African franchise in the looming settler state of South Africa.

The African vote was no longer perceived as a threat to white rule in the Cape, and illiberal as well as liberal factions in parliament were now less hostile to the nonracial franchise. The proportion of African and Coloured voters in the Cape Colony had remained more or less static at 15–16 percent of the total electorate between 1892 and 1910.[41] Thus the ruling political discourse at the Cape came to accept voting rights for Africans, and even the extension of the Cape franchise to the northern provinces, in the waning years of colonial rule.

Economic impoverishment coupled with the cumulated effect of discriminatory legislation helped undermine the African voter's ability to meet the wage and property qualifications. More Africans "can read and write," as one *Izwi* correspondent put it in 1908, but they could not meet the monetary qualifications, whereas Africans who owned property were often illiterate.[42] African political organizations in the Cape remained committed to the principle of participation in white party politics, but by 1910 only a few constituencies in the eastern Cape were still affected by the African vote.

African political leaders would seek alternatives to participation in settler politics in the last fifteen years or so before the end of colonial rule at the Cape. The political culture of the emerging petty bourgeoisie lay beyond the horizons of the mass of the African population, but their political agenda would address the interests of this larger and more combative audience. African politicians also began to reach out to their counterparts outside the region, especially after the South African War when it became clear the British were prepared to sacrifice the basic liberties of all Africans to appease the defeated Afrikaner republicans and unify South Africa's white population.

6

The Beginnings of African Nationalism

African nationalism in the eastern Cape has its roots in the reaction and response to the Cape-Xhosa wars. The prophet Nxele, for example, has been described as the archetype of armed resistance in the struggle against colonialism, and his view prevailed until the Xhosa were subdued. The prophet Ntsikana preached a kind of indigenous Christianity that was open to participation in mission culture and ultimately to accommodation within the new colonial order. His moral vision of a Christianity that would act as a redemptive force in society would be adopted by African modernizers in the postconquest generation.[1]

The mid-Victorian desire to assimilate Africans as individuals into colonial society, however, was losing favor even with the missionaries by the 1880s, and the process of cooption favored by middle-class liberals in metropolitan Britain had been all but abandoned by middle-class liberals in the Cape by the end of the nineteenth century.

The sense of abandonment was particularly painful to the African Christian community. Jonas Ntsiko, a blind catechist from the Anglican station of St. John's at Umtata in the Transkei, expressed the sentiments of an alienated generation in a protest poem first published in *Isigidimi* in 1884:

> Some thoughts till now ne'er spoken
> Make shreds of my innermost being;
> And the cares and fortunes of my kin
> Still journey with me to the grave.
> I turn my back on the many shams
> That I see from day to day;
> It seems we march to our very grave
> Encircled by a smiling Gospel.
> And what is this Gospel?
> And what salvation?
> The shade of a fabulous Hill [i.e., spirit]
> That we try to embrace in vain.[2]

160

Two years earlier, Isaac Wauchope, writing under the pseudonym I. W. W. Citashe, was urging the readers of *Isigidimi* to use the skills they had acquired to fight for their rights:

> Your cattle are gone, my countrymen!
> Go rescue them! Go rescue them!
> Leave the breechloader alone
> And turn to the pen.
> Take paper and ink,
> For that is your shield.
> Your rights are going!
> So pick up your pen.
> Load it, load it with ink.
> Sit on a chair.
> Repair not to Hoho.
> But fire with your pen.[3]

Tiyo Soga exemplified the position of a generation that had rejected the breechloader and taken up the pen. Although he was not a political figure— Soga died in 1871—he was nevertheless far ahead of his time as the proto-type African nationalist of the colonial era. An ardent defender of the mission tradition, Soga also sought to uphold the cultural and territorial integrity of his people. Writing in the early 1860s, Soga was already urging his readers to preserve their heritage:

> Let us bring to life our ancestors. . . . Let us resurrect our ancestral fore-bears who bequeathed to us a rich heritage. All anecdotes connected with the life of the nation should be brought to this big corn-pit our national newspaper *Indaba* [The News].[4]

He admonished his white missionary colleagues to respect the position of the chiefs, and he appealed to *Indaba*'s Xhosa-speaking Christians not to set themselves apart from the non-Christian community. The chiefs received their authority from God, he said, and were entitled to the same respect as Cape officials. Soga also urged his people to differentiate between those whites who were deserving of respect and those who were not:

> Raise your hats to chiefs and respectable people. To White gentlemen bow your heads gently even though you do not utter a word. Do that to White people who deserve this. This is pleasing. But we do not advise this even to poor Whites of no repute who are no better than yourselves. This "Morning Sir" of the Xhosa people whenever they see a White face is very annoying.[5]

Soga was proud of his race. As his biographer and fellow missionary John Chalmers put it:

He would not bow down before any one, because of his own black face. . . . he was not disposed to demean himself, when treated slightingly or shabbily, by a fearful or slavish submission. He seemed at such times to grow taller before you, as if he would say "I am also a man! a gentleman! a Christian!" [6]

Soga kept a notebook entitled "The Inheritance of my Children" that he hoped would serve as a code of conduct. The first of 62 guidelines for his children read:

For your own sakes never appear ashamed that your father was a Kafir, and that you inherit some African blood. It is every whit as good and as pure as that which flows in the veins of my fairer brethren. . . . I want you, for your own future comfort, to be very careful on this point. You will ever cherish the memory of your mother as that of an upright, conscientious, thrifty, Christian Scotchwoman. You will ever be thankful for your connection by this tie to the white race. But if you wish to gain credit for yourselves—if you do not wish to feel the taunt of men, which you sometimes may be made to feel—*take your place* in the world as *coloured,* not as *white* men; as *Kafirs,* not as Englishmen.[7]

Soga had pride in his church, his race, and in the history and culture of his people, but he also articulated a kind of pan-Africanism that embraced all those who were of African origin. In May 1865 Soga wrote a rejoinder to an article written by his colleague Chalmers that first appeared in *Indaba* and was reprinted in the King William's Town *Gazette,* a settler newspaper. Chalmers had written that unless the Xhosa "rise in the scale of civilisation" they would face "extinction." Soga's response, according to Donovan Williams, is the first article on "African consciousness" published by an African in southern Africa:

Africa was of God given to the race of Ham. I find the Negro from the days of the old Assyrians downwards, keeping his "individuality" and "distinctiveness," amid the wreck of empires, and the revolution of ages. I find him keeping his place among the nations, and keeping his home and country. I find him opposed by nation after nation and driven from his home. I find him enslaved. . . . I find him exposed to all these disasters, and yet living—multiplying "and never extinct". . . . returning unmanacled to the land of his forefathers, taking back with him the civilization and the christianity of those nations. . . . Until the Negro is doomed against all history and experience—until his God-given inheritance of Africa be taken finally from him, I shall never believe in the total extinction of his brethren . . . of the land of Ham. . . . How does the extinction of the Kaffir race tally with the glowing prediction . . . "Ethiopia shall soon stretch her hands to God!" [8]

This chapter explores Soga's legacy as it was taken up by African nationalists in the Ciskei region between the 1880s and 1910.

Section 6.1 summarizes the main events in the campaign to unify Britain's

Figure 6.1. Tiyo Soga, a major ecclesiastical and literary figure of the new era.

four South African colonies following the South African War, when Africans, Coloureds, and Indians faced the prospect of being denied any share whatsoever in the negotiations.

Sections 6.2 and 6.3 explore two other issues that captivated African nationalists in the Ciskei and beyond during the later colonial period—the campaign for an African university in South Africa and the separatist church movement.

6.1. The Campaign for and against the Union of South Africa

British South Africa's political priorities were made clear soon after the signing of the Treaty of Vereeniging in May 1902. The authorities returned property to whites that had been seized during the war, compensated white war victims, and allowed Afrikaner republican elites to retain power in the new colonial governments being established north and south of the Vaal River. Money was poured into public works (notably railways), social services, and especially into white commercial agriculture (to expand production and lower food prices in the urban areas). Black war victims received little if any compensation, and those who had rendered support to the British during the conflict were not supported in the postwar dispensation.

African political and economic rights were to be sacrificed on the altar of a new and more powerful white supremacist state. Sir Alfred Milner, the British high commissioner for South Africa who was in charge of postwar reconstruction, essentially ignored the African population. When the Rand gold mines were recaptured, for example, wages remained below prewar levels. When Africans protested against the way they were being treated by trying to withhold their labor, British administrators temporarily solved the problem by importing more than sixty-three thousand Chinese workers on five-year contracts at low fixed wages. By the time most of the Chinese were repatriated in 1908, the Chamber of Mines (through its subsidiary, the Witwatersrand Native Labour Association) was able to satisfy most of its labor needs with African mine workers from Mozambique and British colonies in central Africa like Nyasaland (Malawi).

Britain granted responsible government to ex-republican Transvaal in 1906 and to the Orange River Colony in 1907. Thousands of Africans in Natal were killed or imprisoned in the so-called Bambatha rebellion of 1906, and the subsequent arrest, trial, and deportation of the Zulu king Dinuzulu on charges of treason signaled the end of armed resistance to colonial rule in South Africa.[9]

White Politics and the Pro-Union Campaign

The "closer union" campaign opened in March 1903 with an intercolonial conference to establish a South African customs union embracing Britain's four settler colonies—Cape, Natal, Transvaal, and Orange River (Orange Free State)—and three protectorates—Basutoland (Lesotho), Bechuanaland (Botswana), and Swaziland—in southern Africa.[10] Delegates also expressed concern over the shortage of labor and the need to address the "native question" in South Africa. Some months later, the South African Native Affairs Commission (SANAC) was created under the chairmanship of Sir Godfrey Lagden, a former native commissioner for colonial Basutoland. The SANAC spent sixteen months collecting information and interviewing a cross section of the South African population—African opinion representing both the non-Christian majority and the mission-educated elite.

John Cell points out that the SANAC never used the word "segregation" in its report, which was issued in April 1905, and apparently it did not appear in the volumes recording its proceedings. This commission, however, played a crucial role in crystallizing the ruling ideology of the looming segregationist state of South Africa:

> Products of a racist culture, the commissioners were racists themselves. But they were not fanatics. In an intelligent and even scientific manner they sought to gather information and to base their conclusions on it. Their interest was clear: a compromise that would enable the divided white community at the end of a long and bitter war to unify, modernize, and survive as a white man's country. The SANAC was the surprisingly well-informed base from which the evolution of South Africa's modern Native policy began.[11]

The commissioners anticipated the 1913 Land Act in favoring territorial segregation. They rejected a free market in land: Africans and Europeans should be allowed to buy property only in areas reserved for them. Existing areas set aside for Africans in regions like Natal, the eastern Cape, and Basutoland should be surveyed for individual tenure, while land occupied by Africans elsewhere in South Africa should be protected from white encroachment. White farmers, however, should be discouraged if not prevented from allowing African peasants to occupy their land as sharecroppers or renters rather than wage workers.

The commissioners anticipated segregationist legislation that would finally eliminate a free market in labor. They favored a policy that controlled and manipulated the movement of African workers to areas reserved for whites. Specific categories of African workers—namely, young able-bodied males without land—should be encouraged to migrate for limited periods of time to proclaimed white areas and live in segregated townships. They called for a labor force that was literate in English and had undergone some form of "industrial" training.

While the Transvaal Land Commission in 1903 had concluded that at least three hundred thousand workers were needed to meet the demands of the postwar economy, the commissioners realized that peasants who were self-sufficient on their reservations could not be induced to leave the land to work for whites. Nevertheless, they rejected coercive labor quotas as immoral and less direct measures like a labor tax (as in the 1894 Glen Grey Act) as ineffective. They also rejected arbitrary increases in wages: it would aggravate competition for labor among prospective white employers, and it would not alleviate the labor shortage. Africans would work in the white-controlled capitalist sector only until they had accumulated enough capital to reestablish themselves as peasant farmers. In the end, the majority report offered a contradictory analysis of the labor problem: Africans would remain voluntary participants in the economy, so wages should be allowed to seek their own levels in relation to the supply of labor.

The commissioners rejected any form of power sharing between Europeans and Africans. They favored separate voters' rolls with a fixed number of white legislators representing the interests of blacks in parliament. They also favored a more flexible approach to African authority at the local level. Although "tribalism" was in decay, where practical these institutions should be reestablished and Africans assisted in setting up and maintaining their own systems of local government. Councils with elected as well as appointed members like those created in Glen Grey and some districts in the Transkei could ultimately be made responsible for developing public works projects and maintaining such necessities as roads and schools in the segregated locations. The SANAC's prescription for a unified "native policy" provided a guideline for South African governments after 1910.

Meanwhile, Lord Selborne (William Waldegrave Palmer) had replaced Milner as high commissioner in 1905 and negotiated the granting of responsible government to the ex-Boer republics. He also issued the so-called Selborne Memorandum in January 1907 that for the first time officially proposed the union of South Africa's white settler colonies.

A national convention composed of thirty-three white delegates from Britain's four South African colonies and Rhodesia (they were given the right to speak but not to vote) assembled in Durban in October 1908. The delegations were made up of the four colonial prime ministers and the leading government and opposition members from each of the colonial parliaments. The Cape delegation included such "friends of the natives" as Sir Henry de Villiers, chairman of the legislative council and the colony's chief justice, John X. Merriman, and J. W. Sauer, the main supporters of Jabavu in the South African party. William Schreiner, regarded by European and African politicians alike as the most sympathetic white spokesman for African political and civil rights, had also been included in the delegation but was obliged to withdraw. He had agreed to defend the Zulu king, who was scheduled to go on trial at the same time the National Convention was meeting.

The imperial government played virtually no role in the deliberations of the National Convention, but its views were made known to the delegates through Lord Selborne. He had proposed that a limited franchise for blacks, based on a vague "test of civilisation," be made mandatory in all four colonies. If blacks in these colonies did not have at least some chance of gaining access to the franchise, Britain would be reluctant to turn over its protectorates in southern Africa to a future South African state. Although most delegates had hoped to gain control over the protectorates, they would not accept this condition.

The National Convention decided in the end to preserve the status quo on the franchise issue. Liberal members of the Cape delegation by and large supported their nonracial franchise during the debates, but even if Schreiner had been present it is unlikely they could have influenced the course of events. The existing nonracial franchise in the Cape and the color-bar franchises in the three northern colonies were upheld, but blacks in the Cape who qualified for the vote would not be allowed to sit in parliament. Four white senators in the proposed parliament would be appointed to represent the interests of disenfranchised blacks outside the Cape. Once unity was achieved and the four existing colonies became provinces of the Union of South Africa, black voters could be members of the Cape Provincial Council. The delegates also agreed that no person who was a registered voter at the time would be denied the franchise on the grounds of race or color (outside the Cape, two Africans had been placed on the voters' roll in Natal between 1865 and 1903). But the Cape franchise could be overturned on these grounds in future if two-thirds of the members of both houses of the union parliament sitting together voted to do so.[12]

Although the National Convention appended a twenty-five-point schedule to the proposed South African constitution detailing African rights in the protectorates if they were ceded, the imperial authorities eventually held back on final authorization. They had effectively abandoned the African population in South Africa, but they were under considerable public pressure to retain control over the African population in the protectorates for at least four or five years after union. This temporary reprieve turned out to be permanent. South Africa's repressive racial policies in the next generation rapidly diminished the possibility that Britain would relinquish the protectorates, although the South African government did not finally abandon its claim to these territories until the 1950s.[13]

Lord Selborne indicated that Britain would not oppose the decisions made by the National Convention, and the draft South Africa Act embodied in its report was released to the press in February 1909. The National Convention held its final meeting in Bloemfontein in May, and within a month all four colonial parliaments had approved the report with minor amendments. Only some Cape MPs—notably William Schreiner, who spoke out against the draft act on no less than sixty-four occasions during the course of the debate—tried to revise the legislation or otherwise urged the extension of the Cape franchise to the other colonies. The draft South Africa Act was then sent to the imperial government and after some debate in parliament it was approved. The Union of South Africa came into being on May 31, 1910.

The white parties that had dominated Cape colonial politics in the early 1900s also dominated national politics. The South African party won a majority of seats in the South African parliament in the 1910 elections, but ex-Boer War general Louis Botha (the party leader in the Transvaal) was chosen over Merriman (the party leader in the Cape) as South Africa's first prime minister.

Schreiner and Col. Walter Stanford, a liberal who had been Schreiner's replacement as a delegate to the National Convention and supported the Cape franchise, were two of the four white senators selected to represent black interests in South Africa. Schreiner had been endorsed by all African political factions, while Stanford had received a mixed review (he was nominated only by Jabavu and his group). The other two senators—J. C. Krogh, a Transvaal magistrate and native commissioner, and Frederick Moor, the last prime minister and minister of native affairs in Natal Colony—were not even moderately sympathetic to African interests.

Black Politics and the Anti-Union Campaign

African protest groups in the eastern Cape had been in contact with their counterparts outside the region since the 1880s, and within two decades a thin network of African political organizations and organs of opinion had spread all over British South Africa.[14] Xhosa speakers were among the first Africans to join the wage labor force in numbers, and they played a significant role in the development of a specifically African political culture. They were generally the best educated and obtained the better-paying, higher-status jobs. They had the social skills, and they had the most experience in organized politics.

The South African Native Congress (SANC) emerged from the South African War as the strongest regional political organization west and east of the Kei River. Communication with the colonial authorities was reopened within three months after hostilities ended in May 1902. The SANC held an executive committee meeting in June and sent a petition to the new governor, Sir Walter Heley-Hutchinson, in August. The first postwar conference was held at Lesseyton (the Methodist mission station near Queenstown) in September, and three months later the executive committee interviewed Sprigg, who was again prime minister, at the *Izwi* offices in King William's Town. In February 1903 an SANC delegation led by Thomas Mqanda, who was still president, met Joseph Chamberlain, secretary of state for the colonies, in Grahamstown. He was presented with a petition which, like the one sent to the governor, outlined African hopes for a new deal in the postwar reconstruction period.

The SANC continued to participate in white party politics, but by the early 1900s such participation was only one of many activities and apparently did not feature as a major issue at the yearly conferences. It was discussed mainly during election campaigns at the local iliso lomzi level. Prominent members of the SANC continued to support the Progressive party, but rank-and-file members often voted and sometimes worked for South African party candidates.

The number of branches increased from eighteen in 1902 to an estimated forty in 1908. There were now several branches in urban areas outside the eastern Cape (including Cape Town, Kimberley, and Johannesburg), although the main ones were still in the Ciskeian districts carved out of British Kaffraria and in Glen Grey, in towns like East London, King William's Town, and Queenstown and at mission stations like Lesseyton, Shiloh, and Peelton. New branches were formed after the war at Berlin and Tamara in the King William's Town District and at Wartburg in the Stutterheim District (Map 3). Other branches were located west of the Fish River in towns like Grahamstown, Port Elizabeth, Graaff-Reinet, and Colesberg, and east of the Kei River in rural areas like the Herschel District bordering colonial Basutoland and as far north as Kokstad in East Griqualand. About fifty (ranging up to ninety) delegates were present on average at the SANC's yearly conferences between 1902 and 1909. At least half the branches would be represented, and others would send messages of greetings and support. Attendance at the local iliso lomzi meetings was often greater than at the conferences, especially in the towns. Audiences of eighty to a hundred were not unusual, and four hundred attended a meeting of the East London iliso lomzi in 1906. Odendaal estimates the SANC had at least a thousand members by 1908 with hundreds of others linked informally to the organization.

Local iliso lomzi affiliates to the 1898 Imbumba or to the SANC were now the grassroots African political organizations in the eastern Cape. These viligance associations represented a cross section of supporters from the villages and mission stations in the rural areas, and they were concerned primarily with local issues. Land disputes occupied a more or less permanent position on the agenda, but the new local government bodies created by the 1894 Glen Grey Act, the financial plight of unaided schools, problems with mission education, the activities of separatist churches, and agricultural matters like stock diseases and seed subsidies were also topics for discussion.

Although the SANC was now the most influential African political body in the eastern Cape, it was still weak when compared with white organizations like the Afrikaner Bond. The SANC, like the various Imbumba, was not big or rich enough to support permanent offices or paid, full-time staff. Appeals for funds to send protest delegations to Cape Town, for example, inevitably failed, one in 1908 managing to raise less than four pounds. Fundraising at the grassroots level was generally in the form of tea parties, concerts, and subscriptions, but these efforts were not always enough even to maintain local branches or to send delegates to the regional conferences.

The SANC was controlled by a small group of men who remained in office for long periods of time. Seven of the original thirteen members of the executive committee elected in 1891, for example, were still serving in 1903. Thomas Mqanda, the farmer and headman from Peddie, remained president for more than twenty years, but Walter Rubusana (elected to the executive committee in 1903) emerged as the SANC's key spokesman. Nathaniel Umhalla and James and Meshach Pelem were all vice presidents in the early 1900s. Charles Madosi, a farmer from Berlin (near King William's Town), replaced business entrepreneur Paul Xiniwe (he died in 1902) as chairman of the company that published *Izwi*. Other executive committee members during these years included *Izwi* editor Alan Soga, poet S. E. Krune Mqhayi, Peelton teacher Attwell Maci, who was a major player in the SANC's African university scheme, and F. Jonas, a printer by trade.

Ministers and teachers continued to dominate the organization: at least twenty-five clergymen, many representing separatist churches, attended the yearly conferences during these years. Of the thirty known members of the SANC's executive committee between 1891 and 1913, virtually all were Xhosa (the exceptions being the president Thomas Mqanda, and possibly one or two others) from what was once British Kaffraria in the Ciskei and Gcalekaland in the southern Transkei. Seven of the twelve known regional conferences held between 1891 and 1909, however, were in the Thembu-dominated districts of Queenstown and Glen Grey, where a number of progressive farmers lived. Three conferences were held at the mission stations of Wartburg and Mgwali, which catered largely to the Ngqika Xhosa in the King William's Town District. The executive committee met in King William's Town because most members lived in the district.

The SANC played an important role in coordinating African political groups outside the eastern Cape immediately after the South African War. Xhosa migrants in Cape Town, for example, had formed the Cape Peninsula Native Association, which had links with the SANC. Its president, Thomas Zini, was from Queenstown in the Ciskei. Another leader of Cape Town's African community associated with the SANC was Alfred Mangena, a Zulu who had arrived in the city about 1900 to further his education and became an activist in several court cases protesting discriminatory acts against Africans. Mangena would eventually pursue his legal studies in London and become the first African from South Africa to qualify as a lawyer. Yet another Cape Town–based ally was F. Z. S. Peregrino, a West African–born journalist who was editor of the weekly *South African Spectator* and a major political figure in the western Cape Coloured community. Influential supporters in the northern Cape included Silas Molema, a younger brother of Montshiwa, chief of the Tshidi Barolong, the most powerful Tswana-speaking chiefdom in the region.

Members of the SANC in the Transvaal helped organize the Transvaal Native Congress in 1903, and the Native Press Association was formed in King William's Town in 1904 in a bid to provide a news agency for the fledgling black press. It was enthusiastically endorsed by *Izwi*'s Alan Soga and other leaders of the SANC. Editors from as many as twelve black publications expressed interest in joining the organization, but it collapsed in less than two years in part because Jabavu refused to cooperate.[15]

African political activists did not participate in the campaign to unify Britain's South African colonies, but they were reluctant initially to challenge the colonial authorities on this issue. They had criticized the report of the South African Native Affairs Commission and condemned the granting of responsible government to the Transvaal and the Orange River Colony because both had color-bar constitutions that denied blacks basic political and civil rights. The SANC and the 1898 Imbumba joined their counterparts in the northern colonies, petitioning the British government and the House of Commons and making representations to British authorities in South Africa, in a futile bid to block this decision. A public response to the closer-union movement, however, was not made until after the Selborne Memorandum was published in 1907.

Efforts to coordinate African protest groups in the Cape were formalized initially in November 1907, when more than eighty delegates from twenty-nine centers throughout the colony met at Queenstown. Jabavu and his supporters refused to attend, but for the first time Africans and Coloureds joined forces in protesting the proposed union. The second-largest contingent at this conference after the SANC was the African Political (later People's) Organisation (APO). The APO was by far the most important Coloured political force in South Africa at this time. Within eight years after its birth in Cape Town in 1902, the APO had 111 branches in the four South African colonies as well as Rhodesia (Zimbabwe). It had led the fight for Coloured political rights in the Orange River Colony and the Transvaal, and in 1906 a delegation was sent to London protesting the granting of responsible government to the two ex-republics. The leader of APO after 1905 was Dr. Abdullah Abdurahman, the first black medical doctor in South Africa. A year earlier, he had become the first person of color elected to the Cape Town City Council.

The Queenstown delegates issued a five-point manifesto that envisaged a federal system of government for a future South Africa, the retention of imperial control over the protectorates, and the extension of the Cape franchise to the other settler colonies. The Queenstown resolutions were duly sent to the authorities in Cape Town and London, and to various Cape missionary societies. Nevertheless, African politicians in the Cape, as Odendaal put it, "generally evinced a measure of complacency about their political future." [16] Both white political parties in the colony—the South African party and the Unionists—had pledged publicly to maintain the Cape franchise in any future South African state, and Cape Africans relied on the Cape delegation at the National Convention to uphold these rights.

The anti-union protest movement was organized mainly by African and Coloured groups outside the eastern Cape. When the National Convention finally released its draft version of the South Africa Act in February 1909, the Orange River Colony Native Congress called for an African national convention to meet in Bloemfontein. Regional caucuses were quickly convened throughout South Africa to select delegates, and vocal opposition to the draft act was even expressed by some whites, including J. H. Hofmeyr and the Cape Town branch of the Afrikaner Bond.

Six weeks after the draft act was published, thirty-eight delegates from the four South African colonies—including Rubusana and Alan Soga from the SANC—met in a schoolhouse in Bloemfontein's African location. For the first time in colonial history, the Africans of South Africa were gathering together in a national conference to discuss their mutual grievances and aspirations. The South African Native Convention, as it was called, proposed amendments to the racial provisions of the draft South Africa Act and elected a permanent executive committee. The historic role played by the SANC during this formative period in African national politics was recognized when Rubusana was chosen president and Soga general secretary of the new organization. John L. Dube, the leading African politician in Natal Colony, was elected vice president.

Divisions between African political groups in the Ciskei and elsewhere, however, continued. Jabavu and several key aides had resuscitated *Imvo* (in October 1902) and the 1898 Imbumba in opposition to *Izwi* and the SANC. The Imbumba again canvassed the African vote for the South African party, issued petitions to colonial authorities alongside those of the SANC, and held conferences in 1908 and 1909 in response to those organized by its rival against the looming South Africa Act. More than fifty delegates and three hundred observers attended the first one, a testimony to Jabavu's continued charisma as an opinion leader.

The SANC and the Imbumba would remain apart, even though individuals often changed sides and the two groups made at least five attempts between 1905 and 1911 to reconcile personal and political differences. Jabavu and the Imbumba had refused to attend the South African Native Convention meeting in Bloemfontein, and they held their own Cape Native Convention in King William's Town in April 1909. The meeting was attended by forty-one delegates representing seventeen constituencies, most of them in the Ciskei. Jabavu was elected president of a permanent executive committee, and protest petitions were sent to parliament, which was meeting in Cape Town to debate the draft act, and to the South African National Convention, which was about to reconvene in Bloemfontein. A native rights protection fund was created, and the resolutions passed at this meeting were sent to other African and Coloured protest groups.

An outpouring of petitions protesting the draft act were now being sent to the governing authorities in South Africa and Britain, and Jabavu clearly hoped that his Cape Native Convention might join the APO and the South African Native Convention at Bloemfontein in providing the organizational base for coordinating the anti-union movement. Indeed, the APO appealed to both conventions to form a united front at its own national conference held in Cape Town in April 1909.

The Protest Delegation to London. Meanwhile, the focus of the anti-union movement had begun to shift from South Africa to Britain. Merriman had already undermined white opposition forces in the Cape by persuading Hof-meyr of the Afrikaner Bond to join the official colonial delegation proceeding to London and help pilot the draft legislation through the imperial parliament. Abdurahman and the APO together with members of the Schreiner family and other white sympathizers met in Cape Town to organize their own over-seas protest delegation. William Schreiner agreed to lead this group, whose members were to be selected by the major African and Coloured political organizations in the four South African colonies and the protectorates.

The anti-union delegation, which was ready to proceed by June 1909, consisted of Schreiner, Jabavu (Cape Native Convention), Rubusana, Daniel Dwanya and Thomas M. Mapikela (the SANC),[17] Abdurahman, D. J. Lenders and Matt J. Fredericks (APO),[18] and J. Gerrans (a Mafeking trader who repre-sented the Bechuanaland Protectorate chiefs). The Schreiner group received support from a number of other opinion leaders who were in Britain at this time. Indian organizations in Natal and the Transvaal had sent deputations to London to press for a resolution of various Indian grievances, and Mohandas Gandhi was among these delegates. John Dube was in London ostensibly to raise funds for Ohlange Institute, the secondary school he had founded near Durban. Protest delegates also conferred with three aspirant lawyers who would later play key roles in African nationalist politics—Alfred Mangena, Richard Msimang and Pixley Seme—and with other students in London, including Jabavu's eldest son, D. D. T. Jabavu.

Black political activists achieved a hitherto unprecedented degree of solidarity during the anti-union campaign, and black civil rights became the key issue when the South Africa Act was debated in the British parliament. The protest delegation failed to halt passage of the act, but its members were brimming with optimism when they returned to South Africa: the imperial authorities had been obliged to state publicly that they were not in favor of the color-bar clauses, and the official South African delegation had been obliged to deny publicly that black political and civil rights would be restricted after union.

The South African Native Convention, which had gained considerable credibility during the anti-union campaign, held its second conference in Bloemfontein in March 1910. Rubusana and Dube were again elected president and vice president, respectively, of the five-man executive committee. Strenuous efforts were made to unite the various African political organizations in South Africa behind the banner of the Convention and to establish permanent links with the Coloureds in Abdurahman's APO.

Rubusana's political base in the eastern Cape, however, was rapidly unraveling. The biggest blow to the SANC was the loss of its mouthpiece, *Izwi Labantu,* in April 1909. As with all black protest journals, the newspaper had always struggled financially. It was supported initially by Rhodes, and for at least sixteen months his deputy, C. P. Crewe, a member of the Cape Legislative Assembly, was in charge of *Izwi*'s financial affairs. But when Rhodes died in 1902, the leaders of his party (the Unionists) apparently stopped subsidizing the newspaper. Soga's increasingly anticapitalist editorial line may well have contributed to this decision.[19]

Izwi had rivaled and then supplanted *Imvo* as the most militant African protest journal in the eastern Cape. For more than eleven years it had concretized the ideas and attitudes of its readers and translated them into viable political action programs for the SANC. Rubusana and other members of the executive committee would continue to play an important role as individuals in national politics,[20] but the SANC itself apparently ceased functioning as a political pressure group sometime before or during World War I.

Meanwhile, the South African Native Convention held its third conference in Johannesburg in May 1911 amid a spate of segregationist bills being considered by parliament, including legislation that would make breaches of labor contracts by Africans a criminal offense (Native Labour Regulation Bill, which was based on the Cape's Masters and Servants Acts), reserve certain skilled jobs in mining and engineering for whites (Mines and Works Bill), and discriminate against all Africans but wage laborers on white farms and bar African syndicates from buying land (Native Settlement and Squatters Registration Bill). A permanent white citizen and defense force was also being created for South Africa (Defence Act); more and more African interpreters were being replaced by whites in the courts; and jobs held by Africans on the railways were being given to whites. Afrikaner republican sentiments, more-over, would soon reemerge with the establishment of the National party in January 1914 under the leadership of ex-Boer War general Barry Hertzog.

Very little is known about the South African Native Convention's 1911 conference, but it seems clear that in the years immediately preceding union the center of African political activity in South Africa shifted decisively from the eastern Cape and southern Natal to the southern Transvaal. The executive committee, for example, now included Pixley Seme, who had completed his studies in London and was setting up a law practice in Johannesburg. Alfred Mangena had also returned to South Africa along with Richard Msimang, and both were prominent in the Transvaal Native Congress. The pioneer political bodies in the Ciskei region were in various stages of decay. Rubusana and Soga were prominent members of the Convention, but they no longer commanded an organized following. Jabavu and his Imbumba remained aloof—as always—from any group they could not dominate. Nevertheless, the leadership in the Transvaal discussed the topic of unity at length following the 1911 confer-ence, and Seme circulated a proposal that called for a new African national organization to replace the "Bloemfontein Convention."

The South African Native National Congress. The South African Native National Congress (SANNC) was formed in January 1912 as a permanent national organization to represent African political interests in the new Union of South Africa and in the adjacent British protectorates. About 60 dele-gates participated in the four-day conference held in Bloemfontein's African township: the Transvaal had the largest delegation (25), but there were few representatives from Natal (2) or the Cape (6). Rubusana was the only person in attendance from the eastern Cape. For the first time a number of chiefs and their deputies were present, the biggest contingent being from colonial Basuto-land. John Dube of Natal was elected president in absentia, Solomon Plaatje, a pioneer investigative journalist, literary figure, and political leader from the northern Cape, was elected general secretary, and Rubusana was made an honorary vice president along with twenty-two chiefs. The real powerbrokers in the founding of sub-Saharan Africa's oldest African nationalist organization were Seme, who was elected treasurer, and his colleagues from the Transvaal.

The goals of the SANNC were defined in the draft constitution. Emphasis was placed on African unity, on the political, economic, and cultural advance-ment of the African people, and on the protection of their interests "by seeking and obtaining redress for any of their just grievances." The SANNC would also provide "a central channel between the Government and the aboriginal races in South Africa" and promote "mutual understanding between the Native chiefs and the encouragement in them and their people of a spirit of loyalty to the British crown and all lawfully constituted authorities." [21]

The SANNC was to be organized in two tiers in an obvious attempt to cement a political alliance between the old guard ruling elites and the petty bourgeoisie. The chiefs would have some power in the new national organization: they would comprise an "Upper House" of "nobles" who would counsel the elected committee of twelve "Executive Commoners." The executive committee would administer the organization, and it was made up of the president, seven vice presidents representing various regional groups then affiliated to the SANNC (Transvaal, Orange Free State, Natal, Basutoland, Cape peninsula, northern Cape/Bechuanaland), a general secretary and his assistant, and a treasurer and his assistant. There was considerable dissent, however, over the question of finances and in particular the size of contributions from local branches. A committee headed by Richard Msimang did not produce a draft of the constitution that was approved for official use until September 1919. Women had virtually no representation in the new organization, and the alliance with the chiefs would not be severed until the 1940s.

The SANNC passed several resolutions relating to African grievances and sent a deputation to the minister of native affairs (the Cape liberal J. W. Sauer) to protest the Squatters Registration Bill. A new multilingual weekly newspaper entitled *Abantu-Batho* (The People) was launched to publicize the aims and activities of the Congress, and links were established with the APO. The two organizations agreed to work together on matters of mutual concern and to hold joint meetings at least once a year.

The SANNC's influence remained weakest in the eastern Cape, where the African petty bourgeoisie jealously guarded its franchise rights. Neither the SANC nor the 1898 Imbumba had been represented at the inaugural meeting in 1912, and Jabavu was already well advanced on a new scheme to establish his own national organization. While in London, he and a thousand other delegates from more than fifty countries had attended the inaugural meeting of the United Races Congress, a benevolent association designed to promote international goodwill between peoples of different races and nationalities. Jabavu decided to start a South African branch, and at a conference in King William's Town in May 1911 the 1898 Imbumba was reorganized with a new constitution for this purpose. It was renamed the Imbumba Yezizwe Zomzantsi Afrika or the South African Races Congress in March 1912.

Within the ranks of the 1912 Imbumba were many who had been involved in the earlier Imbumba initiated in Port Elizabeth in 1882 and in King William's Town in 1887 and 1898. Jabavu himself was at pains to stress the continuity of the Imbumba tradition. The new organization was to be open to all races in keeping with its aim of promoting a nonracial South Africa. Those who supported the 1912 Imbumba believed that separate, segregated bodies would isolate and alienate Africans from settler society and thereby further weaken their position in a settler-dominated South African state. Try as they might, however, Jabavu and his lieutenants could not expand the Imbumba's ethnic and geographical support base. It remained essentially an Mfengu organization confined to the Ciskei and southern Transkei. The 1912 Imbumba, like the SANC, apparently collapsed sometime just before or during World War I.

6.2. Launching an African University in South Africa

The bonding of politics, education, and religion was as obvious to modernizers in the eastern Cape as it was to modernizers in other African mission-based communities in southern Africa.[22] There were particularly strong links between the educational and political organizations formed between 1880 and 1910. SANC leaders Rubusana and Tunyiswa were president and vice president, respectively, of the Native Educational Association, for example, in the watershed election year of 1898. Tunyiswa was president in 1902, and the NEA during this period was closely identified with the SANC.

The mission-educated community wanted higher educational standards for African pupils than was acceptable to the settlers or available in the mission schools. Lovedale had only started its first matriculation course in 1882. Almost all the early students in the programs were white males, moreover, and it was apparently not until 1892 that an African actually matriculated from Lovedale.[23] Less than a dozen Africans in the Cape Colony as a whole obtained matriculation certificates between 1887 and 1899. Pass rates for the few mission schools with prematriculation classes were also extraordinarily low. Only 50 of 233 students taking the postprimary examinations at Lovedale, for example, actually passed between 1892 and 1908. The door was finally closed on multiracial education in the Cape's government-aided schools with the passing of the Cape School Board Act in 1905, although in the case of Lovedale Seminary and perhaps a few other mission institutions it was not enforced until some years after 1910.

Lack of access to postprimary schools, the low pass rate, and the increasing impoverishment of poorly paid teachers angered and frustrated the mission-educated elite. Local teachers' organizations together with regional bodies like the NEA in the Ciskei and the Transkei Teachers' Association (comprising mainly teachers from districts in the southern Transkei) continued to seek alternatives to the status quo in African education. Mission-trained Africans were leaving the Cape to improve their educational qualifications, for example, by the late 1890s. Some went to Britain, but a majority of this diaspora preferred the United States, where they attended black colleges—notably Lincoln University (Pennsylvania), Wilberforce University (Ohio), Hampton Institute (Virginia), and Tuskegee Institute (Alabama)—and were often sponsored by independent African and African-American churches. At least a hundred Africans from the Cape Colony alone left to study overseas between

178

1898 and 1908.[24] Consequently, demands for "higher" education were being taken seriously by some missionaries and school officials, who feared their control over African education would be weakened if a college or university for Africans was not established on Cape soil.

H. Isaiah Bud-Mbelle (ca. 1870–1947), a leader of Kimberley's Mfengu community and a member of the SANC, initially proposed a fund-raising campaign to establish a university for Africans in 1901. The SANC took up this proposal during its annual conference at Lesseyton, near Queenstown, in September 1902. The Queen Victoria Memorial, as it was called, became a major project of the SANC in the early 1900s. It was hoped that at least enough money would be forthcoming to offer scholarships for advanced study, but the ultimate goal was a university for Africans located in the eastern Cape.

Even though the project was named in honor of the late Queen Victoria, it was to be completely independent of white control. Bud-Mbelle later felt that Rubusana and the SANC had turned his plan into "an anti-white campaign" that was symptomatic of separatist tendencies emerging in other areas like the "Ethiopian" churches.[25] Rubusana, who stumped the colony in search of African support for the project, confirmed in part this separatist impression at a meeting in East London in 1906:

> I am not an Ethiopian, but I could just as well be one because the Ethiopian says our nation must help itself since no white man will lift up the black nation. . . . every nation is uplifted by its educated members. Africa will also be helped by educated Africans who will work hard and give themselves, with their little education to the nation.[26]

The memorial committee set a target of ten thousand pounds and tried unsuccessfully to interest the governing authorities in their venture.

Meanwhile, the South African Native Affairs Commission had recommended that an African college be established in the South African colonies,

---

Figure 6.2. African members of the Inter-State Native College Executive Committee. Standing *left to right,* Enoch Mamba, Scanlen Lehana, Simon P. Gasa, Isaiah Bud-Mbelle, John Tengo Jabavu, John Knox Bokwe, Isaac Wauchope, and Thomas Mtobi Mapikela. Mamba was a headman from Idutywa in the Transkei and a leader in dissident African politics. Lehana was a chief from Mount Fletcher in the Transkei who helped lead a popular revolt against the Glen Grey council system imposed after 1895. Gasa was one of two Africans (the other being Tengo Jabavu) appointed to the Inter-State Native College Board, which was created in 1907 to negotiate with various South African colonial officials on behalf of the proposed college. Bud-Mbelle, a prominent political figure from Kimberley in the northern Cape, initially proposed a university for Africans in 1901. Jabavu was the major fundraiser and publicist for the proposed college, while his political associates Bokwe and Wauchope were probably the best known advocates of the mission-sponsored scheme in the Ciskei region after Jabavu. Mapikela represented the Orange River Colony Native Congress in the anti-Union protest delegation that was sent to England in 1909.

and missionaries from Lovedale with support from various Cape officials launched the Inter-State Native College fund-raising campaign in April 1905 a few months after the commission's report was published. Jabavu recognized that the Inter-State Native College scheme offered an opportunity to regain some of the prestige he had lost during the South African War, and he helped sponsor a "Native convention" at Lovedale in December 1905 to consider the project. More than 150 delegates from the eastern Cape, Transvaal, and Basutoland attended the conference. South Africa's colonial governments were urged to accept the recommendations of the South African Native Affairs Commission concerning the proposed college, and a committee was organized to supervise the campaign. James Weir, the King William's Town merchant-trader who had helped subsidize the launching of *Imvo* in 1884, was elected chairman. SANC leaders Nathaniel Umhalla and Jonathan Tunyiswa, who had switched sides and thrown their support behind the Inter-State scheme, were also involved along with Jabavu, the separatist church leader James Dwane, and veteran Imbumba supporters like Isaac Wauchope, John Knox Bokwe, and Simon Sihlali.

The SANC was urged to amalgamate their Queen Victoria Memorial scheme with the new Inter-State scheme, but SANC members rejected this option at a conference in Queenstown in April 1906. They refused to abandon the vision of an African university that was free of white control. Although the Queen Victoria Memorial never really got off the ground, the African university issue became another battleground between those who sought an integrated society, albeit on colonial terms, and those who preferred to go it alone on African terms.

Outside the anti-union campaign, no activity undertaken by the petty bourgeoisie in the eastern Cape during this period equaled the effort that was made to mobilize African opinion in support of the Inter-State Native College scheme. No other issue except the closer-union movement received so much coverage in *Imvo* during these years. Jabavu was appointed a paid traveling secretary, and he campaigned strenuously throughout the colonies in an effort to raise funds. An executive committee dominated by the missionaries and their settler allies—Jabavu and Simon P. Gasa were the only Africans on the ten-member board—was formed in 1907 to negotiate on behalf of the proposed college with government officials in the various South African colonies. By 1907–8, Africans had pledged about £18,000 (of which the Transkeian Territories General Council had promised £10,000 and a similar body in Basutoland £6,000) and Europeans (mainly missionary) about £22,000.[27]

A second Inter-State Native College convention was held at Lovedale in July 1908, by which time there were committees in forty-seven magisterial districts representing virtually the entire eastern Cape. More pledges of support were made by African organizations elsewhere in the northern and western Cape and in other British colonies—Natal, Orange River, and the

Transvaal as well as Basutoland, Bechuanaland, and Rhodesia. The college was to be located near Lovedale on ground donated by the parent body of the Presbyterian mission, the United Free Church of Scotland.

Jabavu became so closely identified with the Inter-State Native College that in African eyes it was his college. The credibility of the SANC was severely strained because it refused to drop its Queen Victoria Memorial in favor of the mission-sponsored plan. The debate provoked a schism within the SANC leadership and undoubtedly contributed to its decline as a regional political organization. The Inter-State Native College was temporarily shelved during the debate over union, but after 1910 the educationists at Lovedale reopened negotiations with various colonial and missionary bodies, while African supporters discussed the proposal at South African Native National Congress meetings held in Bloemfontein in 1912 and 1913.

The South African government eventually approved the scheme, and in February 1916 the South African Native College at Fort Hare was officially opened by the prime minister, Louis Botha. It was a far cry from what even the missionaries had envisaged. The new college occupied a few dilapidated buildings on a slender grant of £1,100 a year from the central government and the United Free Church of Scotland. None of the first class of twenty students (eighteen of whom were men, including two whites) had matriculation certificates. It would be eight more years before the Native College was actually graduating students as an African university in South Africa.[28]

6.3. Clergy and Church in Schism and Separation

Before the 1880s the church had been virtually the only institution in Cape colonial society where the African Christian community had experience in governing its own affairs.[29] Religious organizations had proliferated with the expansion of the church, and there was a parallel growth in religious functionaries at every level—catechists and readers, deacons and elders; Sunday school teachers and administrators; officers of children's clubs, temperance societies, and dozens of other church-centered men's and women's associations. Preachers and evangelists who were paid and formally employed in the mission's "native agency" programs, moreover, were reinforced by literally thousands of unpaid volunteers operating in the Ciskei–southern Transkei and beyond. It is not surprising that the ordained clergy, leaders of the church, had a large and relatively sophisticated support group within the Christian community.

The importance of the church in the political life of the Christian community during this period cannot be overestimated. It was probably inevitable that African nationalism would be revealed most militantly in the one institution where Europeans were most vulnerable and Africans had the most opportunity to express themselves relatively free of mission-colonial control.

Three separatist churches had a major impact on the Christian community in the Ciskei region before 1910,[30] and each one is a case study in the strategies that were employed in seeking independence outside the framework of Cape colonial society. The expression of African militancy by the independent church movement in the Ciskei, and elsewhere, also had implications for the non-Christian community.

The Thembu Church

Nehemiah Tile was a highly regarded Wesleyan Methodist evangelist who had served for many years in Thembuland (Transkei) and was a graduate of the mission's theological training school at Healdtown. Four years after returning to Thembuland as a probationer minister in 1879, Tile left the mission following a dispute over his involvement in Thembu politics. Tile had become a confidant of Ngangelizwe, the Thembu paramount, and in 1884 he founded what was apparently the first permanent African independent church in southern Africa.

The Thembu church sought initially to reunify the Thembu people, using as role models the British monarchy and the Church of England. Ngangelizwe, head of state, would also function as head of church. As an adviser to both Ngangelizwe and Dalindyebo, his successor, Tile sought to avoid a colonial takeover of Thembuland. He wanted to retain imperial control because he thought this would allow for greater autonomy, but in 1885 Thembuland was annexed by the Cape Colony.

Under colonial pressure, Dalindyebo withdrew his support of the Thembu church, but in 1890 Tile was apparently restored to favor. He died a year later, shortly after obtaining land to build a church near the paramount chief's main residence. Jonas Goduka, an ordained Wesleyan Methodist minister who had left the mission in 1892, succeeded Tile. The influence of the Thembu church within the chiefdom declined thereafter, but Goduka, an Ngqika Xhosa, expanded its ethnic base. Church membership increased, and new congregations were established in other parts of the Transkei and in the Ciskei. The Thembu church was cited in parliament (by, among others, Cape liberal James Rose-Innes) and in the settler press as a seditious movement.

Dalindyebo withdrew his support from the Thembu church again in 1895 and returned to the mission. Goduka left Thembuland with some members of the Thembu church about 1898 and moved to the Herschel District, where he changed the name of the church to the African Native Mission church and rewrote its constitution. Those who had followed Goduka into the new church named him leader for life about 1904, but more splinter groups broke away after his death in 1919, and membership apparently declined in subsequent years.

The Ethiopian Church

Another Methodist minister, opposed to the mission's segregationist policies and the inferior position accorded to African clergy, launched the most important African separatist church in an urban setting during this period. Mangena

Maake (Moses) Mokone (1851–ca. 1936), an ordained pastor from Natal, founded the Ethiopian church in Pretoria in 1892.

Ethiopia was a symbol of independent Africa and a historic center of African Christianity with roots in the biblical period. One of the proof texts was Psalm 68:31 ("Ethiopia shall soon stretch out her hands unto God"), which Tiyo Soga had cited, it will be remembered, in a letter published in 1865. In the ethnic melting pots of Pretoria and especially in the mining towns centering on Johannesburg, Mokone and his colleagues sought to build an African church under African leaders to evangelize Africa.

Among those in contact with Mokone were Goduka[31] and James Mata Dwane (1848–1916), yet another ordained minister of the Wesleyan Methodist mission. Dwane, a Xhosa from Middledrift in the Ciskei, qualified as a teacher at Healdtown and later studied for the ministry at Healdtown's theological training school. One of his fellow students was Nehemiah Tile. Ordained in 1881, Dwane like Tile became a much-respected leader of the mission church. He was sent to England in 1894–95 to raise money for the church but quarreled with the mission over the disposal of these funds. Dwane's request to use the donations to build a higher educational facility for Africans was denied, and he left the mission in 1895. He established an independent congregation and for several months worked as a journalist on *Imvo Zabantsundu*. He also made contact with Mokone in Pretoria, and in March 1896 he and his followers joined the multi-ethnic separatist church.

The Ethiopian church decided to seek affiliation with the African Methodist Episcopal church (AME church), an independent African-American church that was seeking to gain a missionary foothold in southern Africa. The Ethiopian separatists hoped that among other things the AME church would bring them official recognition from the governing authorities in the Cape and Transvaal. Leaders of the Ethiopian church corresponded with AME church leaders, read their newspaper *Voice of Missions,* and became well acquainted with their activities. Dwane was sent to the United States in 1896 to negotiate a union on equal terms with the AME church. But instead of union, the Ethiopian church was made a district of the AME church with Dwane as presiding superintendent.

The Ethiopian church underwent a dramatic expansion in the next two years. Between 1896 and 1898, when AME church leader H. M. Turner visited his African congregations in South Africa, the Ethiopian church grew from about 70 ministers and 2,800 members to about 140 ministers and 10,800 members. There were now seventy-three congregations affiliated to the AME church in all four settler colonies. Turner impressed President Paul Kruger of the South African Republic (Kruger reputedly told Turner he was the first black person he had ever shaken hands with), and he endorsed the activities of the AME church. Kruger hoped these church separatists would conteract the activities of the British missionaries, who were deemed a potential threat to the republic. Turner appointed Dwane an assistant bishop and bought land in Queenstown—now the regional headquarters along with Pretoria of the AME church in South Africa—to build a university for Africans.

Dwane traveled again to the United States in 1899. AME church leaders had apparently assured him that the money (two thousand pounds) promised by Turner to build the university would be forthcoming, but he returned to the Cape Colony empty-handed. Membership in the Ethiopian church had increased to 12,500 by March 1899—there were also sixteen African students studying at Wilberforce University in Ohio, the AME church's principal training college, and one studying medicine in Tennessee—but Dwane himself had become disillusioned with the African-American church and accused its leaders of being discriminatory to darker-skinned African ministers. He was now convinced the AME church would never support his dream of a higher educational institution for Africans in South Africa.

Dwane was also convinced the AME church would never gain recognition from the Cape government. Colonial officials, alarmed at the spread of the Ethiopian church, had refused to sanction either the church or Dwane as an ordained minister. In what appeared to be an extraordinary volte-face, Dwane concluded that the authority of the AME church was really derived from the Anglican church. Thus he decided to seek a new home for the Ethiopian church with the Church of the Province of South Africa—the white Anglicans—at a special conference held in Queenstown in October 1899. Dwane managed to persuade thirty-five of the thirty-nine church officers present to join him in forming a new, autonomous body—the Order of Ethiopia—under the wing of the Anglicans. Mokone initially voted to secede as well, but he later backed down (the South African War apparently prevented leaders of the church in the Transvaal from attending the Queenstown meeting) and joined those who had decided to remain with the AME church.

The Order of Ethiopia retained its separate identity when it was formally accepted into the Anglican church in August 1900, and Dwane was ordained as a deacon four months later. But relations began to deteriorate soon thereafter over Anglican attempts to control the activities of the separatist church. The Anglicans refused to allow the Order of Ethiopia to remain an autonomous body, and Dwane's quest to become a bishop of the church was denied. A training college was set up in Queenstown's African location under a white priest in May 1901 to prepare the new adherents for confirmation in the Anglican church. Perhaps seven hundred lay members and twelve catechists of the Order of Ethiopia had been accepted by February 1902. Anglican attempts to monitor the activities of the Order received a temporary setback four years later when Dwane and some of his followers began holding separate services, but the schism was resolved with a new constitution in April 1907 giving his church virtual autonomy. Dwane himself was ordained a priest and appointed provincial of the Order of Ethiopia.

The breach between Dwane and the Anglicans had apparently been healed, but membership in the Order of Ethiopia continued to decline. The Order claimed 1,389 adult members in 1903, an insignificant figure when compared with the membership of the Ethiopian church four years earlier. There were only 786 communicants in 1907, following the schism, and 940 in 1908 (although 3,410 adherents were claimed by the Order). About 75 percent of the members were Xhosa living in the Anglican Diocese of Grahamstown, which included most of the Ciskei region. The others were also mainly Xhosa living in the Transkei and in Pretoria. More than one-half of the sixty-three congregations in the Grahamstown diocese in 1907 had been established before the Order of Ethiopia was created in 1900, and there were only 3,230 members, including adherents, by 1914.[32] The Anglicans continued to balk at appointing Dwane a bishop and would not allow the Order to send representatives to the yearly provincial synod. As late as 1915, they believed "the time was not yet ripe for a native episcopate." [33] When Dwane died in February 1916, there was some doubt in missionary circles that the Order of Ethiopia would survive.

The Presbyterian Church of Africa

The Presbyterians were the focal point of the most significant secession from a mission church in the Ciskei during this period. Pambini Mzimba, probably the most able of its African ministers and the first to be ordained in South Africa, left the mission after more than thirty-five years of service to launch the independent Presbyterian Church of Africa in 1898.

Mzimba had links with other separatist leaders prior to breaking away from the mission. He knew Dwane, and he probably also knew Tile since he spent some time in mission work in the Transkei during the 1880s.[34] He was certainly active in advocating churches in the urban areas and helped organize a congregation in Johannesburg in 1891. On Mzimba's advice, the mission placed Edward Tsewu (1856–1930s?), another ordained pastor, in charge of the mission church.[35] When Tsewu and some members of his congregation got involved in the Ethiopian movement in 1896, Mzimba was sent to Johannesburg to investigate, and he undoubtedly made contact with leaders of the Ethiopian church at that time. The mission-dominated Synod of Kaffraria decided to send a European missionary to reopen the church in Johannesburg, and Mzimba, the only African clergyman present at the synod meeting, voted against the resolution. Both Mzimba and the more cautious Elijah Makiwane, senior members of the African clergy, publicly protested these decisions. Tsewu and the Johannesburg dissidents formed the separatist Independent Presbyterian church in 1897.

Control of church funds and property contributed to Mzimba's break with the mission. He had been sent to Scotland to represent the mission in the Free Church of Scotland's jubilee celebrations in 1893, and like Dwane he had raised funds to build a new church that he was not allowed to administer when he returned to the eastern Cape. Mzimba was in charge of the mission's central congregation at Lovedale and responsible for its growing mission-outreach program west and east of the Kei River. Nevertheless, the missionaries did not approve of his choice of a new site and a more elaborate building for the church. Like his colleagues, Mzimba was angered by the fact that the congregations built and maintained the churches and paid a high proportion of the expenses but had no rights when it came to ownership or control of church property.

African church leaders (and some missionaries) were also afraid the mission might allow its congregations in the Synod of Kaffraria to be absorbed by the settler church. The Free Church mission was under heavy pressure to join the settler-dominated Presbyterian Church of South Africa, especially after the parent bodies of the Free Church and United Presbyterian Church in Scotland were reunited in 1900. African Presbyterians might still accept a missionary of their own Free Church as pastor of a congregation—he still had status and in any event his salary was paid by the mission—but they would not accept any form of settler control over an African church.[36]

Mzimba separated from the Presbyterian mission in April 1898, and two-thirds of his congregation—about a thousand communicants, all of whom were Mfengu—followed him into exile. They formed the Presbyterian Church of Africa (PCA) in December 1898. Xhosa church members remained with the mission. Mzimba rapidly recruited Mfengu dissidents from other mission churches, and by 1902 membership in the PCA was more than one-third the membership of the mission's African churches in the Synod of Kaffraria. A year later, the PCA had an estimated seventeen thousand members in congregations spread throughout southern Africa. The ethnic base of the church, moreover, gradually expanded beyond its Mfengu nucleus. When Mzimba died in 1911 the PCA was a multi-ethnic church with more than thirty-nine thousand members. Even the missionaries were impressed by Mzimba's skill as an administrator. The congregations were well organized and generously supported, and the church continued to grow in subsequent years.[37]

The Dynamics of Separatism

The two independent churches founded by Tile and Mzimba were launched along ethnic lines, but like the Ethiopian church they sought a wider African audience. This was reflected in the titles of all three churches. Even in Tile's lifetime, the Thembu church appealed to members of other ethnic groups who sought to identify with a religious organization controlled by Africans.

Nevertheless, African separatist church leaders also sought to reestablish their roots in the precolonial order. Tile tried to link his church directly with the Thembu ruling elite, because a state church would offer a home for the Christian minority and a haven for the non-Christian majority. He believed the Thembu church could be a vehicle for those who resisted colonial attempts to divide and subordinate the Thembu people and take away their land. Mzimba had the support of headmen like Bovani (his Christian name was George) Mabandla, a prominent political activist from Keiskammahoek, who had clashed with Makiwane and other loyal mission clergy in the Synod of Kaffraria over the mission-sponsored African university scheme.[38]

Dwane was a classic example of the independent African who sought to anchor the church in precolonial society. His father was the brother of a chief of the Ntinde Xhosa (the Ntinde had been incorporated into the Rharhabe confederacy during the early Cape-Xhosa wars), who had become a council- lor to Chief Khama of the Gqunukhwebe Xhosa. One of Dwane's sisters had married a brother of William Shaw Kama, the ordained pastor and son of the Gqunukhwebe chief who had followed his father as chief of the Gqunukhwebe in 1874. Kama sympathized with Dwane and the separatists, but he never left the mission. William Shaw's son and successor, however, joined the Order of Ethiopia, and the Gqunukhwebe Xhosa were apparently its main supporters.

Dwane succeeded in moving the Order's confirmation college from Queenstown to Kama's location in 1902. He envisaged a full-fledged theo- logical college that would enroll trainees from two village primary schools he intended to build on land given to the Order by the chief. Dwane wanted to create a self-contained settlement of perhaps a thousand adherents who would live in their own huts, pay a quitrent to farm the land, and grow their own food. This was to be a Christian community that lived in harmony with precolonial values and was isolated as far as possible from the European way of life. Dwane sought a "simpler life for students," who would not be dependent on "large buildings, iron beds, tables, bought food and a quantity of clothing"— or subordinated in any other way to the material demands of the dominant culture.[39] While a school of sorts for the Order did operate in Kama's location between 1902 and 1907, Dwane's dream of a Christian center of learning that followed the old Xhosa way of life was never realized. Instead, various Chris- tian factions continued to fight fiercely for converts and land in the truncated African reservations of the Ciskei and beyond.

The mission's subordination of the ordained clergy, in particular, was a major factor in the schisms. All the separatist church leaders were domi- nant personalities who had exercised positions of responsibility in the mission church. They had taken the greatest advantage of the opportunities offered by the mission and had tried to live lives that conformed to the mission's image of reality. Now they sought a share in the power structure as decision makers— in allocating funds, controlling and administering property, choosing suitable candidates for the ministry and promoting them to positions of authority. In short, the ordained African clergy wanted to become equal partners with the missionaries in the ongoing life of mission and church. When they were denied this role, they felt they had no choice but to separate.[40]

Mission-educated Africans everywhere in South Africa were being drawn to the African-American experience by the late 1880s and early 1890s. The writings of teachers like Booker T. Washington and historians like George Washington Williams, the political struggles of men like Frederick Douglass (the subject of a stirring eulogy in *Imvo Zabantsundu* after his death in February 1895), and occasional visits from musical groups like the Jubilee Singers served as role models for the African Christian community at the time. The Jubilee Singers toured South Africa in 1895, produced their own newspaper in Kimberley (called *The Citizen*), and made a decided impression on the educated African elite.[41] At least two members of the choir were Africans from South Africa, Eleanor Xiniwe, a sister of Paul Xiniwe, the business entrepreneur from the Ciskei, and Charlotte Manye, who would enroll as a student at Wilberforce University in 1895. Manye's uncle was Mangena Mokone, and she was the initial catalyst in establishing a link between the Ethiopian church and the AME church.

Relations between African and African-American separatists, however, would be sustained only when Africans were left firmly in control of their own church organizations. As the experience of the Ethiopian church suggests, African-American churches would be influential when they demonstrated their willingness to help Africans help themselves.

Ethnic rivalry between Mfengu and Thembu and Mfengu and Xhosa also played a role in the independent church movement. The Congregational and Presbyterian mission churches were particularly vulnerable. Congregational churches in East London and King William's Town, for example, split over ethnic differences and lost many members to the separatist churches. Mzimba's secession had been preceded by almost ten years of tension between Mfengu and Xhosa in Lovedale's central church, and ethnic rivalries eventually fragmented the station community.

All the separatists tried to avoid alienating settler opinion in hopes of gaining a semblance of legitimacy for their churches. Government recognition was needed to provide security for the clergy and land for churches and schools. Mzimba, for example, tried but failed to retain control of the property of congregations that had joined the PCA. The courts ruled that all church property was vested in the mission-sponsored Synod of Kaffraria. The decision of the Ethiopian church to join the AME church was prompted in large part by its failure to gain government recognition. Dwane and his followers sought a haven with the Anglicans for much the same reason.

Government approval meant that ordained clergy in the Cape would be recognized as marriage officers, granted railway concessions, and exempted from the pass laws. Approved independent churches, moreover, would be eligible for land grants. Settler hysteria over the "Ethiopian" movement—the settler term for all independent African churches at the time—was at its height between 1896 (when the Abyssinians defeated the invading Italians at Adowa in another corner of European imperialism in Africa) and 1906 (Bambatha's "rebellion" in Zululand). But the South African Native Affairs Commission had urged government recognition for churches that were politically reliable, and the Cape government was relatively benign in its treatment of separatist churches and clergy. The PCA, for example, received official approval in 1908 and the Order of Ethiopia in 1914. After the 1913 Land Act was passed, independent churches recognized by the government could apply for church and school sites in the reserves.

One striking characteristic of the separatist churches was their reluctance to deviate from the doctrines and rituals of the mission. They did not question the philosophical, theological, or ethical assumptions of the missionaries. Hence the African independent church movement during this period was decidedly orthodox in belief and behavior. Most adherents were already Christians from established congregations. Mzimba's converts came from all missionary denominations operating in the Ciskei. Dwane's followers were linked mainly to the Ethiopian church, AME church, and various Methodist mission churches.

The separatists made little effort to seek converts among the non-Christian majority, but they succeeded in recruiting less-educated Christians. Chief Burns-Ncamashe's analysis of the occupational status of forty-three students at the school operated by the Order of Ethiopia in Chief Kama's location in 1903, for example, shows that most had worked at menial unskilled or at best semiskilled jobs and had little formal education.[42] The Gqunukhwebe, moreover, were living mainly in the Middledrift area by this time, one of the poorest districts in the Ciskei. The congregations of the Order of Ethiopia, according to C. E. Tuckey, were generally impoverished, and what little support they provided to the church was in kind rather than cash.[43] Very few members of independent African churches at the time were recruited from the more educated, more prosperous ranks of the Christian community.

The separatist church movement was bitterly attacked by liberal as well as illiberal members of the settler community. European officials, merchants, magistrates, and missionaries were at one in condemning these independent churches. They feared the implications of any African institution that refused to recognize European sovereignty. The modernizing African Christian elite, however, was divided in its response to the separatist churches. Walter Rubusana, Elijah Makiwane, and John Knox Bokwe, all ministers who remained loyal to the mission church, were conspicuously involved in disputes involving separatists. The church leaders all knew one another—Makiwane, for example, was a lifelong friend of Mzimba—and for the personalities involved it must have been a wrenching, traumatic experience.

All the separatist church leaders were involved in African political, educational, and other cultural organizations, and they were critical opinion leaders at the community level. The political links are particularly interesting. Tile, the earliest separatist leader, was the most conspicuous. Active in Thembu politics during the 1880s, he wanted to reunite the old Thembu nation with its territory intact and return to British rule. He lobbied to obtain official recognition for Ngangelizwe as paramount and sought to remove the magistrates who had undermined the power of the chiefs. Arrested for urging the chiefs not to pay the hut tax, he would resist colonial rule until his death.

Edward Tsewu, initially a member of the SANC and politically active later on in the Transvaal, was actually nominated for the presidency of the South African Native National Congress that eventually went to John Dube of Natal. Mzimba, who had once urged his Lovedale parishioners not to get involved in settler politics, was an active participant by the early 1900s. As an SANC member (despite his Mfengu origin), Mzimba served on the 1903 delegation that met with the British colonial secretary to discuss the future status of Africans in the settler states. Jonas Goduka was a prominent SANC supporter in the Herschel District. Dwane was chairman of the SANC conference at Queenstown in 1898, but he became associated with the Inter-State Native College scheme and was elected to the fund-raising committee in 1905. Moses Mokone wrote letters to *Isigidimi* and *Imvo* in support of organizations like the NEA and the Imbumba in the 1880s, and he was politically active in later years in the Transvaal.

Most of the clergy associated with the main separatist churches in the Ciskei region during this period were members of either the SANC or the Imbumba. Some were political leaders in their own right. Mzimba's chief lieutenants included men who were instrumental in organizing opposition against the Glen Grey Act in the Transkei. The long-serving secretary of the South African Native Educational Association, W. W. Stofile, was in charge of PCA churches in the key East London and King William's Town districts. PCA church members who qualified for the franchise generally supported the Imbumba and voted for the South African party, while AME and Order of Ethiopia church members generally supported the SANC and voted for the Progressive party.

The separatist version of a self-supporting, self-governing, self-propagating church embracing all Africans was perhaps the fullest indigenous expression of African nationalism in the eastern Cape during the later colonial period. But at every level of activity the nexus between nationalism and dependency was evident in the actions and reactions of the nationalists. "Dwane's leadership," according to Tuckey, "shows a conflict between the desire to become a bishop acceptable to the white bishops and clergy and the urge to be the leader of a national church acceptable to the African people." Mzimba, as Brock put it, "tried to become a leader in African society without relinquishing his rights in European society."[44] This was the real dilemma of the modernizing elite, and it would constitute the central ambiguity in the development of African nationalism in South Africa in the generation after 1910.

Part 3
Repression and Revolt in South Africa's Periphery

7

The Underdevelopment of
an African Reserve

Popular resistance in the African reserves of South Africa after 1910 was conditioned by the struggle for economic survival. The periodization of under-development in these areas, however, has been the source of some controversy. Economist Charles Simkins, for example, has challenged an assumption held by liberal and radical scholars alike that peasant production steadily declined in the postcolonial era. He says (1) total production valued at constant prices (1946 = 100) remained more or less stable between 1918 and 1965, and (2) the downturn in production per capita began only after 1948.

While Simkins agrees that peasant production in the reserves could not satisfy minimum subsistence needs even before the first agricultural census was compiled in 1918, he contends that the proportion of food requirements met by African producers remained more or less constant between 1918 and 1954. Despite government controls, the surplus population was able to leave the reserves during this period, and overall population density remained rela-tively favorable, increasing only slowly from more than fifty to fewer than sixty persons per square mile in thirty-six years. A relatively stable ratio between peasant and urban wage worker incomes also enhanced the value of peasant production during this period, and the terms of trade actually improved as regards reserve agriculture between the mid-1940s and mid-1950s.

In contrast to this thesis, J. B. Knight and G. Lenta argue that farm pro-duction per capita in the reserves declined steadily between 1918 and 1974. While they agree that real income per capita (adjusted for inflation) did in-crease—at least from 1936 when statistics for the reserves became available— the gain was due entirely to migrant wages. The real incomes of reserve resi-dents even with these remittances, however, did not improve significantly until the 1970s.

Simkins pinpoints the mid-1950s as the start of the decline in peasant agriculture, when the central government made a concerted attempt to reverse migration trends by redirecting surplus African labor in proclaimed white areas back to the reserves. Total production and output per head of population in the reserves fell drastically, and within fifteen years peasant producers were no longer supplying food in significant quantities. Indeed, agriculture, which supplied only about 25 percent of the gross domestic product in the reserves as a whole by 1970, was no longer a dominant form of economic activity. The gap between urban and rural incomes soared, and the reserve population was now largely dependent on remittances from migrants working in the cities.[1]

This chapter focuses on the political economy of the Ciskei reserve between 1910 and 1950, when the implementation of apartheid would inaugurate a new and even more tragic era for the African peoples of this region. The Knight/Lenta thesis with regard to agricultural production and migrant wages in the reserves can be confirmed for the Ciskei reserve. Other indices of dependency are introduced to suggest that the material welfare of the African population continued to worsen, and in reality underdevelopment proceeded apace during this period.

Section 7.1 explores the changes made in land allocated to the reserve and the shifts in the population resident in the Ciskei region between 1910 and 1950.

Section 7.2 offers a profile of the African residents of one key Ciskeian district at the beginning of this period as a benchmark for a survey of the African population in the reserve.

Section 7.3 traces the pattern of economic dependency in the Ciskei reserve between 1920 and 1950.

Section 7.4 describes the central government's efforts to intervene directly in the reserves between 1920 and 1950 in order to boost food production and blunt the exodus of rural family units to the urban areas. The focus is again on the Ciskei, where economic conditions were now officially acknowledged to be the most serious in South Africa.[2]

7.1. Land and Population, 1910–1950

The Ciskei reserve before the apartheid era formed a portion of thirteen of the fourteen magisterial districts (Stockenstrom was excluded) lying between the Fish and Kei rivers. Each of these magisterial districts contained segregated rural African locations that taken together composed the reserve. Two virtually all-African districts outside the old Ciskei frontier zone—Herschel and Glen Grey—would remain part of the Ciskei reserve until 1975 (Map 4).

The Question of Land

South Africa's reserve system was formally created in the Natives' Land Act of 1913. It was the culmination of a long historical process, dating back to the 1830s in the case of the Ciskei region, and it has been widely regarded as the single most important piece of segregationist legislation affecting the

African peasantry since union in 1910. The measure sought to consolidate the efforts made by the settler colonies to prevent Africans from acquiring land and accumulating capital by curtailing the activities of African tenant producers on white-owned farms and by restricting the bulk of the African population to small tracts of land set apart from the white community. These areas were to be regarded as a reservoir of migrant labor for the mines, farms, factories, and homes of white South Africa.

Revisionist scholars have recast the setting, sequence, and significance of the 1913 Land Act in recent years.[3] The legislation was introduced at a critical point in the development of commercial agriculture, which had become increasingly dependent on state subsidies to increase food supplies to burgeoning urban markets along the coast and in the mineral-laden interior. Aid to white (especially Afrikaner) farmers in the form of transport/marketing facilities and loan capital had begun to bear fruit in the years immediately before and after 1910. Money at low interest rates from private as well as public agencies was now available, and more land was brought under cultivation. Drought conditions had eased, and with good rains and greater control over animal diseases there was a rapid increase in the stock population. As production increased, land became more valuable and land prices soared.

Boom conditions intensified competition between black tenant farmers and poor white landholders, who could not compete with white commercial farmers for black labor. The focus of the struggle lay in the northern and eastern districts of the Orange Free State and in the southern districts of the Transvaal, where agricultural production at this time was the most advanced in South Africa.

Lower-ranked members of the rural white petty bourgeoisie used every means at their disposal to undermine the autonomy of black tenant producers. Color consciousness became a potent ideological force in the campaign to drive black tenants off white-owned land. Considerable pressure was brought to bear against speculators and absentee landowners who catered to black commercial sharecroppers. White ranchers also wanted to reduce the African stock population so they could gain more access to increasingly expensive grazing land. Many could now afford to improve the quality of their stock, so they wanted to prevent inferior breeds of cattle and sheep from mixing with their animals, and eliminate African goats which were hard on the grass and trees (especially commercial fruit trees). Production methods at this time, however, were much the same for all farmers. White landholders still needed the resources of African tenant families, especially their draft oxen and plowing spans to cultivate the land and their labor to tend the fields and reap the crops.

There were three essential features to the 1913 Land Act. First, Africans were to have permanent access to land only in reserves set aside for them. White landholders wanted legislation to prevent black tenants from buying or leasing property outside these reservations and competing with whites in commercial agriculture. The principle of territorial segregation was to be extended from the Cape and Natal, where it had been implemented, to the Orange Free State and especially the Transvaal. The reserves at this time constituted about 7.1 percent of South Africa's land mass. In theory, no African would be allowed to buy or lease land in the proclaimed white areas of South Africa, and no white could buy or lease land in the proclaimed African reserves.

Second, the area under individual tenure was to be extended as far as possible in the reserves. The model favored by most lawmakers was the one-man-one-lot rule embodied in the Glen Grey Act, which was designed to reduce social stratification and pack as many people as possible on the land. Along with territorial segregation, the Glen Grey option was endorsed by the 1903–5 South African Native Affairs Commission and incorporated into the 1913 Land Act.

Third, a major attempt was made to prohibit Africans who were not labor tenants from renting white-owned land. Tenants—they were officially called squatters—who paid all or part of their rent in cash or in kind (normally 50 percent of their crops) would be illegal residents. Only 27,600 squatters were recorded on private land in the Cape by 1913, but Natal had an official squatter population (excluding private and crown land in Zululand) of 437,000, the Transvaal had 381,000 (private and crown land), and the Orange Free State had 80,000 (private land). Legislators had tried to resolve the squatter issue two years earlier with the Native Settlement and Squatters Registration Bill, but it was withdrawn in the face of pressure from white farmers who depended on black sharecroppers for survival.[4] Four versions of the Natives' Land Bill were submitted to parliament before agreement was reached, and most disputed clauses related to these tenant farmers.

Solomon Plaatje has provided a graphic description of the plight of African tenants evicted from white farms in parts of the Orange Free State in 1913,[5] but in reality most of them continued to live on white commercial farms even in the heartland of South Africa's maize belt. They also occupied noncommercial farms bought by land companies (especially in the Cape) and continued to settle on what remained of the crown land (except in Natal where tenants were forbidden to buy plots in these areas after 1903). Despite evictions in the Free State, the Land Act's antisquatting clauses could not be enforced, and authorities effectively shelved plans to remove African sharecroppers and other tenant producers from white-owned land.

None of the issues that seemed so crucial to white landowners and lawmakers in 1913 were actually resolved by this legislation. Against the wishes of the Transvaal and Orange Free State farmers, the Land Act provided that the reserves in future should be expanded and consolidated to accommodate the African population. The Supreme Court, moreover, ruled in 1916 (*Rex v.*

Tsewu) that the act should not be applied to the Cape because it would jeopardize African franchise rights. Africans who owned property could qualify for the vote, but it would be difficult to meet this condition if they were subjected to the Glen Grey clauses in the Land Act. The report of the Native Location Surveys in 1922, moreover, concluded that attempts to encourage individual tenure had failed in the African reserves just as attempts to abolish squatters had failed on proclaimed white farms.[6]

Nevertheless, African tenants had fewer options and less mobility after the Land Act. While full-time wage workers were still a rarity on white landholdings, the tenants were now forced to spend more labor time in servicing the needs of those who owned the land. They were also forced to sell more stock and give a larger portion of their crop (up to 80 percent) to the landowner, and they were subjected to greater supervision in their daily activities. Autonomous African tenants continued to occupy white-owned land after 1913, but essentially they lost whatever hopes they might have had of creating a rural petty bourgeoisie outside the reserves.

Once Africans were legally domiciled inside these reservations, moreover, the central government could address more effectively the labor demands of the various fractions of capital that were in need of workers. The 1913 Land Act became the lynchpin in the migrant labor system, and in the end no other legislation promulgated after union seemed more inviolable to those who ruled South Africa.

The Natives' Land Commission, chaired by Sir William H. Beaumont, an ex-army officer, Supreme Court judge, and administrator of Natal, was appointed in 1916 to suggest additional land that might be "released" for African occupation, especially in the Transvaal and Orange Free State where there were very few reserves. The Beaumont Commission's directive to find more land for Africans was not welcomed by white landowners anywhere in South Africa. They also opposed the 1917 Native Affairs Administration Bill, which sought to standardize reserve administration under the central government and implement the Beaumont Commission's land proposals. The bill was dropped, and provincial committees were appointed to review the Beaumont Commission's findings.

The report of the Cape provincial Natives' Land Committee was completed in 1918. While Cape Africans were theoretically excluded from the provisions of the Land Act, the size of the province's African reserves was still determined by these government-appointed bodies. The Appendix to this chapter (Table A7.1, Ciskei Reserve Land Proposals, 1913–1918) provides evidence to support the view that the central government was actually very reluctant to add land to the reserves scheduled under the Natives' Land Act. In reality, most land in the Ciskei region had already been set aside for African or European occupation.[7]

The Cape Land Committee proposed that 100,935 morgen (213,982 acres) be added to the Ciskei reserve scheduled under the 1913 Land Act. It was 44,309 morgen (93,935 acres) more than the Beaumont Commission had proposed and slightly more generous than the actual amount of land already occupied solely by Africans in the Ciskei's fourteen magisterial districts in 1916. Nevertheless, there were important differences between the 1916 Beaumont Commission and 1918 Cape Land Committee proposals, and Africans were threatened with the loss of valuable land they had previously occupied.

Africans in the Ciskei in 1916 actually owned 115,392 morgen (244,631 acres) or 11.4 percent of the land they occupied in the region, and a major portion of these farms (41 percent) were in three districts bordering the Kei River—Cathcart, Stutterheim, and Komgha.[8] They fully occupied almost the same amount of white-owned land in this area, which was concentrated in the valley of the Kei River stretching roughly a hundred miles inland from the Indian Ocean.[9] This was the so-called white corridor between the Ciskei and Transkei reserves, which had been created when the Ngqika Xhosa under Sandile were finally expelled from the Ciskei after the War of 1877–78. Farmers, magistrates, and law enforcement officials were unanimous in wanting to reclaim as much of this land as possible for white occupation, and the few concessions granted to African occupiers by the 1916 Beaumont Commission were reversed by the 1918 Cape Land Committee. Of 104,980 morgen (222,558 acres) owned or otherwise occupied by Africans in the three Kei River districts, only 20,337 morgen (43,144 acres) or 19.4 percent of the total was retained for the reserve. None of this land was in the Kei River valley.

More land for the Ciskei reserve was to be obtained from uneconomic areas for the most part occupied by Africans but owned by whites. In Cathcart, Queenstown, and Stutterheim districts, land added to the reserve had been allocated mainly to missionary societies. In Komgha District, land would be added to an African location specifically created as a labor reservoir for nearby white farmers. In East London District, the biggest single block of relatively unoccupied land would be found near the coast where the soil was too thin to be suitable for cultivation or ranching by white landholders.

Despite the admonition of the Cape Land Committee that in the Ciskeian magisterial districts "Natives and Europeans are so interlocked that their separation is economically impracticable,"[10] whites everywhere who actually occupied land were segregated from their African counterparts. No matter where whites had land in relation to the adjacent reserve, moreover, their rights and privileges were protected. The 1916 Beaumont Commission prevented Africans from gaining access to any land in the relatively prosperous Stockenstrom District and in a number of tiny villages originally founded by German immigrants, for example, in the East London District. Furthermore, the 1918 Land Committee reversed the Beaumont Commission's recommendations in three magisterial districts where whites actually owned/occupied land in the proposed reserve: "highly improved and closely settled" white farms in Victoria East, village plots and required grazing land held by whites in King William's Town, Keiskammahoek, and Middledrift, and high-priced, white-owned land in Stutterheim were to remain white.[11]

Although every inquiry into South Africa's reserves recognized that the Ciskei could not support its population, only about 63,782 morgen (135,218 acres) seems to have been acquired for the Ciskei reserve between 1913 and 1950. The reserve apparently increased in size from 927,771 morgen (1,966,875 acres) to 991,553 morgen (2,102,092 acres), although contemporary estimates of the total area would vary by as much as 100,000 morgen. As the chief native commissioner for the Ciskei observed in 1950, "unless circumstances are exceptional," virtually no more land could be acquired for the reserve.[12] Indeed, the possibility of obtaining more land anywhere in the Cape for African reserves seemed "so slender as to be almost hopeless." The only available land lay in the arid, barren northeast sector of the province, far removed from the "congested" districts of the Ciskei.[13]

Africans themselves could buy land anywhere in the Cape between 1913 and 1936 since property transactions between white and black in the province were still legal. Nevertheless, they actually lost more land than they acquired during this period. Witnesses testifying before the 1916 Beaumont Commission noted that existing African landowners in richer farming districts like Cathcart, Komgha, Stockenstrom, and Stutterheim were in debt and increasingly obliged to sell their land to whites.[14] After the 1936 Native Trust and Land Act, Cape Africans could buy land only in areas set aside for African reserves, which in the case of the Ciskei reserve was not an economic proposition. By 1949, only about 43,197 morgen (91,578 acres) were still owned by Africans in the Ciskei—37 percent of what they had owned in 1916.[15]

The Question of Population

While very few attempts were made to provide a systematic and detailed census of Africans in reserves until after World War II, there is evidence to suggest that the African population resident in the Ciskei reserve had reached saturation point by the early 1900s. As Appendix Table A7.2 (Population of Ciskeian Magisterial Districts, 1911–1951) indicates, eight key districts containing about 65 percent of the Ciskei's African residents—Fort Beaufort, Glen Grey, Herschel, King William's Town–Keiskammahoek-Middledrift, Komgha, and Victoria East—actually declined in population between 1911 and 1921. As Appendix Table A7.3 (African Population in the Ciskei Reserve, ca. 1916–1951) indicates, except for Glen Grey the African reserve population residing in these districts also declined or remained static between 1916 and 1936.

An increase in Glen Grey's reserve population between 1916 and 1936 was almost certainly due to the acquisition of land that lay outside the 1916–18 proposals.[16] After 1936, however, no more land could be obtained outside the released area, and so the reserve population in the district thereafter declined. East London's reserve population increased between 1916 and 1951, but as noted earlier this was also almost certainly due to the acquisition of a relatively large block of unoccupied white farmland near the port city.

The Ciskei reserve population's presumed increase of 27,914 or 11.9 percent between 1916 and 1951, then, can be attributed largely to the addition of land, most of which was already occupied by Africans. Herschel was apparently the only district that did not acquire any land inside or outside the released areas but nevertheless recorded a significant increase in population after 1936. The explanation may lie in the fact that hundreds of peasant families who had gained access to land in the Orange Free State as tenant farmers returned to Herschel after the 1936 Native Trust and Land Act. According to the Tomlinson Commission, the Ciskei's reserve population as a whole again declined between 1946 and 1951.[17]

The African population in the Ciskei's fourteen magisterial districts increased by 134,238 or 42.4 percent, and the total (white and black) population by 174,071 or 45.7 percent, between 1911 and 1951 (Appendix Table A7.2). Africans comprised on average about 82 percent of the total population in the region during this period. While the urban African population increased by 6.8 percent (from 13.8 percent in 1911 to 20.6 percent in 1951), the vast majority remained in the rural areas. If one assumes, extrapolating from the 1911 and 1921 census figures, that the regional African population in 1916 was 319,004, the reserve absorbed only about 21 percent of the increase in the Ciskei region's resident African population between 1916 and 1951. The reserve's capacity to absorb the African population in the Ciskei as a whole, moreover, declined throughout the period. In 1916, about 73.7 percent of the region's resident African population was living in the reserve. In 1936 it was about 63.1 percent, and in 1951 it was 58.3 percent. Other Ciskei Africans— there are no published statistics but they must have numbered in the tens of thousands—left the region each year and never returned.

7.2. Inside the Reserve: A District in Profile

Detailed information on the African population in specific Ciskeian magisterial districts is very difficult to obtain, but one can construct a profile of a key district and use it as a benchmark to examine developments in other districts.

King William's Town (also known as Tamacha) was selected for analysis (Appendix Table A7.4). As noted in earlier chapters, it was the center of African political activity in the Ciskei between 1880 and 1910. Keiskammahoek and Middledrift, moreover, were administered as part of King William's

Town District until 1937. Africans living in this area—a major portion of the old Crown Colony of British Kaffraria and the nucleus of the future Ciskei "homeland"—comprised 36 percent of the reserve population in 1916. Virtually all the evidence from the Ciskei that was presented to the 1903–5 South African Native Affairs Commission came from this district. Detailed evidence on conditions in King William's Town and other districts in the Ciskei was also compiled for the first South African Blue Book on Native Affairs in 1910 and for the 1916 Beaumont Commission.

Production, Income, and Expenditure

Like Africans in other Ciskeian districts, those living in rural locations in the King William's Town–Keiskammahoek-Middledrift District were overwhelmingly dependent on a single crop—maize—as a source of food.[18] The proportion of land devoted to the cultivation of sorghum, the other subsistence food staple, was declining. Other crops were still planted—beans (mainly during periods of drought), pumpkins, peas, oats, and winter wheat in the surveyed locations (where individual tenure was enforced)—but all were marginal activities by the early 1900s.

Everywhere the plow was now employed alongside the hoe in the cultivation of crops, but the type of wooden, single-furrow instrument in use had not really changed since the 1830s when it was first introduced in the Ciskei. White officials complained it did not prepare the land effectively for cultivation and contributed to soil erosion. While there were very few mules, donkeys, or horses for transport in the locations, the number of cattle, sheep, and goats owned by Africans in the King William's Town–Keiskammahoek-Middledrift District had apparently increased dramatically in the early 1900s (Appendix Table A7.4). The peasants had recovered to some extent from the catastrophic stock losses suffered in the 1896–97 rinderpest epidemic, and there was some improvement in quality since they had been forced initially to buy cattle from nearby white farmers to replenish their herds.

Official attempts to mandate cattle-dipping regulations following the outbreak of East Coast fever were opposed by some stockfarmers in the Ciskei (they bore the cost of such measures), but popular protest does not seem to have occurred on a wide scale as it did in the Transkei. Those who had the biggest cattle herds apparently cooperated with government authorities; cattle-dipping fees were paid, and in some cases African syndicates were formed to build cattle-dipping tanks.[19]

Stock estimates for the Ciskei reserve as a whole could not be obtained, but there is considerable evidence from white observers and black residents alike that the reserve was overstocked by 1910 (see Appendix Table A7.4 for Keiskammahoek and Middledrift). The official view, which prevailed between 1913 and 1950, was made clear by the chairman of the 1916 commission, who told African spokesmen from Herschel: "If you did not have so much stock you could put more people on the land, and if you cultivated more land you would keep more people."[20] From this perspective, overstocking not only limited population density but also ruined the land, weakened the quality of the cattle, in particular, and thus reduced the milk yield that was a crucial supplement to maize as a source of food.

The African peasant's perspective, of course, was quite different. Household heads needed to retain as much stock as possible and even reap their mealies before maturity to pay their taxes and debts to the local white trader (there were very few Africans who owned or operated stores in the reserve before the 1970s). In addition, the householder needed stock as collateral to buy food to feed his family when the crops failed. It is difficult to prove this point from the available evidence, but some officials were well aware of the problem. The field cornet for Kamastone and Oxkraal locations in the Queenstown District told the 1916 commission that it was "necessary" to keep these areas overstocked because "that is the only way our people have of obtaining a livelihood—from the sale of wool, etc.—and the only means they have got of paying their taxes."[21]

Estimates of African income and expenditure levels in the Ciskei are both difficult to find and incomplete. They almost always stem from official government sources and are impossible to verify. Nevertheless, Africans themselves occasionally offered estimates of minimum subsistence needs during this period, and African labor statistics compiled by various district magistrates for the Native Affairs Department's first report in 1910 are reasonably detailed.

Nathaniel Umhalla, the prominent eastern Cape politician who was a headman and labor recruiter in the King William's Town District, told the 1903–5 Native Affairs Commission, for example, that roughly forty pounds in cash earnings would keep a migrant worker's family alive in the reserve for one year. Peter K. Kawa, a Church of Ethiopia minister living in King William's Town, told the commissioners that sixty pounds a year would be "a proper wage" for a man working in town.[22]

Rural householders obtained cash from the sale of household stock and produce and from wage labor as migrant workers on the mines or in town and as migrant or day workers on nearby white-owned farms. Estimates of the value of stock and produce sold in the Ciskei's African locations, as we shall see, apparently did not exceed £6 a year per household between 1920 and 1950, and there is no reason to assume that this figure was much greater between 1900 and 1920. African migrants in the Transvaal gold mines earned about £28 10s. a year in 1911, a portion of which would be returned to their families in the reserve.[23]

Wages for Ciskeian farm laborers and domestic workers in 1910 apparently had not improved since the 1870s.[24] They ranged from £3 to £18 a year, with women at the lower end and men at the upper end of this scale. While men in King William's Town (Tamacha) District earned between £9 and £18 a year working on white farms (Appendix Table A7.4), for the Ciskei as a whole the median wage for males in these categories was between £6 and £9. There would be no improvement in farm wages during the next generation.[25] Wages for male laborers in town ranged from £12 to £48 with the median being about £15 to £28 a year in 1910. The median wage for semiskilled and skilled male workers in town was between £24 and £48 a year.

These figures support the view that cash income from the selling of stock and produce and from wages earned in town or on white farms did not meet the perceived minimum subsistence needs of the vast majority of Africans who lived in the Ciskei. Only a few town dwellers (salaried professionals and skilled workers) were earning £60 a year or above, and apparently the vast majority of householders in the reserve had cash incomes well below £40 a year in 1910. It is not surprising residents clung to the land, since it was still their ultimate means of survival.

The Question of Migrant Labor

King William's Town–Keiskammahoek-Middledrift District was very typical for the Ciskei. A significant migrant labor population had been observed since the 1870s, and according to evidence given by the local magistrate before the 1903–5 Native Affairs Commission, only a small portion of the "able-bodied men" avoided work outside the locations.[26]

The trader was still a catalyst in the local labor-recruiting network because he could place pressure on peasants to migrate to the mines to service their debts. "The whole economic life of the people," as one confidential report put it in 1941, "is centered on the trading store."[27] This was often acknowledged but rarely investigated by government officials. In King William's Town in 1910, some traders were known to specialize in giving generous amounts of credit to household heads with sons who were old enough to work. When the debts were not paid, the fathers were forced to turn their sons over to the trader who, in turn, "gets a good commission from the Labour Agent, clothes the boys at a further profit, and finally gets his debt paid, with good interest."[28] According to the 1943 Mine Wages Commission, about 51 percent of the mine workers obtained by the Native Recruiting Corporation, which operated mainly in the eastern Cape, were recruited through traders who received £2 10s. for every signed contract.[29]

Mine labor-recruiting centers were well established in all Ciskeian magisterial districts except Herschel.[30] The youth at this time migrated mainly to mines in the Transvaal (gold), Orange Free State (diamonds at Jagersfontein), and the northern and eastern Cape (diamonds at Kimberley and coal in the Stormberg-Indwe area). The middle-aged sought jobs in nonmining activities—expanding harbors, building railroads, and working in the towns and major cities along the coast and in the interior. Ciskei's white farmers, moreover, employed most of the legal African tenants in the Cape. Of 2,928 household heads who were authorized tenants on white farms in the province in 1910, about 81 percent were employed in the districts of East London (1,021), Glen Grey (94), Peddie (340), Stutterheim (104), and Komgha (822).[31]

Although it was often assumed that white farmers had a severe shortage of labor, the magistrates' reports for the Ciskeian districts in 1910 indicate that only East London specifically cited a shortage of farm workers. In practice, farmers' complaints were based largely on the scarcity of labor during peak wool-shearing and crop-reaping periods. For most of the year, they were well supplied with local workers.[32]

About one-seventh of the African population was deemed suitable for migrant labor, according to an official estimate in 1903.[33] If this assumption is correct, there were an estimated 15,211 potential migrants from the King William's Town–Keiskammahoek-Middledrift District in 1910. According to the magistrates' reports, there were 8,704 registered migrants in the district, excluding Middledrift. Ciskei residents who actually obtained passes to seek outside employment, however, were only a portion of the total migrants. In Middledrift, a "majority of the laborers" migrated to the Reef and to German South-West Africa apparently as nonregistered migrants.[34] If the number of registered migrants from King William's Town and Keiskammahoek is increased by a conservative one-third to include the nonregistered migrants, and Middledrift is included in this estimate, the district already provided perhaps 14,500 migrants in 1910.

Recruiters of African migrant labor were actually not so much interested in trying to find new workers as they were in making more efficient use of the existing work force by trying to increase the amount of time a migrant was employed away from the reserve. Most workers returned after four to six months, fearful of losing access to allotted garden plots, and mining contracts normally lasted six months. Migrant mine workers returned in the spring plowing months to tend their household crops and care for the stock. Recruiters of mine labor, in particular, sought ways of shortening the time the migrant "rested" between contracts so as to maximize the use of a trained and disciplined labor force.[35]

Land Tenure and Authority in the Locations

White magistrates, superintendents of African locations, labor recruiters, farmers, and missionaries generally agreed with black residents: in terms of prevailing patterns of land use, locations in the Ciskei were "fully occupied" or "overcrowded" in 1910.[36] Garden plots in the King William's Town–Keiskammahoek-Middledrift District covered virtually all the designated arable land in 1903, while huts and garden plots on commonage (grazing) land in both surveyed and unsurveyed locations were a matter of "serious" concern by 1910.[37] As the 1916 Beaumont Commission and the 1918 Cape Land Committee made clear, however, very little additional land would be added to the reserve. As far as the governing authorities were concerned, the only way to resolve the population problem was to extend the Glen Grey Act and limit every household to one plot of land.

The peasants continued to resist having their land surveyed because individual tenure gave them even less security than they had under communal tenure.[38] Those who held individual allotments in the surveyed locations had to pay a quitrent that was five shillings more than the hut tax, while those who were officially landless—meaning household heads who had not been allotted residential-cum-garden plots—still had to pay the hut tax. The landless in the surveyed locations were usually absorbed by those who had land, and they shared with their relatives whatever food was produced, but they remained illegal residents. In overcrowded Glen Grey, for example, 50 percent of the householders were residing illegally on the commonage by 1922, and there were even more landless on the commonage in the surveyed locations of King William's Town. Tax delinquents in Glen Grey, which was still the only district where all the African locations had been surveyed, were the highest in the Ciskei region in 1910 (£7,056 in arrears); in Herschel, where there were no surveyed locations, no tax delinquents were reported.[39]

The distribution of land under individual tenure, like the distribution of stock, remained inequitable. In the case of Glen Grey, existing inequalities were maintained after the 1894 act was implemented despite the mandatory limitation of households to a single arable plot. About 40 percent of Glen Grey's registered plots in 1922, for example, were held by household heads who were not the original owners. Others who already held land in the district were presumed to hold a portion of these allotments, since only 16 percent of the original titles had been canceled (for failure to pay the quitrent or improve the property) and awarded to landless householders.

The size of individual allotments in the surveyed locations continued to decrease. Plots surveyed before 1894, as noted in Chapter 3, were relatively larger in size than those surveyed in later years. The Glen Grey Act attempted to standardize individual plots at 4 morgen (8.48 acres), but by 1913 (Proclamation No. 300) the acceptable minimum had been reduced to 3 morgen (6.36 acres). By the 1920s, 3-morgen plots were "an empty dream" in both surveyed and unsurveyed locations in the Ciskei.[40] In the surveyed locations of Keiskammahoek, for example, garden plots averaged 1 morgen (2.12 acres) in the 1920s, while in unsurveyed Herschel they averaged roughly 1.5 morgen (3.18 acres) and in Victoria East about 2.6 morgen (5.51 acres).[41]

Between 1913 and 1950, locations were surveyed and individual tenure adopted in nine of the fourteen districts in the region—East London, Fort

Beaufort, Glen Grey, Herschel, King William's Town, Peddie, Queenstown, Stutterheim, and Victoria East. The only other reserve in South Africa where individual tenure was tried on any scale was the Transkei, where seven districts were surveyed and individual titles issued. In the Ciskei as in the Transkei, however, individual tenure was a failure: most locations in the reserve remained unsurveyed.

Headmen sought to guarantee the right to land in unsurveyed locations, whereas this right was taken away once the land was surveyed and fixity of tenure secured. Headmen provided their followers with land by simply converting more and more of the commonage into garden plots. As poverty levels deepened, however, the wealth and status of the headmen declined. There were numerous contenders for power and patronage inside the locations by the 1920s and 1930s, so it is not surprising that headmen would cling to their right to allocate land: this was perhaps the last symbol of their authority in a way of life that had been more or less maintained since the conquest of Xhosaland.

Government intervention in the locations before the 1940s was aimed primarily at curbing the power of headmen to distribute communal land. The Native Affairs Department had lists of household heads who paid hut taxes, but there were few details on who owned these plots, how they were distributed, how big they were, and where they were located. Thus the authorities decided to apply the Glen Grey one-man-one-lot principle to land held in communal tenure in unsurveyed locations as it had earlier been applied to land held in individual tenure in surveyed locations.

Government Notice 833, which sought to regulate communal tenure in the Ciskei reserve, was actually proclaimed in 1921, and it was a radical departure from prevailing custom in reserve administration.[42] Family holdings in communal locations were to be consolidated into one plot not exceeding five morgen (10.6 acres) in size and registered in the name of the household head. Registered landowners would be given certificates to legitimize their right to the land. Unregistered plots would revert to the commonage after a specified time and be available for reallotment. In theory, local white officials would replace headmen in the allocation of land, and information obtained from the registration certificates would give the government far more control over communal landholders than it had ever had in the past. As we shall see, the regulation provoked considerable resistance in the case of Herschel and presumably in other districts as well because apparently it was not enforced before South Africa's reserves were reorganized in the apartheid era.

Nevertheless, Government Notice 833 highlighted the government's growing conviction that reserve land had to be administered more efficiently if the reserves were to continue to be a reservoir for the African population. According to the Mine Wages Commission, there were 12,814 landless families in the Ciskei's surveyed and unsurveyed African locations, for example, by 1943. If one uses this figure and accepts the estimate of the 1955 Tomlinson Commission that the average size of an African family unit in South Africa's reserves at the time was 6.27 members, more than 80,300 people or 31 percent of the resident population in the Ciskei reserve may have been landless by 1951. This figure correlates with an estimate made by R. W. Norton, assistant director of native agriculture for the Ciskei, who reported in the late 1940s that "nearly 30 percent" of the reserve residents were landless.[43]

7.3. A Mosaic of Dependency, 1920–1950

The Ciskei reserve reached an acute stage of underdevelopment during the 1920s and 1930s. Empirical evidence of economic decay in the 1920s is based on unofficial case studies of two districts—Victoria East and Herschel. The central government made an effort to generate more data on conditions within the reserve from the 1930s: information on crop production, however, was still gathered infrequently, especially in the unsurveyed locations, and it was unreliable as well as incomplete.

Locations in the 1920s: Victoria East and Herschel

A particularly graphic illustration of dependency could be seen in the Victoria East District, where the mission enterprise had first taken root among the Bantu speakers of southern Africa.[44] Lovedale, for example, was only a few miles from where Johannes van der Kemp of the London Missionary Society had made contact with the Ngqika Xhosa in 1799. James Henderson, principal of Lovedale (1906–30), was one of the leading missionary critics of conditions in the reserve. His colleague D. A. Hunter, editor of *South African Outlook,* the most prestigious mission publication in South Africa, regularly published articles on the decline in African living standards in the district during this decade.

Based on information obtained from Native Affairs blue books, Henderson compiled a graph of production and expenditure in the reserve area in 1875 and 1925 and concluded that the reserve economy had deteriorated drastically during the intervening period (see Appendix Table A7.5). African locations in Victoria East, moreover, were "typical . . . of the greater part of Ciskeian areas, some of which are even in a worse condition."[45]

Cash income from production per household in 1925 was about 22 percent of what it had been in 1875 and cash expenditure slightly less than half, without considering inflation or the increase in population during the intervening period. Cash income equaled cash expenditure in 1875, whereas cash income in 1925 (about £4 9s. per household) was less than half cash expenditure (estimated at £9 5s. per household). The proportion spent on food rose from 20 percent of the total in 1875 to 64 percent in 1925. Henderson did not offer an estimate of the gross value of household production (consumed as well as marketed) in 1925, but little if any maize or stock was being sold outside the reserve. Peasants were bartering subsistence rations mainly to pay their debts to traders, who were using the maize for fodder or reselling what they received to other householders in the district. Arable land had been under continuous cropping for up to thirty years. Maize was the only crop in most areas, whereas fifty years earlier a variety of crops had been grown with more than twice the number of plows and other farm tools.

Recurrent drought, disease, and inferior stock due in part to inbreeding and poor (and ever-diminishing) grazing land had steadily reduced the number and quality of African-owned cattle in the district. African farmers had been "compelled" to take up sheep farming, according to Henderson, because the sale of wool—subsidized by the central government as a concession to white farmers—"affords to their owners the means for buying food." [46] For example, there were about 9,500 cattle and 50,000 sheep and goats in Victoria East's African locations in 1923.

Supplementary food, clothing, taxes, quitrent, school and church fees for families who were Christian, and medical, marriage, and funeral costs as well as miscellaneous expenses such as the cost of dipping stock would be paid for with migrant wages. Henderson did not estimate the wages earned by absentee householders in his district, but almost all able-bodied men (60 percent of those between fifteen and fifty in his survey) were migrants in 1925. Women would move in force into migrant labor during the 1930s.

The pattern of dependency outlined by Henderson for Victoria East was supported by the historian W. M. Macmillan in his case study of Herschel published in 1930. The district was situated in the foothills of the Drakensberg bordering colonial Basutoland and was therefore isolated from the rest of the Ciskei reserve. Created as a magisterial district in 1870, it consisted almost entirely of African locations. Herschel experienced relatively severe winters, so few people lived permanently in the mountains, which comprised about one-third of the district. By the 1920s, at least 10 percent of the householders were landless, and up to 75 percent of the men were migrants working outside the area (many on farms in the Orange Free State) for six months or more a year.

Figures compiled by Macmillan and Colin Bundy suggest that the value of production had fallen considerably since the heyday of peasant prosperity in the early 1870s. Cash income from production per household dropped by about 62 percent between 1873 and 1921–29 (the value of stock and produce sold in the district declined from £54,475 to about £35,000 during this period). Cash income from production per household during the 1920s was about £5 8s. or roughly one-half of total cash expenditure (calculated at £10 to £13 per household) [47]—the same as Henderson had estimated for Victoria East. Cash income from migrant labor did not generate enough revenue to balance cash expenditure, and the shortfall was estimated at £25,000 to £32,000 (between £3 1*s*. and £4 per household) a year. Thus each year the debt burden—and the trader's stranglehold over the peasant—increased.[48]

Herschel's peasants no longer provided maize and sorghum for export, and even in good years production met only half the yearly grain requirements. Some wheat, maize, sorghum, stock, and stock by-products (wool, mohair, hides, and skins) was still marketed by the most prosperous households through Lady Grey, a small village in a white farming area outside Herschel, but otherwise there was little commerce with surrounding districts in South Africa. Transportation networks were almost nonexistent. There were virtually no serviceable roads or bridges in Herschel. The "average native," Macmillan commented, was "poor in production and very low in consumption" and the population "seething with discontent." While Herschel was marginally better off than other drier and more densely populated Ciskeian districts, most peasants survived "almost on the very lowest level of bare existence." [49]

The Economic Crisis Worsens, 1930–1950

The Ciskei in the 1920s was a harbinger of the future:

> Poverty, congestion, and chaos, are worst in these districts which were the scene of the first conflicts between European and Bantu. . . . For overcrowding, and its consequences in ill-health and starvation . . . for low and stagnant wages, for an inextricable mix-up of European and Native areas and the impossible administrative difficulties which result . . . for sullen discontent and hopelessness on the part of that most tractable of races, the Bantu—the Ciskei suggests what other parts of the Union are fast drifting to.[50]

As industrialization accelerated during the 1930s, and a flood of non-economic African labor migrating to the white urban areas seemed imminent, more pressure was placed on the central government to intervene in the reserves. Legislative measures were not enough. The burden of accommodating unwanted black families in the cities could be avoided and the supply of wage laborers to the white urban and rural areas regulated only by maintaining the subject population in the reserves. As the 1930–32 Native Economic Commission pointed out, state intervention was necessary "to enable the Natives to develop their Reserves, so as to make these sufficiently productive and attractive to stop the present compulsory migration to the towns." [51]

Grazing as well as arable land in some areas of the Ciskei reserve had become so eroded by the 1930s, according to the commission, that the cost of reclaiming the land exceeded the value of the soil. Erosion, moreover, was just as bad in the surveyed areas as it was in the unsurveyed areas.[52] Norton, the assistant director of native agriculture, observed in the 1940s that soil erosion was "slight" in 10 percent, "bad" in 50 percent, and "nothing less than terrifying" in 40 percent of the reserve's arable land. He recommended that 20 percent of the garden plots be withdrawn from cultivation immediately if they were "to be saved from total destruction." [53]

Overstocking—the perennial theme in official explanations of why land in the reserve had deteriorated—was particularly well documented during this period. The report of the 1930–32 Native Economic Commission cited overstocking in the Ciskei, especially in the Middledrift, Herschel, and Glen Grey districts, as the "worst" in the country and warned the government that if something was not done "the Transkei and the Native areas in the rest of the Union will be to-morrow what that of the Ciskei is to-day." [54] Twenty years later, the Tomlinson Commission said the Ciskei was still "the most heavily over-stocked" reserve in South Africa. [55]

As Appendix Table A7.6 (Livestock Production in the Ciskei Reserve, 1927–1953) suggests, overstocking was endemic—67.4 percent in 1927 and 74.5 percent in 1953. These figures dropped below 60 percent only during years of prolonged drought when stock losses were particularly severe. Although sheep and goats had outnumbered cattle for 50 years or more, in terms of the carrying capacity of the land cattle still dominated. Thus official efforts to reduce stock in the reserve continued to focus on culling cattle. [56]

Stock ownership, moreover, continued to vary widely throughout the reserve. Although 27 percent of 6,896 household heads in the King William's Town locations in 1944, for example, owned 11 or more head of cattle, 42 percent owned less than 5 head, and 35 percent had no cattle. In adjacent Keiskammahoek, 33 percent of the household heads possessed between 1 and 5 head of cattle, and 29 percent had no cattle. As Norton observed, the average householder owned "a sub-economic unit of land and a sub-economic number of stock. Above him is a relatively small favored class of bigger owners with up to 100 head of cattle and 1,000 head of sheep. Below him are thousands who own nothing." [57]

Crop production fluctuated widely from year to year, and most of it was consumed before reaching the market. Only about 20 percent of the land in the reserve was deemed to be arable. Norton told the Fagan Commission in 1948 that the average householder in the Ciskei reserve occupied a garden plot of 2.2 morgen (4.6 acres), which yielded at best 6.9 bags of grain a year. There had been no increase in this yield, moreover, in at least a generation. In essence, the Ciskei reserve could provide at best about 50 percent of the estimated minimum yearly requirement of 13.75 bags of grain per household. [58]

Maize remained the staple crop. In 1936–37, it provided 78.1 percent of the plant food calories consumed by the resident population in South Africa's reserves as a whole. During a prolonged drought in the 1930s, however, maize production plummeted in all the reserves. The Ciskei maize crop in 1939 was still below what it had been five years earlier, and production was intermittent

Table 7.1. Average yearly income and expenditure of a mine
worker's family from the Ciskei in 1943 (in £)

1. Cash income		3. Cash expenditure	
Mine worker's wages	27.9	Clothing	10.3
Sale of stock	2.1	Food	9.6
Sale of produce	2.2	Migrant's expenses	2.6
Total	32.2	Purchase of stock	2.0
2. Value of produce consumed		Miscellaneous articles	2.7
Maize	3.0	Taxes, school and church	
Beans	0.2	fees, school books and	
Sorghum	1.9	stationery	2.6
Pumpkins	0.1	Total	29.8
Milk	3.1		
Meat	1.7		
Total	10.0		

SOURCE: *Report of the Witwatersrand Mine Natives' Wages Commission
for 1943* (UG 21-1944), Appendix J. Although the average number of
persons per kraal was 8.7, the average family unit was estimated at 5
persons. Eighty wage earners, representing 401 persons, were involved
in the survey which was carried out in the districts of Glen Grey, Herschel, Keiskammahoek, Middledrift, Peddie, and Queenstown. Each
family unit contained one wage earner.

during the 1940s. Grain supplies were "less than half" of the subsistence requirement in 1943–44, for example, when the maize crop was described as
"bountiful," and about 42 percent in 1944–45. Grain imports to the Ciskei
soared from 200,000 bags in 1947–48 (when the maize crop was described as
"the best for many years") to 500,000 bags during the 1949–50 drought.[59]

In little more than a generation after the South African War, the number
of migrants working outside the Ciskei reserve at any given time increased
from an estimated one-seventh to one-fifth of the population. Migrants who
worked in the mines for six months in 1903 were averaging nine months by
World War I and 14 months by World War II. Whereas very few females were
working outside the reserve in 1903, they comprised 15.3 percent of this labor
force in 1936. About 63 percent of the reserve's able-bodied males (between
eighteen and fifty-four years of age) were now migrants, and miners comprised
70.3 percent of these wage earners.[60]

The principal mine-recruiting depots in the Ciskei were at Queenstown
and King William's Town. According to a Mine Wages Commission survey in
1943, the average mine worker's family living in the reserve sold stock and
produce worth £4 3s. and spent £29 8s. for clothes, food, and other necessities
(see Table 7.1). Whereas cash income from household production had covered
roughly 50 percent of cash expenditure in the Victoria East and Herschel surveys during the 1920s, it covered only about 13 percent in the 1943 Ciskei

survey. Although migrant incomes were apparently sufficient to meet basic household expenses in this survey, consumption patterns remained extremely low. A confidential report on the Ciskei and Transkei submitted to the Chamber of Mines in 1941 noted that "semi-starvation is a very insecure basis on which to build a permanent labor supply." [61]

Public Health. Public health data for the African population in the Ciskei reserve between 1910 and 1950 are virtually unobtainable, but diseases associated with malnutrition and poor living conditions were unquestionably a major problem. Henderson commented in 1925 that huts in Victoria East's locations were overcrowded and "unfit for human occupation." There was little clothing, and many people could no longer afford even blankets.[62] The Ciskeian Missionary Council in a 1927 survey of the African population in twenty-nine magisterial districts west of the Kei River found that most householders were relying solely on maize as a source of food. In 87 percent of the districts, milk could no longer be obtained as a regular supplement to the diet, and meat was rarely eaten. The consumption of processed food other than tea and coffee was still confined largely to the towns. The missionaries concluded that living conditions for Africans in the region were "unsound, unstable and deteriorating." [63]

Infant mortality—a key index of impoverishment—was extremely high. In a sample of 295 mothers from the rural areas who were interviewed in 1937, for example, it was found that only 43 percent of the children conceived actually survived birth. Of those who survived, the mortality rate (per 1,000 births) was 164 for children up to one year, 80 for children between one and two years, and 130 for children between two and eighteen years. It was estimated that 25 percent of the children in rural Ciskei and Transkei died before they were a year old, 35 percent before they were two years old, and 50 percent before they were eighteen years old.[64] Infant mortality in the towns, as we shall see, was even higher.

Relatively new diseases—especially tuberculosis and venereal infections brought into the reserve mainly by migrants returning from the mines—were spreading rapidly during this period. Outbreaks of traditional diseases associated with endemic poverty, including enteric or typhoid fever, typhus, scurvy, and dysentery, continued to plague the population.[65] Official concern about health conditions at this time, however, was limited to inoculating the peasants when epidemics threatened the adjacent white population.[66]

Mission agencies were primarily responsible for public health services, but mission hospitals were small and dependent on irregular overseas grants.[67] They lacked both staff and equipment, and virtually no preventative work was done. As Appendix Table A7.7 (District Hospitals in the Ciskei Region with Beds for Africans) suggests, nine of the fourteen magisterial districts in the

Ciskei had no hospitals at all for Africans in 1936. While some provincial hospitals began to provide beds for Africans in segregated wings, there were still four or five districts without any medical facilities for Africans in 1945. Mission hospitals provided 77 percent of the African beds in 1936 and at least 56 percent in 1945.[68] The number of hospital beds for general cases in the Ciskei region as a whole was roughly one-half of what the government decreed to be the minimum requirement for Africans in rural areas, but even this was a gross overestimate since the government hospitals were located in white urban areas.[69]

Three hospitals for Africans in the Ciskei in 1936 were training African nurses, but in 1945 there were apparently only 10 African nurses actually working in the reserve. In thirteen of fourteen Ciskeian magisterial districts in 1948, there was one doctor for every 522 whites and 9,579 Africans.[70] The Ciskeian Missionary Council estimated that the locations alone required at least 360 medical personnel (including 160 registered nurses and 40 doctors) to meet the minimum needs of the African population.[71]

The oldest mission hospital in South Africa was at Lovedale mission station. Victoria Hospital, opened in 1898, pioneered nursing education for Africans in the subcontinent (the first courses were established in 1903), and it was among the first to train midwives and provide maternity wards for African mothers. In addition, Victoria achieved a national reputation during the 1930s and 1940s as an orthopedic facility (spinal tuberculosis was particularly widespread in rural Ciskei at the time). Minuscule grants from the government, funded in large part by African tax revenue, were channeled primarily to Victoria as the prestige hospital in the region. The Department of Health agreed to build South Africa's first tuberculosis facility for Africans at Lovedale, and Macvicar Hospital (named after Victoria's medical superintendent from 1902 to 1937) was opened in 1940. The hospital was still staffed and controlled by the mission, but administration costs were subsidized by the government.

The central government, however, began to phase out subsidies to mission hospitals and shift the burden of caring for the medical needs of the African population to the provinces after World War II. Mission hospitals in the Cape, which catered mainly to Africans, were to be defined as "private" hospitals in terms of noninfectious diseases, and the maximum subsidy per patient would be 50 percent of daily hospital costs. The province would provide full subsidies only in cases of infectious disease, and no allowance was made for outpatient care, equipment, buildings, ambulances, and other capital needs. From the mission's perspective, the purpose behind this legislation was clear; the Cape and other provinces were "starving these [mission] hospitals out of existence."[72]

Most missionary agencies, however, could no longer afford to subsidize their hospitals, and they were forced to comply with the new regulations. The

Cape effectively took over administrative control of the mission hospitals in the Ciskei from 1950. Provincial control would have a considerable impact on African medical care in the reserve. As the missionaries had predicted, some rural hospitals would be phased out or reduced to the status of clinics. Health care for those who lived in the reserve would depend on the expansion of clinics in the towns and villages, but funding remained precarious, and health education was virtually nonexistent. Most rural Africans continued to rely on herbalists and their remedies because they had no viable alternative.

Life in the Towns: East London

However faint, the only hope of improving one's living standards lay in towns outside the reserve.[73] There were only four towns of any size in the Ciskei region before the 1950s, and the biggest was East London (see Table 7.2).

East London was established near the end of the War of 1846–47 at the mouth of the Buffalo River, one of the few natural harbors in the eastern Cape. The seaport remained undeveloped until the early 1870s, when the diamond discoveries made funds available to begin construction on the harbor, an ongoing project that would mirror the cycles of growth and decay in the local economy for decades to come.

East London's share of the South African export market rose dramatically from 2.9 percent to 23.1 percent between 1875 and 1890, and its share of the import market reached a high of 18.8 percent in 1895. East London was the major wool-export port, overtaking Cape Town in 1881, Durban in 1894, and Port Elizabeth in 1903. Other export commodities, more dependent on African household production, declined dramatically toward the end of the nineteenth century. Hide and skin exports, for example, reached a peak figure of six thousand tons in 1898, while maize exports virtually ceased between 1875 and 1885 and again between 1892 and 1910.

The Cape economy suffered severe economic depressions in the early–mid-1880s and again between 1905 and 1910, when East London and other major towns in the Ciskei region actually experienced a decline in population (Table 7.2). Maize briefly reemerged as an export crop during and immediately after World War I as prices rose and white farmers, increasingly subsidized by the state, began to enter the commercial market in greater numbers. Maize and maize products helped East London recover as a port, grabbing a record 23.7 percent of South Africa's export market in 1920.

Nevertheless, the seaport's primary exports before the war—wool (including angora hair), maize, hides, and skins—were in more or less permanent decline by the late 1920s. Virtually no maize, for example, was exported through East London between 1930 and 1952, and the port's share of the South African export market had slumped to a low of 4.5 percent by 1945. East London did not develop as an industrial city during this period. Most economic

Table 7.2. Ciskei's urban African population, 1904–1951

	1904	1911	1921	1936	1946	1951
East London						
Total	29,869	26,068	36,571	61,287	80,001	92,103
African	10,821	8,255	12,631	24,855	33,107	40,350
% total	36.2	31.7	34.5	40.6	41.4	43.8
King William's Town						
Total	14,185	13,930	15,654	16,709	17,762	21,768
African	6,091	5,864	6,958	7,636	8,146	11,399
% total	42.9	42.1	44.5	45.7	45.9	52.4
Queenstown						
Total	9,616	9,028	12,868	18,255	23,600	25,880
African	4,923	4,071	6,134	9,662	13,157	14,795
% total	51.2	45.1	47.7	52.9	55.8	57.2
Fort Beaufort						
Total	1,690	4,312	3,988	6,102	8,024	8,293
African	447	2,822	2,499	3,579	5,136	5,242
% total	26.5	65.5	62.7	58.7	64.0	63.2

SOURCE: SA Bureau of Statistics, *Urban and rural population of South Africa, 1904–1960*, Report No. 02-02-01, 129 (Table 4.1.1), 161 (Table 4.1.5).

activity revolved around the harbor and railway depot, the marketing (and to some extent processing) of farm products, and the import of goods destined for the African trade.

African labor built East London, and Africans lived on the fringes of the town from the earliest period of settlement. Nevertheless, they were continually subject to relocation by the authorities, the first of which occurred in December 1849.[74] East London became a municipality in 1873, but the bylaws did not even mention the black population. The city did not actually take formal jurisdiction over its African locations until 1876.

The African population would be subjected to repeated removals in the next fifteen years. An African political elite consisting of voters and other members of the mission-educated community had been established in East London by the 1880s, and they tried to resist relocation and seek a permanent housing site for themselves in the city. Local officials ignored their petitions, and the Cape attorney general ruled in January 1890 that the municipality had the right to move the locations whenever it pleased. East London's African locations, however, had been virtually consolidated by the end of 1890, and there was no need for further removals. The bulk of the African population was now housed in one location known as the East Bank location because it lay on the eastern side of the Buffalo River, and a much smaller community was housed in what was known as the West Bank location west of the river.

Members of the African (and Asian) community who held the franchise

were theoretically exempt from discriminatory legislation, including the location acts, and they had the right to reside in white East London. Local officials,
however, refused to recognize their status and continued to implement regulations that were designed to subordinate and segregate all persons of color in the
city. East London began issuing municipal passes in 1878 (the town was apparently unique in South Africa at the time in forcing women to carry passes),
imposed a night curfew (the only exceptions being African voters and workers
with passes from employers to stay in town), passed regulations barring whites
and American blacks from living in the locations, and appointed a full-time
inspector of locations (in 1880). The city council set the curfew for Africans at
8 P.M. in 1883 (a bell was rung every night for this purpose) and also banned
Africans from carrying knobkerries (sticks that could be used for walking or
fighting). Beer brewing was banned in the location in 1884, public bathing was
segregated in 1888, and all but one of the beaches were reserved for whites.

The African political elite was apparently not numerous enough to challenge these regulations until 1892, when a visitor to the city appealed the stick
rule in court. The local magistrate upheld the by-law, but the city lost on appeal
to the eastern Cape district court. The city then appealed to the Cape Supreme
Court, but again it was turned down.[75] The stick case had serious implications
for East London and other white municipalities because local regulations that
discriminated on the basis of color were not yet protected by parliamentary
statute. The city council, however, sent a private bill to parliament that would
allow municipalities to prevent Africans from carrying sticks and brewing beer,
and it was passed in 1893 (Local Bodies' Increased Powers Act 12 of 1893).

Now laws discriminating against the black community at the local level
could be enacted legally, and East London's city councillors gradually restored
the old regulations and invented new ones, like forbidding persons of color
from walking on municipal sidewalks or using municipal bathing areas (enforced from 1903) and from watching or playing sports on land set aside by
the municipality for recreational purposes (enforced from 1897), and banning
the fledgling black press (in this case *Izwi Labantu*) from attending city council
meetings (1899). There were less than six hundred Asians in East London in
1904, but the city fathers were determined to discourage further settlement
so Asians were forced to live in a concentration camp built during the South
African War. All attempts to reverse this edict failed, even though appeals
were lodged as far away as the British House of Commons. As East London
historian Keith Tankard puts it, "the town gained the reputation of being the
most racist in the Colony."[76]

A vigilance association was established in East London in 1893 as a result
of the stick case. The improvement of conditions in the locations—housing,
water and sewage, rents and roads, education and taxes—and the treatment
of Africans by the supervising authorities were the primary concerns of this

body in subsequent years. Although a road was built linking the location to the town and a pipe was laid to supply drinking water in the early 1890s, in reality very little was done to improve living standards. East London's African locations had virtually no streets, no lighting, sanitation, water facilities (there were eleven water faucets for about 9,500 people in 1916), or public housing until the 1920s.

As in other towns in the eastern Cape, most of the money Africans paid to the municipality in the form of hut taxes and other fees was actually spent on improving amenities for the city's white residents.[77] Irregular reports on the locations were provided by the local police and medical health officer, who were interested primarily in making sure these areas did not pose a crime or health risk to white East London.

African migration to East London ebbed and flowed, depending on economic conditions in the town and adjacent reserve. The official location population (including Khoi-Coloureds and Asians) rose dramatically from 752 in 1885 to 1,939 in 1894 to a peak of 12,111 in 1905 at the onset of the postwar depression. About two-thirds of the location population at the end of the South African War were males, and one half were prosperous enough (many were voters) to build their own huts on lots (forty feet by forty feet) made available to them by the municipality. The rest sought housing as lodgers in these dwellings, which were continually expanded to accommodate the excess population. Only the elite could afford to meet the specifications laid down for erecting a hut and pay the sanitary and water rate (two shillings a month) and the fee for renting out rooms to lodgers (four shillings a month).

A new influx of immigrants occurred during and after World War I, and the population continued to grow thereafter (Table 7.2). Under pressure from the secretary for native affairs, who thought funds obtained from Africans should be spent on African welfare, local authorities finally made a minimal attempt to improve conditions in the locations. The Africans would pay for these amenities under the terms laid down by the Native (Urban Areas) Act of 1923. This crucial measure was intended to control the movement of Africans from rural to urban areas and provide for the territorial segregation of Africans in town just as the 1913 Land Act had envisaged for Africans in the countryside.

Some municipal houses were built in the mid-1920s, and a few public amenities (some toilets, showers, laundry basins, more water faucets and street lights) were installed, but construction stopped abruptly in 1927 when the funds allotted from African taxes for this purpose were exhausted. No municipal houses at all were built for Africans in East London between 1927 and 1940, even though the African population virtually doubled to 24,855 between the official censuses of 1921 and 1936. Unofficial estimates of East London's African population were much larger than the official figures, moreover, throughout this period.[78] Two commissions of inquiry—the 1937 Thornton Commission and the 1949 Welsh Commission—condemned the municipality for its failure to house African residents, but the housing backlog would not begin to improve until the apartheid era.

The physical appearance of the locations before the 1950s was typical of urban African slums everywhere in South Africa. White East London in 1931, for example, was more than 4½ times larger than black East London. The East Bank location (known as Duncan Village), which contained 82 percent of the land set aside for Africans in the port city, housed most of the residents. Wattle-and-daub huts (ranging from one to eight rooms) were being replaced for the most part with shanties built out of wood and corrugated iron. Recreational as well as religious activity was centered in the churches, some of which also served as schools.[79] There were forty-four churches in black East London by 1931, and twenty-seven of these were independent churches not recognized by the government. The unrecognized churches, as we shall see, played a significant role in dissident African politics in the early 1930s.

East London during the interwar period was a depressed economy with a growing surplus of African labor. Wages were low both in terms of the cost of living in town and in relation to wages in other urban centers. Two separate estimates were made of average monthly expenditures (rent, food, clothing, and sundries for a household unit consisting of six persons), for example, in 1929. The figures provided by the Independent Industrial and Commercial Workers' Union of Africa, the dominant African trade union in East London at the time, were considerably higher than those provided by the public health officer—£7 13s. 7d. as opposed to £5 1s. 6d.—but both estimates were above average monthly incomes. Two years later in the midst of the Great Depression, the public health officer revised his estimate upward to £7 14s. 11d. a month.

The African male laborer was earning £4 a month on average or about £48 a year in 1931, virtually the same as he had earned in the early 1900s. A female domestic earned on average between £15 and £18 a year. Even the few semiskilled/skilled workers who earned about £60 a year did not make enough money to cover expenditures. Only some salaried professionals, like ordained mission clergy (£120–£156 a year) and qualified teachers (£60–£138 a year), could pay their bills. In most job categories, then, wages in town did not cover minimum living expenses, unless the family unit contained two or more wage earners and/or members were involved in illegal informal sector activities.

The African labor force (excluding pensioners, infants, and schoolchildren) in East London was estimated at 14,555 in 1931, about 71 percent of the estimated total African population (see Table 7.3). The professional elite comprised an insignificant percentage of the labor force. Most workers were unskilled male wage earners, and most of them continued to find employment in the harbor and on the railways. Stevedores (462), wagon/lorry

Table 7.3. Profile of East London's African
labor force in 1931 ($N = 14,555$)

Category	Number	% of total
Male	9,721	66.8
Unskilled workers	8,572	58.9
Semiskilled workers	695	4.8
Informal sector	402	2.8
Professional	52	0.4
Female	4,834	33.2
Domestic-type jobs	4,675	32.1
Nondomestic jobs	159	1.1

SOURCE: East London, *Report of the medical officer of health* (East London, 1931), 46–47 (adapted from Table 9).

drivers (148), and clerks/messengers/hotel porters (85) were designated as semiskilled wage earners. The nonwage-earning informal sector—the largely self-employed street vendors, artisans and producers of petty commodities—offered a variety of essential goods and services at prices the working poor could afford.

While there were still more men than women in town, female workers now formed one-third of the labor force. Most were formally employed as domestics of one kind or another, but a small number were involved in nondomestic jobs as "fresh produce dealers," wood sellers, tobacco sellers, "eating house keepers," and "boarding house keepers." Others were employed as sack repairers, wool sorters, cooks, waitresses, and midwives. It was the women, above all, who made ends meet by participating in illegal activities, especially the unlicensed hawking of produce and the making and selling of beer. Although 1,992 cases of beer brewing were brought to court in 1931—apparently all were women—this represented "a very small proportion" of those involved in the trade. The medical health officer observed that beer brewing "proceeds merrily" in the locations.[80]

Health conditions in East London's African locations were grim by any standards during this period (see Table 7.4). Vital statistics for the African population had been kept since 1908, and in the first twenty-three years the infant mortality rate fell below 300 (per 1,000 births) only twice. Since the birthrate was not high enough to offset the infant mortality rate, the increase in East London's African population was due mainly to immigration from the rural areas. In the 1940s, the infant mortality rate was apparently even worse, reaching a high of 587 (per 1,000 births) in 1943.

The African and white populations were comparable by the early 1930s—20,602 Africans and 20,672 whites lived in the port city, for example, in 1931.

Table 7.4. East London's African birth, infant mortality, and death rates, 1925–1930 (per 1,000)

Year	Births	Infant mortality	Deaths
1925–26	39.0	338.9	35.0
1926–27	44.0	331.0	43.0
1927–28	41.4	543.0	53.9
1928–29	41.1	322.0	31.9
1929–30	33.2	400.0	29.0

SOURCE: East London, *Report of the medical officer of health* (East London, 1931), 65.

But the African death rate in that year was almost three times higher than the white death rate, and the infant mortality rate more than six times higher. Children died primarily from intestinal and respiratory diseases (enteritis, acute diarrhea, and bronchitis) and adults from various forms of tuberculosis. TB, for example, accounted for 77 percent of the infectious diseases affecting the African population in 1930–31, and the death rate among Africans in the seaport regularly ranked among the highest in urban South Africa.[81]

7.4. State Intervention in the Reserves

The Native Affairs Department (NAD), created in 1910 with the merger of three of the four colonial agencies (the Orange Free State abolished its NAD in 1908), was nominally responsible for administering the reserves. English-speaking officials from the Cape, often the offspring of missionaries or colonial officials active in African affairs on the Cape's eastern frontier, dominated the NAD at this time. Although these officials had more or less abandoned the notion that they were the civilizing agents of Victorian culture, they continued to associate themselves with the Cape liberal tradition.

The NAD was relatively weak and fragmented[82] and without an effective departmental secretary or a full-time minister, but it had considerable autonomy under successive South African party coalition governments led by Louis Botha and his successor Jan Smuts. NAD officials remained committed to a tradition of pragmatic paternalism that had been a feature of African administration in the eastern Cape, and in colonial Natal (under Theophilus Shepstone and his successors). They saw themselves as secular missionaries who were charged with the responsibility to protect Africans as wards of the state and act as their ombudsmen in matters relating to government.

The legislative landmark in this liberal segregationist tradition was the 1920 Native Affairs Act. The all-white Native Affairs Commission was created to advise the authorities on matters involving Africans living outside as well as inside the reserves. Another consultative body, the Native Conference, made up of government-approved Africans from the urban and rural areas, would meet once a year to discuss matters deemed to be relevant to Africans. Local councils as envisaged in the 1894 Glen Grey Act would also be extended beyond the few rural districts in the eastern Cape where they had been implemented. A few years later Africans in town would be given a forum for discussion with the official recognition of location advisory boards. The 1920 act was welcomed by black and white liberals alike as a historic development in race relations, but within a decade the government had virtually derailed its own recommendations.

Saul Dubow has shown how African administration in South Africa was transformed during the interwar period.[83] The supposedly annual Native Conferences were virtually abandoned after 1927, except for one held in 1930 and several regional gatherings hastily put together in 1935 to consider Hertzog's Native Bills (see Chapter 8). Members of the all-white Native Affairs Commission were seriously divided over measures affecting Africans by the mid–late 1920s, but government officials were no longer paying attention to their deliberations anyway. No local councils for Africans in rural areas were established between 1920 and 1926, but several would be created (mainly in the Ciskei) after legislation was passed curtailing the authority of these councils (Act 27 of 1926). Although a number of urban advisory boards for Africans were created during these years, they had virtually no power to affect changes in the administration of African townships.

The NAD was gradually stripped of its Cape legacy and reorganized to meet the needs of a more demanding segregationist state. The department's policies and activities came under increasing scrutiny from the Public Service Commission and the powerful Justice Department during the early 1920s. The NAD's budget was cut, officials were forced into early retirement, and its staff reduced by 17 percent when Major J. F. Herbst, a convinced technocrat and an experienced administrator from South-West Africa, was appointed secretary for native affairs by Smuts in 1923.[84] He was retained when the National party under General J. B. M. Hertzog gained control of the government in 1924.

Personal autonomy and judgment in the conduct of African affairs were downgraded in favor of bureaucratic uniformity. Anthropologists, sociologists, and other academics would be utilized as social engineers to target problems and propose solutions in the reserves. Prospects for higher salaries and promotions would now be linked to proficiency in taking tests and acquiring more education. NAD administration was to become increasingly centralized and authoritarian, and the first full-time minister of native affairs (hitherto the portfolio had been controlled by the prime minister) was appointed in 1929.

The reserves were placed under the microscope with the creation of a subdepartment of native agriculture in 1929 and the appointment of a director and assistant directors for each of the various reserve regions—Northern Areas, Natal, Transkei and Ciskei. Operating on a slender budget of about thirty-seven thousand pounds a year in the 1930s (excluding the Transkei), for example, this agency would seek to establish experimental farms, employ trained African agricultural demonstrators, organize agricultural shows and stock sales, combat soil erosion, and construct irrigation works and various other land-reclamation projects in the reserves.

The Native Administration Act of 1927 offered concrete evidence that Hertzog intended to restore "tribal" authority and impose it on the whole of the African population. Based on precedents established in colonial Transkei and Natal, the chiefs would be reempowered, and customary courts, marriage rites, the *lobolo* system, and other principles of "native law and custom" (as codified by whites) would be standardized throughout the provinces and enforced. The governor-general was made the titular political ruler over all Africans: he could rule by proclamation, and his decisions would not be subject to challenge by the judiciary. The 1927 act would employ the NAD as an agency of social control to repress dissent, promote cultural ethnicity, and distance Africans even further from the rule of law as applied to white South Africa.

The attempt to retribalize the African population, however, was a complex and often a contradictory process. Dubow emphasizes the differences of opinion and emphasis in administering the 1927 act during the interwar period. For example, T. W. C. Norton, chief native commissioner for the Cape, and W. T. Welsh, chief magistrate for the Transkei, argued so forcefully against allowing chiefs and headmen to hear civil or criminal cases arising out of customary law that the Cape was finally excluded from proclamations issued in the name of the governor-general. On the other hand, a return to customary law was welcomed by many Africans, especially rural authority figures and their followers in the reserves "for whom 'tradition' was a means of fending off the demands of a capitalist economy and the incursions of the colonial administration."[85]

The 1927 act, then, returned the Native Affairs Department to a position of power in the administration of African affairs. The governor-general's directives were promulgated in practice by the minister of native affairs acting through the NAD, and these officials were supposed to enforce the state's segregationist policies inside and outside the reserves. Nevertheless, individuals within the department were still committed to the old Cape ideal of assimilation, and Dubow suggests they had a "moderating influence" on the segregationist policies pursued by the state during the interwar period.[86] In addition, the central government refused to spend much money on African administration. A minuscule 1–2 percent of the total budget (1912–36) was set aside for the NAD to carry out its responsibilities.

A uniform code of African administration in South Africa, moreover, would come about only when it could be imposed on the Cape as well as the other provinces. Africans in the Cape were not subject to the proclamations of the governor-general, the "Supreme Chief of all Natives" under the 1927 act, and African voters in the Cape still had a little political clout during white elections. Voters were also protected to some extent from the segregationist policies pursued by the Botha, Smuts, and Hertzog governments between 1910 and 1936: they did not have to carry passes, they were not subject in theory to regulations imposed on Africans in segregated rural and urban locations, and they could buy property anywhere in the province.

These rights were lost with the passing of the Representation of Natives Act (see Chapter 8) and the Native Trust and Land Act. Cape Africans like other Africans were now denied the vote and forbidden to buy land outside the reserves. The Land Act, approved by parliament in May 1936, would subject all Africans in the Cape to the conditions of the 1913 Land Act. The Native Affairs Department was still in charge of day-to-day administration in the reserves, but a new body called the South African Native Trust was created to acquire land the 1916–18 proposals had recommended should be added to these areas. The Native Trust would purchase and maintain control over all land obtained exclusively for Africans—scheduled reserves under the 1913 act, other areas set aside for African occupation between 1916 and 1935, and areas to be released to the reserves under the 1936 act. It would be the registered owner of all land not held in freehold in the reserves.

The policy of strict territorial segregation for Africans as envisaged in the 1913 Land Act, however, was abandoned. Africans would continue to be classified as migrants, and they would be housed separately in proclaimed white urban and rural areas, but Hertzog was not interested in expanding the reserves to accommodate the whole of the African population. Blacks displaced from white cities and farms would be pushed back to the reserves, but the amount of land to be added to these areas was less than either the 1916 Beaumont Commission or the 1918 land committees had envisaged. In theory, the reserves were to be enlarged by 7.25 million morgen (15.37 million acres), until they constituted 13.7 percent of South Africa's total land area. About 21.7 percent of this land had already been acquired for the reserves by 1936. Most of it was either already occupied or in arid areas far removed from the main African population centers.

The 1936 Land Act envisaged a more active role for the central government in terms of land conservation and resettlement inside the reserves. It also placed more restrictions on African sharecroppers and cash tenants on white farms. The farmers would now have to pay punitive fees to retain these "squatters"—the fee scale started at ten shillings per tenant for the first year and increased to five pounds after ten or more years. Africans resident on white farms were to be registered, and they had to provide at least four months of full-time service to the landowner. New nonlabor tenants were barred from taking up permanent residence on white-owned land, and in theory white farmers even had to get permission to have more than five labor-tenant families on their farms. It was an obvious attempt to reduce nonlabor tenants to labor tenants and ultimately to wage labor, and to redistribute African workers more equitably among the white farmers.

This provision (Chapter IV of the 1936 Land Act), however, could not be implemented in the countryside even in the late 1930s. Many if not most white farmers could not pay the fees, and they could not survive without nonwage labor. A mass eviction of "squatters" at this time would have had severe consequences for the farmers as well as their tenants, and the government announced to parliament in April 1936 it would not enforce these regulations. They would not be carried out anywhere in South Africa until the 1950s.

Government Advisory Bodies before the 1950s:
The Ciskeian General Council

The policies of the expanding segregationist state could be implemented only if Africans themselves played a greater role in the administration of areas set aside for them. And when local councils for the reserves were endorsed in the 1920 Native Affairs Act, the topic became a fixture in regional African politics.

Imvo crusaded for years to obtain local councils and a general council for the Ciskei region, even though many political activists were still fearful they might lose their voting rights if they accepted these councils. White-style village management boards had been created for Africans under the 1909 Mission Stations Act,[87] but these were withdrawn in 1920 on the promise that local councils would be provided. Africans in the locations paid taxes to white divisional councils but received virtually no benefits; hence they wanted local councils so they could control their own tax revenue. A native commissioner for the Ciskei was appointed in 1922, but *Imvo* complained bitterly that his "attitude" was "consistently one of opposition" to local councils. The newspaper also claimed he was trying to undermine the credibility of local political organizers by pitting "the intellectuals against the illiterate" and replacing rural leaders "of standing and influence" with "inferiors."[88]

After the powers of African councils were reduced in 1926, however, local councils in the Ciskei were established in King William's Town (Tamacha) and Middledrift (1926), Peddie and Victoria East (1927), Keiskammahoek (1928), Herschel (1930), and East London (1932). These councils were followed by the creation of the Ciskeian General Council in 1934 (a United Transkeian Territories General Council was also created in 1931). The Ciskeian General Council or Bunga represented only the local councils established for Africans in these seven districts and the Glen Grey District Council. One other council was created between 1934 and 1950 when Hewu (its administrative headquarters was the village of Whittlesea) was carved out of the Queenstown District in 1937.

The new councils were responsible for building and maintaining roads and bridges, providing dipping tanks for cattle, installing small dams, drains, and water furrows, improving water supplies, fencing, maintaining garden plots, and destroying poisonous weeds on grazing land. Each local council consisted of six members (they could have up to nine members), four elected and two appointed. An attempt was made to ensure parity between the various ethnic and "tribal" units, but this proved to be impossible because there were not enough funds to support representatives for every chiefdom in the district. All taxpayers except those from the Glen Grey District (an anomaly that was amended in 1943) could vote directly for local council and Bunga representatives.[89]

The Transkei Bunga controlled and dispersed all taxpayer revenue, but the Ciskei depended on a "federal" system in which each council contributed on average 12½ percent of its income to the Bunga, 12½ percent to the white-controlled divisional councils, and controlled the remaining 75 percent.[90] The Ciskei Bunga's already fragile position, then, was weakened further since it had access to only a relatively small percentage of the potential revenue at its disposal.

The revenue obtained from African taxes would be considerably greater after 1925, when the central government finally succeeded in consolidating the provincial tax laws. The previous African hut tax of ten shillings imposed on all married men (heads of households) was now effectively replaced by a tax on all men eighteen years of age and older. They were to pay a twenty-shilling general tax and a ten-shilling local tax each year for each residence owned or otherwise occupied. The local tax and one-fifth of the general tax were paid into a special account to help subsidize African education and provide services in the area where the tax was collected. In the Ciskei, the local tax was paid to the local councils. The portion of the general tax paid into the special account, now called the Native Development Fund, was gradually increased to 80 percent between 1935 and 1943—all earmarked for African education.

The 1925 Native Tax Act effectively tripled the basic tax from 10s. to 30s. a year. In addition, Africans in the Ciskei and other reserves were still subject to other taxes, rents, fines, and fees, in particular, the dog and wagon-wheel taxes,[91] divisional council taxes, and a fee for the right to rent land in areas released to the reserve. Taxes would increase from 12s. to 32s. a hut for communal landholders in the Ciskei reserve. For those with individual tenure, taxes would increase from 15s. 3d. to 35s. 3d. for each allotment.

The Ciskei Bunga made numerous attempts between 1934 and 1950 to obtain a greater proportion of the potential tax revenue and distribute the available funding more equitably, since some councils (Glen Grey being the most favored) generated more revenue than others. In 1939, 1942, and 1943, for example, several councillors sought to reduce the autonomy of the councils and redistribute revenue. A formal "unification" proposal seeking to absorb the local councils and control all revenue, however, was defeated overwhelmingly in 1944. Local bodies simply refused to relinquish what power they possessed to control and distribute their own revenue.[92]

The ineffectiveness of the Bunga as an administrative body became a source of considerable frustration. The councillors met four or five days only each year, usually in September. They were urged to discuss "matters of public interest relating to the economic, industrial or social conditions of the people" and to consider "any proposed legislation or existing law specially affecting the Natives,"[93] but in practice they had some control only over matters affecting public health and sanitation, hospitals and other medical services, afforestation and education. Revenue allocated to the general council, moreover, was "so small," as a special recess committee put it in 1944, "that its sphere of usefulness has been severely circumscribed."[94] As Bunga spokesman Alexander Jabavu once commented: "We do minor things with what we have in hand from the local tax."[95]

Even these minor things were circumscribed. As Appendix Table A7.8 (Ciskeian General Council Financial Statements, 1934–1950) illustrates, most of the money at the Bunga's disposal each year was never spent. The councillors could not create a finance committee to allocate these funds, and in practice the NAD (a white official was Bunga treasurer) controlled the subsidy just as it did at the local council level. The credit balance on expenditure allotted to the Bunga each year ranged from 25.8 percent to 56.1 percent, and the accumulated credit balance between 1934 and 1950 increased by slightly more than eighteen times to £17,105. Most of the money was placed with a government body—the Public Debt Commission—which offered very little interest on this investment and would have charged a penalty if it had been withdrawn. Despite protests from the local councils, it was not until 1950 that the Bunga succeeded in regaining even part of this revenue.[96]

The most important items of expenditure were education, agriculture, and medical care. Educational funds were allocated mainly for scholarships and occasionally to various schools for repairs and equipment. Funds previously earmarked for agriculture were apparently given to mission hospitals in the 1940s to supplement donations from other sources. The Bunga spent virtually nothing on public works after 1934—this was left to the local councils— while responsibility for preserving and extending the forested area was given to the Native Trust after the 1936 Land Act.[97] Administrative costs accounted for a significant proportion of expenditure in some years, reaching a high of 30.6 percent in 1942, but public health was a priority from 1944 when the government became more concerned about malnutrition in the reserve.

The local councils, on the front line in carrying out the central government's attempts to conserve the land and improve farming methods, were in a comparable position to that of the Bunga. The magistrates controlled the ten-shilling local tax paid to the local councils, and they refused to spend what little they received. Thus credit balances (and unpaid taxes) in the local councils also increased each year.[98]

A journalist who worked for the wartime Bureau of Information toured the reserves with NAD officials in 1944 in an attempt to project a more positive image of their activities. He attended a Glen Grey council meeting and made the following observation:

> The white magistrate sat up on his bench, and the Natives in a half-circle at desks down on the floor. . . . They sat there just a drab bunch of dejected-looking old men (most of them) come to hear what the magistrate considered suitable for them to listen to and discuss. . . . I am not lacking in a sense of history, and I was fully conscious that I was present at a session of what the official with me called "the mother and father of all District Councils". . . . I consoled myself with the realisation that soil erosion and the like are only the external part of the Ciskeian problem; soul erosion is the submerged part, and it goes much deeper.[99]

Dominance and Deviancy in the Bunga. The white chairmen of the local councils (all location magistrates had been attached to the NAD by 1928 and were called native commissioners) and the white chairman of the general council (the chief native commissioner for the Ciskei) were nonvoting members, but they controlled the agenda. Councillors (and outsiders who addressed the Bunga) were forbidden to discuss "political" matters, which was translated as anything that might provoke racial animosity.[100] As Bunga chairman, the chief native commissioner monitored debates and chided councillors when he thought they had made intemperate, inaccurate, or even foolish remarks. In a pictorial metaphor of dominance and dependency, black councillors inevitably stood on their feet and white native commissioners sat in chairs in official council photographs.

At one level of discourse, the councillors did conform to the roles they were expected to play in helping to legitimize the state's reserve policies. As the 1930–32 Native Economic Commission had anticipated:

> If recognition is accorded to [African] institutions in the administration of the Reserves, a great deal will be accomplished towards meeting the aspirations of Natives to have a share in their own government. This must inevitably have a favourable influence in their whole outlook in regard to the European.[101]

Undoubtedly their most prominent member between 1934 and his death in 1946, for example, was *Imvo Zabantsundu* editor Alexander Jabavu. The subservience to white authoritarian rule voiced by Jabavu and his colleagues during council debates became a public ritual, as in the following examples:

> Joseph Mphuthing (Herschel) in 1934: "The European is always respected. It is our nature to respect the white man."

Alexander Jabavu (King William's Town-Tamacha) in 1940: "I would like to tell our European friends that the Native mentality does not grasp things so quickly as the European mentality."
H. Tele (Peddie) in 1949: "All that is needed of us is to obey orders from our authorities." [102]

At another level of discourse, however, the councillors provided insight into what was really happening in the reserve, and they defended consistently and sometimes courageously the dignity of their people. Motions were passed urging the government to scrap the pass laws (1943), grant "universal suffrage" to all races in South Africa (1945), and remove "all discriminatory legislation" directed against blacks (1945). The councillors also spoke out against the National party's plans to abolish the native representatives in parliament, who had been created when Cape Africans lost their franchise rights (see Chapter 8). As Councillor Mzazi (Glen Grey) put it in 1949: "We have been deprived of nearly all our rights in this world. Now we learn that even the little thing we had is being taken away from us." [103]

The councillors' priorities as regards reserve matters are illustrated in Table 7.5, which is an attempt to quantify the motions placed before the Bunga and discussed between 1934 and 1950.[104] Members were concerned mainly with questions relating to land, education, transport facilities, and council administration.

The councillors had little authority to deal with land matters, but they spent much of their time debating this issue. They were also concerned with education, and motions were circulated in 1934, 1941, 1945, 1947, and 1949, for example, urging compulsory education for youths seventeen years of age and younger.[105] All appeals were turned down. The councillors were "crying for the moon," as one native commissioner put it, because there was not

Table 7.5. Ciskeian General Council subject agenda, 1934–1950 ($N = 502$)

Subject	Rank Order in %
Land acquisition and "development"	22.9
Education	17.3
Transportation facilities	17.1
Council affairs	16.3
Public health and poverty	9.4
"Tribal" matters	6.6
Taxes	3.4
War-related matters	2.6
Crime and unrest	2.4
White traders and labor recruiters	2.0
Total	100.0

SOURCE: Ciskeian General Council *Proceedings*, 1934–1950.

enough revenue from African taxes to pay for compulsory education.[106] Alexander Jabavu, however, knew where the money could be found: "Education can be subsidised by a share of the profits the Government gets from the mines. These great profits are only made possible by the cheap labour supplied by the Natives." [107]

The virtual absence of a public transport system was the subject of numerous motions, but virtually no money was spent on transport by either the Bunga or the white-controlled divisional councils, which received a portion of the African tax ostensibly to build and maintain roads in the locations. Even the native commissioners admitted: "there is just a suspicion that the Divisional Council loses sight of the fact that the [African] Local Councils are very large contributors to its funds." [108] Councillors repeatedly complained, in vain, about high fares, inadequate shelters, poor conditions of travel, and the limited employment opportunities for Africans in transport services.

Relatively fewer motions were circulated on more provocative issues. The general poverty of reserve residents was noted at nearly every council meeting. As N. Major Makwabe (Middledrift) put it in 1936: "the Native people are poor—they are starving." [109] But specific motions to relieve poverty usually entailed the creation of jobs in government service that would benefit the educated community—clerks in newly segregated post offices, interpreters in the courts, and more posts for educated Africans in the NAD and the Native Trust.

The retribalization of the Ciskei gathered momentum during the 1930s. The government began to recognize Xhosa and Mfengu chiefs for the region, and Ciskeian chiefs began holding yearly meetings in King William's Town.[110] Councillors urged that subsidies paid to chiefs and headmen be increased, and they wanted to give these "tribal" figures more authority in civil matters. As Jabavu put it: "It is a mistake to think that the Ciskei Native reserves have become so detribalized as to cause the chiefs to lose most of their influence." [111]

Councillors also sought relief from the burden of taxation for their most destitute constituents, some of whom were still taxed even though they were legally exempt,[112] and they tried in vain to gain control of miscellaneous taxes (especially the dog tax), court-imposed fines paid by Africans, and that portion of African revenue allocated to the divisional councils. Such long-standing grievances as white traders and labor recruiters operating within the reserve, however, were virtually ignored. Motions referring to crime and unrest were rare until the mid-1940s, when the central government stepped up its campaign to cull stock and control land use in the reserve.[113]

Government-imposed Development before the 1950s:
The "Betterment" Program

Official concern with soil erosion and land conservation in South Africa dates back to the late nineteenth century, and it was directed at white as well as black farmers.[114] Attention was more narrowly focused on the reserves with the Great Depression and the severe droughts of the 1930s, when the decline in food production was linked to what the authorities perceived as poor peasant farming methods and widespread misuse of the land. In reality, economic intervention was virtually inevitable as Africans in the periphery became more closely interwoven into South Africa's developing industrial economy. Traditional methods of conservation were no longer effective in an environment where peasant households were forced to live on subsubsistence holdings and exploit the land more and more intensively in order to survive.[115]

Before World War II, conservationist measures in the reserves focused on attempts to halt the further deterioration of the soil and regulate peasant farming practices. Officials sought initially to protect areas particularly vulnerable to erosion like the banks of streams and rivers and existing forest belts. They tried to establish new forest plantations and fill in eroded areas or build weirs across them. They also tried to get the peasants to use lighter plows requiring less oxen, to shift from plowing up and down hillsides to plowing along natural contour lines with intermittent terracing. African farmers' cooperatives were employed to introduce vegetable- and fruit-growing competitions and organize stock sales, and regulations restricting the entry of stock into locations were initiated as early as the 1920s.[116]

The 1936 Land Act, however, envisaged a much more radical shift in settlement and land use patterns in the reserves by suggesting that so-called Betterment locations be proclaimed and the ground divided into residential, arable, and grazing areas with regulations to limit stock and protect the soil. The first Betterment scheme for the reserves was supposed to demarcate separate grazing areas and seal them off from cultivated land and residences, but it focused only on culling stock. It was presented to the Natives' Representative Council in 1937, and the Ciskei Bunga reluctantly accepted the proposal in 1938.[117]

The Ciskei was regarded as a kind of test case. Livestock Control and Improvement Proclamation No. 31 of 1939 was first introduced in African locations in the King William's Town (Tamacha) District. Stock culling was to take place only after the householders concerned had been consulted and a majority were in favor of the plan. Government officials in conjunction with the local council would determine how many stock were allowed to remain on grazing land in each location. Culled stock—mainly diseased or ill-fed animals and bulls and rams of poor quality—would be sold or otherwise removed from the proclaimed area rather than slaughtered. Officials optimistically hoped to reduce the number of cattle in South Africa's reserves by 50 percent, but voluntary Betterment locations were confined mainly to the Ciskeian districts of King William's Town, Middledrift, Glen Grey, and Herschel, and very little was accomplished after the coming of World War II.

The state intervened again in 1945, and development planning in the later

1940s shifted from stock culling and land conservation to population resettlement.[118] Anticipating the prospect of absorbing a flood of returning soldiers as
well as tenants being displaced from white farms, various African bodies were
informed of a new "Rehabilitation" scheme for the reserves. It was outlined in
detail to councillors at a special session of the Ciskei Bunga in January 1945.[119]

The proposal was very similar to ones that would be implemented under
apartheid in the next generation. Planning committees would be created in the
reserves, and the peasant population would be divided into permanent farmers
and migrant wage laborers. Both groups would be removed from scattered
homesteads and relocated in residential villages. The full-time farmers would
be allotted a single plot of arable land and subjected to the regulations imposed
in the proclaimed Betterment locations. The nonfarm population—peasants
who were not given arable land, other landless peasants, and refugees who
had been forced to return to the reserve—would be resettled as near as possible to existing centers of industrial employment. No stock or separate garden
plots—a key provision—would be allowed in the nonfarm villages, and jobless
workers were subject to eviction.

The Rehabilitation scheme generated considerable debate in the Ciskei
Bunga. Jabavu, for example, acknowledged "that a period of crisis in the
economic and social life of the Natives is at hand," but he and his colleagues
rejected the proposal at the January 1945 meeting.[120] The councillors reiterated
the traditional peasant position that overpopulation rather than overstocking
was the primary factor in "the deterioration of their land." As H. Phooko (Herschel) put it: "If we reduce the stock we deprive the people of food and milk and
they will be left emaciated skeletons. What will happen to them?"[121] Outgoing
secretary of native affairs Douglas L. Smit (1934–45) bluntly told members
there would be no more land for the reserve. His successor, Gordon Mears
(formerly the Ciskei's chief native commissioner and the son of a missionary),
had already warned them in 1938 that if they did not accept the government's
proposals voluntarily, "sooner or later compulsion will be justified."[122]

The Transkei Bunga finally approved the Rehabilitation scheme in April
1945, and the Ciskei Bunga was browbeaten into submission in September.
Although the authority to resettle the population and impose separate residential, arable, and grazing areas in these locations was not given until 1949
(Proclamation No. 116),[123] all released land acquired by the Native Trust for the
reserves was automatically Betterment land. Virtually all locations controlled
by local councils in the Ciskei had accepted the new regulations by the end of
the decade.

The first peri-urban village for industrial workers inside South Africa's
reserves was built in the Ciskei on land purchased by the Native Trust near
King William's Town. The designated occupants for Zwelitsha (New Era), as
the township was somewhat ironically called, were supposed to be landless

peasants from the reserve and tenants who had been forced off white-owned farms. The main source of employment was a cotton textile mill to be built about 3½ miles from the township outside the reserve.

Zwelitsha was a blueprint for future government schemes to promote industries inside and on the borders of existing African reserves. It was financed by state capital in the form of the Industrial Development Corporation (established in 1940). The IDC would train African labor to build the township of Zwelitsha inside the reserve, and Calico Printers Association of Manchester (England) would provide capital and skilled workers to develop the Good Hope Textile Mill outside the reserve. Calico Printers and the IDC would each hold 50 percent of the shares in the new company. Zwelitsha would eventually become the capital of the Ciskei Homeland and the western terminus of a vast complex of black dormitory suburbs stretching from white-owned King William's Town to white-owned East London.[124]

Privileged Farmers. Land released to the reserve after the 1936 Land Act—most of it of marginal value in terms of cultivation—was virtually off limits to local residents.[125] Gibson Maneli's (Victoria East) lament was echoed repeatedly in the Ciskei Bunga during this period:

> We leaders today are taken as people who are not trustworthy, so much so that we old leaders are being regarded as enemies, and the time is approaching when people will not accept anything from us, because there are many things we have promised them because we had been promised by the Government, and the Government has not fulfilled its promises.[126]

The Betterment projects that were implemented inside the reserve before the 1950s favored the few remaining semicommercial farmers, those who still had enough land and capital to participate marginally in the market economy. The privileged elite, moreover, had the best hope of gaining access to land purchased by the Native Trust for the reserve. The Native Affairs Commission noted in 1940 that it would give primary consideration to "the special needs of Natives of an advanced and progressive type" when looking for farmers who would occupy beneficially "newly acquired land." [127]

The first Betterment areas had been proclaimed in the surveyed locations where the mission-educated community predominated. A typical profile of the "progressive" farmer at this time would have included at least a primary school education, adherence to an officially recognized (and preferably mission) church, ties to headmen or chiefs, access to more than the minimal plot of land, and ownership of more than the minimal number of stock, especially cattle and sheep.[128]

The distinction between landed and landless was undoubtedly the most important single factor governing social relationships between groups within the reserve before the 1950s, but other cleavages existed between landowners, their tenants, and communal landholders. Shelton Peteni (Keiskammahoek), for example, told his fellow councillors in 1935: "I have people under me on my farm. I give a man time to make up his hut, but he goes to a beer drink, and I am bound with my wife to put up a hut for him; the man does not do his part." [129] Communal landholders also regarded themselves as superior to the tenants and to those landless who obtained garden plots from the Native Trust after 1936. The landowners dominated political and economic activities, and there was apparently little intermarriage with nonlandowners.[130]

The local councils decided when and where development would take place, and these projects clearly benefited the wealthier farmers and their councillor patrons. They were the ones who attended council meetings and participated in the political process, but they were also severely hampered by the one-man-one-lot rule and could not acquire land outside their magisterial districts.[131]

State support for the growth of a capitalist farming class inside the reserves was minimal during this period. Only the Native Trust could promote Betterment in these areas. The central government would not provide loan capital to Africans for commercial farming or industrial development. They could not even borrow money from the Land and Agricultural Bank, set up in 1912 to assist white farmers, even though African tax revenue helped fund the institution. Opportunities for landless or otherwise displaced peasants to learn trades or acquire businesses within the reserves, moreover, were remote before the 1950s. White entrepreneurs were also effectively prevented from investing inside these areas under the 1913 and 1936 Land Acts because they could not buy or lease land in designated African areas.

The practical impact of the central government's economic intervention in the reserves was negligible before the apartheid era. Legislation was passed and the reserves' role in the South African political economy was more carefully defined and described—especially from the 1930s—but few Betterment regulations were enforced. Even in the Ciskei, the one reserve where everyone concerned agreed that something had to be done, very little in fact was done.

The peasants were not consulted when it came to development planning, and regulations were implemented largely without their cooperation. For the mass of the people, there was no real incentive to support the council system or to cooperate with the coopted councillors in carrying out the government's Betterment/Rehabilitation policies.[132] Grossly inadequate funding, a dearth of administrative and technical expertise, and, above all, peasant opposition would effectively neutralize official attempts to promote Betterment. The authorities acknowledged "a general spirit of non-cooperation," and "in certain areas" there was "active resistance" by the late 1940s. The "rehabilitation program" was "lagging behind" in all the reserves: "deterioration is swiftly outrunning reclamation and the seriousness of the position cannot be exaggerated." [133]

Appendix

Table A7.1. Ciskei reserve land proposals, 1913–1918 (in morgen: 1 morgen = 2.12 acres)

Magisterial district	Scheduled reserve 1913[a]	Land occupied by Africans 1916[b]	Beaumont Commission additions 1916[a]	Cape Committee revisions 1918[c]	Proposed reserve
Cathcart	—	13,436	1,889	—	1,889
East London	11,479	25,763	3,200	+28,743	43,422
Fort Beaufort	15,401	11,216	—	—	15,401
Glen Grey	268,319	245,612	—	—	268,319
Herschel	206,156	206,138	—	—	206,156
Keiskammahoek[d]	—	—	—	—	—
King William's Town	265,347	223,901	2,160	−141 +6,156	273,522
Komgha	3,209	57,469	4,267	+1,400	8,876
Middledrift[d]	—	—	—	—	—
Peddie	63,725	78,745	15,982	+5,483	85,190
Queenstown	64,973	82,435	17,982	+900	83,855
Stockenstrom	—	2,077	—	—	—
Stutterheim	7,860	34,075	8,712	−8,000 +1,000	9,572
Victoria East	21,302	29,600	2,434	−2,434 +11,202	32,504
Total	927,771	1,010,467	56,626	+44,309	1,028,706

[a]Source: *Report of the Natives' Land Commission*, Vol. 1, UG 19-1916, 10–16, 43.

[b]Source: Ibid., Appendix 3. Includes the scheduled reserve areas, mission land, African-owned farms and crown land occupied by Africans that were not yet designated as part of the scheduled reserve, and white-owned land fully occupied by Africans.

[c]Source: *Report of the Local Natives' Land Committee*, Cape Province, UG 8-1918, 10–14, 19.

[d]Keiskammahoek and Middledrift were still part of the King William's Town District.

Table A7.2. Population of Ciskeian magisterial districts, 1911–1951

Magisterial district	1911	1921	1936	1946	1951
Cathcart	12,518	14,266	14,656	18,067	15,662
African	9,418	11,335	12,297	14,847	13,643
% total	75.2	79.5	83.9	82.2	87.1
% rural	92.7	91.0	88.9	86.2	84.4
East London	47,711	61,433	94,122	118,377	133,102
African	27,311	34,360	53,781	67,108	76,121
% total	57.2	55.9	57.1	56.7	57.2
% rural	70.3	63.7	53.2	50.1	46.3
Fort Beaufort	13,987	12,719	17,374	19,219	18,923
African	10,889	9,821	13,424	15,301	14,910
% total	77.9	77.2	77.3	79.6	78.8
% rural	38.8	39.9	67.2	61.0	61.2
Glen Grey	50,736	42,898	64,638	66,688	65,716
African	49,629	41,836	63,624	65,957	65,008
% total	97.8	97.5	98.4	98.9	98.9
% rural	99.7	99.5	99.3	99.0	99.1
Herschel	39,078	38,084	38,644	48,394	50,273
African	37,498	36,622	37,289	46,982	48,777
% total	96.0	96.2	96.5	97.1	97.0
% rural	100.0	100.0	100.0	100.0	100.0
Keiskammahoek (Part of King William's Town District)			18,105	18,391	19,032
African			16,830	17,243	18,029
% total			93.0	93.8	94.7
% rural			93.8	92.9	92.6
King William's Town	106,474	104,590	66,143	68,195	71,055
African	94,303	91,998	55,253	57,213	59,298
% total	88.6	88.0	83.5	83.9	83.5
% rural	88.7	89.3	85.5	85.2	80.3
Komgha	16,355	15,194	17,074	20,099	20,880
African	14,474	13,479	15,082	18,298	18,934
% total	88.5	88.7	88.3	91.0	90.7
% rural	97.9	97.4	96.5	96.2	93.3
Middledrift (Part of King William's Town District)			25,978	25,621	25,149
African			25,564	25,317	24,818
% total			98.4	98.9	98.7
% rural			99.8	99.8	99.6

(table continued on following page)

Table A7.2 Population of Ciskeian magisterial districts, 1911–1951 (*continued*)

Magisterial district	1911	1921	1936	1946	1951
Peddie	20,946	22,382	26,848	27,035	26,917
African	19,210	20,836	25,377	25,822	25,827
% total	91.7	93.1	94.5	95.5	96.0
% rural	94.6	97.9	92.7	90.7	90.4
Queenstown	32,905	39,338	41,893	50,294	52,398
African	22,777	27,845	30,951	37,520	39,131
% total	69.2	70.8	73.9	74.6	74.7
% rural	60.9	69.9	67.1	63.3	60.7
Stockenstrom	10,641	10,751	12,363	11,938	11,370
African	6,531	7,154	8,540	8,612	8,128
% total	61.4	66.5	69.1	72.1	71.5
% rural	91.6	91.4	95.9	94.3	90.9
Stutterheim	13,305	15,237	19,380	24,815	25,329
African	10,595	12,569	16,155	20,966	21,499
% total	79.6	82.5	83.4	84.5	84.9
% rural	72.8	71.8	70.0	67.8	64.6
Victoria East	16,275	15,083	16,645	18,894	19,196
African	14,339	13,179	14,667	16,858	17,089
% total	88.1	87.4	88.1	84.5	89.1
% rural	91.4	88.8	87.0	86.2	82.6
Total	380,931	391,975	473,863	536,027	555,002
African	316,974	321,034	388,834	438,044	451,212
% total	83.2	81.9	82.1	81.7	81.3
% rural	86.2	86.2	84.5	82.2	79.4

SOURCE: Census returns UG 15-1923 (1911 and 1921), UG 21-1938 (1936), UG 42-1955 (1946 and 1951).

Table A7.3. African population in the Ciskei reserve, ca. 1916–1951

Magisterial district	1916[a]	1936[b]	1951[c]
Cathcart	1,322	1,322?	534
East London	7,496	10,000	11,442
Fort Beaufort	3,088	3,088	4,683
Glen Grey	50,320	73,600	64,430
Herschel	39,078	36,300	48,671
Keiskammahoek	—	15,300	16,682
King William's Town	84,280	41,500	44,289
Komgha	5,802	5,802?	1,432
Middledrift	—	25,400	24,650
Peddie	14,605	18,100	18,777
Queenstown	9,376	(included in Glen Grey)	13,273
Stockenstrom[d]	—	—	—
Stutterheim	5,022	5,022?	3,274
Victoria East	14,739	9,800	10,905
Total[e]	235,128	245,234?	263,042

[a] SOURCE: *Report of the Natives' Land Commission (Beaumont Commission)*, UG 19-1916, Vol. 1, Appendix 4. These figures are extrapolated from the 1911 election returns, and they include Africans living on designated locations, on crown land, on mission-owned land, on land owned but not occupied by whites, and on African-owned farms.

[b] SOURCE: *Social and Economic Planning Council Report 9*, UG 32-1946 ("The Native Reserves and their place in the economy of the Union of South Africa"), 8 (Table 1). The number of Africans in locations in three magisterial districts (Cathcart, Komgha, and Stutterheim) apparently did not change between 1916 and 1936.

[c] SOURCE: *Report of the Commission for the Socio-Economic Development of the Bantu Areas within the Union of South Africa (Tomlinson Commission)*, UG 61-1955, Vol. 15, Annexure 1. Locations near Humansdorp, west of Port Elizabeth, with a population of 1,429 Africans, were included in the Ciskei region by the Tomlinson Commission.

[d] Although Stockenstrom had no designated African locations, 176 Africans either owned their own farms or lived as tenant farmers on white-owned farms in the district in 1916.

[e] The official estimates of the Bureau of Census are considerably higher than these figures. According to this evidence, the reserve population increased from 244,884 in 1911 to 334,967 in 1951—a growth rate of 36.8 percent. The sources used by the census are not given. Bureau of Census and Statistics, *Union statistics for fifty years: Jubilee issue*, A-9.

Table A7.4. Profile of King William's Town (including
Keiskammahoek and Middledrift) District in 1910

1. Population and land tenure in the African locations

Population[a]	Land tenure
106,474 (1911 census)	All but eight locations surveyed by 1903

Observed density: overcrowded in all African areas of the district.

2. Grain and stock production in the locations

Grain production unknown. Main crops were maize and sorghum. Stock
included 177,500 cattle, 253,000 sheep, 120,500 goats.[b] Observed density:
overstocked in Keiskammahoek and Middledrift.

3. Taxation[c]: direct taxes (per year).

Unsurveyed locations	Surveyed locations
Hut tax—10s. a hut (household head).	Quitrent—12s. 9d. for each allotment (household head).
Special tax—2s. a hut (Divisional Council).	Special tax—2s. 6d. for each allotment (Divisional Council).

Taxes owed in surveyed and unsurveyed locations totaled £1,356 in 1910.
Each African also paid an estimated 2s. 6d. in *indirect taxes* (custom duties).

4. African wages in the district (per year)

	KWT (Tamacha)	Keiskammahoek	Middledrift
Domestic workers (men/women)	£9–£18 + rations (men)	unknown	£6 + rations
Farm workers	£9–£18 + rations (men)	—	£6 + rations (men)
Semiskilled workers[d]	£28 8s.–£48 no rations	—	£12 no rations

SOURCE: *Blue Book on Native Affairs*, U17-1911, sections on vital statistics,
food supply, agriculture, stock, taxation, and labor.

[a] The African population density for the district was estimated at 49.7 per
square mile in 1891 (tied with Victoria East as the highest in the Ciskei) and
79.4 in 1921. An estimated 129,000 Africans lived in the district in 1903.
South African Native Races Committee, *The Natives of South Africa* (London, 1901), map; *SANAC*, Vol. 2, 787–90 (evidence of Ernest Rein, acting
registrar of deeds for the district); census return for 1921, UG 15-1923.

[b] A few horses but no mules or donkeys were found in the African locations
in this district.

[c] The special tax in unsurveyed locations that went to the divisional council
was essentially a road rate. Quitrents included a stamp duty that varied between 3d. and 6d. for each allotment. In some areas, the quitrent varied for
additional allotments. Most household heads also paid various license fees,
in particular a dog tax that varied from 2s. 6d. to 5s. per dog. Those who
had wagons paid a wheel tax that was 7s. 6d. in the Cape. African tenants
on white farms also paid a hut tax.

[d] Storemen, drivers, and messengers generally made up this subcategory.
Wages paid to unskilled town laborers in this district are unknown.

Table A7.5. African production and expenditure in the Victoria East District location in 1875 and 1925 (in £)

Cash income from grain and stock production[a]		
	1875	1925
Wool	12,541	6,471
	(250,620 lbs)	(157,210 lbs)
Hides	1,317	806
Skins	1,093	922
Horns	47	—
Maize/Sorghum[b]	4,275	2,177
	(372,420 lbs)	(212,875 lbs)
Total	19,273	10,376

Cash expenditure		
	1875	1925
Farm tools (mainly plows & hoes)	1,416	778
Clothing (mainly blankets)	12,000	4,792
Boots and shoes	14,440	532
Household goods	1,708	613
Books/stationery/misc.	220	585
Food	4,289	12,748
Total	21,073	20,048

Cash income from production and cash expenditure per family unit[c]		
	1875	1925
Production	£20 12s. 0d.	£4 8s. 9d.
Expenditure	£20 2s. 0d.	£9 5s. 5d.

SOURCE: James Henderson, principal of Lovedale, as recorded in *S.A. Outlook* 1 July 1927, 130–31.

[a] In 1875 production of hides, skins, and horns was tabulated by number and in 1925 by weight.

[b] The original figure was expressed as 74,484 bags of maize and sorghum. The standard weight of a bag of grain was 200 lbs.

[c] Henderson assumed there were on average six persons per family unit in 1875 and 1925. His estimate excluded the minor children of dependent relatives living in the home.

Table A7.6. Livestock production in the Ciskei reserve, 1927–1953

	1927	1930	1934	1936	1939	1948/49	1949/50	1953
Cattle units [a]	391,763	412,163	329,563	367,163	412,963	394,373	304,465	408,261
% excess carrying capacity (above 234,000 units)	67.4	76.1	40.8	56.9	76.5	68.8	30.1	74.5
Cattle number	190,000	179,000	154,000	188,000	216,000	194,145	130,417	185,331
% cattle units	48.5	43.4	46.7	51.2	52.3	49.2	42.8	45.4
Sheep number	624,000	750,000	514,000	542,000	591,000	560,599	453,702	618,484
% cattle units	31.9	36.4	31.2	29.5	28.6	28.4	29.8	30.3
Goats number	276,000	307,000	255,000	245,000	285,000	331,724	307,723	387,351
% cattle units	14.1	14.9	15.5	13.3	13.8	16.8	20.2	19.0
Horses/donkeys number	21,763[b]	21,800	21,763[b]	22,400[c]	21,763[b]	21,763[b]	21,763[b]	21,090
% cattle units	5.6	5.3	6.6	6.1	5.3	5.5	7.2	5.2

SOURCES: Calculations based on data compiled by the *Social and Economic Planning Council Report 9* (UG 32-1946), *Reports of the Department of Native Affairs* for 1948–49 and 1949–50 (UG 51-1950, UG 61-1951), and the *Tomlinson Commission Report* (UG 61-1955), 79.

[a] One head of large stock (cattle, horses, mules, donkeys) and five head of small stock (sheep, goats) is the equivalent of one "cattle unit." Small stock such as pigs and poultry are not included. The carrying capacity of the land in the Ciskei reserve was estimated at 234,000 cattle units. *Fagan Commission* (UG 28-1948), 15.

[b] Since the number of horses and donkeys in the reserve seems to have remained relatively constant, the figure of 21,763 cattle units (based on the mean for 1930, 1937, and 1953) was used in years where no data were available. There were virtually no mules in the reserve during this period.

[c] 1937 estimate.

Table A7.7. District hospitals in the Ciskei region with beds for Africans in 1936 and 1945

District	No. hospitals, Mission (M)/ Province (P)		No. beds		No. persons per bed	
	1936	1945	1936	1945	1936	1945
Cathcart	—	1 (P)	—	9	—	1,650
East London	—	1 (P)	—	268	—	250
Fort Beaufort	—	1 (P)	—	22	—	696
Glen Grey	—	1 (M)	—	200	—	330
Herschel[a]	1 (M)	?	84	?	444	?
Keiskammahoek	1 (M)	1 (M)	25	55	673	314
King William's Town[a]	2 (M/P)	1 (P)?	102	46?	542	1,244?
Komgha	—	—	—	—	—	—
Middledrift[b]	—	1 (private)	—	12	—	2,110
Peddie	—	—	—	—	—	—
Queenstown[a]	2 (M/P)	1 (P)?	73	69	424	544?
Stockenstrom	—	—	—	—	—	—
Stutterheim	—	—	—	—	—	—
Victoria East	1 (M)	2 (M)	175	250	84	67
Total[c]	7	10?	459	931	847	471?

SOURCES: F. W. Fox & D. Back, "A preliminary survey of the agricultural and nutritional problems of the Ciskei and Transkeian territories," confidential unpublished report, Johannesburg, 1941, 164 (Table 8); *S.A. Outlook* 1 January 1946, 7 (Ciskeian Missionary Council regional medical survey for 1945).

[a] Mission hospitals at Herschel, King William's Town, and Queenstown were reported in 1936 but not in 1945.

[b] A maternity hospital at Middledrift was established by Roseberry T. Bokwe, an African physician with a medical practice in the district. He was the only African district surgeon in South Africa at the time.

[c] The total number of beds in 1936 and 1945 as given in this table differs from the totals recorded by Fox & Back and the *Outlook,* which were 441 and 961, respectively. There is no explanation for the discrepancy, although one mission hospital at Xalanga in the Transkei was incorrectly placed in the Ciskei in 1936.

Table A7.8. Ciskeian General Council financial statements in even-numbered years, 1934–1950

Year	1934	1936	1938	1940	1942	1944	1946	1948	1950
1. Total revenue each year (£)	1,891	6,336	9,324	11,403	14,637	18,424	19,550	21,475	23,060
2. Expenditure each year (£)									
a. Allocated	1,330	4,101	4,349	4,889	4,693	4,803	8,040	6,919	8,016
b. Spent	934	2,191	2,381	2,147	3,066	3,563	3,644	4,715	5,954
3. Payments each year (% of expenditure)									
a. Council matters									
Salaries/transport	0.4	0.2	0.2	0.2	0.1	0.1	0.4	0.1	0.1
Printing/stationery/misc.	17.5	7.6	11.7	6.0	30.6	14.8	12.4	8.9	6.4
b. Education	12.7	18.9	28.2	35.1	23.1	23.0	19.5	27.7	31.1
c. Afforestation	8.4	11.3	10.5	4.9	4.4	5.6	8.6	1.3	1.1
d. Agriculture	22.1	42.0	27.0	19.7	2.9	7.6	10.2	12.7	9.7
e. Hospitals	21.4	19.4	21.8	28.0	30.0	25.9	23.0	17.8	37.8
f. Public health	0.8	0.6	0.6	6.2	8.8	23.0	25.9	31.6	13.9
g. Public works	16.8	0.4	0.1	—	—	—	—	—	—
4. Credit balance each year (£)	957	4,145	6,943	9,256	11,571	14,861	15,906	16,760	17,105
a. % of allocated expenditure	29.8	46.6	45.3	56.1	34.7	25.9	54.7	31.9	25.8
b. % of total revenue	50.6	65.4	74.5	81.2	79.1	80.7	81.4	78.0	74.2

SOURCE: Ciskeian General Council *Proceedings,* financial statements 1934–51. All figures calculated to the nearest pound equivalent, and where available the audited reports were used.

8
Opposition Politics and Popular Resistance I

Class boundaries in African society were neither rigid nor clearly defined in the generation after union in 1910. As a number of scholars have noted, the petty bourgeoisie was fragmenting downward at an accelerated pace, and alliances between social groups that might otherwise have been differentially placed in the relations of capitalist production were increasing.[1]

As discrimination and repression at all levels intensified, more and more Africans on the fringes of the lower middle class descended into the ranks of the impoverished proletariat. Wage scales were so low that even the most educated African white-collar workers had little opportunity to emulate the lifestyles of their European counterparts. It is not surprising that especially in periods of hegemonic crisis alienated fractions of the African petty bourgeoisie would find common cause with industrial workers and peasants in defying the status quo.

Such a crisis occurred in the years immediately following World War I. Soaring food prices, low wages, and job discrimination temporarily galvanized African workers, especially on the Witwatersrand, where a wave of wildcat strikes and boycotts appeared to threaten civil order. Nationalists within the South African Native National Congress (SANNC)—renamed the African National Congress (ANC or Congress) in 1923—were divided over the most appropriate response to take toward industrial strife, and mobilizing workers briefly radicalized African politics in the Transvaal. In the countryside, a malnourished population succumbed to outbreaks of smallpox, typhoid, cholera, and the dreaded 1918–19 influenza epidemic,[2] while fluctuating grain prices, prolonged drought, and plant and animal diseases posed a continuing threat to food and stock production, especially in the reserves.

The ruling South African party responded in part by creating several consultative bodies. As noted in the previous chapter, they included the all-white Native Affairs Commission, the Native Conferences, the promise of more local/regional councils for Africans in rural areas and the recognition of location advisory boards for Africans in urban areas. These measures signaled a

desire on the part of the central government to use moderate African nationalists as intermediaries in the ongoing process of formulating an African public
opinion that would support the existing political order.

The process of cooption in the cities had already begun during World
War I, when white liberals with the backing of mining capital began forming
welfare associations in a bid to improve African living standards. Following
the end of hostilities, a number of social and recreational facilities for Africans
were established, most notably in Johannesburg. These became cultural venues
for the parties, contests, concerts, film shows, speeches, and meetings targeted
specifically at the urban African petty bourgeoisie. Parallel cultural organizations were also created for Africans already segregated in other spheres of
activity. The Pathfinders and Wayfarers, for example, would duplicate the Boy
Scouts and Girl Guides. Clinics and creches, night schools, libraries and reading rooms, and literary, debating, and drama groups for Africans were started
on the Rand. Sports, games, and film shows were also introduced in mining
compounds in and around the golden city.[3]

The joint-council movement was the most important political response
by white liberals to the grievances of the African petty bourgeoisie during the
interwar period.[4] They were modeled initially on interracial committees being
established in the rural areas of some southern U.S. states. In a segregated
society, it was argued, dialogue at the local level moderated racial tension
and offered blacks an opportunity to lobby for limited political and economic
rights. The joint councils and their ideological allies would appeal in particular
to mission-educated Africans, who continued to accept white trusteeship as
the best guarantee that their existing rights and privileges would be protected.

The first joint council was organized in Johannesburg in 1921, a year after
a massive African mine workers' strike on the Witwatersrand. There were
twenty-six joint councils in the major cities and towns of South Africa by 1930
and about forty by 1935. The agents of cooption comprised a cross section of
the white liberal petty bourgeoisie. Clergy were well represented, and it was
the Dutch Reformed church, for example, that took the lead in organizing two
European-Bantu conferences in 1923 and 1927 in conjunction with the joint
councils. University academics, teachers, lawyers, journalists, businessmen,
and even municipal officials and government civil servants joined the councils
and were involved in their activities. Supplementing the councils were various
interracial mission, church, and student welfare–cum–civil rights groups.

While subscriptions were kept low for black members in an attempt to
ensure racial parity, it was clear from the beginning that white members would
provide the leadership in the joint councils. They had the time and money, the
contacts with white officialdom, and the experience in white party politics.
Above all, they were committed to redirecting the liberal discourse toward an
accommodation with the government's segregationist policies.[5]

These policies expanded dramatically after the so-called 1922 Rand Revolt in response to the demands of European blue-collar and lower-ranked white-collar workers. The confrontation pitted capital against white labor in South Africa's industrial heartland and resulted in the death of more than two hundred people (including about thirty blacks, who were killed by white mobs). Striking white mine workers had formed commandos and threatened to take over Johannesburg and adjacent mining towns, and Smuts had employed armed and mounted troops, heavy artillery, and even planes to suppress them. A National party–dominated coalition government under the leadership of Barry Hertzog, another ex-Boer War general and a cabinet minister in Louis Botha's 1910 government, came to power in 1924 and enacted a legislative program in the next fifteen years that was designed to reduce virtually all Africans to the status of minimum wage labor.

The African petty bourgeoisie was now clearly in danger of being pushed wholesale into the ranks of the working poor and unemployed. Some groups found a political haven in the ANC, but personality conflicts, ethnic differences, and tensions between members over the tactics of protest and the suitability of alliances with non-African groups severely weakened its credibility. Congress was a fragile and deeply fragmented organization during the interwar period, poorly administered and without funds to supervise and coordinate branch activities.

Alienated African nationalists found other alternatives in their own independent local and regional political organizations, in a burgeoning African trade union movement that was epitomized during the 1920s by the Industrial and Commercial Workers' Union of Africa (ICU), in the Communist Party of South Africa (the CPSA had resolved in 1924 to concentrate on organizing black workers), in African-American expressions of black unity and independence (the most influential in South Africa at this time being the Garvey movement), and in millennial religious movements originating mainly in the countryside.

This chapter will demonstrate that African nationalists in the Ciskei region embraced most of these strategies in a complex and sometimes volatile mix of discourses with important implications for the resistance movement in South Africa.

Sections 8.1 and 8.2 offer benchmark profiles of protest politics and popular resistance between the world wars.

Section 8.3 highlights the petty bourgeoisie's protracted struggle to preserve African political rights in the Cape. The mission-educated community in the Ciskei would play a national role in the attempt to mobilize African opinion against the central government's campaign between 1926 and 1936 to disenfranchise South Africa's surviving African voters.

Table 8.1. Cape voting population, 1909–1937

Date	White	African	Coloured	Total	% African	% black
1909	121,336	6,637	14,394	142,367	4.7	14.8
1921	156,501	14,282	26,790	197,573	7.2	20.8
1927	173,291	16,481	26,091	215,863	7.6	19.7
1929	167,184	15,780	26,618	208,582	7.6	19.8
1931	352,658	12,271	26,378	391,307	3.1	9.9
1933	369,182	10,776	25,005	404,963	2.7	8.8
1935	382,103	10,628	24,793	417,524	2.6	8.5
1937	396,237	—	26,700	422,937	—	6.3

SOURCE: V. Klein, "African responses in the eastern Cape to Hertzog's Representation of Natives in Parliament Bill, 1926–1936," B.A. Hons. thesis, University of Cape Town, 1978, Appendix A (as modified).

8.1. African Protest Politics between the World Wars

African voters in the Cape—the only Africans who had even qualified franchise rights in South Africa—constituted the most prestigious segment of the petty bourgeoisie during the interwar period. African and Coloured voters constituted about 21 percent of the Cape vote in the peak year of 1921, while a record 16,481 African voters were recorded in the Cape in 1927. But the African electorate declined steadily thereafter under pressure from the central government (see Table 8.1).

The African vote, of course, remained an insignificant factor in provincial politics. Only ten of sixty-one electoral districts in the Cape in 1936 had more than 450 African voters. Nine constituencies (five in the Ciskei) were in the eastern Cape: they contained about 70 percent of the African voting community (an estimated 10,453 of 14,912 African voters in 1926)—the nucleus of the African petty bourgeoisie in the region.[6]

The Petty Bourgeoisie in the Eastern Cape

Africans who had the vote in the eastern Cape were members of a fragile elite—socially isolated, increasingly destabilized, and extremely conscious of their vulnerability. As elsewhere in black South Africa, the petty bourgeoisie in this region were relatively insignificant in terms of numbers and by no means homogeneous as regards occupation, education, or affluence. In an ever-expanding culture of poverty, lower-ranked members who had little formal education and/or low incomes were hardly distinguishable from the nonvoting peasant majority, especially in the reserves.

A particularly poignant illustration of their position was contained in the following report of a voters' meeting in a rural Ciskei constituency during the 1924 general election:

> An old elector with the pessimism of his years complains that everything is going
> wrong and to decay; all their circumstances, even their churches and their schools,
> are falling back, and the Government that should help them they have learned only
> to fear. . . . The Government was represented to them by the magistrates, but
> these local officials they knew only as exactors of taxes and imposers of fines and
> punishments. They feared to go near them.

Apart from a few teachers, a civil servant, and a former policeman on the
mines, the voters were dressed in "mean, worn-out and inadequate clothing."
As the reporter observed, "the indigence of these electors" was not congruent
with "their franchise privilege and responsibility." [7]

Upper-ranked members of the African petty bourgeoisie in the eastern
Cape now included members in key professions (ordained ministers, qualified
teachers, physicians, nurses, journalists, and lawyers), students in mission
boarding schools and at Fort Hare Native College, certain categories of wage
earners (especially court interpreters, policemen, skilled clerks, and artisans),
some self-employed persons (owners of lodging houses and other small businesses as well as affluent traders), educated chiefs and headmen, semicommercial and fully commercial farmers, agricultural demonstrators, and others
with access to wealth and power in the reserves. They were members of the
voting community for the most part, and they remained faithful to what Stanley
Trapido has called the "small tradition" of Cape liberalism. They maintained
existing alliances with white "friends of the natives" who might represent their
material interests. They continued to seek an extension of the Cape's African
franchise to the northern provinces and to promote individual rather than community rights. They continued to assume (at least in their public utterances)
that Britain would intervene on behalf of her former subjects if existing African
political privileges in the Cape were really threatened. And they were pro-
tective, paternalistic, and even discriminatory in seeking to maintain existing
rights and privileges. [8]

The mission-educated elite in the eastern Cape, however, was also being
undermined by the decline in peasant prosperity that had been in evidence
since the closing decades of the nineteenth century. The Ciskeian Missionary
Council's 1927 survey of the African population in twenty-nine magisterial districts west of the Kei River, for example, concluded that the African Christian
community was stagnating in the region. [9] The percentage of African Christians
in the Cape, according to census officials, had risen from 29.2 percent in 1911
to 37.4 percent in 1921. According to the unofficial mission survey, 15 percent
of the African population was affiliated with any kind of mission or separatist
church, and only 22–25 percent could be classified as Christian. [10]

The Cape remained far in advance of the other provinces when it came to
African education. With 34.9 percent of the African population in 1920, for
example, the Cape allocated 76.5 percent of government aid earmarked for

African schools. The province contained 59 percent of the African schools, 60.9 percent of the African pupils, and 63.5 percent of the African teachers in South Africa. White missionaries still controlled most African schools in the Cape, as in the other provinces, but African teachers dominated primary education and were now teaching in many secondary schools. Although subordinate to white officials, African school inspectors were appointed from the 1920s. While the Cape had adopted a separate primary syllabus for Africans in 1922, in practice the curriculum in white and black primary and secondary schools was virtually the same except for the language of instruction at the lower primary level.[11]

Educational opportunities for Africans even in the Cape, however, had changed little since the 1890s. The vast majority of children in school in 1926, for example, were still in Standard III (fifth grade) or under (89.8 percent) and only 0.1 percent (excluding students in teacher-training schools) were above Standard VI (eighth grade). A majority of the pupils, like the church members, were female (63.3 percent and 60.5 percent, respectively, in the 1927 Ciskeian Missionary Council survey), and attendance was very irregular, especially at harvest time.[12] African schools were funded mainly with African taxes that the provinces levied, but the power to tax the African population was transferred to the central government with the 1922 Financial Relations Fourth Extension Act. The provinces thereafter spent no more money on these schools than they received in government subsidies, and funding for African education declined in the next two decades.[13]

The House of Jili. Christian virtues, formal education, and allegiance to churches recognized by the government, however, remained dominant cultural symbols for the African petty bourgeoisie in rural areas like the Ciskei.[14] Most political activity in the region during the interwar era was still associated either directly or indirectly with the family of John Tengo Jabavu, the pioneering figure in Cape African politics. After Jabavu's death in 1921, the House of Jili (Jabavu's clan name) was led by Davidson Don Tengo Jabavu (1885–1959), the eldest of his sons and one of the most influential mediators of African nationalist opinion in South Africa.

D. D. T. Jabavu was perhaps the living embodiment of the ideal New African at this time.[15] His personal Christian piety and lifelong allegiance to the mission church coupled with his compelling belief in the power of the written word gave him a status within the mission-educated community that few others could emulate. After some years of study in colonial Basutoland, Britain, and the United States, Jabavu was appointed the first black faculty member at Fort Hare Native College when it opened in 1916. His vision of the proper Christian environment that would change people's lives embraced nonacademic as well as academic concerns. The students' leisure time would be taken up with organized recreational activities: Jabavu supervised literary and debating societies, conducted choirs, and sponsored the Students' Christian Association and various other religious groups on campus. Cardinal values inherited from the founding fathers of African nationalism in the eastern Cape—individual enterprise, self-reliance, African as opposed to ethnic loyalty—would continue to be instilled in African students inside and outside the classroom.

Jabavu was a great admirer of the native welfare societies and social clubs that were being established by white liberals for Africans in the metropolitan areas, and he urged that similar activities be initiated "in every location, rural, and urban, to heighten the tone of Native life." [16] In association with organizations like the Ciskeian Missionary Council, an attempt was made to provide these amenities for Africans in the eastern Cape.

As a leading proponent of political trusteeship, Jabavu was closely associated with the joint-council movement. The initial stimulus in establishing the joint councils had come from the Phelps-Stokes Commission, a privately endowed U.S. philanthropic body that had sent a team to survey industrial training facilities in Britain's African colonies in 1921.[17] James Aggrey, an African from the Gold Coast (Ghana), was one of the team members to visit South Africa. Aggrey apparently convinced large numbers of African students to persist in seeking peaceful change in dialogue with the whites. Jabavu was impressed by Aggrey's "captivating personality and his versatility as a public speaker" and declared that he had "done more than any other visitor I know of . . . to persuade people in our circumstances of the necessities of racial cooperation between white and black." [18]

Aggrey accepted racial differentiation and sought to channel black political and economic aspirations into rural development. Having spent twenty-five years as a student and teacher in the United States, he was thoroughly familiar with the tradition of black higher education epitomized by such colleges as Hampton Institute in Virginia and Tuskegee Institute in Alabama. Jabavu himself had visited Tuskegee and was much impressed by the performance of its students and the policies of its principal, Booker T. Washington. He admired the efforts being made to promote agricultural enterprise at Tuskegee and other segregated black colleges in the rural U.S. South, and he endorsed these efforts in a subsequent report on his trip to the South African government.

The Tuskegee tradition under Washington ensured that blacks would receive the rudimentary industrial and agricultural skills required of labor in an industrializing economy. As John Cell put it: "Washington, very consciously and deliberately, made himself a collaborator of the 'right type,' played a role largely defined by whites, and raised accommodation to a high art." [19] He died in 1915, but his ideas were embraced by enthusiastic admirers like Thomas

Jesse Jones, a lecturer in sociology at Hampton and educational director of the Phelps-Stokes Commission. Jones led the commission's survey team to Africa in 1921.

Like their white counterparts, Jabavu and other African liberals of this generation feared they were losing control over the civil rights movement. Again, the African-American experience set a precedent for their concerns. Washington's strategy of accommodation for blacks in the United States was being challenged by Harvard-educated W. E. B. DuBois, editor of the National Association for the Advancement of Colored People's newspaper *Crisis* and a leading member of the so-called Harlem Renaissance during the 1920s, and by Jamaican immigrant Marcus Garvey, a black nationalist who advocated a separatist alternative with his "Back to Africa" movement.[20]

The mission-educated community in the eastern Cape at the time probably preferred the strategy represented by Washington as being most appropriate for African protest groups in South Africa. As Jabavu expressed it:

> The coloured races . . . need to substitute for untrained leaders a number of intellectual spokesmen of the type of Booker T. Washington, J. E. K. Aggrey and R. R. Moton [who succeeded Washington at Tuskegee], among the American Negroes, who will call attention in a vigorous but constitutional manner to some of the glaring examples of injustice . . . and who will at the same time furnish constructive schemes for the amelioration of the conditions of their people, on lines of cooperation with the friendly section of the Whites.[21]

Jabavu, like Aggrey, was alarmed by the impact of Garveyism "on our illit-erate people." DuBois was admired for his efforts to establish a pan-African movement, for his contributions to African-American arts and letters, and in particular for his concept of training a "talented tenth" to be the leaders in the struggle for equality. His marxist sympathies, however, were unsettling to men like Jabavu, who had written fearfully in 1920: "Bolshevism and its nihilistic doctrines are enlisting many Natives upcountry. Socialism of the worst calibre is claiming our people." [22]

Jabavu family members would play a prominent role in the government advisory bodies established for Africans during the interwar period. D. D. T. Jabavu himself was the standard bearer for moderate African nationalism in relations with the central government. He was a member of the Native Con-ferences during the 1920s and the African representative on a number of government commissions where African interests were concerned, including Education (1919), Pass Laws (1920), Urban Areas (1923), and Economic and Wages (1925). Alexander Macaulay ("Mac") Jabavu (1889–1946), a younger brother, succeeded their father as editor of *Imvo Zabantsundu* in 1921. He was a founder-member of the national body, the Location Advisory Boards' Congress (established in 1928), the Natives' Representative Council (representing the Cape rural areas from 1937 to 1942), and the Ciskeian General Council.

The Jabavu family was also a driving force behind a number of new African political organizations launched inside and outside the eastern Cape during the interwar period. D. D. T. Jabavu and Abdul Abdurahman of the African People's Organization, for example, organized four Non-European Conferences between 1927 and 1934 that for the first time brought together leading members of the African, Coloured, and Indian petty bourgeoisie to discuss the government's segregationist policies. No permanent body was formed, and the Indians remained on the periphery of proceedings, but a precedent was set for the future. The African liberal tradition in the eastern Cape would eventually coalesce with the All-African Convention in 1935.

Independent African Political Organizations

The African mission-educated community maintained control over most African political organizations in the Ciskei region during the 1920s and 1930s, and at one level protest politics was not much different from what it had been forty years earlier. The protesters formed delegations, wrote petitions, and utilized accessible news media. They reacted primarily to events that were initiated by the dominant political parties and pressure groups in South Africa, and they generally resisted any strategy of protest that promoted racial consciousness or advocated strikes, boycotts, and civil disobedience.

While the key African political groups in the eastern Cape—the 1912 Imbumba and the South African Native Congress (SANC)—had apparently ceased functioning by World War I, new ones were reestablished soon after the war ended in 1918. Organized African political organizations—including Bantu Union, Ciskei Native Convention, Cape Native Voters' Association, Cape Native Voters' Convention, the ANC's eastern Cape branch headquartered at Cradock, and various branches of the ICU in the Ciskei and Transkei— were well represented in the region during the interwar period. These independent political groupings were supplemented by a host of other organizations engaged at some level in protest politics. They included the location advisory boards in the towns, local/district councils and the Ciskeian and Transkeian General Councils in the reserves, the vigilance associations (iliso lomzis), and numerous economic and cultural organizations.

Bantu Union was formally launched in Queenstown in February 1919 by various Imbumba and SANC officials. They wanted to reduce ethnic tensions and promote political unity (remembering that the Mfengu had been aligned mainly to the Imbumba and the Xhosa-Thembu to the SANC before the war), while defending and extending the rights of the African voting community in South Africa.[23] Walter Rubusana, former leader of the SANC and Tengo Jabavu's main political rival, was a member along with Alan Soga, editor of the defunct SANC newspaper *Izwi Labantu*. Jonathan Mazwi and his brother Benjamin, veteran political campaigners who had once been associated with the Imbumba, were also members along with men like James Calata, who was just beginning his political career.

Bantu Union was led by Meshach Pelem (1859–1936), a vice president of the SANC in the early 1900s. Pelem had worked in the Kimberley diamond fields for ten years as a clerk and then as a registered diamond digger before returning to the eastern Cape, where he became a labor agent and established a successful business in King William's Town. The failure of the African National Congress to establish a firm base in the eastern Cape apparently prompted Pelem, now one of the wealthiest Africans in the province, to get involved in the new organization. Bantu Union partially filled the vacuum in regional politics—and became yet another Cape rival to the ANC—in the early 1920s.

Outside of Bantu Union, there was very little organized African political activity in the eastern Cape at this time. Voter complacency was due in part to the various government-approved consultative bodies created since 1920 to represent African interests. Solomon Plaatje had remarked early in 1924: "Government has in the past two years given us less cause for fresh complaints. There is a ring of sincerity about [the] attitude of the Government, which has created a hearing for champions of native rights who formerly had no audience in this Union." [24]

The looming 1924 general election, however, was a source of considerable anxiety to the African voting community. The Ciskei Native Convention had already been organized in King William's Town in September 1923. More than a hundred delegates—"progressive Natives" representing various organizations based in the Ciskei—attended the inaugural meeting, and *Imvo Zabantsundu* declared it was the "most important" function of its kind that had been held in the region "in over 10 years." [25] Meetings were held twice a year. In 1925–26, for example, attendance increased from roughly three hundred to seven hundred "including 'reds' and the civilised." *Imvo* saw the convention as an unofficial Bunga embracing "the leading section of thinking Natives in the rural areas outside of the Transkei territories." [26]

The activities of the Cape Native Voters' Association are more obscure. Although an organization with the same name was reportedly in existence in the 1890s,[27] *Imvo* noted the CNVA's "second inaugural meeting" in 1924, when a branch was formed in Colesberg. The organizing secretary was S. M. Bennett Ncwana, a veteran Cape journalist who was an active member of Congress and an ICU official as well as an election agent for the South African party during the 1920s.[28] Its political agenda was almost immediately overtaken by the Cape Native Voters' Convention (CNVC), launched in King William's Town in May 1924.

The CNVC would become the key regional body in the Cape voting community's fight to preserve its franchise rights, and it attracted most of the active African politicians in the province. The first meeting—dubbed initially an "All African Convention"—was held to consider the African voting community's priorities in view of the upcoming election.[29] As *Imvo* put it: "The proceedings were, in typical Bantu deliberative fashion, slow, protracted, often passionate but always united and determined, taking one's thoughts back to the eighties [the beginnings of African political activity at the Cape]." After an all-night session, the delegates agreed to avoid being a "tool" of white party politics and "face all parties and candidates alike with a manifesto of their own."[30] This manifesto effectively outlined the political agenda of the Cape voting community during the interwar era.

The delegates continued to maintain that the franchise should be extended to Africans in the northern provinces and the "colour bar" clauses in the South Africa Act removed "to enable non-Europeans to have direct representation in the Union Parliament." They called for a return to "the British ideal of complete equality, opportunities, protection and rights to all British subjects without distinction of colour and race . . . a Government of all the people by all the people and for all the people, not a Government of some of the people for some of the people and by some of the people."

They condemned the pass laws and the harsh sentences meted out to Africans in the courts. They urged that Africans be allowed to serve on juries and replace whites as court interpreters when African languages were used. They called on the central government to increase African representation at the Native Conferences, appoint Africans as native commissioners, and include Africans on government commissions of inquiry, appoint a separate, full-time minister of native affairs, and provide more local-government councils for Africans in town and countryside.

Economic priorities included appeals to bar foreign black laborers from working in South Africa, compel employers to provide "a fixed minimum wage for all skilled and unskilled labor irrespective of race and colour," obtain freehold rights for Africans in urban areas, repeal or amend the 1913 Land Act, and allow African farmers to obtain loans from the Agricultural Land Bank. Cultural priorities centered on state control of African schools to ensure "a uniform system of Native education" throughout South Africa. Delegates urged that white and black education be administered by a single superintendent-general and controlled directly by the South African parliament. Existing legal sanctions against "social and sexual intercourse between black and white" should also be amended to include "all classes of the community without discrimination of color or race."[31]

CNVC delegates generally met once or twice a year, in places like King William's Town, Kimberley, and Queenstown, to issue resolutions, petition parliament, mobilize protest delegations, and interview officials at the local as well as the national level. A fund was established to help publicize the grievances of African voters at home and abroad. Attendance at meetings during the mid–late 1920s, for example, varied from 100–200 to more than 3,000, depending on the severity of segregationist legislation directed against the Cape voting community or their allies in the northern provinces.[32]

Regional organizations already in existence associated themselves with the CNVC, and their officials became leaders in the new organization. Pelem and Elijah Makalima of Bantu Union, for example, were the first vice presidents, and Bennett-Ncwana of the Ciskei Native Voters' Association was the first organizing secretary. D. D. T. Jabavu replaced Elijah Mdolomba, a senior Cape ANC official during the interwar period, as president of the organization in 1929. Other activists during the 1920s and 1930s included his younger brother Alexander, who was a secretary-treasurer; A. Frank Pendla, a court interpreter, businessman, and one-time postmaster of Port Elizabeth's African township of New Brighton, who unsuccessfully contested one of the city's provincial council seats in 1929; and Richard H. Godlo (1899–1972), a journalist and one of the most active political figures in the eastern Cape during this generation. He was the principal founder and long-time president of the Location Advisory Boards' Congress, an All-African Congress official during the later 1930s, a lifetime member of the Natives' Representative Council, and a member of the ANC national executive during the turbulent 1940s.

The Cape African voting community characteristically pursued policies that were independent of national bodies like the ANC.[33] In an address delivered at Queenstown in 1919, for example, Sefako Makgatho, the newly elected president-general, had noted that Cape voters did not "appreciate the difficulties under which the Natives are groaning in the Transvaal, in Orange Free State and in Natal." Congress had been given "more help from Europeans than the Natives of the Cape who enjoy the franchise." If Cape voters did not "show a bit of fellow feeling for their own kith and kin," he warned, "their day of reckoning" would come.[34]

Their day of reckoning would not come until they lost the franchise. In the interim, most Ciskeian politicians did participate in the activities of the ANC-affiliated Cape African Congress based in Cradock. They also had intermittent contact with the Bechuanaland–Griqualand West Congress based in Kimberley. But they were wary of the Cape Western Congress based in Cape Town. Its leader, the flamboyant self-styled "professor" James Thaele (1888–1948), spent about ten years studying in the United States and had become a follower of Marcus Garvey and his Universal Negro Improvement Association before returning to South Africa in the early 1920s.[35]

Although somewhat equivocal in their initial response to the ICU, regional political leaders were generally supportive of the trade union and its charismatic leader, Clements Kadalie. Founded in Cape Town in 1919, the ICU moved its headquarters to Johannesburg in 1925 (leaving Thaele, who was also a member of the ICU, and his supporters to organize protesting African and Coloured workers in the western Cape). Membership in the trade union soared to perhaps a hundred thousand in 1927, and most new members were African peasants living on proclaimed white farms. The ICU developed into a rural populist movement and eclipsed Congress as the most influential African political organization in South Africa during the mid–late 1920s.

The ICU leadership, however, could not accommodate the complex and often contradictory needs of its urban and rural constituents. Personality conflicts, organizational weaknesses, factional disputes, allegations of mismanagement and misuse of funds, and the personal extravagances of Kadalie and other officials helped undermine confidence in the ICU. By mid-1929 it was in an irreversible state of disintegration with three main splinter groups centered in East London, Johannesburg, and Durban.

The ICU branch in East London, headquarters of the ICU in the eastern Cape, was organized in 1922. The port city had experienced periodic bouts of labor unrest for a number of years. A strike by African dockworkers in 1911, for example, was followed by work stoppages elsewhere in the city. Food price increases in 1918 triggered more wildcat strikes, and the first recorded workers' organization—the East London Native Employees' Association—was formed in 1920. The dockworkers again went out on strike in 1921.

An African trade union under the leadership of a man named Samuel Masabalala was already in existence in Port Elizabeth, where a major confrontation with the local authorities occurred in October 1920. Masabalala was jailed in the midst of a campaign to mount a general strike over low wages, and the police fired on a crowd of three thousand who were demanding his release. In a night of rioting, twenty-four township residents were killed and eight injured. The incident had reverberations throughout the Ciskei hinterland and beyond. Kadalie and Masabalala joined forces, and within a few years rural eastern Cape—particularly the Transkei—was a major center of ICU activity.[36]

Members of the mission-educated elite controlled the local ICU executive during the 1920s. They included *Imvo* editor Alexander Jabavu, Theo Lujiza, and John Mzaza, all of whom were also members of the national executive committee. Jabavu, who had become a vice president of the trade union, urged his readers to ponder the "wise words" of Kadalie and urged the government to expand African representation on the Natives' Conference to include him. Kadalie was "immensely popular" in the eastern Cape "by reason of his dashing personality and fearless language in expressing the woes of his downtrodden people." His speeches were "strong, brave and outspoken but never seditious nor calculated to arouse anarchy." The ICU would constitute an important element in *Imvo*'s political agenda, even though editorials on occasion would criticize Kadalie for his "provocative" and "intemperate" remarks

and caution that in "politics he lacks judgement and has made mistakes." [37]
D. D. T. Jabavu gave the opening address at the ICU's annual conference
in East London in January 1924, and he "stressed the wisdom of the use of
moderate language and sane objects in a movement destined to play a great
part in the upliftment of Native labourers." [38]

Most union members in East London during the mid–late 1920s were
migrants in town and peasants in the rural hinterland, but branch activities in
the port city do not seem to have had much impact on the laboring poor.[39]
Union demands, ranging from specific calls for higher wages and better working conditions to general appeals for African unity and self-respect, were
expressed primarily in noncombative language. The trade union sidestepped
local grievances and concerned itself primarily with organizational matters,
promoting loyalty to the union and trying to ensure that members paid their
dues. East London's ICU officials did incorporate some agrarian concerns in
their political rhetoric with the dramatic increase in rural membership, but
political linkages between town and countryside in East London, as elsewhere
in South Africa, remained fragile.

Kadalie resigned from the ICU after a series of confrontations with
William Ballinger, a British trade union organizer who had arrived in South
Africa to advise the trade union at Kadalie's request in July 1928. The ICU
branch in East London, now under the control of the faction led by Ballinger,
was represented by Lujiza (who had succeeded Kadalie as general secretary)
and Mzaza. When Kadalie and several lieutenants launched the Independent
ICU in April 1929, however, the parent body effectively collapsed in the
eastern Cape. East London became the headquarters of the new trade union,
and attendance at ICU branch meetings, already below a hundred on average
by mid-1928, dropped to virtually nothing after the Independent ICU was
established.

While Kadalie's presence continued to inspire enthusiasm, dissidents
working through the iliso lomzi (vigilance association), independent churches,
and other organizations provided most of the leadership in the new union. It
became more Africanist and separatist in its ideological orientation, and the
leadership cadre became more diffuse. As the Independent ICU got more involved in popular resistance, it gradually distanced itself from petty bourgeois
politics.

8.2. Popular Resistance in Town and Countryside

The bonding of peasants, semiproletarianized migrants, and permanent town
dwellers was very evident in the Ciskei during the interwar period. Strategies
of popular resistance would continually contest strategies of petitionary protest
in this region as elsewhere in South Africa.

The Independent ICU in East London

African politics in East London was a reflection of the social divisions in urban African townships at this time.[40] Leading members of the petty bourgeoisie controlled the local vigilance committee, and leading members from this body were elected to the location advisory board, which was officially recognized by the municipal authorities in 1921. Although the advisory board theoretically represented all Africans in the city, its members were permanent residents who held salaried middle-class jobs for the most part and had bought or leased most of the property in the locations. The dominant personalities included men like Rubusana, still the acknowledged leader in local politics (he died in 1936), J. J. Vimbe, and Richard Godlo. Those who controlled the advisory board also controlled the local branches of national bodies like Congress and the ICU as well as regional bodies like the CNVC.

The mass of the working population had little influence in local politics except through the iliso lomzi, which represented a broader constituency and was more sympathetic to popular grievances than the advisory board. The iliso lomzi included workers with township permits as well as leaseholders, women as well as men, and it represented rural as well as urban issues and separatist as well as mission churches. The advisory board and the iliso lomzi initially complemented each other, but as the working-class population increased and grievances mounted relations between the two bodies became more contradictory.

As we have seen, conditions in East London for the vast majority of African residents were intolerable during the 1920s. The railways and harbors—the two main sources of local employment—were generating few jobs, and the port city was in the throes of a prolonged economic downturn. The growing African population was increasingly dependent on semilegal and illegal informal sector activities to provide essential household goods and absorb some of the rural exodus.

The Independent ICU recruited members from the iliso lomzi and rapidly attached itself to independent churches that had moved beyond the separatist discourse of the early Ethiopian movement and were searching for a more militant African religious experience. Kadalie was being elevated in some speeches to the status of a "black Moses" who had inherited Ntsikana's mantle or even "the son of Jesus Christ."[41] Popular figures in the iliso lomzi and the independent churches were being placed on the Independent ICU executive committee, and some consideration was even given to establishing an Independent ICU church.

Keable 'Mote, a compelling speaker who had been a national leader in the old ICU and a leading advocate of direct action, spent about two months in mid-1929 helping to organize the Independent ICU in East London.'Mote was soon in contact with local dissidents and their grievances, particularly those involving women, who were heavily involved in illegal informal sector activities. He also tackled the wage issue. In separate reports issued in 1929, the medical officer of health and the Independent ICU had demonstrated a considerable gap between income and expenditure for African male and female workers in East London. Armed with these statistics, Independent ICU leaders tried to negotiate directly with white employers and the official arbitration body, the Wages Board. While a few small factory owners agreed to raise wages, the major employers of African labor—the railways and harbor—claimed their workers were not subject to the jurisdiction of the Wages Board and refused to negotiate.

The Independent ICU held its first yearly conference in East London in early January 1930, bringing the union's most experienced organizers into the port city. Kadalie issued a forty-eight-hour ultimatum to the rail and harbor authorities that went unanswered, and in mid-January the workers walked off their jobs. The strike escalated rapidly during the first week. Attendance at Independent ICU meetings soared from prestrike estimates of 250–500 to between 2,000 and 4,000 sympathizers. Kadalie appealed directly to female workers to join the men and called for a general strike on January 20, 1930. The popular mood became more combative, and on January 22 Kadalie told an enthusiastic crowd: "Talk about law and order; I say damn law and order." [42]

The first phase of the strike ended the next day when the seven-member strike committee was arrested and charged with public violence. Five of the seven had been leaders of the old ICU—Kadalie, Alexander Maduna (at one time the union's provincial secretary in Natal and the Orange Free State), Henry Tyamzashe (editor of the defunct union newspaper *Workers' Herald*), and Alfred Mnika and Joel Magade (formerly interpreters for ICU officials visiting East London). They appeared in court a few days later, and Kadalie produced a letter calling off the strike and urging workers to return to their jobs.

The second phase of the strike generated a breach between the jailed committee and the strikers, while work stoppages continued for another six months. Leadership of the Independent ICU during this period seems to have fallen on various independent church leaders. A preacher named Nonkonyane was the main speaker at public meetings that were attracting up to eight thousand people by mid-February. The strike movement now began to embrace the lowest-paid female workers, the marginally employed, and the unemployed. Long-standing local grievances served to sustain popular resistance. The arrest of twelve strikers who did not have permits to reside in the townships, for example, prompted a march of three thousand angry protesters on the courthouse. Fearful authorities agreed to release the strikers to the marchers, who paid their fines.

Meanwhile, Kadalie and the other strike leaders were found not guilty on

115 of 116 counts of incitement (Kadalie had to pay a twenty-five-pound fine). Their credibility, however, had diminished considerably after Kadalie's attempt to call off the strike. When the strike committee returned to East London in late May 1930, they found that the Independent ICU was a different organization from the one they had known four months earlier.

Two factors were apparently instrumental in the Independent ICU's shift to popular resistance. Women rose rapidly in status to become key leaders of public opinion inside the city's townships. At the same time, the strikers turned to the countryside for help, and rural issues were interwoven into the fabric of urban dissent.

As in the old ICU, women had been assigned passive support roles in the Independent ICU before 1930 and even in the early days of the strike. They met separately, did not speak at mass meetings, and were not elected to union committees. They were expected to provide tea and food and make union badges, support the male strikers, and at most help in picketing. Nevertheless, one of the distinguishing characteristics of the Independent ICU strike in East London was the mobilization of female workers, who made up one-third of the African labor force. Minimum wage demands were set for female domestics as well as male industrial workers, and the women were most active in sustaining the work stoppages during the months when the strike committee was in detention.

East London's authorities now began to enforce regulations against residents who were living in town illegally or were participating in activities that required municipal licenses. The women—breadwinners especially in times of crisis—were the main victims. They operated boarding houses and sold produce without permits, and they brewed and sold beer and liquor illegally. The Independent ICU had opposed beer brewing on the grounds that it weakened support for the union, but by mid-1930 the issue could no longer be ignored. In the aftermath of an unsuccessful strike, the right to brew domestic beer, sell produce, and live in the townships became campaign issues along with the actions of the police.

The resistance movement succeeded for a few years in cementing links between dissidents in town and countryside. Africans who still adhered to the old way of life in districts like King William's Town, Keiskammahoek, and Middledrift in the Ciskei and especially Kentani, Idutywa, and other districts in the southern Transkei were receptive to urban leaders who had moved beyond petty bourgeois politics and were employing a more liberating Africanist discourse to mobilize popular opinion. Visiting chiefs provided gifts of food for the strikers and urged unemployed followers not to take their jobs. Independent ICU leaders in turn supported numerous grievances in rural villages where they had constituents, defending the rights of landholders, condemning the methods of mine recruiters and the low wages paid to farm workers, calling for African traders, and supporting beer drinks, initiation rites, and other traditionalist pursuits.

The rhetoric of Independent ICU politicians now included allusions to the heroic chiefs of the preconquest period. The artefacts of precolonial culture—its rituals and other social practices—provided reference points that would appeal to migrant supporters and confirm the union's commitment to the rural majority. The emblems of the trade union—its badges and membership cards—were embossed with spiritual power just as the emblems of mission culture had been in the nineteenth century.

In responding to popular grievances, however, the Independent ICU had moved far beyond strictly trade union issues, and its leaders had no hope of making good on their promises. Police pressure on brewers, hawkers, and illegal residents in the townships was unyielding, and union officials were soon distancing themselves from the grievances that had sustained the movement. Kadalie's excessive drinking and personal extravagances coupled with allegations of union mismanagement and misuse of funds—problems that had beset the old ICU in the late 1920s—were also undermining confidence in the Independent ICU. By 1933, the trade union was a spent force in regional politics. Virtually all Kadalie's lieutenants but Tyamzashe had deserted him, and at least one partisan group had set up a rival union.[43] In the rural hinterland, the Independent ICU was largely absorbed in the millennial movement.

Millenarianism in Rural Ciskei

The message of millenarianism had formed part of the reaction to conquest since the early Cape-Xhosa wars.[44] It was proclaimed by war doctors like Nxele and Mlanjeni and above all by the prophets of the cattle killing, and it remained a potent force in rural Ciskei, as elsewhere in rural South Africa, in the generation after 1910. Decades of endemic poverty, moreover, were accompanied by a vacuum in leadership. The precolonial political order had been shattered, and especially in the Ciskei reserve the new authority figures—councillors associated with local governing bodies created by the 1894 Glen Grey Act, rural representatives of the mission-educated elite, and even the headmen and other government-appointed authority figures—had limited influence. Alternative patrons were found in the leaders of independent churches, who espoused a millennial solution to the many problems besetting the depressed peasantry.

Mgijima and the Israelites. The most dramatic example of millenarianism in the 1920s involved a prophet figure by the name of Enoch Josiah Mgijima (1868–1929). His family stemmed from the Mfengu diaspora: they had crossed the Kei River with the British into the Ciskei and moved initially to Peddie and then to the Herschel District before settling finally in the African location of

Kamastone about twenty-five miles southwest of Queenstown (Map 3). Africans who had sided with the British received about 12 percent of the land taken from Thembu dissidents in the Queenstown District after the 1850–53 war; the rest went to the white settlers. The main African locations developed around the mission stations at Oxkraal and Kamastone, sites of the largest individual land tenure scheme for Africans in South Africa prior to the Glen Grey Act.

The Christian community at Oxkraal and Kamastone was relatively large, a number were voters (about 20 percent of the eligible population at Kamastone, for example, in 1921), and in the early decades of settlement a significant proportion were actively involved in surplus production for the market. Nevertheless, by World War I most peasants had been reduced to a marginalized existence. Land titles were in chaos, most of the cattle had been wiped out by disease, and the population density was one of the highest in the Ciskei. Mgijima would have been an eyewitness to the rise and fall of peasant prosperity in the district.

Mgijima's parents were relatively affluent members of the modernizing mission-educated (Wesleyan Methodist) community: they possessed cattle, sheep, and other stock, and held land in individual tenure. His father had established the household at a place known by the Europeans as Bulhoek below a hilltop called Ntabelanga ("the mountain of the rising sun"), which was where Enoch, the youngest of nine children, was born. Although educated at the village school to Standard III (fifth grade), he complained of severe headaches and did not proceed to a boarding school for more instruction as his older brothers had done. Instead, Mgijima became a farmer and a lay preacher in the local Wesleyan Methodist Church. At Ntabelanga in April 1907 he had a visionary experience that would transform his life: he was told to teach the people to worship God according to the old traditions, to tell them a war was coming, and to prepare for the end of the world. Mgijima began holding evangelistic meetings at Ntabelanga, where he attracted a considerable following with his prophetic utterances.

The Queenstown District was fertile ground for separatist church activities at this time. Nehemiah Tile's renamed African Native Mission church had a strong congregation along with Pambini Mzimba's Presbyterian Church of Africa. The AME church also maintained a small congregation of protesters, who had rejected James Dwane's appeal to affiliate with the Anglican church as the Order of Ethiopia. Mgijima shared their grievances with respect to the mission churches. As an unordained preacher he had no power, no control over church funds or property, and no access to land on the mission station.

The content of Mgijima's message was typically millennial. It centered on the early biblical image of Jehovah as the angry, vengeful god of a chosen people who had been miraculously released from bondage and restored to their land. If Jehovah's instructions were obeyed, the spiritual heirs of Israel—the followers of Mgijima—would also be freed and the land returned to them. His identification with the Israelites eventually embraced a number of Jewish rituals, including the Passover service.

Mgijima's evangelical activities were welcomed initially by the Methodists and other established mission churches in the district, but relations cooled considerably when Africans and Coloureds who were agitating for a more equitable distribution of mission land began flocking to Mgijima. The prophet's followers were denied permission to build a church on land held by the mission, and Mgijima began baptizing his own converts in 1912. He also established contact with the Church of God and Saints in Christ, an African-American church founded by William Saunders Crowdy in Kansas in 1896. Crowdy was convinced that Africans in Africa and the diaspora were the descendants of the original tribes of Israel. By the time Crowdy died in 1908, his church had several missionaries and a number of congregations in South Africa. Mgijima broke all ties with mission churches in November 1912 and joined Crowdy's church. A few months later he had become the titular leader of Crowdy's church in the eastern Cape.

Mgijima embraced Crowdy's teachings, but his increasingly violent apocalyptic visions disturbed leaders of the church in the United States. His first prediction that the end of the world would take place on Christmas Day 1912 went unfulfilled, but his vision of a catastrophic war came to pass with the coming of World War I. He also envisaged a race war from which the Israelites, as his followers were now called (they regarded themselves as descendents of the lost tribes of Judah and Benjamin), would be spared. Mgijima was finally excommunicated when he refused to renounce these teachings, but most members of Crowdy's church in the region followed him into the wilderness.

The Israelites would withdraw from the world and create an alternative society at Ntabelanga. Mgijima proclaimed a Day of Judgment sometime in 1919, which was a signal to his followers to congregate at Ntabelanga in anticipation of the millennium. Mgijima, having failed to persuade mission authorities to grant him a site to build a church, would now provide a home for his followers illegally on the commonage. It was a propitious historical moment: a severe drought that would last several years began in 1919, almost a thousand Africans had died in the Queenstown District during the 1918–19 influenza epidemic, and workers in the city were protesting low wages and the carrying of passes.

The community of believers had constructed a small village on the commonage by September 1920, complete with brick houses, streets, a school for bible study, a police force and religious court, a nursing brigade and a church called the Tabernacle, where members worshiped four times a day. The community had several skilled workers, including a surveyor, saddle maker, cobbler, butcher, blacksmith, and a number of builders. Ntabelanga was a steadily expanding, self-contained, self-sufficient communal settlement. It confronted landless Africans in the overcrowded location who were not Israelites as well as white farmers and government officials, who saw the community as a threat to European administrative control in the African reserves.

Local officials issued court orders in a vain attempt to stop the converts from building and occupying these houses, and an armed police force was organized in December 1920 to pressure the Israelites to leave the commonage. But the police were told to avoid a confrontation, and the show of force did not work. They beat a hasty retreat, leaving behind tents, food, and equipment, when a body of marching Israelites approached them, and Mgijima claimed a moral victory.

The central government then got involved and sent a delegation (half of whom were police and army officers) led by the secretary for native affairs to Queenstown to negotiate with the separatists. An African delegation consisting of Tengo Jabavu, Meshach Pelem, and two other members of Bantu Union was also asked to intervene. These official and unofficial mediators failed to persuade the Israelites to abandon the commonage. The Israelites asked for the personal intervention of the prime minister, but he refused to enter the discussions.

Mgijima told his people to isolate themselves from the outside world and expect the worst: "Tell these children [i.e., converts] that they have come to face death." [45] God's chosen were gathering at Ntabelanga for the coming Armageddon. Adherents were urged to live chaste lives (which included proscriptions against drinking, smoking, and immorality), and obey the Ten Commandments and the Seven Keys, a set of beliefs drawn from various parts of the Bible that had originally been codified by Crowdy for his church. The millennial promise proclaimed that the Israelites would be the martyred remnant, the "Fifth Seal," revealing "the souls of them that were slain for the word of God" (Revelation 6:9 Authorized Version).

No government officials were allowed to enter Ntabelanga and no church leaders were allowed to leave for fear they might be arrested or otherwise harmed. In early January 1921, the district surgeon was refused entrance to investigate a reported outbreak of typhus. In early April, members of the newly appointed Native Affairs Commission were sent to negotiate, but the Israelites refused to abandon their Jerusalem. Another African delegation from Mgijima's home district also tried but failed to reach a compromise. In the meantime, the community had increased rapidly from about 1,650 adherents in April to almost 3,200 by late May 1921. Finally, the commissioners recommended that an armed force be sent to remove the Israelites from the commonage at Ntabelanga.

An 800-man police contingent drawn from all parts of the country and equipped with rifles, artillery, and machine guns—the largest peacetime force

Figure 8.1. Prophets of African nationalism: *On this page,* the Israelite leader Enoch Mgijima and, *on the facing page,* the leader of the "Wellingtonites," Elias Buthelezi.

ever assembled up to that time in South Africa—gathered at Ntabelanga on May 24, 1921. Mgijima had already given his followers the option of leaving the community, but they refused, and more recruits actually arrived the night before the police raid. About 500 white-robed, shaven-headed Israelite men, armed only with knobkerries (sticks) and a few spears and knives, confronted the police while their women and children gathered in the Tabernacle, praying and singing hymns. When the shooting finally ceased, at least 183 Israelites were dead and 100 wounded; one policeman suffered a stab wound.

The authorities placed 150 Israelites on trial, including Enoch Mgijima and his brother Charles (he was the main spokesman during the negotiations and the commander of the Israelite force during the police raid). The prison sentences ranged from twelve to eighteen months of hard labor for ordinary members to six years of hard labor for the Mgijima brothers, but most were released before their terms expired. Charles died in prison, and Enoch was freed in 1924: he returned to his home district and spent the last few years of his life ministering to those who had survived the massacre.

The Native Churches Commission was appointed to investigate the Bulhoek affair, and its findings were published in 1925. In part, the report reflected the fact that white control inside the reserves was still very tenuous. African acquiescence was obtained primarily through negotiation and very rarely by

Figure 8.1. Elias Buthelezi.

using force, since the authorities simply did not have enough police to impose unilateral decisions. The location inspector at Kamastone, for example, had been impressed with Mgijima, who was apparently more influential in administrative matters than government-appointed headmen. The only way to avoid similar incidents in future, the commissioners concluded, was to increase the number of government advisory bodies "on Native matters," to agree on "a permanent Native policy," and to institute "a proper system of Native administration." This report was an important stimulus to Hertzog's subsequent efforts to reinforce the authority of rural-based collaborative structures, centralize African administration, and expand the segregated African consultative bodies in urban and rural areas.[46]

The Israelites represented a new stage in the transition to a fully Africanist political and ecclesiastical tradition. Unlike the Ethiopian separatists of the late Victorian period, they were not orthodox Christian reformists. Israelites stopped paying taxes, refused to work for neighboring white farmers, and above all would not recognize the authority of the government over their church. Particularly interesting was Mgijima's success in attracting farmworkers, landless peasants, migrant workers, and converts from the non-Christian community.

Most adherents were Mfengu and Xhosa from the Ciskei and Transkei, but a broad range of ethnic groups inside and even outside South Africa were represented. In terms of geographical origin, the Israelites ranged from the eastern Cape to colonial Nyasaland. As they embraced more Africans from the most alienated sections of the peasantry, church leaders apparently moved further away from conventional Christian doctrines and rituals. Mgijima and his contemporaries, moreover, accepted precolonial authority figures when they were not used against their churches. A restored and rejuvenated chiefship was more acceptable to millennialists like Mgijima than mission-educated politicians.

The Bulhoek massacre was undoubtedly the most dramatic example of popular resistance in South Africa's reserves before the 1950s. Like other millennial groups during this period, however, the Israelites did not resist the government to hasten the advent of the millennium. Salvation would come through divine intervention. An alternative African society would be created, but popular resistance in this context had no broader political goals. The Israelites defended their City of God against government encroachment, but they did not move beyond it to confront white rule in South Africa.

The Prophetess Nonteta. Prophets littered the landscape of the eastern Cape during the interwar period. Another influential figure to emerge in the Ciskei during the 1920s was a woman known as Nonteta. Unlike Mgijima, she never attended school and spoke no English (or Afrikaans, which was the main European language spoken by Mfengu in the Queenstown District). Nonteta was born about 1875 near King William's Town, trained as an herbalist, and eventually became a celebrated psychic. During the influenza epidemic, she apparently had a millennial experience that changed her life. Although Nonteta never joined a church, her children were baptized Wesleyan Methodists and she became a traveling evangelist. Her circuit covered the district embracing King William's Town, Keiskammahoek, and Middledrift, where she addressed audiences, sometimes numbering in the thousands, at open-air meetings.

Nonteta relied on literate followers to communicate Scripture, and her messages focused on the purity of the Christian life, laying down numerous proscriptions against drinking, smoking, immorality, traditional dancing, circumcision ceremonies, and witchcraft. Adherents were urged to avoid pork and the meat of animals that were not slaughtered. Chiefs and headmen were distinguished guests, and School people as well as Reds attended her services. Nonteta's millennial vision embraced an eschatology that featured a looming day of atonement in which Christ would appear in a cloud to judge the living and dead. The ancestors would remain in their graves until this event occurred.

Nonteta's messages apparently had no specified political goals. Like Mgijima, she rejected the world ruled by whites, but she did not preach resistance against the government, and she urged her followers to obey their chiefs and headmen. She seems to have had no plans to create a new church, but converts did establish one after she was detained in 1922.

Nonteta's relationship to Mgijima is unknown, but she certainly equaled him in popularity, and authorities feared her influence, especially after the massacre at Bulhoek. Consequently, she was committed to a mental institution. at Fort Beaufort. Although released in January 1923 on condition she cease preaching, Nonteta disobeyed the order and was again committed to the mental facility. She continued to maintain contact with her followers, and government officials finally transferred her to a mental institution in Pretoria in 1924, where she died eleven years later.

Buthelezi and the Wellingtonites. The career of Elias "Wellington" Buthelezi, a Zulu born near Melmoth in Natal about 1895, is another example worth mentioning because it illustrates how millennial messages, Africanist-oriented separatist churches, African-American images, and local grievances could be fused to broaden the discourse of popular resistance in the rural areas.

Buthelezi initially appeared in the Ciskei in 1921 as a Standard VII (ninth grade) student at Lovedale. He left the school after one term and apparently spent the next several years in a series of jobs—insurance salesman, clerk in a labor-recruiting firm, patent medicine peddler, and herbalist—in Basutoland, East Griqualand, and Natal. By the mid-1920s, Buthelezi had taken on a new persona: he was now calling himself a medical doctor and he had changed his name to Dr. Butler Hansford Wellington. He claimed he was an American, subsequently disavowing his African origins even in court, and would speak only English at public meetings. He had also become a preacher in the African-American AME church and had joined the Garvey movement.

Buthelezi's millennial message was an amalgam of black unity and liberation from white rule. He rejected government authority and stressed political and religious autonomy. Liberation in this case was to be achieved not by divine intervention but by an army of African-Americans who would reach South Africa mainly by air and hurl down fiery balls of charcoal on all whites and nonbelieving Africans. Those who accepted the message were told to reject European-made goods, paint their houses black, and purify themselves by slaughtering all pigs and refraining from the use of candles and other products derived from pigs.

There was nothing particularly new in Buthelezi's vision. Pig taboos symbolizing the sacrifices that believers must make were common, and rumors of black Americans intervening on behalf of the peasants had been circulating in the eastern Cape for some years (the rumors had reached Mgijima's followers in Queenstown and Nonteta's followers in King William's Town). Many rural Africans believed the United States was controlled by blacks and were convinced they played a pivotal role in world politics. The Garveyites and various African-American churches operating in the region would certainly have contributed to this myth.

The Wellingtonites, as the disciples of Buthelezi were called, attracted converts from Red and School communities, and most had little or no formal education. Like Mgijima, who had used educated lieutenants to communicate with outsiders, Buthelezi sought organizers who were literate and had reached Standard V (seventh grade) in school. Members paid a fee equivalent to twenty-five cents to join the movement and wore a symbolic red, green, and black button.

The Wellington movement found its most receptive audience among impoverished, debt-ridden peasants in East Griqualand and in the northeastern districts of the Transkei. Wellingtonites set up their own churches and "American" schools and solidified their role in opposition politics through links with Garvey's Universal Negro Improvement Association and the ICU during the later 1920s. Buthelezi claimed that 200 churches and 181 schools had been opened in the eastern Cape by 1930. Most schools were housed in the homes of adherents, but few teachers had any formal education beyond Standard II (fourth grade). While the curriculum was apparently the same as in the mission schools, it embraced an Africanist ideology that sought to free the peasant from dependence on European culture.

Buthelezi himself was banned from the Transkei in March 1927, but by then leadership in the Wellington movement was firmly in the hands of local organizers. It would remain a potent force in the countryside during the interwar period. While the Wellingtonites were strongest in the Transkeian Territories, they also appeared in such Ciskeian districts as Queenstown, King William's Town, Komgha, and especially in Herschel, where local authorities were being challenged by dissident peasants at numerous levels during the 1920s.

The Amafela Movement in Herschel

Numerous ethnic groups (Hlubi and other Mfengu, Thembu, Sotho, and some Griqua) lived in Herschel, and a majority of the population by the 1920s was apparently Christian.[47] The mission-educated elite dominated local politics—they controlled the farmers' and teachers' associations, the mission churches and schools, and the local branch of the ANC—but there were deep social and economic divisions within this community of believers.

Dissident politics in Herschel centered on a combination of local grievances, directed against the African political elite and their mission schools, and white traders and government officials who wanted to establish a local council, control the distribution of communal land, and enforce the new uniform tax system imposed on all Africans in South Africa in 1925. As noted in the previous chapter, a portion of these taxes was to be used to fund local councils and schools, the two institutions favored by leaders of the mission-educated community.

While the 1920 Native Affairs Act made the extension of advisory councils in the reserves desirable, the authorities were fearful of establishing one in Herschel because the peasants were so divided on the issue. An educated man named Joseph Fanana, who had once been an interpreter and jail warder, gained control of the local iliso lomzi and joined forces with an alienated sub-headman named Makobeni Mehlomakhulu to lead the dissidents against the council system.

Local authorities were empowered to control the distribution of communal land, it will be remembered, under a proclamation (Government Notice 833) issued in 1921. Officials could now register all land held in communal areas, limit each family to one arable holding, and issue certificates of occupation to registered landholders. The iliso lomzi mobilized opposition against this regulation which, in turn, was linked to the proposed local council. Fanana and Mehlomakhulu led a protest deputation to Pretoria to discuss these grievances in September 1921, and concerned members of the mission-educated community warned the local magistrate they could no longer control public opinion.

The prices paid for goods bought and sold by the traders was also a sensitive topic in Herschel. The women were most concerned because they carried the major burden of providing for their families in a district where most able-bodied males were now migrants. Christian women were particularly well organized in the Anglican and Methodist *manyano* or women's leagues, and they were prepared to defy the traders. Food prices that had increased steadily during World War I had begun to decrease in the urban areas by the early 1920s. In rural areas like Herschel, however, the traders refused to reduce prices, even though the district was still plagued by drought. A multi-ethnic group of impoverished School and Red women organized a boycott against the traders in March 1922. The women stopped picketing after nearly two months when the traders agreed to lower the prices of some goods, but the boycott continued sporadically until mid-1922. Passive resistance against white trading practices also spread to adjacent districts in the Transkei and East Griqualand.

Government authorities in Herschel sought to proceed with the registration of communal land a few months later. Opposition centered once again in the iliso lomzi, and it was so intense that new officials had to be dispatched to the district in mid-1924 to seek compliance. Even so, the campaign to force communal landowners to register their garden plots met with little success, and officials in other Ciskeian districts apparently made no effort to impose this regulation.

While the dissidents in Herschel maintained a facade of legality—the iliso lomzi fought land registration, for example, primarily on the grounds that it was a proclamation and not a law passed by parliament—resistance was hardening by the mid-1920s. The popular Mehlomakhulu, who had been appointed a headman in 1923, was dismissed in 1925 along with others who had attacked the land registration measure. New opposition leaders emerged in the form of preachers like Timothy Mngqibisa, who arrived in March 1925 as minister of the AME church, one of two (with the African Native church) independent congregations in the district. Mngqibisa incorporated existing grievances into his preaching, and he soon had a large following. He also replaced Fanana, who had clashed with Mehlomakhulu in 1925 and moved away from dissident politics, as the leading spokesperson in the iliso lomzi.

The women's movement, the other wing of popular resistance in Herschel during the 1920s, established links with the iliso lomzi and threw its support behind the deposed Mehlomakhulu, who was now making a bid to become a chief headman in the district. Women in considerable numbers were now leaving the Anglican and Methodist mission churches and joining Mngqibisa and the AME church. Religious separatism was associated directly with political protest, and the AME church became a key mediator between the iliso lomzi and the women's movement.

The women directed their attention against the mission schools, an important agency of social control in the rural areas. Since the teachers supported land registration and the proposed council, the children were removed from the classroom. The school boycott, which lasted from October 1925 to about June 1926, helped target new grievances and publicize the activities of the resisters. The term *Amafelandawonye* (we who die together) or *Amafela* was now being used to describe the resistance forces at Herschel—the alliance between the women's movement and the iliso lomzi.

Mehlomakhulu, whose overall leadership was now recognized by both groups, made a trip to Cape Town in March 1926 and persuaded the secretary for native affairs to come to Herschel to discuss the peasants' grievances. The SNA used the occasion, however, to confirm existing Native Affairs Department policies and refused (despite an appeal from the local magistrate) to compromise. The boycotters retaliated by taking possession of one of the schools, and in the ensuing confrontation twenty-seven women were arrested and later fined. Police reinforcements called in to restore order were stoned by the defiant women, but these arrests marked the end of the school boycott and the beginning of a new phase in Herschel's resistance movement.

Boycotts against the traders and schools had expanded into a popular front against any interference from white administrators or the local African mission-educated elite. The dissidents became more entrenched in their support of popularly elected headmen who would protect their right to the land. Having no rights in a common society, many Christians were already moving beyond recognized separatist bodies like the AME church in their search for a fully Africanist religious experience.

At this juncture, the millennialist preacher Buthelezi became involved in the Herschel disturbances. Mngqibisa, leader of the iliso lomzi, had quarreled with Mehlomakhulu and left the district in March 1926. Buthelezi arrived a few months later to take his place as minister of the AME church, married a local woman, and was quickly absorbed in the Amafela movement. As with the Israelite Mgijima, his version of Africanist separatism was almost as antagonistic to the black political elite as it was to white rule. Unlike Mgijima, he was quickly confronted by local authorities and forced to leave the district permanently in December 1926.

Buthelezi nevertheless established a base in the vicinity of Lady Grey near the Herschel border and held meetings periodically in the late 1920s. He maintained his links with the Amafela leadership—especially the women— and helped them set up separate schools in several locations inside Herschel. Eighteen independent schools were reportedly in existence by December 1928, but most of them were closed by the end of the decade. Even with Buthelezi's help, the peasants couldn't afford to keep them going, especially when local officials in Herschel finally began collecting the new African tax levy in 1928. His influence with the Amafela, moreover, was being undermined by a number of ANC factions who had become involved in the internal affairs of the Herschel dissidents during the mid–late 1920s.

Mehlomakhulu, who was instrumental in publicizing Amafela activities to the outside world, had made contact with Thaele, the leader of the Cape Western Congress, in 1925. Thaele, who was trying to secure a foothold in the eastern Cape, urged ANC leaders in Johannesburg to render support, and two representatives were sent to Herschel. Mehlomakhulu returned with them to the Transvaal early in 1926 for further meetings and attended the ANC's yearly conference in Bloemfontein. President-General Zaccheus Mahabane[48] visited the district early in 1927, and his successor, Josiah Gumede, joined Mehlomakhulu in July in another unsuccessful effort to gain concessions from NAD officials in Pretoria.

Congress leaders had one advantage over the Wellingtonites: they were relatively free to hold meetings in Herschel. Thaele also established a branch of his Cape Western Congress in the district in 1928, thereby challenging the leadership of the rival ANC organization controlled by the local mission-educated elite, but his followers could not contain the dissidents. The Thaele-aligned branch of Congress was virtually defunct by the end of the decade.

The resistance movement in Herschel, apparently the best organized and most sustained in the Ciskei reserve during the interwar period, began to fragment soon after Mehlomakhulu died in 1928. The iliso lomzi lost the support of those who had joined the Amafela alliance through the women's movement and the separatist churches. These groups preferred the uncompromising Africanism of the Wellingtonites. Local officials renewed their campaign to register communal land in 1929, and the hated local council, dominated by the mission-educated elite, was finally installed in 1930.

Resistance groups undoubtedly existed elsewhere in rural Ciskei during the interwar period. Africans in the reserve were prohibited in 1935, for example, from carrying arms and other weapons regarded as dangerous, and all work projects authorized by the councils were provided with security. Peasant intransigence did help to delay official attempts to register communal plots, reduce stock, and control land use in the rural locations until the end of the 1930s, when state intervention would again provoke widespread disaffection in the Ciskei.

The African petty bourgeoisie in the eastern Cape at this time steadfastly refused to recognize any political action that called for confrontation with the state. Tengo Jabavu was critical of the Israelites even before the Bulhoek incident: "These people are fanatics. The best course seems to be for the Government to sell them a farm where they can go on with their worship forever and not trouble other people." [49] Imvo relied on official reports of the massacre and exonerated the government of any wrongdoing: "That the people were demented there remains no room to doubt; and no inquiry, however searching, can reveal anything. . . . There are always elements ag'in the Government. These are irresponsible. . . . At the bottom it is a political movement identified with worship. The main object being to drive the whiteman from the country." [50] D. D. T. Jabavu described Mgijima as an example of "an untrained intellect, the undisciplined mind," who "failed in the end to adapt his religion to the conditions imposed by Government." Mgijima's followers were "unsophisticated rustics" who accepted his prophecies "with typical innocence and gullibility." [51]

Imvo regarded Wellington Buthelezi's apparent failure to gain a foothold in the Queenstown District as a victory. As D. D. T. Jabavu put it: "imposters of the type of Wellington would cut no ice with Ciskei Natives, thanks to the [Ciskei Native] Convention, where the educated men led their backward fellow citizens on lines of economic wisdom and loyalty to authority." [52] Joseph Fanana, the one-time spokesman for Herschel's dissidents, was classed with Mgijima as "the so-called leader of the unintelligent people. . . . who suspect everything that leads to better educational facilities, progress and civilisation." [53]

8.3. The Crusade against Hertzog's Native Bills

Popular resistance in any form was unacceptable to African politicians who held the franchise, but a significant shift in government policy on African voting rights had already occurred with the National party's victory in the 1924 election.[54] As noted in Chapter 7, Hertzog was intent on expanding the boundaries of the segregationist state, but he could not do so until Africans in the Cape—the province that supplied most of the indigenous mine labor and contained (with Natal) most of the land set aside as reserves—were subjected to the controls that prevailed in the other provinces. Once South Africa had a single African land and franchise policy, other aspects of the state's segregationist program could be enforced more effectively.

The Franchise Question

The challenge posed by Hertzog's ten-year campaign to disenfranchise the Cape's African voters brought the petty bourgeoisie in the eastern Cape back into the mainstream of African national politics in South Africa. His plan for the Cape African voting community was first revealed in November 1925—seventeen months after the election that had brought the National party to power—during a speech he made to his constituents at Smithfield in the Orange Free State.

The initial proposal would expand Coloured voting rights (they were to be included in a white-dominated "civilised labour" policy), provide Africans with a partially elected and permanent native council to replace the Native Conference set up under the 1920 Native Affairs Act, extend the area set aside for Africans in the reserves, and—the real motive for the speech, as *Imvo* later noted—remove Cape Africans from the common voters' roll in exchange for a few white representatives in parliament.[55]

The importance of the Smithfield speech was made clear by Hertzog when he spoke for the first time to African delegates at the Native Conference held in Pretoria in early December 1925. The first of these conferences had been organized in 1922, a year after the first joint council was founded in Johannesburg. The number of Africans appointed by the government to attend the 1925 conference was increased from twenty-five to fifty, including nineteen chiefs. Hertzog outlined his proposals and told delegates they would be given a chance to respond at the next conference.[56]

Four bills—three relating to Africans and one to Coloureds—were tabled in parliament in July 1926. The main provision of the Native Lands Further Release and Acquisition Bill made available for African purchase the area set aside for the reserves by various provincial land committees in 1918. The Union Native Council Bill created a consultative native council with thirty-five of its fifty members elected by Africans. The Representation of Natives in Parliament Bill removed African voters from the common voters' roll in the Cape. Seven whites in the House of Assembly would represent the African population, and they could vote only on legislation affecting Africans. The whites, in turn, would be elected by a small group of Africans nominated by the central government. The Coloured Persons' Rights Bill extended existing Coloured voting privileges in the Cape to the rest of South Africa. They would now be distinguished from Africans, but the process of cooption stopped far short of giving them equality with whites.[57]

Hertzog's "Native Bills" were integral to his segregationist program, but they hinged on the Representation of Natives in Parliament Bill. The Native Council Bill and the Land Bill were to be offered in exchange for the loss of African voting rights in the Cape. Hertzog insisted the bills be treated as a single legislative package, which meant that public attention would be focused on the African and Coloured franchise bills. Any change in African or Coloured voting rights in the Cape, it will be remembered, required a two-thirds majority vote in a joint sitting of both houses of parliament.

Initial attempts to gain African support for these measures ended in failure. Members of the Native Affairs Commission toured some of the reserves—they addressed Africans, for example, at meetings in Herschel, Queenstown, Lady Frere, King William's Town, and Alice in the Ciskei—but there was little enthusiasm for Hertzog's proposals. Delegates at the Native Conference held in Pretoria in November 1926 passed resolutions strongly condemning the legislation. While some support was expressed for the Native Council Bill, the Land Bill was rejected, and "voteless" Africans from the northern provinces, as D. D. T. Jabavu noted in *Imvo Zabantsundu,* led the debate against the African franchise bill.[58] After this rebuff, Hertzog waited until 1930 before calling another Native Conference, and delegates were forbidden to discuss the Native Bills.[59]

The Cape's African voters won a temporary respite when the House of Assembly rejected Hertzog's four bills at their first reading in March 1927 and referred them to a select committee of parliament. After almost two years and two select committees, a report on Hertzog's bills was finally presented to parliament in January 1929. Hertzog decided to withdraw temporarily the Native Council and Land bills in February and submit revised and more restricted versions of the Coloured and African franchise bills to a joint sitting of parliament. He tried to woo Smuts and the South African party in a bid to obtain bipartisan support for the legislation, but the bills failed to gain the necessary majority.

The prime minister again submitted the Coloured and African franchise bills to a joint sitting of parliament in February 1930, but again they failed to obtain the necessary majority. Hertzog then referred the four bills to a new interparty select committee, whose meetings were closed to the public. Between 1930 and 1935, this joint select committee worked on revising and reformulating these bills. The Coloured franchise bill was finally abandoned (very few Nationalists were in favor of extending the vote to Coloureds in the Orange Free State and Transvaal), and in May 1930 the committee voted to reject "common representation in Parliament for Europeans and Natives."[60]

Meanwhile, universal white suffrage in South Africa was assured with the Women's Enfranchisement Act of 1930, giving white females the vote, and the Franchise Laws Amendment Act of 1931, removing all property and literacy tests for white voters. At the same time, electoral officials continuously challenged the voting rights of existing African franchise holders and sought to limit the registration of new voters. Despite the efforts of the Cape Native Voters' Convention and other civil rights groups, who defended individual cases at considerable cost in court, the number of African voters continued to decline (Table 8.1). By 1933, they represented only 2.7 percent of the electorate in the Cape and 1.2 percent in South Africa.

Smuts and Hertzog agreed to form a coalition government in the aftermath of the Great Depression, and the two ex-Boer War generals and their followers joined forces in 1934 to form a new United party with Hertzog as prime minister and Smuts as his deputy. Those African politicians who still believed Britain would intervene if their franchise rights were really threatened lost that guarantee with the Statute of Westminster, which was passed by the British parliament in 1931 and embodied in South Africa in the Status of the Union Act 69 of 1934. Even in theory, legislation discriminating against blacks was no longer subject to appeal to the Crown.[61]

The fate of the African voter in the Cape was sealed when the joint select committee's final report on Hertzog's Native Bills was presented to parliament in April 1935. The four original bills had now been reduced to the Native Trust and Land Bill and the Representation of Natives Bill. Hertzog announced that the two revised bills would be presented to a special joint sitting of parliament in 1936.

The Liberal Opposition

The Cape African voting community responded to these developments by mounting a massive publicity campaign of resolutions, petitions, pamphlets, and public prayers. In other words, the tactics employed by Cape African voters in protesting Hertzog's Native Bills were virtually the same as those employed by Tengo Jabavu and his contemporaries in the 1880s and 1890s, when the African franchise was weakened to the point where it was no longer even a potential threat to Cape colonial rule.

African politicians worked through white voluntary organizations, government-sponsored consultative bodies, and their own political organizations. The first of the four Non-European Conferences organized by D. D. T. Jabavu and Abdul Abdurahman, for example, was held in Kimberley in June 1927. It was attended by 114 African, Coloured, and Indian delegates, and resolutions were passed rejecting both the Coloured and African franchise bills.[62] Leading white members of the joint-council movement meeting under the auspices of the European-Bantu Conference in Cape Town in February 1929 expressed the same sentiments as African members in condemning legislation that discriminated on the basis of color. A motion was passed deploring "any alteration of the law which would result in depriving the Natives of the Cape Province of the franchise in its present form."[63]

The liberal resolve to resist Hertzog's discriminatory legislation, however, was largely a facade. As Saul Dubow points out in a detailed analysis of these events, liberal responses to Hertzog's Native Bills were "ambivalent." The franchise debate in particular illustrated "the confusion and powerlessness of the extra-parliamentary opposition." [64]

The opposition South African party was divided over the Cape franchise from the beginning. MPs especially from the eastern Cape supported the 1910 constitution and believed the African vote was still important in a number of constituencies, but MPs in Natal and the other northern provinces opposed a separate Cape franchise. Smuts was a white supremacist who hardly differed from Hertzog when it came to the mechanisms to be used in subordinating the black population. He had no real alternative to Hertzog's proposals, so he sent out mixed messages in a bid to maintain party unity. Those S.A.P. members most antagonistic to the Cape franchise, led by men like G. N. Heaton Nicholls, a Natal sugar baron, and Col. C. F. Stallard, party leader on the Rand, were placed on the joint select committee that reviewed this legislation between 1930 and 1935. In the absence of public debate, the S.A.P. was essentially committed to abolishing the African vote by May 1930.

White and black liberals were also divided over the Cape franchise, which was supported in public but increasingly subject to negotiation in private. Heaton Nicholls, J. S. Marwick, and other Natal hardliners were among those who believed the African political elite would swap the franchise for more land in the reserves. D. D. T. Jabavu apparently rejected a deal on these terms, but several prominent ANC leaders were prepared to consider it in the early 1930s. These included Pixley Seme, the ANC president-general (1930–37), who was buying land in the eastern Transvaal and had several cooperative business ventures in Johannesburg, and John Dube, who was also involved in land purchases and had firm links with the Natal sugar barons. Nicholls actually recruited Dube to canvass African opinion on this issue, and Dube traveled to Johannesburg, Kimberley, Bloemfontein, and the eastern Cape to promote a land bill that Nicholls had written for the joint select committee. Dube claimed several African opinion leaders, including ANC officials in the Transvaal like H. Selby Msimang and *Bantu World* editor Selope Thema, had actually signed a document supporting the measure. The land bill presented to parliament in 1935 was based on Nicholls' proposal.[65]

Even leading members of eastern Cape regional bodies were willing to compromise on the Cape franchise bill. Meshach Pelem of Bantu Union claimed erroneously before the first select committee in 1927 that his organization favored "separate representation for Natives," [66] and Bennett Ncwana, secretary of the Cape Native Voters' Convention, broke ranks and supported Hertzog's franchise plan in a letter to *Umteteli Wa Bantu* in 1930. The reaction of chiefs, headmen, and other leaders in the rural areas was equally contradictory. The Transkeian Territorial Council expressed its opposition to Hertzog's proposals, attacking the African franchise bill on several occasions, but there were virtually no references to this legislation in the Ciskeian General Council.[67]

Meanwhile, white liberals in Cape Town, including James Rose-Innes, one of Tengo Jabavu's major benefactors, who had retired as South Africa's chief justice in 1927, formed the Non-Racial Franchise Association (NRFA) in April 1929 "to resist any measure differentiating between franchise rights of the Cape Province on account of race or color" and "to promote a policy of making a certain standard of civilization a qualification for the franchise throughout the Union."[68] The NRFA was a throwback to the mid-Victorian ideal that emphasized the bonds of common citizenship between "civilised" Africans and "civilised" Europeans. It was "the authentic voice," as Dubow put it, "of nineteenth-century Cape liberalism." Although the NRFA and allied groups like the National Franchise League had little support outside the Cape, their uncompromising stand on African voting rights embarrassed Smuts and the South African party, especially during the 1929 election.[69]

The interracial joint councils and their surrogates helped mobilize protest against the Native Bills, but the doctrine of segregation tended to permeate the rhetoric of white-sponsored groups that sought to promote African political and civil rights.[70] Hertzog's policies provoked dissension between key players like J. D. Rheinallt Jones and Howard Pim, who accepted segregation but opposed the African franchise bill, and Charles T. Loram, who accepted this measure and felt the joint councils should not get involved in politics.[71] The joint councils set up the South African Institute of Race Relations (SAIRR) in 1929 to oversee council activities and collect data on race relations,[72] and four years later SAIRR director Rheinallt Jones created a committee to coordinate the political activities of the joint councils. This committee would play a key role in organizing the campaign against Hertzog's bills when they were reintroduced in parliament in 1935.

White-dominated organizations like the NRFA, the joint councils, and the SAIRR, the Non-European Conferences chaired by Jabavu and Abdurahman, and regional and national African bodies like the Cape Native Voters' Convention and the ANC never developed a long-term strategy to fight the Native Bills during the five years they were locked up in parliamentary committees. Despite the publicity surrounding the fundamental issue of the Cape African franchise, the limits of constitutional protest were hardly tested. The liberal petty bourgeoisie never managed to mount a unified nonracial front against Hertzog's segregationist policies, and the mass of African peasants and industrial workers remained on the periphery as far as these events were concerned.

Figure 8.2. African modernizers of the new order after 1910: political activists in the Ciskei region included men like, *left*, Z. K. Matthews, *right*, James Calata and, *on the facing page*, D. D. T. Jabavu photographed in 1921, when he was a lecturer at Fort Hare. Matthews and Calata were key ANC leaders in the eastern Cape during the 1930s and 1940s.

The All-African Convention

Parts of the revised franchise bill submitted to parliament in April 1935 were more restrictive than any previous version. Africans in the Cape and South Africa's three other provinces would be represented in parliament by four white senators, but African interests would not be represented in the House of Assembly as envisaged in the 1926 franchise bill. A twenty-two-member Natives' Representative Council would be established as a national consultative body—instead of the fifty members envisaged in the 1926 Native Council Bill—consisting of sixteen Africans (twelve elected and four nominated by the government) and six whites. The secretary for native affairs would chair the NRC and have a casting vote. The five native affairs commissioners would sit on the NRC but they would not be able to vote.

The official African reaction to Hertzog's revised bills came from a series of conferences hastily convened by the secretary for native affairs and members of the Native Affairs Commission in Pretoria, Pietermaritzburg, Mafeking, Kimberley, King William's Town, and Umtata in September 1935. About a thousand Africans—selected chiefs, headmen, and leaders of the main political organizations—were invited to discuss these bills on the eve of their

presentation to parliament. Jabavu noted that Hertzog's proposals had not been translated into the vernacular languages or distributed to African representatives before the meetings. He feared the meetings were being held "to divide us into sections so that we may contradict each other," [73] and the African response in fact was ambiguous.

The land bill was favored by many because it proposed to increase the area set aside for Africans. Similar opinions were expressed with regard to the Natives' Representative Council, which provided some representation for Africans at the national level. Delegates in Pretoria did not comment on the franchise bill, while delegates in Pietermaritzburg apparently limited their comments to rejecting "a European representative in Parliament." The Cape delegations (Mafeking, Kimberley, King William's Town, and Umtata) were predictably the most outspoken in condemning the franchise bill. The King William's Town delegation offered twenty-five points in support of its position that the African vote be retained. For the Kimberley delegates, the bill was "indefensible from every ethical point of view . . . uncharitable as it is unjustifiable." [74]

Soon after the Representation of Natives Bill was published, moderate African nationalists in the Transvaal called for a national convention under the chairmanship of D. D. T. Jabavu that embraced all non-European groups opposed to Hertzog's segregation policies. On December 16, 1935, more than four hundred African and Coloured delegates from an estimated seventy-three organizations convened in the African township in Bloemfontein, the chosen venue for African national conferences since the South African Native Convention had met there in 1969 to protest the impending Act of Union. [75] It was probably the most representative body of African political opinion ever brought together in one place up to that point in South African history.

The All-African Convention (AAC) rejected political separation as envisaged in the franchise bill because it would create "two nations in South Africa, whose interests and aspirations must inevitably clash in the end and thus cause unnecessary bitterness and political strife." Loss of a "common citizenship" would endanger the possibility of participating in the political process "through constitutional channels." All racial groups were "bound together by the pursuit of common political objectives," and delegates insisted that "the rights of citizenship" must be extended "to all" in South Africa. But they also accepted the necessity for a qualified franchise—a "civilisation test" based on an "educational or property or wage qualification"—to protect the whites "in whose favor the dice are already heavily loaded." And they agreed that "the various racial groups may develop on their own lines, socially and culturally."

In keeping with previous tactics, they called for a national day of prayer ("a day of universal humiliation and intercession"), asked sympathetic members of parliament to oppose the legislation, requested that the governor-general refuse the franchise bill should it be passed by parliament, and appealed to King George V and the British parliament "for an expression of their opinion" on the loss of the Cape African franchise. They also accepted a suggestion from John Gomas, a Coloured member of the Communist party from Cape Town, that committees in the urban areas be formed to organize "protest meetings" against the franchise bill.

The AAC rejected the Natives' Representative Council because it was "a substitute for the Cape Native franchise." While delegates "welcomed" the government's willingness to consider making more land available to Africans, the amount of land envisaged was unacceptable for present and future needs. Delegates deplored the deteriorating position of Africans employed on white farms and condemned a wide range of "repressive legislation" which "tended to emasculate the Africans and to relegate them to a position bordering on slavery." The delegates resolved to make the Convention a permanent federal body and appointed a deputation to present the resolutions passed at the conference to parliament.[76]

While virtually every segment of organized African political opinion was represented at the Convention, the delegates actually represented "very little but themselves," as Eddie Roux later put it.[77] Those Africans most in sympathy with the joint-council movement were in fact the ones who had proposed the Convention through their regional and national bodies, and Rheinallt Jones of the SAIRR helped finance the proceedings.[78] The AAC executive committee would work very closely with the joint councils in the final campaign—communicated for the most part through SAIRR pamphlets and the English-language press—to convince parliament to reject the franchise bill. A conference was organized in Cape Town in January 1936 to coincide with the opening of the franchise bill debate in parliament, and the joint councils joined forces with the AAC deputation (headed by Jabavu), which had arrived in Cape Town to present its resolutions to sympathetic legislators.

At this juncture, a group of MPs from the eastern Cape offered a so-called compromise on the franchise bill. The original measure had allowed registered African voters to remain on the common roll, but new voters would be placed on a separate roll. The revised measure would place all African voters on a special Cape voters' roll: they could vote for three white members to the House of Assembly and two white members to the Cape Provincial Council in addition to the four white senators. Hertzog accepted the proposal and presented it to the AAC deputation, because he assumed the new franchise bill would be acceptable to the African voting community as well as the liberal wing of his party in the Cape. Jabavu summoned the AAC's executive committee to Cape Town, and Hertzog apparently did persuade some members to support his proposal.[79] After two days of private discussions, however, the Africans unanimously rejected this alternative: they "could not bargain nor compromise with the political citizenship of the African people by sacrificing the franchise." [80]

Hertzog and his deputy Smuts, of course, were not deterred. They went forward with the new Representation of Natives Bill, and it was approved 169–11 at a joint sitting of both houses of parliament on April 6, 1936—"Black Monday" as it would be remembered by the Cape African voting community.[81] The Native Trust and Land Bill was approved in parliament the following month without revision.

The AAC under Jabavu's leadership was not really prepared to contest the legislation. The mass protests that had been envisioned did not materialize. Individual Africans raised objections to the removal of their names from the common roll and disputed the validity of the franchise act in court, but these attempts to postpone or overturn the measure failed. The AAC's second conference was held in Bloemfontein in June 1936 following the passage of the Native Bills. Jabavu urged delegates to adopt what he described as "an intermediate policy of using what can be used and fighting against all that we do not want." [82]

The conference approved a "Programme of Action" recording its "profound disappointment" at the passage of the land and franchise bills. Delegates reiterated their appeal for "common and citizenship rights for all" and instructed the executive committee to enlist affiliated organizations "to devise ways and means . . . for the attainment of these objectives." A vocal minority—mainly Coloured and African Trotskyites from Cape Town—tried to convince the delegates to boycott the newly created Natives' Representative Council, but Jabavu won in the end. The AAC would rely on the NRC and the white parliamentary representatives to defend what remained of African political rights in South Africa.[83]

The date of the first elections under the Representation of Natives Act was set for June 1937. Every African opposition group, including the Communist party, participated in the election campaign, but the AAC returned thirteen of the twenty-one candidates who won seats in the NRC, parliament, and the Cape Provincial Council.[84] NRC representatives from the eastern Cape included CNVC officials Alexander Jabavu and Richard Godlo and the veteran Transkei politician Charles Sakwe. Bertram B. Xiniwe, a lawyer from King William's Town and eldest son of the eastern Cape's best-known African entrepreneur at the turn of the century, was also elected. Margaret Ballinger, a university lecturer, beat her AAC-sponsored opponent in the eastern Cape parliamentary contest primarily because she had pledged to fight for the restoration of the Cape franchise and its extension to the three northern provinces.[85]

Thus the AAC now embraced the segregated institutions that had been rejected at the first conference in June 1935. Delegates who met in Bloemfontein for the third conference in December 1937—thirty-nine organizations attended, including three ANC provincial bodies—were faced with a fait accompli. Six white representatives in parliament and the Cape Provincial Council along with at least four members of the NRC were present to endorse the AAC's new statement of policy, and all those elected were "recognised as the accepted mouthpiece of Africans." [86]

The voting community felt it had no option but to continue participating in the few segregated consulting bodies that had been set aside for Africans. The tactics of constitutional protest had ultimately failed to preserve a space for the African petty bourgeoisie in South Africa's political order. As an anonymous correspondent to the *Cape Times* observed in 1933:

the confidence in European assistance and sympathy, which it is the policy of the Joint Councils to foster in the native mind, will merely blind both the natives and the Europeans to the truth. . . . the European population as a whole is implacably determined upon the permanent subjection of the native races. . . . Any attempt to inform natives of the causes of their sufferings, any attempt to organise them into bodies by which they may bring about the removal of those causes will inevitably lead to banishment, prison, or deportation. It is, in fact, impossible, to achieve reform within the framework of South African constitutional and criminal law.

The letter ended with a prophetic warning: "This is the dilemma which confronts South African liberals—the law gives the Government power. . . . to make effective action illegal; while activities which can be carried on in the sunshine of Government approval must always be those which are ineffective." [87]

9

Opposition Politics and Popular Resistance II

A resurgence in black opposition politics and popular resistance at the national and regional level occurred during the 1940s and 1950s, and these activities were accompanied by an unparalleled expansion in South Africa's industrial economy.[1] The most significant economic development was in secondary industry, especially manufacturing. As a contribution to the national income, manufacturing had already moved ahead of agriculture by 1930; fueled by the war economy, it passed mining in 1943. The demand for African industrial workers increased dramatically, especially during the war years when the labor pool contracted as hundreds of thousands of black and white South Africans were serving in the armed forces. The number of Africans employed in manufacturing alone more than doubled from 151,889 in 1939/40 to 369,055 in 1949/50.

The plight of rural dwellers in the Ciskei was now the plight of rural dwellers almost everywhere in South Africa. The number of African peasant families migrating out of necessity to the cities rose steadily during the 1930s and dramatically during the 1940s and 1950s. For the first time women as well as men were being employed extensively in the factories, and the permanent urban African population doubled from roughly 1.2 million in 1936 to 2.4 million in 1951. More Africans than whites were living in town by 1946. Urban Africans comprised 18.5 percent of the total African population in 1936 and 27.8 percent in 1951. Johannesburg had the largest African population with 513,726 in 1951—an increase of 109.4 percent in fifteen years. Growth rates in the port cities were even more impressive: African populations in Durban, Cape Town, and Port Elizabeth, for example, increased by 129.0, 268.9, and 142.2 percent, respectively, between 1936 and 1951.

As Africans flooded the cities, living conditions worsened for most industrial workers. Municipal officials were unable to provide housing, and so-called squatter camps sprang up everywhere as Africans seized vacant land and built their own makeshift homes. The price of essential foods, moreover, rose 91 percent between 1939 and 1944 and almost 50 percent between 1944 and 1950.

Even relatively high paid workers were below the minimum subsistence level, and according to one survey food alone accounted for 87 percent of an urban African family's budget.[2]

Popular resistance grew in town and countryside. Although Africans were forbidden to strike, there was a dramatic increase in unorganized as well as organized work stoppages during the war by workers in Johannesburg and other Rand towns and in the major port cities.[3] Mass protests in Johannesburg's black townships, in particular, were also evident during the 1940s: community action groups organized a series of bus boycotts in the African township of Alexandra between 1940 and 1945, and the desperate housing shortage triggered a squatters' rights movement in several townships between 1944 and 1947. Unrest in South Africa's peripheral reserves rose to the surface again in the early 1940s, and sporadic outbreaks of violence continued for two decades.

The African petty bourgeoisie was largely unprepared for this upsurge in popular consciousness. Fearful of Afrikaner nationalism and powerless in any event to alter the course of events, black political opposition groups with varying degrees of enthusiasm supported the policies of General Smuts, who had lobbied vigorously in support of South Africa's entry on the side of Britain and her allies at the outbreak of World War II. This split the ruling United party, and Smuts again became prime minister in September 1939. Hertzog and his followers, who wanted South Africa to remain neutral, merged with dissident Afrikaner nationalists under Daniel Malan to form the opposition "Reunited" National party in January 1940. The ANC, the communists (after the German invasion of the Soviet Union in 1941), and virtually every other organized protest group rejected the tactics of direct action in the interests of maintaining the war effort.

The United party government under Smuts (1939–48) did respond to some extent to African grievances. Various economic interests (represented primarily by commerce and manufacturing) and their advocates within the United party were beginning to think that productivity would be enhanced if a permanent African labor force enjoying an improved standard of living was housed in the cities. Allied defeats in the early years of the war and the activities of several pro-Nazi groups in South Africa, moreover, convinced many leaders in government and industry that they should respond more positively to African trade union demands. Such views were in conflict with other economic interests (represented primarily by mining and agriculture), and their advocates within the opposition National party, who could not compete with secondary industry in attracting workers and continued to rely heavily on migrant labor.

The prime minister himself publicly endorsed the principles enshrined in the 1941 Atlantic Charter, which had outlined the postwar aims of the allies and anticipated the United Nations,[4] and in a widely reported speech at a South African Institute of Race Relations meeting in March 1942 he declared that "segregation has fallen on evil days." [5] The pass laws controlling African migration to the cities were temporarily relaxed during the early years of the war, and some urban workers (especially in manufacturing) succeeded in gaining significant wage increases. The minister of labor had expressed support for some kind of recognition for African unions as early as 1939, and this was reinforced in various government commissions and reports in the 1940s.[6] The 1941 Workman's Compensation Act offered limited benefits to black workers, and the 1945 Native Education Act made more money available for African schools and established an eleven-member national advisory board that included two Africans. Free school meals were introduced in 1943, and in the following year the Old Age Pensions Act (1926) and Blind Persons Act (1936) were amended to include Africans. Unemployment and disability grants were also extended to Africans in 1946.

But social welfare and educational benefits for Africans remained glaringly unequal and discriminatory. Strikes were banned in 1942 (War Measure 145), and a regulation prohibiting meetings of more than twenty persons on ground "proclaimed" as off limits by the authorities (Proclamation 201 of 1939) was reinforced with specific reference to property owned by mining companies (War Measure 1425 of 1944). Officials stopped talking about recognizing African trade unions,[7] the pass laws were tightened up again toward the end of the war, and the government again sought to intervene in the reserves in an effort to control the use of the land. The major confrontation between African labor and the state during this decade ended in disaster for the workers, their leaders, and the unions, when the Smuts government brutally repressed a strike by 70,000–100,000 mineworkers in Johannesburg in August 1946.

Effective cooperation between white and black liberals also declined in the 1940s. The joint councils, operating mainly as welfare organizations after the failure of the African franchise crusade, experienced a drastic drop in African membership, even though leading ANC officials continued to serve on these bodies. The SAIRR lost almost 50 percent of its African members between 1944 and 1947, and interracial contacts between volunteer student and church groups were also apparently much less frequent in the 1940s and 1950s.

Historians have interpreted these decades as being one of increasing violence and mass mobilization against a unified, monolithic state. The ANC and/ or its allies launched a series of nonviolent strikes, boycotts, and stay-at-home campaigns centering in the cities, and elite politics faded away in the crusade for full democratic rights. The shift to violent resistance began a year after the Sharpeville-Langa shootings and the outlawing of Congress and its Africanist offshoot the Pan-Africanist Congress in March–April 1960. The last vestiges of legal protection were swept aside, political dissidents detained and imprisoned, and most black and radical white opposition groups driven into exile. There was no other alternative but armed struggle.

Two assumptions informing this interpretation—the solidarity of the resistance movement and the unity and efficiency of the state—have recently been subjected to revisionist critiques. Moderate petty bourgeois dominance over African nationalist politics has now been extended to the early 1960s by most scholars and even to the 1980s by some who questioned the ANC's commitment to a strategy of resistance that would bring the working classes to power.[8]

Dennis Davis and Bob Fine contend that African leaders in the 1940s and 1950s continued to rely on agitation from above that essentially marginalized or attempted to coopt popular grievances. They remained isolated from the mass of industrial workers and peasants during a critical period in the history of the African nationalist movement.[9] The turn to armed struggle in 1961 was made prematurely and without reference to the alienated workers, who as one participant put it "were left on the threshold, fascinated bystanders of a battle being waged on their behalf." [10] This decision effectively increased the credibility of the ruling Afrikaner Nationalists among white voters and allowed them to strengthen the central government's repressive apparatus at a turning point in South African history. It took more than a decade before the workers were ready once again to confront the regime.

Chapter 10 will consider the role of the state in the apartheid era. This chapter continues to examine the contradictions in petty bourgeois politics and popular resistance at the national and regional level during the 1940s and 1950s.

Section 9.1 outlines the resurgence of the ANC and the leadership of the Congress Youth League in African nationalist politics during the 1940s, the role of the Communist party in the revived African trade union movement, and the All-African Convention's new strategy of noncollaboration following the loss of the Cape African franchise.

Section 9.2 chronicles opposition politics at the national level during the 1950s. The ANC-inspired mass resistance movement is highlighted by three events—the 1952 Defiance Campaign, the 1955 Freedom Charter, and the separation of the Africanists from Congress at the end of the decade.

Section 9.3 focuses on those events in opposition politics at the national level that acted as lightning rods for converging local grievances in rural Ciskei during the 1940s and 1950s. Mass mobilization against the state in the 1952 Defiance Campaign and in the agitation against Bantu education during the mid–late 1950s was reified in the experiences of dissidents in the Ciskei, but popular resistance was sustained by local issues centering on the government's continued attempts to intervene in the reserve.

9.1. The Resurgence of the ANC in National Politics

The ANC had perhaps 1,000 members when Alfred Bitini Xuma (1893–1962), a physician with a practice in Johannesburg, was elected president-general in December 1940.[11] In the next nine years, he would employ his considerable talents as an administrator to reassert central control over the organization, strengthen financial accountability, and cooperate more effectively with sympathetic white, Coloured, and Indian protest groups.[12] ANC membership would increase more than five times between 1940 and 1947 to a record 5,517 members (more than half in the Transvaal) for the decade.[13]

Xuma and the other moderates who still controlled the ANC became increasingly more demanding in their political rhetoric. Congress was now calling for African representation at all levels of government, individual and/or collective land rights in the urban and rural areas even if segregated reserves were retained, and the recognition of African trade unions. ANC resolutions also included a minimum wage for all workers, equal pay for equal work and an end to the color bar in employment, trading rights, equal social welfare benefits, a single progressive tax system applicable to all races, free and compulsory primary education, and the removal of all forms of statutory discrimination. These resolutions were first codified in a bill of rights manifesto entitled "Africans' Claims in South Africa," which was adopted by Congress in December 1943. Among the points were two calling for "full citizenship rights" and "redistribution of the land." [14]

Xuma also initiated a new, streamlined constitution to replace the detailed, twenty-eight-page document drafted in 1919. Key changes involved the chiefs, who finally lost their special privileges, and female members, who were given full equality. Membership in the organization was now extended in theory to anyone of any race who was "willing to subscribe to the aims of Congress." Branch responsibilities (especially in financial matters) were set out in some detail, and authority was centralized in a new working committee consisting of members who lived within fifty miles of the national headquarters in Johannesburg.[15]

Congress continued to promote the various government-sponsored consultative bodies in the rural and urban areas. At the national level, members mobilized support for the native representatives in parliament and especially the Natives' Representative Council, a "black parliament" to militants and moderates alike.[16] Z. K. Matthews (1901–68), then a lecturer at Fort Hare and a Xuma supporter, replaced the ailing Alexander Jabavu as NRC representative for the Cape rural areas in 1942 and was elected chairman of the NRC caucus after the death of John Dube, the Natal leader, in 1946.[17] Bertram Xiniwe would retain the other NRC seat for the rural Cape until his death in 1949, while Richard Godlo would hold the Cape urban areas seat until the NRC was disbanded in 1951. Margaret Ballinger remained the native representative for the eastern Cape until African representation in parliament in any form was abolished in 1960.

Xuma's chief collaborator in the Cape was James Calata (1895–1984), head of the eastern Cape branch at Cradock and ANC secretary-general for thirteen years during this turbulent period.[18] Calata's major task was to unify the various Congress factions in the province—he had been elected Cape ANC president in 1930—and to strengthen its links with regional politicians who were traditionally reluctant to commit themselves to the national movement. He was aided in these efforts by a dedicated group of ANC advisers in the eastern Cape. These included men like Matthews, who had joined the ANC in 1940, and Matthews' brother-in-law Roseberry T. Bokwe (1900–63), a physician (and the only African district surgeon at the time in South Africa) from Middledrift.

Calata, however, was not able to unify the many splinter groups of the Cape ANC during the 1940s. A year after Xuma was elected, Calata himself lost the Cape presidency to Frank Pendla, the unsuccessful candidate for the Cape provincial council seat of Port Elizabeth in the 1929 general election. The Pendla faction wanted to print its own ANC membership cards and retain control of the fees, affiliate with the All-African Convention, but also sponsor its own native representative in parliament. Xuma suspended the separatist leaders in September 1942 and Calata was again elected president, but re-covery thereafter was slow. Congress membership in the Cape—pressured by police (the Cape ANC's biggest branch at Cradock, for example, was raided in 1943), personality clashes between ANC members, and factional disputes with the AAC—would lag far behind those of the other provincial congresses in the 1940s.[19]

The resurgence of the ANC in South Africa depended not so much on numbers as on the quality of a new group of alienated political activists drawn from a population that was more literate and more varied in religious and vocational composition than the previous generation. Between 250,000 and 500,000 Africans, for example, were believed to be reading newspapers and other periodicals by 1946. About 21.3 percent of the adult African population was regarded as literate in 1946 and 23.8 percent in 1951, when the first white-controlled mass-circulation magazines and newspapers aimed at the African market such as *Drum* and *Golden City Post* were launched.[20]

Although the ANC's leadership cadre would include semi-educated artisans, clerical and industrial workers, and even domestics by the 1950s, it was still largely a professional elite trained in mission boarding schools. Xuma and his colleagues, however, were well aware of the need for more effective leadership in Congress. They worked hard to recruit younger members, and the ANC Youth League was formally established in Johannesburg with Xuma's blessing in April 1944. While the Youth Leaguers were drawn for the most part from the same social class that had produced most of the politicians since the 1880s, it is significant that none of them were clerics and few, if any, had been educated overseas. They had fewer illusions about the nature of white rule in South Africa, and they were not so dependent on the tactics of moral suasion characteristic of the nationalist movement in the past.

The Youth Leaguers were suspicious of alliances with non-African organizations, and their links with dissident African worker and peasant groups were also tentative, except in certain regions like the Ciskei in the early 1950s. Nevertheless, they were convinced Congress could provide the leadership needed to direct a mass movement. They envisaged a new organization that would appeal to all Africans. Men like Anton Lembede, the Youth League's leading theoretician until his premature death at the age of thirty-three in July 1947, preached an African consciousness that transcended ethnic, socio-economic, and cultural boundaries.

Like those who had launched the Gaelic League in Ireland two generations earlier, the Youth League sought to cleanse African nationalism of elitism and dependence on others. A few Youth Leaguers—particularly those with marxist sympathies—urged alliances with all racial groups that rejected white domination, but for Lembede and his followers even cooperation with Coloureds and Indians was "a fantastic dream." [21] Most members in the mid–late 1940s accepted the view that formal alliances with outside groups were premature. Africans themselves had to be organized before they could consider links with other groups.

The founders of the Youth League were teachers, skilled clerks, and upper-ranked professionals, and all were under forty years of age. Patrick Mda, a university graduate who became a teacher and eventually qualified as an attorney, succeeded Lembede as president of the organization. Mda was the son of a progressive peasant family—his father was a headman and shoemaker by trade and his mother a teacher—from the Herschel District. Jordan Ngubane, a journalist who was editor of the Youth League's unofficial organ *Inkundla ya Bantu* (Bantu Forum), was born near Ladysmith in Natal, the son of a policeman-cum-landowner. William Nkomo, a graduate of Fort Hare who later qualified as a medical doctor, was born near Pretoria, the son of a Methodist minister. Only a few stemmed from more humble origins. Lembede himself was the son of poor tenant sharecroppers who had worked on a white farm near Durban, but he eventually acquired three degrees, became a teacher, and also qualified as an attorney. Walter Sisulu, a factory worker and later a real estate agent, was born in Xuma's home district of Engcobo in the Transkei and raised by his mother and an uncle, who were impoverished members of the local Christian community. [22]

The Youth League had expanded to virtually all the major cities and towns and to some rural districts in South Africa by the end of the 1940s. Youth League branches, for example, were formed in Port Elizabeth, Cradock, East London, and several towns in the Ciskei hinterland. The main branch in the region, however, was at Fort Hare, the university that was now furnishing the bulk of the nation's African professional elite.

Nelson Mandela and Oliver Tambo had both gone to Fort Hare—Mandela was suspended after a student protest in 1940 and Tambo graduated in 1941— and they were among the founding fathers of the Youth League in Johannesburg. The All-African Convention had been active at Fort Hare for more than a decade, and there was an established tradition of dissident politics at the university when the Youth League branch was established in 1948.[23] Godfrey Pitje, a lecturer in anthropology, was elected president, and Joe Matthews, the eldest son of Z. K. Matthews, was his secretary. Duma Nokwe, a future ANC secretary-general, was also a founding member.[24]

The Youth League branch at Fort Hare would become an important center of ANC activity in the Ciskei hinterland during the early 1950s. Many Africanists had grown up in rural communities—the Youth League's first branch in the Ciskei was founded by Mda at Herschel—and Youth Leaguers at Fort Hare shared the AAC's interest in mobilizing popular resistance in the African reserves.

The AAC and the Rhetoric of Noncollaboration

Although the All-African Convention was established as a permanent federal body in December 1937, the first national conferences were held only once every three years. The executive was dominated by men like D. D. T. Jabavu (who would remain president of the organization until December 1948) and old guard officials of Congress. Zaccheus Mahabane, a Methodist minister and former ANC president-general (1924–27), succeeded A. B. Xuma as vice president of the Convention in 1937 and kept this post when he replaced Pixley Seme to serve a second term as president-general of Congress (1937–40). When Xuma beat him by one vote to become the new ANC leader in 1940, Mahabane retained his membership in both organizations—as chaplain of Congress and vice president of the Convention (a post he would not relinquish until 1954). James S. Moroka, a physician with a practice in the rural area of Thaba 'Nchu in the Orange Free State, was AAC treasurer in 1936, and he would succeed Xuma as president-general of the ANC in 1949.[25] Other activists in the AAC during the late 1930s who would play crucial roles in Congress in the next decade included the two moderate nationalist leaders from the eastern Cape, Anglican priest James Calata and Fort Hare academic Z. K. Matthews.

The AAC also contained a relatively vociferous group of African and Coloured militants, who were unwilling to accept the tactics of collaboration that had characterized black protest politics during the interwar period. The leaders of this group were teachers associated with the Cape African Teachers' Association (CATA), the largest African professional body in the Cape at the time, and other salaried professionals active in various left-wing discussion groups (especially those associated with the Trotskyites) in and around Cape Town.[26]

Isaac B. Tabata, one of the AAC's most prominent African activists, grew up in Lesseyton (the Methodist station) near Queenstown and attended Fort Hare before settling in Cape Town in 1931. Tabata was a delegate to the AAC's first conference along with associates like the physician Goolam Gool, a prominent member of the Coloured community in Cape Town. He married Gool's sister Janub, another AAC activist. CATA would join the AAC officially in 1948, largely due to the efforts of men like Wycliffe Tsotsi, a teacher and later an attorney who lived in the Ciskei's Glen Grey District, and Nathaniel Honono, a teacher and businessman from Umtata, capital of the Transkei. Tsotsi, who married Tabata's sister, would succeed Jabavu as president of the AAC in 1948, and he would be followed by Honono in 1959.[27]

Coloured leaders, who had hitherto played a marginal role in African politics, were adopting an increasingly militant posture in the AAC by the early 1940s. They were galvanized into action when the government set up a separate body, the Coloured Affairs Department (CAD), in 1943. Anti-CAD forces, led by men like Gool, Tabata, and Benjamin Kies, a teacher from Cape Town, issued a "call for unity" to the AAC and the South African Indian Congress (SAIC) to join together to fight the government's segregation policies.

The AAC's executive committee, meeting in August 1943, agreed "to enter into negotiations for a unification of all Non-European peoples in the struggle against segregation, a struggle for full citizenship rights." [28] The anti-CAD coalition and the SAIC were invited to attend the AAC's triennial conference in December 1943, where a "Draft Declaration of Unity" and a "10-Point Programme" were approved by the delegates. The anti-CAD coalition and the AAC were to comprise a new federal body called the Non-European Unity Movement (NEUM). As a comprehensive bill of rights, the ten-point program established several important precedents for the democratic movement. The qualified franchise, for example, was dropped in favor of a universal franchise for all men and women above the age of twenty-one, and individual rights (including the right to compulsory, free, and uniform education for all children to the age of sixteen) were to be guaranteed. The manifesto also called for sweeping changes in land ownership, workers' rights, taxation, and the legal system.[29]

The AAC executive committee met in Johannesburg in July 1944 and issued a statement ("Along the New Road") detailing a new strategy of noncollaboration that would be ratified, together with the unity plan and the ten-point program, at the AAC conference in December. The Convention would henceforth boycott the NRC (African councillors were urged "to resign collectively and immediately"), the native representatives in parliament, and all other "segregatory institutions" (local/district and general councils in rural Ciskei and Transkei and the urban location advisory boards), and seek "Unity with the other sections of the non-Europeans." [30]

Although moderate African nationalists remained at the head of the AAC's executive committee, the organization was effectively absorbed by the militant NEUM. Control shifted to the anti-CAD faction centered in Cape Town. The Unity movement, as it would be called, contained 102 affiliated organizations with "a very conservative estimate" of almost sixty thousand members by January 1945.[31] National conferences would now be held once a year with branches established in all the provinces. Like the AAC, however, the Unity movement was restricted mainly to the Cape.

The Communist Party and the Trade Union Movement

Members and former members of the Communist Party of South Africa (CPSA) played a prominent role in the second phase of African trade union activity beginning in the mid-1930s (the first phase began in World War I and ended with the Great Depression). The party's marginal existence in South African politics also improved dramatically with the coming of World War II. Government officials became more conciliatory after the Soviet Union entered the war, and the CPSA was then able to oppose fascism at home and abroad with equal vigor.

The party contested elections reserved for whites and blacks at all levels of government and became fully involved in organizing black workers in Johannesburg and in several port cities during the war years. To a much lesser extent, party activists also helped organize community-action campaigns in the urban townships and in the reserves (the most notable at this time being Alpheus Maliba, who worked with peasant dissidents in the Venda area of the Zoutpansberg).

Although communist trade union activities were centered in Johannesburg and other towns along the Rand in the southern Transvaal, the CPSA was very active in Cape Town, Port Elizabeth, and East London during the 1940s. Party officials in Port Elizabeth, for example, effectively established themselves as leaders in the local trade union movement during World War II. The unions, which included African laundry workers and other domestics, were organized under the umbrella of the Council for Non-European Trade Unions (CNETU), a coordinating body based in Johannesburg and dominated by the communists. The CNETU claimed 158,000 members—including 30,000 in Port Elizabeth and 15,000 in East London—who were organized in 119 unions by 1945. This figure was undoubtedly inflated, and, in any event, CNETU's membership would drop drastically in the wake of a 1946 miners' strike. Nevertheless,

CNETU had briefly succeeded in attracting perhaps 40 percent of the Africans employed in commerce and manufacturing in South Africa by the mid-1940s.

The CPSA also gained considerable credibility within African nationalist circles, and three organizers were eventually elected to the ANC national executive—John B. Marks (chair of the African Mineworkers' Union) and Moses Kotane (the party's general secretary) in 1946 and Daniel Thloome (vice president of the CNETU) in 1949. Yusuf Dadoo, Ismail Meer, and J. N. Singh, leaders of the Transvaal Indian Congress, were CPSA members, and G. M. Naicker, head of the Natal Indian Congress, was closely associated with party stalwarts.[32] In addition, the CPSA had links with African and Coloured radicals in Cape Town who controlled the Unity movement and affiliated organizations like the AAC.

As far as the eastern Cape was concerned, CPSA trade unionists dominated opposition politics in Port Elizabeth during the 1940s, whereas members of the mission-educated elite held sway in East London. They still controlled the local ANC and what remained of the ICU; surviving leaders of the breakaway Independent ICU, ever fearful of the communists, had also moved back to mainstream middle-class politics. CPSA officials controlled most trade unions in East London and competed in location advisory board elections with older ANC members and labor leaders like Kadalie who could still command some support, but they had little success in revamping local politics.

The political vacuum was partially filled by the Youth Leaguers, who seemed to be particularly sensitive to the urban-rural mix that was so pervasive in this port city. The Youth League would use East London as a base to mobilize popular resistance in the Ciskei hinterland in the early 1950s, just as the Independent ICU had done in the early 1930s.

9.2. The Beginnings of a Mass Movement

Congress leaders were under increasing pressure from younger militants in the Youth League and the rival AAC to challenge the government's segregationist policies by the mid-1940s.[33] Although they opposed an alliance with the AAC—repeated attempts were made to reconcile differences between the two organizations during this decade[34]—they defied Youth League militants and cooperated to some extent with the communists and the Indian congresses.[35] ANC leaders, however, still had little sympathy for the politics of direct action, whether it emanated from workers' groups, community action groups, or political groups controlled by the petty bourgeoisie.

The timidity of the ANC in the 1940s is illustrated by its response to a national antipass campaign sponsored by the CPSA toward the end of the war and to an Indian passive resistance campaign that continued sporadically between 1946 and 1948. Congress never went further than pledging moral solidarity with the Indians, who were protesting legislation limiting Indian land and trading rights in the Transvaal and Natal. ANC leaders rejected repeated calls for militant action against South Africa's pass laws by the CPSA and other dissident groups following massive police raids in April 1943. Xuma waited thirteen months after this incident before he agreed to preside at a meeting where a resolution condemning the pass laws was finally passed. Congress members participated in an antipass parade in downtown Johannesburg on a Sunday afternoon when the city was virtually empty, and a national antipass signature campaign launched after this demonstration proved to be equally futile. The acting prime minister (Smuts was out of the country) refused to accept the petition containing the signatures (far fewer than the million promised) when it was finally presented to parliament in June 1945, and the leaders of the antipass delegation were arrested and fined for leading an unlawful procession.

Congress took its first tentative steps toward confrontation politics in the wake of the 1946 African miners' strike. The Africans on the Natives' Representative Council suspended their discussions in the midst of the strike, and the ANC meeting in emergency session two months later approved a resolution calling for a boycott of all elections conducted under the 1936 Representation of Natives Act. Meanwhile, Xuma (accompanied by Hyman Basner, leader of the short-lived African Democratic party,[36] and two members of the Indian passive resistance council) made a trip to the United Nations where the world body was alerted for the first time to the grievances of the black population in South Africa. The ANC at its national conference in December 1946 declared it would "consider the possibilities of closer cooperation with the national organisations of other non-Europeans in the common struggle." Delegates called for a "nationwide campaign" to boycott the 1948 NRC election.[37]

The ANC endorsed the boycott option again at its national conference in December 1947, but a month later the decision was reversed. Africans on the NRC wanted to participate in the 1948 NRC election, which coincided with South Africa's whites-only general election, and Congress leaders did not want to provide the National party with an issue that might embarrass the Smuts government. The communists also agreed to participate, supporting the moderates against the Africanists in the ANC, but the All-African Convention stuck by its 1943 boycott decision.

The Youth League's influence in African nationalist politics increased enormously after the abortive 1946 mine workers' strike.[38] Six of its members were elected to the ANC's executive committee at the December 1949 conference, including Mandela, Tambo, and Sisulu, who became secretary-general. Xuma was replaced as president-general by James Moroka, a compromise candidate who was more acceptable to those in sympathy with the politics of direct action.[39] A policy statement drafted by the Youth League a year earlier[40] formed part of a "Programme of Action" manifesto adopted by Congress. This was a triumph for militant nationalists within the ANC, which for the first time agreed to employ the tactics of noncollaboration—boycotts, strikes, noncooperation, and civil disobedience—in the struggle against white domination.[41]

The Youth League's rapid rise to power in the ANC and the adoption of the Programme of Action was also prompted in part by the National party's victory in the 1948 general election. The challenge of Afrikaner nationalism and its apartheid policies would ignite the African nationalist movement, and in a few regions of South Africa—notably the Ciskei—sectional and petitionary protest would give way to various forms of collective resistance during the early 1950s.

The Defiance Campaign

The African and Indian Congresses set up a joint planning council in mid-1951 to coordinate a civil disobedience campaign in response to the spate of repressive legislation pushed through parliament after 1948 by the Afrikaner Nationalists.[42] The protesters initially sought to repeal six "unjust laws." The Group Areas Act, which imposed separate areas for Coloureds, Indians, and whites as well as Africans, and the Suppression of Communism Act, which outlawed the CPSA (the central committee in anticipation had already dissolved the party) and virtually silenced what was left of CNETU-sponsored trade union activity, were enacted in 1950. The Suppression of Communism Act was particularly significant because it was framed very broadly: virtually any individual or institution actively opposed to the ruling National party could be censored by this legislation.

The Coloured Voters Act, which removed Coloureds from the common voters roll in the Cape as the Africans had been removed fifteen years earlier, and the Bantu Authorities Act, which abolished the NRC and reorganized local government in the reserves, were passed in 1951. Two other grievances—the pass laws and stock-limitation measures—were not limited to a single legislative act. The pass laws, tightened up considerably during the early years of Nationalist rule, had major implications for industrial workers seeking permanent residence in the cities, while government intervention in the reserves triggered a resurgence in the rural protest movement. The Population Registration Act (1950) and the bans placed on sexual and other forms of social intercourse between designated racial groups would fuel these grievances during the early 1950s.

The Defiance Campaign, the most successful attempt at nonviolent mass action ever conducted by the ANC, was launched in June 1952. Modeled on the passive resistance campaigns initiated by Mohandas Gandhi in South Africa almost two generations earlier, it was to be carried out in three stages. Trained volunteers in the major cities would deliberately defy designated laws

Table 9.1. Arrest profile in the 1952 Defiance Campaign

Region	Number	%
Eastern Cape	5,941	71.4
Port Elizabeth	2,007	
East London	1,322	
Other towns and villages		
west of the Kei River	1,094	
west of the Fish River	1,518	
Transvaal	1,578	19.0
Western Cape	490	5.8
Natal	192	2.3
Orange Free State	125	1.5
Total	8,326	100.0

SOURCE: T. Lodge, *Black politics in South Africa since 1945* (London & New York, 1983), 46–47 (as adapted).

and invite arrest until all metropolitan areas were involved in the civil rights struggle. These efforts would then be extended to other urban areas and finally to the rural areas—the white farms and African reserves. Even Africanists could participate since multiracial groups would be formed only in exceptional cases. Each racial group would remain separate from the others and oppose legislation directed against that specific group.

The Defiance Campaign was concentrated in the metropolitan areas, and it lasted more than six months. The crucial role played by eastern Cape dissidents during this campaign is revealed in Table 9.1.

Despite appeals to continue from rank-and-file volunteers in the eastern Cape and southern Transvaal, the political leadership called a halt to the campaign several weeks after East London's African locations were savaged by riots in November 1952. In the aftermath of the 1952 campaign, legislation was enacted that allowed the central government to suspend all civil rights (by declaring a state of emergency) and enact stiff penalties against those protesting the law.

The ANC in the Mid–Late 1950s

The Defiance Campaign was the most dramatic event in African national politics during the 1950s. ANC membership had soared in roughly six months from seven thousand to a hundred thousand. Sixty percent of the members were now in the Cape, where the number of local branches had risen from fourteen to eighty-seven between 1952 and 1953. Paid-up membership fell to below thirty thousand in 1953, but it was still more than four times what it had been before the campaign. Membership would increase rapidly again in the last three years before the organization was banned. Throughout this period, moreover, the number of Congress activists was actually much larger than the membership lists revealed. The All-African Convention, which had refused to participate in the Defiance Campaign, apparently declined rapidly in numbers and influence even in the Cape during the 1950s.

A Congress-inspired mass movement, however, required a much more effective organization than appeared to be possible at the time. An attempt was made to equip local branches, for example, with a street-level political structure (called the Mandela plan), but it was not really carried out except in some eastern Cape towns. Even in this region, the thirty-five full-time organizers needed to implement the plan could not be paid. Indeed, the ANC as a whole could afford only one full-time organizer (Walter Sisulu) before it was forced into exile in 1960.

Congress leaders were largely in Johannesburg, but the strongest centers of ANC activity now lay outside the Transvaal. Policy decisions were still not implemented by some provincial congresses, and links with local branches remained fragile. Congress was extremely vulnerable to pressure from the governing authorities, since it had no press of its own and continued to operate as if it functioned in a democratic society, relying on mass meetings, yearly conferences, the issuing of pamphlets, sporadic bulletins, and newsletters, and making statements to the white-controlled press.

Interpreters of African nationalist politics during the 1950s have stressed that the ANC remained essentially a reformist organization. Congress focused on mass action in the cities: civil disobedience in the form of stay-at-home protests was the main tactic used by protesters because it didn't involve direct confrontation. As Gail Gerhart suggests, ANC leaders did not indulge in racial rhetoric, and democracy was not perceived simplistically as majority rule: "spokesmen for Congress at the national level continued to call upon whites to 'share' power, to 'extend' freedom, and to allow nonwhites to participate as 'partners' in government within the system as it stood." [43]

Congress leaders still preferred moral protest to mass mobilization. Despite the demand for noncollaboration as expressed in the 1949 Programme of Action, they continued to compete for seats on the urban location advisory boards and other local bodies, virtually the only government-approved political venues left open to the African petty bourgeoisie during the 1950s. Their actions were still determined in large part by fears that the resistance movement was not strong enough to confront the state. They continued to hope that white voters would respond to African grievances if they were expressed in nonviolent, nonthreatening terms. They accepted the white liberal view at the time that industrial capitalism and apartheid were incompatible, and they continued to believe political and economic rights would be won if antigovernment whites could defeat Afrikaner Nationalists at the polls.

Nevertheless, the ANC maintained links with other groups in the resistance movement after the Defiance Campaign. The highlight of the mid-1950s was the forging of the multiracial Congress Alliance between the ANC, South African Indian Congress, South African Coloured People's Organisation (later renamed the Coloured People's Congress), and the white South African Congress of Democrats. The South African Congress of Trade Unions (the successor to the Congress of Non-European Trade Unions) joined the alliance after it was organized in March 1955.[44]

The historic Freedom Charter drafted in June 1955 was essentially a reformist liberal-democratic document. Racial and other forms of discrimination were to be eliminated and civil rights for all racial groups in South Africa guaranteed. As the preamble declared, "South Africa belongs to all who live in it, black and white." [45] The document, as Sean Archer suggests, was open-ended on the question of economic objectives, opting neither for socialism nor capitalism. But as interpreted by Mandela himself at the time, the vanguard for reform would be the aspirant black middle class:

> The breaking up . . . of these monopolies will open up fresh fields for the development of a non-European *bourgeois* class. For the first time in the history of this country the non-European *bourgeoisie* will have the opportunity to own in their own name and right mills and factories and trade and private enterprise will boom and flourish as never before.[46]

The ANC continued to rely primarily on urban stay-at-home campaigns to mobilize opposition in the later 1950s, although popular resistance was manifested in a variety of other forms, sometimes with and sometimes without the aid of Congress and its allies. Multiracial solidarity was strengthened as the Congress Alliance leadership cadre was decimated by bannings, detentions, and a marathon treason trial for 156 accused that began in 1956 and actually lasted more than four years.

The Africanists Separate from Congress

Africanists within the ANC who believed that racial conflict was inevitable became increasingly disenchanted with events following the Defiance Campaign.[47] The issue of collaboration with non-African organizations—in particular, the growing influence of some whites in African politics—was unsettling to hard-liners in the Youth League. Congress leaders, moreover, seemed unwilling to adhere strictly to the 1949 noncollaboration policy. They were perceived as being too timid and too compromised to provide the dynamic leadership that was needed to mobilize resistance.

As the Africanists became more estranged from mainstream African politics, they became more vociferous in their demands. More and more youth who were victims of apartheid, moreover, turned to them for leadership. The key Africanist strongholds were in the Cape peninsula, a haven for thousands of legal and illegal refugees from the Ciskei and Transkei reserves, and in several African townships in the industrial heartland of the southern Transvaal.

The Africanists broke away from the ANC to form the Pan-Africanist Congress (PAC) in April 1959. Their leader was Robert Mangaliso Sobukwe (1924–78), a Xhosa who was born in Graaff-Reinet and educated at Healdtown and Fort Hare. A prominent activist in the Youth League and a militant supporter of the ANC's 1949 Programme of Action, Sobukwe eventually emerged as a skilled interpreter of the Africanist perspective (he contributed to the *Bureau of African Nationalism* bulletin in East London during the Defiance Campaign and later edited *The Africanist* in Johannesburg) and a passionate public orator.

The PAC had an immediate impact on the African nationalist movement. In less than a year (August 1959), the leadership claimed a membership of 24,664 in 101 branches. While this was far less than the target of 100,000 members, it rivaled the ANC's paid-up membership at the time. The Transvaal led with 13,324 members in 47 branches, and the Cape claimed a somewhat distant second with 7,427 members in 34 branches. PAC's membership consisted almost entirely of males who were on average at least ten years younger than their ANC counterparts. While Congress apparently had a greater hold over industrial workers, the PAC had broad support from youths at all social levels. On the whole, the Africanists were better educated and more successful in attracting the growing number of unemployed and underemployed literates in the townships.

The separation of the Africanists from Congress would have significant implications for the resistance movement, but African divisional politics were almost immediately overtaken by the events of 1960. The antipass campaign that ended in the Sharpeville-Langa shootings, the declaration of a state of emergency that allowed the government to detain nearly two thousand political activists, the banning of Congress and the PAC, and a white referendum that resulted in South Africa's becoming a republic and leaving the Commonwealth are well known and do not require elaboration. The banned ANC and PAC regrouped in exile, formed underground guerrilla units inside South Africa, and moved into the first stage of armed struggle.

Virtually all the underground groups, however, had been destroyed by 1964 (although isolated attacks would continue until the end of the decade). Aided by informers, forced confessions, intercepted plans, and an ill-conceived public statement by PAC deputy leader P. K. Leballo, the police infiltrated the outlawed organizations and captured most of the major participants. The Rivonia trial, which ended in June 1964 with life sentences for Mandela, Sisulu, and other leaders of the Congress Alliance, was just the beginning. Arrests, detentions, bannings, and trials would continue for several more years in the campaign to root out and destroy all vestiges of independent African political and trade union activity in South Africa.

9.3. Ferment in the Ciskei

There have been two major cycles of popular resistance in rural South Africa in the twentieth century. African tenants on white-owned farms were in the vanguard of the struggle during the 1920s, and African peasants in the reserves were in the vanguard of the struggle for roughly two decades between the early 1940s and early 1960s.

The reserve peasants were provoked to action by the central government's repeated attempts to cull stock and enforce other restrictions on the use of the land, reorganize the population, and impose a new system of government in the form of Bantu Authorities. The major flashpoints were in the Zoutpansberg (now Venda) and Sekhukuniland (now Lebowa) reserves in the northern Transvaal between 1941 and 1944, in the Witzieshoek (now Basotho QwaQwa) reserve in the Orange Free State in 1950, in the Marico (now western Bophutatswana) reserve in 1957–58, in Sekhukuniland again in 1958–59, in the Natal (now KwaZulu) reserve in 1958–59, in Mpondoland (northern Transkei) in 1960, and in Thembuland (southern Transkei) in 1962–63. And, as Tom Lodge puts it, "throughout this period the Ciskeian territories were in a state of almost constant ferment." [48]

Phase I of the Struggle, 1945–1953

The Ciskei reserve was no longer isolated from the outside world by the 1940s. The war opened up new opportunities for vast numbers of residents but especially for men who joined the armed forces and for women who trekked to the cities as never before in search of work. Migrant workers absorbed the militant rhetoric of urban opposition groups and employed their tactics, using the boycott weapon and the courts against oppressive authorities in the rural locations. Migrant associations were involved in coordinating activists in town and countryside, and female migrants were playing an influential role in these events. Increasing numbers of Africans, moreover, were being removed from the cities and white farms and resettled in the reserves by the 1950s, another potential radicalizing force in rural areas like the Ciskei.

Mission schools in the reserves were perennial sites of resistance. In the ten years between 1937 and 1946, for example, 28 out of 46 mission schools in South Africa and the two British protectorates of Basutoland and Swaziland experienced a total of 49 student disturbances, 31 of which were regarded as serious by the authorities. Virtually all these disturbances occurred in the boarding institutions, and it is significant that they increased dramatically after World War II, 20 major incidents being recorded between 1945 and 1947. [49]

The Ciskei was a focal point of student unrest in the 1940s and 1950s: Ciskei Bunga members, for example, commented on disturbances in several prestige mission boarding schools, in a government vocational-training school at Zwelitsha, and at Fort Hare. [50] The riots at Lovedale and Healdtown in

August 1946 offer a case study in militant student politics at this time. About 50 percent of the Africans who passed the Cape Senior Certificate exam came from Lovedale and Healdtown, and these two schools supplied a majority of the students to Fort Hare, now the alma mater of virtually all black university graduates in South Africa.

Missionary education was beginning to break down even in the elite African schools by the 1940s. The Cape like other provinces was still willing to subsidize only teachers' salaries, while mission agencies continued to pay for the salaries of nonteaching employees, administrative costs, medical services, buildings, equipment, and upkeep. The missions could no longer finance their schools, and the schools could no longer absorb the increasing numbers of students seeking secondary education. Fueled by wartime inflation, Lovedale was thirty thousand pounds in debt by 1946, but the missionaries were unable (and in many cases unwilling) to impose ever-higher increases in school fees on a deeply impoverished population.

The missionaries were also at a crossroads in their relations with the students. Scholars are generally agreed on the parochial issues that triggered student unrest during these years, key themes being the quality of food served to students and resistance to discipline administered by school authorities. Food problems were aggravated by rationing during and immediately after the war, by the drastic decline in food production in the reserves, and by the high cost of certain foodstuffs. Food ranked high on the lists of student grievances at Lovedale and Healdtown: there were periodic shortages of bread, vegetables, fruit, milk, tea, and other items, and the meals were bland and sometimes uneatable. As Jonathan Hyslop suggests: "for the students the inferior quality of their food became a symbol of the forms of social domination they experienced in their daily lives. . . . food became a metaphor for power." [51]

The authority of the missionaries in the administration of the boarding schools was challenged as never before by the students during this period. They rebelled against mission paternalism and against the racist comments of individual missionaries.[52] They rebelled against the student prefects, whose authority was sanctioned by the missionaries, and they rebelled against compulsory manual labor regulations enforced by the prefects.[53] The prefect system in South African schools was modeled on that of the English public school: prefects were given numerous privileges in return for which they policed the students. This was particularly resented in black boarding establishments, where in contrast to white schools the range in ages was wider at almost every grade level, especially after the war when many veterans returned to school to improve their educational qualifications. Students had to channel their complaints to the prefects, who were often younger and usually more compliant. Ex-soldiers at Lovedale, for example, apparently masterminded the 1946 riot.[54]

Students in mission boarding schools were also influenced by the grievances of urban opposition groups during the 1940s. Left-wing publications like the *Guardian,* which supported the Communist party, and the *Torch,* official organ of the Unity movement, surfaced in schools like Lovedale and Healdtown, and militant pamphlets and newsletters produced by students at Fort Hare also circulated in these institutions. Some African teachers, who were subordinate to their white counterparts even in mission schools, discussed political issues with their pupils, and in the case of Lovedale a few resorted to "passive resistance" and refused to enforce new regulations imposed after the 1946 riot.[55]

Nevertheless, there is no evidence to suggest that student agitation in the mission boarding schools had any impact on the rural peasantry during the 1940s. The peasants initially rose in revolt against the Rehabilitation scheme introduced in 1945. They cut fences, set fire to commonages, threatened land surveyors, boycotted cattle-dipping facilities, refused to cooperate with agricultural fieldworkers from the Native Affairs Department, and aired their protests at public meetings sponsored by the Native Trust. Householders in Glen Grey and Herschel threatened their Bunga representatives—one Glen Grey councillor had his trading store burned down—and boycotted the local councils after they voted in favor of Rehabilitation. Angry residents in Middledrift and Keiskammahoek argued that local councillors had accepted the plan without their approval. Violence erupted in the King William's Town District where three policemen were killed.[56]

Betterment/Rehabilitation antagonized Ciskeian peasants more than any other single issue during the 1940s and 1950s, because it threatened their already precarious existence as rural landholders. As Anne Mager notes, however, there were distinct differences in male and female perceptions of this threat, and communities were divided by age and class as well as by gender in responding to government intervention. Patriarchal relations were already strained by the steady deterioration of the reserve economy, by the decline in the value of female labor power, and by the effects of migrant labor which removed women as well as men from their rural villages and at least temporarily freed unmarried females from the controls imposed on them by their male guardians. While urban opposition groups like the AAC and Congress Youth League were in solidarity with the peasants in resisting government intervention, they did not recognize these divisions or their impact on the local population.[57]

Women with access to men who had cattle and land enjoyed a measure of status and security in the patriarchal system, and they tended to support the men in resisting Rehabilitation. The struggle for land, however, was much worse in the 1940s than it had been in previous decades. Groups of starving people, a high proportion of whom were women with children, were now moving about the rural districts in search of food and shelter. Widows no longer had access to their husbands' garden plots, and women without husbands as well as illegitimate sons had no hope of obtaining land. Escape to town in the absence of jobs and tightened pass controls was not an easy option, but many landless women living on the fringes of the rural economy found their way to Native Trust land. As Mager puts it: "If collaboration with the Trust meant access to land, if co-operation with the authorities allowed women to work, if acceptance of Trust regulations meant women could feed their children and retain their self-respect, then this was an option they would exercise." [58]

The focus of resentment against Betterment/Rehabilitation was the culling of cattle—the crucial link, it will be remembered, in the precolonial power system. The protesters initially were older men, often from traditionalist Red households, who saw in cattle "the key to male power and control over women" and the "base of rural production." [59] Women in this situation defended men with cattle because it was also the basis of their security. The early leaders in this struggle were the rural elite—chiefs, headmen, and privileged farmers with surplus sheep and cattle—who were immediately threatened by the move to cull stock, fence land, and change plowing habits.

The ANC opposed government intervention in the reserves during the 1940s, but members were focused on urban issues and apparently did not attempt to get involved in rural politics until the Congress Youth League began organizing branches in the Ciskei/Border region toward the end of the decade. AAC organizer Isaac Tabata, however, toured the Transkei in 1945 and produced a pamphlet in English and Xhosa (*The Rehabilitation Scheme: A New Fraud*) suggesting that the real motive behind culling cattle and restricting the right to land was "the regimentation of African labour." Transkei and Ciskei residents were urged to boycott the government councils and sabotage the Rehabilitation scheme. The AAC was involved in peasant politics in the Transkei in the mid–late 1940s, but little is known about their activities in the Ciskei at this time. [60]

While older men with wealth and power were in the forefront of resistance to Betterment/Rehabilitation in the mid–late 1940s, a new leadership cadre arose during the early 1950s. These were younger men—poorer, more dependent on migrant wages, and more interested in pursuing an urban lifestyle. Unlike their fathers, they were often unable or unwilling to participate in the lobola system, which continued to sustain gender relations in the countryside. Marriage no longer guaranteed land, and a woman's labor power had little value when there was no land or cattle. Most young men in the Ciskei could no longer afford the bride price (the average dowry had remained constant at 7.4 cattle or their equivalent since 1890), and the marriage age for both sexes was steadily increasing. [61] One solution was to seek permanent residence in town: men might avoid the bride price entirely, and women might escape their male guardians and earn money for themselves.

Younger men and women in town opposed stock culling and other aspects of Betterment/Rehabilitation for a variety of reasons. Some men hoped eventually to be able to afford a wife, and stock still provided a measure of financial security for their rural relatives. Urban slum cultures would subject single women to extreme levels of violence and degradation, and where possible they sent their children (most of whom were born out of wedlock) to their home villages to be raised. The burden of having to support parents and children would be eased if they had access to stock and garden plots in the reserve.

The Congress Youth League in the Ciskei/Border region at this time was made up of many first-generation wage workers in town. They were better educated than the previous generation (although most had not taken the Junior Certificate exams—equivalent to the tenth grade—as had their counterparts in the All-African Convention) and more antagonistic to the obligations placed on them by the old patriarchal order. Government intervention in the form of Betterment/Rehabilitation offered the ANC a golden opportunity to gain access to the reserve and fuel the African nationalist movement.

Local resistance hardened with the introduction of the Bantu Authorities Act of 1951 and two amendments to the pass laws promulgated in 1952—the Natives (Abolition of Passes and Coordination of Documents) Act and the Native Laws Amendment Act. The Bantu Authorities Act formally abolished the Natives' Representative Council and the local/district and general councils that had been created in the Ciskei and Transkei. A three-tiered hierarchy of administrative authority was established for the reserves. Tribal and/or Community Authorities[62] at the local level were appointed by the chiefs and the white native commissioners (now called Bantu commissioners). Each Tribal Authority would consist of a chief (or someone acting in this capacity) and a varying number of councillors.

Chiefs were appointed in much greater numbers than before, which would have considerable impact in reserves like the Ciskei where local authority had been vested in headmen and subheadmen. Their salaries as government officials increased, and they gained enormously in political status. They were not accountable to their subjects, and they could be deposed only by the central government. The other two tiers were not even theoretically based on the old precolonial political hierarchy. Regional Authorities were responsible for two or more Tribal Authorities, and Territorial Authorities supervised the Regional Authorities. Chiefs were the dominant power brokers at all three levels along with the white Bantu commissioners, who retained their veto power.

Political activists who were not associated with the Tribal Authority lost whatever power they still had in the reserves. The impoverished rural petty bourgeoisie vigorously opposed this measure. Even the would-be beneficiaries, the chiefs and their allies, were apprehensive. After all, they would now be expected to enforce Betterment/Rehabilitation and other government edicts inside the reserves. Those who were not compliant would be deposed and others—often with little or no evidence that they were members of a royal lineage—elevated to power.

The new pass laws sought to consolidate, update, and extend the procedures regulating the movement of African labor from the reserves to the proclaimed white agricultural and industrial areas. Severe constraints were placed on all Africans working in cities, and South Africa was divided into "prescribed" and "nonprescribed" regions. Africans who were not "exempted" could no longer remain in "prescribed" white urban areas, for example, for more than seventy-two hours. They would be "endorsed out" to the "nonprescribed" white rural areas and African reserves. Labor bureaus to control and distribute migrant labor had been established in the reserves beginning in 1949, and the pass books that Africans had to carry would now have photographs and fingerprints as well as a record of employment. In a very significant amendment, the pass laws were also extended to African women in 1952.

Resistance to Rehabilitation, Bantu authorities, and the pass laws provided considerable ammunition for the Congress Youth League and the AAC in the Ciskei region between 1951 and 1953. According to Mager, the ANC was strongest in the Ciskei's southern districts where the rural villagers were most dependent on wage earners.[63] The Port Elizabeth branch, for example, mobilized peasants in the Peddie District, and the East London branch was influential in the King William's Town District. Villagers directed their anger at the Native Trust, which was responsible for implementing the Rehabilitation regulations, and local issues ignited the resisters during the 1952 Defiance Campaign.[64]

The ANC hierarchy might deplore the tactics of Youth Leaguers from the cities who incited "semi-educated" School and "red-blanket natives" to defy the law, but they were also very active in the Ciskei during the early 1950s. The older ANC generation was represented by the privileged class in the reserve: they relied on the boycott weapon and were "strictly non-violent." The Defiance Campaign in Middledrift, for example, was led by people like D. D. T. Jabavu, District Surgeon Roseberry Bokwe, and local teachers and their wives—and the Youth Leaguers deferred to them at public meetings.

In northern districts like Glen Grey, the ANC was not as active as the All-African Convention. The local population was well organized with constituent groups of parents, women, farmers, voters, and teachers. Wycliffe Tsotsi, president of the Cape African Teachers' Association, was the main figure in AAC-sponsored activities. While the AAC was opposed to the Defiance Campaign, it was actively involved in organizing resistance to Rehabilitation. Noncollaboration tactics were used in confronting the Native Trust, but peasants were also sabotaging conservation programs. AAC's organizational base apparently did not extend much beyond Glen Grey, but Tsotsi and his colleagues used existing ties with local iliso lomzis, CATA, and the National Council of African Women to influence events in Queenstown, Keiskammahoek, and possibly other districts.

Mager maintains that rural resistance in the Ciskei during this period was characterized by "gender specific responses to the form of proletarianisation set in motion by the Rehabilitation strategy." Unprecedented numbers of women of all ranks, for example, defied the authorities, but they did not play a role as activists apart from their men. Single women and their families along with tenants displaced from white farms continued to cooperate with the Native Trust as a matter of survival. In the face of these and other contradictions, the rural struggle "remained uneven, incomplete and partial."

The Urban Struggle: East London. Nevertheless, the Ciskei was the only region in South Africa during the 1952 Defiance Campaign where the ANC succeeded in forging alliances between the working poor in town and countryside. This brief moment of collective action was achieved in Port Elizabeth, East London, and the rural hinterland. Port Elizabeth and East London were peopled mainly by Xhosa speakers, there were no single-sex dormitories, and the ratio between men and women was now roughly equal. Both cities had experienced a rapid growth in African population during and especially after the war, when there was an upsurge in the regional economy. A large proportion of the newcomers were migrants from impoverished, drought-stricken locations in the southern Transkei and Ciskei reserves.

There were also important differences in living and working conditions for blacks in the two port cities. Africans in East London were forced to carry up to 25 passes day and night and observe a curfew, whereas Port Elizabeth was the last major city in South Africa to impose curfew and influx-control regulations on African residents. In contrast to East London, municipal officials provided housing until the late 1940s, when the tide of immigrants began to overwhelm available facilities. African migrants seeking to escape restrictions placed on them in other municipal areas tended to favor Port Elizabeth, whereas migrants to East London were almost all first-generation town dwellers who continued to maintain ties with their rural villages. Red-School tensions, moreover, continued to divide urban African slum cultures like East London during the 1950s.[65]

Everyday life for Africans in East London had hardly improved since the generation of the 1920s. Population densities in proclaimed black and white areas were 141.4 and 6.4 per acre, respectively, according to the Border Regional Survey in 1955. Most Africans still lived in makeshift wood-and-iron shacks, the African infant mortality rate in East London that year was between 370 and 381 (per 1,000 births), and the city still had one of the highest tuberculosis rates in South Africa. Most Africans (more than 70 percent in the 1955

Table 9.2. Profile of East London's African male
labor force in 1955 ($N = 1,356$)

Category	Number	% of total
Working class	1155	85.2
Unskilled	918	67.7
Semiskilled and skilled	237	17.5
Middle class	68	5.0
Unemployed	133	9.8

SOURCE: D. H. Houghton (ed.), *Economic development in a plural society: studies in the border region
of the Cape Province* (Cape Town, 1960), 225–28
(arithmetical errors in Table 126 corrected). The
sample population was based on a random survey
of 18,632 African males issued with new reference
books between August and November 1955. Designated middle-class categories included the professional elite, clerks, self-employed persons, proprietors, managers, and government officials.

survey) continued to live in the East Bank location, where there were eighty
public toilets at the beginning of the decade and the streets were reportedly
polluted with human excrement. One high school (with room for 350 pupils)
and eight primary schools served an African population that was now estimated
unofficially at 78,000. Perhaps 40 percent of the male (and 30 percent of the
female) work force had four years of formal schooling or less.[66]

The African labor force in East London totaled 22,675 in the official 1951
census, and 37.6 percent of these workers were female. The port city had
established an industrial base during the 1940s, and about 42 percent of the
male workers were employed in designated industrial enterprises (manufacturing, construction, and transport). Virtually all African women (and 25 percent
of the men) were employed in service industries, most in domestic-type jobs.
A survey four years later examined the designated occupational categories of
male workers, two-thirds of whom were unskilled (see Table 9.2). White male
workers were earning about five times more a year than African workers: 15
percent of the whites were in the lowest white-income category of less than
£200 a year, whereas 90 percent of the Africans were in an income category of
no more than £180 a year. Most African workers were classified as migrants (78
percent in a survey of 193 male employment histories in 1955), who returned
to their rural villages at least once a month.[67]

East London's African residents were almost completely alienated from
the dominant white-mediated, middle-class culture, according to a recent study
of the 1952 East London riots by Anne Mager and Gary Minkley.[68] The realities of location life were rooted in "an extremely violent patriarchal society

and a slum culture which . . . rejected female children and sent male children to the streets for learning." [69] African women moved independently to East London from the adjacent rural locations and white farms in the Ciskei's southern districts, while most African men were migrants from the Transkei. Duncan Village—the East Bank location—now housed the poorest and least stable portion of East London's African population. The men were generally older, part-time workers still linked closely to rural society.

Both sexes were brutalized by urban life, but women were far more vulnerable:

> Men regularly beat and not infrequently stabbed their wives and lovers. . . . Babies strapped to their mothers' backs not infrequently absorbed the blows. Rape was extraordinarily common and often women going to the aid of a rape victim were overpowered and sexually assaulted themselves. . . . Pregnancy was difficult to avoid and paternity hard to prove. . . . With rural links ever more tenuous, and child maintenance almost impossible to enforce, young mothers were constantly thrown on their own resources. . . . Utterly alone, and often very young, many mothers resorted to killing their newborn infants—particularly baby girls. . . . infanticide was both commonplace and well known in the locations.[70]

Single mothers composed the majority of African women living in East London's locations. They often started out in wage labor and later got involved in informal sector activities. The female infant mortality rate was highest in the West Bank location, where young women competed with each other for men until they were too old (the age limit being about thirty) or had too many children. Then they would often move to the East Bank location to do household chores for older men who were in need of their services.

Mager and Minkley paint a grim picture of criminal life in East London at this time.[71] The *tsotsi*, meaning a male member of a criminal gang, was not bound either by traditional patriarchal or middle-class authority: "Alcohol, gambling and sex filled leisure time for boys from an early age," and most youths were "not yet circumcised or married, with little prospect of acquiring *lobola* and a homestead, or an urban job." Tsotsis and their *tsotsikazis* (female members of criminal gangs) had their own language and dress codes, and a lifestyle that inspired terror in the locations. The tsotsi gangs offered a way out for the most alienated young men in the locations: "*Tsotsi* identity enabled youths to wield a certain power as 'men' in a patriarchal society where they could not become patriarchs and in a capitalist, racist society where they could not become high income earners." Tsotsi mothers, typically unmarried and living in unstable households themselves, identified closely with their sons, who were usually the only permanent male figures in their lives: "as mothers stood by their sons, they drew support from their power as men."

Hardcore tsotsi and tsotsikazi youths would be at the center of the East London disturbances that virtually ended the Defiance Campaign in South

Africa. Riots had occurred at Kimberley and Port Elizabeth in October 1952, and police reinforcements had been sent to East London in a futile attempt to prevent unrest from spreading to this port city. The central government had banned demonstrations and restricted fifty-two campaign leaders in the eastern Cape under the Riotous Assemblies and Suppression of Communism Acts. Two leaders of the East London branch of the Youth League, including local president Skei Gwentshe, a musician and shopkeeper then in his mid-forties who had been orphaned in the 1920 Bulhoek massacre, were among those restricted. Gwentshe had received permission to hold a Sunday prayer meeting in Duncan Village in the second week of November to protest the government's actions, and it was white police who initiated the riots when they fired on the crowd of about fifteen hundred black protesters.

It was the tsotsis who initiated the violence that followed. By Sunday evening, nine people were dead (including a white Roman Catholic nun, who was killed in circumstances that shocked the middle-class white and black community), twenty-seven wounded by gunshot, and three policemen injured. Virtually every building associated with whites in the East Bank and West Bank locations—mission churches and schools, a new teacher-training college, a reform school, a milk depot, a municipal hall, and various other structures—was burned down in the next twenty-four hours. These events were followed by massive police raids, the arrest of 178 persons (of whom 91 were charged with various counts of murder, arson, and public violence), and the eventual deportation of most of the alleged tsotsi population (estimated at 6,000) to their homes in the reserves. The average age of those charged with crimes was 17½; more than half had no secondary education, only one-quarter had jobs, and one-third had criminal records.

Although ANC leaders held the police responsible for initiating the riots, they sought to disassociate Congress from these events, and the local branch of the Youth League "turned their backs on the women and *tsotsis.*"[72] East London's municipal officials initially tried to shift responsibility for the riots to the state and its implementation of the Riotous Assemblies Act. They urged that talks be held with Congress, but the central government demanded that the city council stay away from politicians and consult only with tribal leaders empowered under the Bantu Authorities Act. Local ANC, Youth League, or trade union officials were not invited to a special "consultative" conference sponsored by the white authorities on the so-called tsotsi problem.

Conditions did not improve, but city officials declared the locations "no longer loathsome" when the tsotsi gangs were destroyed.[73] Six years after the riots, however, youth gangs were once again in evidence in East London. The crime rate in the locations rose sharply in November 1958, and this time old-guard traditionalists took matters into their own hands. Arming themselves with sticks and clubs, they went on a rampage, beating up young men and women all over the locations who were suspected of being tsotsis or the mothers of delinquent children. The police eventually intervened, but confrontations between the old rural patriarchal order and the new urban youth culture would continue to surface in East London (and other South African cities) for years to come.

The Congress Youth League had strained to represent all the elements of urban African culture in East London during the Defiance Campaign—young women without husbands, young men without fathers, radical tsotsi gangs, newly arrived migrants, fully proletarianized factory workers, the urban petty bourgeois elite—but this alliance of competing interests and needs was doomed from the beginning. The rituals and rhetoric of Congress, with its khaki-colored uniforms and rosettes, thumbs-up salute, and strident hymns of defiance, papered over these differences at a crucial moment in the early 1950s, but the riots brought them out again. The tsotsis were subordinated or driven out of East London's African slums by a combination of forces—older ANC members with roots in middle-class culture, older male migrants with roots in precolonial culture, and East London's white authorities—but the radical underpinnings of this excluded underclass would reappear in the student uprisings of the 1970s and 1980s.

Phase II of the Struggle: The Mid- to Late 1950s

Rehabilitation and the reorganization of local government under the Bantu Authorities Act of 1951 remained major grievances in rural Ciskei during the mid- to late 1950s, but a new issue arose when the central government took over mission schools with the implementation of the 1953 Bantu Education Act.[74]

State-controlled schools would ensure that Africans received training in the skills that were needed to make them more effective workers in the developing industrial economy. The tribal authorities would also receive training to make them more effective administrators in the reserves and managers in the proliferating number of government-approved enterprises for Africans in white and black South Africa. Hence the missionaries were removed and the mission's boarding school traditions destroyed, while the central government embarked on a massive program to provide the rudiments of a primary education taught in ethnic languages to the bulk of the African school-going population.

Legislation like the Bantu Education Act benefited uneducated chiefs and headmen but tended to undermine the status and authority of the mission-trained teachers, while efforts to pack the reserves with unwanted labor had much the same impact on the indigenous peasantry. Thus it is not surprising that resistance to Bantu education during the mid- to late 1950s extended to Bantu Authorities in their role as collaborators who enforced Betterment/Rehabilitation, policed the schools, and facilitated the labor control system.

The teachers, it will be remembered, were potent but ambiguous power brokers in regional politics. Alienated, lower-ranked members of the profession in particular could perform an important leadership role in rural resistance. The Cape African Teachers' Association, which still controlled most of the teachers in the eastern Cape's mission schools, had been attacking the central government's reserve policies and the Cape's administration of African schools since the 1940s. When Bantu Education was implemented, the AAC began to mobilize public opinion in the eastern Cape against this legislation. In retaliation, the government refused to recognize CATA as the official teachers' association in the province and transferred authority to a puppet organization called the Cape African Teachers' Union. Local school boards were then told to fire CATA-affiliated teachers.

The AAC opposed the boycott of schools since most of their members were teachers who would have been subject to dismissal, but members favored the boycott of school committees and boards. Even so, teachers and parents appear to have acted on their own, keeping their children at home, holding protest meetings, organizing demonstrations, and in rare cases setting fire to school buildings.

Meanwhile, Congress also decided to mobilize opposition against Bantu Education. But the ANC campaign was not approved until April 1955, when mission schools were to be transferred to the Native Affairs Department, and it was a disaster. Leadership was divided: the planned withdrawal of children from the schools and the boycott of the school committees and boards were badly organized and never really implemented. An abbreviated attempt was made to provide alternative educational facilities, but only a few of these independent schools, culture clubs, and home education programs could be sustained for more than a year.

A definitive account of this struggle must await further research, but there is no preliminary evidence to suggest that the AAC or Congress (or the Congress Youth League) played a leadership role in rural Ciskei during the Bantu Education boycotts. The mission schools in this region, however, emerged as one of two focal points of resistance to Bantu Education (along with African schools in Johannesburg and other industrial townships in the southern Transvaal) during the mid- to late 1950s. School boycotts in rural Ciskei lasted intermittently for almost three years, long after protests had ended elsewhere in South Africa.

10

African Labor and the State in the Apartheid Era

As South Africa became increasingly vulnerable to pressure from within and without in the later 1970s and 1980s, critical scholars gradually abandoned a long-held position that the state was an all-powerful instrument of homogeneous ruling-class interests. In essence, the looming hegemonic crisis called into question the nature of the state in modern South Africa.

Stanley Greenberg's study of the labor control system has been employed in this chapter as a framework for analyzing the role of the state under apartheid.[1] Labor remains central to any understanding of why and how the state exercised so much power over the everyday lives of South Africa's black population. The state's labor control policies, however, generated increasing conflict within the ruling bloc and intensified resistance from the mass of black workers and peasants, which ultimately led to a breakdown of the apartheid system.

Section 10.1 periodizes the central government's attempts to modernize the labor control system. Virtually all legislation directed at the African, Coloured, and Indian population had the effect of increasing state control over black workers. Thus labor became a crucial site in the internal struggle against apartheid. A major attempt was made to redistribute personal income from white to black and accommodate privileged fractions of the African working and middle classes with the decentralization of the labor control system in the 1970s and 1980s.

Section 10.2 explores the ramifications of a modernized labor control system for South Africa's reserves. The state intervened decisively inside these areas to resettle unwanted African labor, establish new mechanisms of political control, improve food production, and provide employment.

Section 10.3 focuses on the Ciskei reserve, which served as the principal dumping ground for unwanted Xhosa-speaking workers and their families. The segmented territory was gradually consolidated, political control was ensured through the establishment of Bantu Authorities, and new development strate-

313

gies were pursued. The result was a disaster for all who were forced to live in this small corner of the South African periphery.

10.1. Modernizing the Labor Control System in South Africa

The restraining influence of dissident middle-class politics was finally broken in the aftermath of the state's attempts to destroy the resistance movement in the early 1960s. Attempts by the ANC to mobilize dissent in the cities had been tentative and sporadic. Peasant unrest in the reserves had been contained for the most part without spilling over into the urban areas, and mainstream African nationalist groups had little influence over these events. The contemporary struggle for a democratic South Africa really begins during a period when there is very little organized African political activity, and it is triggered by the state's labor control policy.

The Pattern of Labor Control, 1937–1976

The development of the labor control system in modern South Africa has been divided by Greenberg into three periods.[2] The "formative" period is somewhat loosely positioned between 1937 and 1948, when the first steps were taken to impose limits on African migration to and from the cities. Local authorities were urged to supply information on the African labor market, help workers find jobs, and compel them to leave if they had no work. These "influx control" measures had been authorized before 1937, mainly by the Native (Urban Areas) Act of 1923 (with amendments in 1930 and 1937), but they were applied intermittently, and only eleven municipalities had actually begun restricting African migrants. The Native (Urban Areas) Consolidation Act of 1945 placed more restrictions on African claims to permanent residence in urban areas, but enforcement was still left to the local authorities. By 1948, only five municipalities—and Johannesburg was not one of them—had agreed to accept this responsibility.

Meanwhile, pass law arrests, which had risen in the early war years, dropped to prewar levels in 1942 as the demand for industrial workers soared. While various commissions and committees of inquiry appointed by the Smuts government criticized the migrant labor system and implicitly or explicitly endorsed a permanent (and upwardly mobile) African labor force in the cities, as noted earlier the ruling United party did not move to implement these proposals during the 1940s.

The National party came to power in 1948 and moved quickly to gain control over the labor market. Legislation passed during the "innovative" period (1948–60) laid the foundations for modernizing the control and distribution of African labor. Pass laws before the 1950s had been used primarily to facilitate the flow of black labor to proclaimed white urban and rural areas, but now pass laws would be used to push unwanted labor out of the cities and back to the white farms (until they were no longer needed) and reserves. Pass law arrests in the metropolitan areas rose steadily during the 1950s, but the African population in these areas increased even faster—a growth rate of more than 60 percent during the decade (Appendix Table A10.1a: Domestic African population in South Africa, 1950–1980).

The central government continued trying to get municipalities to police the labor market during the "innovative" period—to establish labor bureaus, enforce the registration of workers, and prevent illegal migrants from living in the segregated African townships—but there was considerable resistance. Johannesburg, for example, refused to cooperate until 1953, and even then the staff assigned to do the policing was too small to have much impact. The new apartheid laws generated opposition from white municipalities and commercial and manufacturing interests, who would have benefited from a permanent urban labor force. Above all, they generated opposition from African workers and thus helped to accelerate the shift to civil disobedience in the cities during this decade.

At the same time, white farmers especially in Natal and the Transvaal continued to frustrate the central government's efforts to force their tenants into wage labor. The Prevention of Illegal Squatting Act of 1951 and a 1954 amendment to Chapter IV of the 1936 Land Act allowing local authorities to remove squatters from white farms, for example, were not enforced. The Bantu Laws Amendment Act of 1964 would finally prohibit all forms of tenancy on white farms, but even this landmark legislation was not actually applied until 1967.

Thus official efforts to control labor in the 1950s were only partially successful. When the National party succeeded in temporarily blunting white as well as black opposition to its policies in the early 1960s, however, a much more vigorous attempt was made to control the labor market. This was the "repressive" period (1960–76), when a master plan was devised for reclassifying, redistributing, and ultimately relocating the entire black labor force in South Africa. It was gigantic in conception and ruthlessly repressive in application.

Africans, Coloureds, and Indians were to be separated from each other as well as from whites, and Africans in the urban areas and reserves were to be resettled according to ethnic group. All movement within and between urban areas as well as between rural and urban areas was to be strictly controlled. Urban African townships were built or rebuilt so they could be sealed off from surrounding white areas by the police or army. They were also built outside city and industrial areas and where possible close to existing reserves. Permanent resident rights for Africans in the cities were eliminated for all but a privileged minority, and vigorous attempts were made to prevent African women from entering the urban areas. Migrant labor assumed a new form as Africans were forced to become "contract" (temporary migrant) workers in ever-growing numbers. The government established labor bureaus outside the control of the municipalities from 1957. The powers of the labor bureau were extended to cover all Africans—permanent and contract laborers—working in white urban areas.

African/white labor ratios were established for companies operating in the main industrial regions of the Cape and Transvaal, and the number of Africans to be employed in any category was drastically curtailed (initially 2.5 and later only 2 Africans could be hired for every white hired). An existing Coloured "labor preference" area in the western Cape would now be enforced, making it even more difficult for Africans to obtain legal employment in the region, and an Indian "labor preference" area was envisaged for parts of Natal. Government housing for Africans in proclaimed white areas—almost the only subsidized housing available—was virtually frozen between 1968 and 1974, and contract workers were barred from gaining residential rights. The bulk of the money allocated to African housing thereafter was spent on urban townships located in the reserves.

Since cities had been the focal point of African political agitation, labor control on this scale offered enormous political advantages, and few economic disadvantages. Mining and various segments of secondary industry (such as construction and smaller, labor-intensive manufacturing concerns often owned by the Afrikaner petty bourgeoisie) would benefit from an enlarged migrant labor force, while the larger manufacturing concerns (especially those involved in the production of consumer goods) would be given at least some access to a permanent urban labor force. White entrepreneurs would reap considerable profits from these removals, especially during the 1960s when thousands of Coloured and Indian traders and commodity producers who operated in white areas were forced to relocate.[3]

At the same time, new controls were devised for regulating African labor at its source in the reserves. Tribal labor bureaus were set up in 1968, and reserve migrants now had to apply for work permits from these local officials and take the jobs that were offered; they could no longer seek work outside the reserve on their own. Contract workers were also forced to return to the reserves at least once a year to ensure that links with their "place of origin" would not be severed. "Call-in cards" were issued to allow migrants to get their jobs back in the urban areas, if employers still needed their labor.

White municipal and employer control over the labor process was completely eliminated with the establishment of the Bantu Affairs Administration Boards in 1971. These agencies—initially twenty-two but later reduced to fourteen—largely took over the administration of African affairs outside the reserves and centralized the control and allocation of African labor in white urban and rural areas.[4] The hierarchical bureaucracy of labor control—the Native Affairs Department, the administration boards, labor bureaus, and tribal labor bureaus—expanded rapidly and became increasingly expensive to maintain. The staff of the administration boards, for example, doubled to 52,000 between 1971 and 1977. The labor control system alone consumed at its height about 14 percent of the national budget, in contrast to the 1–2 percent spent on the entire Native Affairs Department between 1912 and 1936.

A massive increase in the police, security and prison forces gave effect to the labor control measures, and convicts were increasingly exploited as the cheapest form of labor. Pass law prosecutions, for example, soared to an average of 621,600 a year between 1965 and 1970, peaking at 693,700 in 1967/68. In 1969/70, it was estimated that 4.1 percent of the total African population (10.2 percent of the African population of working age) was actually in jail.[5]

The ultimate goal in the expansion of the labor control system during the "repressive" period was to eliminate African population growth in the cities and relocate as many nonessential workers as possible to the reserves. South African agriculture was finally mechanized during the 1960s, so there was no longer a need to retain sharecroppers or even labor tenants. Surviving tenants and other illegal squatters as well as casual labor on white farms were replaced by a permanent wage-labor force during the 1960s and 1970s, and for the first time in history massive numbers of Africans in proclaimed white farming areas were expelled to the reserves.[6]

The Ambiguities of Labor Control

The removals, as they are called in South Africa, were conducted on a scale that was unparalleled anywhere else in Africa.[7] According to the Surplus People Project, at least 3,548,900 people were forcibly removed or obliged to flee their homes between 1960 and mid-1983, and another 1,943,650 were scheduled for "resettlement." Those subject to removals were mainly Africans, but they also included hundreds of thousands of Coloureds and Indians and even some whites (who were usually well compensated). These estimates do not include numbers of people forced to leave towns *outside* metropolitan areas and resettled in the reserves.[8]

South Africa's African labor policy was dictated by the need to maintain a small but permanent industrial work force in the urban areas, establish select categories of migrant contract workers to serve the capitalized sector in town and countryside (especially the mines, commercial farms, and state-owned corporations), and contain so-called redundant and contract workers and their families in the reserves. The state was partially successful in this effort. The *percentage* of the African population in white urban and rural areas apparently did decrease between 1960 and 1980 by 2.6 percent and 11.5 percent, respectively (Appendix Table A10.1a). There were also more African males than females in the white urban and rural areas and more African females than males in the reserves. The proportion of African males to females after 1960 increased rapidly in towns outside the metropolitan areas, increased slightly in the reserves, and gradually decreased in the white rural areas as farmers shifted from tenant and casual labor to full-time wage labor (Appendix Table A10.1b). At the same time, foreign workers (mainly in mining) were displaced by domestic workers (Appendix Table A10.1c).[9]

Nevertheless, the *number* of Africans in proclaimed white urban and rural areas continued to increase. The urban African population rose from 2.2 million in 1950 to 5.6 million in 1980 and the rural African population from 3 million to 4.3 million during the same period (Appendix Table A10.1a). The percentage decrease, moreover, was accounted for in part by incorporating urban African townships in adjacent reserves wherever possible and forcing large numbers of other Africans to commute daily to work from homes in the reserves. As anticipated, the number of Africans in the reserves rose from 3.4 to 11 million between 1950 and 1980 (Appendix Table A10.1A).

Masculinity ratios in the metropolitan areas decreased steadily between 1950 and 1980, which suggests the central government could not stop African females from migrating to South Africa's main employment centers (Appendix Table A10.1b). The trend was particularly noticeable in the 15–29 age group during the 1950s and 1960s, and women in virtually all the older working-age categories (35 years and above) were defying the law to gain entrance to the cities by the 1970s.[10] The urban African population in proclaimed white areas was about 33 percent in 1980, but no less than 50 percent if "closer settlements" in the reserves are included (rural sites where refugees were resettled without access to arable or grazing land).[11]

The state displaced enormous numbers of workers from the core to the periphery, moreover, only to lose control over this huge, congested surplus labor force. As Greenberg makes abundantly clear, the lower echelons of the labor control network were breaking down completely by the 1970s. The six hundred tribal labour bureaus in the reserves "virtually disintegrated" as desperate work seekers bypassed them and migrated directly to metropolitan areas.[12] Labor bureau officials in the white urban and rural areas also ignored government directives in supplying workers to local employers. Employers themselves often ignored the regulations and hired workers whenever they needed them. Indeed, workers and employers alike often bypassed the labor bureaus.

Despite the enormous power at their disposal, the officials charged with responsibility for controlling the movement of migrants between the reserves and cities were unable and often unwilling to do so. Part of the reason lay in the fact that the labor bureaucracy still lacked money and manpower to enforce regulations at the local level. Prosecution was intermittent and uncertain— much depended on who the offender was and where the offense occurred. Corruption at the lower levels of administration, moreover, was increasingly pervasive.

The most visible signs that the labor control system had broken down were the illegal squatter communities emerging in the recesses of Soweto and Alexandra in Johannesburg and virtually encircling the other metropolitan areas—places like Crossroads (Cape Town), Inanda (Durban), Onverwacht (Bloemfontein), and Wintervelt (Pretoria). Although ignored in the census reports, they probably housed between two and three million people and were emerging as folk cultures of resistance in urban African society by the early 1980s.

The State Turns to Decentralization

The "repressive" period marked the beginning of mass mobilization against the state in South Africa, and it was directed against the labor control system. Although more research needs to be done on this topic, it would appear that the gap between popular resistance in town and countryside was gradually closed during these years. A majority of the African population was officially landless and fully proletarianized by the 1970s, and local leadership cadres emerged that were more truly representative of their interests and concerns. Resistance from below was now expressed within organized political structures that had once been the exclusive preserve of the petty bourgeoisie. Militant discourse was displayed in an expanding cycle of strikes and work stoppages, school boycotts and other forms of noncollaboration, and civil disobedience at the community level.

The state tried to contain the resistance movement from the later 1970s by depoliticizing and deracializing the labor control system. The plan, in broad outline, was to fragment the old Native Affairs Department and restructure the language of control to make it more palatable to domestic and foreign critics. Repressive measures would be applied to a few targeted areas and relaxed when and where they could not be defended. Government officials hoped to phase out direct coercion, delegate responsibility to white employers and recognized black authorities in the urban black townships and reserves, and provide incentives for privileged strata within the black community to support the state in its efforts to maintain the apartheid order.

The Department of Natives Affairs (1910–58) had become the Department of Bantu Administration and Development (1958–78), the Department of Plural Relations and Development (1978), the Department of Cooperation and Development (1978–84), and eventually the Department of Constitutional Development and Planning (1985–). The reserves in the 1950s had been renamed Bantustans; now they would be called homelands and ultimately (on being given "independence") national states. As labor control was fragmented, other government departments were also renamed, as were agencies at middle and lower echelons of the state bureaucracy: Bantu Affairs Administration Boards, for example, became Development Boards in 1985.

Many responsibilities of the renamed Department of Cooperation and Development shifted to other government departments in the early 1980s.

Job placement went to the renamed Department of Manpower Utilization. The prosecution and punishment of pass law offenders was undertaken by the Department of Justice, while control over the movement of African commuters and contract workers from the reserves to South Africa's white urban and rural areas was given to the Department of Foreign Affairs. The renamed Development Boards were placed under the authority of the renamed Department of Constitutional Development and Planning in 1985.

Local government was gradually transferred to African officials operating in the African reserves and segregated townships within proclaimed white urban areas. The urban location advisory boards, created in 1921, were reconstructed as Bantu councils in 1961 and renamed community councils from 1977. The Black Local Authorities Act of 1982 sought to develop a local government system for the 299 segregated urban African townships in white South Africa that would be comparable to that of other racially segregated municipalities. The Bantu Affairs Administration Boards (now Development Boards) would still have some responsibilities at local-government level (especially housing), but the new town and village councils would be essentially autonomous.[13]

The government also began to phase out the most overt forms of labor repression—arbitrary searches and arrests of Africans in the streets and in their homes. Pass law prosecutions, for example, actually started declining from 1968, and they were reduced even further in 1984; two years later, the pass laws were abandoned altogether. They were no longer needed because the government already had alternative, not easily detectable, and less costly methods of maintaining labor control. Instead of confronting workers out in the open, the government selected three agencies to police the system. Two were located in the white urban areas and one was located in the reserves. Employers would now be constrained to adhere to pass-control regulations with fines up to 500 rand (about $463 in 1983) for each illegal employee and scheduled court appearances. Workers who had jobs were required to prove that they had legal access to housing in the townships, and the new African local councils were assigned the task of enforcing this regulation. With Africans in control, harsh search-and-seizure measures to root out illegal residents were again introduced inside the townships.

Tribal labor bureaus for contract workers would be administered by African officials in the reserves. A confidential agreement was concluded in 1975 with several homeland leaders, who agreed to take over these "efflux control" centers. African officials would also be responsible for policing their own "frontier commuters." In return, the South African government released funds for African housing in reserve townships that were now deemed to be outside the boundaries of white South Africa. As these townships expanded, the number of daily and weekly commuters crossing the borders of the reserves increased from 290,000 in 1970 to 739,700 in 1981—from 5.2 percent to about 13 percent of the total African labor force.[14]

Privileged Elites in the Apartheid Era

Decentralization of the labor control system in the 1970s and 1980s was accompanied by a significant shift in the government's racial policies. Afrikaner Nationalists now controlled virtually the entire state apparatus. Afrikaner capital had achieved a modus vivendi with English capital in mining, business, commerce, and industry, and the need to discriminate in favor of Afrikaner labor was no longer as urgent as it had seemed a generation earlier. Mounting African resistance, moreover, was accompanied by mounting international pressure (especially after 1974 when Portugal pulled out of Mozambique and Angola) to improve the living and working conditions of the black population.

A concerted attempt would be made to create privileged fractions of African blue- and white-collar workers and integrate these elites into the social order, desegregate public- and private-sector services, decriminalize social relationships between the races, and deracialize the language and culture of oppression. Nevertheless, key social components of the apartheid system— racially defined and segregated housing and education—remained virtually undisturbed in the 1980s.

The right of African labor to form trade unions was recognized in 1979 following the Wiehahn Commission proposals, but most workers, especially domestics, rural laborers, and wage earners inside the reserves, remained unorganized. While attempts were made to decentralize the economy and increase personal mobility, key economic components of the apartheid system also remained undisturbed. Since Africans were still forbidden in most cases to own or control property outside the reserves, for example, they were effectively prevented from gaining access to capital in South Africa's industrial economy.

Political dissent from pressure groups outside the framework of separate development was again permitted and initially even encouraged. Nevertheless, the key political components of the apartheid system did not change in the 1970s and 1980s. Africans remained essentially outside the decision-making process at the local, provincial, and national level, and exiled political organizations remained in exile.

The necessary preconditions for the growth of an African middle-class culture formed an increasingly important subtext in the wider debate over attempts to reform the apartheid system. Census reports, for example, did suggest that Africans were entering the white-collar job market in increasing numbers after World War II. The major expansion was between 1960 and 1980, when Africans in designated middle-class occupations increased from 102,373 to 569,894—from 2.6 percent of the economically active African population to 10.2 percent in twenty years (Appendix Table A10.2).

The redistribution of personal income from white to black first became noticeable in the 1970s: white income levels dropped 9.7 percent to 61.5 percent of the total income, whereas African income levels rose 8.5 percent to 29 percent of the total income between 1970 and 1980 (Appendix Table A10.3a). The proportion of income earned by the top 20 percent of South Africa's population—virtually all white—declined from an estimated 77 percent of the total in 1970 to 61 percent in 1980. According to the Bureau of Economic Research at Stellenbosch, real average African earnings (adjusted for inflation) increased by 56 percent between 1971 and 1979, while real average white earnings declined by 5 percent during the same period. But these figures excluded agriculture.[15]

The mining industry sparked the wave of wage increases during this decade. Mine owners had to make wages more competitive if they were to attract domestic workers to replace foreign migrants. Greater reliance on domestic workers during the 1970s led to increased wages, improved working conditions, and more vigorous attempts to establish a permanent African labor force. Mine owners could now improve wages and working conditions without risking a commensurate loss in surplus profits because the price of gold, which had been fixed at thirty-five dollars an ounce, rose dramatically from the late 1960s when it was allowed to float in the open market. Real average African mine wages, which had not improved between 1910 and 1971, rose about 216 percent between 1971 and 1979. Mine wages, however, were still below the mean for African wages in other nonagricultural sectors of the economy.[16]

The labor control system preserved social divisions between privileged industrial workers who lived permanently in the cities and the mass of contract and redundant industrial workers who were confined to the reserves.[17] The ratio of urban to rural incomes among African wage earners by the mid-1970s was 8.3 to 1—a ratio of inequality comparable to the wage differentials normally encountered between whites and Africans in the urban areas.

Those with permanent residential rights in the white areas now had considerable job mobility. They could ignore the labor bureaus and change jobs without the risk of being forced to leave the cities. Since they enjoyed preferred market status, they were usually better educated, had more opportunities to improve their job-training skills, and were better paid. Commuters and contract workers were still restricted in terms of housing—they generally couldn't obtain residential rights in proclaimed white areas outside the reserves—and many were forced to travel long distances (in some cases, up to eight hours a day) to and from work. But they had virtually the same employment rights as those who had permanent residential rights in the cities, and they could seek employment without fear of harassment.

Economic and social deprivation was most extreme in three lower-ranked labor categories. Africans living in squatter communities on the edge of metropolitan areas couldn't get jobs legally unless they were hired off the street, given legal accommodation, and the employer formally applied for legal exemption from the Tribal Authorities in the reserve where the work seeker was supposed to be living. Male Africans living in the reserves, who were forced to rely on recruiters and Tribal Authorities for gaining necessary job permits, were in an even worse position. In a market with a growing labor surplus, there were few jobs advertised at this level. African women living in the reserves ranked at the bottom of the labor force. They were actively discriminated against at every level of employment, and they were the most desperate work seekers. Women, for example, represented 13 percent of those arrested for breaking the pass laws in 1977 and 26 percent in 1982.

There was considerable debate during the 1980s over whether the state would succeed in depolarizing South Africa's racial caste system in favor of a nonracial class system. Inflation, for example, had a disproportionate impact on Africans in the lower- and middle-income categories, and some scholars thought real African incomes were being reduced more substantially than white, Coloured, and Indian incomes. Most African workers, moreover, still remained below the minimum subsistence levels compiled for the urban and rural areas during the 1970s.[18]

Most economic sectors were capitalizing at an accelerated rate, in part because of labor unrest, increases in labor costs, and low productivity, and relatively fewer workers (especially in unskilled categories) were being recruited into the wage labor market. The number of Africans in the economically active population actually decreased by about 111,000 between 1970 and 1980. Africans constituted 70.3 percent of the total work force in 1970 and 64.4 percent in 1980 (Appendix Table A10.3b). While African wages may have increased in several job categories, so did African unemployment, which was estimated at 11.8 percent in 1970 and 21.1 percent in 1981. As one might expect, unemployment tended to be lowest in the metropolitan areas and highest in the reserves.[19]

10.2. The Transformation of the Periphery

The development of the labor control system coincided with a radical reorganization of the authority structures inside the reserves.[20] Ethnicity would be employed to discourage racial solidarity between people of color and prevent participation in a nonracial society. Each African ethnic group would now be categorized as a national unit with its own language, culture, and history. Each group, in turn, would be allocated a specific territory, and even the segregated urban townships outside the reserves would be segmented along ethnic lines.

The Politics and Economics of Dependency

Before the National party came to power in 1948, only the Transkei and Ciskei reserves in the eastern Cape had limited local government bodies for Africans, and the reserve populations were represented at the national level only through the Natives' Representative Council.[21] Under apartheid, the central government abandoned any pretense of attempting to provide a national forum for African political opinion. As noted earlier, the NRC was abolished, and local government in all the reserves was reorganized along ethnic and pseudotraditionalist lines with the 1951 Bantu Authorities Act. The government proceeded cautiously, however, in the face of mounting resistance from the peasant population. The Ciskei and Transkei Bunga were not disbanded until 1955, and Tribal Authorities were established in only a few reserves during this decade. Little was done to develop Regional and Territorial Authorities outside the Transkei (its Territorial Authority was established in 1957) until the labor control system was perfected in the 1960s.

The Promotion of Bantu Self-Government Act of 1959 provided the legislative framework for establishing autonomous ethnic units in the reserves (now called Bantustans). Eight Bantu Authorities (later increased to ten) were created in the 1960s to represent the designated African ethnic groups of South Africa. These Bantu Authorities were initially established on the basis of language and culture rather than the reserves they occupied—hence the Ciskei and Transkei were part of the Xhosa ethnic unit—but South African government officials remained firmly in control. The white native representatives, the African population's only remaining link to parliament, were eliminated, and white commissioners-general were appointed as agents of the central government for each Bantu Authority (their counterparts at the local level in the reserves were the white Bantu commissioners).

The National party began to address the issue of self-government for the reserves during the 1960s. Despite widespread opposition, government-appointed leaders in the Transkei were persuaded to accept home rule in 1963. Transkeian citizenship was defined, and the boundaries of the territory were formally delineated. Other ornaments of the nation-state were also established, including an executive cabinet and a unicameral legislative assembly, and provision was made for a flag and national anthem. Although the Transkeian experiment would not be repeated in the 1960s, the constitutions of the Territorial Authorities were revised and they were given more authority. Regional Authorities, however, were downgraded to advisory status. Political power in the reserves was to be centralized in the Territorial Authorities.

South Africa's rulers were now ready to persuade their African acolytes to accept home rule. The Bantu Homelands Citizenship Act of 1970 and the Bantu Homelands Constitution Act of 1971 established a standardized legislative mechanism for proceeding to eventual independence for the Bantustans, or homelands as they would now be called. Prompted in part by the Transkei experiment, self-government in the other homelands would be achieved in two stages rather than one. In the first stage, legislative assemblies and executive councils would be established, but they would have no power to amend or repeal South African legislation. In the second stage, the councils would be replaced by legislative assemblies and executive cabinets with full autonomy.

All Africans were to be registered as citizens of one of the homelands—hence any rights they might have outside these areas was in doubt—and the central government could provide the Bantu Authorities with all the accoutrements of self-government without recourse to parliament. Urban African townships in white areas, as noted earlier, would be amalgamated with adjacent homelands, and a concerted attempt would be made from the early 1970s (especially with the Bantu Laws Amendment Act of 1973) to consolidate these fragmented territories.

The Transkei became the first homeland to accept independence in 1976, and three other homelands would become national states in the next five years. The retribalization of the reserves was the National party's political response to African nationalism and to the problem of resettling the labor refugees in these territories. The Tribal Authorities would be obliged to accept these surplus people as the price to be paid for acquiring power and for funds to stay in power.

The National party's economic policy for the reserves was first articulated in the report of the Tomlinson Commission, which was published in 1955. Five years in the making, it was the most comprehensive government document ever produced on South Africa's reserve system. The commissioners approved a land-use plan that was very similar to the Betterment/Rehabilitation schemes devised by the United party government and first introduced in the Ciskei in the 1940s. The principle of one-man-one-lot—virtually all official pronouncements on land distribution in the reserves had been couched in these terms since the 1894 Glen Grey Act—was finally abandoned. Only a proportion of the families in the reserves would be settled as full-time farmers, and the surplus farm population would be resettled in villages without access to stock or arable or grazing land. The nonfarm population would be employed either inside the reserve or as migrant workers.

The villages were supposed to "fulfill all the functions normally expected of an urban centre" [22] with housing, schools, clinics, recreation facilities—and employment opportunities. Efforts would be made to stimulate commercial agriculture—sugar cane, fiber, and forest plantations were specifically examined in the report—and the African farm population would finally have access to credit facilities. While most farm units would be situated on dryland plots, roughly 63,000 morgen (76,320 acres) of irrigated land would be developed to sustain 36,000 progressive farmers.

The commissioners presented a master plan for transforming the economic environment of the reserves that would cost £104.5 million for the first ten years—35.3 percent for agriculture and forestry, 29.7 percent for industry and mining, 23.9 percent for urban development and "basic facilities," and

11.1 percent for health, education, and welfare. If the plan was to be implemented successfully, the government would have to provide the necessary infrastructure and ensure that sufficient capital and technical expertise were made available. The plan would require substantial expansion and reorganization of the NAD and support from other government agencies not involved in reserve administration.

Phasing out Peasant Communities in the Reserves

To establish a class of permanent farmers, the commissioners estimated that each family farm unit would have to earn £120 a year to survive in full-time employment, and 80 percent of the resident reserve population would have to be resettled in nonfarm townships. Since a relocation of the resident reserve population on this scale was politically unacceptable, the commissioners *arbitrarily* reduced the self-sufficiency figure to about £60 per farm unit ("the present low standard of productive efficiency in Bantu agriculture") and the surplus farm population to just under 50 percent of the 1951 reserve population.[23]

The commissioners intended that each dryland plot, absorbing up to 97 percent of the full-time farmers, would comprise 5.7 morgen (12.1 acres) of arable land, of which 3.9 morgen (8.3 acres) would be cultivated on a yearly basis. Dryland farmers were also supposed to have access to grazing land, so that the total area available to them would be 54 morgen (114.5 acres). Irrigated plots would average 1.75 morgen (3.71 acres). Each economic farm unit, they estimated, would have the equivalent of 12 cattle units and a yearly harvest of 18.7 bags of grain. The market value of the surplus livestock and crops in the mixed-farming areas was estimated at £62 12s. a year. Even with these figures, the Tomlinson Commission accepted as fact that 55 percent of the cattle units (based on the 1951/52 livestock census) would have to be culled and that some of the farmers would actually be cultivating subeconomic plots (which were not to be less than 2 morgen or 4.24 acres). The 307,000 families who were supposed to be settled as full-time farmers, then, included about 47,200 families (15.4 percent of the total) who would actually have incomes of less than £60 a year.[24]

The commissioners recommended that freehold tenure (on a voluntary basis) should be revived and eventually replace all other forms of tenure. All reserve land (including mission and freehold land), moreover, should be proclaimed as Betterment land. Residents should be able to buy more than one arable plot, but the Native Trust should retain its authority to reclaim plots not being used effectively and resell them to more efficient farmers.

The Tomlinson Commission provided a plan for the consolidation of the fragmented reserves and pinpointed a hundred sites for the proposed nonfarm villages and towns (each residential plot would be roughly ¼ morgen or slightly more than ½ acre in size). The industrial potential of reserves and border industries adjacent to these territories was assessed, and specific growth points were described in detail. But the commissioners favored industries within the reserves over border industries in white South Africa.

The Tomlinson Commission, of course, accepted separate development. The reserves were examined essentially in isolation from the rest of South Africa, and the commissioners' proposals were based on the assumption that a large proportion of the African population would continue to reside in these territories. Its prescriptions for restoring the land, developing agricultural productivity, stimulating industry, and maintaining even the existing population in the reserves were subjected to widespread criticism, but in the midst of the removals the state actually had no intention of implementing these recommendations.

The possibility of creating a large class of permanent farmers in viable farm units was never seriously contemplated. As a program fostered at various levels since the 1930s for conserving the land and improving the quality of life in the reserves, Betterment/Rehabilitation was effectively abandoned from the mid-1950s. The Tomlinson Commission's initial budget recommendation was reduced drastically from £104.5 million to £36.6 million in 1957. A reduction in government expenditure was possible, it was claimed, because Africans would now be paying higher taxes.[25] Communal tenure was retained because government officials thought freehold tenure would undermine the authority of the chiefs. White entrepreneurs, moreover, were still not allowed to invest inside the reserves.

The division of land into economic farm units and nonfarm residential villages was supported, but removing even 50 percent of the peasant population to nonfarm villages was rejected as politically unacceptable. Residential villages in the rural areas, moreover, would not be built specifically to house the projected nonfarm population, and no provision was made for future growth. Very few villages to house the nonfarm population were actually built before the 1970s.

The poorest sections of the farming population fared worst when the land was subdivided into farm and nonfarm units. The peasant's spatial environment was drastically altered: social relationships were severed and ceremonial and ritual activities abandoned in many rural areas. The privileged farmers were mainly those who were favored by the Tribal Authorities, had access to credit facilities, and could buy multiple dryland plots or obtain irrigated land. Marginal dryland plot holders, peasants forced to live in nonfarm villages, and younger members of the resettled refugee population bitterly resisted the new dispensation. Since most surplus farmers had not been placed in residential villages, very few designated farm units received even the Tomlinson

Commission's scaled-down version of an economic holding. The sixty-pound minimum income per year, moreover, was still being used as a yardstick for economic farm units in the early 1970s when dryland plots actually averaged less than 2 morgen (4.24 acres).[26]

Betterment/Rehabilitation in the post–Tomlinson Commission era, like Bantu Authorities, would be used mainly to promote a pro-homeland elite. The policy of preserving the reserve population as an undifferentiated class of peasants-cum–migrant industrial workers was scrapped, and social stratification was now endorsed as a matter of urgency. In the process, farming would now become little more than a marginal activity for most of the reserve population.

The Strategy of Industrial Decentralization

The attempt to decentralize industry, prompted in part by the need to redress the economic imbalance between South Africa's core and periphery, ease rural unemployment, and thereby slow down African migration to the cities, gathered momentum during the 1960s. The strategy was to establish factories outside rather than inside the reserves, and it was based on the precedent initiated by the United party in the Ciskei. The first border industry in South Africa, it will be remembered, was the Good Hope Textile Mill built near King William's Town outside the reserve in 1946. The dormitory township of Zwelitsha was constructed inside the reserve to supply workers to the mill.

A permanent government committee was set up in 1960 to consider the creation of various industrial enterprises or their relocation to the borders of the existing African reserves. The policy of decentralization was extended to other racial groups from the mid-1960s, and industrial growth points encompassing the whole of South Africa were enumerated and refined. At the same time, state corporations were created—initially the Bantu Investment Corporation (1959)—to promote economic development inside the reserves. Development corporations for each ethnic unit were established in the wake of the Bantu Homelands Development Corporations Act of 1965, which led to the creation of the Xhosa Development Corporation for the Ciskei and Transkei reserves in 1966 and a separate Ciskei National Development Corporation ten years later. The border industry program, however, did not really materialize, and the central government's attempt to promote economic development inside the reserves during this decade was a failure.

A new strategy of decentralization was launched in 1968 when white entrepreneurs were finally allowed to invest inside the reserves. In the same year, the Promotion of Economic Development of Homelands Act was passed to encourage investment in different economic sectors (such as mining) inside the reserves. The government also tried to limit the growth of the metropolitan areas with the Physical Planning and Utilisation of Resources Act of 1967.

Official efforts to improve the quality of African labor were instituted after the report of the Inter-Departmental Committee on the Decentralisation of Industries (the Riekert Committee Report) and a subsequent white paper were issued in 1971. Africans could now be trained as artisans in the reserves and adjacent border areas. Following the proposals of the Riekert Commission in 1979, greater efforts were made to improve the training and employment of African workers, although the reformist image projected by Riekert and its counterpart, the Wiehahn Commission (1979), was undermined by critics in the 1980s.[27]

Legislation alone, however, was not enough. Even with extravagant subsidies and the cheapest possible labor, white capitalists could not be induced to leave South Africa's existing industrial areas for the reserves. The development corporations were still ineffective inside the reserves, and only a small number of border industries had been established outside these territories. African entrepreneurs were now being heavily subsidized by the state, but the African business community was still too small, too inefficient and undercapitalized, and often too corrupt to provide much stimulus to local development.[28]

The central government's efforts to stimulate the economies of the reserves did have some success in the 1970s. Economists noted that gross domestic production (production generated within the reserves) and gross national incomes (income generated by contract labor, commuters, and residents working inside the reserves), for example, increased rapidly in real terms. Nevertheless, job opportunities for reserve migrants and residents alike were declining by the end of the decade. And the gap in personal income levels between urban and rural residents inside the reserves was widening. Rapid urbanization fostered these inequalities because the growth that did occur in commerce, industry, and public sector activity occurred mainly in the urban areas. At the same time, agricultural production (and the number of reserve residents involved in subsubsistence farming) continued to decline.

The state made overtures to the white business community from the later 1970s to get more actively involved in reserve development, and a new industrial decentralization policy was unveiled with the so-called Good Hope Plan in 1981. South Africa was to be divided into eight economic regions; specific "growth points" in or near the reserves were to be targeted and numerous concessions given to investors. The political and economic boundaries of the new regional development strategy, however, did not coincide. Reserves cut across the economic regions, and growth points were often selected for noneconomic reasons. Critics pointed out that the new policy would increase the dependence of the reserves on white South Africa for capital, technology, skilled personnel, raw materials, and markets. Above all, white businessmen, ever more wary of being identified with apartheid policies, remained largely aloof. The strategy of promoting decentralization through regional industrialization made little headway in the 1980s.

10.3. The Ciskei from Reserve to National State

The Ciskei remained a desperately impoverished enclave in South Africa's periphery as it moved from truncated reserve to national state in the apartheid era.[29] State intervention came in the form of the post-Tomlinson version of Betterment/Rehabilitation, the implementation of Bantu Authorities, homeland consolidation, and the forced resettlement of Xhosa pushed out of white South Africa.

A New Political and Territorial Dispensation

The Ciskei's local councils and *Bunga* were dissolved in 1955, and the three-tiered system of Bantu Authorities to be administered by chiefs—Tribal and/or Community Authorities, Regional Authorities, and Territorial Authorities—was gradually introduced between 1957 and 1959.[30] Chiefs in the Ciskei in the postconquest era, it will be remembered, had been replaced by government-appointed headmen and subheadmen, and they had essentially governed the reserve under the authority of white resident magistrates. Thus there were not enough recognized chiefs initially to operate the new system of local government in the Ciskei.

Nevertheless, the Ciskei Territorial Authority consisting of twenty-two members (some of whom had been connected in one way or another with the previous local councils and Bunga) was established by proclamation in 1961. New chiefs were simply appointed—often on very dubious grounds[31]—until they controlled all levels of local government. The Ciskei had thirty-five Tribal and three Community Authorities by 1968 and forty-two Tribal Authorities by 1980. Nine Regional Authorities, representing African locations in the districts of Glen Grey, Herschel, East London, King William's Town, Keiskammahoek, Middledrift, Peddie, and Victoria East, together with the subdistrict of Hewu (carved out of the Queenstown District), were also created in the late 1960s.

Regulations governing the Ciskei's Tribal-Regional-Territorial Authority structure were formally repealed and the Ciskeian "constitution" was revised to strengthen the Territorial Authority in 1968. The Ciskei Territorial Authority (CTA) became a quasi-legislative body containing elected as well as nominated members, and for the first time all Tribal/Community Authorities were represented. An executive council was also created with a chairman and five members, who were given responsibilities for various government departments.

Each ethnic unit was supposed to be represented proportionally on the CTA executive council—two Rharhabe Xhosa, two Mfengu (they had successfully petitioned the government to be recognized apart from the Xhosa), one Sotho, and one Thembu. Rharhabe Xhosa paramount Velile Sandile, who had been the nominal head of the Territorial Authority from 1961 to his death in 1968,[32] was succeeded by Justice Mabandla, an educated Mfengu chief. Native Trust income derived from the Ciskei, pension funds, and disability grants were transferred to the CTA, which could now establish its own budget. The CTA had a shadow executive and legislative body as well as its own civil service, but real control remained in the hands of South African government officials.

The upper tier of the Bantu Authority system in the Ciskei, as in the other reserves, effectively dominated administration at the local and regional level. Tribal and Community Authorities were too small to be self-supporting, and from 1969 the finances of these local bodies were handled by the Territorial Authority. All secretaries of these local bodies, moreover, were made civil servants of the Ciskei government. The intermediary Regional Authorities in the Ciskei were also effectively stripped of executive power in 1969. The trend by the end of the decade, then, was to centralize reserve administration at the level of the Territorial Authority.

The first step toward self-government for the Ciskei was implemented in May 1971 when the Territorial Authority was replaced by a unicameral legislative assembly with a separate executive cabinet. The second step was reached fourteen months later when the Ciskei was formally proclaimed a self-governing homeland. In February 1973 elections were held for the reconstituted Ciskei Legislative Assembly (CLA), which met for the first time in May.

Chiefs had dominated the CTA and they would dominate the CLA. Their importance in modern Ciskei politics can be seen most clearly with the emergence of political parties in the homeland during the 1970s. The sixty-three candidates in the first general election in 1973 were aligned for the most part with various pressure groups dominated by personalities who had been members of the CTA. The two most important were Justice Mabandla, chair of the CLA executive council, and Lennox Sebe, a member of Mabandla's cabinet.

The key perceived difference between these candidates was their ethnic origin: Mabandla was Mfengu and Sebe was Rharhabe Xhosa. Ethnic conflict, relatively quiescent during the period when the ANC and other African political bodies were active in South Africa, had resurfaced in the Ciskei and in other reserves during the 1960s. It was encouraged by the central government and linked to Bantu Authorities, Betterment/Rehabilitation, and resettlement. A majority of the refugees, for example, were Xhosa who had entered the reserve as the land was being subdivided into farm and nonfarm units. A majority of the indigenous farmers were designated Mfengu: they had received land in exchange for siding with the British during the later Cape-Xhosa wars but had few historic claims to chiefships. The exploitation of ethnic loyalties, aided and abetted by Hans Abrahams, commissioner-general for the Ciskei, would be a major factor in Ciskeian political life in the 1970s.

Sebe's followers won thirteen of the twenty elected seats, but Sebe himself

Table 10.1. Political affiliation of CLA members, 1973–1981

Legislators	1973		1974		1975		1976		1978		1981	
	CNIP	CNP	CNIP	CNP	CNIP	CNP	CNIP	CNP	CNIP	CNP	CNIP	CNP
Chiefs	11	19	16	17	18	18	15	12	27	6	33	—
Elected	15	5	16	4	16	4	14	1	22	—	22	—

SOURCES: N. Charton & G. R. kaTywakadi, "Ciskeian political parties," in N. Charton (ed.), *Ciskei: economics and politics of dependence in a South African homeland* (London, 1980), 145–47; South African Institute of Race Relations, 1981 *Survey*, 301. These figures exclude one or two chief's deputies, who were nominated members of the CLA, and two short-term fringe parties formed by individuals who opposed the CNIP before 1980. In addition to the nominated chiefs and elected members, the CLA at independence included the Rharhabe Xhosa paramount and five members nominated by President Sebe.

required the allegiance of two independent legislators and eleven of the chiefs to be elected chief minister by a margin of two votes. Sebe could strengthen his party in the CLA only by establishing new chiefships. Nine were created between 1973 and 1976—including one for Sebe—and eight were Xhosa (one pro-Sebe Mfengu chief was also recognized). The Thembu and Sotho had little political significance as ethnic groups in the Ciskei once Herschel and Glen Grey were ceded to the Transkei in 1975. The South African government favored Sebe (several officials linked to the Department of Bantu Administration and Development were charged with voting irregularities following the 1973 election), and most of the new pro-Sebe chiefships were carved out of locations hitherto administered by Mabandla's supporters.

The Ciskei's two major political parties—Mabandla's Mfengu-dominated Ciskei National party (CNP) and Sebe's Rharhabe Xhosa–dominated Ciskei National Independence party (CNIP)—were formed after the 1973 elections (see Table 10.1).

In the absence of political alternatives, the CNIP obtained a measure of grassroots support, especially in the rural areas and among members of the local petty bourgeoisie dependent on the party for support—civil servants, teachers, medical personnel, traders, semicommercial farmers, and the new, heavily subsidized industrial and commercial entrepreneurs. Sebe's faction had a more effective party apparatus—100 as opposed to 11 (mainly urban) branches for the opposition CNP in 1976—and gradually gained control over the Tribal and Regional Authorities. There was little sympathy or understanding for the concept of an opposition party, especially among rural constituents, and voters did not distinguish between the ruling party and the government.

Nor was there much opposition within the CLA. Only 50 percent of the bills prepared by the public service and approved by the executive cabinet between 1973 and 1976, for example, were contested at any level, and only two minor amendments were passed. In reality, the CLA had no power: chiefs and elected members had little or no experience as legislators; white advisers were rapidly withdrawn,[33] and the parliamentary committee system, which might have provided some training in the art of government, was virtually undeveloped. The legislature, as Nancy Charton put it, was "a rubber stamp for the executive arm of government." [34]

The CNIP quickly consolidated its power base after the 1973 elections. In addition to packing the CLA with pro-CNIP chiefs, Sebe's faction sought to influence the appointment of CNIP officials in the rural and urban areas. With 53 percent of the eligible voters casting ballots and most of the opposition candidates either in detention or in hiding, Sebe's party won an overwhelming victory in the 1978 elections. What was left of the CNP opposition was virtually forced to cross the floor of the legislative assembly and join the CNIP,[35] and Sebe himself was proclaimed president for life. Within seven years after becoming a self-governing homeland, the Ciskei had become the political fiefdom of one man and one party. Sebe now sought to broaden his support: ethnic rivalries were downplayed, Xhosa and Mfengu days of celebration (yearly events since the early 1900s) were suppressed, and selected Mfengu were promoted to positions of power in the government.

The CNIP's popular mandate was largely illusory in the urban townships and among Xhosa living outside Ciskei. Surveys of political attitudes among the Xhosa population in the eastern Cape during the mid–late 1970s, for example, consistently revealed a preference for a unified nonracial South Africa with access to political power vested in a single franchise open to all segments of the population. These surveys suggested that African political aspirations had not changed since Bantu Authorities were initially imposed in the 1950s. While Sebe did enjoy some legitimacy—in the absence of permissible alternatives—he was also perceived as a leader controlled by the South African government.[36]

Communication with the majority of CNIP constituents in the rural areas was authoritarian and hierarchical, from legislators and bureaucrats in Zwelitsha, the capital, through the chiefs in the Tribal Authorities, to the headmen and local councils (*inkundla*) in the villages. The CNIP did not launch a youth wing until January 1980 when it was in full control of the state apparatus—an important consideration, given the crucial role that African youth have played in the resistance movement—and women as well as youth were unrepresented in the political process during the 1970s. Nevertheless, rural residents still identified with the CNIP, and Sebe's faction regularly won most of the contested seats at election time. As Philippa Green and Alan Hirsch suggest, CNIP membership, payment of party dues, and loyalty to the local (CNIP) chief or headman was the only way most rural or resettled Ciskeians could secure housing plots, pension money, unemployment benefits, local jobs, or migrant labor contracts.[37]

Sebe and the CNIP initially claimed historic Ciskei between the Kei and Fish rivers and between the Indian Ocean and the Stormberg Mountains as their territory. The South African government, however, was interested only in consolidating the existing reserve, and this became an urgent priority after the Ciskei was declared a self-governing territory in 1972.

The Ciskei reserve at the time comprised about nineteen separate pieces of land (Map 4). Plans for the partial consolidation of the reserve in five separate tracts (four large and one small) were tabled in parliament in April 1972: additional land was to be obtained mainly from the Peddie District (52.7 percent) and an adjacent area along the coast in the East London District. The consolidation of the Ciskei would entail the removal of Africans from fourteen locations (referred to as "black spots") in the so-called white corridor between Ciskei and Transkei and from other locations that had now been designated as part of the Ciskei reserve west of the Fish River in the Port Elizabeth–Humansdorp area. White villages that had been preserved within the reserve since the 1913 Land Act, moreover, would now be under African control.[38]

New consolidation proposals for the Ciskei were outlined in 1975 and refined slightly in 1977. The reserve area was reduced temporarily by 45 percent when Glen Grey and Herschel were ceded to the Transkei to make territorial independence more palatable. The Ciskei was to be compensated with better agricultural land obtained from the Peddie, Queenstown, Stockenstrom, Victoria East, King William's Town, and Keiskammahoek districts.[39] In the process, the reserve would become a single block of land with its own redrawn magisterial districts—Mdantsane, Zwelitsha, Victoria East, Peddie, Keiskammahoek, Middledrift, and Hewu. The 1975 consolidation proposals were well on the way to being implemented by the early 1980s (Appendix Table A10.4). Although more than 40 percent of the consolidated reserve was new, the size of the reserve was about the same as it had been a generation earlier—and there were now at least 2½ times more people living on the land.

The Ciskeian government was advised by an autonomous commission of inquiry early in 1980 against seeking independence. The homeland lacked "virtually all the attributes of a viable economy," and independent statehood was rejected by "a clear majority of Xhosa."[40] Sebe and his party, however, were already in the process of negotiating independence. A referendum of sorts was held in accordance with the Ciskei Commission's recommendations on December 4, 1980.[41] The CNIP monitored the polling booths, and virtually all who voted—59.5 percent of the registered voters—opted for independence.[42] Exactly one year later, it was accomplished. Appropriately enough, the flagpole bearing the symbol of independence fell, broke, and was finally supported by South African soldiers during the proclamation ceremony.

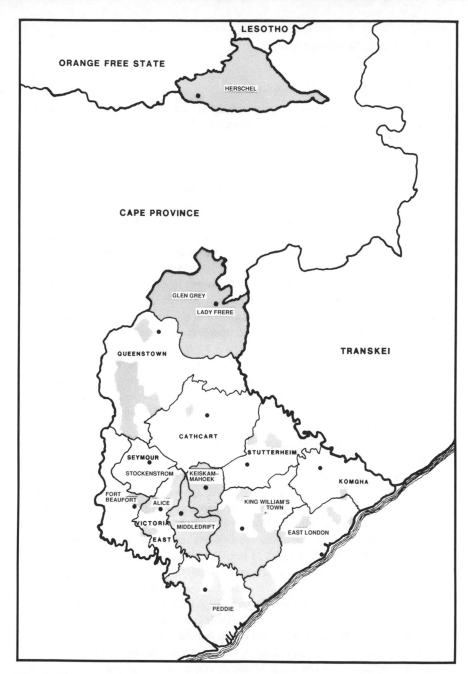

Map 4. Ciskei magisterial districts and reserves (shaded areas) before consolidation. Courtesy of C. B. Freeman, "An assessment of the territorial development of the Ciskei with special reference to independence," unpublished honours thesis, Rhodes University, 1981.

335

A Dumping Ground for Xhosa Refugees

As the Ciskei reserve was being consolidated and separated politically from the rest of South Africa, it was also forced to absorb most of the Xhosa being removed from proclaimed white areas outside the territory. The Xhosa ethnic unit was split between the Ciskei and Transkei in 1976, but the Transkei successfully avoided having to accept a major portion of the refugees because it was the showcase reserve in the new era of Bantu Authorities.

They poured into the Ciskei from four main regions. Farm consolidation and mechanization in rural eastern Cape during the 1960s had helped to trigger a relatively heavy migration of white farmers and town dwellers to the metropolitan areas. Redundant African farm workers and their families, especially casual labor, the aged and disabled, and minor children, were forced for the most part to move to the reserve.[43] The Coloured labor preference area, which initially comprised the western Cape, was steadily widened during the 1960s until it reached the boundaries of the Ciskei at the Fish River. Africans from the western and central Cape were systematically removed and relocated in the reserve from the mid-1960s.

A third group was removed from African locations in the East London metropolitan area and relocated in the rapidly expanding African township of Mdantsane beginning in the 1960s.[44] African refugees from the districts of Glen Grey and Herschel composed the fourth group. Perhaps 37,500 voluntarily fled to the Ciskei between 1976 and 1977, for example, because they either feared reprisals (Glen Grey residents had voted against inclusion in the Transkei in a 1971 referendum) or were promised land by Ciskeian officials.[45] As boundaries were redrawn, Africans owning land or living in locations or on historic nineteenth-century mission stations between the Fish and Kei rivers outside the reserve would also be subject to resettlement inside the reserve along with Africans residing west of the Fish River.

The Ciskei reserve alone absorbed two-thirds of the Xhosa refugees between 1970 and 1980. The resident population increased by an estimated 76 percent (designated rural inhabitants increased by 54 percent and the urbanites by 230 percent), and officially refugees composed about 26 percent of the Ciskei's population in 1980 (Appendix Table A10.5a). When broken down into specific magisterial districts (Appendix Table A10.5b), the refugees composed 54 percent of the population in rural Hewu (which absorbed the Africans from Glen Grey and Herschel) and 42 percent in urban Mdantsane (which absorbed the Africans from East London). Middledrift was the only district in the Ciskei that apparently did not have a resettlement camp and did not absorb refugees during the decade. The refugee population in other districts ranged from 3 percent (rural Peddie) to 33 percent (urban Zwelitsha). According to the Surplus People Project, there were at least forty-four resettlement sites of various kinds in the Ciskei reserve by 1982 (Map 5).[46] These figures do not measure the impact of resettlement on the reserve before the 1970s or resettlement within the reserve. According to Charton, at least 383,236 refugees—60.8 percent of the Ciskei's official population in 1980—were removed to the reserve between 1960 and 1980.[47]

Removal and resettlement had a particularly devastating impact on the Ciskei reserve. Population density more than doubled from an estimated 48.1 to 118.9 persons a square kilometer between 1970 and 1980. The Ciskei Commission actually estimated the population density at 126 persons a square kilometer in 1980, when the reserve was only 617,500 morgen (1,309,100 acres). In the proclaimed white corridor between the Ciskei and Transkei reserves it was 33, and in white South Africa outside the reserves it was 13.5 persons a square kilometer. Most peasants became landless, existing inequalities between residents deepened, and unemployment soared. As the Ciskei Commission put it, the reserve was "perhaps the most overcrowded rural area in South Africa." [48]

The population density was supposed to drop to an estimated 87 persons a square kilometer when the reserve was fully consolidated under the 1975 boundary proposals, but Ciskei Xhosa living outside the reserve and subject to resettlement were variously estimated at 443,094 (Department of Statistics) and 1,433,000 (Ciskei Commission).[49] The reserve population was increasing by 5.8 percent a year between 1970 and 1980 (Appendix Table A10.5b), whereas the natural increase (based on the national average) was estimated at 2.7 percent a year. Resettlement had more than doubled the population growth rate in the Ciskei in a single decade.[50] Forced removals in the 1980s would focus on Africans living outside the reserve in the Ciskei/Border region and in Cape Town, an employment center for Xhosa speakers since the mid-nineteenth century.

The refugees moved mainly from a rural to an urban or peri-urban setting. According to official statistics, the Ciskei reserve's urban population increased from 26.8 percent to 36.2 percent between 1970 and 1980. If the nonfarming population (residents living in peri-urban areas, rural villages, and resettlement camps) is included, at least 60.8 percent of the Ciskei's population (383,021 residents) in 1980 was urban, the highest in South Africa's reserve system.[51]

Mdantsane, Zwelitsha, and the other designated urban townships within the reserve were essentially dormitory suburbs for adjacent white urban areas. Municipal infrastructures were poorly developed—Mdantsane functioned at the level of a country town a tenth its size[52]—and there were very few economic opportunities for local residents. Official figures continued to underestimate the urban population; the Ciskei Commission's estimate of Mdantsane's population in 1980, for example, was 250,000 or 60 percent above the official figure. In contrast to the rural areas, public housing was available but there

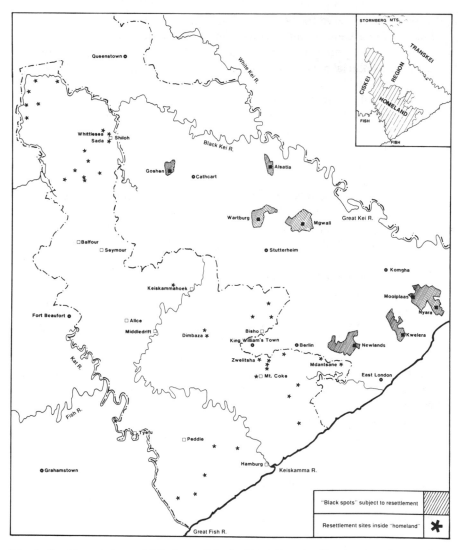

Map 5. Resettlement sites and "black spots" in the Ciskei "homeland" and region after consolidation. Courtesy of Surplus People Project, *Forced Removals in South Africa, Vol. 2: The Eastern Cape*. Copyright January 1983 by Surplus People Project.

Table 10.2. Ciskei reserve medical services in 1980

Magistrial district	Hospitals	Beds	Persons /bed	Beds /1000	Clinics	Persons /clinic
Mdantsane[a]	1 (C. Makiwane)	638	280	3.5	18	9,931
Zwelitsha	1 (Mt. Coke)	300	558	1.7	18	9,301
V. East[a]	1 (Lovedale)	182	378	2.6	6	11,472
K'kammahoek	1 (St. Matthews)	215	181	5.5	13	2,988
Peddie	1 (Nompumelelo)	156	380	2.6	8	7,399
Hewu	—	—	—	—	12	6,209
Middledrift	—	—	—	—	6	8,006
Total	5	1,491	426	2.3	81[b]	7,847

SOURCE: Community Health Research Project, "Health and health services in the Ciskei," unpublished paper, University of Cape Town, SALDRU, 1983, 24, 26 (adapted from Tables 2 and 4).
[a] Cecilia Makiwane Hospital had expanded to 840 beds by 1981. Macvicar Hospital, the tuberculosis facility at Lovedale, was closed by the Ciskei Health Department in October 1977.
[b] There were also a few mobile or subclinics that brought the total figure to about 90 (or 7,063 persons per clinic) in 1980.

was an acute shortage. Nevertheless, the urban areas offered the best chance for survival in the Ciskei.[53]

Residential villages for the nonfarming population in the rural areas— three had been built in the Ciskei by 1960—offered some food in the form of gardening activities, but they did not become market centers or attract industry as the Tomlinson Commission had hoped. For many years, they lacked even basic services like schools, clinics, and trading stores. Conditions were worst in rural resettlement camps, where housing was extremely primitive and even modest facilities like public toilets and reticulated water were sometimes missing.

Resettlement would have a devastating impact on the mental and physical well-being of the Ciskei's impoverished population.[54] There had been some improvement in basic medical services in the postwar generation. Ten mission and provincial hospitals provided, it will be remembered, about 931 beds for Africans in the Ciskei region in 1945 (Appendix Table A7.7), while the consolidated reserve in 1980 had five hospitals with 1,491 beds. Nevertheless, the number of beds per person was about the same. The Ciskei region had roughly 2.1 beds per 1,000 Africans in 1946 (population 438,044), and the reserve had 2.3 beds per 1,000 Africans in 1980 (population 630,353), still virtually one-half the minimum of four beds set by South Africa's Department of Health (see Table 10.2).[55]

The doctor-population ratio had not improved much in the interim. There was roughly one doctor for every 9,570 Africans in 1948 in the region as opposed to one doctor for every 8,707 Africans in 1980 in the reserve.[56] The major change in health services during this period was the provision of clinics in rural villages, but the geographical distribution of these clinics remained uneven. The clinic-population ratio in most districts, moreover, was far above the norm set by the South African Department of Health for community health centers (clinics), which was one examination room for every 2,000–5,000 people.

The Ciskei Department of Health and Welfare was established in 1975, and health along with education and the creation of domestic employment was a top priority in terms of state expenditure. The health budget, however, could fund at best only 60 percent of the Ciskei's minimum welfare needs.[57] The hierarchical system of health-care administration in the Ciskei, as in the other reserves, was critically understaffed and almost totally dependent on South Africa.[58]

As always, a high percentage of those afflicted with diseases relating to poverty were the very young. Infant and child mortality figures were still scarce in the Ciskei during the 1970s and 1980s, but one estimate placed the infant mortality rate (up to one year) for the reserve as a whole at 200 (per 1,000 births) in the early 1980s. Health-care worker Trudi Thomas estimated the infant mortality rate at 100 (per 1,000 births) in Mdantsane and 250 (per 1,000 births) in the rural areas. Infant mortality in Mdantsane was apparently much lower than it had been in East London's African townships during the interwar period, but in the rural areas it was more than 50 percent higher than in the only other survey of infant mortality rates recorded for the Ciskei (the 1937 Ciskei-Transkei survey).

Life remained grim for children who survived infancy. In a malnutrition survey conducted by a group of doctors for the Ciskei government in 1978, for example, it was found that 50 percent of children between the ages of two and three were malnourished. In the rural areas one in six and in the urban areas one in ten children was suffering from a specific malnutrition disease such as kwashiorkor or marasmus.[59] In a sample of African patients from seven Ciskeian hospitals in 1977, for example, about 57 percent suffered from diseases attributable to poverty.[60] Ciskei's health problems in the 1980s, especially in the rural villages and among the refugees in the resettlement camps, were similar to what they had been at the beginning of the century— an undernourished and malnourished population without minimum preventive or curative health care services.

Economic Incentives: the Industrial Program

As noted earlier, the resettlement crisis did help to activate two regional development strategies in the 1960s and 1970s, one based on border industries outside the reserve and one based on capital-intensive agricultural and industrial projects inside the reserve.[61]

The first strategy was to establish border industries in the so-called white corridor between the Ciskei and Transkei reserves. East London was one of the designated growth points, and the border industry program did provide a temporary boost to the local economy. The Industrial Development Corporation (IDC) in conjunction with a firm from Lancashire, England, built another textile factory near the new township of Mdantsane, and a number of existing manufacturing firms in East London received assistance from the IDC to expand their facilities. Most of the industrial land in the city had been developed, and various job-training schemes had been initiated and jobs created for about eight thousand Africans by 1969. The East London industrial zone was extended to the nearby town of Berlin, where a few more factories were in production by 1972. The Good Hope Textile Mill next to Zwelitsha was enlarged (it is now one of the biggest factories of its kind in the southern hemisphere) and absorbed by the reserve under the 1975 consolidation proposals, and some small firms in King William's Town were given financial assistance.

Nevertheless, East London remained the only real economic growth point as far as border industries in the Ciskei region were concerned. The raw materials were largely imported, and production was largely exported to South Africa's metropolitan areas.[62] The city's industries could not survive without the subsidies and rebates provided by the South African government. Industrial development, moreover, was brief as well as artificial. The local economy was in the doldrums again by the mid-1970s, and African unemployment increased steadily as the South African economy entered a prolonged period of recession in the late 1970s.

The shift in development strategy from border industries to the reserves did not take effect in the Ciskei reserve until self-government status was granted in 1972. The South African government offered major incentives to attract investors,[63] and the Ciskei National Development Corporation (CNDC) was created to stimulate economic growth,[64] but there was little to show for these efforts. CNDC-promoted industries created on average only 416 jobs a year, for example, between 1974 and 1981, providing work for about 5 percent of the estimated yearly increase in the Ciskeian labor force. Development projects from all sources (CNDC, Bantu Investment Corporation, private entrepreneurs) had generated an estimated 8,096 new jobs by 1980, half of them with the Good Hope Textile Mill.[65]

The Ciskei became a focus of international attention with such infamous "closer-settlement" camps as Sada (near Whittlesea), Ilinge (near Queenstown), and above all Dimbaza (near King William's Town), which was the subject of the BBC documentary film *Last Grave at Dimbaza*. Thus it was no coincidence that Dimbaza (created in 1968) was selected as the primary industrial growth point inside the reserve. Removals were stopped in 1974 when the industrial program was initiated, and soon thereafter Africans were moving voluntarily to the township seeking work. The population had increased from about 4,000–5,000 in 1969 to 18,000 by 1980. Dimbaza was promoted as an industrial showpiece for the reserves in the 1970s just as Zwelitsha had been promoted as a model township for border industries next to the reserves thirty years earlier.[66]

The problems involved in establishing an industrial base in the Ciskei were summed up in the Dimbaza experience. The cost per industrial job in 1980 ranged from R2,667 for wood products to R29,455 for fabricated metal products, and metals were the fastest-growing manufacturing sector in Dimbaza.[67] The South African subsidy, then, was apparently attracting capital-intensive rather than labor-intensive industry to the Ciskei. Factory workers were mainly women (almost 70 percent of the workforce between 1977 and 1979), the cheapest, most stable, and docile form of labor (from the employers' perspective) in the reserve. Even so, an estimated 30–35 percent of the working population was unemployed.[68]

Commerce in the Ciskei reserve remained undeveloped. Rural incomes were too low to support more than a limited number of traders, although virtually all white businesses in the countryside were now owned by Africans. Most commercial activity was located outside Ciskei in the East London–King William's Town border industrial area. Inside Ciskei, the CNDC had licensed only 774 commercial undertakings (almost all CNIP-aligned family businesses) employing about two thousand people by 1977.

Economic Incentives: the Agricultural Program

Ciskei's farmers, like their counterparts in other reserves, continued to suffer in the post–Tomlinson Commission era.[69] Conservation policies were downgraded in favor of demarcating the land and dividing the rural population into nonfarm and farm units. The profound impact these changes had on village life in the Ciskei is illustrated by Chris de Wet's study of Chatha in the Keiskammahoek District (see Table 10.3).

Official planning committees did not consult the residents when drawing up a Betterment plan for Chatha in the early–mid 1950s. All the local authorities, including the village headman, agricultural officer, and even the native commissioner, warned against implementing the scheme. If economic farming units along the lines envisaged by the Tomlinson Commission were to be achieved, only 64 families would actually retain a right to farm the land. A key to implementing the new Betterment plan in Chatha, as in other villages in the reserve, was the provision of funds to buy land and erect a village for the surplus nonfarm residents. Money for this purpose was not made available, and in 1961 local planners were forced to drop even subeconomic farm units and provide all households with at least a garden plot.

Nevertheless, all land in the location was to be demarcated into arable, grazing, forest, and residential areas. Beginning in the early 1960s, the demarcated zones were fenced in and families moved to their new housing sites. Dryland and irrigation plots were allotted in the mid–late 1960s. Betterment would separate many farmers from their fields and force householders to spend

Table 10.3. Chatha village before and after Betterment

Category	1948–1950	1980–1981
Population	2,325	2,800
Number of households	375	415
Households with access to arable/pasture land	97%[a]	62%
Land under cultivation (in morgen)	887 (dryland)	235 (dryland)
		24 (irrigated)
Average size of family holding (in morgen)	2.4 (dryland)	0.5 (dryland)
		1.5 (irrigated)
Grazing per cattle unit (in morgen)	1.8	2.3
Families without stock	17%[a]	23%

SOURCES: M. E. E. Mills & M. Wilson, *Land tenure*, Vol. 4, *Keiskammahoek Rural Survey* (Pietermaritzburg, 1952), 42–44; C. J. de Wet, "Betterment planning in a rural village in Keis-kammahoek, Ciskei," *Journal of Southern African Studies* 15 (2), January 1989, 329, 339–40; idem, "Betterment and trust in a rural Ciskei village," *Social Dynamics* 6 (2), 1981, 28. The pre-Betterment survey of Chatha village, undertaken by researchers from Rhodes University in Grahamstown, formed part of the four-volume Keiskammahoek Rural Survey.
[a] Almost 30 percent of the eligible household heads (all married men and widows) were actually landless, but virtually everyone in Chatha had access to fields and stock: "the land is sub-divided in practice even further . . . for most of them [the landless families] acquire some portion of a field [and] they are not prevented from grazing stock on the commonage." Mills & Wilson, *Land tenure*, 44.

more time carrying water and wood for fuel. The designated boundaries were inflexible, so more and more families had to be squeezed into the residential area as the population increased. Households without any access to arable land rose from 3 percent in 1948–50 to 38 percent in 1980. Officials removed about 71 percent of the most debilitated arable land from cultivation, so the average dryland plot shrank to 21 percent of what it had been a generation earlier. Land holdings in peasant communities like Chatha were more uniform than in the past, but the yield from dryland plots was too low to make a real difference between farm and nonfarm incomes.

De Wet shows clearly how conditions worsened for Chatha's peasant farmers after the Tomlinson Commission's version of Betterment was intro-duced. Cash incomes for migrant and commuter workers, however, rose about 169 percent in real terms in the generation between the 1950s and the 1980s. Thus more money circulated in Chatha, and a small group of commercial entrepreneurs emerged alongside the drylanders and those with irrigated plots. The local bureaucracy under Tribal Authorities also expanded, and there were more potential patrons available to residents. CNIP-appointed officials were now the arbiters of power and wealth in the village. The distinctions dividing these communities in the past—between pagans and Christians, Reds and School people, landed and landless, those with stock and those with no stock, those who had and those who did not have access to strong headmen—were no longer relevant.

For the Ciskei reserve as a whole, dryland plots constituted 95 percent of the cultivated land in 1980, but these plots were now so small they could not be regarded as even marginal production units. They averaged less than 1.17 morgen (2.47 acres), as opposed to 2.17 morgen (4.6 acres) in the 1940s, and virtually no crops were marketed. The production of maize—the primary food crop—was about 29 percent of estimated requirements in 1980. Production (consumed and marketed) constituted only 15 percent of the average rural household income in 1980 as opposed to about 34 percent in 1943 (Table 7.1: Ciskei mine workers' survey). Almost all farm income was obtained from livestock, but in 1980 the reserve carried only about 281,000 cattle units. In the drought-stricken 1930s with little more than one-third the population, the reserve carried on average about 370,000 cattle units.

Arable, grazing, and residential land had been demarcated for 80 percent of the Ciskei's designated farm units by 1980, but farmers now constituted only about 25 percent of the homeland's total population. Roughly 10 percent of these rural households were viable economic units. While 64 percent of the reserve population were officially rural in the 1980 census, less than 5 percent were making a full-time living as farmers, and agriculture generated only 13 percent of the national income (1976). Most white farms absorbed by the reserve when it was consolidated were turned over to commercial African farmers loyal to the CNIP, or they remained with the Ciskei government.

Agricultural development was promoted with considerable vigor from the mid-1970s, but most of the money allocated to farming was spent on irrigation projects (in part, to reestablish a dairy scheme) and pineapple plantations that benefited only a small group of pro-CNIP farmers. The goal of development in rural as in urban areas was now "the creation of a new middle class of farmers firmly entrenched in the cash economy." [70] John Daniel warned that if rural development continued to focus on capital-intensive projects for the benefit of the few and ignored dryland agriculture which employed virtually all the farmers, "the Ciskei can have no agricultural future." [71]

Green and Hirsch argued that the real importance of the Ciskei government's agricultural and industrialization policy was political and ideological rather than economic. The new enterprises provided some ideological support for Sebe's claim that he would provide a procapitalist, free-enterprise environment for development. They also benefited some components of the resident petty bourgeoisie—nonmanual workers in industry and peasants who had gained access to irrigated land and/or were involved in commercial farming—who might be expected to support the ruling CNIP. In terms of employment, roughly 18 percent of the Ciskei's economically active population were believed to have a stake in preserving the Sebe regime by the early 1980s.[72]

The Ciskei had the dubious distinction of having the lowest economic growth rate and the second fastest population growth rate in South Africa's reserve system during the 1970s. Per capita income rose by only 1.8 percent a year, the second lowest in the reserves in 1970 (after Kwangwane) and 1977 (after Qwa Qwa).[73] South Africa provided roughly 75 percent of the Ciskei's budget requirements through direct and indirect aid during the 1970s, and it was more than 80 percent by the 1980s.[74] The major shifts in employment between 1970 and 1980 were a sharp decline in the number of persons involved in agriculture (from ca. 81,000 to ca. 50,000), and an increase in the percentage of commuter workers (from 8 to 19 percent of the labor force). About 35 percent of the labor force inside the reserve remained unemployed throughout the decade, and the increase in total employment was marginal.[75] Most commuting (92 percent in 1979) was between Ciskei's main dormitory suburbs—Mdantsane and Zwelitsha—and East London and King William's Town. The commuter growth rate, however, slowed down considerably from the mid-1970s with the economic downturn in this industrial zone.

Reserve commuters and contract workers (or migrants) working outside the Ciskei constituted at least 45 percent of the economically active population (15–64 years of age) in 1970 and 64 percent in 1980. Estimates of dependency on income derived from commuters and contract workers combined were high: about 65 percent of the Ciskei's income in 1976, for example, was earned outside the homeland. The average industrial wage for Africans in East London was R160–R200 a month in 1980—only 47 percent (1976) of the average industrial wage in other metropolitan areas but far higher than wages for contract workers or for industrial and agricultural workers inside the reserve. Industrial workers at Dimbaza, for example, were making on average R73 a month (1980), and agricultural workers on the irrigation schemes were receiving between R36 (women) and R72 (men) a month (1980)—among the lowest wages paid to Africans in South Africa's reserve system.[76]

The Ciskei's desperate economic position dictated a shift in priorities soon after independence in 1981. The Ciskei government had hitherto dominated the formal sector of the economy, but employment in this sector—plot holders and laborers in dryland and irrigated farm units, industrial workers and civil servants employed inside the reserve, and commuters and contract workers employed outside the reserve—had reached saturation point by the early 1980s. In future, a concerted attempt would be made to decentralize and privatize the whole of the homeland economy in conjunction with the central government's equally desperate attempt to decentralize the national economy.[77]

South Africa's regional development plan inaugurated in 1981 (the Good Hope Plan) placed the Ciskei hinterland and adjacent white corridor at the core of Region D, which embraced the eastern Cape from the Port Elizabeth–Uitenhage metropolitan complex to the southern Transkei. Of the eight development regions envisaged for South Africa, Region D was to receive top priority since it was regarded as the most depressed in the country.[78]

Table A10.1a. Domestic African population in South Africa,
1950–1980 (in nos. and %s)

Location	1950	1960	1970	1980
White urban	2,204,300	3,375,800	4,191,400	5,606,700
	25.4	29.3	27.1	26.7
Metropolitan[a]	1,452,800	2,325,400	2,808,600	3,915,600
Other towns	751,500	1,050,400	1,381,800	1,691,100
White rural[a]	3,025,700	3,690,900	3,794,800	4,310,000
	34.9	32.1	24.5	20.6
African reserve[a]	3,439,400	4,440,200	7,481,900	11,055,600
	39.7	38.6	48.4	52.7
Total	8,669,400	11,506,900	15,468,100	29,972,300

Table A10.1b. African masculinity ratios (per 100 females)
in South Africa, 1950–1980

Location	1950	1960	1970	1980
White urban				
Metropolitan	166	140	130	128
Other towns	116	104	131	139
White rural	117	112	110	107
African reserve	72	76	79	84

Table A10.1c. Foreign African population in South Africa,
1950–1980 (in nos.)

	1950	1960	1970	1980
Total	603,200	586,600	516,000	201,600

SOURCE: C. A. W. Simkins, "Four essays on the past, present and possible
future of the distribution of the black population of South Africa," unpublished paper, University of Cape Town, SALDRU, 1983, 53–56 (Table 1),
57 (Table 2), 82 (Table 8). Simkins' figures represent adjustments for
undernumerations of the African population in the census reports.
[a] The metropolitan and reserve populations for 1960 and 1970 were adjusted
to reflect the merging of urban African townships into adjacent reserves.
So-called "black spots"—African freehold farms and mission station land
leased to Africans that lay outside the reserves after the 1913 Land Act—
were included as part of the white rural area in 1960.

Table A10.2. African middle-class occupations in South Africa

Occupation	1946	1960	1970	1980
Professional/technical/related	43,369	48,487	91,996	190,089
Administrative/managerial		5,716	2,306	5,108
Clerical	⎰ 12,784	19,276	95,359	206,814
Sales	⎱	28,894	78,939	167,883
Total	56,153	102,373	268,600	569,894

SOURCES: The 1946 census was used as a baseline, but job categories were standardized only from 1960. The "professional" category (excluding "entertainment" and "sports") in 1946 comprised mainly policemen, teachers, clergy (ordained and nonordained), herbalists, prison warders, hospital attendants, nurses, and "other professional"—83 percent of the total. Occupations categorized as clerical and sales from 1960 were found in the "commercial and financial" category in 1946: salespersons and shop assistants, small traders, clerks, hawkers, vendors and other sellers of petty commodities made up 94 percent of the total. Union of South Africa, *Population Census for 1946*, Vol. 5 (Occupations and Industries), UG 41-1954, 183–87, 190–93; Republic of South Africa, Department of Statistics, *Population Census for 1960*, Vol. 8, No. 1 (Occupations), 3 (Table 1); *Population Census for 1970*, Report No. 02-05-04 (Occupations), 1 (Table 1); *Population Census for 1980*, Report No. 02-80-05 (Occupation by statistical region and district), 510.

Table A10.3a. Distribution of income in South Africa by race, 1960–1980 (in %)

Year	White	Coloured	Asian	African
1960	71.9	5.6	1.9	20.5
1970	71.2	6.7	2.4	19.8
1976	65.7	6.4	2.7	25.1
1980	61.5	6.5	3.0	29.0

Table A10.3b. Distribution of economically active population in South Africa by race, 1970–1980 (in %)

Year	White	Coloured	Asian	African
1970	18.6	8.8	2.3	70.3
1980	22.0	10.7	2.9	64.4

SOURCES: S. Devereux, "South African income distribution 1900–1980," unpublished paper, University of Cape Town, SALDRU, 1983, 4 (Table 1), 36 (Table 3); Republic of South Africa, *South African Labour Statistics* (Pretoria, 1986), D1, D6, 21–22. Devereux cites income distribution figures based on estimates by McGrath (1960 and 1970), Simkins (1976), and Devereux (1980). The economically active African population declined by 110,965 from 1970 to 1980.

Table A10.4. Ciskei reserve consolidation proposals, 1971–1981
(in morgen: 1 morgen = 2.12 acres)

Year	Blocks of land	Proposed additions	Proposed reserve
1971	19[a]	—	1,070,306
1972	5	215,991	not specified
1975–77	1	361,179[b]	967,028
1981	1	159,618	1,126,646[c]

SOURCE: Surplus People Project, Vol. 2, *The Eastern Cape* (Cape Town, 1983), 33–39. Figures were originally expressed in hectares. Daniel noted that the confusion over the Ciskei reserve's total area between the 1950s and the 1970s was no different than it was before 1950. The Tomlinson Commission Report (1955) offered two different areas—922,575 morgen (1,955,860 acres) and 1,023,221 morgen (2,169,228 acres)—for the reserve. Unpublished data from the Department of Bantu Administration and Development indicated that the reserve comprised 904,113 morgen (1,916,720 acres) at the end of 1974, but Benbo's figure for 1975 was 1,097,607 morgen (2,326,928 acres). Benbo, *Ciskei Economic Review* (Pretoria, 1975); J. B. McI. Daniel, "Agricultural development in the Ciskei: review and assessment," *S. A. Outlook*, January 1982, 4–5 (Table 1).

[a] Daniel's figure was 21 and the Ciskei Commission's figure was 20 separate pieces of land for the reserve in 1973 and 1980, respectively (several locations in the Port Elizabeth–Humansdorp area were included as part of the Ciskei reserve). Daniel, "Agricultural development in the Ciskei," 6; 1980 *Quail Report*, 49.

[b] The reserve was reduced by 489,340 morgen (1,037,401 acres) when Glen Grey and Herschel were transferred to the Transkei. Roughly one-third of the proposed addition, then, was to compensate for the loss of land outside the consolidated reserve.

[c] The 1981 consolidation plan included the King William's Town–Berlin industrial zone and some mountain resort areas, but white residents protested vigorously. Few of the 1981 land proposals were actually carried out.

Table A10.5a. Resident African population in the Cape, 1970–1980

Area	1970	1980	Net migration
A. White urban			
E. Cape region	241,421	236,690	−79,808
E. London	59,908	32,892	−45,646
Other towns	181,513	203,798	−34,162
Rest of Cape	403,533	555,276	+26,252
B. White rural			
E. Cape region	358,163	343,671	−125,874
Rest of Cape	89,996	67,115	−50,868
C. African reserves			
Ciskei [a]	357,801	630,353	+161,283
Transkei	1,961,341	2,621,000	+50,420
Other reserves			
Xhosa only	48,712	96,916	+33,056

SOURCE: Surplus People Project, Vol. 2, *The Eastern Cape*, 29. The Xhosa-speaking population outside the Cape increased from 674,418 to 843,162 between 1970 and 1980, and net migration was −47,542 for this period.

[a] The population of Glen Grey and Herschel, ceded to the Transkei in 1975, was not included in this table so that a base line could be established to determine the impact of resettlement on the Ciskei between 1970 and 1980. If these districts are included, the resident reserve population was 534,732 in 1970 (census). Estimates of the resident population in 1980 ranged from 630,353 (Department of Statistics) to about 666,000 (1980 *Quail Report*, 19).

Table A10.5b. African migration to specific magisterial
districts within the Ciskei reserve, 1970–1980

District	Population (nos.)		Growth per year (%)	Net immigration (nos.)
	1970	1980		
A. Urban				
Mdantsane	66,380	149,621	8.5	+55,250
Zwelitsha	24,662	48,503	7.0	+14,273
Hewu	10,671	17,825	5.3	+3,385
Subtotal	101,713	215,949	7.8	+72,908
B. Rural				
Mdantsane	18,975	29,122	4.4	+3,747
Zwelitsha	68,402	118,495	5.7	+25,438
Hewu	19,574	56,240	11.1	+26,989
Victoria East	42,303	65,616	4.5	+8,966
Keiskammahoek	26,800	38,280	3.6	+2,777
Peddie	43,300	58,725	3.1	+1,730
Middledrift	36,734	47,926	2.7	−205
Subtotal	256,088	404,335	4.9	+69,442
Total	357,801	630,353	5.8	+142,350[a]

SOURCE: Surplus People Project, *The Eastern Cape*, 68. Based on a reserve
population (excluding Glen Grey and Herschel) of 350,741 in 1970, the
resettled population was calculated at 172,537 for the decade. P. Green &
A. Hirsch, "The impact of resettlement in the Ciskei: three case studies,"
unpublished paper. University of Cape Town, Second Carnegie Inquiry into
Poverty and Development in Southern Africa, 1984, 16 (Table 1).
[a] On the basis of these figures, 18,933 children were born to Africans
resettled in the Ciskei between 1970 and 1980.

11

The Legacy of the Ciskei in South Africa

The history of the Ciskei has been the history of South Africa in microcosm. The Xhosa who came to dominate this region occupied an intermediate position in terms of what constituted power and wealth before the age of capitalism. They were stockfarmers who had developed a surplus cattle-keeping economy, and they lived in segmentary states that contained a varying number of autonomous political units led by chiefs who were members of the same royal lineage. But the homestead production units did not produce a significant surplus of goods and services, and Xhosa chiefs never achieved conspicuous economic or political advantages over their subjects before the Europeans arrived. Most surplus cattle-keeping cultures apparently had developed segmentary states like the Xhosa. They were stronger than the polities of San hunters and Khoikhoi herders, but they were much weaker than the centralized states that developed in a few presumably Bantu-speaking regions of southern Africa during the precolonial Iron Age.

In retrospect, this does not seem to have been a disadvantage when the Xhosa came into permanent contact with Europeans from the 1770s. No other African society in southern Africa fought harder to maintain their independence. The Xhosa held their own against the Dutch, and it took the British, who were the most powerful nation-state in Europe at the time, more than forty years to gain permanent control over the region. Nine Cape-Xhosa wars were fought in the conquest of Xhosaland, and it was truly a battleground of immense significance in the period of primary resistance against colonial rule.

As a result, no other region in the subcontinent was as thoroughly subjected to the economic, political, and social practices of the new cultural order. The economic implications were profound: Xhosa-speaking householders were among the first Africans to be subjected to a monetarized economy and subordinated to the mercantile system. The precolonial homestead production units disintegrated, and there was no longer enough food to feed the population by the 1830s. While a few peasant farmers were competing in the market economy as early as the 1820s, peasant prosperity was evident only in a minority of households. It was fading by the late 1870s—even before the impact of the mineral discoveries—and it was in permanent decline by the 1890s.

The growing impoverishment of African peasants in the locations of rural Ciskei and southern Transkei toward the end of the nineteenth century would set a precedent for African peasants elsewhere in rural southern Africa in the first half of the twentieth century. These were the first Africans in the subcontinent to enter the migrant labor force in large numbers. They were also among the first to live permanently in town, where they would form the core of the urban working class in the Cape's major port cities and to some extent even in the mining settlements of the northeastern Cape and southern Transvaal from the earliest stages of the mineral revolution.

These proletarians in the making were molded by the Cape colonial experience, where the first attempts were made to control everyday life in the reserves (with the Glen Grey Act), reduce the number and status of black tenants on white-owned farms (with the Location Acts), and establish contracts that bound black workers in virtual perpetuity to their white employers (with the Masters and Servants Acts). Job mobility was gradually extinguished in the closing decades of colonial rule, and migrants were forced to work at the lowest levels of employment in the developing economy.

The political and social implications were equally profound. The precolonial rulers—represented by the chiefs and their councillors—were stripped of authority beginning in the 1850s and replaced by government-appointed headmen. The first headmen were selected from Xhosa who did not join the cattle killing, from collaborators collectively designated as "Fingo" (Mfengu) by the settlers, and from the mission-educated community. As the key administrators in the African locations, they were answerable to no one but the resident white magistrates. The Ciskei was the only region in South Africa where the precolonial ruling elites were deposed in this way during the period of conquest.

Africans in the Ciskei region were probably the earliest in southern Africa to experience the expansionist middle-class culture that accompanied the advent of industrial capitalism. The mission enterprise first took hold among Bantu-speaking Africans in the Ciskei region in the early nineteenth century, and British Protestant missionaries were influential communicators of the culture of modernity to the fledgling African Christian community. Participation in the new social order was conditioned by a personal conversion experience, formal education, and the adoption of Western middle-class social practices that favored individual enterprise over all collective, precolonial forms of belief and behavior. Mission-educated Africans who responded in a positive way to these admonitions were the key facilitators of change in African society during the later colonial period.

The African genesis of the Cape liberal tradition was in the Ciskei, where Africans who qualified for the franchise first began to participate in settler politics. This was also the region where the first independent African religious, educational, and economic organizations in the postconquest era were launched. Above all, it was the locus of independent African political activity in the last three decades of colonial rule, a crucial period in the birth of African oppositional politics in South Africa. For example, the basic African political organization at the grassroots level in the Ciskei from the end of the 1880s—the iliso lomzi or vigilance association—was the prototype for hundreds of similar bodies developed in later years in other regions of South Africa. Xhosa speakers were more widely dispersed geographically than any other African ethnic group, and they would play a significant role in the development of a specifically African political culture in the last two decades or so of colonial rule.

The modernizing, mission-educated elite had now emerged as a distinct social class—an African petty bourgeoisie—within Cape colonial society. They would represent the interests of the majority population and be a mediating force between black and white as the vanguard of an African middle-class culture. They would maintain alliances with white "friends of the natives," because these liberals were essential to the democratic process—and to the political survival of African voters. There were no substantive political or ideological differences between the various African political groups operating in the Cape at this time. They employed the same strategy of petitionary protest in seeking to redress African grievances. They used the political options that were open to them, and they operated strictly within the discriminatory legal and legislative framework imposed on all persons of color by the Cape authorities.

Nevertheless, divisions were beginning to appear within the ranks of the African petty bourgeoisie over their declining status in colonial society. The major political bodies in the Ciskei—the various Imbumba and the South African Native Congress—reflected these divisions toward the end of colonial rule. The SANC became more Africanist in its extrapolitical orientation, whereas the Imbumba were increasingly unwilling to become involved in organizations or activities that were independent of settler influence. In part, this reflected a growing division between moderate nationalists, who continued to cling to the Cape liberal ideal of assimilation in a future nonracial society, and militant nationalists, who were prepared to encourage the development of independent African organizations that were free from colonial interference.

The assimilationists achieved a victory with their African university scheme. Fort Hare was actually South Africa's first nonracial university—and the only one until this door was finally closed in the apartheid era. The independent church movement was the clearest manifestation of militant African nationalism during this period, because the church was virtually the only African institution in colonial society where Africans themselves had experience in governing their own affairs. African clergy in the Ciskei region were among the first to establish independent churches in South Africa, and each one was a case study in the strategies used to establish an African identity outside the framework of the existing social order. The African church would be the earliest and one of the most fundamental sites of struggle between the agencies of power and resistance in South Africa in the generation after 1910.

African-American political, educational, and religious role models would be another potent but ambiguous source of inspiration to Africans of all classes who were seeking space for themselves in a racially stratified society. African-American discourses that sought to counter and confront the prevailing social order would be especially significant in the eastern Cape as elsewhere in South Africa between the 1890s and 1930s—and again in the 1970s with the Black Consciousness movement.

The initial focus of African political activity in South Africa during the colonial era had been in the eastern Cape and southern Natal, but it began to shift northward during the campaign in 1908 and 1909 against the impending South Africa Act. The South African Native National Congress of 1912—the African National Congress—was dominated from the beginning by mission-educated elites who now lived in Johannesburg and adjacent towns in the emerging industrial heartland of South Africa.

As the guardians of organized African politics, however, members of the petty bourgeoisie were becoming more impoverished and more fragmented in the early decades of postcolonial rule. The mediators of African political and civil rights in South Africa found themselves increasingly marginalized as the new segregationist state steadily expanded its power over the black population.

African nationalists in the Cape jealously guarded their franchise rights, because as voters they were immunized to some extent against the white supremacist policies pursued by various South African party coalition governments between 1910 and 1924. Africans with franchise rights inside the Cape were exempt from key segregationist laws (like the 1913 Land Act) imposed on Africans outside the Cape. They did not have to carry passes (at least in theory); they could buy property anywhere in the province and join trade unions.

This would change when the National party coalition government came to power in 1924. African political organizers in the Ciskei region were in the forefront of the protracted ten-year national struggle to preserve African voting and land rights in the Cape. The strategy of petitionary protest, however, could not preserve even a subordinant position for the African petty bourgeoisie in the new South Africa.

African politicians in the Ciskei would become much more involved in the national movement after they lost the franchise in 1936, and opposition politics would seek more militant options in the campaign to broaden and democratize the struggle for human rights in South Africa. African leaders of the post–1910 generation were gradually replaced by a new breed of young men and women drawn mainly from the ANC's Youth League, the All-African Convention, the Communist party, and a resurgent black trade union movement. Appeals for noncollaberation and civil disobedience signaled a dramatic shift away from the politics of petitionary protest, especially after the National party election triumph in 1948 that inaugurated the apartheid era.

The mass of the African population—peasants in the reserves, tenants on white farms, migrant laborers and industrial workers living permanently in town—had little access to the political culture of the petty bourgeoisie before the 1950s, but the independent African was most visible and potentially most explosive in these communities. The urban and rural poor were often propelled into action by circumstances that were not anticipated and could not be controlled by mainstream African political and trade union organizations.

The Ciskei was the textbook example of popular resistance at the local-regional level during the first half of the twentieth century. This was apparently the only region in South Africa where alliances were sustained between dissidents in town and countryside, as in East London and the rural hinterland with the Independent ICU in the early 1930s and the ANC Youth League in the early 1950s. Other disturbances were confined essentially to the Ciskei reserve, as in the millenarian movements of the 1920s (Mgijima and the Israelites, the prophetess Nonteta, and Buthelezi and the Wellingtonites) and the Amafela movement in Herschel District that lasted for about ten years between the early 1920s and early 1930s. The struggles waged by the impoverished peasantry against the central government's repeated attempts to modernize racial domination in the reserve would gather momentum from the mid-1940s and last for almost two decades, while student agitation in various mission boarding schools and at Fort Hare would continue intermittently into the 1980s.

The Ciskei became a focal point of popular resistance, because the underdevelopment of the African reserve in this region was more advanced than that in any other in the South African periphery. The political economy of the Ciskei reserve and adjacent East London, the region's main urban center, between 1910 and 1950 formed a complex but revealing case study of the labor control policies of the South African state before the apartheid era. The National party's future economic policies for the reserves, for example, were first envisaged in the 1930s and tested in the Ciskei reserve during the 1940s.

Labor would become the crucial site of struggle inside South Africa between the 1960s and the 1980s, a struggle that eventually pitted the state against the mass of the African population. Nowhere was this more evident than in the Ciskei, which remained the most impoverished reserve in South Africa during this period.

The state had to intervene decisively in the reserves if these areas were to contain millions of designated migrant workers, surplus workers, and their families, who were deemed to be draining the resources of the new industrial economy. The labor-control system had to be modernized, but to achieve this goal the state had to consolidate the reserves, establish a cadre of black political collaborators with enough authority to control the residents, and devise new development strategies to feed and employ the redundant population. The impact of these policies on South Africa's periphery is revealed in the experiences of those who lived in the Ciskei. The state did not succeed, and the reserves finally collapsed: more than any other single factor this led to the breakdown of the apartheid system.

Violence escalated as Ciskeian and South African authorities sought to compel the civil population to accept the new political and economic order. The Ciskei was the fourth reserve to accept independence, but it was perceived as a pariah nation even in comparison to the other homelands. The Surplus People Project declared in 1985: "The level of repression is so harsh in the Ciskei . . . that it is almost impossible to undertake research there."[1] Political control would be maintained by using brute force and by reallocating economic resources to reward CNIP loyalists.

The most vocal critics of the Ciskei homeland and its rulers in the 1970s and early 1980s were students aligned with the Black Consciousness movement and workers aligned with the revived black trade union movement. The two groups developed apart from each other, and there was little interaction during this period.

The Black Consciousness Movement

The origins of Black Consciousness lay in the political vacuum that was created in the 1960s when the main black opposition groups were banned and armed resistance was crushed by the state. This vacuum was filled in part by white liberals, who by this time had segmented into two fairly distinct camps.[2] Members of the liberal establishment had inherited the old Cape liberal tradition. They were concerned primarily with the social welfare of the black population, and they were represented in this generation by the South African Institute of Race Relations, English-speaking Protestant churches, and missionary societies and related organizations allied mainly to the South African Council of Churches and the Liberal party (launched in 1953 and disbanded in 1968 when multiracial political parties were prohibited in South Africa). They had few political allies and were largely estranged from those liberals who had rallied around the Freedom Charter when it was adopted in 1955.

Disenchanted liberal churchmen who were committed to the Freedom Charter helped give birth to the Black Consciousness movement. The interdenominational Christian Institute (1963–77) under Beyers Naude, for example, maintained close contact with African churches and clergy, helped establish the Council of African Independent Churches, the Women's Association of African Independent Churches, and the ecumenical Federal Theological Seminary of Southern Africa (FTS), an autonomous theological college that had been built next to Fort Hare with funds from the Ford Foundation. The students at FTS were among the earliest and most ardent supporters of Black Consciousness. The Christian Institute together with the South African Council of Churches also sponsored the Study Project on Christianity in Apartheid Society (Spro-Cas), which produced the first comprehensive review of apartheid's impact on the Christian witness in South Africa. Although Spro-Cas was dominated by moderate white academics and clergymen, it did launch several black welfare projects, out of which was formed Black Community Programmes (BCP) in 1972. Under the leadership of Bennie Khoapa, an ex-YMCA organizer, BCP was quickly absorbed into the Black Consciousness movement.

The most important Black Consciousness body was the South African Students' Organization (SASO), which was first proposed in December 1968 at Mariannhill College (a Roman Catholic boarding school) in Natal. The liberal English-speaking National Union of South African Students (NUSAS) nominally represented black students, although NUSAS was not allowed to operate on segregated black campuses. SASO was officially inaugurated at the University College of the North, an apartheid era "tribal" college located at Turfloop in the northeastern Transvaal, in July 1969.

The events that led black students to separate themselves from NUSAS are well known, but it is worth remembering that they found a more congenial haven initially in the University Christian Movement (UCM), established in 1966 as a militant alternative to the mainstream liberal Students' Christian Association. UCM, which had a majority of black members by 1968, provided a sympathetic forum for the discussions that would result in the formation of a black-only students' organization. UCM would also furnish a significant proportion of SASO's leadership cadre, including people like Steve Biko of King William's Town, SASO's most prominent leader, and Barney Pityana, an ex–Fort Hare student from Port Elizabeth, who was his chief lieutenant in the eastern Cape.

SASO activists stemmed mainly from the Turfloop campus, from the Transvaal College of Education (a teacher-training institution for Indians) in Johannesburg, from another SASO branch in Johannesburg that brought together black students affiliated with the University of South Africa and various other colleges in the Transvaal, from the University of Natal's medical school in Durban (the only institution in South Africa where African, Coloured, and Indian students could be trained and housed together), the University of Durban-Westville (designed for the Indian community), and the University of the Western Cape at Bellville outside Cape Town (designed for the Coloured community). There were also a number of student leaders from the Federal

Theological Seminary and Fort Hare University at Alice in the Ciskei, although the Sebe regime opposed the movement from the beginning.[3]

Black Consciousness (BC) developed in two stages during the 1970s. In the first stage between 1969 and 1972, BC attempted to establish an alternative to the dominant liberal discourse that had engaged generations of African nationalists.[4] In part, it interrogated the Eurocentric assumptions that conditioned the liberal vision of a common society. White liberals were attacked by Pityana as "a farcical non-racial front that enjoys little support,"[5] and Biko declared in 1970:

> The role of the white liberal in the black man's history in South Africa is a curious one. Very few black organisations were not under white direction. True to their image, the white liberals always knew what was good for the blacks and told them so. The wonder of it all is that the black people have believed in them for so long. . . . Does this mean that I am against integration? If by integration you understand a breakthrough into white society by blacks, an assimilation and acceptance of blacks *into an already established set of norms and code of behaviour set up by and maintained by whites,* then YES I am against it. . . . When the blacks announce that the time has come for them to do things for themselves and all by themselves all white liberals shout blue murder! [But] one cannot be a racist unless he has the power to subjugate. . . . The liberal must understand that the days of the Noble Savage are gone; that the blacks do not need a go-between in this struggle for their own emancipation.[6] (My italics)

BCP leader Khoapa pointed out to whites who felt Black Consciousness was just another form of racial apartheid: "History has charged us with the cruel responsibility of going to the very gate of racism in order to destroy racism— to the gate not further."[7]

The term "black" was to be reified at all levels of private discourse and substituted for "nonwhite," "Bantu," and on occasion even "African" in public discourse. The students were inspired by the writings of numerous political and literary figures in black Africa and the African diaspora in developing the philosophical underpinnings of Black Consciousness.[8] Although similar in many respects to the Lembede-led Youth League Africanists of the 1940s (SASO's main slogan: "Black man, you are on your own"), the movement embraced all persons of color. BC tried to raise up "a culture of the oppressed," as Robert Fatton put it, "as a means of transforming the whole of society into a new and superior ethical order."[9] The invocation of a "black liberation theology" and identification with a common "African culture" provided a moral reference base, and the concept of "black communalism" provided the outlines of an economic strategy (although hardly a program for "African socialism") for those who stressed the needs of the community above the needs of the individual consumer.[10]

The first stage of the Black Consciousness movement, then, was devoted primarily to deconstructing the language of subordination in the process of constructing a new ideology of alienation. According to Biko:

> Black Consciousness is an attitude of mind and a way of life. . . . Its essence is the realisation by the black man of the need to rally together with his brothers around the cause of their oppression—the blackness of their skin—and to operate as a group to rid themselves of the shackles that bind them to perpetual servitude. . . . At the heart of this kind of thinking is the realisation by blacks that the most potent weapon in the hands of the oppressor is the mind of the oppressed.[11]

Biko and his colleagues were determined to derail the government's attempt to modernize the discourse of racial domination. As Sam Nolutshungu put it: "Even the way in which it [Black Consciousness] defined 'the oppressed' and 'the people' as *black* isolated the one line of differentiation in South Africa which was most consistent—the political one between Whites who had . . . a privileged relation to the state and the Blacks, who did not." [12]

As an ideology, however, Black Consciousness was always open-ended: It could mean "different things to different people." [13] Many militant white liberals (especially some university students, clerics, and academics), members of the black petty bourgeois elite (including business leaders, professionals, and white-collar workers whose salaries were increasing), and even some African homeland leaders (such as Gatsha Buthelezi of KwaZulu) sought to identify with the new movement in the beginning. BC organizations operated in the open and espoused nonviolence. Indeed, the apartheid regime tolerated and in some cases actually encouraged BC activities during these years.

SASO tried to widen the movement's support base and establish a more specifically political organization with the launching of Black People's Convention (BPC) in 1971. Two years later BPC had forty-one branches throughout South Africa with perhaps four thousand members, although most recruits were "SASO alumni" and there were divisions within the leadership.[14] SASO also started recruiting younger students, and high school or nonuniversity branches of the organization existed in seven cities by early 1972. As the rhetoric of Black Consciousness began to pervade urban township culture, numerous other youth groups were established, the most important being the South African Students' Movement (set up by high school students in Soweto, the cluster of African townships near Johannesburg) and the National Youth Organisation (a federation of youth groups in Natal, Transvaal, and the Cape).[15]

Black Community Programmes employed virtually all the full-time workers in the Black Consciousness movement.[16] After Biko was banned in March 1973, for example, he directed BCP activities in the eastern Cape for more than 2½ years from his home in King William's Town.[17] BCP, which focused on self-reliance projects, was more active in this region than in any other in South Africa. Education in the rural areas was a priority, and there were classes in literacy, homemaking, and health education. A fund was set up

Figure 11.1. *Left,* Steve Biko, leader of the Black Consciousness movement and, *right,* Ciskei "homeland" president Lennox Sebe.

for political prisoners (the Zimela Trust Fund), and a "compassion day" was set aside "to get students to develop a social conscience, to see themselves as part of the community." [18] The largest and most successful of BCP's three clinics was the Zanempilo Community Health Clinic five miles outside King William's Town.

Although Black Consciousness became the rallying point for political activists during the 1970s, little was said or done about specific political or economic programs. SASO and Black People's Convention had limited contact with industrial workers,[19] and Black Community Programme's links with peasant groups were tenuous at best. Most student activists and their audiences lived in South Africa's urban metropolitan areas, the major port cities and the industrial townships centering on Johannesburg in the southern Transvaal. They were middle-class in occupation and intellectual persuasion. Once again, the movement's only real urban-rural link was established by Biko in the triangle embracing Port Elizabeth, East London, and the Ciskei hinterland, the historic heartland of African politics and popular resistance in South Africa.

The second stage in the evolution of the Black Consciousness movement between 1973 and 1977 was conditioned by government directives targeting individual activists, by the events surrounding the decolonization of Angola and Mozambique, and by a resurgence of guerrilla activity inside South Africa. Banning orders were issued against Biko, Pityana, and six other BC leaders in early 1973, and the movement's first martyr was created in February 1974 when Abraham Tiro, a SASO activist expelled from the University College of the North who had fled to Botswana, was killed by a parcel bomb apparently planted by South African security agents. The government also confiscated the land and buildings of the Federal Theological Seminary in the Ciskei on the pretext they were needed for Fort Hare University.

External pressure against the apartheid regime—the resistance movements in South-West Africa (Namibia) and Rhodesia (Zimbabwe) and the new African socialist governments in Angola (where South African military forces experienced a severe setback after invading the country in 1975) and Mozambique—was increasing dramatically in the 1970s. Campus protests and marches in support of these struggles, especially in the case of neighboring Mozambique, prompted more bannings and the seventeen-month trial of nine BC leaders charged under the Terrorism Act. This trial, widely reported by the South African and overseas press, provided an unprecedented public platform for the Black Consciousness movement.[20]

BC's confrontationist rhetoric became more pronounced during these years. Black business and ethnic cultural leaders who had attempted to use the movement for their own ends were ostracized, and BC leaders moved rapidly away from accommodation with Bantustan officials (especially after SASO President Temba Sono was expelled from the organization in July 1972 when he urged that members adopt a "realist" position on this issue). The influence of a specifically marxist critique of capitalism and neocolonialism in South Africa was evident in increasingly harsh attacks on the professional elite: these "darlings of the white liberals" were "obsessed with capitalist values" and sought "the exploitation of their own people."[21]

The second stage was supposed to train BC members for the armed struggle, but it never got off the ground. BC leaders did establish contact with banned black political organizations in 1974: Ranwedzi Nengwekhulu, SASO's only full-time organizer, had talks with the ANC in Botswana, and a committee under Biko's leadership was supposedly set up to recruit and train guerrillas inside South Africa. The movement, however, was simply not organized for armed resistance.[22]

Black Consciousness created the ideological conditions for a resurgence of armed struggle in South Africa. The violence that erupted in the 1976 Soweto uprising, however, was triggered by the state against higher primary and secondary students who did not have close personal or organizational ties to parent BC groups. Student agitation, hitherto concentrated in mission boarding schools and mainly in the eastern Cape, had shifted dramatically in

the 1970s to government day schools in urban townships located largely outside this region. The Soweto students were linked mainly to the South African
Students' Movement (SASM), which was a national organization by March
1976 with branches in Johannesburg (and other urban townships in the southern Transvaal), Cape Town, and Durban as well as the eastern Cape. Although
SASM developed independently of SASO, these students were more sophisticated in their political grievances, more organized, and far more determined
to succeed than the previous generation trained in mission boarding schools.[23]

The events leading up to the Soweto student revolt of June 1976 and its
aftermath opened up a new era in the resistance movement. The violence would
continue at varying levels of intensity for eighteen months and spread throughout the country. More than six hundred persons—mainly the young—would
be killed and three thousand wounded during this period. At least twenty-five
hundred others had been detained by mid-1978—and a number were killed in
detention (including Biko)—but four thousand had also left South Africa to
join the ranks of Umkonto we Sizwe, the ANC's guerrilla army.[24] Eighteen
organizations (including the Christian Institute) were banned in October 1977
along with *The World* (a black newspaper distributed mainly in Soweto), as
police and security forces tried to destroy Black Consciousness in the same
way they had tried to destroy the ANC and other opposition groups in the
previous generation.

This time it did not work. Although their moment had passed, new organizations rooted in the BC tradition would emerge, most notably the Azanian
People's Organisation (formed in May 1978) and the National Forum (formed
in June 1983).[25] The scale of attacks on selected targets inside South Africa
would rise dramatically during the 1980s, and the ANC in exile (represented
in South Africa by the United Democratic Front, formed in May 1983) would
reemerge as the most popular political force in the country.

The Revived Trade Union Movement

The African trade union movement resurfaced in Ciskei and in South Africa
following an upsurge in strikes and other work-related disturbances in the early
1970s. The most important trade union in the region was the South African
Allied Workers' Union (SAAWU), which was formed initially in Durban in
March 1979. SAAWU, a nonracial body that sought to represent all industrial
workers, shifted its base of operations to East London early in 1980 and soon
emerged as the fastest-growing trade union in South Africa, claiming more
than seventy thousand black members by early 1982.

SAAWU stressed collective leadership, workers' control of union activities, and cooperation with community-based groups. Membership was drawn
from virtually every workplace in the industrial zone between East London and

King William's Town. SAAWU set up committees in the factories and sought recognition from employers when 60 percent of the workers had joined the union. Refusing to be registered with the South African government under the Labour Relations Act, SAAWU at this time was in the forefront of attempts to establish a national federation of unregistered trade unions.

Closely linked with SAAWU in East London were two smaller nonracial and unregistered trade union bodies, the General Workers' Union (GWU) and the African Food and Canning Workers' Union (AFCWU). The GWU originated in Cape Town (as the Western Province General Workers' Union) in 1978 and shortened its name when branches were formed outside the western Cape in 1981. The AFCWU was the eastern Cape branch of the Food and Canning Workers' Union, formed initially in the western Cape in 1940. All three unions operated out of the same offices in East London and were linked with other local political and cultural organizations engaged in the resistance movement.

The boycott was used as a potent weapon of protest during these struggles, and all racial groups were involved in consumer boycotts against the products of companies that refused to negotiate with the trade unions. SAAWU's membership soared, and its charismatic leader, Thozamile Gqweta, had become a household name throughout the region by the early 1980s. Bus boycotts—especially one in 1983 that pitted the Ciskei government (which owned the buses) against the commuters—were also resurrected, and they gained considerable support from urban township residents.

The Ciskei and South African authorities worked together in attempting to repress all activities linked to trade unions inside and outside the homeland. Security legislation was tightened up during the 1970s and used to banish or otherwise relocate suspected activists to various parts of the reserve.[26] The CNIP government's repressive apparatus, which included paramilitary vigilantes or "Green Berets" recruited from the rural areas as well as police, military, and security forces, became a major item in the budget, especially in the 1980s. Lennox Sebe relied heavily on his brother Charles, head of Ciskei's notorious Central Intelligence Service, to stamp out opposition, until he got involved in an assassination plot against the president and was imprisoned in June 1983.

SAAWU, now the effective mouthpiece of the Ciskei's urban commuter population, was singled out for attack. With help from South Africa, a concerted attempt was made in the early 1980s to destroy the burgeoning trade union movement in the East London–King William's Town area bordering the homeland. Hundreds of union members were detained, interrogated, and tortured, relatives and friends assaulted, homes looted and burned. As casualties mounted, the Ciskei government declared a state of emergency in 1983, and a large section of the civil population in Mdantsane and other urban townships was subjected to a campaign of random violence lasting several months.[27]

Ciskeian police also cooperated with South African authorities in attempting to curb resistance from residents living in "black spots" in the region's proclaimed white areas (Tiyo Soga's old mission station at Mgwali was a center of opposition), who were slated for removal to the reserve. Ciskei's youth were pitted against the Sebe-run homeland state in an upsurge of riots and boycotts in the schools and at Fort Hare. At least thirteen clashes between the students and CNIP authorities were reported in various parts of the homeland, for example, between 1978 and 1980, and a number of students were killed and injured.[28] In the wake of this revolt, Lovedale and Healdtown—the prestige mission boarding schools of South Africa—were forced to close down permanently. The CNIP tried to blunt opposition inside the homeland by placing even greater controls over domestic and contract workers.[29] Repression, however, did not silence Sebe's opponents. Rural as well as urban dissidents now formed part of an increasingly vocal opposition inside the reserve-cum-homeland. Existing political cleavages were becoming blurred, and even the beneficiaries of government policies were now considered marginal supporters of the Sebe regime.

This study effectively ends when the Ciskei homeland became "independent" at the end of 1981, and the local resistance community was fully engulfed in the context of events overtaking South Africa as a whole. Within a decade, Mandela and other political prisoners would be freed, the ANC and allied organizations would be allowed to resume political activities, thousands of men and women would return from exile, most apartheid laws and statutes would be repealed, and negotiations would begin to seek a new political dispensation for South Africa. The Sebe regime in the Ciskei, one of the most brutal and corrupt of South Africa's puppet states, would also be overthrown. In a land where the burden of the past is always the burden of the present, for the first time in living memory apartheid's children had reason to hope for a future.

Notes
Index

Notes

Introduction: A Case Study of the Ciskei Region

1. The earliest known reference to the term Ciskei is in a dispatch from Sir Harry Smith, soon after he became governor of the Cape Colony in December 1847, to the colonial secretary, Earl Albert Grey. Smith refers to the "Cis-Keian chiefs" in this letter. *Imperial Blue Book* (Cape of Good Hope) No. 946 (1848), 24, Smith to Grey 23 December 1847. This citation was first pointed out to me in 1984 by Keith Tankard, a Rhodes University graduate student in history at the time.

2. H. J. Deacon, *Where hunters gathered: a study of Holocene Stone Age people in the eastern Cape,* South African Archaeological Society Monograph Series No. 1 (Claremont, 1976).

3. R. G. Klein, "The ecology of early man in southern Africa," *Science,* 197 (4299), July 8, 1977, 115–26. For interpretations of early hominid occupation of the subcontinent, cf. J. D. Clark (ed.), *The Cambridge history of Africa* (Cambridge, 1982), 206–13 (G. L. Isaac), 296–312 (J. D. Clark), 452–62 and 820–26 (D. W. Phillipson); R. R. Inskeep, *The peopling of southern Africa* (New York, 1979).

4. J. Banaji, "Modes of production in a materialist conception of history," *Capital and Class,* 7, 1977, 1–44. The modes-of-production debate is a central feature in the literature on development as underdevelopment. For recent summaries, see A. Foster-Carter, "Can we articulate artriculation?" in J. Clammer (ed.), *The new economic anthropology* (London, 1978), 217–31; J. G. Taylor, *From modernization to modes of production: a critique of the sociologies of development and underdevelopment* (New York, 1979); H. Wolpe (ed.), *The articulation of modes of production* (London, 1980); R. H. Chilcote and D. L. Johnson (eds.), *Theories of development: mode of production or dependency?* (Beverly Hills, 1983).

5. J. Guy, "Analysing pre-capitalist societies in southern Africa," *Journal of Southern African Studies,* 14 (1), October 1987, 33–37.

6. Underdevelopment theory assumes that the material forces and social relations associated with the capitalist sector develop or expand at the expense of an underdeveloping precapitalist sector. This critique moves beyond the debate over the forms that capitalism takes in promoting dependency (especially in relations of exchange) to its content as a mode of production that can develop only by generating dependent underdevelopment. For a brief outline of this position, see L. Switzer, *Media studies and the critique of development* (Durban, 1987), 10–17.

7. This term has more explanatory power than the term "underclass" used by many American scholars. E.g., H. Veltmeyer, "Surplus labor and class formation on the Latin America periphery," in Chilcote & Johnson, *Theories of development*, 201–29.

8. Q. Hoare & G. N. Smith (eds.), *Selections from the prison notebooks of Antonio Gramsci* (New York, 1971), 244, 258.

9. J. Femia, "Hegemony and consciousness in the thought of Antonio Gramsci," *Political Studies*, 23 (1), 1975, 29–48. For a discussion of the role of persuasive and coercive agencies in relation to the state, see L. Althusser, *Lenin and philosophy and other essays* (New York and London, 1971), 127–86.

10. T. J. J. Lears, "The concept of cultural hegemony: problems and possibilities," *American Historical Review*, 90 (3), June 1985, 574.

11. Ibid., 570.

12. As outlined by Marx and Engels in *The German ideology*, Part 1, in R.C. Tucker (ed.), *The Marx-Engels reader*, 2d ed. (New York, 1978), esp. 172–74 and 187.

13. Some structuralists suggest that the state may function in a semi-autonomous manner, but this still leaves open the question of whether or not these semi-autonomous institutions are not actually masking the power of a ruling class behind the appearance of objectivity. E.g., L. Althusser, *For Marx*, trans. B. Brewster (London, 1969; reissued by New Left Books, 1977), 106–7, 110–11, 238, 240–41. For Althusser and others, the "classical" position as outlined in *The German ideology* was greatly enriched by Engels' letter to Joseph Bloch (21–22 September 1890), in Tucker, *Marx-Engels reader*, 760–65.

14. A major statement on the instrumentalist position is Ralph Miliband's *The state in capitalist society* (New York, 1969), esp. chaps. 7–8. The structuralist position is elucidated by Nicos Poulantzas in several books beginning with *Political power and the social classes* (London, 1973). For a summary of this debate, see D. A. Gold, C. Y. H. Lo & E. O. Wright, "Recent developments in marxist theories of the state," *Monthly Review*, 27 (5), 1975, 29–43, and 27 (6), 36–51. As far as South Africa is concerned, the instrumentalist view prevailed until at least the early 1980s, even though most scholars claimed a Poulantzian position. For a critique of the literature, see H. Wolpe, "Towards an analysis of the South African state," *International Journal of the Sociology of Law*, 8 (4), November 1980, 399–421.

15. On ideology as a concept in critical cultural studies, see J. Larraine, *The concept of ideology* (London, 1979) and *Marxism and ideology* (London, 1983).

16. S. Hall, "The problem of ideology—marxism without guarantees," in B. Matthews (ed.), *Marx: a hundred years on* (London, 1983), 59.

17. This has been labeled the "discursive" position in critical cultural studies. E.g., L. Grossberg, "Strategies of marxist cultural interpretation," *Critical Studies in Mass Communication*, 1 (4), December 1984, 392–421. The pro-ideology position is argued by John Thompson in a seminal study on ideology and language: "To study ideology . . . is to study the ways in which meaning (or signification) serves to sustain relations of domination." J. B. Thompson, *Studies in the theory of ideology* (Berkeley & Los Angeles, 1984), 4. For an anti-ideology position, see D. J. Sholle, "Critical studies: from the theory of ideology to power/knowledge," *CSMC*, 5 (1), March 1988, 16–41. For discursive scholars, especially those writing in the "deconstructionist" tradition of French philosopher Jacques Derrida and his disciples, the meaning of a "text" (a term that embraces all forms of social activity) cannot be determined with finality

because it is experienced individually, it is always indeterminate, and it cannot be separated from its own frame of reference. E.g., J. Derrida, *Of grammatology*, trans. G. Chakravorty Spivak (Baltimore, 1976).

18. The following quotations are taken from S. Hall, "Signification, representation, ideology: Althusser and the post-structuralist debates," *Critical Studies in Mass Communication*, 2 (2), June 1985, 104–5.

19. Hall, "Problem of ideology," 78.

20. F. J. Corcoran, "Ideology and consciousness: the construction of social meaning," in S. Thomas (ed.), *Studies in communication*, Vol. 3 (Norwood, 1987), 13–15 (with reference to the work of Freudian psychoanalysts Wilhelm Reich and Jacques Lacan).

21. For the application of such approaches to the rituals of resistance in South Africa, see J. Comaroff, *Body of power, spirit of resistance: the culture and history of a South African people* (Chicago & London, 1985), 6–9.

22. The word *amaqaba* means "heathens," and it stems from the word *ukuqaba* which refers to people who smear themselves with red or ochre-colored clay mixed with fat. Reds use the root *qaba* when referring to themselves, but non-Reds use it in a derogatory fashion when referring to primitive behavior. The word *ukugqoboka* literally means to be pierced through or to make a hole. As opposed to heathenism, it refers to the process of being converted to Christianity. P. Mayer (ed.), *Black villagers in an industrial society: anthropological perspectives on labour migration in South Africa* (Cape Town, 1980), 72 (fns. 1–2).

23. Cf. M. Hunter, *Reaction to conquest: effects of contact with Europeans on the Pondo of South Africa* (London, 1936); D. Hammond-Tooke, *Bhaca society: a people of the Transkeian uplands, South Africa* (Cape Town, 1962); B. B. Keller, "The origins of modernism and conservatism among the Cape Nguni," Ph.D. diss., University of California, Berkeley, 1970; P. & I. Mayer, *Townsmen or tribesmen: conservatism and the process of urbanization in a South Africa city* (Cape Town, 1967, 1971).

24. E.g., W. Beinart & C. Bundy, *Hidden struggles in rural South Africa: politics and popular movements in the Transkei and eastern Cape, 1890–1930* (London, 1987), 26–30ff.

25. James Scott argues persuasively that the peasantry's "anonymous, quiet acts of routine practical resistance" are largely "removed from the institutional circuits of symbolic power. Living outside the cities where the agencies of hegemony are quartered . . . being an old class (unlike the proletariat) with its own cultural traditions and patterns of resistance, and having its own shadow institutions . . . the peasantry is simply less accessible to hegemonic practice." J. C. Scott, *Weapons of the weak: everyday forms of peasant resistance* (New Haven & London, 1985), 321.

Chapter 1. The Precolonial Past

1. This interpretation of Later Stone Age hunting and herding societies in southern Africa is based on the following sources: M. Wilson, "The hunters and herders," in M. Wilson & L. Thompson (eds.), *The Oxford history of South Africa*, Vol. 1 (New York & Oxford, 1969), chap. 2; R. M. Derricourt, *Prehistoric man in the Ciskei and Transkei* (Cape Town, 1977), chaps. 10–12; D. W. Phillipson, *The later prehistory of eastern and southern Africa* (London, 1977), chaps. 10–11; R. Elphick, *Kraal and castle* (New Haven, 1977), part 1; P. T. Robertshaw, "The origin of pastoralism at the Cape,"

South African Historical Journal, 10, November 1978, 117–33; R. B. Lee, *The !Kung San: men, women and work in a foraging society* (Cambridge, 1979); Inskeep, *The peopling of southern Africa,* chap. 4; D. R. Yesner, "Maritime hunter-gatherers: ecology and pre-history," *Current Anthropology,* 21 (6), December 1980, 727–35; J. E. Parkington, "Southern Africa: hunters and food gatherers," in G. Mokhtar (ed.), *General history of Africa,* Vol. 2 (Berkeley, 1981), 639–70; C. Ehret, "The first spread of food production to southern Africa," in C. Ehret & M. Posnansky (eds.), *The archaeological and linguistic reconstruction of African history* (Berkeley, Los Angeles & London, 1982), 158–81; A. J. Hausman, "Holocene human evolution in southern Africa," and R. G. Klein, "The prehistory of Stone Age herders in South Africa," in J. D. Clark & S.A. Brandt (eds.), *From hunters to farmers: the causes and consequences of food production in Africa* (Berkeley, Los Angeles & London, 1984), 261–71, 281–89; J. Deacon, "Later Stone Age people and their descendants in southern Africa," in R. G. Klein (ed.), *Southern African prehistory and paleoenvironments* (Rotterdam & Boston, 1984), chap. 7; J. Denbow, "A new look at the later prehistory of the Kalahari," *Journal of African History,* 27 (1), 1986, 3–28; J. R. Denbow & E. N. Wilmsen, "Advent and course of pastoralism in the Kalahari," *Science,* 234 (4783), December 1986, 1509–15.

2. The meaning of San is uncertain. It was used by Khoikhoi herders when referring to hunters, who were regarded as the original settlers, but it was also a negative term applied to stockraiders and people of low status.

3. The literature on the Iron Age in southern Africa is uneven in quality, but the following sources proved useful in writing this synthesis: D. Birmingham & S. Marks, "Southern Africa," in R. Oliver (ed.), *The Cambridge history of Africa,* Vol. 3 (Cambridge, 1977), 567–620; S. Marks & A. Atmore, Introduction, in Marks & Atmore (eds.), *Economy and society in pre-industrial South Africa* (London, 1980), 8–13; T. Maggs, "The Iron Age sequence south of the Vaal and Pongola rivers: some historical implications," *Journal of African History* 21 (1), 1980, 1–15; D. N. Beach, *The Shona and Zimbabwe, 900–1850* (New York, 1980), chaps. 1–3; D. W. Phillipson, "The beginnings of the Iron Age in southern Africa," in Mokhtar, *General history,* 671–92; T. Maggs, "The Iron Age south of the Zambezi," in Klein, *Southern African prehistory and paleoenvironments,* chap. 8; P. Maylam, *A history of the African people of South Africa* (New York, 1986), chaps. 1, 5; J. Parkington & M. Hall, "Patterning in recent radiocarbon dates from southern Africa as a reflection of prehistoric settlement and interaction," *Journal of African History,* 28 (1), 1987, 1–25; G. Connah, *African civilizations: precolonial cities and states in tropical Africa* (Cambridge, 1987), chap. 8; M. Hall, "Archaeology and modes of production in pre-colonial southern Africa," *Journal of Southern African Studies,* 14 (1), December 1987, 1–17; idem, *The changing past: farmers, kings and traders in southern Africa, 200–1860* (Cape Town & Johannesburg, 1987), chaps. 3–12. See also references to Derricourt and Denbow in note 1.

4. E.g., M. Hall & A. Morris, "Race and Iron Age human skeletal remains from southern Africa: an assessment," *Social Dynamics,* 9 (2), 1983, 29–36.

5. Three radiocarbon dates from an iron site at Mpame (Elliotdale District) in the Transkei suggest that Iron Age groups were in what is now the southern Transkei in the seventh, eighth, and fifteenth centuries. Evidence for Early Iron Age smelting sites has also been found in the vicinity of Port St. Johns and near the Mthatha River mouth in

the Transkei (Map 1). Interviews with Michael Cronin, formerly of the Albany Museum (Grahamstown, South Africa) in December 1978.

6. J. D. Lewis-Williams, "The social and economic context of southern San rock art," *Current Anthropology*, 23 (1982), 429–49; Hall, *Changing past*, 69–72.

7. E.g., W. D. Hammond-Tooke, "Descent groups, chiefdoms and South African historiography," *Journal of Southern African Studies*, 11 (2), April 1985, 305–19; T. M. Evers & W. D. Hammond-Tooke, "The emergence of South African chiefdoms: an archaeological perspective," *African Studies*, 45 (1), 1986, 37–41.

8. The cities that flourished along the coast of eastern Africa during the second millennium of the Christian era have traditionally been linked to Arab and other Muslim merchant-trader colonizers from the Persian Gulf area, who maintained what was essentially an export trade with the Asian states of the Indian Ocean basin. But this scenario is being revised by critical scholars, who suggest the eastern African coastline was much more densely populated than previously believed and the settlements were African rather than Arab or Asian in origin. They point to the diversity of the coastal environment and to the range of indigenous resources, to the number of smaller mud, wood, and thatch settlements (suggesting an African origin) alongside the few stone settlements originally believed to have been built by Arab colonizers, and to the complex patterns of economic interaction apparently developed with the interior. While the Islamic influence and the presence of Arab immigrants in the larger cities on the coast were undoubtedly important in opening up the export trade, these African trade diffusion centers had survived for thousands of years (some settlements may extend backward in time to the first millennium before the Christian era) on internal trade networks and a strong subsistence economy that undoubtedly made the transition to surplus production. Connah, *African civilizations*, chap. 7.

9. The names and dates for the major centralized states of Zimbabwe during the Later Iron Age are taken from D. N. Beach, "The Zimbabwe plateau and its peoples," in D. Birmingham & P. M. Martin (eds.), *History of central Africa*, Vol. 1 (London & New York, 1983), 249–50.

10. The term in Zulu-Xhosa translates roughly as "the crushing"; its counterpart in Sotho-Tswana is *Difaqane* or *Lifaqane* or "the scattering."

11. A variation on this theme is the attempt by some contemporary scholars to invert the caricature and portray Shaka as a hero. As a recent reviewer points out, this does not resolve the problem. See C. A. Hamilton, " 'An appetite for the past': the re-creation of Shaka and the crisis in popular historical consciousness," *South African Historical Journal*, 22 (1990), 141–57.

12. E.g., C. A. Hamilton, "Ideology, oral traditions and the struggle for power in the early Zulu kingdom," M.A. thesis, University of the Witwatersrand, 1986; J. R. D. Cobbing, "The *Mfecane* as alibi: thoughts on Dithakong and Mbolompo," *Journal of African History*, 29 (1988), 487–519; J. Wright, "Political mythology and the making of Natal's *Mfecane*," *Canadian Journal of African Studies*, 23 (2), 1989, 272–91; J. Wright & C. Hamilton, "Traditions and transformations: the Phongolo-Mzimkhulu region in the late eighteenth and early nineteenth centuries," in A. Duminy & W. Guest (eds.), *Natal and Zululand from earliest times to 1910: a new history* (Pietermaritzburg, 1989), chap. 3; J. Wright, "The dynamics of power and conflict in the Thukela-Mzimkhulu region in the late 18th and early 19th centuries: a critical reconstruction," Ph.D. diss.,

University of the Witwatersrand, 1990; J. Cobbing, "Grasping the nettle: the slave trade and the early Zulu," J. Wright, "A. T. Bryant and the 'wars of Shaka,' " D. Wylie, "Utilizing Isaacs: one thread in the development of the Shaka myth," unpublished seminar papers, University of Natal, 1990.

This critique is not without its critics. Leonard Thompson, for example, rejects it completely in *A history of South Africa* (New Haven & London, 1990), 83–84. Others support with some qualification the labor thesis but reject other aspects of the revisionist position. The critique generated a colloquium entitled "The 'Mfecane' aftermath: towards a new paradigm" at the University of the Witwatersrand in September 1991 (hereafter Mfecane colloquium, 1991).

13. These raiding communities present an interesting though controversial case study. The raiders themselves—whether European, African, or of mixed descent— were increasingly dependent on the commodities produced by the European mercantile system. Raiding networks would eventually traverse the western and eastern zones of Stone Age and Iron Age occupation between the mid-eighteenth and mid-nineteenth centuries. Existing trade relations would be disrupted and/or distorted by the demand for labor to service the expanding colonial economies. Cf. J. Richner, "Eastern frontier slaving and its extension into the Transorangia and Natal, 1770–1843," J. B. Gewald, "Untapped sources: slave exports from southern and central Namibia up to the mid-nineteenth century," C. Gorham, "Port Natal: a 'blind' darkness," B. Lambourne, "A chip off the old block: Moletsane's Taung and the false history of the early nineteenth-century 'Interior,' " unpublished papers, Mfecane colloquium, 1991.

14. The literature on the Xhosa in the precolonial era is also uneven in quality, but the following sources proved useful in writing this synthesis: M. Wilson, "The early history of the Transkei and Ciskei," *African Studies,* 18 (4), 1959, 167–79; idem, "The Nguni people," in Wilson & Thompson, *Oxford history,* 1, 75–130; R. M. Derricourt, "Settlement in the Transkei and Ciskei before the *Mfecane,* " in C. Saunders & R. Derricourt (eds.), *Beyond the Cape frontier: studies in the history of the Transkei and Ciskei* (London, 1974), chap. 2; idem, "Early European travellers in the Transkei and Ciskei," *African Studies,* 35 (3–4), 1976, 273–91; J. B. Peires, "A history of the Xhosa, ca.1700–1835," M.A. thesis, Rhodes University, 1976; idem, "Chiefs and commoners in precolonial Xhosa society," and M. Wilson, "Nguni markers," in J. B. Peires (ed.), *Before and after Shaka: papers in Nguni history* (Grahamstown, 1981), 125–57; idem, *The house of Phalo* (Johannesburg, 1981), chaps. 2–3; J. Lewis, "The rise and fall of the South African peasantry: a critique and reassessment," *Journal of Southern African Studies,* 11 (1), October 1984, 1–24; Maylam, *History of the African people,* chaps. 2, 5; Guy, "Analysing pre-capitalist societies in southern Africa."

15. E.g., S. Marks, "The traditions of the Natal 'Nguni': a second look at the work of A. T. Bryant," in L. Thompson (ed.), *African societies in southern Africa* (London, 1969), 126–44; J. B. Wright, "Politics, ideology and the invention of the 'Nguni'," in T. Lodge (ed.), *Resistance and ideology in settler societies* (Johannesburg, 1986), 96–118.

Wright suggests that the term Nguni had three regionally distinct meanings in the nineteenth century: it was used south of the Tugela (or Thukela) River with reference to the Xhosa, north of the Tugela with reference to the Zulu kingdom's ruling lineage, and by the Sotho and Thonga (or Tsonga) outside Zululand with reference to those ruled by the Zulu or associated with the Zulu in terms of language and culture. Other coastal peoples were being included within the meaning of the term, however, by the early twentieth century. For most academics, Nguni became the generic reference for the peoples of southeastern Africa with the publication of *Olden times in Zululand and Natal* (London, 1929), a seminal work by the Catholic missionary-scholar A. T. Bryant. Native Affairs Department officials adopted the term in the 1930s, and in a later generation it was associated with the language of apartheid. In essence, the term Nguni fit in with government-approved notions of ethnicity during an era when African history was being contextualized as tribal history.

16. Quoted by R. H. Davis, "Nineteenth-century African education in the Cape colony: a historical analysis," Ph.D. diss., University of Wisconsin, Madison, 1969, 13.

17. Hammond-Tooke now discounts segmentary lineages as the basis for power in Nguni society (see "Descent groups, chiefdoms and South African historiography"). Once territorial-based chiefdoms were established, he says, there was no more room for kinship-based authority structures.

18. Guy, "Analysing pre-capitalist societies in southern Africa," 25.

19. Peires, *House of Phalo*, 39–40. Xhosa chiefs ate more, lived in better houses, and had more wives and concubines than their subjects. The chiefs also had more cattle and these were of superior quality.

20. Peires, "History of the Xhosa, ca.1700–1835," 61. On the genealogies of the main Xhosa chiefs, see Peires, *House of Phalo*, 18, 45, 48–49.

21. J. A. Hopper, "Xhosa-colonial relations, 1770–1803," Ph.D. diss., Yale University, 1980, 261.

22. J. H. Soga, *The south-eastern Bantu* (Johannesburg, 1930), 124–25, 128–29.

23. Peires, *House of Phalo*, 46–50.

24. The first documented contact between Portuguese traders on their way to the East Indies and the African population along the Cape coast was in 1488. The Portuguese were replaced by the Dutch and English as the dominant merchant interests in the region during the 1590s.

25. The processes that shaped the Dutch settler community at the Cape in the seventeenth and eighteenth centuries are examined in detail by various authors in R. Elphick & H. Giliomee (eds.), *The shaping of South African society, 1652–1820*, 2d ed. (Middletown, Ct., 1988), esp. 66–108, 184–323, 521–66; H. Giliomee, "Eighteenth century Cape society and its historiography: culture, race, and class," *Social Dynamics*, 9 (1), 1983, 18–29; L. Guelke, "The anatomy of a colonial settler population: Cape colony, 1657–1750," *International Journal of African Historical Studies*, 21 (3), 1988, 453–73.

Chapter 2. Frontier Zones in a Colonial Setting

1. A brief outline of South African frontier historiography can be found in C. Bundy, *Re-making the past: new perspectives in South African history*, University of Cape Town, Department of Adult Education and Extra-Mural Studies, 1986, 18–25.

2. H. Lamar & L. Thompson (eds.), *The frontier in history: North America and Southern Africa compared* (New Haven & London, 1981), 7.

3. This section is based on G. Harinck, "Interaction between Xhosa and Khoi: emphasis on the period 1620–1750," in Thompson, *African societies in southern Africa*,

145–70; Elphick, *Kraal and castle,* chaps. 8–12; R. Ross, "Ethnic identity, demographic crisis and Xhosa-Khoikhoi interaction," *History of Africa,* 7, 1980, 259–71; Hopper, "Xhosa-colonial relations," chap. 3; Peires, "History of the Xhosa, ca.1700–1835," esp. 60–61, 158–62; idem, *House of Phalo,* 22–24, 95–98; P. Delius & S. Trapido, "Inboekselings and Oorlams: the creation and transformation of a servile class," *Journal of Southern African Studies,* 8 (2), April 1982, 214–42; R. Elphick & V. C. Malherbe, "The Khoisan to 1828," in Elphick & Giliomee, *Shaping of South African society,* 3–65, 184–239; A. B. Smith, "The origins and demise of the Khoikhoi: the debate," *South African Historical Journal,* 23, 1990, 3–14.

4. The volume of trade was apparently not significant enough to have much impact on the Xhosa before the colonial era. While they needed iron, Peires claims the trade was largely speculative. The Xhosa bartered not to obtain essential commodities or to diversify the existing economy but primarily to accumulate more wealth in cattle. *House of Phalo,* 98.

5. Peires suggests the process of absorption moved from "informal influence" to "direct penetration" in Khoikhoi affairs to "incorporation" in Xhosa society. The process of incorporation initially involved Khoikhoi becoming clients of the Xhosa—apparently an obligatory condition "in the transition from free non-Xhosa to full-fledged Xhosa." "Xhosa expansion before 1800," in *The societies of Southern Africa in the 19th and 20th centuries,* Vol. 6, University of London, Institute of Commonwealth Studies, October 1974–May 1975, 1–14.

6. Peires, "History of the Xhosa, ca.1700–1835," 49.

7. Peires, *House of Phalo,* 13.

8. Elphick, *Kraal and castle,* 50–52; Peires, *House of Phalo,* 22.

9. E.g., Elphick & Malherbe, "Khoisan to 1828," 22–28. Khoisan resistance to European settlement at the Cape would last, as Shula Marks has observed, for almost two centuries. S. Marks, "Khoisan resistance to the Dutch in the 17th and 18th centuries," *Journal of African History,* 13 (1), 1972, 55–80.

10. This section is based on Hopper, "Xhosa-colonial relations," chaps. 5, 7, 9, 11; Peires, *House of Phalo,* 98–99, 104.

11. For details on the extension of the Cape's eastern frontier during the eighteenth century, see J. S. Bergh & J. C. Visagie, *The eastern Cape frontier zone, 1660–1980: a cartographic guide for historical research* (Durban, 1985), 4–15.

12. Settler-inspired histories of the early wars on the Cape's eastern frontier have been altered considerably by revisionists in recent years. E.g., M. Oloyo, "The Cape eastern frontier in the early 19th century," in *The societies of Southern Africa in the 19th and 20th centuries,* Vol. 3, University of London, Institute of Commonwealth Studies, October 1971–June 1972, 1–12; W. Freund, "The Cape under the transitional governments, 1795–1814," and H. Giliomee, "The eastern frontier, 1770–1812," in Elphick & Giliomee, *Shaping of South African society,* 324–57, 421–71; Hopper, "Xhosa-colonial relations," chaps. 2, 4, 6, 8, 10–11; Peires, *House of Phalo,* 53–58, 140–43. On the War of 1799–1803, see S. Newton-King & V. C. Malherbe, *The Khoikhoi rebellion in the eastern Cape (1799–1803),* University of Cape Town, Centre for African Studies, Communications No. 5, 1981.

13. On the War of 1811–12, see B. Maclennan, *A proper degree of terror: John Graham and the Cape's eastern frontier* (Johannesburg, 1986), chaps. 15–16.

14. On settler historians, see K. Smith, *The changing past: trends in South African historical writing* (Johannesburg, 1988), 31–49; C. Saunders, *The making of the South African past: major historians on race and class* (Totowa, N.J., 1988), 9–44.

15. These wars were originally designated "Caffer wars," Caffer being a corruption of "Kaffir," a pejorative Arabic term meaning unbeliever and used by the settlers mainly with reference to the Xhosa. The term "Kaffir wars" was still used in standard histories of South Africa in the early 1960s. E.g., E.A. Walker, *A history of southern Africa*, 3d ed. (London, 1957, with corrections in 1962). It was eventually replaced by another nonneutral term, "frontier wars." Some scholars have named specific wars after a major personality, such as "Nxele's War," "Maqoma's War," or "Mlanjeni's War," but this compounds the problem. I am using the term "Cape-Xhosa wars" with reference to the period as a whole, and I have adopted Alan Webster's suggestion that the wars be designated by year only (although I am using the standard dates to indicate a beginning and ending to these wars). A. C. Webster, "Land expropriation and labour extraction under Cape colonial rule: the war of 1835 and the 'emancipation' of the Fingo," M.A. thesis, Rhodes University, 1991, 72 (fn. 2).

16. On the liberal school, see Smith, *Changing past*, chap. 4; Saunders, *Making of the South African past*, chaps. 5–15; J. Butler, R. Elphick & D. Welsh (eds.), *Democratic liberalism in South Africa* (Middletown, Ct., Cape Town & Johannesburg, 1987), chaps. 7–8. Liberal historians produced a number of studies on colonial policy during the Cape-Xhosa wars. There is much of value in this literature, although it is essentially Eurocentric and the perspectives of some scholars do not always reflect a liberal view of history. See W. M. Macmillan, *Bantu, Boer and Briton: the making of the South African native problem* (1929; 2d ed., London, 1963), chaps. 5–6, 9–11, 15–16; A. E. du Toit, *The Cape frontier: a study of native policy with special reference to the years 1847–1866*, Archives Year Book for South African History, Vol. 1 (Pretoria, 1954); J. Rutherford, *Sir George Grey: a study in colonial government* (London, 1961), chaps. 21–26; J. S. Galbraith, *Reluctant empire: British policy on the South African frontier, 1834–1854* (Berkeley, 1963), chaps. 6–8, 10–11; A. K. Millar, *Plantagenet in South Africa* (Cape Town, London & New York, 1965), esp. part 2, chaps. 7–10; M. Wilson, "Co-operation and conflict: the eastern frontier," in Wilson & Thompson, *Oxford history of South Africa*, 1, 233–71; L. Thompson, "The subjection of the African chiefdoms," in Wilson & Thompson, *Oxford history of South Africa*, 2, 257–59.

African liberals were also attacking settler versions of South African history in print from at least the 1920s. E.g., R. V. Selope Thema, "From Cattle-herding to the Editor's chair," unpublished manuscript, University of the Witwatersrand, ca.1935, Chap. 6 ("The Veil is lifted"), 24–28ff.: "the history of the African people was often written with prejudice. There was nothing that our ancestors did which was not severely criticised and stigmatised as barbarous and cruel. . . . Their [historians of South Africa] primary object seems to have been to impress the world with the wickedness and cruelty of the African race, and to enhance the prestige of the white race." Thema was editor of *Bantu World*, flagship of Bantu Press, the first white-owned chain of black commercial publications, between 1932 and 1952.

17. Radical broadsides attacking settler histories of South Africa were also in evidence from the 1920s. See Saunders, *Making of the South African past*, chap. 13. Two publications inspired by the Non-European Unity Movement are used in this study:

"Mnguni" (the pseudonym of Hosea Jaffe), *Three hundred years* (Cape Town, 1952); N. Majeke (the pseudonym of Dora Taylor), *The role of the missionaries in conquest* (Johannesburg, 1952).

18. T. Ranger, "The invention of tradition in colonial Africa," in E. Hobsbawm & T. Ranger (eds.), *The invention of tradition* (Cambridge, 1983), 227.

19. On the War of 1818–19, see Maclennan, *Proper degree of terror,* chaps. 23–25.

20. J. B. Peires, "The British and the Cape, 1814–1834," in Elphick & Giliomee, *Shaping of South African society,* 480–84. For a perceptive reading of Ngqika, see Peires, "Ngqika c.1779–1829," in C. Saunders (ed.), *Black leaders in southern African history* (London, 1979), 15–30.

21. As evidence, Webster points to legislation that sought to encourage free blacks within and beyond the borders of the Cape to enter the colonial labor market, to the activities of raiding parties in the interior who were selling increasing numbers of captive Africans to farmers in the eastern Cape during this period, and to settler commando raids against the Xhosa in which women and children were being seized in addition to cattle. The emancipation of the slaves in 1834 also heightened the demand for labor. Webster, "Land expropriation," chap. 2.

22. Missionaries at the time, for example, were employed as political agents by the Cape government to report on the activities of the chiefs. Cf. Majeke, *Role of the missionaries in conquest,* chap. 5; D. Williams, *When races meet* (Johannesburg, 1967), chap. 4.

23. Webster, "Land expropriation," 73.

24. On the War of 1834–35, ibid., chap. 3; Peires, *House of Phalo,* 89–94, 109–15, 145–50. Both studies contrast sharply with the settler and liberal schools of history, but Webster in particular shows the extent to which officials at the time and apologists in subsequent generations tried to reconstruct these events to suit their own interests. The tactics they used included the censoring and apparently even the destruction of key official documents (see Webster's thesis, especially 219–22).

25. Peires, *House of Phalo,* 105.

26. The term "Fingo" or Mfengu is derived from the verb *ukumfenguza,* which means "to wander about seeking service." Peires, *House of Phalo,* 88.

27. Cf. Cobbing, *"Mfecane as alibi,"* 514 and fn. 139. The standard work on the Mfengu by Richard Moyer, for example, does not critique the primary texts: see R. A. Moyer, "A history of the Mfengu of the eastern Cape, 1815–1865," Ph.D. diss., University of London, 1976. Although Peires rejects Ayliff's claim that the Mfengu were slaves of the Gcaleka, he accepts the settler view that they were Mfecane refugees resettled largely at Peddie as a buffer against the Xhosa. See *House of Phalo,* 86–89, 110–11, 224–25 (fn. 65).

28. Webster, "Land expropriation," 118–19. The figure of 80,000 for the Gcaleka Xhosa population in 1837 is probably too high. The Xhosa nation has been estimated at anything from 40,000 to 80,000 in the early 1800s and 100,000 in 1824, but there were at least as many Xhosa west of the Kei as there were east of the river. The Rharhabe Xhosa population was estimated at more than 55,000 in 1835. Cf. Peires, *House of Phalo,* 2–3, 114, 159; Maclennan, *Proper degree of terror,* 228.

29. Webster, "Land expropriation," 131–32.

30. The "Fingo" story is deconstructed in ibid., chap. 4.

31. The Khoikhoi, for example, were good marksmen and provided most of the military intelligence (and supplied the menial labor) to Dutch and British expeditions alike against the Xhosa between the 1770s and 1830s. The Cape Regiment fought effectively alongside British regular troops and Boer militia in four frontier wars.

32. The Mfengu uncovered grain depots, disrupted internal communications, foiled battle plans, and became skilled in guerrilla tactics during the Cape-Xhosa wars. Led mainly by white missionaries, they were grudgingly accepted by their protectors, but while campaigning they ate and slept apart from them. Mfengu chiefs were created by the Cape authorities, provided with a fake history, and coopted into the colonial system from the beginning. Webster, "Land expropriation," 145–48 (on the chiefs).

33. On the War of 1846–47, see Peires, *House of Phalo,* 117, 150–58, 251 (fn. 110).

34. On the War of 1850–53, see Peires, *The dead will arise: Nongqawuse and the Great Xhosa cattle-killing movement of 1856–7* (Johannesburg, London & Bloomington, Ind., 1989), chap. 1.

35. On the grievances of the Kat River settlers, see T. Kirk, "Progress and decline in the Kat River settlement, 1829–54," *Journal of African History,* 14 (3), 1973, 411–28. About 250 Khoi/Coloureds from Kat River and perhaps 1,000 from other settlements joined the Xhosa.

36. Quoted by Rutherford, *Sir George Grey,* 334.

37. Ibid., 328–29, 438.

38. On Grey's policies in British Kaffraria before the cattle killing, see Peires, *Dead will arise,* chap. 2.

39. On the cattle-killing movement, see ibid., chaps. 3–6. See also J. Hodgson, *The God of the Xhosa* (Cape Town, 1982), esp. chaps. 3–4; Peires, " 'Soft' believers and 'hard' unbelievers in the Xhosa cattle-killing," *Journal of African History,* 27 (3), 1986, 443–61; idem, "The central beliefs of the Xhosa cattle-killing," *Journal of African History,* 28 (1), 1987, 43–63.

40. On Nxele, see J. B. Peires, "Nxele, Ntsikana and the origins of the Xhosa religious reaction," *Journal of African History,* 20 (1), 1979, 51–61; idem, *Dead will arise,* chap. 1.

41. These included Nongqawuse's cousin Nombanda, a girl between eight and ten years old who had been with Nongqawuse when she had her first vision, and another young (aged about eleven) prophet named Nonkosi, who lived in British Kaffraria in Mhala's district. Mhala, the senior chief of the Ndlambe Xhosa, was another influential believer among the chiefs during the cattle killing.

42. On the chiefs' plot, see Peires, *Dead will arise,* chap. 7; idem, "The late, great plot: the official delusion concerning the Xhosa cattle-killing, 1856–1857," *History in Africa,* 12, 1985, 253–79.

43. The one private attempt to feed, clothe, and house destitute Xhosa inside British Kaffraria—the Kaffir Relief Committee launched in King William's Town in July 1857—was effectively undermined by Grey and his officials. Autonomous agencies that provided indiscriminate relief, however small and submissive to government, might compromise the governor's efforts to make aid available only to potential migrant labor. J. B. Peires, "Sir George Grey versus the Kaffir Relief Committee," *Journal of Southern African Studies,* 10 (2), April 1984, 145–69; *Dead will arise,* chap. 8.

44. The first settlers were 2,300 former members of the German Legion who had fought in the Crimean War. Most of them were unmarried, and the scheme was a disaster. Grey then recruited about 4,000 more settlers from Germany.

45. Maqoma, now an old man, refused to stay in his designated location and sought twice to return to his home near Fort Beaufort. In 1871 the authorities sent him back to Robben Island without even a hearing, and he died there eighteen months later.

46. On Cape-Thembu relations, see E. J. C. Wagenaar, "A history of the Thembu and their relationship with the Cape, 1850–1900," Ph.D. diss., Rhodes University, 1988, chap. 8.

47. Quoted by C. C. Saunders, "The hundred years war: some reflections on African resistance on the Cape-Xhosa frontier," in D. Chanaiwa (ed.), *Profiles of self-determination: African responses to European colonialism in southern Africa, 1652–present* (Northridge, CA., 1976), 64.

48. On the War of 1877–78, see J. Meintjes, *Sandile: the fall of the Xhosa nation* (Cape Town, 1971), chap. 13; M. W. Spicer, "The war of Ngcayecibi 1877–8," M.A. thesis, Rhodes University, 1978.

49. Nearly four thousand men, women, and children were transported to the western Cape between April 1878 and January 1879 and indentured for three years to work in Cape Town and nearby farm districts. Workers were not paid wages for the first six months, and wages thereafter were generally below the minimum paid to African farm laborers at the time. Living conditions were poor, and desertions especially in the country districts increased with the end of the winter season in 1878. Some workers tried to walk back to Xhosaland, while others sought to rejoin friends and relatives in Cape Town. The labor distribution center in the port city, called the Kafir Depot, was closed down after criticism over the treatment of unemployed women and children sent back to Xhosaland by ship in May 1879. C. Saunders, "Africans in Cape Town in the nineteenth century: an outline," in C. Saunders & H. Phillips (eds.), *Studies in the history of Cape Town*, Vol. 2 (Cape Town, 1980).

Chapter 3. Peasants and Proletarians in a Transitional Economy

1. This section is based mainly on C. Bundy, *The rise and fall of the South African peasantry* (London, 1979), chap. 2; S. Newton-King, "The labour market of the Cape Colony, 1807–28," and T. Kirk, "The Cape economy and the expropriation of the Kat River settlement," in Marks & Atmore, *Economy and society in pre-industrial South Africa,* 171–207, 226–46; Peires, *House of Phalo,* chap. 7; J. Lewis, "An economic history of the Ciskei, 1848–1900," Ph.D. diss., University of Cape Town, 1984, chap. 2; R. Ross, "The origins of capitalist agriculture in the Cape Colony: a survey," in W. Beinart, P. Delius & S. Trapido (eds.), *Putting a plough to the ground: accumulation and dispossession in rural South Africa, 1850–1930* (Johannesburg, 1986), 56–100; R. Ross, "The Cape of Good Hope and the world economy, 1652–1835," and J. Peires, "The British and the Cape, 1814–1834," in Elphick & Giliomee, *Shaping of South African society,* chaps. 5, 10. See also Macmillan, *Bantu, Boer and Briton,* chap. 6; M. Wilson, "Co-operation and conflict: the eastern Cape frontier," and T. R. H. Davenport, "The consolidation of a new society: the Cape Colony," in Wilson & Thompson, *Oxford history of South Africa,* 1, 241–42, 297–311.

2. Holland and later Britain partially made up the shortfall with regular grants to cover the costs of civilian and military administration at the Cape.

3. The authorities sought to channel paper currency into two government banks established in 1793 and 1808 to extend credit mainly to the merchant community. Promissory notes or *slagters briefjes* were also issued by traveling butchers to their clients (mainly stockfarmers and traders) in the frontier districts. These notes were an alternative source of money in the interior, but they could be cashed only in Cape Town and there was no protection in the event a butcher went bankrupt. The British authorities finally allowed a private bank to be established in Cape Town in 1837 (Cape of Good Hope Bank), and in subsequent years numerous others were launched in Cape Town and in the interior. The Cape government formally abandoned banking operations in 1843.

4. The West African slave trade was insignificant. Only two shiploads of slaves (from Angola and Dahomey) were sent to the Cape. On the subject of slavery, see J. C. Armstrong & N. A. Worden, "The slaves, 1652–1834," in Elphick & Giliomee, *Shaping of South African society,* 109–83.

5. Robert Ross argues that the treatment of slave and Khoisan labor in the eastern frontier districts was directly related to the farmers' ability to prosper in a cash economy and gain access to an outside market. "Cape of Good Hope and the world economy," 271.

6. Jeff Peires offers numerous examples of corrupt practices in the frontier districts. These involved the allocation of land and labor, the calculation of quitrents and taxes, and the use of public funds to bankroll family and friends. "British and the Cape," 493.

7. Ibid., 490–99.

8. As a percentage of the total export trade in agricultural products, wine exports fell from 41 to 8 percent while wool exports rose from 11 to 62 percent between 1838 and 1850. Lewis, "Economic history of the Ciskei," 78 (Table 2).

9. On the Mantatee story, cf. Cobbing, "*Mfecane* as alibi," 492–500; Webster, "Land Expropriation," 29–30; G. Hartley, "The battle of Dithakong and 'Mfecane' theory," and Richner, "Eastern frontier slaving," *Mfecane* colloquium, 1991.

10. Peires, *House of Phalo,* 106; Lewis, "Economic history of the Ciskei," 86. There were 35,000–40,000 black workers in the colony by 1839. According to Macmillan, the employment of Bantu-speaking migrants was "established custom" by the 1840s. *Bantu, Boer and Briton,* 88.

11. Afrikaner farmers owned virtually all the estimated 6,600 slaves in the eastern frontier districts in 1828, and they were being denied new land in the "ceded" territory because they had slaves.

12. Peires, "British and the Cape," 499–510.

13. On the rise of the British gentry in the eastern Cape, see C. C. Crais, "Gentry and labour in three eastern Cape districts, 1820–1865," *South African Historical Journal,* 18, 1986, 125–46.

14. Ivory peaked at 107,000 pounds in 1825, while horn exports rose from 509 pounds in 1820 to more than 95,000 pounds in 1828. Hide exports, which had not been above 6,000 pounds before 1822, rose to more than 75,000 pounds in 1827. Xhosa exports of aloes (a plant native to South Africa) were also significant before 1802. Lewis, "Economic history of the Ciskei," 65 (Table 1).

15. On defining the peasantry, cf. Bundy, "Re-making the past," 34–41; S. Feierman, *Peasant intellectuals: anthropology and history in Tanzania* (Madison, 1990), 24.

16. The following paragraphs are based on Bundy, "The emergence and decline of a South African peasantry," *African Affairs,* 71 (285), October 1972, 369–88; idem, *Rise and fall,* chaps. 2–3.

17. Bundy, *Rise and fall,* 92.

18. Quitrent tenure for Africans was endorsed in the 1879 Native Locations Act and in the report of the 1883 Cape Native Laws Commission.

19. Surveyed allotments on mission stations, however, were generally less than 4.7 morgen or 10 acres.

20. *Report of the South African Native Affairs Commission,* 1903–1905, Vol. 2 (Minutes of evidence taken in the Cape Colony), e.g. 620–22 (evidence of King William's Town solicitor Richard Rose Innes).

21. *Report on Native Location Surveys,* UG 42–1922, 3–4. Householders living in overpopulated locations surveyed in the Queenstown District, for example, were soon forced to reorganize their land holdings. Survey beacons were torn down and the commonages cultivated. Virtually none of the building lots and only about one-third of the garden lots were occupied by the original owners in 1922. A representative of the South African Native National Congress had told the 1916 Natives' Land Commission: "the natives of Oxkraal and Kamastone are packed like sardines; they cannot move." *Report of the Natives' Land Commission,* UG 19–1916, Vol. 2, 118 (evidence of Ema Makalima, a landowner from Hackney in the Queenstown District).

22. Quoted by Bundy, *Rise and fall,* 71.

23. For a useful survey of the literature on peasant studies in Africa, see A. Isaacman, "Peasants and rural social protest in Africa," *African Studies Review,* 33 (2), September 1990, 1–120.

24. Bundy, "Re-making the past," 40. Bundy responded to his critics in the preface to the second edition of *Rise and fall* (Cape Town, Johannesburg & London, 1988).

25. Unless otherwise noted, the following paragraphs are based on Lewis, "Economic history of the Ciskei," chaps. 5, 6, 9, 10, conclusions; idem, "The rise and fall of the South African peasantry: a critique and reassessment" [hereafter "Rise and fall critique"]. All percentages are rounded off to the nearest whole number.

26. Lewis, "Economic history of the Ciskei," 275. His calculations are based on local grain sales, whether or not ox wagons were used to transport the grain to market, and the number of Mfengu households in the main Mfengu locations west of the Keiskamma River. He assumes the larger producers owned the oxen and wagons.

27. R. B. Beck, "Bibles and beads: missionaries as traders in southern Africa in the early nineteenth century," *Journal of African History,* 30, 1989, 211–25.

28. Bundy, *Rise and fall,* 42.

29. Disparities in terms of wealth were apparently even greater among the Ngqika Xhosa at this time. In an 1864 survey of their locations in the Ciskei, about 12,665 households comprising 59,727 people had a total of 675 plows (18 households per plow) and 225 wagons. Charles Brownlee, who was Sandile's magistrate, observed that the "distribution of stock"—39,037 cattle and 36,303 sheep in the 1864 survey— "leaves the mass of people entirely destitute and they have nothing but their grain for subsistence and the payment of their taxes." Lewis, "Rise and fall critique," 19–20 (citing Brownlee letter 17 May 1865).

30. Single families who lived in more than one hut were initially charged a single tax, but in cases where more than one family occupied a hut an additional ten-shilling

tax was charged for each family. Those who built European-style rectangular houses paid only a single tax even if more than one family lived on the premises. A ten-shilling tax was introduced for extra huts (House Duty Act of 1878), but it is not clear that this legislation was actually enforced.

31. Each village was to contain no more than 200 families. British Kaffraria had 164 villages by the end of 1858 and 242 by 1861, but the population was so low that the number of family huts per village remained below 200 for many years thereafter. Returning migrants had increased the number of Xhosa in British Kaffraria by December 1865 to about 64,000 or 61 percent of what it had been eight years earlier. Regulations introduced in May 1860 required Africans to produce receipts proving all taxes had been paid before they could move from one district to another in the Cape.

32. As quoted by Lewis, "Economic history of the Ciskei," 638.

33. Regulations introduced in September 1864 allowed headmen to receive a commission of three pence on each five shillings they collected in hut taxes (these taxes were supposed to be paid in two installments). At first, they were not given a commission in cases where the taxpayer was delinquent, but in January 1865 this restriction was removed and headmen were allowed commissions on arrear taxes as well. K. P. T. Tankard, "East London: the creation and development of a frontier community, 1835–1873," M.A. thesis, Rhodes University, 1985, 185.

34. Lewis cites several examples where headmen challenged Cape officials during the 1880s and 1890s. "Economic history of the Ciskei," e.g., 674–75 (opposition to the Abakweta and Intonjane Dances Prohibition Act No. 19 of 1892, a law prohibiting beer drinks during initiation ceremonies); 685 (William Shaw Kama of Middledrift); 692–94 (Bovani Mabandla of Keiskammahoek).

35. On discrimination against African farmers in the eastern Cape, see Bundy, *Rise and fall*, chap. 4.

36. This section is based mainly on the following sources: S. T. van der Horst, *Native labour in South Africa* (London, 1942), 79–81, 96–97, 100–104, 128–31, 140–41, 145–47, 163–67, 205–8, 234–39; P. Kallaway, "Labour in the Kimberley diamond fields," *South African Labour Bulletin*, 1 (7), 1974, 52–61; T. J. Keegan, "African responses to the implementation of the Glen Grey policy," B.A. (Hons), University of Cape Town, 1975; R. Edgecombe, "The Glen Grey Act: local origins of an abortive 'Bill for Africa,'" in J. A. Benyon, C. W. Cook, T. R. H. Davenport & K. S. Hunt (eds.), *Studies in local history: essays in honour of Prof. Winifred Maxwell* (Cape Town, 1976), 89–98; K. Gottschalk & J. Smalberger, "The earliest known strikes by black workers in South Africa," *South African Labour Bulletin*, 3 (7), 1977, 73–75; Bundy, *Rise and fall*, 78, 80, 128, 133–37; M. Lacey, *Working for Boroko: the origins of a coercive labour system in South Africa* (Johannesburg, 1981), 14–18; R. Turrell, "Kimberley: labour and compounds, 1871–1888," in S. Marks & R. Rathbone, *Industrialisation and social change in South Africa: African class formation, culture, and consciousness, 1870–1930* (London & New York, 1982), 45–76; A. Mabin, "Strikes in the Cape Colony, 1854–1899," unpublished paper, University of the Witwatersrand, African Studies Institute, 1983; A. Odendaal, "African political mobilisation in the eastern Cape, 1880–1910," Ph.D. diss., University of Cambridge, 1983, 150–53; P. Warwick, *Black people and the South African War, 1899–1902* (Cambridge, 1983), chaps. 6–7; W. R. Nasson, "Moving Lord Kitchener: black military transport and supply work in the South African War, 1899–1902, with particular reference to the Cape Colony," *Journal of South-*

ern African Studies, 11 (1), October 1984, 25–51; Lewis, "Economic history of the Ciskei," chap. 11; W. Beinart, " 'Jamani': Cape workers in German South-West Africa, 1904–12," in Beinart & Bundy, *Hidden struggles,* chap. 5; Wagenaar, "History of the Thembu," chap. 7.

37. Lewis, "Economic history of the Ciskei," 654. Droughts averaging once every six years plagued South Africa between 1882 and 1925. C. W. de Kiewiet, *A history of South Africa: social and economic* (London, 1941), 189.

38. See C. van Onselen, "Reactions to rinderpest in southern Africa," *Journal of African History,* 13 (3), 1972, 473–88.

39. African peasants had supplied oxen and wagons used in building the railroads, sold food to the workers, and found work themselves at these sites. This market was closed to them once the railroad system was completed.

40. These figures refer specifically to prices peasants paid for maize bought in the drought years of 1885–86 and 1893, and prices peasants received for maize sold in the harvest years of 1886–87. Lewis, "Economic history of the Ciskei," 661; Wagenaar, "History of the Thembu," 356–57. Traders were selling grain back to the peasants at double or triple the price between the 1910s and 1940s, and the secretary for native affairs estimated in 1937 that "one-third to one-half of the Native-grown maize is sold and re-purchased at higher prices from traders by the Native producers of that maize." 1910 Blue Book (Native Affairs), 111–12 (Glen Grey and Herschel); Ciskeian General Council (CGC), 1934 *Proceedings,* 69 (Herschel); *South African Outlook* 1 February 1945, 125 (Victoria East); M. Goldberg, "Underdevelopment in the Ciskei," B.A. Hons., University of Cape Town, 1977, 56 (citing speech by the secretary for native affairs at an agricultural conference in September 1937).

41. According to one resident magistrate, tax collectors were seizing "even the very cooking pots" from the huts of delinquent taxpayers. Lewis, "Economic history of the Ciskei," 673 (as cited).

42. Bundy, *Rise and fall,* 140.

43. African peasant activity in the commercial sector outside the Ciskei occurred mainly after 1870, and some rural communities were able to compete in the market economy until the 1950s. For recent interpretations of black rural life elsewhere in South Africa, cf. Beinart, Delius & Trapido, *Putting a plough to the ground;* T. J. Keegan, *Rural transformations in industrialising South Africa: the southern highveld to 1914* (Johannesburg, 1986); H. Bradford, *A taste of freedom: the I.C.U. in rural South Africa, 1924–1930* (New Haven, 1987); C. van Onselen, "Race and class in the South African countryside: cultural osmosis and social relations in the sharecropping economy of the south-western Transvaal, 1900–1950," *American Historical Review,* 95 (1), February 1990, 99–123.

44. A "Tambookie Location" was initially proclaimed for a section of the Thembu people who had been allies of the British during the 1850–53 war. The location was divided into two sections and absorbed by the adjacent white districts of Dordrecht and Queenstown in 1870, but eight years later most of it was reassembled as the Glen Grey District. The turbulent history of the Thembu people during this period is examined by Wagenaar, "History of the Thembu," chaps. 2–5.

45. Ibid., 316.

46. On Rhodes and the Glen Grey Act, see R. I. Rotberg, *The founder: Cecil Rhodes and the pursuit of power* (New York & Oxford, 1988), 467–77.

47. Cape Colony, House of Assembly, 1894 *Debates*, 366.

48. Africans on mission stations in Glen Grey District prior to the 1894 act had paid a quitrent of ten shillings a year for plots up to ten morgen in size.

49. On African voters in the Cape Colony, see Chapter 5.

50. A survey of eleven locations by the 1892 Glen Grey Land Commission indicated about 36 percent of the landholders in the district were not in favor of individual tenure, but the respondents were told they could lose their land if they rejected this provision. There was no provision for polygamous households in these single-plot allotments. Wagenaar, "History of the Thembu," 318.

51. No residential plots were surveyed in the Glen Grey scheme, and African title holders were allowed to build their kraals next to their garden plots.

52. No provision was made for widows and other women in the family if there were no male descendants, and there was no guarantee allotments would remain in families without male heirs. These grievances were resolved in amending legislation in 1905.

53. Quoted by Keegan, "African responses to the implementation of the Glen Grey policy," 57 (citing article by J. Brownlee Ross in *Christian Express*).

54. Ibid., 66 (as cited).

55. Ibid., 68.

56. Ibid., 11 (citing *Imvo Zabantsundu* 9 April 1895).

57. Ibid., 13 (citing *Imvo Zabantsundu* 15 August 1894).

58. For details on African reactions to the labor tax, see Keegan, "African responses to the implementation of the Glen Grey policy," chaps. 2, 4.

59. As Charles Pamla, an ordained pastor and a prominent member of the Christian community, put it: "This shuts out all improvements and industry of some individuals who may work and buy. . . . Surely Mr. Rhodes can't expect that all the Natives will be equal. He himself is richer than others; even trees differ in height." Bundy, *Rise and fall*, 136 (citing *Imvo Zabantsundu* 5 September 1894).

60. Quoted by Lacey, *Working for Boroko*, 16–17.

61. Van der Horst, *Native labour in South Africa*, 123–24.

62. Four of six strikes recorded in the Cape in the 1850s occurred in these coastal towns. Two were initiated by boatmen and stevedores in Cape Town.

63. Lewis, "Economic history of the Ciskei," 652–53.

64. Peasant entrepreneurs in the Ciskei, for example, were able to buy 20,000 acres in the Komgha District between 1902 and 1907, and 16,500 acres in the Peddie District in 1906.

Chapter 4. The Mission Enterprise

1. For a useful outline of the main themes in the development of a middle-class culture in England during the nineteenth century, see the *Encyclopaedia of the Social Sciences* (New York, 1933), 9, 435–41. On mission culture in South Africa, see especially James Cochrane, *Servants of power: the role of English-speaking churches in South Africa, 1903–1910* (Johannesburg, 1987), chaps. 1–2.

Donovan Williams paints an ambiguous profile of the 28 male missionaries who served in Xhosaland between 1799 and 1853 (the few women involved in mission work were apparently lay teachers). All the Presbyterian and most of the LMS missionaries had at least some university training, but the Wesleyan Methodists—and they were in the majority—had little postprimary education. The missionaries also came from families with little surplus income and few ties to the privileged elites. Williams stresses the personal idiosyncracies—lack of conviction, emotional instability, and mental stress—that "blunted the missionary thrust" in Xhosaland during this period. "The missionary personality in Caffraria, 1799–1853: a study in the context of biography," *Historia,* May 1989, esp. 23–35.

2. A new wave of foreign evangelical Protestant groups arrived in the eastern Cape from the late 1890s and focused primarily on African migrants in town. These included Baptist, Apostolic, and Holiness churches, Assemblies of God, Seventh Day Adventists, the South Africa General Mission, and the Salvation Army. B. A. Pauw, *Christianity and Xhosa tradition* (Cape Town, London & New York, 1963), chap. 2.

3. For a comparison with Natal, see N. Etherington, *Preachers, peasants and politics in southeast Africa, 1835–1880: African Christian communities in Natal, Pondoland and Zululand* (London, 1978).

4. This section is based mainly on the following sources: J. du Plessis, *A history of Christian missions in South Africa* (New York, 1911), chaps. 18–19, 22, 26, 29, 35–38; Majeke, *Role of the missionaries in conquest,* chaps. 5–6; Pauw, *Christianity and Xhosa tradition,* chaps. 4, 10; Williams, *When races meet,* chaps. 5–7; Davis, "Nineteenth-century African education in the Cape colony," chaps. 3, 5; Keller, "Origins of modernism and conservatism among the Cape Nguni," chaps. 2–3; N. Etherington, "Mission station melting pots as a factor in the rise of South African black nationalism," *International Journal of African Historical Studies,* 9 (4), 1976, 592–605; M. J. Ashley, "Universes in collision: Xhosa, missionaries and education in 19th century South Africa," unpublished paper, Rhodes University, 1978; idem, "The features of modernity: missionaries and education in South Africa, 1850–1900," unpublished paper, Rhodes University, 1979; M. M. Goedhals, "Anglican missionary policy in the diocese of Grahamstown under the first two bishops, 1853–1871," M.A. thesis, Rhodes University, 1979; Peires, *House of Phalo,* 106–8; P. H. Lyness, "The life and influence of William Shaw, 1820–1856," M.A. thesis, Rhodes University, 1982; Cochrane, *Servants of power,* 16–39.

5. There were about 16,000 Africans living on 32 stations in the eastern Cape in 1850. The total African population was perhaps 400,000. Bundy, *Rise and fall,* 40.

6. John Philip (1775–1851), head of the Cape's LMS missions and this generation's most influential champion of the "native" population, believed round huts encouraged promiscuity and were not conducive to individual enterprise. Ashley, "Universes in collision," 7. The Lovedale missionaries, in the words of Timothy White, believed "the hut—small, low and dark—symbolised the primitive state of the African." T. R. H. White, "Lovedale 1930–1955: the study of a missionary institution in its social, educational and political context," M.A. thesis, Rhodes University, 1987, 52–53.

7. This was so important to the missionaries and their African disciples that it was inscribed in the language. The work week ended with Saturday, which was called the "finishing day" (*uMgqibelo*), and Sunday was called "Church Day" (*iCawa*). S. Kopke, "Xhosa concepts of time," in R. C. Fox & J. B. McI. Daniel (eds.), *Fifty years of*

geography at Rhodes University: essays in honour of J. V. L. Rennie (Grahamstown, 1989), 247. For a comparison with the Zulu in Natal, see K. E. Atkins, " 'Kafir time': preindustrial temporal concepts and labour discipline in nineteenth-century colonial Natal," *Journal of African History,* 29, 1988, 229–44.

8. "The Kafir customs of parents requiring cattle from those to whom they give their daughters in marriage, may be defended in theory . . . in practice, it is the source of fearful evils, as it makes it the interest of every Kafir father to dispose of his girls to any old polygamist who can offer many cattle for a new concubine." Goedhals, "Anglican missionary policy," 110 (citing the head of the Grahamstown Diocese in 1862).

9. For a brief but intriguing discussion of female sexual codes in eastern Cape mission circles, see S. Marks (ed.), *Not either an experimental doll: the separate worlds of three South African women* (Bloomington & Indianapolis, 1987), 22–24.

10. The missionaries had no authority to enforce regulations that contravened colonial edicts. E.g., Goedhals, "Anglican missionary policy," 110–11 (on an abortive attempt in 1862 to outlaw the payment of cattle in marriage), 120–21 (on an abortive petition in 1866 asking the Cape authorities not to honor customary marriage contracts).

11. An excellent example is the so-called Blue (and Red) Ribbon Army temperance societies in southern Natal and the eastern Cape in the later nineteenth century. For details, cf. L. E. Switzer, "The problems of an African mission in a white-dominated, multi-racial society: the American Zulu Mission in South Africa, 1885–1910," Ph.D. diss., University of Natal, 1972, 35–37; W. G. Mills, "The roots of African nationalism in the Cape colony: temperance, 1866–1898," *International Journal of African Historical Studies,* 13 (2), 1980, 205–6.

12. Two other mission agencies—the Roman Catholics at Mariannhill in Natal and the Paris Evangelical Missionary Society at Morija in Lesotho—also established major printing and publishing facilities in southern Africa before 1910.

13. For details, see J. Hodgson, *Ntsikana's 'great hymn': a Xhosa expression of Christianity in the early 19th century eastern Cape* (Cape Town, 1980).

14. Peires, *House of Phalo,* 108.

15. The earliest Xhosa-English periodical was apparently *Isitunywa Sennyanga* (The Monthly Messenger), launched by the Methodists at Mount Coke mission station near King William's Town between August and December 1850. It lasted only five issues, a victim of the 1850–53 war.

16. L. & D. Switzer, *The black press in South Africa and Lesotho, 1836–1976* (Boston, 1979), 247 (citing *Indaba* August 1862).

17. For information on these correspondents, see Odendaal, "African political mobilisation in the eastern Cape," 30–31.

18. T. S. N. Gqubule, "An examination of the theological education of Africans in the Presbyterian, Methodist, Congregational and Anglican churches in South Africa from 1860 to 1960," Ph.D. diss., Rhodes University, 1977, 32.

19. Between 1876 and 1882, production at Lovedale Press rose from 6,000–7,000 to more than 12,800 books a year, virtually all hymnals and textbooks for the elementary schools. Davis, "Nineteenth-century African education in the Cape colony," 263, 265.

20. For details on *Isigidimi Sama Xosa,* see Switzer & Switzer, *Black press,* 45–

46; Odendaal, "African political mobilisation in the eastern Cape," 49–53ff.; A. C. Jordan, *Towards an African literature: the emergence of literary form in Xhosa* (Berkeley & Los Angeles, 1973), 64–68.

21. E.g., Jordan, *Towards an African literature,* 103–16 (posthumous appendix: Jordan's tribute to Mqhayi that appeared originally in *South African Outlook*); P. E. Scott, *Samuel Edward Krune Mqhayi, 1875–1945: a bibliographic survey* (Grahamstown, 1976); J. Opland, "The isolation of the Xhosa oral poet," unpublished paper, Rhodes University, 1983.

22. Cf. Peires, "The Lovedale press: literature for the Bantu revisited," *History in Africa,* 6, 1979, 155–75; Opland, "Isolation of the Xhosa oral poet," 8–9. For a more positive interpretation of Lovedale's role in the development of an ethnic African literature, see White, "Lovedale 1930–1955," 73–96.

23. This section is based primarily on S. M. Brock, "James Stewart and Lovedale: a reappraisal of missionary attitudes and African response in the eastern Cape, South Africa, 1870–1905," Ph.D. diss., University of Edinburgh, 1974, chap. 3; W. G. Mills, "The role of African clergy in the reorientation of Xhosa society to the plural society in the Cape colony, 1850–1915," Ph.D. diss., University of Southern California at Los Angeles, 1975, chaps. 2–3; Gqubule, "Examination of the theological education of Africans," chaps. 1–3.

24. The Wesleyan Methodists, for example, brought out an evangelist from the United States in 1866–67 by the name of William Taylor, and he conducted a series of revivals in African and European congregations in the Cape. Taylor had only limited success with the settlers, but in the eyes of the missionaries he helped to legitimize the revivals that were already taking place in their African churches.

25. Bundy, *Rise and fall,* 43.

26. The theological school was transferred from Healdtown to Lesseyton in 1883, but the Wesleyans gave virtually no support to the training of their African pastors. There was little supervision, and admission and performance standards were very low compared with those of the Presbyterians. The mission could afford only one full-time teacher-administrator, who was also the superintendent and minister for the local church circuit. In addition, the theological teacher at Lesseyton was in charge of the mission's industrial and teacher-training school for girls.

27. Pamla is regarded as the most outstanding product of the Methodist mission during the nineteenth century. His parents were refugees from the Mfecane—his father was a member of the Zulu royal lineage—who had settled in the Cape Colony. Pamla was an interpreter (apparently he played a key role as a translator during the revivals of the mid-1860s) and for more than fifty years the mission's main evangelist in church outreach programs in the Cape and Natal.

28. Kama was unquestionably the most prominent of the Christian chiefs ordained to the ministry in the Ciskei. His father, a Christian and the second-ranking chief of the Gqunukhwebe Xhosa, had refused to participate in the cattle killing. Kama quit the ministry when he assumed the chiefship in 1874.

29. On early Zonnebloem, see J. Hodgson, "A history of Zonnebloem College, 1858–1870: a study of church and society," M.A. thesis, University of Cape Town, 1975; idem, "Zonnebloem College and Cape Town: 1858–1870," in C. Saunders (ed.), *Studies in the history of Cape Town,* Vol. 1 (Cape Town, 1979), chap. 5.

30. Canterbury was too costly, and the Africans themselves were not deemed suitable for mission work when they returned home. As the head of the Grahamstown Diocese remarked in 1865: "they most decidedly observe European habits, so much so that we found at first that they would not stay with their friends." Goedhals, "Anglican missionary policy," 140 (as cited).

31. The course lasted six years for those who had not graduated from high school (the matriculation certificate). Since no African had this qualification at the time, no one completed the full course. Hebrew, Greek, Latin, philosophy (logic), science, higher mathematics, history, and literature were required in addition to subjects like biblical studies, theology, and church history.

32. Rubusana wrote a lengthy anthology, for example, called *Zemk' Inkomo Magwalandini* (Preserve Your Heritage). This five-hundred-page literary and historical work was printed privately in London in 1906 with a second edition in 1911.

33. Mills, "Role of African clergy," 170.

34. The Glasgow Missionary Society was split in two in 1838, and one of these branches (the Glasgow African Missionary Society) was absorbed by the United Presbyterian church when it was established in 1847. The United Presbyterians continued to send missionaries to South Africa, and the African churches controlled by these missionaries joined the settler-dominated Presbyterian Church of South Africa (PCSA) in 1897. Three years later, the parent bodies of the Free Church and the United Presbyterian church in Scotland were reunited as the United Free Church of Scotland. D. E. Burchell, "The origins of the Bantu Presbyterian Church of South Africa," *South African Historical Journal*, 9, November 1977, 39–58.

35. Mzimba was educated at Lovedale, completed an apprenticeship as a printer, and was employed as a teacher and a telegraph operator at the Lovedale Post Office before entering the theological school. He was ordained in 1875, the first African ordained by the Presbyterian mission in South Africa. Makiwane was also educated at Lovedale, and in addition to his work as editor of *Isigidimi* he taught in the primary school and was in charge of the telegraph office before entering the theological school. Makiwane was ordained in 1876.

36. For the temperance movement, see Mills, "Role of African clergy," 160–71; idem, "Roots of African nationalism in the Cape colony"; Odendaal, "African political mobilisation in the eastern Cape," 273–76.

37. Like the Good Templars, the IOTT claimed to be an interracial body, but it was also composed of separate African and Coloured Grand Temples. White IOTT members, virtually all missionaries, did not play a significant role in the organization.

38. This section is based primarily on Davis, "Nineteenth-century African education in the Cape colony," chaps. 6–7; idem, "1855–1863: a dividing point in the early development of African education in South Africa," in *The Societies of Southern Africa in the 19th and 20th Centuries*, Vol. 5, University of London, Institute of Commonwealth Studies, October 1973–March 1974, 1–15. See also L. A. Hewsen, "Healdtown: a study of a Methodist experiment in African education," Ph.D. diss., Rhodes University, 1959, chaps. 4–7; D. E. Burchell, "A history of the Lovedale missionary institution, 1890–1930," M.A. thesis, University of Natal, 1979, chaps. 1–3; White, "Lovedale 1930–1955," chap. 1.

39. They had been given English first and last names when they were baptized, a

fairly common practice with Christian converts during this period. Balfour (his Xhosa names were Makhaphela Noyi) was a writer and composer of hymns and a contributor to the mission journal *Ikwezi*.

40. The Presbyterian mission was also apparently the first in the eastern Cape to appoint African teachers to the outstation schools. John Muir Vimbe and Tente, a son of Ngqika, began teaching in the Burnshill outstation schools in 1838.

41. Quoted by Davis, "Nineteenth-century African education in the Cape colony," 197.

42. After a few years as an outstation teacher at Burnshill, Vimbe was sent for further training to Lovedale Seminary. He replaced the European schoolmaster at Burnshill in 1843, probably the first mission African to achieve this position in the eastern Cape. Vimbe built a new mission station near the Kei River in 1846 but was forced to abandon it during the 1846–47 war. He then joined the Wesleyan Methodists in Natal, where he was a teacher and evangelist for many years and also a correspondent for *Isigidimi Sama Xosa*.

43. On the Kafir Institution, see Goedhals, "Anglican missionary policy," 140–42.

44. The Cape Colony appointed a superintendent-general in 1838 to reorganize the school system. The curriculum was standardized, and schools that received government aid were rated as first or second class, depending on the courses offered. Only a few African mission schools, however, received colonial grants before the 1850s.

45. Lovedale would launch an astonishing number of industrial-training classes in subsequent decades. According to R. H. W. Shepherd, the school's last principal before the apartheid era, these included courses in "agriculture, horticulture, carpentry, building and plastering, wagon-making, black-smithing, printing, book-binding, shoe-making, domestic science (housekeeping, cooking, sewing and laundry work), nursing, telegraphy, basket- and mat-making, rug-making, tin-ware, bee-keeping and poultry-farming." White, "Lovedale 1930–1955," 51, fn. 7 (as cited). Industrial training courses apparently were not perceived as inferior to academic courses in terms of prestige, and vocational training was not regarded by the school as an alternative for students who could not cope with academic coursework. The two main problems in maintaining these courses—the relatively high costs involved (in terms of equipment, materials, and salaries for qualified teachers) and the difficulty in finding employment for black artisans in a racist society—were never resolved.

46. The Methodists in 1861, for example, recorded an average of 3,573 pupils attending Sunday schools as opposed to 2,148 in the station and outstation schools.

47. When some African mission schools were upgraded to Order B category, there was a corresponding drop in government funding. Order B schools received 35.1 percent of the educational grant in 1874 and 18.8 percent in 1884. White Order A schools received on average about 60 percent of the colonial government's educational grants, for example, between 1882 and 1887. Order B and C schools each received roughly 20 percent during these years. From the late 1880s, there was a further decline in the proportion of government aid to African Order C schools. The average government expenditure per pupil is equally revealing. Order A schools (they were subdivided into three classes) received between £2 1s. 3d. and £3 17s. 5d. per pupil in 1900. Order B schools and Order C nonboarding day schools received 13s. 4d. and 12s. 3d. per pupil, respectively, in 1900.

48. As Dale put it: "I am inclined . . . to assist only in the training of a sufficient number of native teachers to occupy the various school-stations at the kraals. . . . To the educated Kafir there is no opening . . . either there is no demand for such persons, or prejudice operates against persons of colour being so employed." Goedhals, "Anglican missionary policy," 138 (as cited).

49. Lovedale Seminary was probably the only boarding school that actually increased enrollment in the decade after the Grey plan was terminated—from 82 students in 1864 to 432 students in 1874.

50. Only 3.8 percent of the African pupils passed Standard IV (sixth grade) and 2 percent Standard V (seventh grade) in 1885. Africans were not allowed to take the Standard VI (eighth grade) examination until 1900. The relevance of these inspection examinations in the later colonial period as a test for evaluating functional literacy is questionable. They were normally conducted in English using standard British school texts like the *Royal Reader*. Thus Africans were being tested in a foreign language using culturally biased reading material.

51. Davis, "Nineteenth-century African education in the Cape colony," 279.

52. The percentage of African teachers in inspected schools who had government certificates remained static—15.5 percent in 1876 and 15.4 percent in 1890.

53. Literacy figures cited by Davis, "Nineteenth-century African education in the Cape colony," 297–300 (Appendix B, Tables 1–2); see also Keller, "Origins of modernism and conservatism among the Cape Nguni," Appendix I (The Mfengu). A majority of the Cape Mfengu stated they were Christian—156,767 out of a population (including the Transkei) of 310,720—in the colony's last official census in 1904. The literacy rate among adult Mfengu (fifteen years and older who could read and write) had risen to 20.4 percent. There are no comparable figures for the Xhosa, but the combined literacy rate for Xhosa and Tswana at this time was 4.8 percent. Of the Cape Colony's total African population (more than 1.1 million), 26.2 percent (291,608) were returned as Christians in the 1904 census. Cape of Good Hope, 1904 *Census*, G 19-1905, Tables 6, 16, and 18, 152–55, 226–27.

54. For Lovedale at this time, see Brock, "James Stewart and Lovedale," chaps. 2, 4.

Chapter 5. African Christians and the Cape Liberal Tradition

1. On the ambiguities of the Cape liberal tradition, cf. P. Lewsen, "The Cape liberal tradition—myth or reality?" *Race,* 13 (1), July 1971, 65–80; M. Legassick, "The rise of modern South African liberalism: its assumptions and its social base," unpublished paper, University of London, Institute of Commonwealth Studies, 1973; S. Trapido, " 'The friends of the natives': merchants, peasants and the political and ideological structure of liberalism in the Cape, 1854–1910," in Marks & Atmore, *Economy and society in pre-industrial South Africa,* 247–74; R. Parry, " 'In a sense citizens, but not altogether citizens . . .': Rhodes, race, and the ideology of segregation at the Cape in the late nineteenth century," *Canadian Journal of African Studies,* 17 (3), 1983, 377–91.

2. On the Afrikaner Bond, see T. R. H. Davenport, *The Afrikaner Bond: the history of a South African political party, 1880–1911* (Cape Town, 1966).

3. Cecil Rhodes in particular used the issue of race to build an alliance with the Bond during his two premierships between 1890 and 1895. According to biographer Robert Rotberg, he made racial legislation respectable at the Cape in the waning years of colonial rule and helped prepare the ground for the postcolonial segregationist state. For details, see Rotberg, *The founder,* chaps. 14, 17.

4. Dukwana, who continued his preaching ministry during the hostilities, was a particularly influential moral figure. He and the pioneer modernizer Zaze Soga were killed in the fighting. Gonya Sandile and Nathaniel Umhalla, who as students at Zonnebloem had lobbied for the release of their fathers from Robben Island following the cattle killing, would be imprisoned on the same island following this war. *Isigidimi* was slated for "siding with the whites" at the time, and "hardly any of the leading [African] writers had a good word to say for it." Brock, "James Stewart of Lovedale," 134. The ambiguities in the response of mission-educated Africans to the colonial world of the later nineteenth century are revealed to some extent in a diary that Umhalla kept during this war. C. Saunders, "Through an African's eyes: The diary of Nathaniel Umhala [*sic*]," *Quarterly Bulletin of the South African Library,* 34, 1979–80, 24–38.

5. Odendaal, "African political mobilisation in the eastern Cape," 45 (citing *Christian Express* May and October 1880).

6. Ibid., 47.

7. On the Govan-Stewart debate and Lovedale's educational policy during this period, see Brock, "James Stewart of Lovedale," chap. 3; Burchell, "History of the Lovedale missionary institution," chaps. 1–2.

8. Brock, "James Stewart of Lovedale," 128.

9. Quoted by Burchell, "History of the Lovedale missionary institution," 20.

10. Quoted by Goedhals, "Anglican missionary policy," 138.

11. Stewart dominated students and staff alike at Lovedale Seminary. The only known case of student unrest during Stewart's tenure occurred when he was overseas. Although John Knox Bokwe was Stewart's personal secretary for some years and a few other church leaders served for brief periods as assistant instructors, the boarding school had no permanent African members of staff.

12. Brock, "James Stewart of Lovedale," 137.

13. For an excellent study of British colonial thinking about race and its meaning *before* the publication of Charles Darwin's *Origin of Species* in 1859, see P. D. Curtin, *The image of Africa: British ideas and action, 1780–1850* (Madison, 1964), esp. chap. 15. European images of Africa, according to Curtin, were hardened by the experiences of British imperialism in West Africa in the early nineteenth century: "race as the crucial determinant, not only of culture but of human character and of all history," was "common knowledge" as far as the "educated classes" were concerned before the social Darwinists arrived to justify and even make necessary the conquest of Africa in the later nineteenth century.

14. This section is based mainly on S. Trapido, "African divisional politics in the Cape Colony, 1884 to 1910," *Journal of African History,* 9 (1), 1969, 79–98; idem, "White conflict and non-white participation in the politics of the Cape of Good Hope, 1853–1910," Ph.D. diss., University of London, 1970, chaps. 5–7; D. R. Edgecombe, "The non-racial franchise in Cape politics, 1853–1910," *Kleio,* 10 (1 & 2), June 1978, 21–37; and Odendaal, "African political mobilisation in the eastern Cape," chap. 2. See also G. W. Eybers (ed.), *Select constitutional documents illustrating South*

African history, 1795–1910 (New York, 1918), 48–49 (voting rights under the 1853 constitution).

15. R. H. Davis, "School vs. blanket and settler: Elijah Makiwane and the leadership of the Cape school community," *African Affairs,* 78 (310), January 1979, 28 (citing *Imvo Zabantsundu* 26 January 1885).

16. Ibid., 29–30.

17. Makiwane reflected the experiences of an older generation in cautioning would-be militants in 1885: "The rising generation forgets that the natives are an inferior race." Odendaal, "African political mobilisation in the eastern Cape," 58 (citing *Imvo Zabantsundu* 26 January 1885 and 2 February 1885).

18. Like the NEA, the Imbumba saw the Afrikaner Bond both as a threat to African interests and as an example of how to organize an ethnic group and develop a power base. Members of the Imbumba in later years saw themselves as an authentic Afrikaner Bond, whereas the ethnic Afrikaner organization was only a "Boeren Bond" (farmers' association). Odendaal, "African political mobilisation in the eastern Cape," 60 (citing *Isigidimi Sama Xosa* 18 July 1883).

19. Ibid., 59 (citing *Isigidimi Sama Xosa* 1 March 1884). Gaba (people of the water) was the clan name of both Ntsikana and Tiyo Soga.

20. Ibid., 62 (citing *Isigidimi Sama Xosa* 18 July 1883 and 1 November 1883). Imbumba leaders also prayed for the chiefs in public and sought to obtain freedom for those who were still in prison as a result of the 1877–81 wars.

21. Odendaal, "African political mobilisation in the eastern Cape," 88–91 (citing correspondents in *Isigidimi Sama Xosa* and *Imvo Zabantsundu* between 1883 and 1885).

22. This section is based mainly on L. D. Ngcongco, "*Imvo Zabantsundu* and Cape 'native' policy, 1884–1902," M.A. thesis, University of South Africa, 1974, chaps. 3–7; idem, "John Tengo Jabavu 1859–1921," in Saunders, *Black leaders in southern African history,* 142–55; and Odendaal, "African mobilisation in the eastern Cape," 103–15.

23. Trapido, "White conflict and non-white participation," 286 (citing *Imvo Zabantsundu* 3 November 1884).

24. J. Stewart (comp.), *Lovedale: past and present* (Lovedale, 1887), 533–34.

25. Trapido, "White conflict and non-white participation," 286 (citing *Imvo Zabantsundu* 3 November 1884).

26. For brief biographical sketches of these men, see *Dictionary of South African Biography,* Vol. 6, 102–3 (James Rose-Innes); Vol. 7, 339–41, 496–97 (Merriman, Molteno); Vol. 9, 496, 509, 529 (Sauer, Scanlen, Schreiner); and Vol. 10, 52–53, 320 (Solomon, Stretch).

27. On the pursuit of Victorian sports, see A. Odendaal, "South Africa's black Victorians: sport, race and class in South Africa before union," *Africa Perspective,* n.s., 1 (7 & 8), 1989, 72–93. Mission-educated Africans in the eastern Cape played the dominant role in introducing and popularizing Western sports elsewhere in South Africa. They were involved in informal cricket matches in places like King William's Town by the 1850s, and there were irregular matches between mission schools in the Ciskei by the 1860s and 1870s. Cricket was the most popular male sport, followed by soccer and rugby (from the 1890s). Sport was essentially segregated by the 1880s, and blacks were developing their own separate (and subordinate) organizations at the local, provincial, and even the national level by the end of the century.

28. E.g., G. Baines, "The origins of urban segregation: local government and the residence of Africans in Port Elizabeth, c. 1835–1865," *South African Historical Journal*, 22, 1990, 61–81. The first to arrive were Mfengu, who displaced the Khoikhoi as beach laborers loading and unloading the surfboats that carried goods from ships anchored in Algoa Bay to the landing beach. Blacks (Khoikhoi, Mfengu, and Xhosa) constituted 35.6 percent of the population in the 1865 census.

29. This section is based mainly on Odendaal, "African political mobilisation in the eastern Cape," chap. 3. See also Trapido, "White conflict and non-white participation," chaps. 7–8.

30. Not all African political organizations, moreover, had reacted against the 1887 Registration Act. The Mfengu organizer Andrew Gontshi insisted it did not affect most voters, and his newly formed Union of Native Opinion in Fingoland did not protest the legislation.

31. Odendaal, "African political mobilisation in the eastern Cape," 164 (citing *Imvo Zabantsundu* 14 August 1890).

32. Ibid., 166.

33. Ibid., 174 (citing *Imvo Zabantsundu* 7 January 1892, 27 July 1898).

34. This section is based mainly on J. L. McCracken, *the Cape parliament, 1854–1910* (Oxford, 1967), chap. 6; Trapido, "White conflict and non-white participation," chaps. 8–9; Odendaal, "African political mobilisation in the eastern Cape," chap. 4; idem, *Black protest politics in South Africa to 1912* (Totowa, N.J., 1984), chap. 2.

35. For the story of Rhodes as an imperial adventurer during the 1880s and 1890s, see Rotberg, *The founder,* chaps. 8, 11–13, 16, 19, 20–21.

36. The impact of the Cape's discriminatory policies on the African petty bourgeoisie during these years is epitomized by the careers of people like Alan Soga. Educated like his father in Scotland, he became a qualified lawyer and was appointed assistant magistrate at St. Mark's in the southern Transkei. Soga seemed destined to become South Africa's first African magistrate when he was abruptly removed from this post in 1895 and transferred to the colonial Labour Office. *Imvo* blamed Soga's removal on the Afrikaner Bond. Jabavu's brother-in-law Benjamin Sakuba, a court interpreter in King William's Town, was replaced by a European in 1897. W. G. Mills, "The rift within the lute: conflict and factionalism in the 'school' community in the Cape colony, 1890–1915," *The Societies of Southern Africa in the 19th and 20th Centuries,* Vol. 15, University of London, Institute of Commonwealth Studies, 1990, 34, 39 (fn. 41).

37. He used the phrase in a speech at Kimberly during the 1898 election campaign.

38. *Imvo Zabantsundu* was closed down from August 1901 to October 1902 and plagued thereafter by financial problems. The newspaper did not show a profit until 1905, and within a few years it was in debt again. In 1909 there were so many delinquent accounts that the company publishing *Imvo* was forced to cut circulation in half (from about 4,000 to 2,000 a week) and demand advance payment from subscribers.

39. Mills, "Rift within the lute," 33. Mills suggests that ethnic conflicts surfaced first in the mission churches. The most vulnerable were those established by the Congregationalist and Presbyterian missionaries, who believed most strongly in the autonomy of local congregations and were most dependent on African contributions for survival. As Christian households became poorer, church contributions declined, building programs were curtailed, and stipends paid to preachers, evangelists, and ordained pastors

were cut off or reduced. Ethnic tensions within the churches spilled over into politics at a critical point in time for the struggling petty bourgeoisie.

40. Jabavu was actually asked by the Afrikaner Bond to be its candidate for Fort Beaufort in the 1904 elections. The offer may have been insincere, as Jabavu's supporters claimed, but he declined in any case.

41. The number of registered African voters, however, steadily declined from 8,117 in 1903 to 6,637 in 1909. Registered Coloured and white voters, respectively, increased from 12,601 and 114,450 in 1903 to 14,394 and 121,336 in 1909. *Report of the South African Native Affairs Commission, 1903–1905*, Vol. 1, 93; Cape of Good Hope, 1909 *Statistical Register*, 15. Coloured in these sources includes the racially designated categories of Chinese, Indian, Malay, Hottentot, and "other."

42. Trapido, "White conflict and non-white participation," 252 (citing *Izwi Labantu* 16 April 1908).

Chapter 6. The Beginnings of African Nationalism

1. Peires, "Nxele, Ntsikana and the origins of the Xhosa religious reaction"; idem, *House of Phalo*, 67–74.

2. Ntsiko wrote under the pseudonym uHadi Waseluhlangeni (Harp of the Nation). For the translation, see Jordan, *Towards an African literature*, 96. The original is in *Isigidimi Sama Xosa* 1 February 1884.

3. For the translation, see A. S. Gerard, *Four African literatures: Xhosa, Sotho, Zulu, Amharic* (Berkeley & Los Angeles, 1971), 41, fn. 32. The original is in *Isigidimi Sama Xosa* 1 June 1882. Hoho, in the Ciskei's Amathole Mountains, was reputedly the place where Sandile was killed during the 1877–78 war.

4. Tiyo Soga wrote under the pseudonym Nonjiba Waseluhlangeni (Dove of the Nation), and the original is in *Indaba* August 1862. Quoted by D. Williams (ed.), *The journal and selected writings of the Reverend Tiyo Soga* (Cape Town, 1983), 153.

5. Ibid., 175. The original is in *Indaba* June 1864.

6. J. A. Chalmers, *Tiyo Soga: a page of South African mission work*, 2nd ed. (Edinburgh, 1878), 435 (citing missionary Robert Johnston).

7. Ibid., 430 (italics in original). The notebook has been lost.

8. Quoted by Williams, *Journal of Tiyo Soga*, 178–82. The original is in *King William's Town Gazette and Kaffrarian Banner* 11 May 1865 ("What is the destiny of the kaffir race?" by "Defensor"). Soga initially recorded his response to Chalmers' article in his journal 25 April 1865.

9. On the Bambatha rebellion, see S. Marks, *Reluctant rebellion: the 1906–1908 disturbances in Natal* (Oxford, 1970).

10. The most detailed study on the closer-union movement is L. M. Thompson, *The unification of South Africa, 1902–1910* (Oxford, 1960).

11. J. W. Cell, *The highest stage of white supremacy: the origins of segregation in South Africa and the American south* (Cambridge, 1982), 211.

12. The South Africa Act had six racially discriminatory clauses—24, 26 (re Senate), 34, 35, 44 (re House of Assembly), 137 (re official languages). For details, see Eybers, *Select constitutional documents*, 524–28, 552.

13. Ibid., 555–58 (re Schedule to the South Africa Act). For a sympathetic view of Britain's role in attempting to protect African interests during the negotiations

over union, see R. Hyam, "African interests and the South Africa Act, 1908–1910," *Historical Journal*, 13 (1), 1970, 85–105.

14. This section is based mainly on Odendaal, *Black protest politics*, chaps. 3–11; idem, "African political mobilisation in the eastern Cape," chap. 4.

15. The possibility of resuscitating the NPA was mooted in 1908. Several journals expressed interest (including the Sotho weekly *Naledi ea Lesotho* and the Zulu-English weekly *Ilange lase Natal* as well as *Izwi* and the *Spectator*), but no formal organization emerged from these discussions.

16. Odendaal, *Black protest politics*, 113–14.

17. Dwanya (died 1922), a law agent from the Ciskei's Middledrift District, had chaired the 1907 Queenstown conference, and Mpikela represented the Orange River Colony Native Congress.

18. Lenders was vice president and Fredericks general secretary of the APO.

19. *Izwi* regarded SANAC chairman Godfrey Lagden, for example, as a tool in the hands of the mining magnates. On *Izwi*'s tirades against South African capitalism, see Odendaal, *Black protest politics*, 66, 68–69, 81, 95, 153. *Izwi*'s price was cut by half (from 13s. to 6s. 6d. a year) in 1906, but there was no significant increase in subscribers. In 1907 the price rose again, and two hundred new shares in the publishing company (at £1 each) were offered to the public. *Izwi*'s paying readership, however, remained small, and the newspaper was never able to gain much advertising support.

20. Rubusana contested the Thembuland seat in the Transkei for the Cape Provincial Council in the 1910 elections—the highest governmental body accessible to Africans in the new South Africa—and he became the first African member in its history. *Imvo* refused to endorse Rubusana, who was running as an independent, but the APO in Thembuland actively campaigned on his behalf. In the interests of black unity, Rubusana tried but failed to get Jabavu to contest the Fort Beaufort seat in the Ciskei, and in Cape Town Abdurahman also declined to run. Jabavu, however, decided to compete with Rubusana for the Thembuland seat in the 1914 elections, and in the ensuing campaign the African vote was split. Both candidates were defeated, and Cape Africans would never again win a seat at this level. Abdurahman was elected to the Cape Provincial Council in 1914, and he would serve on this body (as well as the Cape Town City Council) until his death in 1940.

21. Quoted by Odendaal, *Black protest politics*, 274–75.

22. This section is based on M. O. M. Seboni, "The South African Native College, Fort Hare, 1903–1954," Ed.D. thesis, University of South Africa, 1959, chaps. 1–4; A. Kerr, *Fort Hare 1915–48: the evolution of an African college* (New York, 1968), chaps. 1–6; Burchell, "History of the Lovedale missionary institution," chap. 4; Odendaal, "African political mobilisation in the eastern Cape," 186–89, 211–15, 223–26.

23. Simon Sihlali matriculated from Lovedale in 1880, the first African to receive this certificate, but presumably he studied privately. Burchell, "History of the Lovedale missionary institution," 98 (fn. 7).

24. Tengo Jabavu's son D. D. T. Jabavu is a good example. Refused entrance to Dale College, a white school in King William's Town, he completed high school in Wales and went on to complete a B.A. in English at the University of London and a teaching diploma at Birmingham University.

25. Odendaal, "African political mobilisation in the eastern Cape," 188 (citing I. Bud Mbelle to K. A. Hobart Houghton of Fort Hare 30 October 1906).

26. Ibid., 189 (citing *Izwi Labantu* 13 February 1906).

27. The combined total was estimated at £43,500 in 1907 and £40,000 in 1908. About £11,600 (including £3,000 to buy the land and erect buildings on the proposed site) of a promised £40,250 had actually been paid by 1910. Only £300 of £1,750 pledged by individual Africans had been collected. Seboni, "South African Native College," 50, 64, 71, 107.

28. The Education Department contributed £600, the Native Affairs Department £250 (to support an agricultural program), and the United Free Church £250 (to provide accommodation for the students). The faculty consisted of the principal, Alexander Kerr, who had been recruited from Scotland, and Tengo Jabavu's eldest son, D. D. T. Jabavu. The first degrees were awarded in 1924 in association with the University of South Africa.

29. This section is based mainly on the following sources: On the Thembu church, see C. C. Saunders, "The new African elite in the eastern Cape and some late nineteenth century origins of African nationalism," in *The Societies of Southern Africa in the 19th and 20th Centuries,* Vol. 1, University of London, Institute of Commonwealth Studies, October 1969–April 1970, 44–55; idem, "Tile and the Thembu church: politics and independency on the Cape eastern frontier in the late 19th century," *Journal of African History,* 11 (4), 1970, 553–70; Wagenaar, "History of the Thembu," chap. 5.

On the Ethiopian church, see C. E. Tuckey, "The Order of Ethiopia: a study in African church independency, 1900–1916," B.A. Hons. thesis, University of the Witwatersrand, 1977; W. R. Johnson, "The AME church and ethiopianism in South Africa," *Journal of Southern African Affairs,* 3 (2), April 1978, 211–24; idem, "The Afro-American presence in central and southern Africa, 1880–1905," *Journal of Southern African Affairs,* 4 (1), January 1979, 29–44; J. M. Chirenje, *Ethiopianism and Afro-Americans in southern Africa, 1883–1916* (Baton Rouge & London, 1987), esp. chaps. 2–3; S. Dwane, *Issues in the South African theological debate: essays and addresses in honour of the late James Mata Dwane* (Johannesburg, 1989), 83–101.

On the Presbyterian Church of Africa, see Brock, "James Stewart and Lovedale," chap. 5; Mills, "Role of African clergy," chaps. 4–5; Burchell, "Origins of the Bantu Presbyterian Church of South Africa"; idem, "History of the Lovedale missionary institution," chap. 5.

30. There were a few other separatist African churches in the Ciskei—the Melchizedek Ethiopian church, for example, was formed in the Queenstown District about 1890—but they were very small and localized.

31. Mokone, apparently inspired by Tile's success, visited Goduka on at least two occasions, but attempts to amalgamate the two churches failed.

32. Dissidents from the Order of Ethiopia had organized at least three new separatist churches by 1926.

33. Tuckey, "Order of Ethiopia," 44 (citing Archbishop W. M. Carter to Dwane 6 February 1915).

34. Shortly before Mzimba decided to leave the mission in 1898, Dwane was his houseguest. Mzimba also undoubtedly met Simungu Shibe, a Congregational minister with the American Board Mission in Natal who spent eight months at Lovedale in

1896. Shibe was the leader of the first significant independent church in Natal, the Zulu Congregational church established in 1898. On the ZCC, see D. P. Collins, "The origins and formation of the Zulu Congregational Church, 1896–1908," M.A. thesis, University of Natal, 1978.

35. Tsewu, ordained in 1885, was originally supposed to replace the missionary in charge of the station church at Idutywa in the Transkei, but he was denied this post on the advice of the presbytery's clerk: "There is a sluggishness and inertia about our native brethren that militates against them." Quoted by Gqubule, "Examination of the theological education of Africans," 81.

36. The Free Church mission's Synod of Kaffraria was divided over the issue, but a majority of its members voted against joining the PCSA. To complicate matters even further, a rump of the Scottish Free Church known as the "Wee Frees" (or "the 24") refused to sanction the reunion of the parent church and began sending missionaries to the eastern Cape as well in the early 1900s. Burchell, "Origins of the Bantu Presbyterian Church of South Africa."

37. African Presbyterian congregations that remained with the mission church (the Synod of Kaffraria) eventually established their own Bantu Presbyterian Church of South Africa in 1923.

38. Mabandla was a founder member of the local vigilance association. He also tried to start a branch of the Empire League in the belief that Africans would be better off if they were ruled by Britain. He opposed the migrant labor system and organized boycotts in his district in an attempt to force local employers to raise wages. Lewis, "Economic history of the Ciskei," 692–94.

39. Tuckey, "Order of Ethiopia," 83 (citing Order of Ethiopia report for 1914). As a youth, Dwane had been expelled from the government school at Fort Beaufort when white parents were angered because he passed the exams at the top of his class. He strongly supported separate church schools for Africans, and the Order of Ethiopia had established nine in the Cape with more than five hundred pupils by 1912.

40. As the South African Native Affairs Commission put it: "almost without exception secessions have been led by church officers who have been unable to cooperate smoothly with their European counterparts." *Report of the South African Native Affairs Commission,* 1903–1905, Vol. 1, 63.

41. T. Couzens, *The new African: a study of the life and work of H. I. E. Dhlomo* (Johannesburg, 1985), 87 (citing *Imvo Zabantsundu* 30 May 1895).

42. Cited by Tuckey, "Order of Ethiopia," 60. Most of the students in the theological school were at Standard III (Grade 5) or below.

43. Ibid., 61–62.

44. Ibid., 47; Brock, "James Stewart and Lovedale," 345.

Chapter 7. The Underdevelopment of an African Reserve

1. C. Simkins, "Agricultural production in the African reserves of South Africa, 1918–1969," *Journal of Southern African Studies,* 7 (2), April 1981, 256–83; J. B. Knight & G. Lenta, "Has capitalism underdeveloped the labour reserves of South Africa?" *Oxford Bulletin of Economics and Statistics,* 42 (3), August 1980, 161, 169, 172, 194.

2. The chief native commissioner for the Ciskei in 1938: "The Ciskei is the most

over-populated and over-stocked of the native areas," and the reserve had been steadily deteriorating "for 50 years." CGC, 1938 *Proceedings,* 46.

3. On the 1913 Natives' Land Act, see P. Rich, "African farming and the 1913 Natives' Land Act: towards a reassessment," unpublished paper, University of Cape Town, 1976; Bundy, *Rise and fall,* 212–16, 230–36, 241–43; P. L. Wickins, "The Natives Land Act of 1913: a cautionary essay on simple explanations of complex change," *South African Journal of Economics,* 49 (2), June 1981, 105–29; T. Dunbar Moodie, "Class struggle in the development of agrarian capitalism in South Africa: reflections on the relevance of the Natives' Land Act, 1913," unpublished paper, Rhodes University, 1982; and especially T. Keegan, "Crisis and catharsis in the development of capitalism in South African agriculture," *African Affairs,* 83 (336), July 1985, 371–98; idem, *Rural transformations in industrialising South Africa* (London, 1987), chap. 6.

4. Black tenants were preferred over white tenants because they could be evicted more easily and they were less expensive to maintain. The kinship system made their labor more productive, and they could take care of themselves more effectively in hard times. White tenants, moreover, were almost always sharecroppers rather than laborers.

5. S. Plaatje, *Native life in South Africa* (London, 1916).

6. *Report on Native Location Surveys,* UG 42-1922, 6.

7. Only one magisterial district in the Ciskei—Queenstown with 1,463 morgen (3,102 acres)—still contained unoccupied crown land in 1916. *Report of the Natives' Land Commission,* Vol. 1, UG 19-1916, Appendix 3 (Cape Province), 3 (hereafter, 1916 *Beaumont Commission*).

8. Ibid. This constituted in area about 45 percent of the African-owned farms in the Cape. Africans owned or fully occupied (individual tenure, reserve land, crown land, white-owned land) 5.5 percent of the farmland in the Cape in 1916.

9. Ibid., Vol. 2, 175–77 (evidence of Stutterheim magistrate A. W. H. R. Preston and law agent F. C. Bousfield).

10. *Report of the Local Natives' Land Committee,* Cape Province, UG 8-1918, 2 (hereafter 1918 *Cape Land Committee*).

11. Ibid., 10–14.

12. *Report of the Department of Native Affairs,* 1949–50, UG 61-1951, 39 (hereafter 1949–50 *NAD*).

13. *Report of the Native Affairs Commission,* April 1946–December 1947, UG 15-1949, 11 (hereafter 1946–47 *Native Affairs Commission*).

14. 1916 *Beaumont Commission,* Vol. 2, e.g., 164 (evidence of Komgha headman Steven Bongco), 175 (evidence of Stutterheim magistrate A. W. H. R. Preston), 184 (evidence of Stockenstrom magistrate O. C. H. Strong). Although Cape Africans bought 30,448 morgen (64,550 acres) between 1916 and 1926, for example, they lost 147,225 morgen (312,117 acres) during the decade. The amount of land owned by Africans in the Cape declined from 397,973 morgen (843,703 acres) in 1916 to 250,748 morgen (531,586 acres) in 1926. Lacey, *Working for Boroko,* Appendix A.4(b), note c, 386, and A.4(e)–A.4(f), 388.

15. Percentage is based on 1916 *Beaumont Commission,* Appendix 3; *Report of the Department of Native Affairs,* 1948–49, UG 51-1950, 5 (hereafter 1948–49 *NAD*).

16. Between 1919 and 1928, for example, more than two-thirds of the 20,786 morgen (44,066 acres) bought for the Ciskei reserve (about 22 percent of the total land

acquired for reserves in the Cape during this period) was in the severely congested Glen Grey District, which had not been allotted more land in the 1916–18 proposals. Lacey, *Working for Boroko*, Appendix A.5, 389–90.

17. *Report of the Commission for the socio-economic development of the Bantu areas within the Union of South Africa*, UG 61-1955, 53 (hereafter, 1955 *Tomlinson Commission*).

18. No crop production records were kept for the Cape reserves. According to Samuel H. Roberts, chief inspector of native locations in the Cape Colony in 1903, no records were kept on stock either, but officials occasionally did estimate the number of domesticated animals in some rural locations. *Report of the South African Native Affairs Commission*, 1903–5, Vol. 2 (Minutes of evidence taken in the Cape Colony), 812 (hereafter, *SANAC*, Vol. 2).

19. *Blue Book on Native Affairs* for 1910, U17-1911, 157–60 (hereafter 1910 *Blue Book*). On the resistance in Transkei to the cattle-dipping regulations, see C. Bundy, " 'We don't want your rain, we won't dip': popular opposition, collaboration and social control in the anti-dipping movement, 1908–1916," in Beinart and Bundy, *Hidden struggles*, chap. 6.

20. 1916 *Beaumont Commission*, Vol. 2, 124 (evidence of Sir William H. Beaumont).

21. Ibid., 116 (evidence of G. H. Barnes).

22. *SANAC*, Vol. 2., 504 and 616–17 (Umhalla and Kawa wage estimates summarized for the year).

23. F. Wilson, *Labour in the South African gold mines, 1911–1969* (Cambridge, 1972), 46 (Table 5).

24. The following estimates are based on figures obtained from the 1910 *Blue Book* (Native Affairs), 216–24 (Labour: Cape of Good Hope).

25. ̈Sheila van der Horst, writing in the early 1940s, noted that cash wages for African farmworkers in the eastern Cape "appear to have changed little during the last fifty years." *Native labour in South Africa*, 285.

26. *SANAC*, Vol. 2, 429, 452, 454, 487–88 (evidence of R. J. Dick, special magistrate for King William's Town District).

27. F. W. Fox & D. Back, "A preliminary survey of the agricultural and nutritional problems of the Ciskei and Transkeian territories (with special reference to their bearing on the recruiting of labourers for the gold mining industry)," unpublished report, Johannesburg, 1941, 24. For a case study of trading practices in the 1930s and 1940s, see A. B. Forsdick, "The role of the trader in the economy of a native reserve: a study of the traders in the Keiskama Hoek district," M. Comm. thesis, Rhodes University, 1953.

28. 1910 *Blue Book* (Native Affairs), 219.

29. *Report of the Witwatersrand Mine Natives' Wages Commission* 1943, UG 21-1944, 4 (hereafter 1943 *Mine Wages Commission*).

30. 1910 *Blue Book* (Native Affairs), 218–19 (Herschel).

31. Ibid., 377 (table).

32. The farmers were satisfied in part because they had far more Africans on the land than was revealed in the official reports. *Christian Express* 1 July 1918, 104 (citing communication with W. C. Scully, chairman of the 1918 Cape Land Committee).

33. *SANAC*, Vol. 2, 492 (evidence of R. J. Dick).

34. 1910 *Blue Book* (Native Affairs), 219–20.

35. *SANAC*, Vol. 2, 424–537 (evidence of R. J. Dick and Nathaniel Umhalla).

36. Information in this section is based on *Report on Native Location Surveys* (1923); see also T. R. H. Davenport & K. S. Hunt, *The right to the land* (Cape Town, 1974), section 3.

37. *SANAC*, Vol. 2, e.g., 424–501 (evidence of R. J. Dick), 501–37 (evidence of Nathaniel Umhalla), 597–602 (evidence of J. G. Verity, assistant magistrate for Middledrift); 1910 *Blue Book* (Native Affairs), 258–59.

38. Two-thirds of the resident plotholders had to give their consent before a location could be surveyed. *Report of the Native Economic Commission, 1930–32*, UG 22-1932, 23 (para. 151; hereafter 1932 *Native Economic Commission*).

39. 1910 *Blue Book* (Native Affairs), 194–95.

40. W. M. Macmillan, *Complex South Africa: an economic footnote to history* (London, 1930), 210.

41. Ibid., 149; *S.A. Outlook* 1 July 1927, 131.

42. It was based on a precedent set two years earlier in the Transkei. See Beinart & Bundy, *Hidden struggles*, 231–32.

43. 1955 *Tomlinson Commission*, 54; *Report of the Native Laws Commission, 1946–48*, UG 28-1948, 46 (hereafter, 1948 *Fagan Commission*).

44. The information on Victoria East is based on data compiled by James Henderson and published in *S.A. Outlook* 1 August 1925, 175–76; 1 September 1925, 199–201; 1 July 1927, 127–33. The information on Herschel is based on Macmillan, *Complex South Africa*, chap. 11; Bundy, *Rise and fall*, chap. 5.

45. *S.A. Outlook* 1 July 1927, 132. In Victoria East as in other Ciskeian districts, household production varied considerably from year to year. The biggest single contributory factor accounting for these variations was the recurrence of drought. Only a few cultivated areas received enough water to get by without irrigation. Lovedale had recorded local rainfall figures for 44 years (1880–1927), and only twenty years had produced enough rain to assure good crops. The 1932 *Native Economic Commission* regarded Henderson's data for 1875 as "too meagre and unreliable to afford any useful basis for comparison." Victoria East District, the commissioners noted, was one-third smaller in 1925 than it had been fifty years earlier. Nevertheless, they agreed that Henderson's report accurately reflected "the deep poverty existing to-day among the Natives in Victoria East." 1932 *Native Economic Commission*, 183 (para. 68).

46. *S.A. Outlook*, 2 January 1928, 13. Progressive farmers argued that the government should subsidize the sale of cattle in African areas as one way of reducing stock without penalizing the peasant, e.g., *S.A. Outlook* 1 December 1932, 243.

47. Macmillan assumed there were 10,000 household units (10,401 taxpayers) representing 40,000 people in Herschel at the time of his survey in 1925. Total cash expenditure in any given year during the 1920s was estimated at between £80,000 and £100,000. Macmillan apparently accepted an average of four persons per family, and thus he calculated cash expenditure at roughly £8–£10 per household. Estimates of the size of African families between 1910 and 1950, however, indicate there were no less than five and probably more than six persons per household in the reserves. The estimate on expenditure per household in the text assumes there were five persons per family or roughly 8,000 household units at the time of Macmillan's survey.

48. There were thirty-two trading sites—one every four miles—and at least twenty separate traders in Herschel at the time of Macmillan's survey. The traders claimed that debts owed to them by African householders equaled between 10 percent and 25 percent of their yearly gross incomes.

49. Macmillan, *Complex South Africa,* 150, 185.

50. Ibid., 138.

51. 1932 *Native Economic Commission,* 183 (para. 73).

52. Ibid., 21 (para. 136), 22–24 (paras. 148–58).

53. 1948 *Fagan Commission,* 15. The 1932 *Native Economic Commission* observed: "In Middledrift there are large areas where the surface soil has been entirely eroded and no grass whatever grows. . . . In Herschel and Glen Grey the vegetation of the mountainsides having almost disappeared, the rainstorms send torrents down the slopes which wash away periodically large parts of very valuable and fertile soil [and contain] some of the worst *donga* [gully] erosion in the Union." 1932 *Native Economic Commission,* 11 (paras. 72–73).

54. 1932 *Native Economic Commission,* 11 (paras. 72–73).

55. 1955 *Tomlinson Commission,* 80.

56. While the resident reserve population remained more or less static at 95.4 a square mile between 1926 and 1936, for example, the number of cattle units rose from 139.3 to 158.3 a square mile during this decade. *Social and Economic Planning Council Report 9* of 1946, 24 (Table 12). The actual number of cattle per household in the Ciskei, however, was the lowest in South Africa's reserve system. There were 3.53 cattle per household in the 1936 census and 2.09 in the 1951 census. Simkins, "Agricultural production in the African reserves of South Africa," 275 (Table 6).

57. *Social and Economic Planning Council Report 9* of 1946, 23 (Table 11); 1948 *Fagan Commission,* 15 (R. W. Norton).

58. 1943 *Mine Wages Commission,* 12; 1948 *Fagan Commission,* 15. According to Simkins, African peasants in the Ciskei reserve were producing 25–50 percent of their food requirements in 1927 and less than 25 percent in 1960. "Agricultural production in the African reserves of South Africa," 266–70 (Figures 2–4).

59. *Social and Economic Planning Council Report 4,* "The future of farming in South Africa," UG 10-1945, 22 (hereafter 1945 *Social and Economic Planning Council Report 4*); 1946 *Social and Economic Planning Council Report 9,* 14 (Table 5), 15 (Table 7), 49; CGC, 1948 *Proceedings,* 19; 1948–49 *NAD,* 3; 1949–50 *NAD,* 39; O. Walker, *Kaffirs are lively* (London, 1948), 44. The maize yield on white farms was about 6.36 bags a morgen (3 bags an acre) between 1935 and 1939, for example, as opposed to 4.24 bags a morgen (2 bags an acre) for the reserves between 1939 and 1944. White farms averaged 6.98 bags a morgen (3.29 bags an acre) in 1949–50 as opposed to 2.47 bags a morgen (1.16 bags an acre) for the reserves in the same year. *Social and Economic Planning Council Report 9* of 1946, 17 and fn. 2; 1955 *Tomlinson Commission,* 84.

60. 1943 *Mine Wages Commission,* 15; 1946 *Social and Economic Planning Council Report 9,* 45 (Table 34). Migrants composed 67 percent of the adult male population in 1941–43 but only about 41 percent in 1951 according to the Tomlinson Commission, presumably because more migrants had settled permanently in the cities. CGC, 1944

Proceedings, 68 (W. R. Norton); 1955 *Tomlinson Commission,* Vol. 10, chap. 23, 31 (Table 5).

61. Fox & Back, "Preliminary survey," 65. Fox and Back were sent by the Chamber of Mines to investigate the living conditions of mine labor recruits and their families in these reserves in 1937.

62. *S.A. Outlook* 1 September 1925, 199.

63. *S.A. Outlook* 1 March 1928, 49.

64. Fox & Back, "Preliminary survey," 191(Table 11)–193. The infant mortality rate for South African whites up to 1 year was 62 (per 1,000 births) in 1933–35. Mortality rates (per 1,000 births) in a sample of 259 African mothers (aged 17 to 60) in Keiskammahoek in 1946 were 288 for children up to 1 year and 453 for all others. D. H. Houghton & E. M. Walton, *The economy of a native reserve,* Vol. 2 of *Keiskammahoek rural survey* (Pietermaritzburg, 1952), 46.

65. At least 45 percent of the Africans treated at Lovedale in 1925, for example, suffered diseases that could be directly attributed to impoverishment. They included tuberculosis (171), "debility" and scurvy (117), dysentery and enteritis (61), typhus (19), and enteric fever due to polluted water supplies (8). *S.A. Outlook* 1 July 1927, 132.

66. Official neglect was also linked to the low number of young African males who failed the mining physical. The rejection rate at the mine-recruiting depots in the Ciskei averaged 13 percent in 1936. Fox & Back, "Preliminary survey," 314.

67. Information on mission medical facilities is based on *S.A. Outlook* 2 January 1945, 105; 1 March 1945, 48; 1 January 1946, 5, 7–8; 1 November 1946, 165, 171; 1 September 1948, 132–35, 153; 1 February 1949, 20, 27, 82–83; 2 June 1952, 83.

68. About 47 percent of the hospital beds in Ciskei in 1945 were for general cases and at least 37 percent for infectious disease (mainly tuberculosis).

69. The National Health Commission set the ratio at one general bed for every 200 persons (all races) in the urban areas and one general bed for every 500 persons in rural African areas. If one assumes that 47 per cent of Ciskei's hospital beds were for general cases, there was one bed per 1,001 Africans in the region in 1946. South Africa's Department of Health eventually set a minimum for all races at four beds per 1,000 population. If this measure is used, the Ciskei region with 931 beds still had only 2.13 beds per 1,000 Africans in 1946.

70. 1955 *Tomlinson Commission,* Vol. 15, chap. 41, annexure 3. These estimates are based on the 1946 census and the 1948 medical register. The number of whites per doctor in the Ciskei ranged from a ratio of 1/73 in Middledrift to 1/1,165 in Stutterheim. Comparable figures for Africans ranged from a ratio of 1/907 in East London to 1/25,822 in Peddie. There were an estimated 157 doctors in the Ciskei region at this time.

71. *S.A. Outlook* 1 January 1946, 7.

72. Ibid., 1 September 1948, 135.

73. The section on East London is based on the *SANAC,* Vol. 2, 821–39 (evidence of Charles A. Lloyd, inspector of East London's locations from 1901 to the mid-1930s); *Christian Express* 1 August 1914, 117–18; *S.A. Outlook* 1 March 1927, 52–54; 1 August 1931, 142; 1 April 1933, 70–71; 1 July 1933, 123–24; 2 October 1933, 187; 1 January 1944, 4; 1 April 1950, 52; East London, *Reports of the medical officer of health* (East

London, 1930, 1931); 1932 *Native Economic Commission,* 66–67 (paras. 442–49); 1948 *Fagan Commission,* 10 (population tables); H. H. Smith, "The transport system of the border," Ph.D. diss., Rhodes University 1958, chap. 2 and appendix (Tables A.1–A.9); R. H. Reader, *The black man's portion: history, demography and living conditions in the native locations of East London, Cape Province* (Cape Town, 1961), chap. 2; K. Helliker, "Towards a materialist analysis of the South African state policy of urban relocation—with particular reference to Mdantsane," B.A. Hons., Rhodes University, 1981, 50–61; K. P. T. Tankard, "The development of East London through four decades of municipal control, 1873–1914," Ph.D. diss., Rhodes University 1990, chaps. 2–3, 10–11.

74. Tankard, "East London: the creation and development of a frontier community," 172.

75. Although the regulation was regarded as "unreasonable," the court ruled that city officials did have the right to confiscate sticks within municipal boundaries, including the locations. Tankard, "Development of East London," 398.

76. Ibid., 426.

77. Only about 50 percent of the money East London's municipal authorities obtained from African residents during a ten-month period in 1911, for example, was spent on African locations. Reader implies that African revenue was used for the benefit of white East London until at least the late 1930s. In Fort Beaufort, according to the 1918 Cape Land Committee, African residents contributed 80 percent of the municipal rates, but "nothing is done in the Natives' interest." *Christian Express* 1 August 1914, 117; 1918 *Cape Land Committee,* 6 (paras. 40–42); Reader, *Black man's portion,* 14; see also Tankard, "Development of East London," 416 (Table 28 on hut revenues, 1895–1915).

78. Census officials consistently underestimated the urban African population. Fort Beaufort's resident African population, for example, must have been underestimated in 1904 since there is no other explanation for the sudden increase seven years later. The unofficial estimate of the African population in East London in 1951 was 78,000 or more than double the official figure. Reader, *Black man's portion,* 42–43.

79. An estimated 60 percent of the children in the locations in 1931 attended seven church schools up to Standard VI (eighth grade). Most of them left school, however, by Standard IV (sixth grade).

80. 1930–31, *Report of the East London Medical Officer of Health,* 51.

81. It was second only to Port Elizabeth in 1948–49 and the highest in urban South Africa, for example, in 1949–50.

82. In the Cape, there were significant differences in the administration of the Transkei and Ciskei, the province's two principal African reserves. Magisterial rule was centralized under the authority of a chief magistrate in the Transkei, and all the magistrates were controlled by the NAD. In the Ciskei, administrative authority was divided between ex-colonial "superintendents of natives" or "inspectors of locations" controlled by the NAD and magistrates controlled by the Justice Department.

83. S. Dubow, "Holding 'a just balance between white and black': the Native Affairs Department in South Africa, c. 1920–1933," *Journal of Southern African Studies,* 12 (2), April 1986, 217–39; Idem, *Racial segregation and the origins of apartheid in*

South Africa, 1919–36 (New York, 1989), esp. chaps. 3–4; see also Lacey, *Waiting for Boroko*, chap. 3.

84. *Report of the Native Affairs Department*, 1922–26, UG 14-1927, 1. The NAD staff was reduced to 1,211 Europeans and Africans—a loss of 246 posts.

85. Dubow, *Racial segregation*, 114.

86. NAD officials were not in favor of helping white farmers recruit African labor during the 1920s, refused to administer the 1932 Native Service Contract Act (a "draconian" measure imposed on African farm labor in Natal and the Transvaal), and sought to make available as much land as possible to Africans under the 1913 Land Act. Although the 1923 Urban Areas Act was designed to control the movement of Africans to the cities and towns, municipalities were made responsible for providing these workers with adequate housing and sanitation. NAD officials tried with less success to moderate amendments to the 1923 act in 1930 and 1937. Ibid., 119–25.

87. Under the 1909 act, all residents of mission stations could obtain individual tenure and some measure of local government (albeit under the authority of the divisional councils) with the establishment of village management boards. Some station communities in Ciskei used this legislation to complete land surveys and set up village councils in the next decade.

88. *IZ* 14 April 1925, 5; 12 August 1925, 5; 9 February 1926, 5; 15 June 1926, 5. The issue of local councils was a staple on the English-language editorial page throughout the 1920s.

89. CGC, 1940 *Proceedings*, 54–57; 1941 *Proceedings*, 41 (A. M. Jabavu); 1943 *Proceedings*, 63–65 (Minute No. 39).

90. Local/district councils could contribute a minimum of 10 percent and a maximum of 15 percent to the general council. Between 1946 and 1950 contributions to the Bunga dropped to 10 percent, and a motion was approved in 1950 that local councils could pay less than 10 percent if they could not afford the minimum contribution. CGC, 1950 *Proceedings*, 64–65 (Minute No. 34), 81 (Report of the treasurer).

91. Despite appeals from Bunga councillors, Africans in East London, Hewu, and districts without local councils were still subject to wheel taxes in the 1930s. CGC, e.g., 1934 *Proceedings*, 68 (Minute No. 39).

92. CGC, 1939 *Proceedings*, 43–47, 48–52 (Minute No. 20); 1942 *Proceedings*, 40–43 (Minute 24); 1943 *Proceedings*, 84 (Minute No. 53); 1944 *Proceedings*, 21–26 (Report of the Recess Committee on the amalgamation of district and local councils in the Ciskei), 49, 56–63 (Minute No. 10—Report of the Select Committee on the amalgamation of district and local councils in the Ciskei).

93. CGC, 1934 *Proceedings*, 26 (chairman's address).

94. CGC, 1944 *Proceedings*, 22 (Report of the Recess Committee).

95. CGC, 1937 *Proceedings*, 60.

96. CGC, 1950 *Proceedings*, 66–67 (Minute No. 34).

97. The Bunga controlled only about 150 acres of forests in Glen Grey and Herschel districts. 1946 *Social and Economic Planning Council Report 9*, 26.

98. The 1934–43 credit balance, for example, amounted to £24,760 (42.5 percent of the total revenue available for 1943). Unpaid taxes in 1943 amounted to £16,196. CGC, 1944 *Proceedings*, 30 (Appendix B), 32 (Appendix G).

99. Walker, *Kaffirs are lively,* 52–53.

100. In 1938, for example, the chairman reemphasized the "strictly non-political complexion of this body." CGC, 1938 *Proceedings,* 22 (chairman's address). See also 1945 *Proceedings,* 69–70 (Minute No. 50—Definition of political terms).

101. 1932 *Native Economic Commission,* 31 (para. 205).

102. CGC, 1934 *Proceedings,* 60 (Joseph Mputhing); 1940 *Proceedings,* 59 (Alexander Jabavu); 1949 *Proceedings,* 45 (H. Tele).

103. CGC, 1943 *Proceedings,* 71–72 (Minute No. 48); 1945 *Proceedings,* 34–35 (Minute No. 5), 69 (Minute No. 48); 1949 *Proceedings,* 29–31 (Minute No. 2).

104. All motions presented to the Bunga were included except for opening speeches, congratulatory messages and replies, retirements, condolences, nomination and appointment notices, and reports of committees. Each motion was counted as a unit in the analysis. Motions were coded in twenty subject subcategories in the initial investigation and then recoded in ten subject categories.

105. CGC, 1934 *Proceedings,* 88–91 (Minute No. 50); 1941 *Proceedings,* 31–33 (Minute No. 14); 1945 *Proceedings,* 33 (Minute No. 2); 1947 *Proceedings,* 36–38 (Minute No. 20), 1949 *Proceedings,* 46–48 (Minute No. 20). The councillors also urged that the central government assume administration of the schools—at least until the National party victory in the 1948 general elections. Interdenominational rivalry and the increasing number of churches involved in school activities, among other things, were causing dissension. As *S.A. Outlook* put it: "Nepotism, sectarianism and arbitrary methods in administration have shown their ugly faces, thus evoking the resentment of the people." Seven local councils in 1934, for example, recommended that the central government take over African education. CGC, 1934 *Proceedings,* 87–88 (Minute No. 49); *S.A. Outlook* 1 June 1936, 133.

106. CGC, 1934 *Proceedings,* 89 (F. C. Pinkerton).

107. CGC, 1938 *Proceedings,* 74.

108. CGC, e.g., 1938 *Proceedings,* 68–69 (J. J. Yates of King William's Town and D. G. Hartmann of East London).

109. CGC, 1936 *Proceedings,* 47.

110. Seven Xhosa chiefs were officially recognized by 1934 and three Mfengu chiefs a year later. CGC, 1934 *Proceedings,* 34–48 (Minute No. 12); 1935 *Proceedings,* 68–69 (Minute No. 36), 79–80 (Minute No. 42). See also *S.A. Outlook,* e.g., 1 April 1943, 43.

111. CGC, 1937 *Proceedings,* 43; 1938 *Proceedings,* 36.

112. Motions were passed in 1935 and 1943, for example, urging exemption from general and local taxes for all African males aged sixty-five years and older. CGC, 1935 *Proceedings,* 86 (Minute No. 46); 1943 *Proceedings,* 31–33 (Minute No. 4).

113. References to the rights of African war veterans were also made mainly during World War II. The councillors urged that African soldiers be given arms, prisoners be given more relief packages, and veterans be recognized for their contributions to the war effort with higher pay and land when they were released from service.

114. South Africa, moreover, was merely a reflection of a much wider concern with the environment that gathered momentum especially in Britain's African colonies in the first half of the twentieth century. Whites in Nyasaland (Malawi), for example, firmly believed that African farm methods increased soil erosion. J. McCracken,

"Experts and expertise in colonial Malawi," *African Affairs,* 81 (322), 1982, esp. 110–14. For a discussion of the wider conservation movement in sub-Saharan Africa, see D. Anderson & R. Grove (eds.), *Conservation in Africa: people, policies and practice* (Cambridge, 1987), esp. parts 1 and 3.

115. For background information, see W. Beinart, "Soil erosion, conservationism and ideas about development: a southern African exploration, 1900–1960," *Journal of Southern African Studies,* 11 (1), October 1984, 52–83; idem, "Introduction: the politics of colonial conservation," *JSAS,* 15 (2), January 1989, 143–62.

116. Cape officials tried to restrict access of "inferior" stock to grazing land in the Ciskei reserve from 1934 (Proclamation 198).

117. Although the motion calling for the compulsory culling of stock was passed, it triggered a long and at times heated debate. One speaker (Gibson Maneli of Victoria East), for example, was censored for questioning the government's motives, while another (R. J. Time of East London) scolded his "educated" colleagues who had "absolutely nothing to do with cattle" and "do not care about them. . . . I would not be strong enough to go to these people [the peasants] with this request unless I had something in my hand to substitute for what I was taking from them." CGC, 1938 *Proceedings,* 52 (Time), 54 (Maneli), 79–80 (Draft proclamation: Limitation of stock in Native locations and reserves).

118. For information on the government's Betterment projects between 1939 and 1949, see 1946 *Social and Economic Planning Council Report 9,* 7–65; 1946–47 *Native Affairs Commission,* 8–9, 11, 17–18; 1948–49 *NAD,* 3–18, 33–36; 1949–50 *NAD,* 2–19, 38–42.

119. On the 1945 proposals, see CGC, 1944 *Proceedings,* 66–77 (Minute No. 13); 1945 *Proceedings* (Special Session, January 1945), 1–22 (address by the secretary for native affairs and ensuing debate); 1945 *Proceedings* (General Session), 22–31 (address by the secretary for native affairs and ensuing debate); Z. K. Matthews' critique of the scheme in *S.A. Outlook* 1 November 1945, 166–70; 1946 *Social and Economic Planning Council Report 9,* 48–49.

120. Cf. CGC, 1944 *Proceedings,* 76 (comments by A. Jabavu); 1945 *Proceedings* (Special Session, January 1945), 16–18 (comments by W. Majola, G. Maneli, H. Phooko, A. Ngxoweni).

121. CGC, 1945 *Proceedings* (Special Session, January 1945), 17.

122. CGC, 1938 *Proceedings,* 48, 53 (Mears); 1945 *Proceedings,* 6, 12 (Smit); 1945 *Proceedings* (General Session), 22–29 (Mears).

123. Proclamation No. 31 of 1939 was amended in 1944 (Proclamation No. 92), 1947 (Proclamation No. 76), and 1948 (Proclamation No. 66). All previous Betterment proclamations were replaced by Proclamation No. 116 of 1949.

124. On the establishment of Zwelitsha and the local textile industry, see CGC, 1946 *Proceedings,* 15 (minister of native affairs); 1950 *Proceedings,* 56–58 (Minute Nos. 24–25); 1954 *Proceedings,* 33 (Minute Nos. 17, 30); 1946 *Social and Economic Planning Council Report 9,* 59, 61; 1946–47 *Native Affairs Commission,* 18; 1948–49 *NAD,* 34–35; 1949–50 *NAD,* 41; *S.A. Outlook* 2 July 1945, 100; 2 September 1946, 137; B. du Toit, *Ukubamba amadolo: workers' struggles in the South African textile industry* (London, 1978), 34–36; A. Mager, "Moving the fence: gender in the Ciskei and border textile industry, 1945–1986," *Social Dynamics,* 15 (2), 1989, 46–62.

125. By 1941, for example, only 491 Ciskeian peasant families had been given land released to the reserve under the 1936 Land Act. CGC, 1941 *Proceedings*, 13 (chairman's address). Councillors complained that land bought by the Native Trust was retained by Africans already living there, distributed to Africans displaced from white areas, set aside as experimental farms, or left vacant in an effort to revitalize the soil.

126. CGC, 1949 *Proceedings*, 31. H. Phooko (Herschel) commented in 1945: "whatever is being done by the Government . . . we are ignored. . . . we are always excluded." 1945 *Proceedings* (Special Session, January 1945), 17.

127. Quoted by *S.A. Outlook* 1 May 1940, 89.

128. Cf. Goldberg, "Underdevelopment in the Ciskei," 65–78ff.

129. CGC, 1935 *Proceedings*, 46.

130. D. H. Houghton, *Life in the Ciskei: a summary of the findings of the Keis-kammahoek rural survey, 1947–1951* (Johannesburg, 1955), 10–11.

131. CGC, 1945 *Proceedings*, 44–45 (Minute No. 17—Teachers' lands), 45, 52–53, 55–56 (Minute Nos. 18, 32, 34—Land allotments).

132. An agricultural school, for example, was established at Fort Cox in the Middledrift District on 1,200 morgen (2,544 acres) of choice land bought from a white farmer in September 1930. Fort Cox was the only training facility for African farmers established by the central government before the apartheid era (the Transkei Bunga funded three farm schools in their reserve). The school was supposed to train model farmers and agricultural demonstrators for the reserves, but it was not supported by the African population. For details, see CGC, 1934 *Proceedings*, 85 (H. J. Every); *Report of the Interdepartmental Committee on Native Education*, 1935–36, UG 29-1936, 17–18 (paras. 33–37); 1946 *Social and Economic Planning Council Report 9*, 38–39; *S.A. Outlook* 1 October 1930, 197 (editorial); 1 December 1932, 242; 1 July 1937, 146; 1 July 1949, 106–7; 1948–49 *NAD*, 15–16; 1949–50, *NAD*, 16–117.

133. 1949–50 *NAD*, 40; *S.A. Outlook* 1 July 1949, 99, 106.

Chapter 8. Opposition Politics and Popular Resistance I

1. E.g., P. Bonner, "The Transvaal Native Congress, 1917–1920: the radicalisation of the black *petty bourgeoisie* on the Rand," and D. Coplan, "The emergence of an African working-class culture," in Marks & Rathbone, *Industrialisation and social change*, 270–313, 358–75; H. Bradford, "Mass movements and the *petty bourgeoisie:* the social origins of ICU leadership, 1924–1929," *Journal of African History*, 25, 1984, 295–310; Bradford, *Taste of freedom*, chap. 3. The most detailed study of the black petty bourgeoisie during this period is by A. G. Cobley, *Class and consciousness: the black petty bourgeoisie in South Africa, 1924 to 1950* (New York, 1990).

2. South Africa's per capita death rate during the Spanish influenza pandemic was actually one of the highest in the world. The official death toll was 139,471 (of which 11,726 were white), but this figure was rejected even at the time so far as the black population was concerned. At least 300,000 people are believed to have died: the majority of victims were rural blacks (Africans and Coloureds), and the death toll was highest in the Cape. This epidemic would have a decided impact on the demographic profile of the African population during the interwar period. H. Phillips, "South Africa's worst demographic disaster: the Spanish influenza epidemic of 1918," *South African Historical Journal*, 20, 1988, 57–73.

3. Couzens, *New African,* chap. 3.

4. On the joint councils, see B. Hirson, "Tuskegee, the Joint Councils, and the All African Convention," in *The Societies of Southern Africa in the 19th and 20th Centuries,* Vol. 10, University of London, Institute of Commonwealth Studies, October 1978–June 1979, 65–76; P. B. Rich, *White power and the liberal conscience: racial segregation and South African liberalism, 1921–60* (Johannesburg, 1984), chap. 1.

5. On the liberal tradition in the generation after 1910, see P. Kallaway, "F. S. Malan, the Cape liberal tradition, and South African politics, 1908–1924," *Journal of African History,* 15 (1), 1974, 113–29; P. B. Rich, "The appeals of Tuskegee: James Henderson, Lovedale, and the fortunes of South African liberalism, 1906–1930," *International Journal of African Historical Studies,* 20, 1987, 271–292; R. Elphick, "Mission Christianity and interwar liberalism," and J. Butler, "Interwar liberalism and local activism," in Butler, Elphick & Welsh, *Democratic liberalism,* 64–97; Dubow, *Racial Segregation.*

6. V. Klein, "African responses in the eastern Cape to Hertzog's Representation of Natives in Parliament Bill, 1926–1936," B.A. Hons. thesis, University of Cape Town, 1978, 20. For a brief analysis of the black voting population in the Cape, see N. Garson, "The Cape franchise after union: the Queenstown by-election of December 1921," *African Studies,* 45 (1), 1986, 61–79.

7. *S.A. Outlook* 1 July 1924, 154–55.

8. On the "great" and "small" tradition in Cape liberalism during the colonial period, see Trapido, "Friends of the natives," esp. 251–62. On the elitism of this community, see J. & R. Simons, *Class and colour in South Africa, 1850–1950* (Harmondsworth, 1969), 621–23; P. Walshe, *The rise of African nationalism in South Africa: the African National Congress, 1912–1950* (London, 1970), 223–24; D. Chanaiwa, "African humanism in southern Africa: the utopian, traditionalist, and colonialist worlds of mission-educated elites," in A. T. Mugomba & M. Nyaggah (eds.), *Independence without freedom: the political economy of colonial education in southern Africa* (Santa Barbara, 1980), chap. 1.

9. The Ciskeian Missionary Council was formed in 1925. It consisted intially of mission churches and secondary schools, representatives of native welfare societies and the Students' Christian Association, and African independent churches recognized by the government like the Order of Ethiopia, AME church, and the Presbyterian Church of Africa. It would include officials from the Cape Education Department and the NAD as affiliate members, and delegates from the local/district councils and the Ciskeian General Council. Ciskeian Missionary Council, *Minutes,* October 1925–November 1951.

10. *S.A. Outlook* 1 August 1925, 175; 1 December 1927, 226–227 (citing Ciskeian Missionary Council report for November 1927).

11. Cape dominance in African education did not really decline until the 1950s. R. Hunt Davis, Jr., "The administration and financing of African education in South Africa, 1910–1953," in P. Kallaway (ed.), *Apartheid and education: the education of black South Africans* (Johannesburg, 1984), 130–37.

12. *S.A. Outlook* 1 December 1927, 226–27.

13. It would not improve until the 1945 Native Education Act. Unnamed author, "The historical roots of Bantu education," *Africa Perspective,* No. 24, 1984, 45.

14. For a case study of the impact of mission education on the African elite in the Ciskei during the interwar period, see J. A. M. Peppeta, "A portrait of a school: Heald-

town missionary institution (1925–1955) through the eyes of some of its ex-pupils," M.Ed. thesis, Rhodes University, 1989.

15. Tim Couzens' exploration of the term New African, based on the portrait biographies of living and dead Africans recorded by T. D. Mweli Skota in his famous reference guide to the African elite published in 1930, would certainly have applied to the mission-educated community in the eastern Cape. Skota's "progressive" African was a male who (with luck) had a royal pedigree, got involved in his people's welfare, and was a hard worker (if he was a farmer, he plowed his own fields and worked the land in individual tenure). He was a "true, kind-hearted Christian gentleman, respected by Europeans and Africans alike, a good speaker, who does not drink, and who starts as a teacher or interpreter and becomes a clergyman or lawyer." Couzens, *New African*, 5–19.

16. Quoted by Hirson, "Tuskegee, the Joint Councils, and the All African Convention," 71. East London, King William's Town, and Port Elizabeth acquired native welfare societies during the 1920s. *IZ*, e.g., 24 January 1928, 5.

17. The 1921 Phelps-Stokes Commission was funded by the Carnegie Corporation, a U.S. transnational interested in supporting African education. Nevertheless, about two-thirds of the money Carnegie actually earmarked for Africa before 1940 was spent on poor whites in South Africa. J. Bottaro, "Education and development: Carnegie Commissions and South Africa," *Africa Perspective*, No. 25, 1985, 5.

18. Quoted by Couzens, *New African*, 83. On Aggrey, see *IZ*, 19, 26 April 1921, 5; 10 May 1921, 5; 7, 14 June 1921, 5; 8 July 1924, 5; 30 October 1928, 5.

19. Cell, *Highest stage of white supremacy*, 258.

20. Garvey's newspaper *Negro World* was read in South Africa. On the Garveyites, see R. A. Hill & G. A. Pirio, " 'Africa for the Africans': the Garvey movement in South Africa, 1920–1940," in S. Marks & S. Trapido (eds.), *The politics of race, class and nationalism in twentieth century South Africa* (London, 1987), 209–53.

21. Quoted by Hirson, "Tuskegee, the Joint Councils, and the All African Convention," 71; see also *IZ* 9 January 1923, 5.

22. D. D. T. Jabavu, *The black problem* (Lovedale, 1920), 15. Communist Party leader Sydney Bunting, with his wife, Rebecca, and colleague Gana Makabeni, did campaign in the Transkei in a futile bid to win the Thembuland seat during the 1929 general election, but communist organizers would not begin to work extensively on behalf of workers and peasants in the eastern Cape until the 1940s.

23. African voters met initially to select a Cape contingent to accompany the SANNC delegation to London and the Paris peace talks. On Bantu Union, see *IZ* 14 January 1919, 5; 4, 18 February 1919, 5; 15 June 1920, 5; 27 July 1920, 5; 10 August 1920, 5; 3 July 1923, 5; T. Karis & G. Carter (eds.), *From protest to challenge*, Vol. 1 (Stanford, 1972), Document 29 (Pelem's presidential address to Bantu Union 26 February 1919), 101–4; Vol. 4 (Stanford, 1977), 126 (Pelem); Klein, "African responses in the eastern Cape," 18–19.

24. *IZ* 26 February 1924, 5.

25. *IZ* 11 September 1923, 5.

26. *IZ* 22, 29 July 1924, 5; 30 September 1924, 5; 20, 26 January 1925, 5; 28 July 1925, 5; 26 February 1929, 5.

27. Garson, "Cape franchise after union," 72.

28. *IZ* 15 January 1924, 5; 22 April 1924, 5.

29. The ICU issued the initial appeal for a convention, and it was addressed to African, Coloured, and Indian groups in all four provinces. *IZ* 15 April 1924, 5.

30. *IZ* 27 May 1924, 5.

31. *IZ* 20, 27 May 1924, 5; 3 June 1924, 5; *S.A. Outlook* 2 June 1924, 128–29.

32. On the CNVC, see *IZ,* e.g., 3, 10 June 1924, 5; 23, 30 December 1924, 5; 22, 29 December 1925, 5; 26 January 1926, 5; 23 March 1926, 5; 25 May 1926, 5; 3 August 1926, 5; 28 December 1926, 5; 3, 10 January 1928, 5; 25 September 1928, 5; 8 January 1929, 5; 26 February 1929, 5; 11 June 1929, 5.

33. Walshe, *Rise of African nationalism,* 224–27ff.

34. Karis & Carter, *From protest to challenge,* Vol. 1, Document 32 (Makgatho's presidential address to the SANNC 6 May 1919), 110.

35. *Imvo* criticized the Cape Western Congress for claiming to represent all Africans in the province and for its "exaggerated pretensions and extravagant language." *IZ* 15 January 1924, 5.

36. On Masabalala and the Port Elizabeth strike, see G. F. Baines, "The Port Elizabeth disturbances of October 1920," M.A. thesis, Rhodes University, 1988. On the ICU in the Transkei, see Bradford, *Taste of freedom,* chap. 7.

37. *IZ* 9 May 1922, 5; 14 August 1923, 5; 20 January 1925, 5; 13, 20 April 1926, 5; 26 January 1926, 5; 11 May 1926, 5; see also 17 January 1928, 5; 17 April 1928, 5; 30 October 1928, 5.

38. *IZ* 22 January 1924, 5.

39. On the ICU in East London, see W. Beinart & C. Bundy, "The union, the nation and the talking crow," in Beinart & Bundy, *Hidden struggles,* chap. 8.

40. On the Independent ICU in East London, see P. L. Wickins, *The Industrial and Commerical Workers' Union of Africa* (Cape Town, 1978), chap. 12; Beinart & Bundy, *Hidden struggles,* chap. 8.

41. Quoted by Beinart & Bundy, *Hidden struggles,* 294.

42. Ibid., 297.

43. Kadalie, who was banned from addressing meetings on the Witwatersrand after the strike trial, had moved to East London in December 1930. Like Tyamzashe and several other ICU officials, he became active in local advisory board politics in the years before his death in 1951.

44. This section is based mainly on R. R. Edgar, "Garveyism in Africa: Dr. Wellington and the 'American movement' in the Transkei, 1925–40," in *The Societies of Southern Africa in the 19th and 20th Centuries,* Vol. 6, University of London, Institute of Commonwealth Studies, October 1974–May 1975, 100–110; idem, "The fifth seal: Enoch Mgijima, the Israelites and the Bullhoek [*sic*] massacre, 1921," Ph.D. diss., University of California at Los Angeles, 1977; idem, "The prophet motive: Enoch Mgijima, the Israelites and the background to the Bullhoek massacre," *International Journal of African Historical Studies,* 15, 1982, 401–22; idem, "African educational protest in South Africa: the American school movement in the Transkei in the 1920s," in Kallaway, *Apartheid and education,* 184–91; idem, *Because they chose the plan of God: the story of the Bulhoek massacre* (Johannesburg, 1988); Hill & Pirio, " 'Africa for the Africans,' " 238–42; Bradford, *Taste of freedom,* chap. 7.

45. Quoted by Edgar, "Fifth seal," 109.

46. *Report of the Native Churches Commission,* UG 39-1925, 16–17, 31–32, 35–38.

47. On resistance in Herschel, see W. Beinart, "*Amafelandawonye* (the Die-hards): popular protest and women's movements in Herschel district in the 1920s," in Beinart & Bundy, *Hidden struggles,* chap. 7.

48. Mahabane, born at Thaba Nchu in the Orange Free State in 1881, attended the Methodist mission's theological school at Lesseyton near Queenstown and was ordained in 1914. He had been a Methodist minister in Herschel between 1910 and 1916.

49. *IZ* 3 May 1921, 5.

50. *IZ* 31 May 1921, 5.

51. On the Israelites, see *IZ* 21 December 1920, 4–5; 10, 17, 24, 31 May 1921, 5; 7, 21 June 1921, 5; 19 July 1921, 3; *Christian Express* 1 July 1921, 105–6.

52. *IZ* 29 January 1929, 5; see also 15 January 1929, 5; 14 May 1929, 5.

53. *IZ* 11 April 1922, 5.

54. The most comprehensive analysis of Hertzog's campaign to disenfranchise the Cape's African voters is by Dubow, *Racial segregation,* chaps. 5–6. In addition, this section is based on a reading of *Imvo Zabantsundu*'s English-language editorial pages between 1925 and 1937 and on various pamphlets written by D. D. T. Jabavu (cited below); C. Tatz, *Shadow and substance in South Africa: a study in land and franchise policies affecting Africans, 1910–1960* (Pietermaritzburg, 1962), chaps. 4–6; J. W. Horton, "South Africa's Joint Councils: black-white cooperation between two world wars," *South African Historical Journal,* 4, 1972, 29–44; Karis & Carter, *From protest to challenge,* Vols. 1–2; Klein, "African responses in the eastern Cape"; R. Haines, "The opposition to General Hertzog's segregation bills," unpublished paper, University of the Witwatersrand, 1978.

55. *IZ* 24 November 1925, 5.

56. For details, see Karis & Carter, *From protest to challenge,* Vol. 1, Document 39c (1925 Native Conference), 172–80. Many delegates joined the CNVC at a conference in King William's Town to protest Hertzog's proposals. *IZ* 22, 29 December 1925, 5.

57. Coloureds in the Transvaal and Orange Free State "who conformed to European standards of life and passed an education test" could elect one white representative to the House of Assembly in the next general election. Seven years thereafter, if both houses of parliament agreed, Coloureds would be given the qualified franchise in these provinces as well. Walker, *History of southern Africa,* 619–21.

58. *IZ* 14, 21, 28 December 1926, 5; Karis & Carter, *From protest to challenge,* Vol. 1, Document 39d (1926 Native Conference), 180–96. The ANC at its 1926 conference refused to acknowledge the government-sponsored Native Conferences and called for the Cape franchise to be extended to the northern provinces. Even though Kadalie had flirted with segregation and supported Hertzog in the 1924 election, ICU leaders tried unsuccessfully to coordinate with the ANC in mounting a national protest campaign in 1926, and spent much space in the union newspaper *Workers' Herald* and much time at the 1926 and 1927 national conferences condemning the "Native Bills." S.W. Johns III, "Trade union, political pressure group or mass movement? The Industrial and Commercial Workers' Union of Africa," in R. I. Rotberg & A. A. Mazrui (eds.), *Protest and power in black Africa* (New York, 1970), 718, 729.

59. *Imvo* now referred to the Native Conferences as "little more than interesting debating exhibitions on Native affairs." *IZ* 2 November 1926, 5.

60. Quoted by Haines, "Opposition to General Hertzog's segregation bills," 155.

On the joint select committees' debates between 1930 and 1935, see Tatz, *Shadow and substance*, 66–72.

61. G-M. Cockram, *Constitutional law in the Republic of South Africa* (Cape Town, 1975), 21–22. *Imvo* in desperation suggested that Africans in the Cape (and Natal "by way of tradition") should appeal to London "to be allowed to secede from the Union." In an equally futile gesture, the CNVC at an emergency meeting in Queenstown in July 1934 petitioned King George V to veto the Status Act. *IZ* 24 April 1934, 5; 17 July 1934, 5.

62. Abdurahman played a key role in rallying the Coloured and Indian delegates. Karis & Carter, *From protest to challenge*, Vol. 1, Document 44 (Non-European Conference June 1927), 257–67.

63. Quoted by Klein, "African responses in the eastern Cape," 47.

64. Dubow, *Racial segregation*, 133, 172.

65. For details on Nicholls' proposals, see R. Davenport, *South Africa: a modern history* (London & Johannesburg, 1977), 219–20. On his relationship with Dube, see Rich, *White power and the liberal conscience*, 63–66.

66. More than five hundred delegates at a Bantu Union conference in Middledrift in December 1926 had rejected the African franchise bill. Virtually all the African testimony before the 1927 select committee dealt with the African franchise bill. Karis & Carter, *From protest to challenge*, Vol. 1, Documents 40a–40b (Minutes of evidence, *Select Committee on Native Bills*, May 1927), 196–212.

67. Klein, "African responses in the eastern Cape," 74–75, 127. Klein found a single reference to the franchise bill in the proceedings of the Ciskeian General Council between 1934 and 1937. Dubow noted "substantial evidence of active African support for Hertzog" in the state archives (Pretoria), but it was impossible to determine how representative these letters were of African opinion. Dubow, *Racial segregation*, 152 and fn. 18.

68. Quoted by Haines, "Opposition to General Hertzog's segregation bills," 166–67.

69. Dubow, *Racial segregation*, 159–60.

70. Segregationist rhetoric was particularly evident in the proceedings of the European-Bantu conferences during the 1920s and 1930s, which were sponsored by the Dutch Reformed church. E.g., Karis & Carter, *From protest to challenge*, Vol. 1, Document 42b (1927 conference), 233–39.

71. Loram was a member of the Native Affairs Commission during the 1920s and chief inspector of native education in Natal. Rheinallt Jones, a prominent figure in Johannesburg's liberal intellectual community, was a founding father of the Johannesburg council along with Pim, who was an accountant with the Chamber of Mines and a city councillor.

72. Initial funding came from the Phelps-Stokes Fund and the Carnegie Corporation in the United States together with the Rhodes Trust in Britain. P. Rich, "The South African Institute of Race Relations and the debate on 'race relations,' 1929–1958," *African Studies* 40 (1), 1981, 15.

73. *IZ* 3 September 1935, 5.

74. For details on these regional conferences, see D. D. T. Jabavu, *Native views on native bills* (Lovedale, 1935).

75. The Cape delegation dominated with more than two hundred members. There

were one hundred delegates from the Transvaal, seventy from the Orange Free State, thirty from Natal, ten from Basutoland, and one from Swaziland. Eastern Cape representatives on the executive committee included D. D. T. Jabavu (as president), Richard Godlo (as recording secretary), Alexander Jabavu, Charles Sakwe, a veteran of Transkei politics, and James M. Dippa, a former ICU official from Port Elizabeth.

76. For details on the AAC conference in 1935, see D. D. T. Jabavu, *The findings of the All African Convention* (Lovedale, 1935).

77. E. Roux, *Time longer than rope: a history of the black man's struggle for freedom in South Africa* (Madison, 1964), 289. Militants were also heard during the debates, but they could not persuade their colleagues to consider the merits of mass action. Jabavu, *Findings of the All African Convention*, 34.

78. Horton, "South Africa's Joint Councils," 42.

79. "We were divided," A. B. Xuma claimed. "Some were leaning to compromise and others were against it." Quoted by Klein, "African responses in the eastern Cape," 95.

80. *IZ* 22 February 1936, 8.

81. *IZ* 11 April 1936, 7.

82. D. D. T. Jabavu, *All African Convention: presidential address* (Lovedale, 1936).

83. For details on the 1936 Convention, see Karis & Carter, *From protest to challenge*, Vol. 2, Document 12 (AAC conference 29 June–2 July 1936), 54–55.

84. Three senators, two members of the House of Assembly, one member of the Provincial Council and seven of the twelve members of the NRC were AAC candidates.

85. Her opponent was William H. Stuart, a lawyer with an African clientele (he represented Kadalie and other ICU leaders on several occasions) who had held the Thembuland (Transkei) seat in parliament for ten years. More than 75 percent of the eligible African electorate in the eastern Cape voted in the election.

86. The AAC's 1937 Statement of Policy, however, was considerably stronger and more detailed than the 1936 Programme of Action. In addition to African franchise rights, resolutions referred to land rights, wages and working conditions, education, social amenities, the role of chiefs, and economic development. The Convention also rejected Hertzog's attempts to incorporate the three protectorates—Basutoland (Lesotho), Swaziland, and Bechuanaland (Botswana)—into South Africa. For details, see Karis & Carter, *From protest to challenge*, Vol. 2, Document 14 (AAC Policy statement December 1937), 61–64.

87. *Cape Times* 11 July 1933, 8.

Chapter 9. Opposition Politics and Popular Resistance II

1. The following statistical information is taken from S.A. Bureau of Statistics, *Urban and rural population of South Africa, 1904–1960*, Report No. 02-02-01, xxxi (Table IV), 5 (Table 1.5), 158 (Table 4.1.5); Walshe, *Rise of African nationalism*, 300–303; C. E. W. Simkins, "Four essays on the past, present and possible future of the distribution of the black population of South Africa," unpublished paper, University of Cape Town, South African Labour and Development Research Unit, 1983, 39 (Appendix 2). Simkins' adjusted figures were used in establishing proportionate increases for the African population in major cities between 1936 and 1951.

2. Baruch Hirson cites the case of the African Commercial and Distributive Workers Union, whose members were the highest paid unskilled workers in the Transvaal in 1944. The minimum monthly subsistence level for a family of five in that year was still at least four pounds above what these workers were making. *Yours for the union: class and community struggles in South Africa, 1930–1947* (London, 1990), 98.

3. The number of blacks involved in strikes—they were the main strikers during the war years—reached a peak of 12,800 in 1942 (with 58 strikes) and 14,700 in 1945 (with 63 strikes). Ibid., 87 (Table 7.1).

4. The minister of native affairs told members of the NRC in December 1942 that the "Freedoms" in the Atlantic Charter were applicable to Africans in South Africa. Karis & Carter, *From protest to challenge,* Vol. 2, Document 29b (Africans' Claims in South Africa manifesto 16 December 1943), 211.

5. Quoted by Walshe, *Rise of African nationalism,* 269.

6. These included the 1941 Industrial and Agricultural Requirements Commission (Van Eck Commission), the 1942 Interdepartmental Committee on the Social Health and Economic Conditions of Urban Natives (chaired by secretary for native affairs D. L. Smit), the 1946 Social and Economic Planning Council, and the 1946–48 South African Native Laws Commission (Fagan Commission).

7. Although the Smuts government had accepted in principle that African workers could organize unions and participate marginally in the collective bargaining process, the Industrial Conciliation (Natives) Bill introduced in 1947 would have granted only limited recognition to African unions and placed restrictions on their activities. The bill was dropped when it received little support from industry and was rejected by the main nonracial trade union coordinating body, the South African Trades and Labour Council, and most independent African trade unions.

8. E.g., R. Fatton, Jr., "The African National Congress of South Africa: the limitations of a revolutionary strategy," *Canadian Journal of African Studies,* 18 (3), 1984, 593–608.

9. D. Davis & R. Fine, "Political strategies and the state: some historical observations," *Journal of Southern African Studies,* 12 (1), October 1985, 25–48. The authors offer as evidence the African political elite's weak responses to trade union activity in the years immediately preceding the 1946 miners' strike, to the call by the South African Congress of Trade Unions for a national strike in the 1958 elections, and to the massive demonstrations following the Sharpeville-Langa shootings in 1960.

10. Ibid., 45 (citing political activist and historian Ben Turok). See also R. Lambert, "Black resistance in South Africa, 1950–1961: an assessment of the political strike campaigns," *The Societies of Southern Africa in the 19th and 20th Centuries,* Vol. 10, University of London, Institute of Commonwealth Studies, October 1978–June 1979, 112–20.

11. This section is based mainly on Roux, *Time longer than rope,* chaps. 24–30; Simons & Simons, *Class and colour,* chaps. 23–25; Walshe, *Rise of African nationalism,* chaps. 11–14; Karis & Carter, *From protest to challenge,* Vol. 2, part 2; G. M. Gerhart, *Black power in South Africa: the evolution of an ideology* (Berkeley, 1978), chap. 3; T. Lodge, *Black politics in South Africa since 1945* (London & New York), chap. 1.

12. For biographical details, see Karis & Carter, *From protest to challenge,* Vol. 4, 164–66.

13. ANC membership dropped to an average of about four thousand members in 1948–49.

14. The 1943 manifesto was forwarded to Prime Minister Smuts, but he rejected its contents. For details, see Karis & Carter, *From protest to challenge*, Vol. 2, Document 29b (Africans' Claims in South Africa manifesto 16 December 1943), 209–33.

15. Ibid., Document 29a (ANC constitution adopted 16 December 1943), 204–8. The ANC leased its first permanent office next to Pixley Seme's law practice in 1943.

16. See M. Roth, "Domination by consent: elections under the Representation of Natives Act, 1937–1948," unpublished paper, University of the Witwatersrand, 1983.

17. For biographical details, see Karis & Carter, *From protest to challenge*, Vol. 4, 79–81; M. Wilson, *Freedom for my people: the autobiography of Z. K. Matthews* (Cape Town, 1983), esp. chap. 7. Matthews, who was born in Kimberley of Tswana parentage (his father, a mine worker, became a cafe owner and qualified for the vote), graduated from Fort Hare in 1923 as the first African to receive a B.A. degree from a South African university. He taught at Adams College in Natal and took advanced degrees in law and anthropology before returning to teach at Fort Hare in 1936. On D. D. T. Jabavu's retirement in 1944, he was appointed professor of African studies.

18. For biographical details, see Karis & Carter, *From protest to challenge*, Vol. 4, 16–17; Butler, "Interwar liberalism and local activism," 90–91ff. Cradock was the largest ANC branch in the Cape with one hundred members in 1940. Calata, who was born near King William's Town and educated at St. Matthew's, served as a parish priest in Cradock for more than forty years.

19. The Cape had only 519 ANC members (10.8 percent of the total), for example, in 1946 and 376 (6.8 percent of the total) in 1947.

20. For Africans aged ten and above, the literacy rate in 1946 and 1951 was about 27.6 percent and 30.9 percent, respectively. *Union statistics for fifty years*, A-22; Walshe, *Rise of African nationalism*, 384.

21. Gerhart, *Black power*, 76 (citing Lembede in 1943).

22. For biographical details, see Karis & Carter, *From protest to challenge*, Vol. 4, 55–57 (Lembede), 85–86 (Mda), 114–15 (Ngubane), 119–20 (Nkomo), 143–45 (Sisulu).

23. The AAC attempted to counter the influence of the Youth League by establishing a rival student group at Fort Hare—the Society of Young Africa—in December 1951.

24. Pitje succeeded Mda as president of the Youth League in 1949 and also gained a seat on the ANC's executive committee, but he withdrew from active politics in the early 1950s. Joe Matthews would play an important role in the 1952 Defiance Campaign and take over as head of the Youth League in the mid-1950s. Nokwe, elected national secretary of the Youth League in 1954, was secretary-general of the ANC from 1958 to 1969. For biographical details, see Karis & Carter, *From protest to challenge*, Vol. 4, 79 (Joe Matthews), 120–21 (Nokwe), 127 (Pitje).

25. Karis & Carter, *From protest to challenge*, Vol. 4, 97–99 (Moroka).

26. The Trotskyites in Cape Town apparently embraced a number of factions in addition to those which followed the teachings of Leon Trotsky: they included communists expelled from the CPSA and socialists opposed to Stalinism. C. Bundy, "Resistance in the reserves: the A.A.C. and the Transkei," *Africa Perspective*, No. 22, 1983, 61 (fn. 4).

27. Karis & Carter, *From protest to challenge,* Vol. 4, 33–34 (Goolam and Janub Gool), 37–38 (Honono), 150 (Tabata), 160–61 (Tsotsi).

28. Ibid., Vol. 2, Document 64 (AAC executive committee manifesto 26 August 1943), 351.

29. Ibid., Document 65 (AAC and anti-CAD conference 17 December 1943), 352–57.

30. For details, see I. B. Tabata, *The awakening of a people* (Nottingham, 1974), 61–67. The anti-CAD coalition had already endorsed these measures at a conference in January 1944. The SAIC was included in the unity plan even though its leaders, preoccupied with anti-Indian legislation, did not attend the conference. The conservative merchant group controlling the SAIC, however, backed out of the commitment after meeting with AAC and anti-CAD leaders in July 1944. Militants who took over in 1945 preferred to align the Indian Congress with the ANC.

31. Karis & Carter, *From protest to challenge,* Vol. 2, 129 (fn. 91).

32. Ibid., 4, 21–22 (Dadoo), 50–52 (Kotane), 75–76 (Marks), 107–8 (G. M. Naicker), 158 (Thloome).

33. E.g., Gerhart, *Black power,* 81 (Lembede in 1944 was attacking the moderate ANC leadership as "traitors and quislings" who had to be "purged"); Tabata, *Awakening of a people,* chap. 11 (on the AAC's relationship with Congress).

34. The differences between the two organizations are summarized in Karis & Carter, *From protest to challenge,* Vol. 2, 117–19.

35. Youth League attempts to oust CPSA members from the ANC in 1945 and 1947, for example, were blocked by higher-ranked moderates.

36. The African Democratic party was launched in Johannesburg in 1943 apparently out of sheer frustration with the ANC's unwillingness to get involved in the Alexandra bus boycotts. Its leaders were Paul Mosaka, who won a seat on the NRC as its youngest member in 1942, and Basner, an ex-CPSA member who won a Senate seat as a native representative in the same election. The party folded in 1944 after a dispute over tactics in the bus boycott.

37. Karis & Carter, *From protest to challenge,* Vol. 2, Document 37 (ANC conference resolutions 14–17 December 1946), 263–66.

38. Some evidence of the Youth League's prestige in African nationalist circles at this time can be discerned from the circulation figures of the ANC-aligned newspaper *Inkundla ya Bantu.* In 1943, the newspaper was attracting 500 subscribers a month. It became an unofficial (but not uncritical) organ of the Youth League from mid-1944, and two years later circulation was 7,000 a month—about 2,000 more than the official ANC membership. Bokwe, the district surgeon from Middledrift, distributed *Inkundla* in the Ciskei. Switzer & Switzer, *Black press,* 43–44.

39. The Youth League preferred Matthews as president-general, but he wanted to focus on rebuilding the ANC in the Cape. Matthews had replaced Calata as head of the Cape Congress in June 1949.

40. Karis & Carter, *From protest to challenge,* Vol. 2, Document 57 (Basic Policy of the Youth League manifesto issued in 1948), 323–31.

41. Ibid., Document 60 (Programme of Action adopted 17 December 1949), 337–39. A number of moderates, including Calata, refused to accept the new strategy and withdrew from active politics.

42. On the 1952 campaign, see D. Carter, "The Defiance Campaign—a compara-

tive analysis of the organization, leadership, and participation in the eastern Cape and the Transvaal," *The Societies of Southern Africa in the 19th and 20th Centuries*, Vol. 2, University of London, Institute of Commonwealth Studies, October 1970–June 1971, 76–97; Gerhart, *Black power*, chaps. 4–5; Lodge, *Black politics*, chap. 2.

43. Gerhart, *Black power*, 94.

44. On the ANC and the various congresses in the mid–late 1950s, see Gerhart, *Black power*, 101–23; Lodge, *Black politics*, chap. 3.

45. Karis & Carter, *From protest to challenge*, Vol. 2, Document 11 ("The Freedom Charter" adopted by the Congress of the People, 25 June 1955), 205. Gerhart stresses the liberal-democratic perspective. Gerhart, *Black power*, 93–101ff.

46. Quoted by Lodge, *Black politics*, 73; S. Archer, "Economic means and political ends in the Freedom Charter," in Butler, Elphick & Welsh, *Democratic liberalism in South Africa*, 335–52.

47. Cf. Gerhart, *Black power*, chaps. 6–7; Lodge, *Black politics*, chaps. 9–10.

48. Lodge, *Black politics*, 268. For an overview of events in South Africa's reserves during the period, see Lodge, *Black politics*, chap. 11; M. Chaskalson, "Rural resistance in the 1940s and 1950s," *Africa Perspective*, New Series 1 (5–6), December 1987, 47–59. Colin Bundy offers a brief comparison between the "hidden struggles" of the 1920s and the early 1940s–early 1960s in *Remaking the past*, 50–57.

49. Unless otherwise noted, the following paragraphs are based on J. Hyslop, "Food, authority and politics: student riots in South Africa, 1945–1976," *Africa Perspective*, New Series 1 (3 & 4), June 1987, 3–41; White, "Lovedale 1930–1955," chap. 4; J. Bolnick, "Preparing the *petty-bourgeoisie* for privilege—mission school education in the 20's, 30's and 40's," unpublished paper, University of Cape Town, 1988, esp. 10–17.

50. CGC, e.g., 1946 *Proceedings*, 19–20 (Minute No. 11—Strikes at native colleges and institutions); 1949 *Proceedings*, 53 (Minute No. 31—Disturbances at native institutions); 1950 *Proceedings*, 54–55 (Minute No. 21—Expulsion of Zwelitsha vocational school trainees); 1953 *Proceedings*, 40–41 (Minute No. 20, Item No. 44—Disturbances at native educational institutions).

51. Hyslop, "Food, authority and politics," 16–17.

52. There were instances of teachers addressing their students as "baboons" and "kaffirs." Bolnick, "Preparing the *petty-bourgeoisie* for privilege," 13.

53. As D. D. T. Jabavu had perceived in the case of Lovedale as early as 1920: "in our schools 'manual labour' consists of sweeping yards, repairing roads, cracking stones, and so on, and is done by boys only as so much task work, enforced by a time keeper, and under threats of punishment. It is defended because 'it makes for character training.' The inevitable result is that the boys grow up to hate all manual work as humiliating." White, "Lovedale 1930–1955," 50 (as cited).

54. Tim White accepts the view that war veterans with their "egalitarian notions" led the students, but tensions at Lovedale had been building for at least two years before the 1946 riot. Ibid., 112.

55. Hyslop, "Food, authority and politics," 14. The mission authorities in almost every case used harsh methods to quell the riots. The police were brought in, students were arrested and expelled. In the case of Lovedale, the riot lasted for three days, and 237 students (representing more than two-thirds of the student body) were involved. All

but 40 of the 197 pupils temporarily expelled from Lovedale were arrested by the police and charged with public violence, and the school was closed for nine weeks in the aftermath of these disturbances. Nevertheless, the missionaries at Lovedale employed lawyers to represent their students and provided those in jail with food and blankets. Most expelled students were allowed to return to school when it was reopened.

56. CGC, e.g., 1947 *Proceedings*, 31–32 (Minute No. 16—Fencing of Betterment areas); 1951 *Proceedings*, 29–33 (Minute No. 1, Item No. 42—Rehabilitation of native reserves: consent of natives a prerequisite); Walker, *Kaffirs are lively*, 183–85; M. Wilson, S. Kaplan, T. Maki & E. M. Walton, *Social structure*, Vol. 3, *Keiskammahoek Rural Survey* (Pietermaritzburg, 1952), 180–81, 185; Tabata, *Awakening of a people*, 68–70.

57. Unless otherwise noted, the following paragraphs are based on A. Mager, " 'Things of the Trust': gender, rehabilitation and the South African Native Trust in the Ciskei, 1945–1953," unpublished paper, University of Natal, 1991.

58. Ibid., 23.

59. Ibid., 29.

60. On the AAC in the Transkei, see Tabata, *Awakening of a people;* Lodge, *Black politics*, 86–87; Bundy, "Resistance in the reserves," 51–61. The role of Govan Mbeki in the revival of dissident politics in the Transkei during the 1940s is briefly summarized by Colin Bundy in his introduction to *Learning from Robben Island: the prison writings of Govan Mbeki* (London, Athens, Ohio, & Cape Town, 1991). Mbeki became a national figure in the resistance movement during the 1950s and 1960s.

61. The average age at marriage for men increased from 24.3 to 30.1 and for women from 19.3 to 23.6 between 1890 and 1949. Mager, " 'Things of the Trust,' " 30 (fn. 15).

62. Councillors could be substituted for chiefs in locations where there were no chiefs. In instances where these authorities did not exist—which included many locations in the Ciskei reserve—adult male members of the community could elect their own representatives.

63. The following quotations are from Mager, " 'Thing of the Trust,' " 13, 15–16, 20–21, 29.

64. The peasants in Peddie District, for example, resisted the dipping of goats. As "poor men's cattle" in the *lobola* system, goats were also a source of food and ritual sacrifice "in times of sickness, death or hardship," and a weapon "empowered with 'Xhosa magic' " when confronting the authorities.

65. E.g., Mayer & Mayer, *Townsmen or tribesmen*, esp. part 2 ("Resisting urbanization").

66. Reader, *Black man's portion*, 23, 42–43, 51–52, 161 (Table 17).

67. Houghton, *Economic development in a plural society*, 212 (Table 106), 247 (Table 149), 248, 317 (Table 169); cf. Reader, *Black man's portion*, chap. 4.

68. Unless otherwise noted, the following paragraphs are based on A. Mager & G. Minkley, "Reaping the whirlwind: the East London riots of 1952," unpublished paper, University of the Witwatersrand, History Workshop, 1990.

69. Ibid., 8. Police intimidation made matters even worse. Predawn raids were commonplace, since lucrative activities like beer brewing were still illegal. Residents were also subject to random inspections that were gross invasions of privacy. If lice

were found on one person in a household, for example, all inhabitants would be forced to have their bodies sprayed with disinfectant, their heads shaved, and their clothes boiled.

70. Ibid., 9.

71. Ibid., 8–13.

72. Ibid., 15.

73. Ibid., 16.

74. This section is based on E. Feit, *African opposition in South Africa* (Stanford, 1967), chap. 5; Karis & Carter, *From protest to challenge,* Vol. 3, 29–35; Lodge, *Black politics,* chaps. 5, 11.

Chapter 10. African Labor and the State in the Apartheid Era

1. S. B. Greenberg, *Legitimating the illegitimate: state, markets, and resistance in South Africa* (Berkeley, Los Angeles & London, 1987), 13–26. See also D. du Toit, *Capital and labour in South Africa* (London & Boston, 1981), chap. 10; P. Frankel, N. Pines & M. Swilling (eds.), *State resistance and change in southern Africa* (London, 1988), chap. 1.

2. Greenberg, *Legitimating the illegitimate,* chap. 2; see also L. Platzky & C. Walker (comps.), *The surplus people: forced removals in South Africa* (Johannesburg, 1985), chap. 3.

3. The Group Areas Act (1950), which established segregated residential areas for all designated racial groups in South Africa, was applied mainly to Coloureds and Indians from the 1960s.

4. The only labor-recruiting agency operating outside the control of the administration boards was The Employment Bureau of Africa (TEBA), the mine-recruiting organization run by the Chamber of Mines.

5. M. Savage, "Pass laws and the disorganisation and reorganisation of the African population of South Africa," unpublished paper, University of Cape Town, Second Carnegie Inquiry into Poverty and Development in Southern Africa, 1984, 9–11, 20; Greenberg, *Legitimating the illegitimate,* 48.

6. The increase in food production in white rural areas due to mechanization and the use of fertilizers and insecticides actually had an ambiguous impact on the labor force. The area under cultivation between 1937 and 1971 virtually doubled, and by the end of the 1960s more than 50 percent of South Africa's agricultural exports were being processed by secondary industry inside the country. The number of white farming units decreased about 24 percent (1937–1974), and there was a corresponding decrease in the white rural population. Coloured and Indian workers also abandoned white farms in record numbers at this time, since very little money was being spent on improving the quality of the labor force and wages remained very low. The percentage of African farm workers and farm domestics continued to increase. Africans constituted 72.6 percent of the total agricultural labor force on white farms, for example, in 1960 and 78.9 percent in 1969. R. Africa, "Mechanisation in South African agriculture, 1936–1974," unpublished paper, University of Cape Town, Southern Africa Labour and Development Research Unit (hereafter SALDRU), 1976; Platzky & Walker, *Surplus people,* 30–32.

7. A. Baldwin, "Mass removals and separate development," *Journal of Southern African Studies,* 1 (2), 1975, 215–27; H. Joffe, "Rural resettlement in South Africa,"

Africa Perspective, No. 6, August 1977, 13–31; G. Mare, *African population relocation in South Africa: an overview of the 1970s* (Johannesburg, 1980); G. Mare, "Processes, policies and African population relocation," and C. E. W. Simkins, "The economic implications of African resettlement," in D. Thomas (ed.), *Resettlement* (Johannesburg, 1981), 1–45; E. Walt, *South Africa: a land divided* (Johannesburg, 1982); N. Muller, "Rural welfare and constrained urbanisation in South Africa," in P. H. Spies (ed.), *Urban-rural interaction in South Africa* (Stellenbosch, 1983), 45–76; Simkins, "The economic implications of African resettlement," unpublished paper, University of Cape Town, SALDRU, 1981; idem, "Four essays"; Platzky & Walker, *Surplus people*, chap. 2; Greenberg, *Legitimating the illegitimate*, chaps. 3–4.

8. About 1.1 million were removed from white farms, roughly 1.3 million from rural "black spots," white metropolitan areas, and land incorporated in various reserves, and 860,000 were evicted under the Group Areas Act (1950). A small percentage of Africans were also resettled to secure South Africa's northern and eastern borders, to make way for highways and dams, or to preserve conservation areas (mainly wild game parks).

9. The shift to domestic mine labor was prompted in part by the actions of other African states. Tanzania banned recruitment in 1962 and Zambia in 1966. Malawi suspended recruitment in 1974 following a plane crash in which 74 Malawian miners were killed, and the crucial migrant miner population from Mozambique declined by almost 60 percent within a year after independence in 1975. D. Yudelman & A. Jeeves, "New labour frontiers for old: black migrants to the South African gold mines, 1920–85," *Journal of Southern African Studies*, 14 (1), October 1986, 116–18ff.

10. Simkins, "Four essays," 59–61 (Table 3).

11. Ibid., 118, 153. Between 1960 and 1980, the "closer settlement" population—resettled, nonfarm communities—rose from "virtually nothing" to 3.7 million or an estimated one-third of the population in the reserves.

12. Greenberg, *Legitimating the illegitimate*, 64.

13. For developments in local government, see R. Omond, *The apartheid handbook* (New York, 1986), 47–52. Coloured and Indian local authorities were upgraded with the Promotion of Local Government Affairs Act (1983).

14. Greenberg, *Legitimating the illegitimate*, 95.

15. Quoted by S. Devereux, "South African income distribution, 1900–1980," unpublished paper, University of Cape Town, SALDRU, 1983, 35.

16. The other trendsetters in raising African wages during the 1970s were manufacturing and government services. The wage gap between whites and Africans apparently declined slightly in real terms for mining and government services but increased slightly for manufacturing. Africans also replaced poor whites in government service. An estimated 58 percent of the African work force was employed in the public sector, for example, by 1977. Ibid., 43–49.

17. Class divisions within South Africa's black population in the 1970s are discussed in S. C. Nolutshungu, *Changing South Africa: political considerations* (Cape Town, 1983), chap. 4; Devereux, "South African income distribution"; S. Schneier, "Occupational mobility among blacks in South Africa," unpublished paper, University of Cape Town, SALDRU, 1983.

18. Cf. Devereux, "South African income distribution," 50–61; Schneier, "Occupational mobility among blacks," 51–52, 56.

19. Devereux, "South African income distribution," 55 (citing Simkins).

20. This section applies an aspect of dependency theory—the concept of internal colonies within nation states—to South Africa and its peripheral reserves. See especially H. Wolpe, "The theory of internal colonialism: the South African case," in I. Oxaal, T. Barnett & D. Booth (eds.), *Beyond the sociology of development: economy and society in Latin America and Africa* (London, 1975), 229–52; M. Legassick & H. Wolpe, "The bantustans and capital accumulation in South Africa," *Review of African Political Economy*, No. 7, September–December 1976, 87–107; A. M. D. Humphrey, "The changing role of the reserves," *Africa Perspective*, No. 6, August 1977, 32–45; F. Molteno, "The historical significance of the bantustan strategy," *Social Dynamics*, 3 (2), 1977, 15–33; and R. J. Hind, "The internal colonial concept," *Comparative Studies in Society and History*, 26 (3), July 1984, 543–68.

21. There is a vast literature on South Africa's reserves during the apartheid era. For this section, see 1955 *Tomlinson Commission;* J. P. Nieuwenhuysen, "Economic policy in the reserves since the Tomlinson report," *South African Journal of Economics*, 3 (1), 1964, 3–25; M. Horrell, *The African homelands of South Africa* (Johannesburg, 1973); R. Blausten, "Foreign investment in the black homelands of South Africa," *African Affairs*, 75 (229), April 1976, 208–23; B. Rogers, *Divide and rule: South Africa's bantustans* (London, 1980); Knight & Lenta, "Has capitalism underdeveloped the labour reserves of South Africa?"; W. H. Thomas, "Financing socio-economic development in the black homelands of South Africa," *Journal of Contemporary African Studies*, 1 (1), October 1981, 141–65; J. Yawitch, *Betterment: the myth of homeland agriculture* (Johannesburg, 1982); S. van den Berg, "An overview of the position in the black national states," N. Muller, "Rural welfare and constrained urbanisation in South Africa," H. B. Giliomee, "The impact of the flow of migrant and commuter labour in the development and underdevelopment of the black reserves and homelands," in Spies, *Urban-rural interaction in South Africa*, chaps. 3–5; Platzky & Walker, *Surplus people*, chaps. 5, 9; A. Lemon, *Apartheid in transition* (Boulder, 1987), chap. 8.

22. 1955 *Tomlinson Commission*, 200.

23. The commissioners surveyed 900 reserve farmers, of whom 111 were presumed to be engaged in full-time farming with an average gross income of £56.6 a year. Estimates of minimum incomes required for full-time farming in the reserves at the time ranged from £100 to £200. Ibid., 113–14.

24. The commissioners estimated the permanent farming population would eventually comprise 357,000 farm units (or 2.14 million people), when the reserves were expanded to the limits imposed under the 1936 Land Act. Ibid., 114–18.

25. The Natives' Taxation and Development Act of 1958 raised the general tax imposed on all adult African males (18–64 years of age) from 20 to 35 shillings. Men and women earning above £180 a year would pay a higher tax rate, and special "tribal" levies would be enforced in individual reserves. Nieuwenhuysen, "Economic policy in the reserves since the Tomlinson report," 11–13. Chiefs were now responsible for tax dodgers in the reserves, and convictions rose from 48,000 to 179,000 between 1950 and 1960. Lodge, *Black politics*, 266.

26. Yawitch, *Betterment*, 41 (citing reserves in the northern Transvaal).

27. *South African Labour Bulletin* provided an ongoing critique of the government's labor edicts. On the Riekert Commission, for example, see *SALB*, 5(4), November 1979.

28. Critics offered additional reasons for the lack of industrial development inside the reserves. Resources were being drained to feed the border industries, money available for loans to promote African entrepreneurs was limited, the criteria used in selecting candidates were too restrictive, and interest rates were too high. The development corporations were also controlled by white officials who rarely consulted their African counterparts when establishing economic priorities for the reserves.

29. Most Ciskeians lived at or below the minimum subsistence levels established for African households in South Africa. In two rural Ciskei districts (Victoria East and Middledrift) surveyed in December 1964–January 1965, for example, 91 percent of household incomes were below this level. Up to 50 percent of 300 urban households were below this level in a 1976 survey (Mdantsane). J. Maree & P. J. de Vos, *Underemployment, poverty and migrant labour in the Transkei and Ciskei* (Johannesburg, 1975), 22 (Table 4); N. Charton, "The legislature," in N. Charton (ed.), *Ciskei: economics and politics of dependence in a South African homeland* (London, 1980), 21.

30. On political and territorial developments, see University of Fort Hare, *The Ciskei, a Bantu homeland: a general survey* (Alice, 1971), chap. 9 (C. C. S. Holdt); J. Peires, "Continuity and change in Ciskei chiefship," *The Societies of Southern Africa in the 19th and 20th Centuries*, Vol. 8, University of London, Institute of Commonwealth Studies, October 1976–June 1977, 133–42; G. R. Tywakadi, "The development of the political party system in the Ciskei," M.A. thesis, Rhodes University, 1977; Charton, *Ciskei;* 1980 *Report of the Ciskei Commission,* Government Notice No. 14, 1980 (hereafter 1980 *Quail Commission*); P. Green & A. Hirsch, "The Ciskei—the political economy of control," *South African Labour Bulletin,* 7 (4 & 5), February 1982, 65–85; L. Switzer, *Media and dependency in South Africa: a case study of the press and the Ciskei "homeland"* (Athens, OH, 1985); D. J. A. Edwards, "Political identity among South African blacks in and near a contemporary homeland," *International Journal of Psychology,* 22, 1987, 39–55; unnamed author, "Ethnicity and pseudo-ethnicity in the Ciskei," in L. Vail (ed.), *The creation of tribalism in southern Africa* (London, Berkeley & Los Angeles, 1989), 395–413.

31. Competing claims to chieftaincies in the Ciskei were difficult to resolve because government ethnologists rarely had empirical evidence. Chiefly allegiances did not always correspond to location boundaries, and a significant number of people within the reserve were not formally subordinate to any "tribal" authority figure.

32. The successors to the Ngqika chief Sandile were still the acknowledged paramounts of the Rharhabe Xhosa. Exiled to the Transkei following the War of 1877–78, the family (*sans* territory and subjects) was returned to the Ciskei in 1961 to promote the policy of Bantu Authorities.

33. The proportion of seconded white officials in the Ciskei government declined from 25 percent in 1969 to 3.1 percent in 1977. D. M. Groenewald, "The administrative system in the Ciskei," in Charton, *Ciskei,* 93.

34. N. Charton, "The legislature," in Charton, *Ciskei,* 155.

35. Sebe allegedly withheld development funds from Tribal/Community Authorities represented by opposition chiefs. SAIRR, 1981 *Survey,* 297.

36. For a summary of African political opinion surveys conducted in the mid–late 1970s in the eastern Cape, see Switzer, *Media and dependency,* 19–27.

37. Green & Hirsch, "The Ciskei—the political economy of control," 74.

38. There were 11 proclaimed white towns or villages in the reserve in 1960,

including Seymour, Braunschweig, Whittlesea, Frankfort, and the magisterial seats of Alice, Keiskammahoek, Peddie, and Middledrift. G. P. Cook, "Scattered towns or an urban system?" in Charton, *Ciskei,* 34 (Table 3.1).

39. 1980 *Quail Commission,* 53. Stockenstrom District was absorbed by the reserve.

40. Ibid., 115, 118, 123–26.

41. Sebe did not need a referendum. Judge D. Cloete of the Grahamstown Supreme Court ruled that South Africa's parliament had the right to confer independence on the Ciskei regardless of whether the Ciskeians wanted it or not! Surplus People Project, *Forced removals in South Africa,* Vol. 2, *The Eastern Cape* (Cape Town, 1983), 34, 39.

42. About 80 percent of those eligible inside Ciskei and 45 percent outside Ciskei voted in the referendum. Students and trade union leaders were detained, and the voters, roughly 50 percent of whom were illiterate, cast their ballots in the presence of a CNIP-aligned polling officer and two witnesses. N. Charton, "The decision for independence," *South African Outlook,* 112 (1327), January 1982, 3; Human Awareness Programme, *Ciskei: an assessment,* Johannesburg, Special Report No. 2, September 1981, 46–47.

43. Unlike other regions of rural South Africa, only a small percentage of Africans removed from white farms in the eastern Cape were illegal squatters.

44. Mdantsane was established in 1962, and proclaimed a town and absorbed by the reserve in 1966. Africans from King William's Town and Queenstown, the other main urban settlements in the Ciskei region, were moved, respectively, to Zwelitsha and to a site (Ezibeleni) that is now in the Transkei.

45. Charton, "The legislature," 165. According to the Surplus People Project, estimates ranged from 32,000 to 40,000. According to Green and Hirsch, about 50,000 from these districts (including Sotho speakers who felt they were discriminated against in the Transkei and impoverished migrants who lived a tenuous existence on white farms in the Orange Free State) were resettled in Ciskei. They were relocated in the Hewu District on sheep farms formerly occupied by seventeen white families. Surplus People Project, *Eastern Cape,* 108; P. Green & A. Hirsch, "The impact of resettlement in the Ciskei: three case studies," unpublished paper, University of Cape Town, SALDRU, 1983, 15.

46. For details, see Surplus People Project, *Eastern Cape,* 65–111.

47. N. Charton, "Resettlement in the Ciskei," unpublished paper, University of Stellenbosch, Unit for Futures Research, Workshop on Urban-Rural Interaction in South Africa, June 1982, Table 4.

48. Ibid., 11; 1980 *Quail Commission,* 15 (Table 1), 19 (Table 2), 20; Walt, *South Africa: a land divided,* 23.

49. Estimates of the so-called de jure population (Africans regarded as part of the Ciskei Xhosa ethnic group regardless of where they lived) differed dramatically because there was no agreement on the definition of a Ciskei Xhosa. The Ciskei Commission based its figure on the number of Ciskeian migrants employed in the gold mines (17,000), legally resident in white cities and towns (753,000) and on white farms (397,000), and illegally resident or otherwise living in designated white rural areas (265,000). By 1982, for example, removals were pending for at least 477,000 people in the eastern Cape alone, a major portion of whom would probably be resettled in the

Ciskei reserve. 1980 *Quail Commission,* 79 (Table 14); Surplus People Project, *Eastern Cape,* 166–71.

50. Surplus People Project, *Eastern Cape,* 41.

51. According to Charton, 78,629 persons were living in "closer-settlement" camps, 96,066 in peri-urban areas, and 208,326 in designated urban townships in 1980. "Resettlement in the Ciskei," Table 4 (as summarized).

52. J. B. McI. Daniel, "Agricultural development in the Ciskei: review and assessment," *South African Geographical Journal,* 63 (1), 1981, 20.

53. Mdantsane contained at least 70 percent and Zwelitsha about 23 percent of the urban population. Five African townships were proclaimed before the 1975 consolidation proposals. They included two "closer-settlement" camps (Dimbaza and Sada) and three villages that did not qualify as urban areas in terms of the census. With consolidation, there were apparently seventeen urban townships in the Ciskei, including the new capital of Bisho (about 4 ½ miles from King William's Town) established in 1981. Cook, "Scattered towns or an urban system?" 38; 1980 *Quail Commission,* 33–34, 67. See also G. Cook & J. Opland (eds.), *Mdantsane: transitional city* (Grahamstown, 1980).

54. For information on health services in the Ciskei, see H. Engelbrecht, R. Fincham & D. Selvan, "Health facilities and socio-economic aspects of disease in the Ciskei region," unpublished paper, University of Cape Town, SALDRU, 1978; Community Health Research Project, "Health and health services in the Ciskei," unpublished paper, University of Cape Town, SALDRU, 1983; G. Ellis, D. Muir & D. Budlender, "Ciskei health survey," B. Schweitzer, "Gastro-enteritis in the Ciskei," R. J. Fincham & G. C. Thomas, "Nutritional intervention: a Ciskei and eastern Cape perspective," M. Roberts & M. Rip, "Black fertility patterns: Cape Town and the Ciskei," unpublished papers, University of Cape Town, Second Carnegie Inquiry into Poverty and Development in Southern Africa, 1984; R. J. Fincham, "A geographical analysis of nutrition in the eastern Cape and Ciskei," Ph.D. diss., Rhodes University, 1984, part 2.

55. Whites had 5.03 hospital beds per 1,000 population in the Cape, 6.27 in the Transvaal, 7.07 in the Orange Free State, and 7.50 in Natal in 1979. Community Health Research Project, "Health and health services in the Ciskei," 25.

56. This calculation assumes the equivalent of 72 full-time doctors in the reserve in 1980, although there were actually 53 full-time and 19 part-time doctors. The Ciskei government claimed it had 90 doctors (71 full time and 19 part time) in 1981. At least 53 percent of the white population in the Ciskei region lived in communities where the doctor-population ratio was 1:1,900 or less. Ibid., 24–26.

57. An estimated R1 million was needed in 1980, for example, to provide fortified maize and milk to malnourished schoolchildren, but only R60,000 was available. Human Awareness Programme, *Ciskei: an assessment,* 25, 30–31 (Table 3); Surplus People Project, *Eastern Cape,* 56 (Table 8).

58. For an evaluation of health-care administration in the Ciskei, see Community Health Research Project, "Health and health services in the Ciskei," 17–33.

59. Ibid., 34–39; SAIRR, 1981 *Survey,* 398.

60. Engelbrecht, Fincham & Selvan, "Health facilities and socio-economic aspects of disease in the Ciskei region," 49. Two of the five hospitals—Grey (King William's Town) and Fort Beaufort—were located outside the homeland. The figure is based on a 10 percent sample of all diseases recorded by these hospitals in 1977.

61. This section is based mainly on Horrell, *African homelands of South Africa,* 109–11; 1980 *Quail Commission,* section 3 (Economics), 66–71; Surplus People Project, *Eastern Cape,* parts 1, 3; Green & Hirsch, "The Ciskei—the political economy of control"; idem, "The impact of resettlement in the Ciskei," unpublished paper, University of Cape Town, Second Carnegie Inquiry into Poverty and Development in Southern Africa, 1984.

62. According to a survey conducted in 1979, East London's manufacturers, producing mainly food, textiles, and radio-television equipment, imported at least 70 percent of their materials from outside the Ciskei region. More than 50 percent of all industrial goods were exported to other metropolitan areas. D. Dewar, A. Todes & V. Watson, "Theories of urbanization and national settlement strategy in South Africa," unpublished paper, University of Cape Town, 1982, 70.

63. Two major incentives were offered to potential domestic and foreign investors. First, most of the start-up costs would be subsidized with ready-made factories (often built to specifications) at low rents, loans (up to 50 percent) at low interest rates, paid moving expenses, rail and harbor rebates for goods moving to and from the reserve, tax rebates, price preferences on government tenders, and full indemnity in the unlikely event of nationalization. Second, minimum wage and working conditions applicable to workers in South Africa for the most part were suspended, and trade unions were banned from the reserve in 1980.

64. The CNDC was still financed by the Bantu Investment Corporation (renamed the Corporation for Economic Development). The Ciskei and South African governments each selected five of the ten CNDC directors. The Native Trust (now the Development Trust) was still responsible for buying land and developing the reserve's infrastructure.

65. Surplus People Project, *Eastern Cape,* 51; SAIRR, 1981 *Survey,* 316–17.

66. Plautsky & Walker, *Surplus people,* 347; Green & Hirsch, "Impact of resettlement in the Ciskei," 29 (Table 5), 33 (Table 7).

67. The average cost per job was R10,523 for CNDC-subsidized activities in the Ciskei as a whole that year. SAIRR, 1981 *Survey,* 316.

68. Green & Hirsch, "Impact of resettlement in the Ciskei," 32, 125–28 (Appendix B).

69. There is an extensive literature on agricultural conditions in the Ciskei reserve for this period. See Houghton & Walton, *The economy of a native reserve;* and M. E. E. Mills and M. Wilson, *Land tenure,* Vol. 4, Keiskammahoek Rural Survey (Pietermaritzburg, 1952); R. R. Baker, "Agricultural progress in the Ciskei," *Bantu,* 7, 1960, 139–45; O. F. Raum & E. J. de Jager, *Transition and change in a rural community* (Alice, 1972); 1980 *Quail Commission,* Section III (Economics), 71–76; C. W. Manona, "Labour migration, marriage and family life in a Ciskei village," M.A. thesis, Rhodes University, 1981; J. B. McI. Daniel & N. L. Webb, "The image of agriculture in two Ciskeian rural communities," in Charton, *Ciskei,* chap. 4; BENSO, *The republic of Ciskei: a nation in transition* (Pretoria, 1981); J. B. McI.Daniel, "Agricultural development in the Ciskei," and G. G. Antrobus, "Irrigation farming," *South African Outlook,* January 1982 (special issue on the Ciskei); Green & Hirsch, "The Ciskei—the political economy of control"; Surplus People Project, *Eastern Cape,* parts 1, 3; *Report of the Commission of Inquiry into the Economic Development of the Republic of Ciskei,* Decem-

ber 1983 (hereafter 1983 *Swart Commission*); Green & Hirsch, "Impact of resettlement in the Ciskei," J. Daniel, "Man-land relationships in the eastern Cape," and S. Bekker, "Levels of living in Ciskei: a quantitative and qualitative analysis," unpublished papers, University of Cape Town, Second Carnegie Inquiry into Poverty and Development in Southern Africa, April 1984; S. Bekker, "The new regional development policy: some comments from an eastern Cape perspective 'Region D,'" Bekker, P. A. Black & A. D. Roux, "Development issues in Ciskei," and Bekker & C. E. B. Hughes, "Perspectives on rural development in Ciskei," unpublished papers, Rhodes University, Institute of Social and Economic Research, 1982–84; C. J. de Wet, "An analysis of the social and economic consequences of residential relocation arising out of the implementation of an agricultural development scheme in a rural Ciskei village," Ph.D. diss., Rhodes University, 1985; C. de Wet & S. Bekker (eds.), *Rural development in South Africa: a case-study of the Amatola Basin in the Ciskei* (Pietermaritzburg, 1985).

70. Surplus People Project, *Eastern Cape*, 54 (citing pamphlet issued by the Ciskei's Department of Agriculture and Forestry).

71. Daniel, "Agricultural development in the Ciskei," 19.

72. Green & Hirsch, "The Ciskei—the political economy of control," 71, 73–74 (percentage is drawn from their assessment of estimated employment in various sectors of the economy).

73. 1980 *Quail Commission*, 60 (Table 7); Surplus People Project, *Eastern Cape*, 44.

74. 1980 *Quail Commission*, 82 (Table 15); SAIRR, 1983 *Survey*, 320–21, 340–41. Indirect aid was in the form of company taxes, development loans, limited borrowing on South Africa's capital markets, and customs duties collected on behalf of the Ciskei by the South African government.

75. It is impossible to gauge accurately the distribution and employment of labor and the unemployment rate inside the reserve between 1970 and 1980. Cf. N. D. Muller, "Spatial and racial dimensions of selected socio-demographic indicators in South Africa," unpublished paper, University of Stellenbosch, Unit for Futures Research, 1982, 20 (Table 2.1); Surplus People Project, *Eastern Cape*, 57–58; Green & Hirsch, "The Ciskei—the political economy of control," 69, 74; Bekker, "Levels of living in Ciskei," 7.

76. 1980 *Quail Commission*, 63; Surplus People Project, *Eastern Cape*, 47, 51; Green & Hirsch, "Impact of resettlement in the Ciskei," 39 (rural wages per month); 1983 *Swart Commission*, 9.

77. On the Sebe regime's economic policies in the 1980s, see P. A. Black, P. J. McCartan & P. M. Clayton, "The industrial development policy of the Ciskei," unpublished paper, Institute of Social and Economic Research, Rhodes University, 1986; R. Tomlinson, "From decentralisation concessions to a tax free option: changing industrial decentralisation policy in the Ciskei," M.B.A. research report, University of the Witwatersrand, 1986. New economic strategies pledged funding for dryland farmers and entrepreneurs in the hitherto unrecognized informal sector, which embraced perhaps one-third of the Ciskei's economic activities.

78. J. de Villiers (ed.), *The Good Hope Plan for southern Africa* (Pretoria, 1981), 70–73.

Chapter 11. The Legacy of the Ciskei in South Africa

1. Platzky & Walker, *Surplus people*, 374.

2. For details, see P. Rich, "Liberals, radicals and the politics of black consciousness, 1969–76," unpublished paper, University of Cape Town, 1989.

3. Ciskei employees, for example, were prohibited from joining BC organizations or participating in their activities. Nolutshungu, *Changing South Africa*, 202 (fn. 13).

4. Adopting Gramsci's term "war of position" to define the new discourse, Robert Fatton writes: "In this war of position, the fundamental objective is not the conquest of state power as such, but the frontal assault on the cultural and ideological hegemony of the ruling classes. . . . Black Consciousness . . . diffused a counter-hegemony which transformed hitherto apathetic men and women into potentially revolutionary subjects." R. Fatton, Jr., *Black consciousness in South Africa* (Albany, N.Y., 1986), 128.

5. Ibid., 69 (as quoted).

6. S. Biko, *I write what I like* (London, 1978), 20, 24–25.

7. Fatton, *Black consciousness*, 77 (as quoted).

8. These included representatives of the Negritude movement in West Africa (especially Leopold Senghor and Cheikh Ante Diop), Zambian President Kenneth Kaunda's concept of African "humanism," and Tanzanian President Julius Nyerere's commitment to *Ujamaa* and the spirit of cooperative self-reliance. The writings of Frantz Fanon (especially *Wretched of the earth*) and American Black Power advocates like Eldridge Cleaver, Stokely Carmichael, Charles Hamilton, and James Cone (on black theology) were widely read. Gerhart, *Black power*, 270–81.

9. Fatton, *Black consciousness*, 67.

10. For a critical analysis of Black Consciousness as an ideology, cf. Nolutshungu, *Changing South Africa*, chap. 5; Fatton, *Black consciousness*, chaps. 4–5.

11. Biko, *I write what I like*, 91–92.

12. Nolutshungu, *Changing South Africa*, 193.

13. Ibid., 173.

14. Ibid., 169, 191; see also Gerhart, *Black power*, 270, 293. SASO claimed four thousand subscribers for its *SASO Newsletter*.

15. Gerhart, *Black power*, 296–97.

16. BCP had a staff of fifty and a payroll of about R66,000 (about $92,400) in 1978. Another four hundred workers were indirectly dependent on the organization's activities. BCP was funded mainly by European church groups, and it had an operating budget of more than R500,000 (about $700,000) just before it was banned. Nolutshungu, *Changing South Africa*, 203 (fn. 16).

17. Biko worked for BCP in its Durban office for seven months until he was banned in March 1973. He was forced to resign in December 1975, when he was served with another restriction order. D. Woods, *Biko* (New York, 1987), 150–51 (citing Biko).

18. Ibid., 160–61 (citing Biko).

19. Nolutshungu, *Changing South Africa*, 188–93, 202 (fn. 12). Drake Koka, a trade unionist, was recruited by SASO and placed on the BPC executive committee to help organize industrial workers, and a Black Workers' Project was set up in 1971. Differences within the leadership over the most appropriate models and methods to employ in setting up unions led to a breakaway effort by Koka to establish the Black

Allied Workers' Union. This body was not as politicized or as class conscious as the Black Workers' Council, which was created by SASO in 1972 to organize workers. The students, however, had very little success. Their main achievement was the Union of Black Journalists, which was limited almost entirely to newspaper men and women working in Johannesburg.

20. The defendants were finally convicted in December 1976 and received sentences of five to ten years on Robben Island.

21. Fatton, *Black consciousness*, 92 (citing Njabulo Ndebele in 1972 *Black Viewpoint*). One paper at the Black Renaissance Convention organized in 1974, for example, distinguished between the "discrimination" experienced by the black petty bourgeoisie and the "exploitation" experienced by black workers: "An end to discrimination . . . might only mean that there would be equal competition between black and white for positions among the exploiters . . . the functionaries have an interest in the abolition of discrimination while the workers have an interest in the abolition of exploitation." Fatton feels this distinction marked a fundamental shift in the discourse of Black Consciousness. Ibid., 90.

22. Biko told a visiting journalist in August 1976 that Black Consciousness did not have an "armed struggle wing"—this would be left to Congress and the PAC. Woods, *Biko*, 127 (citing John Burns of the *New York Times*). The attempt by Woods to depict Biko and his colleagues as nonviolent liberal reformists, however, has been rejected by scholars who have studied the movement. E.g., Nolutshungu, *Changing South Africa*, chap. 7.

23. For a critical perspective on student politics in the 1970s and 1980s, see Hyslop, "Food, authority and politics," 34–38. A revised version of this paper was published as "School student movements and state education policy: 1972–87," in W. Cobbett & R. Cohen (eds.), *Popular struggles in South Africa* (London, 1988), 183–209.

24. Lodge, *Black politics*, 339–41.

25. On BCM in the 1980s, see D. Hirschmann, "The Black Consciousness Movement in South Africa," *Journal of Modern African Studies*, 28 (1), 1990, 9–22.

26. Security legislation—especially the second Bantu Laws Amendment Act (No. 71) of 1974—allowing the central government to banish persons, prohibit publications and speeches, and outlaw organizations was applied to the Ciskei. The Black States Constitution Act of 1979 also allowed homeland authorities to ban individuals within their territories. Key security legislation promulgated by the Ciskei government included Proclamation R252 of 1977, which allowed detention without trial for ninety days (and it was renewable). This proclamation was replaced by the Ciskei National Security Act of 1982, which repackaged and even strengthened existing South African security legislation and made it applicable to the newly independent homeland. On Ciskei's vigilantes, see N. Haysom, *Apartheid's private army: the rise of right-wing vigilantes in South Africa* (Johannesburg, 1986), esp. 46–61.

27. The pattern of violence in the Ciskei in the early 1980s is chronicled in N. Haysom, "Ruling with the whip: report on the violation of human rights in the Ciskei," unpublished paper, University of the Witwatersrand, Centre for Applied Legal Studies, 1983.

28. Human Awareness Programme, *Ciskei: an assessment*, 47.

29. The government established the Manpower Development Center alongside the tribal bureaus in 1980, for example, to monitor the behavior of workers employed inside and outside the Ciskei. Pension and disability payments as well as drought and poverty relief aid were allegedly subject to manipulation by CNIP chiefs and headmen in the rural areas.

Index

AAC (All-African Convention), 294, 312; and Natives' Representation Council, 278–83, 411n75, 412nn84, 86; noncollaboration policies, 291–93; in rural betterment resistance movement, 306–7; Youth League activities at Fort Hare, 291, 414n23

Abantu-Batho (newspaper), 176

Abdurahman, Abdullah, M.D., and fight for Coloured rights, 171, 173, 174, 251, 275

Abrahams, Hans, 331

Advisory boards, urban, 298

African-Americans: colleges educating Africans, 177, 184, 188, 249–50; influences in African churches, 183–84, 188, 262; perceived as role models, 245, 250, 267, 354

African Commercial and Distributive Workers' Union, 413n2

African Democratic party, 295, 415n36

African Food and Canning Workers' Union (AFCWU), 363

Africanist, The (newspaper), 300

Africanists, separation from the ANC, 299–301

African Methodist Episcopal church. *See* AME church

African National Congress. *See* ANC

African Native Mission church, as successor to Thembu church, 182, 261

African Political (People's) Organization (APO), as Coloured protest group, 171, 173, 174, 176, 251

Africans' Claims in South Africa (1943 manifesto), 288

Afrikaner Bond: alliance with Tengo Jabavu, 156–57, 159, 393n40; anti-temperance stance, 126; opposition in, for unification, 172; relations with African organizations, 144, 145, 391n18; in Cape politics, 137, 390n3

Afrikaner Nationalists, control of national government, 287, 296, 321

Afrikaners: the Great Trek, 79; in Cape politics, 137, 147. *See also* Trekboers

Aggey, James, 249–50

Agriculture, 80, 221–22, 406n132; African productivity in 1860s in, 90–91; crops, 24–33, 210–11, 409n59; economic incentives in the Ciskei for, 342–44; during Iron Age, 22–32; and irrigation, 65–66, 325, 342–43; loan unavailability to Africans, 233, 253; plow use by peasants, 87, 92, 93, 201, 203; in Tomlinson Commission report, 325; wages, 202–3, 285, 418n6; and white farmers, 7, 195, 223–24, 317, 344, 418n6. *See also* Land; Land grants; Livestock; Plots; Tenants

Alexandra (Johannesburg squatter community), 319

All-African Convention. *See* AAC

Althusser, Louis, 8

Amafela movement, in Herschel, 268–72, 355

Amalinde, Battle of (1818), 53

AME (African Methodist Episcopal) church (U.S.), ties in Africa, 183–84, 188, 261, 270

Amiens, Treaty of (1802), 49

Amulets, as Christian symbols, 118

ANC (African National Congress), 304, 314, 354, 362; banning of, 300; franchise proposal opposition by, 276, 277, 410n58; pressures on, by militants, 294–95; role in

429

Fingerprints, for new pass system, 306

Fingo Emancipation Day, 158

Fingoland, created for the Mfengu, 73

Fingo/Mfengu: and introduction into the Ciskei, 56, 58–60, 62, 352, 376nn26, 27, 32. *See also* Mfengu

Firearms: Gun Act of 1878, 75, 137–38, 155; use of, by Xhosa during War of 1877–78, 74

Food, 27, 302, 339, 351; maize as staple, 27, 88, 201, 208, 212; meat in diet, 19–20, 89, 212; milk as staple, 19–20, 28, 202, 208; prices of, in urban areas, 284–85; requirements and population in the reserves, 193–94

Forested areas, in the reserves, 226, 230, 403n97

Fort Hare Native College/University, 247, 248, 358; as Congress Youth League center, 291; student disturbances following WW II at, 301–3

Franchise

—African: during Cape colonial period, 136, 151–52, 157–58, 352–53, 392n30; demands by AAC in 1943, 292; and 1913 Land Act, 196–97; proposed in Union of South Africa, 167; registration, 141, 143, 152–53, 159, 393n41; struggle to keep, during the 1920's–30s, 246–56, 272–83, 410n58

—Coloured, 246, 273, 274, 296; before Union, 136, 153, 159, 393n41

—white: of ex-Boers, 159; voting qualification laws of 1930s, 274

Franchise and Ballot Act (1892), voting qualifications of, 152–53, 155

Franchise Laws Amendment Act (1931), 274

Free Church of Scotland, Synod of Kaffraria, 125, 185–86, 387n4, 396nn36, 37

Freedom Charter (1955), 299, 356

Frontier thesis, comparison of South African and American, 42

Frontier wars, in South African historiography, 52, 375nn15–17

Fundraising: for African university, 179, 180, 395n27; as SANC financial effort, 170

Gamtoos-Fish frontier zone, 86; conflicts between Dutch and Xhosa in, 44–52; loss of, to Khoisan hunters, 43–44; settlement of, by English sheep ranchers, 56

Gandhi, Mohandas K., 150, 173, 296

Ganya, Nana, 154

Garvey, Marcus, movement's effect in South Africa, 245, 250, 254, 267–68

Gasa, Simon Peter, 120

Gawler, John, 144

Gcaleka (Xhosa chief), 39–40

Gcaleka Xhosa: land losses following cattle-killing period, 72–73, 94; population in 1837, 59, 376n28; role in War of 1850–53, 64

General Workers' Union (GWU), 363

Gerhart, Gail, 298

German South-West Africa, in-migration of Ciskei workers, 111, 204

Glasgow Missionary Society (GMS), 113–14, 387n34

Glen Grey Act (1894), 166, 169, 221, 260, 325; and effect on land tenure, 51, 52, 89, 102–3, 146, 155, 352, 383nn50, 51, 52; plot size recommendation in, 89, 205, 380n19

Glen Grey district: and effect of 1894 Act, 101–6, 382–83nn44, 48; and increases in reserve population, 199–200, 397–98n16, *tables* 234, 235, 237; soil erosion in, 400n53; and transfer to the Transkei, 332, 334

Glen Grey District Council, 103–4

Glen Grey Teachers' Association, 146

Goats, 99, 195

God: Israelite concept of, 261–62; missionary concept of, 116–17

Godlo, Richard H., 254, 257, 282, 288

Goduka, Jonas, and Thembu church, 182, 183, 190, 395n31

Gold: impact of discovery and mining of, on peasant farmers, 96, 101; and influence on Zimbabwe's trade in Iron Age, 29–30; and miners' wages, 202, 322

Golden City Post (magazine), 289

Goliath, William (Mhlakaza), 68–69

Gomas, John, 280

Gonaqua Khoikhoi, 44, 46

Gontshi, Andrew, 151, 392n30

Good Hope Plan (1981), as inducement for border industries, 329, 345

Good Hope Textile Mill (border industry), 232, 328, 341

Gool, Goolam, 292

Govan, William, 129, 138

422*nn45, 49;* in urban areas, 215, 217–20, 284, 307, 317, 402*n78, table* 346; of Xhosa after cattle-killing period, 72, 99
Population Registration Act (1950), 296
Port Elizabeth, 108; African migration to, 150; communist activity in, trade unions, 293–94; conditions for African residents in, 307; riots in, 255, 310
Portugal: and influence of early trading missions to Africa, 29, 30, 32; withdrawal from Mozambique, 321
Post office, trading station as, 100
Potatoes, as cultivated food, 27
Pottery, 21, 23; cattle designs on, 30; Iron Age, 26–27
Poverty: in the Ciskei reserves, 209, 212, 229, 401*n65;* as factor in Red-School dichotomy, 11
Power: in cattle-keeping cultures, 28, 36, 304; of chiefs, 4, 29, 222, 229; configurations with resistance, 8–12; Europeans as having, 166; manifestations of, 4–8
Presbyterian Church of Africa (PCA), 185–86, 189, 190, 261
Presbyterian Church of South Africa, 186
Presbyterians: and creation of separate African churches, 185–86; early mission stations, 113–14; education of Africans, 128–29; education of early white missionaries, 383–84*n1;* ordination of Africans, 124–25, 389*n26;* racial separation of temperance temples, 127; use of African teachers, 128, 387–88*nn39, 40*
Prevention of Illegal Squatting Act (1951), 315
Printing press, use by early missionaries, 118–19, 385*n12*
Production: by homesteads, 4; during the Iron Age, 26–32; in the reserves, 193–94, 207–8, 399*n45*
Programme of Action (1949), ANC stand on, 298
Progressive party, 155, 156, 169
Promotion of Bantu Self-Government Act (1959), 324
Promotion of Economic Development of Homelands Act (1968), 328
Property. *See also* Land
—church: after schisms, 186, 188
—private: as alien concept to Xhosa, 36; as concept to Dutch trekboers, 42; as voting qualification, 141, 152

—transactions between whites and Africans, 199
Prophets, Xhosa: fusing of Christianity with Xhosa religion, 67–68
Protectorates, under new union, 165, 167, 412*n86*
Protest(s): campaigns of Africans against unification, 168–73; against 1935 Native Representation Bill, 280, 281–82; petitionary, 3, 353; politics of, 150, 151, 392*n30;* by urban Africans during WW II, 285
Public Debt Commission, as depository for Bunga revenues, 226
Public Service Commission, scrutiny of NAD's policies, 221

Queen Adelaide Province, (re. Ciskei), 60, 63
Queenstown resolutions (1907), as protest against unification, 171–72
Queen Victoria Memorial, as African university fund-raising project, 179–80
Quitrent tenure, 205; under the Glen Grey Act, 102, 383*n48;* provisions for native farmers, 89, 93, 101, 380*n18;* provisions for trekboers, 83

Racial policies, in South Africa. *See* Education; Labor; Segregation
Racism, in South Africa, 139, 390*n13,* 392*n36*
Raiding communities, fostered by European trade demands, 32, 372*n13*
Raids: for forced labor captives, 62, 84, 376*n21;* by trekboers against San, 46
Railway(s): construction, 99–100, 382*n39;* jobs given to whites, 174–75; African worker wages, 258
Rand Revolt (1922), 7, 245
Rape, in African urban areas, 309
Reality, missionary concept of, 117–18
Recruiters, labor, 95, 115, 203–4, 229
Red folk culture: conversion to Wellingtonite millennial sect, 267–68; as stemming from Xhosa millennial movement, 71
Red-School dichotomy, 11–12, 369*n22;* in East London, 307
Referendum, Ciskei independence, 334, 422*nn41, 42*
Refugee(s): consideration of mission stations as asylums, 115, 123; independent Ciskei as dumping grounds, 336–40